STRE[ET]

West Sussex

Bognor Regis, Brighton, Chichester, Crawley, Horsham, Hove, Worthing

www.philips-maps.co.uk

First published in 1994 by

Philip's, a division of
Octopus Publishing Group Ltd
www.octopusbooks.co.uk
2–4 Heron Quays, London E14 4JP
An Hachette Livre UK Company
www.hachettelivre.co.uk

Fourth colour edition 2008
First impression 2008
WSUDA

ISBN 978-0-540-09272-7 (pocket)

© Philip's 2008

OS Ordnance Survey®

This product includes mapping data licensed
from Ordnance Survey®, with the permission of
the Controller of Her Majesty's Stationery Office.

© Crown copyright 2008. All rights reserved.
Licence number 100011710

Data for the speed cameras provided by
PocketGPSWorld.com Ltd.

Ordnance Survey and the OS symbol are
registered trademarks of Ordnance Survey, the
national mapping agency of Great Britain

Printed and bound in China by Toppan

Contents

II List of mobile speed cameras

III Key to map symbols

IV Key to map pages

VI Route planning

VIII Administrative and Postcode boundaries

1 Street maps at 2⅔ inches to 1 mile

213 Street map of Brighton city centre at 5⅓ inches to 1 mile

214 Index of towns, villages, streets, hospitals, industrial estates, railway stations, schools, shopping centres universities and places of interest

Digital Data

The exceptionally high-quality mapping found in this atlas is available as digital data in TIFF format, which is easily convertible to other bitmapped (raster) image formats.

The index is also available in digital form as a standard database table. It contains all the details found in the printed index together with the National Grid reference for the map square in which each entry is named.

For further information and to discuss your requirements, please contact james.mann@philips-maps.co.uk

On-line route planner

For detailed driving directions and estimated driving times visit our free route planner at www.philips-maps.co.uk

Mobile speed cameras

The vast majority of speed cameras used on Britain's roads are operated by safety camera partnerships. These comprise local authorities, the police, Her Majesty's Court Service (HMCS) and the Highways Agency.

This table lists the sites where each safety camera partnership may enforce speed limits through the use of mobile cameras or detectors. These are usually set up on the roadside or a bridge spanning the road and operated by a police or civilian enforcement officer. The speed limit at each site (if available) is shown in red type, followed by the approximate location in black type.

Mike Harrington / Alamy

A27
- 40 Lancing, near Grand Avenue, Upper Brighton Road
- 70 Shoreham, Holmbush
- 70 Angmering, East of Dappers Lane, Hammerpot

A29
- 30 Aldingbourne, Westergate Street
- 40 Bognor Regis, Shripney Road

A259
- 30 Saltdean, Marine Drive
- 30 Fishbourne, Main Road
- 30 Lancing, Brighton Road
- 30 Brighton, Black Rock
- 30 Bognor Regis, Hotham Way

A280
- 40 Patching, Long Furlong

A281
- 30 Horsham, Guildford Road

A283
- 30 Northchapel, nr Pipers Lane
- 30 Pulborough, Lower Street (East)

A285
- 30 Petworth, Station Road
- 40 Halnaker, Stane Street

A2032
- 30 Worthing, Littlehampton Road, Poulter's Lane

A2038
- 30 Hove, Hangleton Road

B2066
- 30 Hove, New Church Road

B2070
- 40 Rake, London Road

B2111
- 30 Lindfield, Lewes Road

B2123
- 30 Brighton, Woodingdean, Falmer Road

B2138
- 30 Fittleworth, Lower Street

B2166
- 30 Bognor Regis, Aldwick Road

UNCLASSIFIED
- 30 Horsham, Pondtail Road
- 30 Bognor Regis, Chalcraft Lane
- 30 Crawley, near Hazlewick Flyover, Gatwick Road
- 30 Worthing, Marine Parade
- 30 Worthing, The Boulevard
- 30 Crawley, Gossops Drive
- 30 Crawley, Manor Royal
- 30 Eastbourne, Brodrick Road
- 30 Brighton, Carden Avenue
- 30 Hove, Shirley Drive

Key to map symbols

III

Motorway with junction number (22a)	◆	Ambulance station
Primary route – dual/single carriageway	◆	Coastguard station
A road – dual/single carriageway	◆	Fire station
B road – dual/single carriageway	◆	Police station
Minor road – dual/single carriageway	✚	Accident and Emergency entrance to hospital
Other minor road – dual/single carriageway	Ⓗ	Hospital
Road under construction	✛	Place of worship
Tunnel, covered road	🖻	Information Centre (open all year)
Speed cameras - single, multiple (30) (30)	🛒	Shopping Centre
Rural track, private road or narrow road in urban area	P P&R	Parking, Park and Ride
Gate or obstruction to traffic (restrictions may not apply at all times or to all vehicles)	PO	Post Office
	🏕 🚐	Camping site, caravan site
Path, bridleway, byway open to all traffic, road used as a public path	▶ ✕	Golf course, picnic site
Pedestrianised area	Prim Sch	Important buildings, schools, colleges, universities and hospitals
Postcode boundaries DY7		Built up area
County and unitary authority boundaries		Woods
Railway, tunnel, railway under construction	River Medway	Water name
Tramway, tramway under construction		River, weir, stream
Miniature railway		Canal, lock, tunnel
Railway station Walsall		Water
Private railway station		Tidal water
Metro station South Shields	Church	Non-Roman antiquity
Tram stop, tram stop under construction	ROMAN FORT	Roman antiquity
Bus, coach station	87	Adjoining page indicators and overlap bands

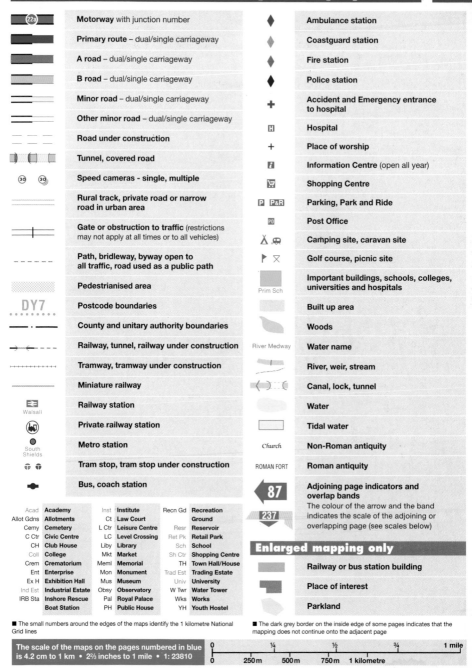

Acad	**Academy**	Inst	**Institute**	Recn Gd	**Recreation**
Allot Gdns	**Allotments**	Ct	**Law Court**		**Ground**
Cemy	**Cemetery**	L Ctr	**Leisure Centre**	Resr	**Reservoir**
C Ctr	**Civic Centre**	LC	**Level Crossing**	Ret Pk	**Retail Park**
CH	**Club House**	Liby	**Library**	Sch	**School**
Coll	**College**	Mkt	**Market**	Sh Ctr	**Shopping Centre**
Crem	**Crematorium**	Meml	**Memorial**	TH	**Town Hall/House**
Ent	**Enterprise**	Mon	**Monument**	Trad Est	**Trading Estate**
Ex H	**Exhibition Hall**	Mus	**Museum**	Univ	**University**
Ind Est	**Industrial Estate**	Obsy	**Observatory**	W Twr	**Water Tower**
IRB Sta	**Inshore Rescue**	Pal	**Royal Palace**	Wks	**Works**
	Boat Station	PH	**Public House**	YH	**Youth Hostel**

237

The colour of the arrow and the band indicates the scale of the adjoining or overlapping page (see scales below)

Enlarged mapping only

	Railway or bus station building
	Place of interest
	Parkland

■ The small numbers around the edges of the maps identify the 1 kilometre National Grid lines

■ The dark grey border on the inside edge of some pages indicates that the mapping does not continue onto the adjacent page

The scale of the maps on the pages numbered in blue is 4.2 cm to 1 km • 2⅔ inches to 1 mile • 1: 23810	0 ¼ ½ ¾ 1 mile 0 250m 500m 750m 1 kilometre
The scale of the maps on pages numbered in red is 8.4 cm to 1 km • 5⅓ inches to 1 mile • 1: 11900	0 220 yards 440 yards 660 yards ½ mile 0 125m 250m 375m ½ kilometre

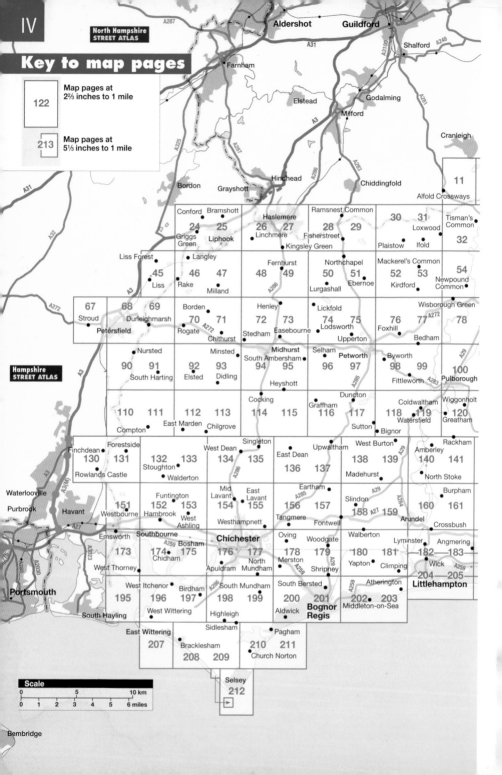

IV

North Hampshire STREET ATLAS

Key to map pages

	Map pages at 2⅔ inches to 1 mile
122	

	Map pages at 5⅓ inches to 1 mile
213	

Hampshire STREET ATLAS

Aldershot   Guildford

Shalford

Farnham

Elstead   Godalming

Milford

Cranleigh

Bordon   Grayshott   Hindhead   Chiddingfold   11
Alfold Crossways

Conford Bramshott   Haslemere   Ramsnest Common   30 31 Tisman's Common
24 25   26 27   28 29   Loxwood   32
Griggs Liphook   Linchmere Fisherstreet   Plaistow Ifold
Green   Kingsley Green

Liss Forest   Langley   Fernhurst   Northchapel   Mackerel's Common   54
45 46 47   48 49   50 51   52 53   Newpound
Liss   Rake   Milland   Lurgashall Ebernoe   Kirdford   Common

67 68 69   Borden   Henley   Lickfold   Wisborough Green
Stroud   70 71   72 73   74 75   76 77   78
Petersfield Durleighmarsh   Rogate   Stedham Easebourne Lodsworth   Foxhill   Bedham
Chithurst   Upperton

Nursted   Minsted   Midhurst   Selham   Petworth   Byworth
90 91   92 93   South Ambersham   96 97   98 99   100
South Harting   Elsted Didling   94 95   Pulborough
Heyshott   Fittleworth

Cocking   Duncton   Coldwaltham Wiggonholt
110 111   112 113   114 115   Graffham   118 119 120
Compton   East Marden Chilgrove   116 117   Watersfield Greatham
Sutton Bignor

Finchdean   Forestside   Singleton   Upwaltham   West Burton   Rackham
130 131   132 133   West Dean   East Dean   138 139   Amberley
Rowlands Castle   Stoughton   134 135   136 137   Madehurst   140 141
Walderton   North Stoke

Waterlooville   Mid   East   Eartham   Burpham
Purbrook   151   152 153   Lavant Lavant   156 157   Slindon   160 161
Westbourne Hambrook   154 155   Tangmere   158 159   Crossbush
Havant   West   Westhampnett   Fontwell   Arundel
Ashling

Emsworth   Southbourne   Bosham   Chichester   Oving Woodgate   Walberton   Lyminster   Angmering
173   174 175   176 177   178 179   180 181   182 183
West Thorney   Chidham   North   Merston   Yapton Climping   Wick 205
Apuldram Mundham   Shripney   Littlehampton

Portsmouth   West Itchenor   Birdham   South Mundham   South Bersted   Atherington
195   196 197   198 199   200 201   202 203   Middleton-on-Sea
South Hayling   West Wittering   Highleigh   Aldwick   Bognor Regis

East Wittering   Sidlesham   Pagham
207   208 209   210 211
Bracklesham   Church Norton

Scale
0   5   10 km
0 1 2 3 4 5   6 miles

Selsey
212

Bembridge

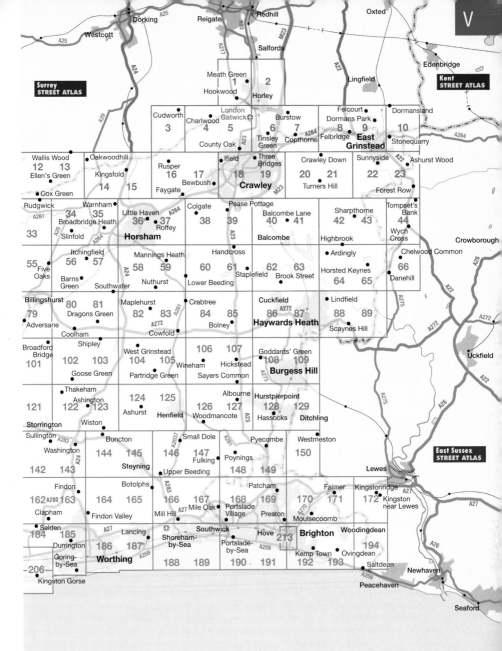

Route Planning

Scale

0 ——— 5 ——— 10 km
0 1 2 3 4 5 6 miles

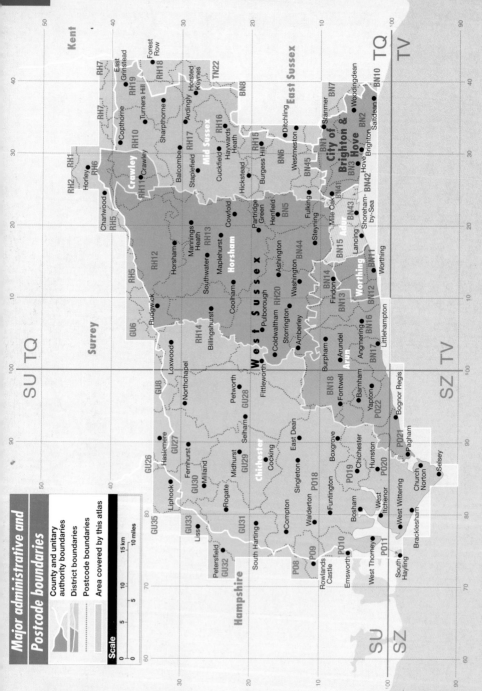

Major administrative and Postcode boundaries

County and unitary authority boundaries
District boundaries
Postcode boundaries
Area covered by this atlas

Scale
0   5   10   15 km
0   5   10 miles

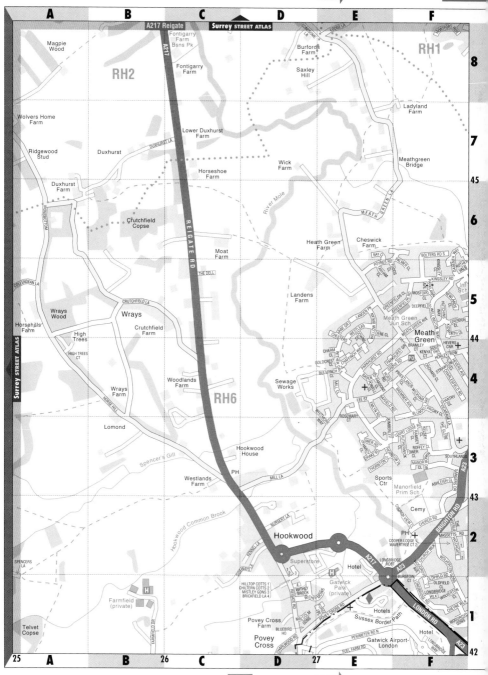

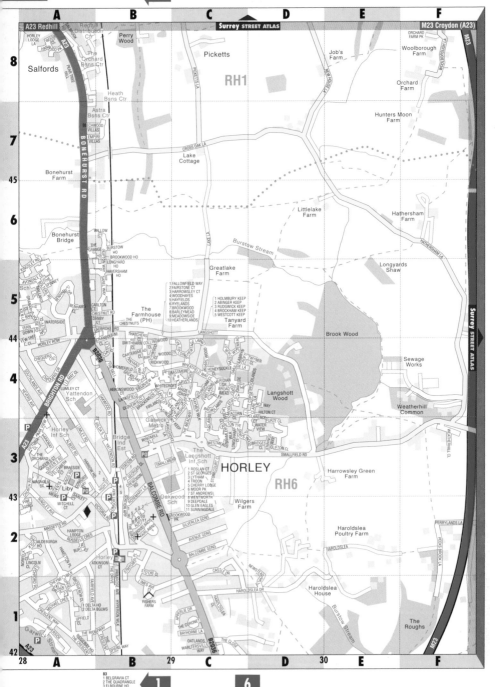

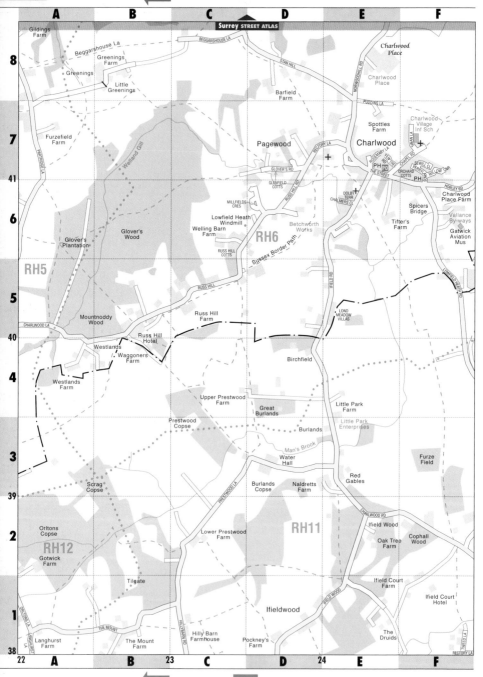

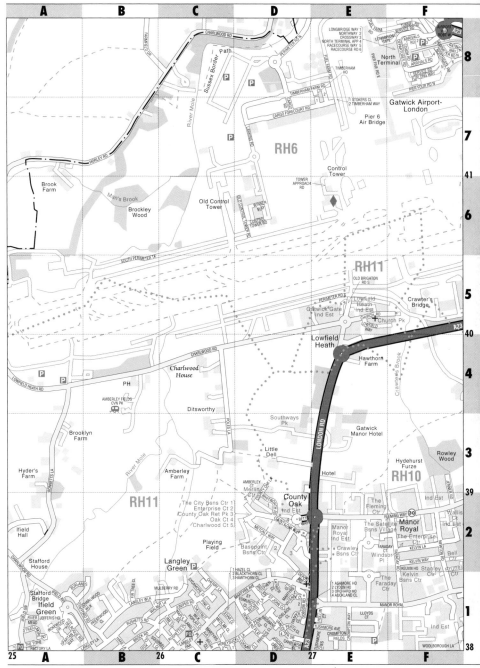

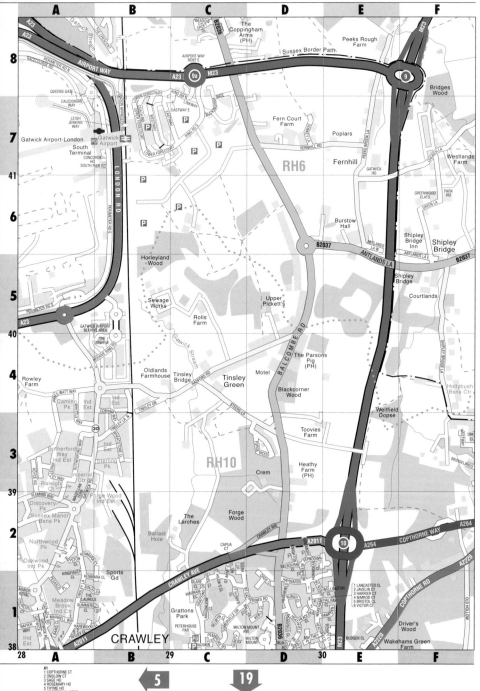

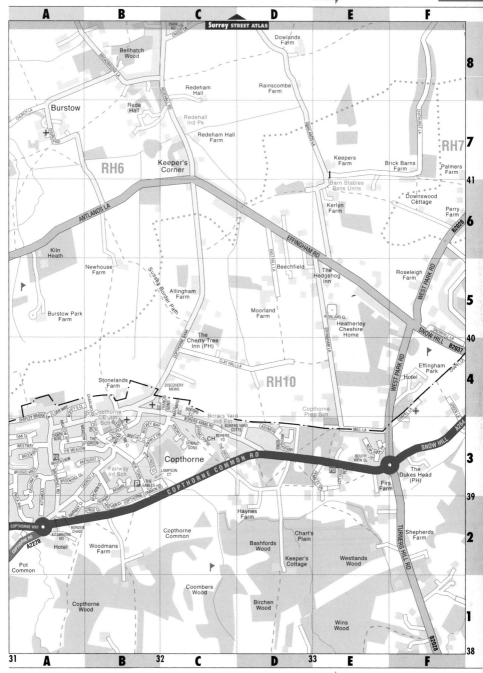

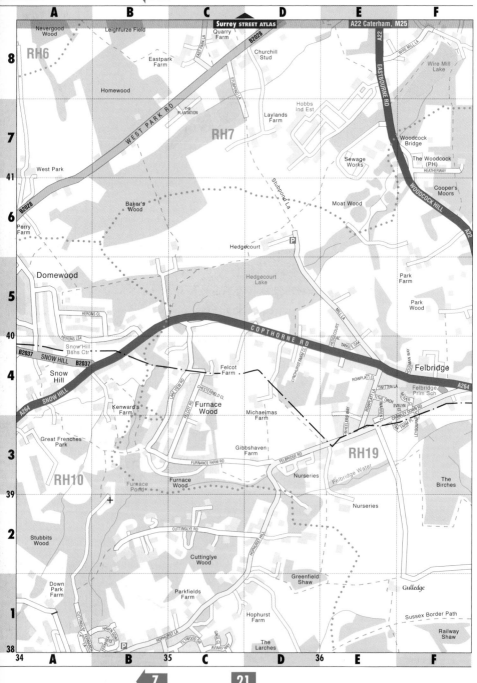

Surrey STREET ATLAS

A22 Caterham, M25

A **B** **C** **D** **E** **F**

Nevergood Wood

RH6

Leighfurze Field

Eastpark Farm

Quarry Farm

B2028

Churchill Stud

WIRE MILL LA

Wire Mill Lake

8

Homewood

EASTBOURNE RD

West Park Rd

THE PLANTATION

RH7

Laylands Farm

Hobbs Ind Est

Woodcock Bridge

7

West Park

Sewage Works

The Woodcock (PH)

HEATHERWAY

41

B2028

Baker's Wood

Stubpond La

Moat Wood

Cooper's Moors

WOODCOCK HILL

A22

Perry Farm

6

Domewood

Hedgecourt

P

Hedgecourt Lake

Park Farm

Park Wood

5

HERONS CL

COPTHORNE RD

MILL LA

HEDGECOURT

TANGIER OAK

40

HERONS LEA

Snow Hill Bshs Ctr

Felbridge

B2037

SNOW HILL

B2037

Felcot Farm

LYNDHURST FARM CL

ROWPLATT CL

Felbridge Prim Sch

A264

4

Snow Hill

SNOW HILL

Kenward's Farm

CHESTERFIELD CL

Furnace Wood

Michaelmas Farm

WHEELERS WAY

ROWPLATT LA

TWITTEN LA

TITHE ORCH

EVELYN CL

CRAWLEY DOWN RD

A264

FELCOT RD

LAKE VIEW RD

3

RH10

Great Frenches Park

FURNACE FARM RD

Furnace Wood

Gibbshaven Farm

FELBRIDGE RD

Nurseries

Felbridge Water

RH19

The Birches

39

Furnace Pond

Nurseries

2

Stubbits Wood

CUTTINGLYE RD

HOPHURST HILL

Greenfield Shaw

Gulledge

Cuttinglye Wood

1

Down Park Farm

CUTTINGLYE LA

HAMMERWOOD RD

Parkfields Farm

HOPHURST LA

TILGATE WOOD CL

Hophurst Farm

Sussex Border Path

Railway Shaw

38

P

AVIARY RD

The Larches

A **B** **C** **D** **E** **F**

34

35

36

Surrey STREET ATLAS

41

10

22

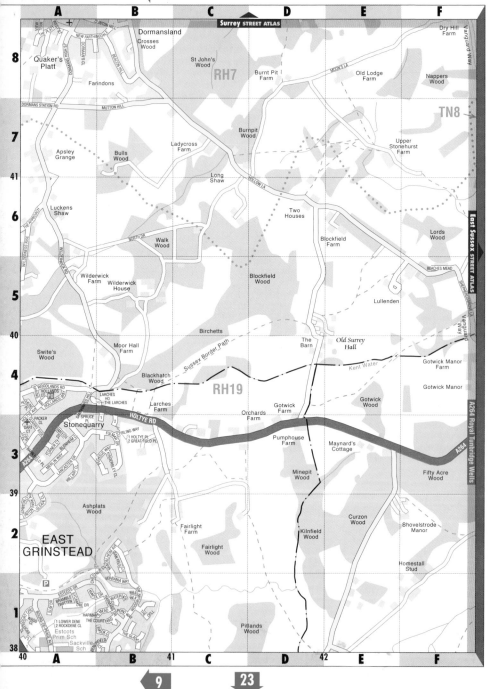

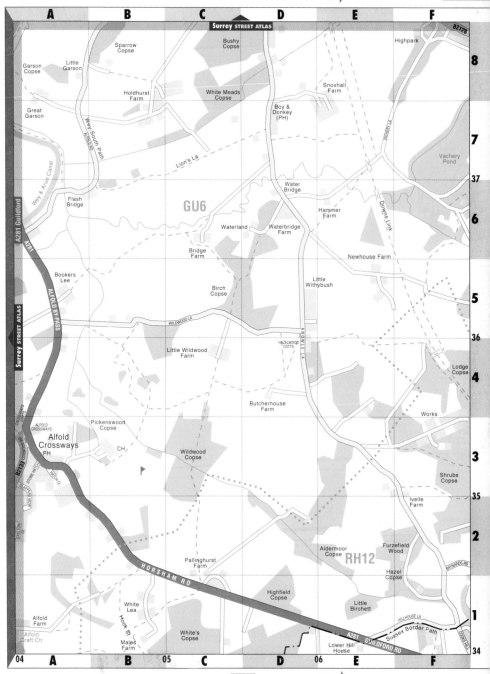

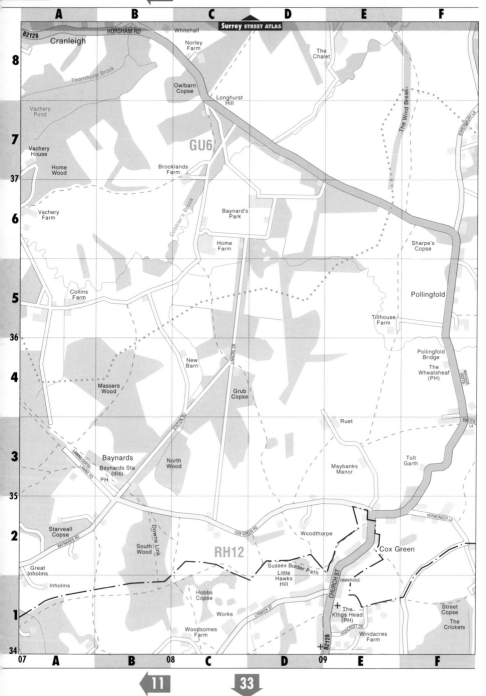

Surrey STREET ATLAS

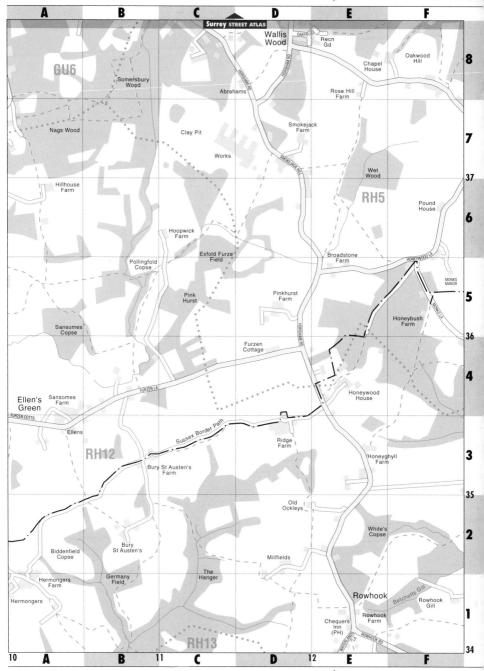

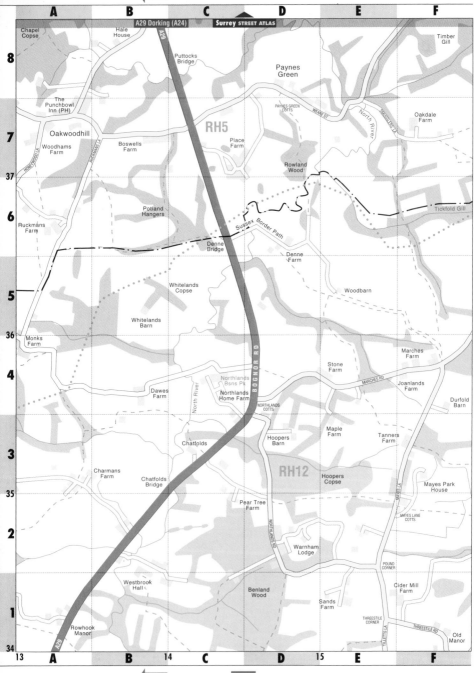

13

A29 Dorking (A24)

Surrey STREET ATLAS

A B C D E F

8

Chapel
Copse

Hale
House

Puttocks
Bridge

Timber
Gill

Paynes
Green

The
Punchbowl
Inn (PH)

RH5

PAYNES GREEN
COTTS

WEARE ST

North River

SNOAKLES LA

Oakdale
Farm

7

Oakwoodhill

Woodhams
Farm

Boswells
Farm

Place
Farm

37

Rowland
Wood

HONEYWOOD LA

RIKEMANS LA

Sussex Border Path

Tickfold Gill

6

Potland
Hangers

Denne
Bridge

Denne
Farm

Ruckmans
Farm

Whitelands
Copse

Woodbarn

5

Whitelands
Barn

36

Monks
Farm

BOGNOR RD

Marches
Farm

4

Dawes
Farm

Northlands
Bsns Pk

Northlands
Home Farm

North River

Stone
Farm

MARCHES RD

Joanlands
Farm

NORTHLANDS
COTTS

Durfold
Barn

Chatfolds

Maple
Farm

Tanners
Farm

3

Charmans
Farm

Chatfolds
Bridge

Hoopers
Barn

RH12

Hoopers
Copse

MAYES LA

Mayes Park
House

35

Pear Tree
Farm

2

NORTHLANDS RD

MAYES LANE
COTTS

Warnham
Lodge

POUND
CORNER

Cider Mill
Farm

Westbrook
Hall

Benland
Wood

Sands
Farm

THREESTILE
CORNER

TILLETTS LA

THREESTILE RD

1

Rowhook
Manor

Old
Manor

34

A B C D E F

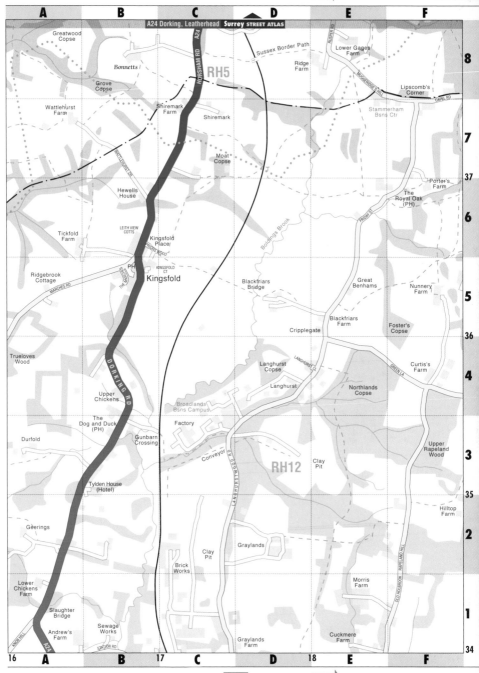

A24 Dorking, Leatherhead **Surrey** STREET ATLAS

8

7

37

6

5

36

4

35

3

2

1

34

Greatwood Copse

Bonnetts

Grove Copse

Wattlehurst Farm

Shiremark Farm

RH5

Sussex Border Path

Ridge Farm

Lower Gages Farm

Lipscomb's Corner

Shiremark

Moat Copse

Stammerham Bsns Ctr

Porter's Farm

Tickfold Farm

Hewells House

LEITH VIEW COTTS

The Royal Oak (PH)

Kingsfold Place

Boldings Brook

Ridgebrook Cottage

PH

KINGSFOLD CT

Kingsfold

Blackfriars Bridge

Great Benhams

Nunnery Farm

Trueloves Wood

DORKING RD

Upper Chickens

Cripplegate

Blackfriars Farm

Foster's Copse

Curtis's Farm

Langhurst Copse

Langhurst

Northlands Copse

Durfold

The Dog and Duck (PH)

Gunbarn Crossing

Broadlands Bsns Campus

Factory

Conveyor

RH12

Clay Pit

Upper Rapeland Wood

Tylden House (Hotel)

Hilltop Farm

Geerings

Clay Pit

Graylands

Brick Works

Morris Farm

Lower Chickens Farm

Slaughter Bridge

Sewage Works

STATION RD

Andrew's Farm

Graylands Farm

Cuckmere Farm

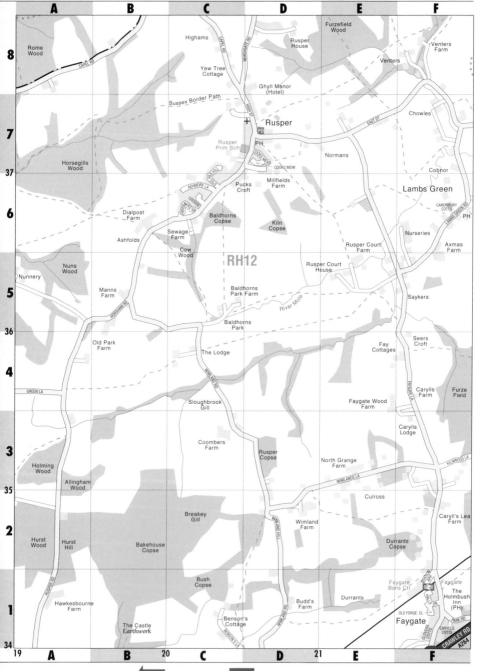

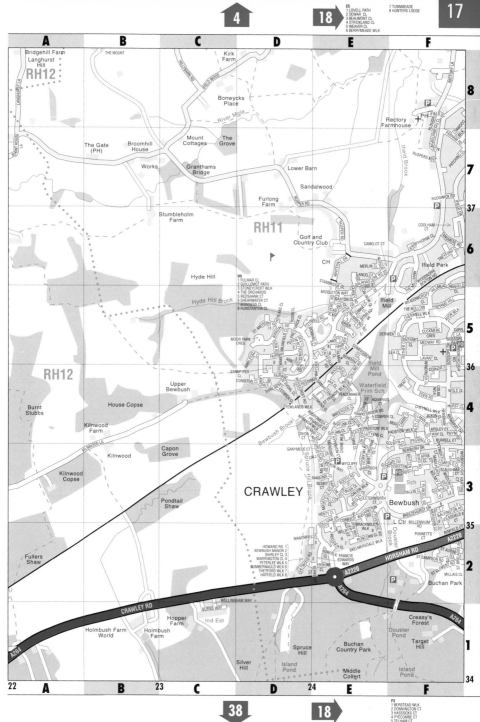

18
E5
1 LOVELL PATH
2 DEWAR CL
3 BEAUMONT CL
4 STRICKLAND CL
5 WEAVER CL
6 BERRYMEADE WLK
7 TUNNMEADE
8 HUNTERS LODGE

8

7

37

6

5

36

4

3

35

2

1

34

Bridgehill Farm
Langhurst Hill
RH12

THE MOUNT

Kirk Farm

Bonwycks Place

River Mole

The Gate (PH)

Broomhill House

Mount Cottages

The Grove

Works

Granthams Bridge

Rectory Farmhouse

PH

Ifield Brook

RUSPERS KEEP

Lower Barn

Sandalwood

RUDGWICK RD

Furlong Farm

Stumbleholm Farm

RH11

COOLHAM CT

CAMELOT CT

Golf and Country Club

CH

MERLIN CL

Ifield Park

Hyde Hill

D5
1 FULMAR CL
2 GUILLEMOT PATH
3 STONEYCROFT WLK
4 THE ORCHARDS
5 REDSHANK CT
6 SHEARWATER CT
7 BOWNESS CL
8 HUNSTANTON CL

Hyde Hill Brook

Ifield Mill

THE HOLLOW

CUCKMERE CRES

CAPEL

GOSSOPS

MOOR PARK CRES

FAIRWAY

DERWENT CL

MEDWAY RD

LAVANT CL

RH12

SANDPIPER

FAIRWAY

Ifield Mill Pond

CONISTON CL

Upper Bewbush

House Copse

Waterfield Prim Sch

PEACEMAKER

AQUARIUS

Kilnwood Farm

YEWLANDS WLK

Bewbush Brook

Kilnwood

Capon Grove

PADSTOW CL

PADSTOW WLK

ORION CL

BEWBUSH DR

Kilnwood Copse

GANYMEDE CT

Spruce Hill Brook

Sch

CRAWLEY

WYCLIFFE

Bewbush

Pondtail Shaw

Bewbush L Ctr

MILLENNIUM

Fullers Shaw

MANORFIELDS

HOWARD RD 1
BEWBUSH MANOR 2
SHIRLEY CL 3
WARRINGTON CL 4
PETERLEE WLK 5
CUMBERNAULD WLK 6
THETFORD WLK 7
HATFIELD WLK 8

SKELMERSDALE WLK

FRANCIS
EDWARDS
WAY

Douster Brook

PUNNETTS CT

HORSHAM RD

A2220

ST SAMPSON RD

MILLAIS CL

ERSKINE

A2220

Buchan Park

A264

Crawley RD

WELLINGHAM WAY

BURNS WAY

A2220

BUCHAN RD

Creasy's Forest

Douster Pond

Hopper Farm

Ind Est

Target Hill

Holmbush Farm World

Holmbush Farm

A264

Silver Hill

Spruce Hill

Island Pond

Buchan Country Park

Middle Covert

Island Pond

22

23

24

18
F3
1 BERSTEAD WLK
2 DONNINGTON CT
3 HASSOCKS CT
4 PYECOMBE CT
5 TELHAM CT
6 WARBLETON HO
7 CALDBECK HO
8 HALNAKER WLK
9 ICKLESHAM HO

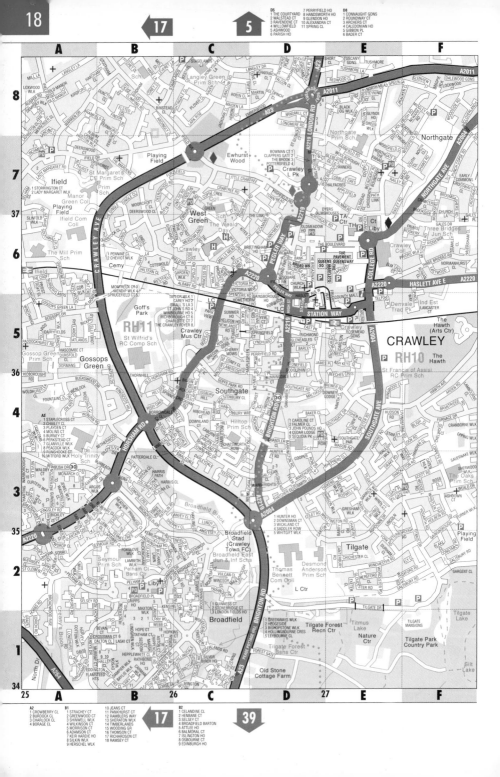

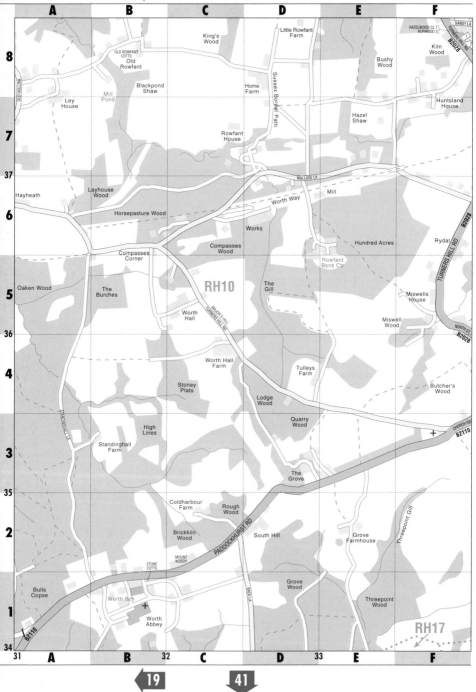

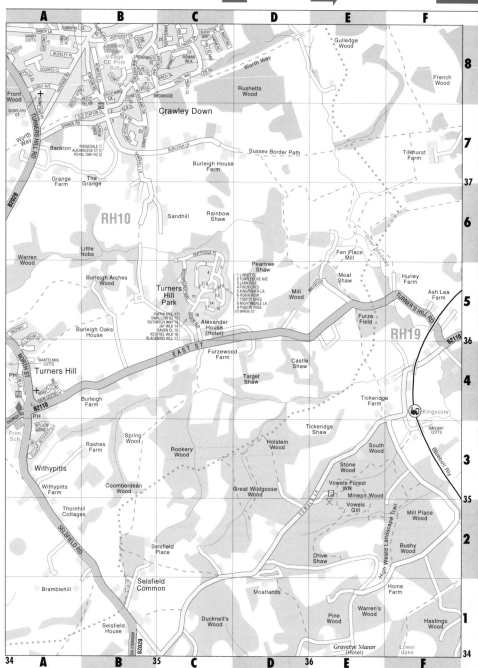

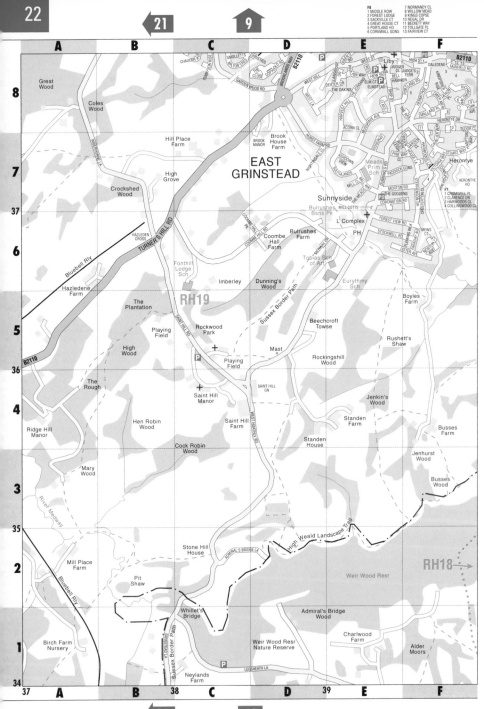

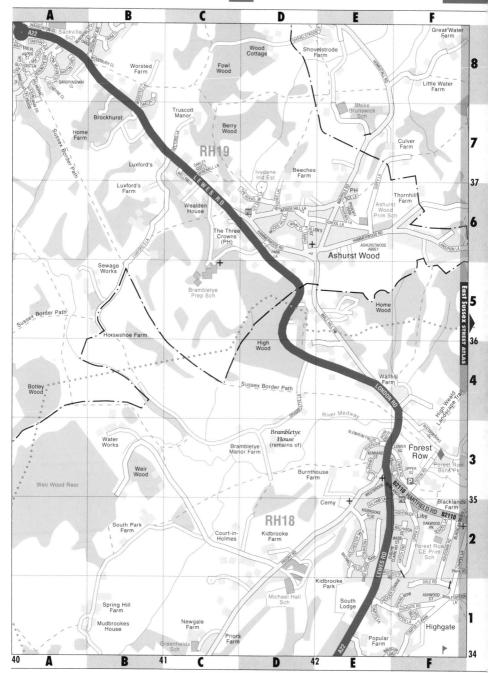

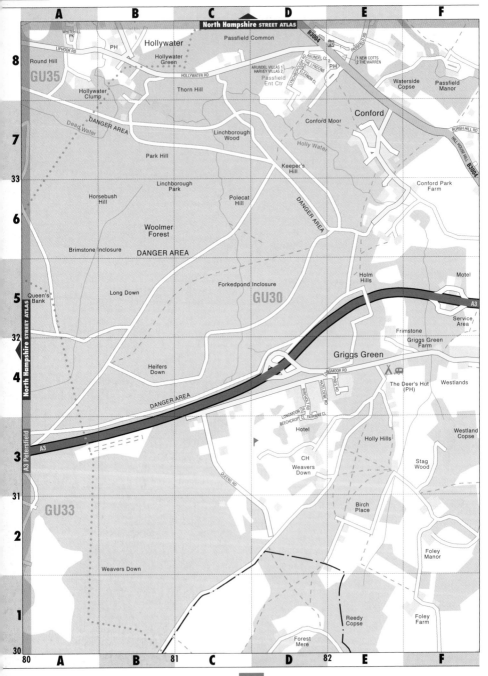

North Hampshire STREET ATLAS

A B C D E F

8

Round Hill

GU35

WHITEHILL PK

LIPHOOK RD

PH

Hollywater

Hollywater Green

Hollywater Clump

Passfield Common

Hollywater Rd

Thorn Hill

ARUNDEL VILLAS 1
HARVEY VILLAS 2

Passfield Ent Ctr

ARUNDEL CL 1
THE LYNDONS 2
ELEANOR CL

PH

1 NEW COTTS
2 THE WARREN

Waterside Copse

Passfield Manor

7

DANGER AREA

Dead Water

Park Hill

Linchborough Wood

Conford Moor

Conford

Holly Water

BURGH HILL RD

B3004

33

Horsebush Hill

Linchborough Park

Keeper's Hill

Conford Park Farm

6

Woolmer Forest

Brimstone Inclosure

DANGER AREA

Polecat Hill

DANGER AREA

5

Queen's Bank

Long Down

Forkedpond Inclosure

GU30

Holm Hills

Motel

A3

32

Service Area

Frimstone

Griggs Green Farm

4

Heifers Down

DANGER AREA

LONGMOOR RD
BEECHCROFT CL
PINE RD
BIRCH PL
HAZELDENE RD
FAIRWAY CL
HILL SIDE RD

Griggs Green

The Deer's Hut (PH)

Westlands

Hotel

Holly Hills

Westland Copse

3

A3 Petersfield

A3

QUEENS RD

CH

Weavers Down

Stag Wood

31

GU33

Birch Place

Foley Manor

2

Weavers Down

1

Reedy Copse

Foley Farm

30

80 A B 81 C D 82 E F

46

North Hampshire STREET ATLAS

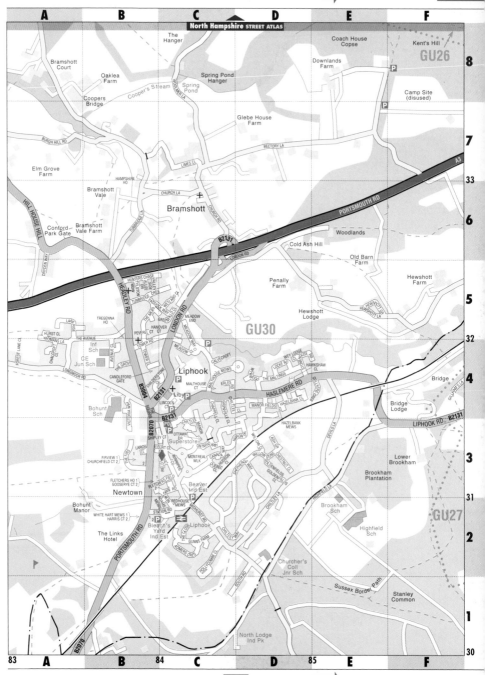

North Hampshire STREET ATLAS

GU26

GU30

GU27

Bramshott Court

Oaklea Farm

Coopers Bridge

Cooper's Stream

The Hanger

Spring Pond Hanger

Spring Pond

Coach House Copse

Downlands Farm

Kent's Hill

Camp Site (disused)

Glebe House Farm

BURGH HILL RD

Elm Grove Farm

RECTORY LA

HAMPSHIRE HO

Bramshott Vale

CHURCH LA

LIMES CL

Bramshott

CHURCH LA

PORTSMOUTH RD

A3

Conford Park Gate

Bramshott Vale Farm

HILL HOUSE HILL

DRYDEN WAY

TUNBRIDGE LA

B2131

LONDON RD

Woodlands

Cold Ash Hill

Old Barn Farm

Hewshott Farm

HEDLEY RD

HUNTERS CHASE

ALDER CL

TUNBRIDGE CRES

GREEN CL

Penally Farm

Hewshott Lodge

HEWSHOTT LA

HEWSHOTT GR

TREGENNA HO

HURST CL

LARK RISE

YEOMANS LA

THE AVENUE

MEADOW END

MEADOW CL

WEY LODGE

HAWKSHAW CL

32

FOREST LANE CL

CAMP GATE

LONGMOOR RD

Inf Sch

CE Jun Sch

CANDLEFORD GATE

THE GROVE

AVENUE CL

PEVEREL CT

HANOVER CT

TOWER RD

LONDON RD

MEADOW CL

CALICECROFT

MALTHOUSE MEWS

UCK RD

THE MALTINGS

Liphook

HASLEMERE RD

Bridge

Bridge Lodge

Bohunt Sch

B3004

B2131

Lib'y

LINCOLN CT

MALTHOUSE CT

CHAPELL LA

PENFOLD CL

MANOR FIELDS

HAZELBANK LA

ESILES RD

LIPHOOK RD · B2131

B2070

SHIPLEY CT

OTTAWAY DR

COURT CL

CHELLE MANOR

SANSON RD

WILLOW RD

HAZELBANK MEWS

DEVILS LA

HIGHFIELD LA

Lower Brookham

FIRVIEW CL

CHURCHFIELD CT 2

LARONS

MONTREAL WLK

CAM LA

WEAVER MEADOW

Brookham Plantation

FLETCHERS HO 1

GOOSERYE CT 2

Newtown

Bohunt Manor

WHITE HART MEWS 1

HARRIS CT 2

The Links Hotel

STATION RD

REDHOUSE MEWS

JOHN RD

Beaver Ind Est

SHEPHERDS WAY

CANAL WAY

LOW MEAD

GOLDEN HILL

CHELTSEY CL

CHELTSEY LA

CHELTSEY RD

Brookham Sch

Highfield Sch

GU27

PORTSMOUTH RD

B2070

Bleach's Yard Ind Est

GUNNS QUAY

HOLLYCOMBE CL

POMERS CRES

SOUTH RD

Churcher's Coll Jnr Sch

Sussex Border Path

Stanley Common

North Lodge Ind Pk

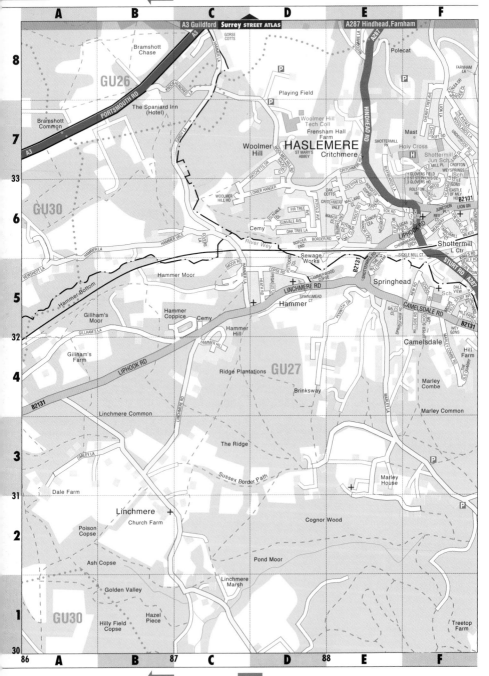

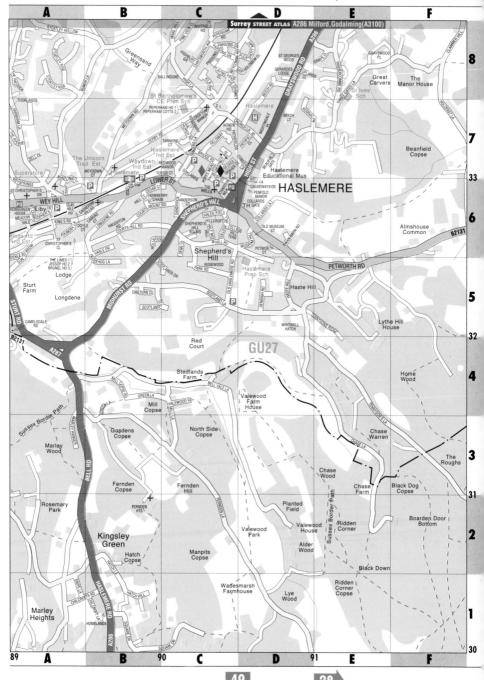

Surrey STREET ATLAS A286 Milford,Godalming(A3100)

HASLEMERE

GU27

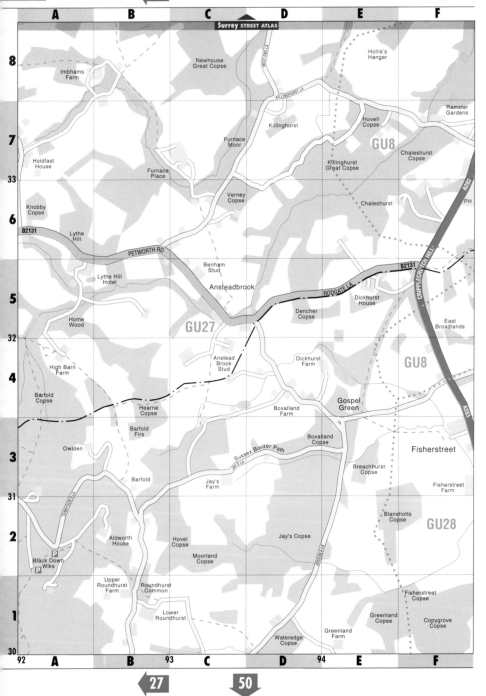

Surrey STREET ATLAS

GU8

GU27

GU8

GU28

A283 Milford

Surrey STREET ATLAS

Chiddingfold

Windmill Copse
Great Copse
Sparkes Copse
Tugley Farm

Hungry Corner
Rovehurst Wood
Fisherlane Hanger

Gostrode Farm
Griggs Bottom
Fisher Lane Nursery
Little Tugley

Sussex Border Path
GOSTRODE LA
Surrey Copse
Robins Farm

Ramsnest Common
White's Hill
Works

Redlands Farm
Furze Field
Surrey Belt
Surrey Rough

GU8
Downlands

Big Copse
Potlane Farm
Upper North Pond
Walk Copse
Shillinglee Park
Downlands Wood

Parkgate
Lower North Pond
HOME FARM CT
Manorhill Copse

Stilland Farm
SHILLINGLEE RD
Newhouse Farm

Gaston's Farm
Turnour's Wood
Deer Tower
Nine Acre Rew
Beanfield Copse
Little Hayman's Farm

Eastland Farm
New Copse
Twenty Four Acres
Raymans Farm

China Bridge
The Lake
RH14

Pond Bay
Mill Copse

GU28
Frith Lodge
The Plantation
Park Mill Farm

Frith Wood
Frith Hill
Dale's Farm Hanger
Dale's Farm

Mitchell Park Farm

Surrey STREET ATLAS

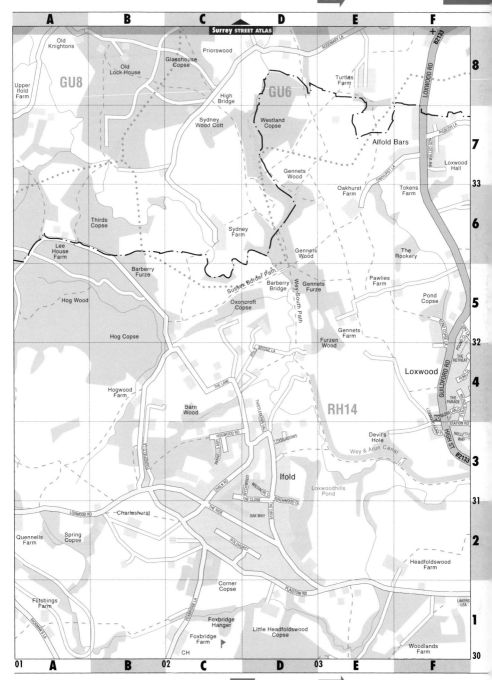

Surrey STREET ATLAS

Old Knightons

Upper Ifold Farm

GU8

Old Lock-House

Glasshouse Copse

Priorswood

High Bridge

ROSEMARY LA

Turtles Farm

8

GU6

Westland Copse

Sydney Wood Cott

Alfold Bars

PYEBUSH LA

THE WALLED GDN

LOXWOOD RD

B2133

7

Loxwood Hall

Gennets Wood

Oakhurst Farm

Tokens Farm

33

Thirds Copse

Sydney Farm

OAKHURST LA

6

Lee House Farm

Gennets Wood

The Rookery

Barberry Furze

Sussex Border Path

Barberry Bridge

Gennets Furze

Pawlies Farm

Pond Copse

5

Hog Wood

Oxoncroft Copse

Way-South Path

Gennets Farm

LONG COPSE LA

32

Hog Copse

Furzen Wood

THE RETREAT

B2134

Loxwood

GUILDFORD RD

Hogwood Farm

TOLL BRIDGE LA

THE LANE

BRIDGE LA

THE PARADE

4

Barn Wood

RH14

Devil's Hole

STATION RD

B2133

GLEBELANDS RD

LOXWOOD FARM PL

PINDARS RD

HIGH ST

WILLETT'S WAY

POUNDFIELD LA

HOGWOOD RD

LOXMEADOWS

Wey & Arun Canal

3

CHALK RD

THISTLEDOWN VALE

PANNELLS ASH

Ifold

Loxwoodhills Pond

31

LOXWOOD RD

Charleshurst

THE RIDE

WILDACRE CL

THE CLOSE

BURCHWOOD DR

THE DRIVE

OAK WAY

Quennells Farm

Spring Copse

FOLDHURST

2

Headfoldswood Farm

FOXBRIDGE LA

Corner Copse

PLAISTOW RD

LAKERS LEA

1

Flitchings Farm

ROMAN S LA

Foxbridge Hanger

Foxbridge Farm

CH

Little Headfoldswood Copse

Woodlands Farm

30

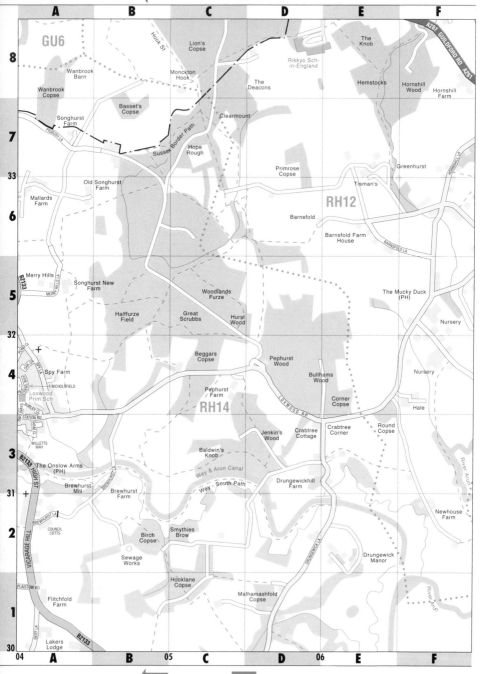

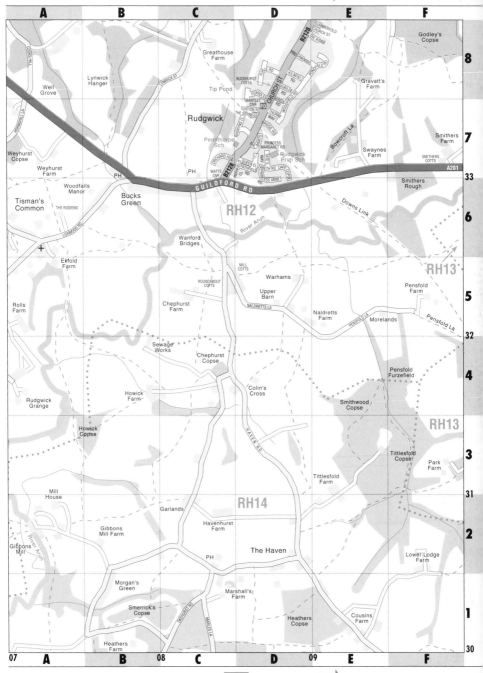

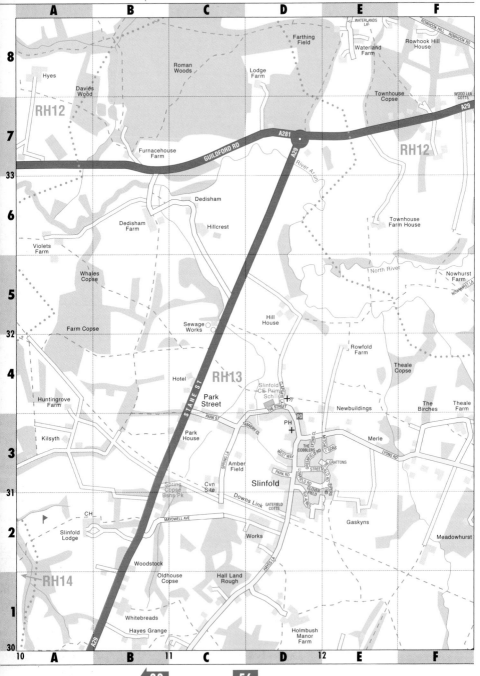

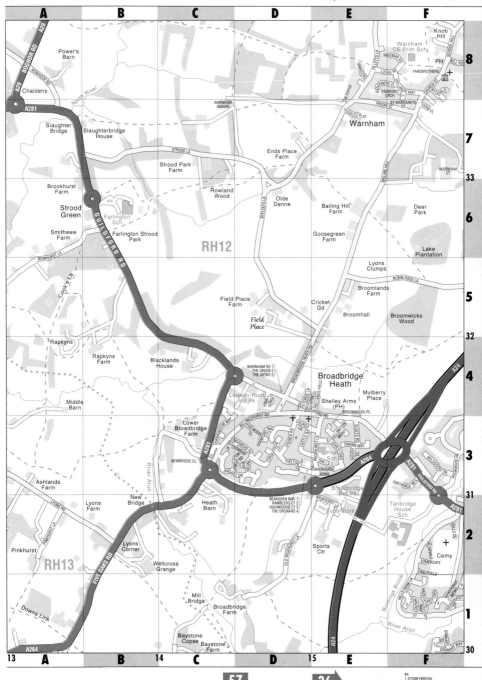

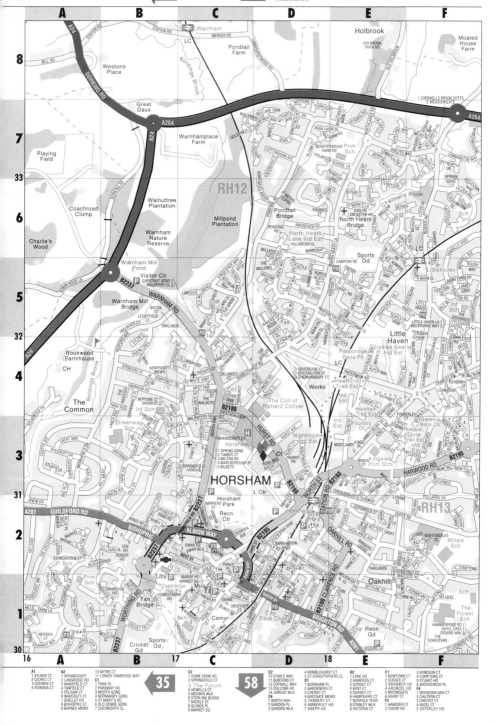

35

15

D5
1 WISTON CT
2 NUTBOURNE CT
3 ARWINGTON CT
4 WARMINGHURST CT
5 MARLBOROUGH CL
6 WOODMANCOTE CT

8

Holbrook

Warnham

Westons
Place

STATION RD
MERCER RD
Pondtail
Farm

MOATED
HOUSE
FARM

Moated
House
Farm

1 CHENNELLS BROOK COTTS
2 MEADOWGATE

A264

Great
Daux

A264

Warnhamplace
Farm

7

Playing
Field

Quarterbrass Prim
Sch

RH12

33

Coachroad
Clump

Walnuttree
Plantation

Millpond
Plantation

Pondtail
Bridge

North Heath
Bridge

Channells Brook

6

Charlie's
Wood

Warnham
Nature
Reserve

North Heath
Lane Ind Est
HOLMBUSH CL

Sports
Gd

Warnham Mill
Pond
Visitor Ctr

The
Willows

LC

Littlehaven

B2237

32

Warnham Mill
Bridge

BROOK
LEGGYFIELD
OAKLANDS

Little
Haven

James Searle
2nd Est

Rookwood
Farmhouse
CH

Parsonage
Bsns Pk

4

The
Common

LC

1 ADVERGANE CT
2 CHILTINGTON CT
3 SHERMANBURY CT

Hawthorn
Trad Est

Works

The Coll of
Richard Collyer

Horsham
Trad Est

B2195

RAVENSCROFT
Horsham

1 SPRING GDNS
2 TIMBER CT
3 MILTON RD
4 MARLBOROUGH CT
5 BILBETS

H

HURST RD

Ind
Est

3

Nightingale
Ind Est

Greenway
Sch

The
WALNUTS

B2180

Foundry
Ct

Genesis
Bsns Ctr

31

HORSHAM

Horsham
Farriers
Park

Kings
Kingsley
Prim Sch

HARWOOD RD

A281

GUILDFORD RD

BISHOPRIC

ALBION WAY

B2231

B2195

STATION RD

B2180

Oakhill

RH13

Nightingales

Millais
Sch

2

B2237

WORTHING RD

WEST ST

MAZURKA
AVE

NORTH ST

CLARENCE RD

OAKHILL RD

Oakhill

The
Forest
Sch

Liby

Tan
Bridge

Manor Ho
Market Ho
Mus

BRIGHTON RD

Recn
Gd

1

Prim
Sch

Tanbridge
Homestream

Cemy

The
Foresters

30

A

B

17

C

D

18

E

F

35

58

A1
1 AYLWIN CT
2 CEDRIC CT
3 GODWIN CT
4 ROWENA CT

B2
1 ARRANCOURT
2 LANGRIDGE HO
3 WAKEFIELD CT
4 TANFIELD CT
5 PELHAM CT
6 WAVERLEY CT
7 SHELLEY HO
8 BISHOPRIC CT
9 BARNES MEWS

10 MITRE CT
11 LOWER TANBRIDGE WAY

C1
1 PARK PL
2 PARKWAY HO
3 MORTH GDNS
4 NORMANDY GDNS
5 ST MARY'S HO
6 OLD DENNE GDNS
7 CHESWORTH CL

C2
1 HOME FARM HO
2 SPRINGFIELD CT
3 The Forum
4 HEWELLS CT
5 MEDWIN WLK
6 STERLING BLDGS
7 MIDDLE ST
8 GLYNDE PL
9 MARKET SQ

10 STAN'S WAY
11 BURTONS CT
12 COPNALL WAY
13 DULCIMA HO
14 JUBILEE WLK

C4
1 NORTH ASH
2 GARDEN PL
3 GARDEN WLK

D2
4 WIMBLEHURST RD
5 ST CHRISTOPHERS CL

D1
1 BURNHAM PL
2 GARDENERS CT
3 CHERRY CT
4 EASTGATE MEWS
5 TANNERY CT
6 AMBERLEY HO
7 KNEPP HO

D2
1 LANE HO
2 HAMPERS CT
3 DORSET CT
4 KENT CT
5 SURREY CT
6 HAMPSHIRE CT
7 NORFOLK TERR
8 STANLEY WLK
9 VICTORIA CT

E1
1 NEWTOWN CT
2 SUSSEX CT
3 BRAMBER HO
4 ARUNDEL HO
5 MOONSGATE
6 ASHBY CT

F3
1 HANOVER CT
2 TUDOR HO

3 WINDSOR CT
4 COMPTONS CT
5 STUART HO
6 WATERCRESS PL

F4
1 MOUNTAIN ASH CT
2 CHELTERN CT
3 CHEVIOT CT
4 HAZEL CT
5 OSTERLEY HO

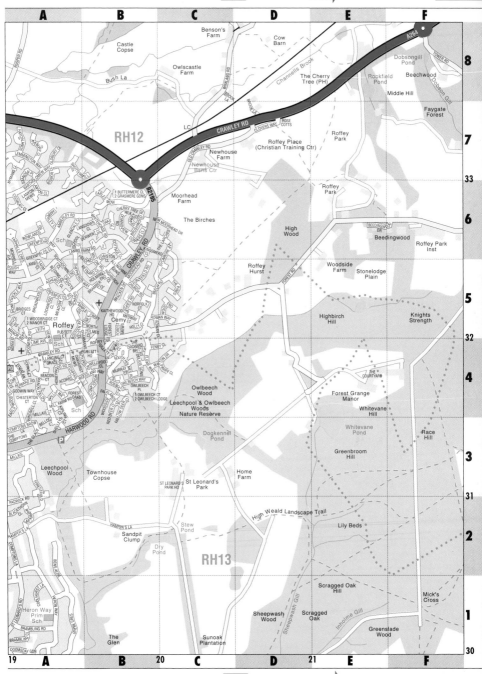

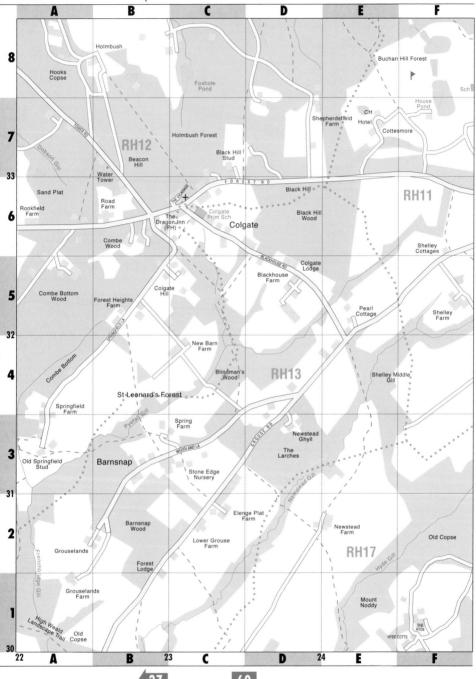

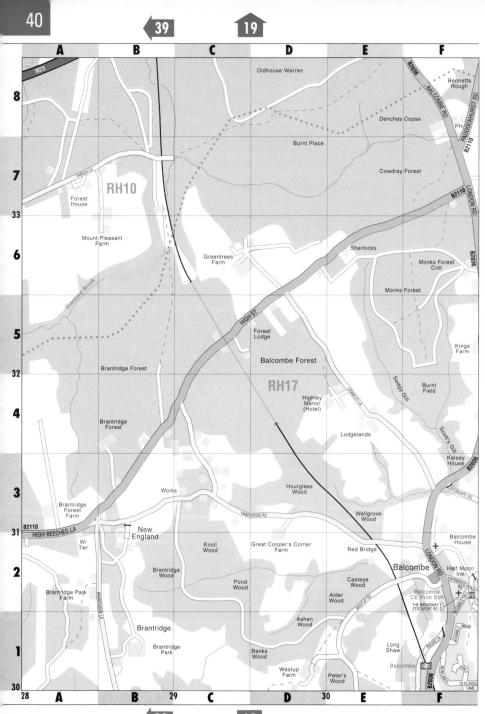

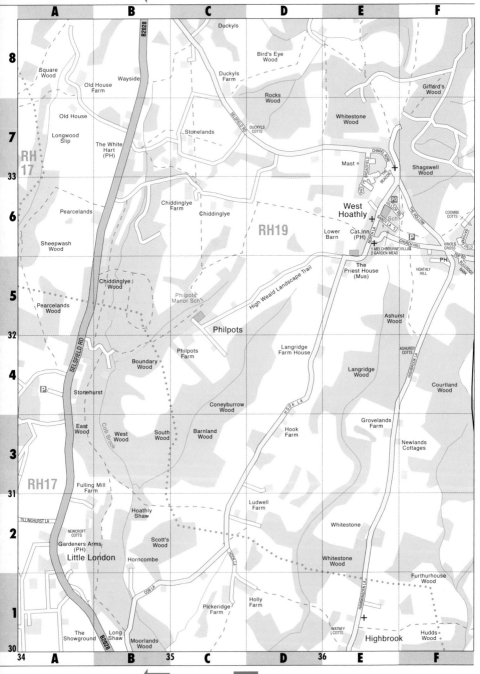

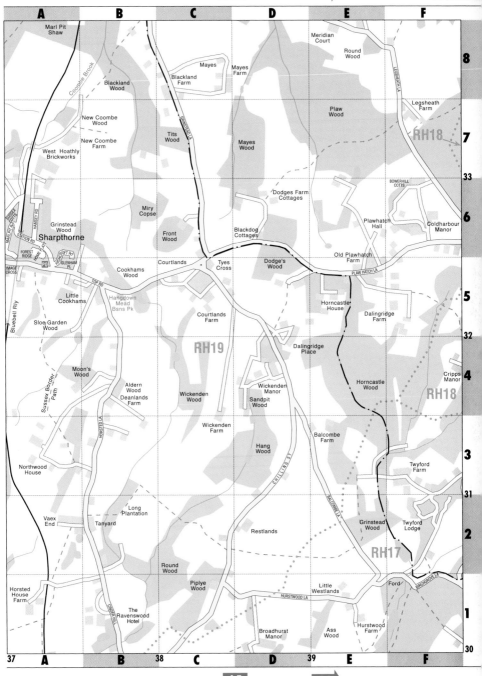

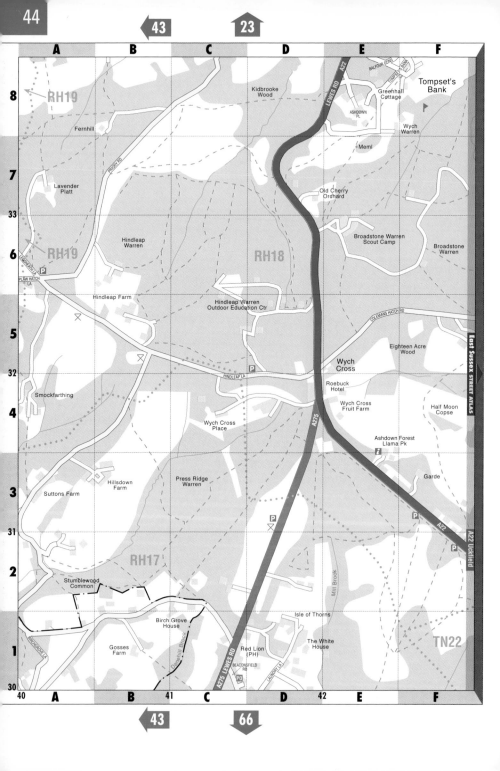

A **B** **C** **D** **E** **F**

8

RH19

Kidbrooke
Wood

LEWES RD

A22

BALFOUR GDNS

TORPES BANK

Greenhall
Cottage

Tompset's
Bank

Fernhill

ASHDOWN
PL

Wych
Warren

7

Lavender
Platt

PRIORY RD

Meml

Old Cherry
Orchard

Wych
Warren

33

Hindleap
Warren

RH19

RH18

Broadstone Warren
Scout Camp

Broadstone
Warren

6

LEWES RD

P

PLAW HATCH
LA

Hindleap Farm

Hindleap Warren
Outdoor Education Ctr

COLEMANS HATCH RD

Eighteen Acre
Wood

East Sussex STREET ATLAS

5

P

HINDLEAP LA

Wych
Cross

32

Smockfarthing

Roebuck
Hotel

Wych Cross
Fruit Farm

Half Moon
Copse

4

Wych Cross
Place

A275

Ashdown Forest
Llama Pk

i

Garde

3

Suttons Farm

Hillsdown
Farm

Press Ridge
Warren

P

P

A22

A22 Uckfield

31

RH17

P

2

Stumblewood
Common

Mill Brook

Isle of Thorns

TN22

1

SPRINGETT LA

Gosses
Farm

Birch Grove
House

Ditchling Brook

A275 LEWES RD

Red Lion
(PH)

BEACONSFIELD
RD

LASHOFT LA

The White
House

30

40 **A** **B** **41** **C** **D** **42** **E** **F**

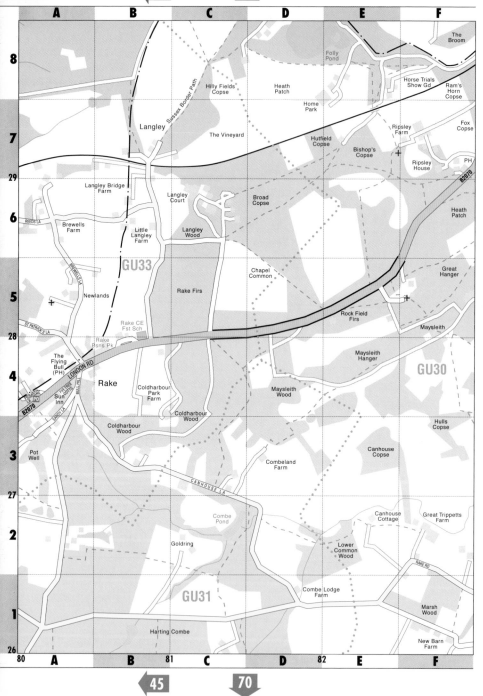

A **B** **C** **D** **E** **F**

8

Wheatsheaf
Enclosure

Iron Hill

Lower End
Plantation

B2070

Sussex Border Path

Shufflesheeps

CH

Hollycombe
Steam
Collection

VICTORIA PL

7

Wheatsheaf
Common

Hatch Birch Piece

Hollycombe

Hatch
Fir

Hatch
Farm

Hillands
Plantations

29

Hollycombe
Hanger

Wardley
Hanger

Hirtwell

6

Wardley
Moor

Upper
Wardley

Home
Farm

Tank Copse

Milland
House

Milland
Place
(Hotel)

Hatch
Hanger

GU30

Becksfield
Farm

5

Ford

Elmers
Copse

28

MILLARD LA

Crockers
Wood

Wardley

WARDLEY
COTTS

Bembrook

4

Wardley
Farm

Wardley
Marsh

Hollycombe
Prim Sch

Northend
Farm

Northend
Copse

Hammer Stream

Mill Farm

FERNHURST RD

Old Moor
Copse

3

Square
Copse

Martin's
Copse

Alfords
Farm

Slathurst
Pond

VANN VALE MDWS

Cartersland

The
Rising
Sun
(PH)

Milland
Marsh

27

Slathurst
Farm

FERNHURST RD

2

STRETTONS CL

FIELD PLACE CL

FIELD VIEW

HARBUER LA

Milland

Hurst
Farm

Lambourne
Copse

Churchfield
Row

Chorley
Common

RAKE RD

Waldergrove
Farm

PINE RD

Inholms
Copse

1

Cook's
Pond

GU29

COOK'S POND RD

Weston's
Farm

Lyford
Farm

26

83 **A** **B** 84 **C** **D** 85 **E** **F**

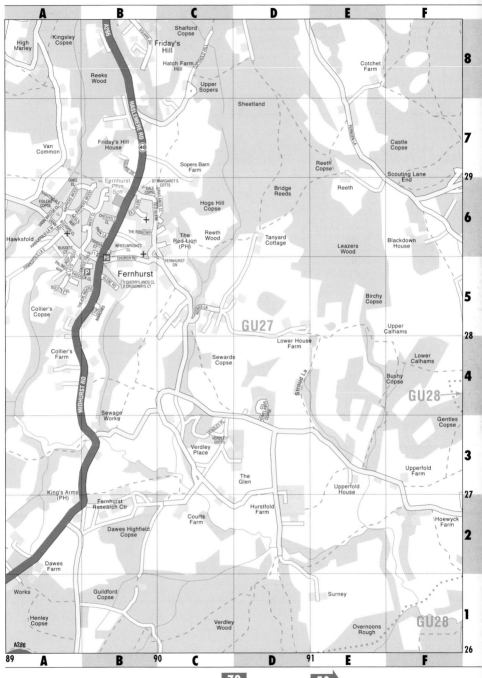

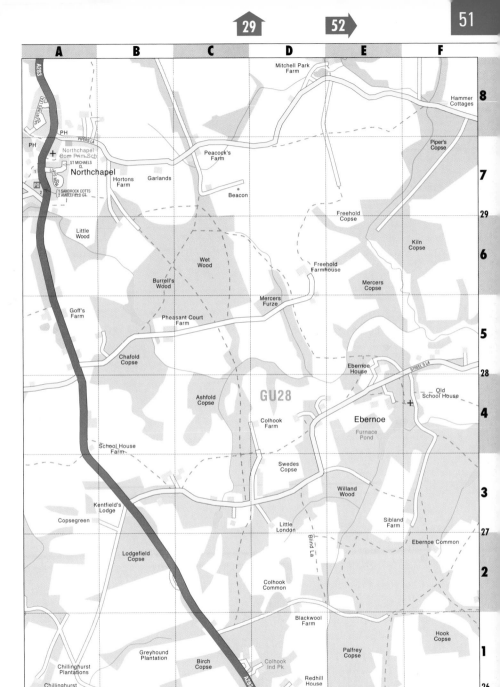

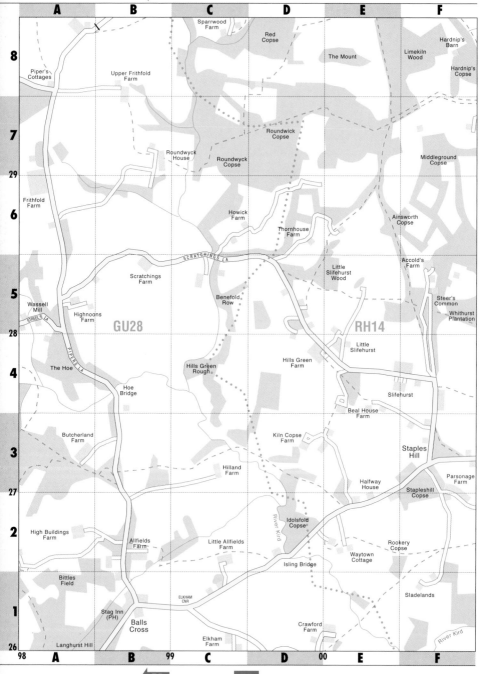

A   **B**   **C**   **D**   **E**   **F**

Sparrwood Farm

Red Copse

Hardnip's Barn

Limekiln Wood

The Mount

Hardnip's Copse

8

Piper's Cottages

Upper Frithfold Farm

Roundwick Copse

Middleground Copse

7

Roundwyck House

Roundwyck Copse

29

Frithfold Farm

Howick Farm

Ainsworth Copse

6

Thornhouse Farm

SCRATCHINGS LA

Little Slifehurst Wood

Accold's Farm

Scratchings Farm

Benefold Row

Steer's Common

5

Whithurst Plantation

Wassell Mill

STREEL'S LA

Highnoons Farm

GU28

Little Slifehurst

RH14

28

The Hoe

PIPER'S LA

Hills Green Rough

Hills Green Farm

Slifehurst

4

Hoe Bridge

Beal House Farm

Butcherland Farm

Kiln Copse Farm

Staples Hill

3

Parsonage Farm

Hilland Farm

Halfway House

Stapleshill Copse

27

High Buildings Farm

Idolsfold Copse

Rookery Copse

2

River Kird

Waytown Cottage

Allfields Farm

Little Allfields Farm

Isling Bridge

Bittles Field

Sladelands

1

ELKHAM CNR

Stag Inn (PH)

Balls Cross

Crawford Farm

River Kird

26

Langhurst Hill

Elkham

98   **A**   **B**   **99**   **C**   **D**   **00**   **E**   **F**

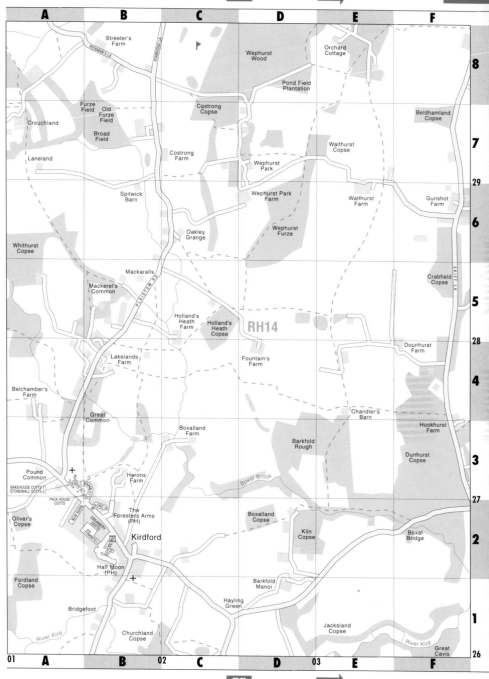

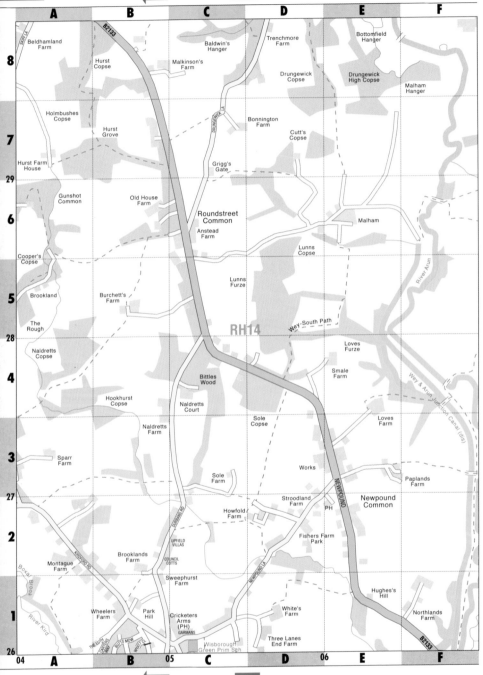

A   B   C   D   E   F

8

Beldhamland
Farm

Hurst
Copse

Baldwin's
Hanger

Malkinson's
Farm

Trenchmore
Farm

Bottomfield
Hanger

Drungewick
Copse

Drungewick
High Copse

Malham
Hanger

Holmbushes
Copse

Hurst
Grove

Bonnington
Farm

Cutt's
Copse

7

Hurst Farm
House

Grigg's
Gate

29

Gunshot
Common

Old House
Farm

Roundstreet
Common

Anstead
Farm

Malham

6

Cooper's
Copse

Lunns
Copse

Brookland

Burchett's
Farm

Lunns
Furze

5

The
Rough

RH14

Wey-South Path

28

Naidretts
Copse

Loves
Furze

Bittles
Wood

Smale
Farm

4

Hookhurst
Copse

Naidretts
Court

Loves
Farm

Naidretts
Farm

Sole
Copse

Sparr
Farm

Works

Paplands
Farm

3

Sole
Farm

27

Stroodland
Farm

Newpound
Common

Howfold
Farm

PH

Brooklands
Farm

UPFIELD
VILLAS

Fishers Farm
Park

2

Montague
Farm

COUNCIL
COTTS

Sweephurst
Farm

Hughes's
Hill

Wheelers
Farm

Park
Hill

Cricketers
Arms
(PH)

White's
Farm

Northlands
Farm

1

GARMANS

Wisborough
Green Prim Sch

Three Lanes
End Farm

26

04   A   B   05   C   D   06   E   F

B2133

River Arun

Wey & Arun Junction Canal (dis)

Boxal Brook

River Kird

NEWPOUND

NEWPOUND LA

DUNGATE LA

KIRDFORD RD

DURBANS RD

B2133

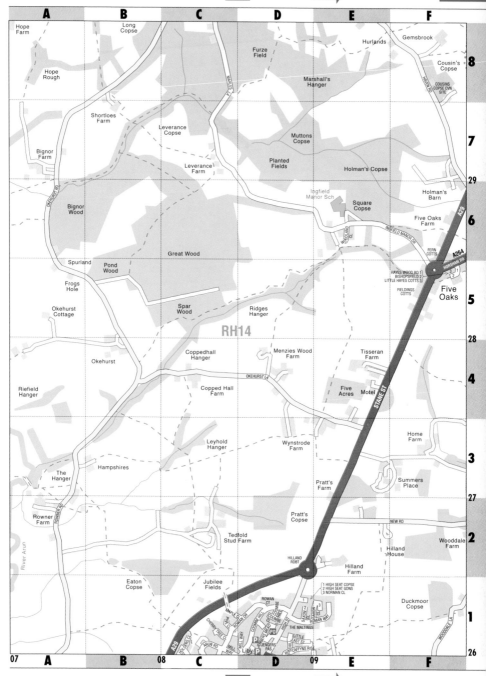

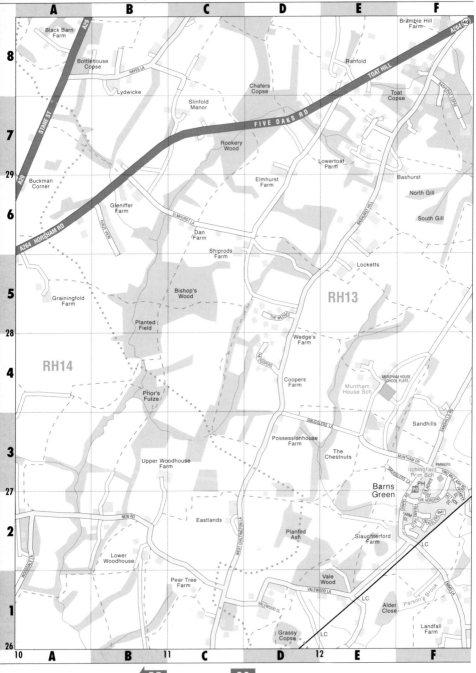

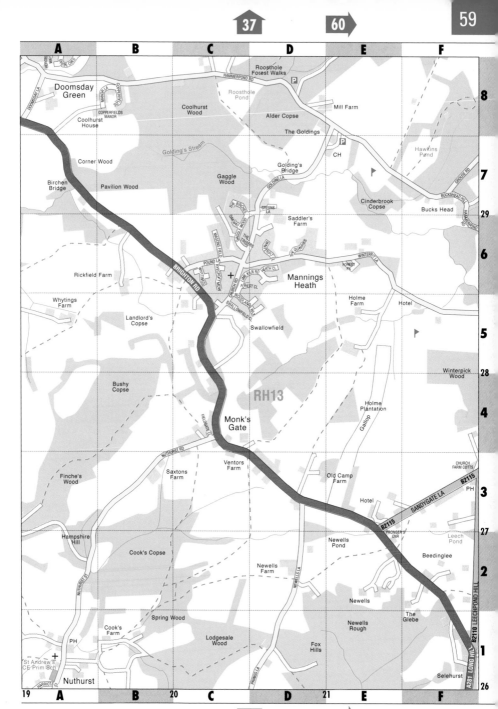

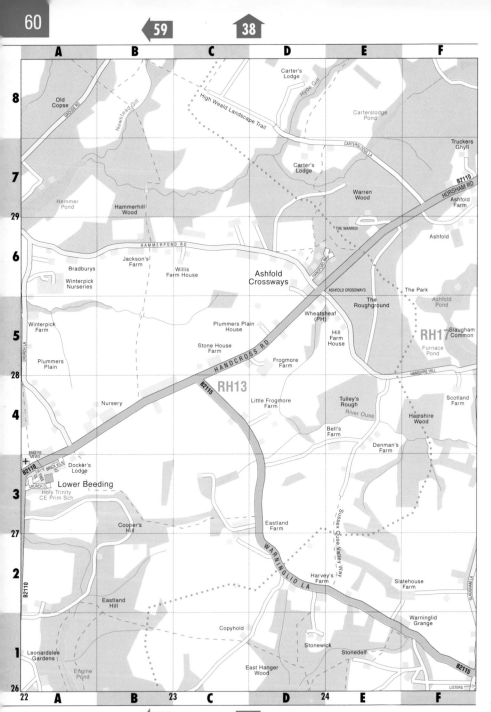

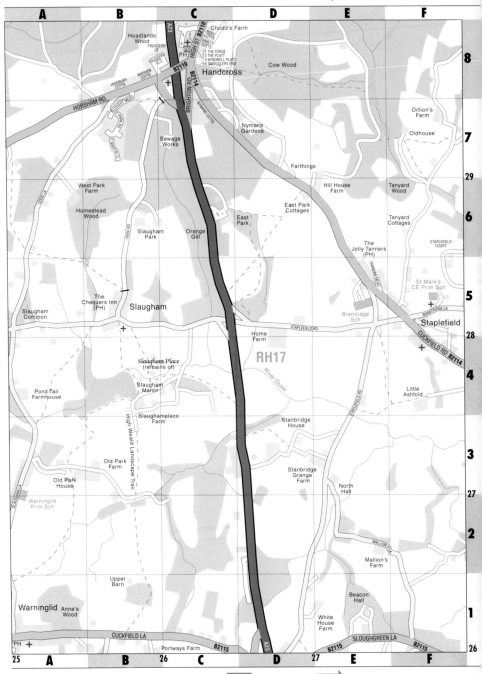

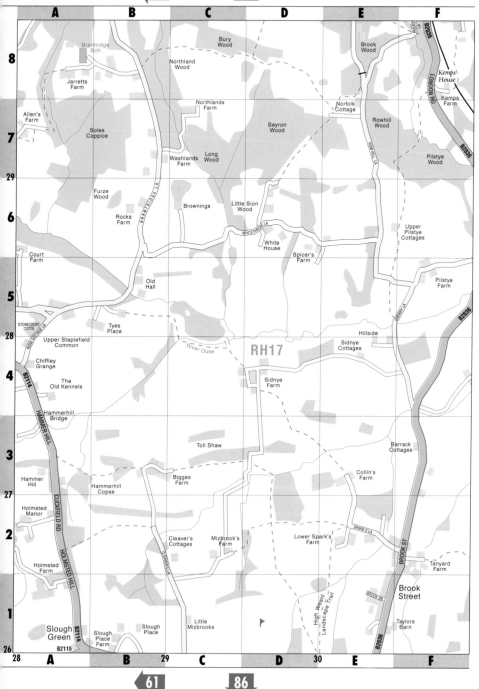

A   B   C   D   E   F

8

Brantridge Sch

Northland Wood

Bury Wood

Brook Wood

Kemps House

LONDON RD

Jarretts Farm

Northlands Farm

Norfolk Cottage

Kemps Farm

B2036

Allen's Farm

7

Soles Coppice

Seyron Wood

Rowhill Wood

Pilstye Wood

29

Furze Wood

Washlands Farm

Long Wood

6

Rocks Farm

Brownings

Little Sion Wood

WHITETHORN LA

Upper Pilstye Cottages

BRANTRIDGE LA

White House

Spicer's Farm

Court Farm

Old Hall

Pilstye Farm

5

STONECOURT COTTS

Tyes Place

Hillside

28

Upper Staplefield Common

River Ouse

RH17

Sidnye Cottages

Chiffley Grange

Sidnye Farm

4

B2114

The Old Kennels

HAMMER HILL

Hammerhill Bridge

Toll Shaw

Barrack Cottages

3

Hammer Hill

Hammerhill Copse

Bigges Farm

Collin's Farm

27

Holmsted Manor

CUCKFIELD RD

2

Cleaver's Cottages

Mizbrook's Farm

Lower Spark's Farm

SPARK'S LA

BROOK ST

Tanyard Farm

Holmsted Farm

HOLMSTED HILL

BROOK GN

Brook Street

1

Slough Green

B2114

Slough Place Farm

Slough Place

Little Mizbrooks

High Weald Landscape Trail

Taylors Barn

26

B2115

B2036

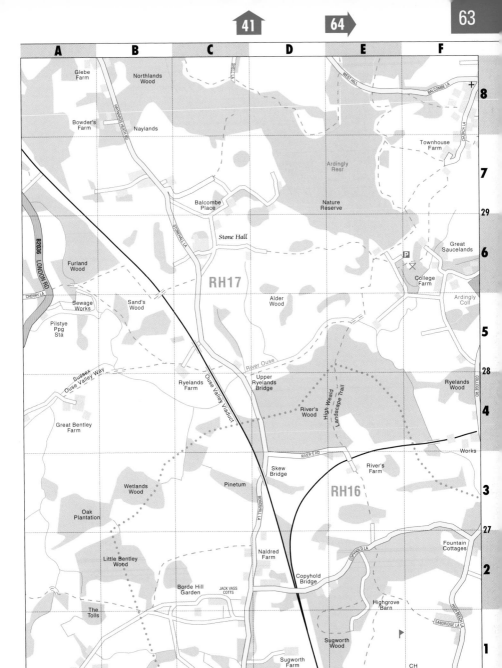

8

7

29

6

5

28

4

3

27

2

26

1

A B C D E F

Glebe Farm

Northlands Wood

WEST HILL

BALCOMBE LA

Bowder's Farm

Naylands

HAYWARDS HEATH RD

Townhouse Farm

Ardingly Resr

Nature Reserve

Balcombe Place

STONEHALL LA

Stone Hall

RH17

Great Saucelands

College Farm

Ardingly Coll

B2036 LONDON RD

Furland Wood

Sewage Works

Sand's Wood

Alder Wood

CHURCH LA

CHERRY LA

Pilstye Ppg Sta

P

River Ouse

Sussex Ouse Valley Way

Ryelands Farm

Upper Ryelands Bridge

River's Wood

High Weald Landscape Trail

Ryelands Wood

COLLEGE RD

Great Bentley Farm

Ouse Valley Viaduct

Works

RIVER'S RD

River's Farm

Skew Bridge

Wetlands Wood

Pinetum

RH16

BORDE HILL LA

Oak Plantation

Fountain Cottages

COPYHOLD LA

Little Bentley Wood

Naldred Farm

Copyhold Bridge

Highgrove Barn

HIGH BEECH LA

Borde Hill Garden

JACK VASS COTTS

SANDRIDGE LA

The Tolls

Sugworth Wood

CH

Lullings Farm

Sugworth Farm

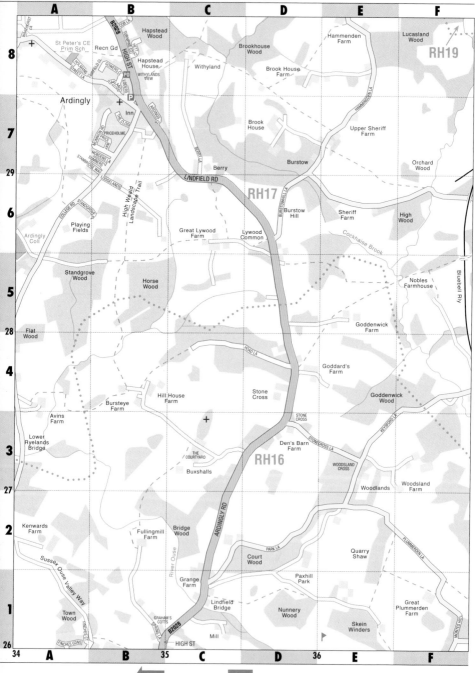

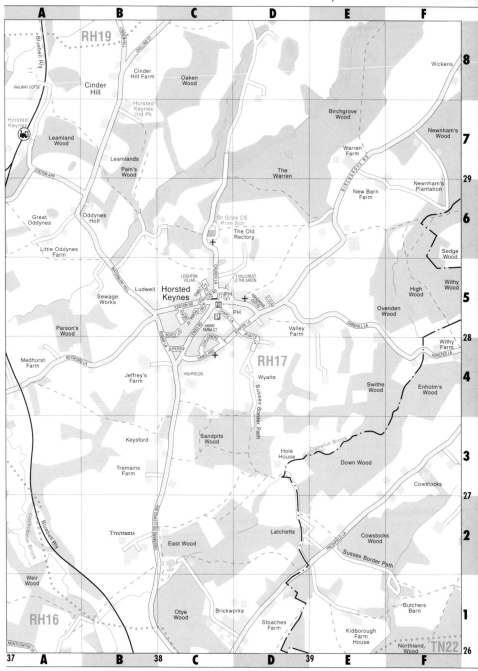

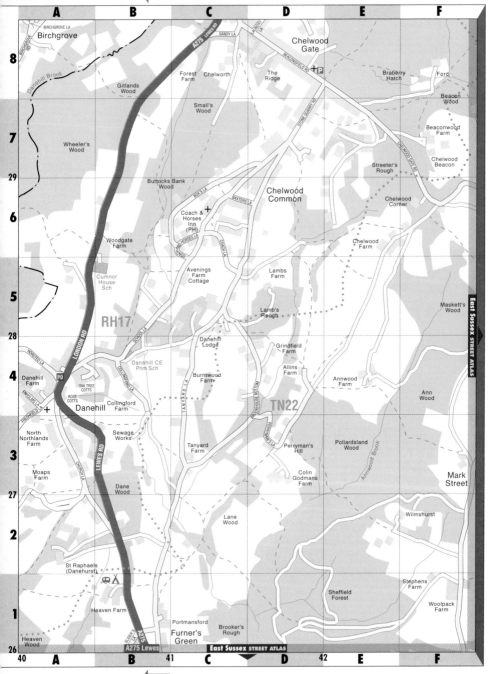

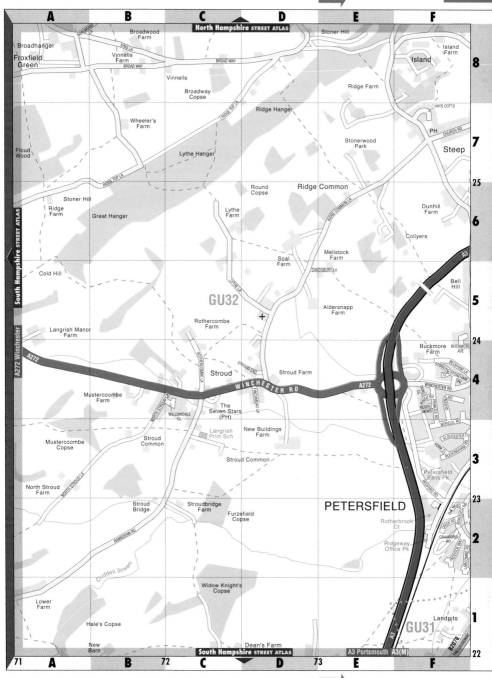

A   **B**   **C**   **D**   **E**   **F**

Broadhanger

Froxfield
Green

Broadwood
Farm

Stoner Hill

Island
Farm

Island

8

Vinnells
Farm

Broad Way

Broad Way

SOALWOOD LA

KING LA

Vinnells

Broadway
Copse

Ridge Farm

HAYS COTTS

PH

CHURCH RD

Steep

7

Wheeler's
Farm

Ridge Hanger

Stonerwood
Park

RIDGE TOP LA

Flood
Wood

Lythe Hanger

Round
Copse

Ridge Common

RIDGE COMMON LA

Dunhill
Farm

25

Stoner Hill

RIDGE TOP LA

Ridge
Farm

Great Hanger

Lythe
Farm

Collyers

6

South Hampshire STREET ATLAS

Cold Hill

Soal
Farm

Mellstock
Farm

SANDISBURY LA

Bell
Hill

A3

5

GU32

LYTHE LA

Aldersnapp
Farm

+

Langrish Manor
Farm

Rothercombe
Farm

Buckmore
Farm

BUCKMORE
AVE

STONEHAM

STONEHAM LA

BECKHAM LA

24

A272 Winchester

A272

ROTHERCOMBE LA

STROUD END

Stroud Farm

Stroud

WINCHESTER RD

A272

FINCHDEAN RD

WINCHESTER RD

DRUM LA

PRINCES RD

REGENT
MEWS

NOREUIL RD

4

Mustercoombe
Farm

NORTH STROUD LA

WILLOWDALE
CL

The
Seven Stars
(PH)

New Buildings
Farm

GLOUCESTER C

YORK CL

BUCKINGHAM C

Mustercoombe
Copse

Stroud
Common

Langrish
Prim Sch

Stroud Common

Petersfield
Bsns Pk

3

North Stroud
Farm

NORTH STROUD LA

Stroud
Bridge

Stroudbridge
Farm

Furzefield
Copse

PETERSFIELD

BEDFORD RD

THE MEAD RD

23

RAMSDEAN RD

Rotherbrook
Ct

LOWER RD

CRANFORD
RD

LARKHAM CL

2

Criddell Stream

Ridgeway
Office Pk

PADDOCK WAY

Lower
Farm

Widow Knight's
Copse

Landpits

GU31

1

Hale's Copse

New
Barn

Dean's Farm

A3

B2070

THE HANGERS

22

A3 Portsmouth A3(M)

71   **A**   **B**   **72**   **C**   **D**   **73**   **E**   **F**

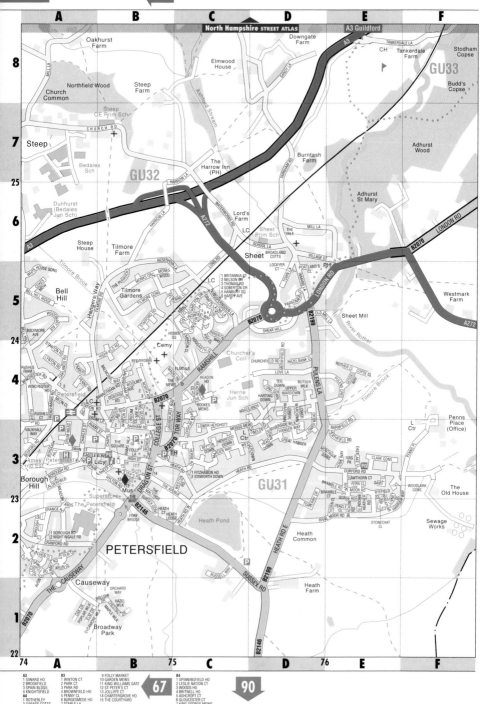

67

A3 Guildford

GU33

Oakhurst Farm

Downgate Farm

Elmwood House

CH Tankerdale Farm

TANKERDALE LA

Stodham Copse

Northfield Wood

Steep Farm

8

Budd's Copse

Church Common

Steep CE Prim Sch

Ashford Stream

Adhurst Wood

CHURCH RD

7

Steep

Burntash Farm

The Harrow Inn (PH)

GU32

25

Adhurst St Mary

Bedales Sch

HARROW LA

Dunhurst (Bedales Jun Sch)

Lord's Farm

WATERLOO RD

Sheet Prim Sch

MILL LA

LONDON RD

B2070

6

Steep House

A272

LC

The Vale

Sheet

MILL LA

Tilmore Farm

SCHOOL LA

Village St

Broadland Cotts

PH

A3

WELL HOUSE GDNS

Tilmore Brook

Hangers Way

Bell Hill

Tilmore Gardens

MONKS WOOD

LC

1 BRITANNIA ST
2 NELSON RD
3 THOMAS RD
4 SOBERTON DR
5 HANBURY SQ
6 HARDY AVE

Lockyer CT

Portland's CL

B2199

OLD MILL LA

Sheet Mill

Westmark Farm

A272

5

BUCKMORE AVE

B2070

SHEAR HILL

River Rother

PARSONS

24

STANTON RD

Cemy

HOBBS SQ

Churcher's Coll

Churchfield RD

HAZEL BANK CL

ROTHER CL

COPSE CL

Tilmore Brook

RUSHES FARM

WINCHESTER RD

WINCHESTER

BELVEDERE CL

ELMDALE

RAMSHILL

Love La

TEG DOWN

BUTSER DOWN

UPPER WARDOWN

Penns Place (Office)

4

Petersfield

STATION RD

READON HO

Herne Jun Sch

HARTING DOWN

HEADLAND

L Ctr

B2070

The Mews

MOGGS MEAD

Hanger Way

LOWER HEYSHOTT

RIVERSIDE WLK

GREAT HANGER

BARNFIELD RD

EASTLAKE CL

CLARE GDNS

3

Borough Hill

SWAN

Liby

Inf Sch

HIGH ST

1 FITZHAMON HO
2 IDSWORTH DOWN

Heath RD

GU31

HAWTHORN CT

DURFORD RD

FERN CL

WOODLARK GDNS

The Old House

Mus

COLLEGE ST

TOR WAY

DRAGON ST

Superstore

The Petersfield Sch

B2146

FORE BRIDGE

Heath CT

Heath Lodge

BRAMBLE RD

MOOR RD

STONECHAT CL

Sewage Works

23

2

1 BOROUGH RD
2 NIGHTINGALE RD

CRANFORD RD

GRANGE RD

Heath Pond

HEATH RD E

Heath Common

PETERSFIELD

THE CAUSEWAY

B2070

Causeway

ORCHARD WAY

WILLOW

HAZEL WLK

B2199

SUSSEY RD

Heath Farm

1

RUSSELL WAY

Broadway Park

B2146

22

67

90

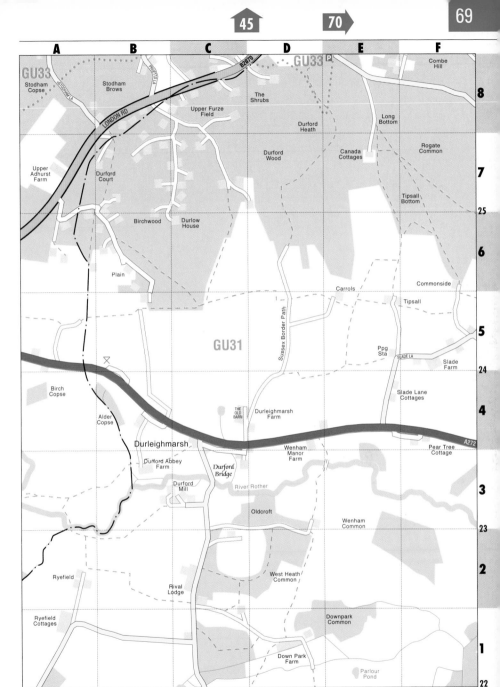

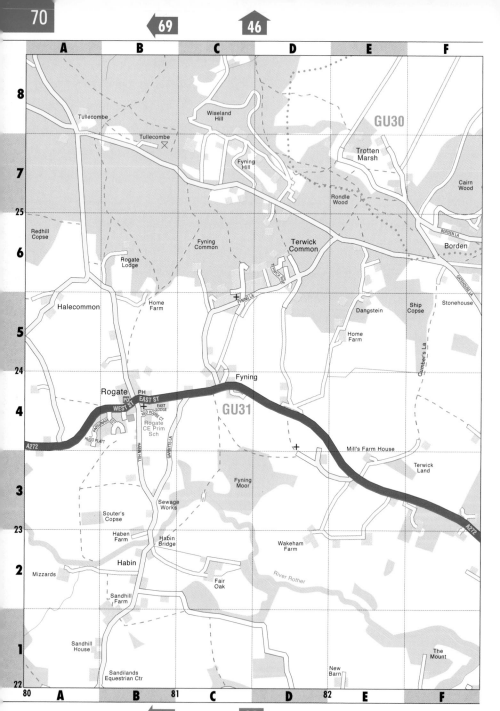

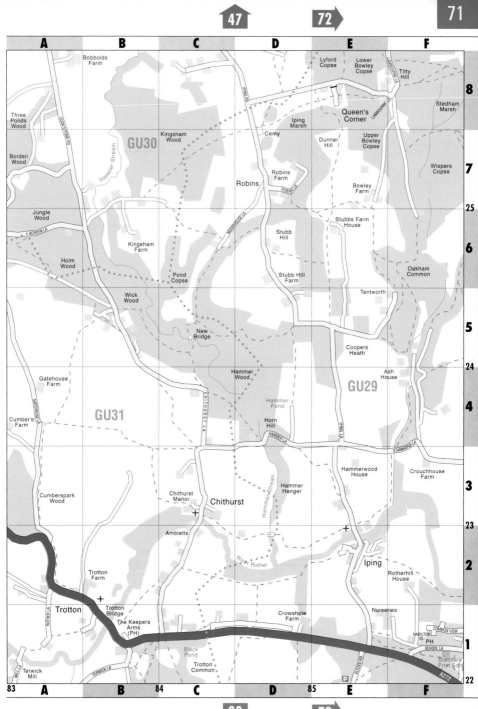

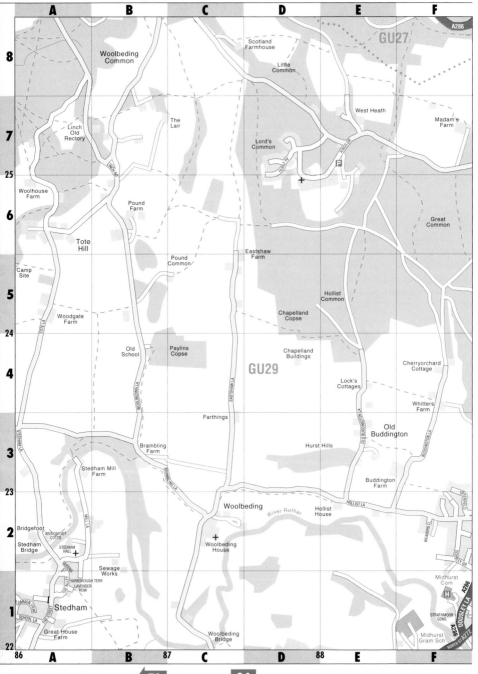

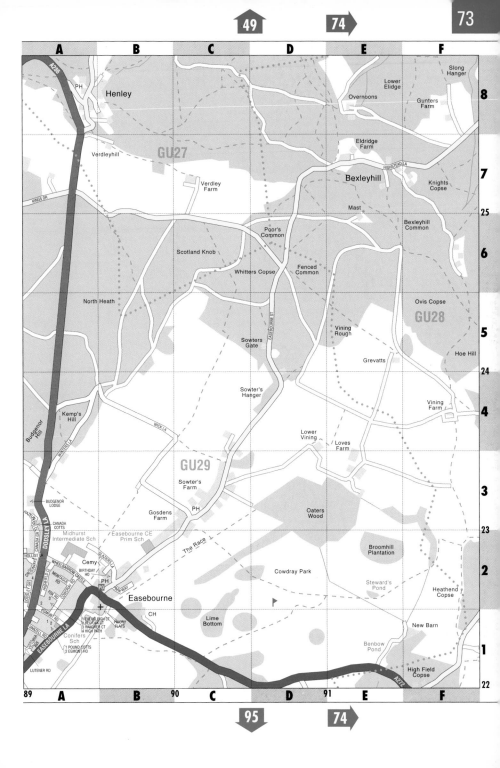

A   B   C   D   E   F

8

GU27

Henley

PH

Verdleyhill

Verdley
Farm

7

25

Lower
Elidge

Overnoons

Slong
Hanger

Gunters
Farm

Eldridge
Farm

HIGHSTEAD LA

Bexleyhill

Mast

Knights
Copse

Bexleyhill
Common

Poor's
Common

Scotland Knob

Whitters Copse

Fenced
Common

6

North Heath

Ovis Copse

GU28

Sowters
Gate

EASEBOURNE ST

Vining
Rough

5

24

Grevatts

Hoe Hill

Sowter's
Hanger

Vining
Farm

4

Kemp's
Hill

WICK LA

Lower
Vining

Loves
Farm

BUDGENOR Hill

WINTERS LA

GU29

Sowter's
Farm

PH

Oaters
Wood

3

23

BUDGENOR
LODGE

CANADA
COTTS

Gosdens
Farm

Midhurst
Intermediate Sch

Easebourne CE
Prim Sch

The Race

Broomhill
Plantation

Cowdray Park

Steward's
Pond

Heathend
Copse

2

DODSLEY LA

HAZELWT

CANADA GR

CROSSFIELD

HIGHFIELD CT

MONTAGUE
RD

FOX RD

Cemy

BIRTHDAY
HO

WHEELBARROW
CASTLE

PH

BLAXERS LA

PO

ST ANNS WAY

Easebourne

CH

Lime
Bottom

New Barn

HOLLIST

DODGE LA

EGMONT RD

VICTORIA

VANCELL RD

EASEBOURNE LA

Conifers
Sch

1 EVERSLEIGH CT
2 REDOAK CT
3 HADLEIGH CT
4 HIGH PATH

1 POUND COTTS
2 EGMONT HO

PRIORY
FLATS

A272

Benbow
Pond

High Field
Copse

1

22

LUTENER RD

89   A   B   90   C   D   91   E   F

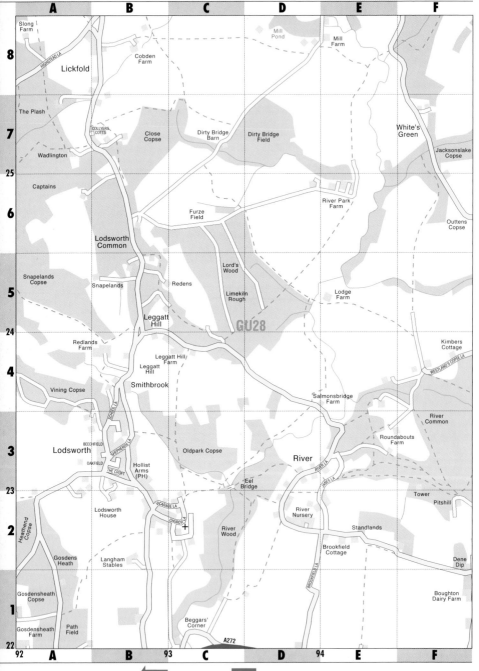

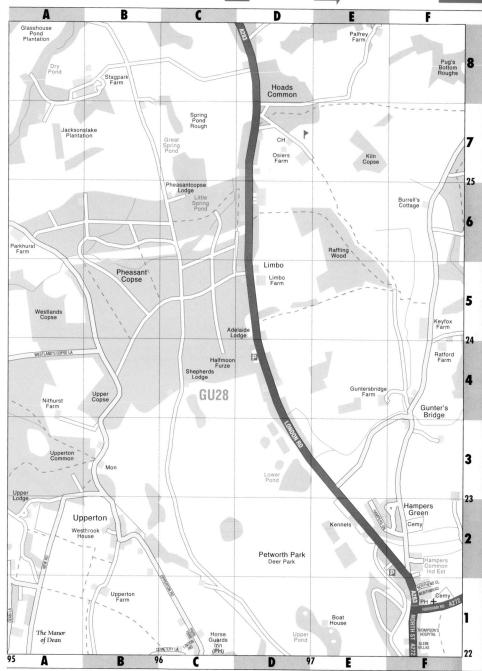

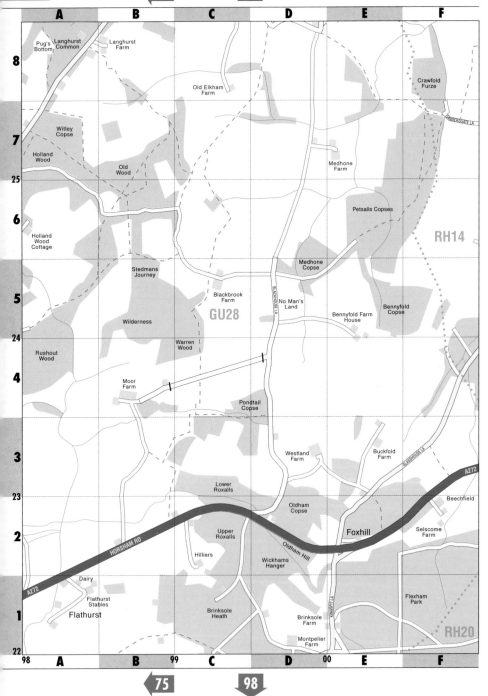

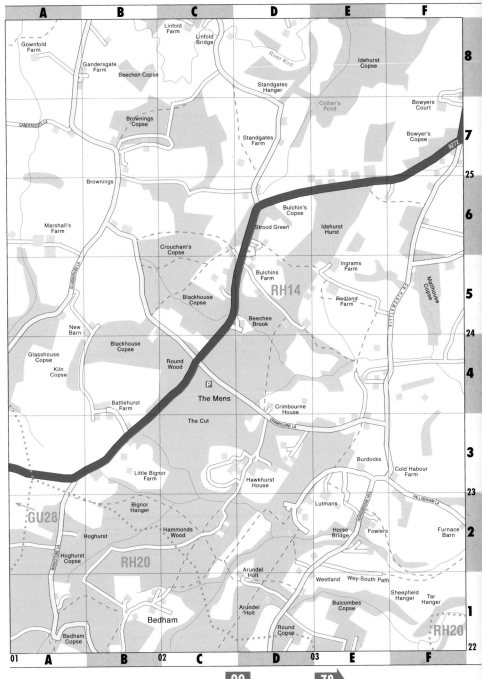

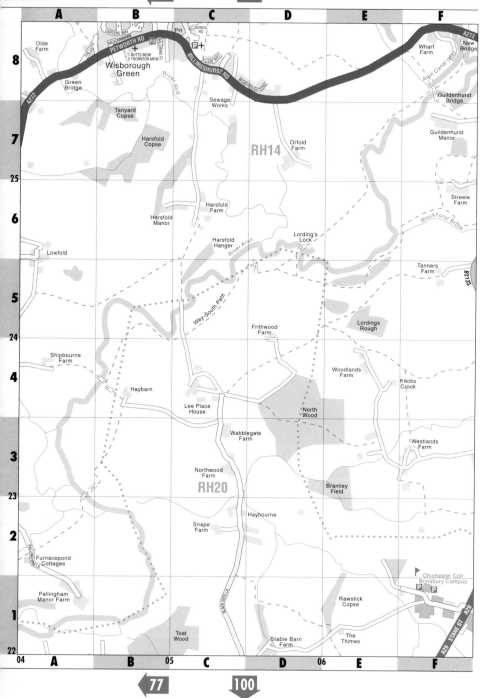

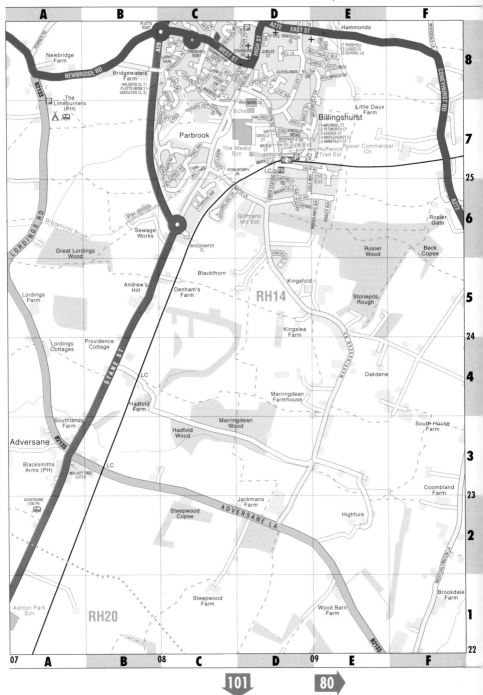

A B C D E F

8

Rowfold
Grange

Woodhouse
Copse

Duncan's
Farm

Hook
Farm

Bullbrook
House
Farm

Courtland's
Farm

BASS LA

BROOKS
GREEN
PK
(CVN PK)

Ten Acre
Copse

Bouges
Farm

7

Rowfold
Farm

25

Valelands
Farm

Brooks Green

LACKENHURST LA

THORN LA

6

A272

Fewhurst
Farm

Palmer's
Farm

RH14

WEST CHILTINGTON LA

Emmetts
Farm

Chivers
Farm

CONEYHURST RD

Kettles
Bridge

5

Court
Farm

Court
Plantation

Purveyor's
Farm

Copyhold
Farm

24

Coneyhurst

RH13

Rainbow
Farm

COOLHAM RD

4

Daniels
Farm

Coolham
House

Slaughter
Bridge
Farm

WEST CHILTINGTON LA

Coneyhurst
Farm

Thornhill
Farm

Lower
Barn

River Adur

Hoe's
Farm

Balls
Green

3

Mast

Snowhill
Farm

Bailey's
Farm

MILL LA

23

The
Blue Idol

Hillside
Farm

WISTERIA
PL

William Penn
Sch

Hoe's
Bridge

A272

OLDHOUSE LA

Patman's
Farm

DORSET
HO

St Cuthmans

2

Coolham

B2139

The
Selsey Arms
(PH)

Oldhouse
Farm

1

Bridge Hill
Farm

COOLHAM RD

Goringlee

22

B2139

Oldhouse
Gorse

10 A B 11 C D 12 E F

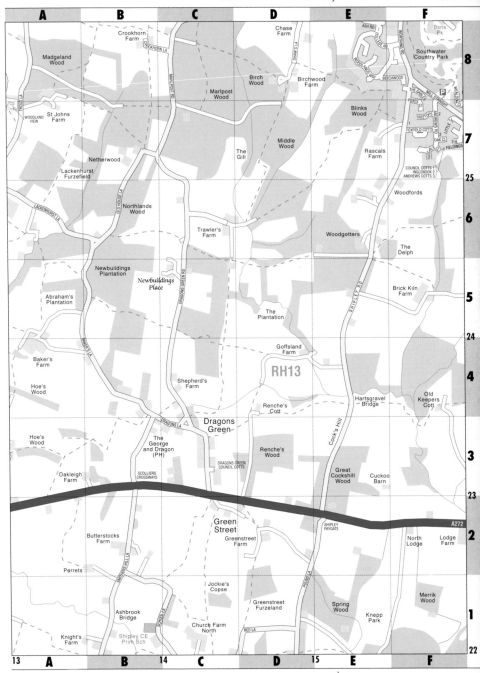

81
58

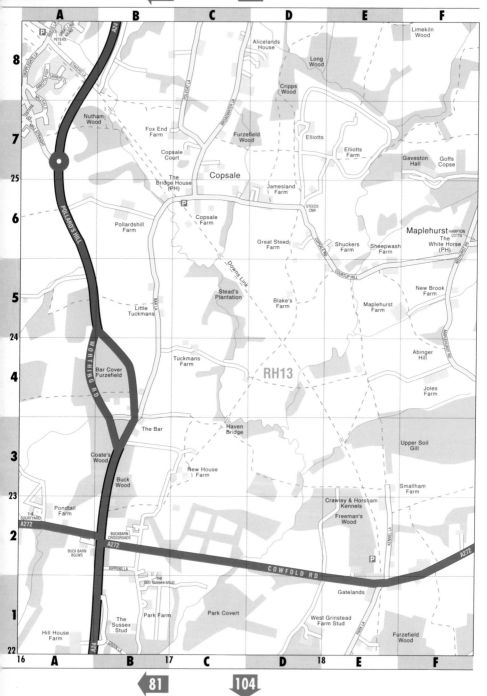

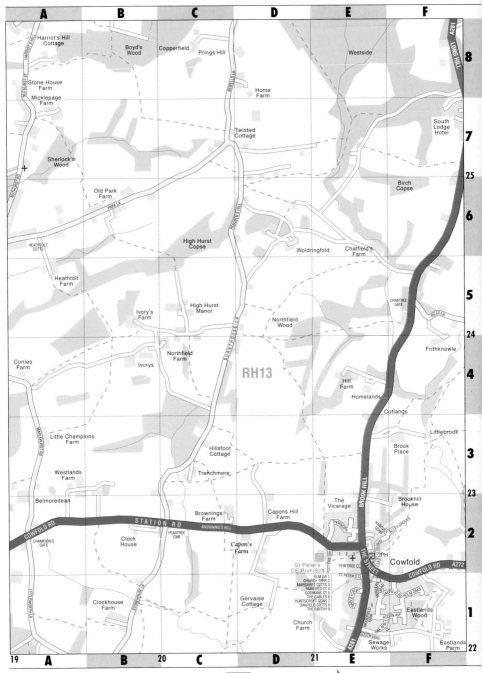

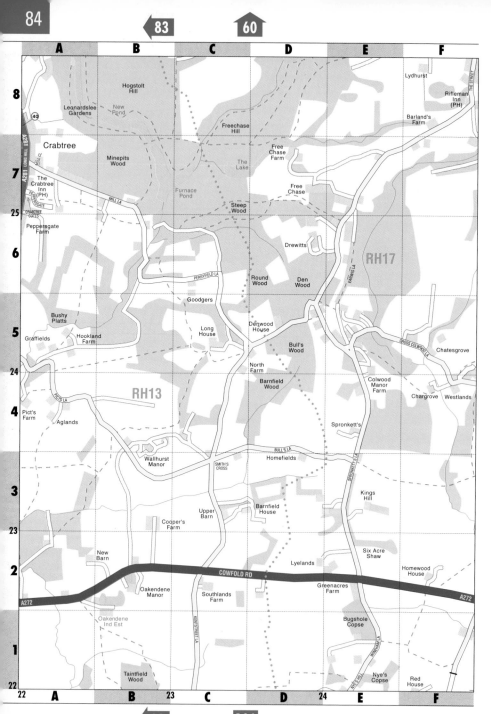

83
60

A **B** **C** **D** **E** **F**

8

Lydhurst

Hogstolt
Hill

Rifleman
Inn
(PH)

THE STREET

Leonardslee
Gardens

New
Pond

Freechase
Hill

Barland's
Farm

40

Crabtree

Minepits
Wood

Free
Chase
Farm

The
Lake

RH17

7

MILL CL

A281

LONG HILL

The
Crabtree
Inn (PH)

MILL LA

Furnace
Pond

Free
Chase

PECKSGATE

CRABTREE
DELLS

25

Steep
Wood

Peppersgate
Farm

Drewitts

6

PERRYFIELD LA

Round
Wood

Den
Wood

BARING LA

Goodgers

Bushy
Platts

Long
House

Denwood
House

Bull's
Wood

CROSS COLWOOD LA

Chatesgrove

5

Graffields

Hookland
Farm

North
Farm

Barnfield
Wood

Colwood
Manor
Farm

Chargrove

Westlands

24

RH13

PIC'S LA

Spronkett's

4

Pict's
Farm

Aglands

BULL'S LA

Homefields

SPRONKETT'S LA

Kings
Hill

3

Wallhurst
Manor

SMITH'S
CROSS

Upper
Barn

Barnfield
House

23

Cooper's
Farm

New
Barn

Six Acre
Shaw

Homewood
House

2

A272

COWFOLD RD

Lyelands

Greenacres
Farm

A272

Oakendene
Manor

Southlands
Farm

KENT STREET LA

Bugshole
Copse

Oakendene
Ind Est

NYE'S HILL

WINEHAM LA

1

Taintfield
Wood

Nye's
Copse

Red
House

22

A 23 **B** **C** 24 **D** **E** **F**

83
106

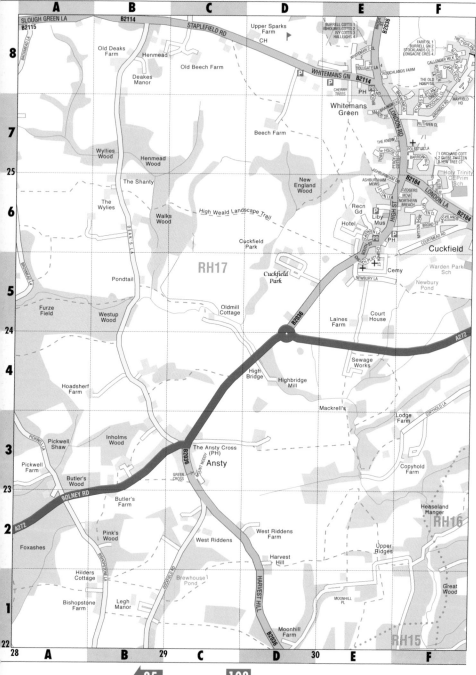

85
62

A **B** **C** **D** **E** **F**

SLOUGH GREEN LA

B2115

B2114

STAPLEFIELD RD

Upper Sparks Farm

CH

BURRELL COTTS 1
INHOLMES COTTS 2
IVY COTTS 3
HALLEIGHS 4

B2036

FARR GN 1
BURRELL GN 2
STOCKLANDS CL 3
LONGACRE CRES 4.

CALLENDER W LK

8

Old Deaks Farm

Henmead

Deakes Manor

Old Beech Farm

WHITEMANS CL

COLLEGATE LA

CRUNCHLANDS FARM

THE HIGHLA

MAYFIELD HO

THE OLD HOSPITAL

WHITEMANS GN

P

CHERRY TREES

B2114

PH

7

Wyllies Wood

Henmead Wood

Beech Farm

Whitemans Green

LONDON RD

THE KNOWL

HOSPITAL

25

The Shanty

New England Wood

ASHBURNHAM DR

POLESHITUILLA

BARROM

Holy Trinity CE Prim Sch

1 ORCHARD COTT
2 GLEBE TWITTEN
3 YEW TREE CT

6

The Wylies

Walks Wood

High Weald Landscape Trail

LEDGERS
MOW
NORTHERN BREACH

B2184

B2184

Recn Gd

P

Liby Mus

Hotel

PH

Cuckfield

25

DELL S LA

Cuckfield Park

Pondtail

Cuckfield Park

Cemy

Warden Park Sch

Newbury Pond

5

Furze Field

Westup Wood

Oldmill Cottage

NEWBURY LA

24

BRIDGE LA

B2036

Laines Farm

Court House

A272

4

Hoadsherf Farm

High Bridge

Highbridge Mill

Sewage Works

Mackrell's

Lodge Farm

3

Pickwell Shaw

Inholms Wood

B2036

MOUNT NOODY

The Ansty Cross (PH)

Ansty

Copyhold Farm

Pickwell Farm

GREEN CROSS

23

Butler's Wood

BOLNEY RD

Butler's Farm

Heeseland Hanger

RH16

2

A272

Pink's Wood

West Riddens Farm

West Riddens

Upper Ridges

Foxashes

Harvest Hill

1

Hilders Cottage

Legh Manor

Brewhouse Pond

HARVEST HILL

MOONHILL PL

Great Wood

Bishopstone Farm

Moonhill Farm

B2036

RH15

22

28 **A** **B** **29** **C** **D** **30** **E** **F**

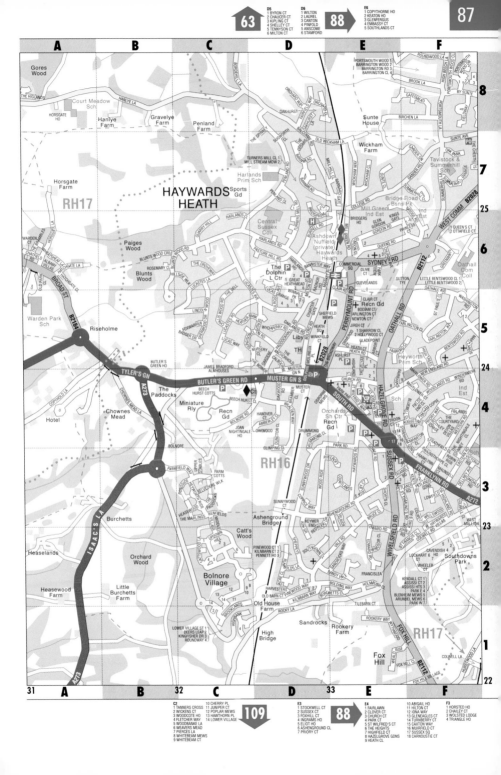

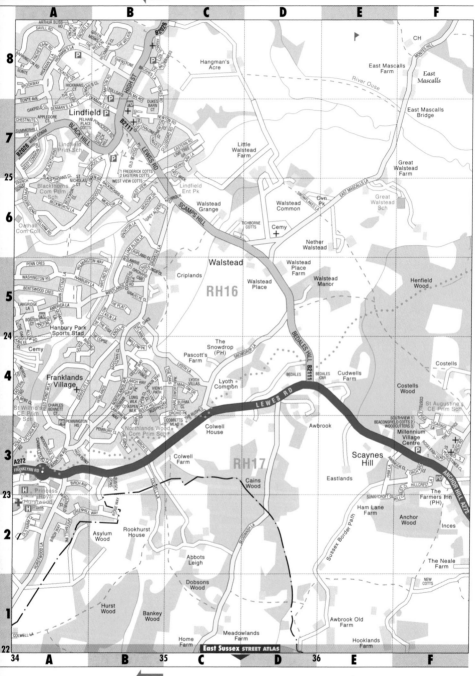

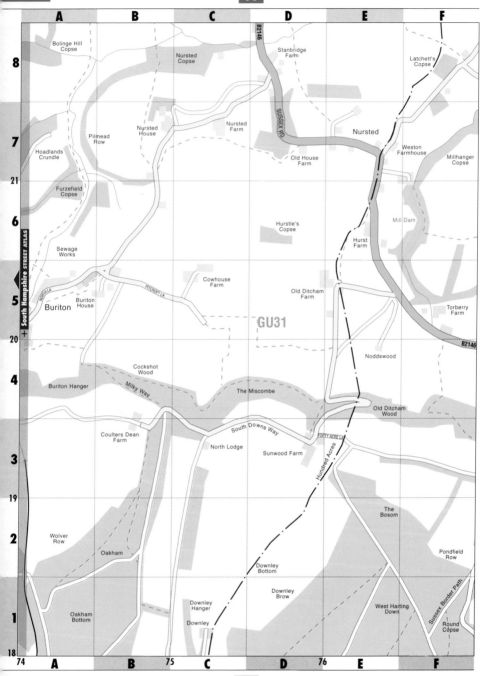

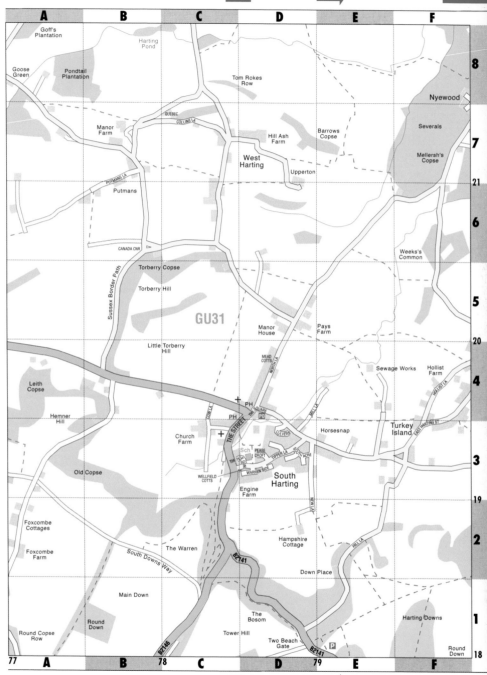

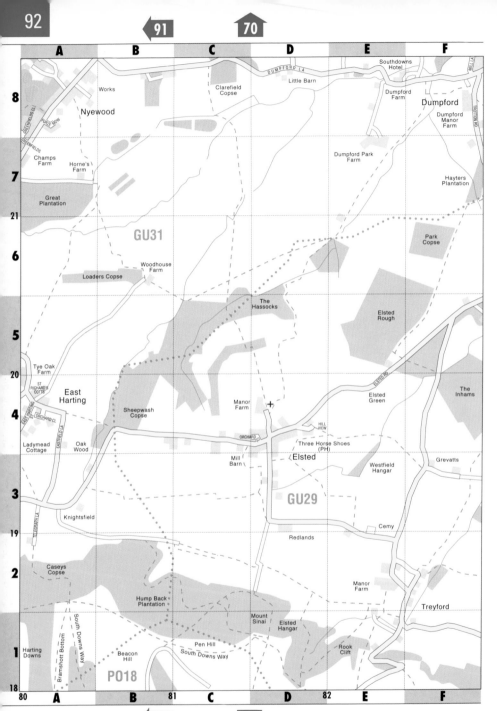

A **B** **C** **D** **E** **F**

8

DUMPFORD LA

Southdowns Hotel

Little Barn

Works

Nyewood

Clarefield Copse

Dumpford Farm

Dumpford

Dumpford Manor Farm

7

Champs Farm

Horne's Farm

Dumpford Park Farm

Hayters Plantation

Great Plantation

21

GU31

Park Copse

6

Woodhouse Farm

Loaders Copse

The Hassocks

Elsted Rough

5

Tye Oak Farm

20

ST RICHARD'S COTTS

East Harting

Sheepwash Copse

Manor Farm

Elsted Green

The Inhams

4

ORCHARD CL

HILL VIEW

Ladymead Cottage

Oak Wood

ORCHARD

Three Horse Shoes (PH)

Grevatts

Mill Barn

Elsted

Westfield Hangar

3

GU29

Knightsfield

TELEGRAPH LA

19

Cemy

Redlands

2

Caseys Copse

Hump Back Plantation

Manor Farm

Treyford

1

Harting Downs

South Downs Way

Bramshott Bottom

Beacon Hill

Pen Hill

South Downs Way

Mount Sinai

Elsted Hangar

Rook Clift

PO18

18

80 **A** **B** 81 **C** **D** 82 **E** **F**

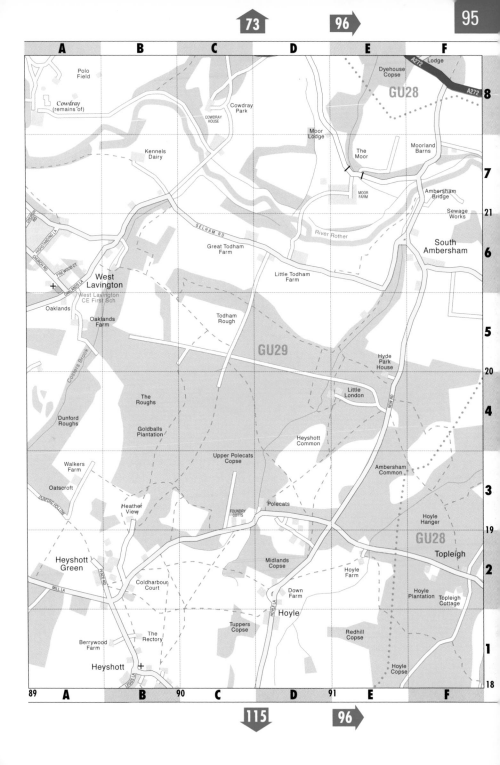

95
74

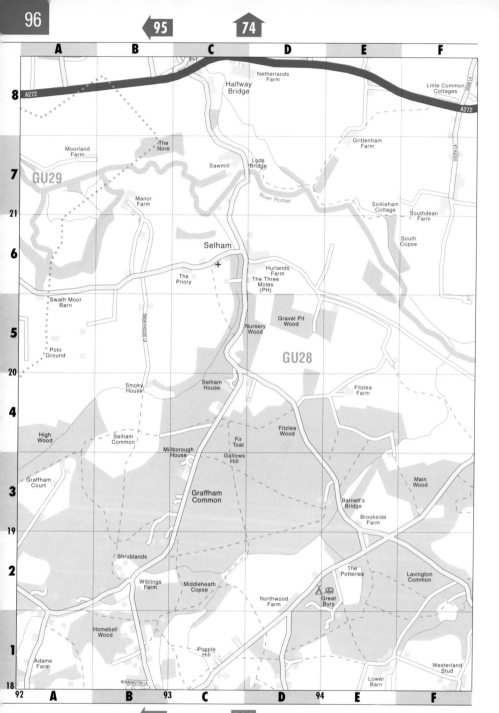

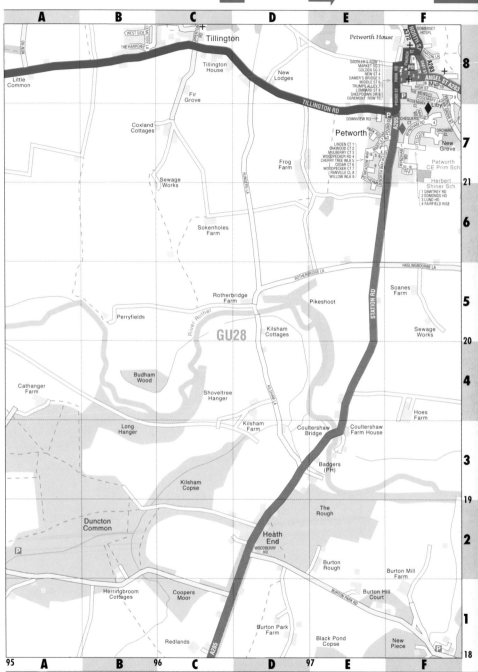

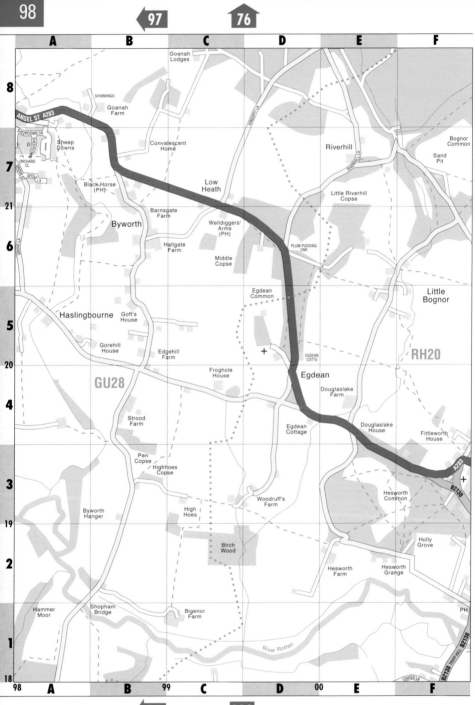

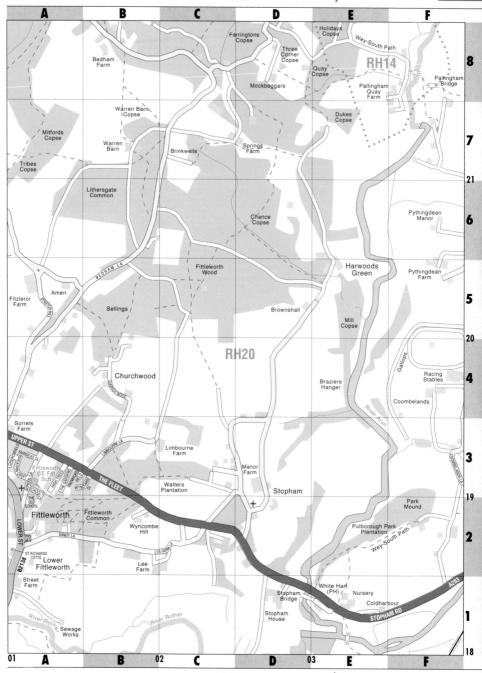

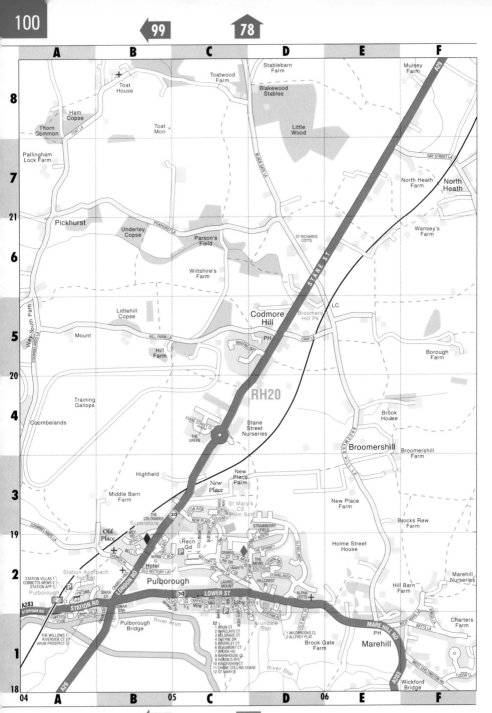

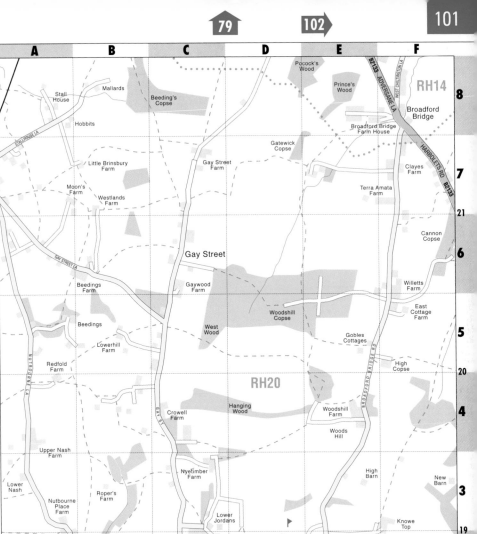

RH14

8

Pocock's Wood

Prince's Wood

Broadford Bridge

Broadford Bridge Farm House

Stall House

Mallards

Beeding's Copse

Hobbits

Gatewick Copse

Little Brinsbury Farm

Gay Street Farm

Clayes Farm

7

Moon's Farm

Terra Amata

Westlands Farm

21

Cannon Copse

Gay Street

6

Beedings Farm

Gaywood Farm

Willetts Farm

East Cottage Farm

Beedings

West Wood

Woodshill Copse

5

Lowerhill Farm

Gobles Cottages

Redfold Farm

High Copse

20

RH20

Hanging Wood

Woodshill Farm

4

Crowell Farm

Woods Hill

Upper Nash Farm

High Barn

New Barn

3

Nyetimber Farm

Lower Nash

Roper's Farm

Lower Jordans

Knowe Top

19

Nutbourne Place Farm

CH

Huntleys Fruit Farm

Nutbourne Place

Oakwood Farm

2

Windmill (dis)

Nutbourne Vineyards

Dennis Marcus Farm

Kings & Princes Farm

Hatches House

West Chiltington

The Rising Sun (PH)

Nutbourne

Hatches Cotts

West Chiltington Com Fst Sch

Nursery

Nurseries

Stream Farm

Meer's Farm

PH

PH

East St

1

Mill Farm Barn

Windmill

Churchfield Farm

Southlands La

Juggs La

18

Nutbourne Common

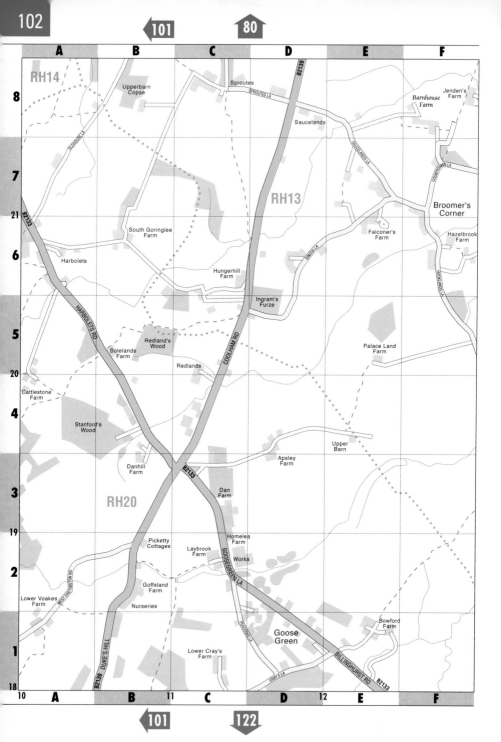

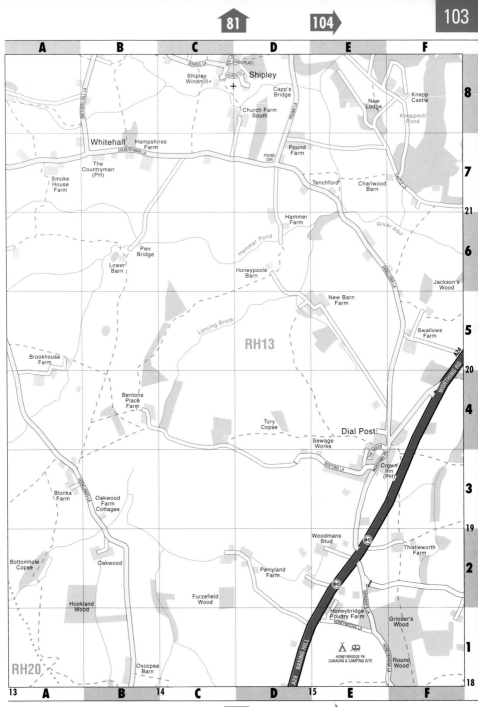

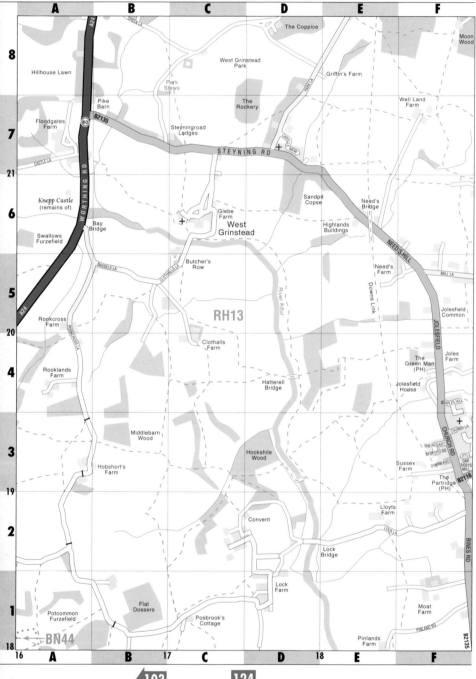

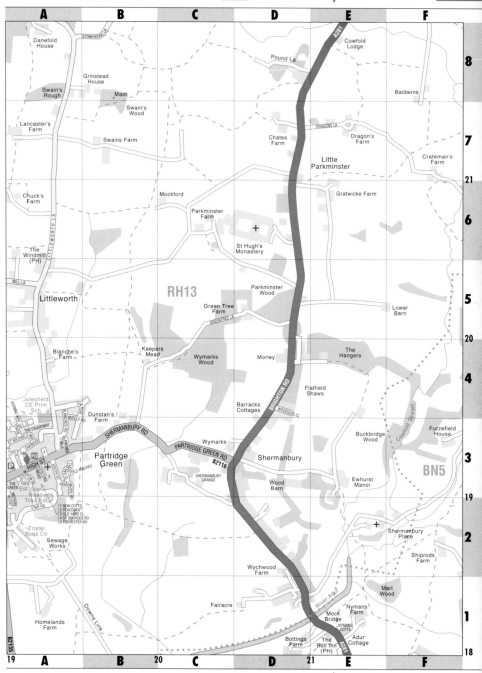

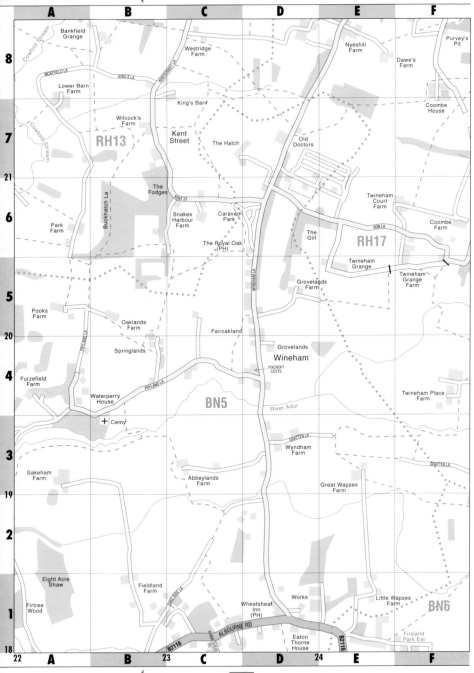

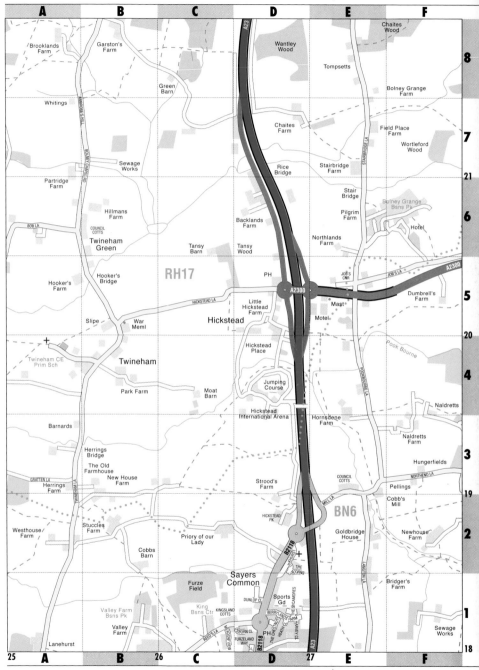

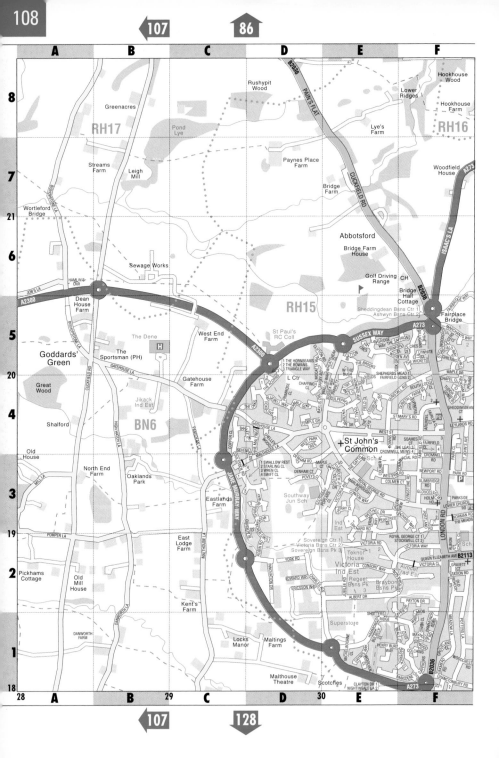

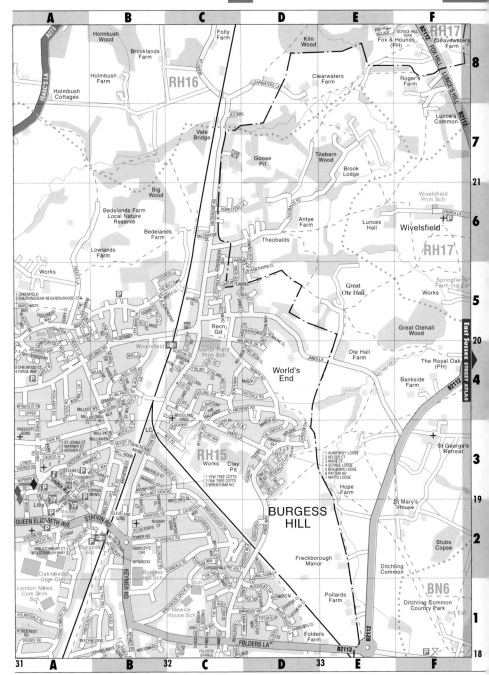

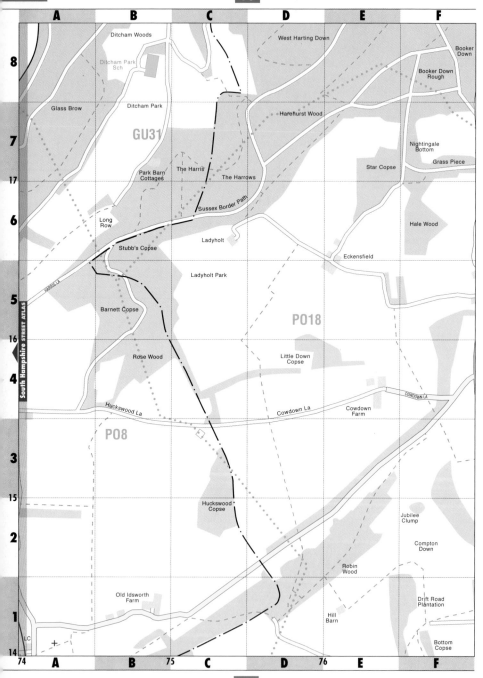

A B C D E F

Ditcham Woods

West Harting Down

Booker Down

Ditcham Park Sch

Booker Down Rough

Glass Brow

Ditcham Park

Harehurst Wood

GU31

Nightingale Bottom

Grass Piece

Park Barn Cottages

The Harris

The Harrows

Star Copse

Long Row

Sussex Border Path

Hale Wood

Stubb's Copse

Ladyholt

Eckensfield

Ladyholt Park

Barnett Copse

PO18

Rose Wood

Little Down Copse

Huckswood La

Cowdown La

Cowdown La

Cowdown Farm

COWDOWN LA

PO8

Huckswood Copse

Jubilee Clump

Compton Down

Robin Wood

Old Idsworth Farm

Hill Barn

Drift Road Plantation

LC

Bottom Copse

74 A B 75 C D 76 E F

HARRIS LA

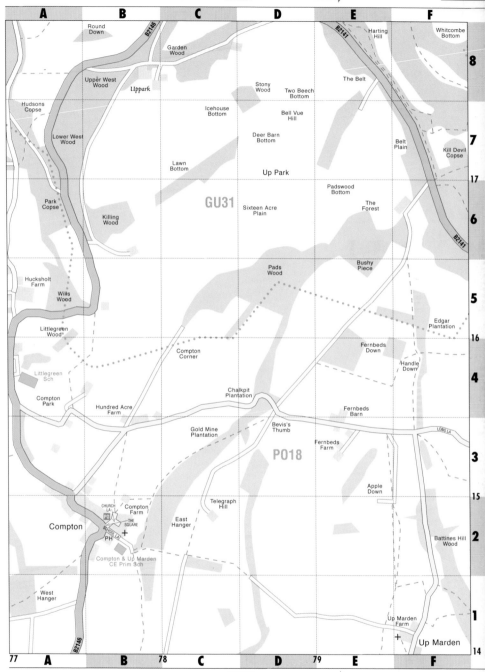

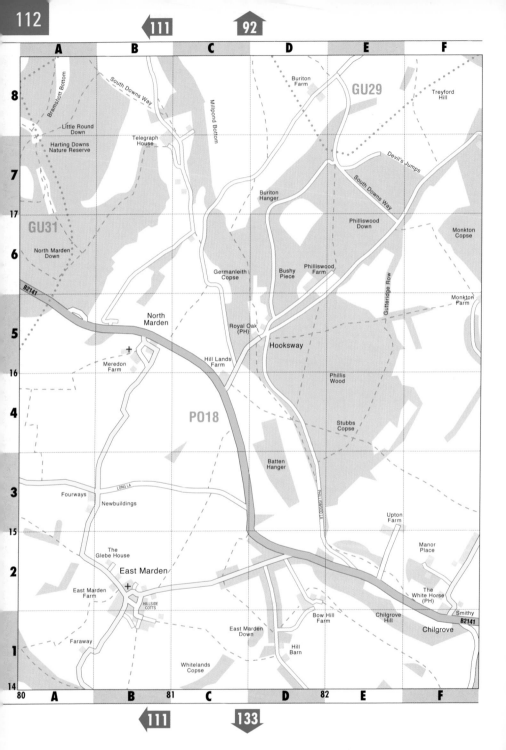

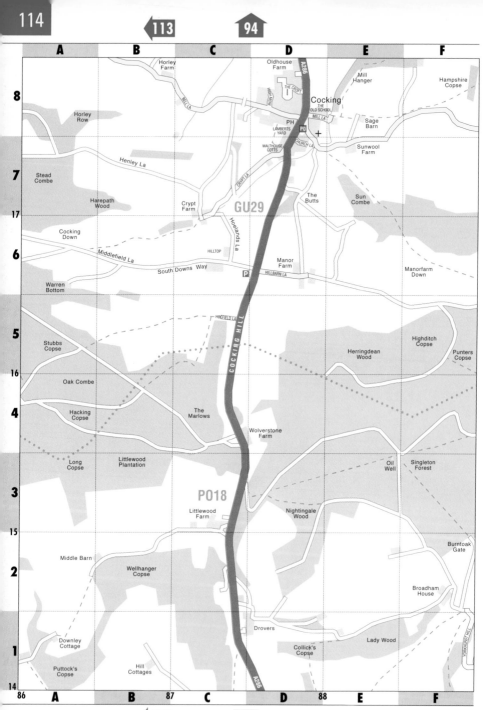

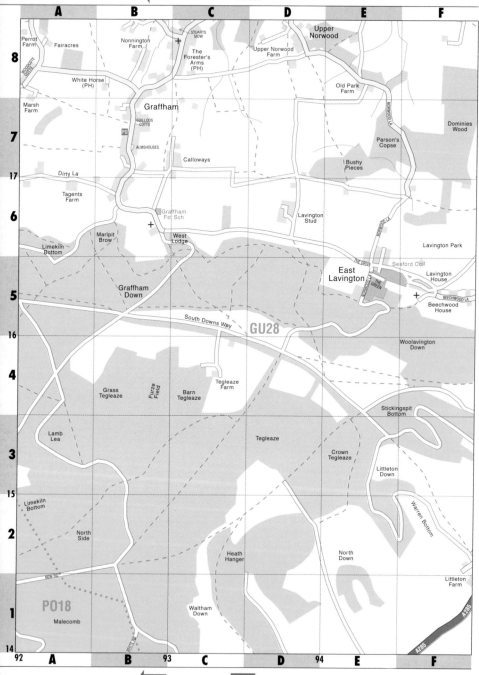

	A	B	C	D	E	F

8

Perrot Farm

Fairacres

Nonnington Farm

STUARTS MDW

Upper Norwood

White Horse (PH)

The Forester's Arms (PH)

Upper Norwood Farm

Old Park Farm

NORWOOD LA

Marsh Farm

Graffham

GUILLODS COTTS

Dominies Wood

7

PO

ALMSHOUSES

Parson's Copse

17

Dirty La

Calloways

Bushy Pieces

Tagents Farm

Lavington Stud

6

Graffham Fst Sch

West Lodge

NORWOOD LA

Marlpit Brow

Lavington Park

Limekiln Bottom

Graffham Down

THE DRIVE

Seaford Coll

Lavington House

5

South Downs Way

East Lavington

NORWOOD LA

THE GREEN

Beechwood House

BEECHWOOD LA

GU28

16

Woolavington Down

4

Grass Tegleaze

Furze Field

Barn Tegleaze

Tegleaze Farm

Stickingspit Bottom

Lamb Lea

Tegleaze

Crown Tegleaze

3

Littleton Down

15

Limekiln Bottom

Warren Bottom

2

North Side

Heath Hanger

North Down

NEW RD

Littleton Farm

1

PO18

Malecomb

Waltham Down

A285

14

92	A	B	93	C	D	94	E	F

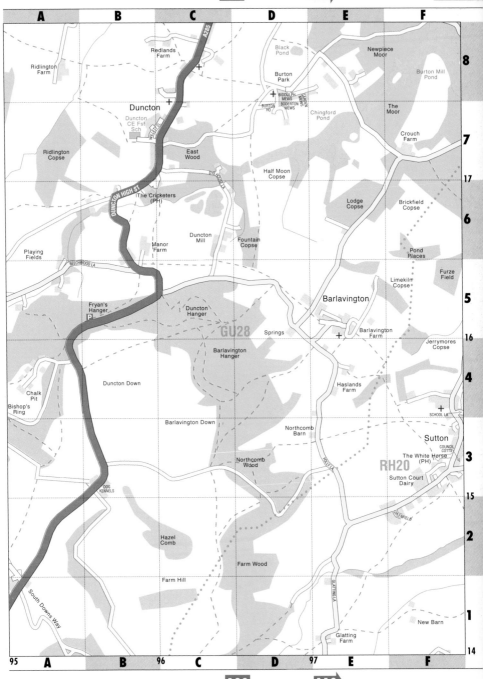

117
98

Ravesland Copse
BURTON PARK RD

GU28

Coates
GATES LA

Lower Horncroft

Tripphill Farm

B2138

8

Welchs Common

COATES CASTLE

Coates Common

TRIPP HILL

Horncroft Farm

7

The Warren

Broad Halfpenny

Lord's Piece

Sutton Common

Coldwaltham Park Wood

17

Tooths Plantation

WALTHAM PARK RD

Horncroft Common

6

Keyzaston Farm

Collumn Hill

Bignor Park Cott

Badland Wood

Horncroft Common

Sutton End

Decoy Copse

Newoods Farm

Bury Gate House

5

Winters Copse

RH20

BIGNOR PARK RD

16

Hospital Copse

Bowler's Crab Wood

Ridge Copse

Bury Gate Farm

4

The Swares

Bignor Park

Bowler's Copse

Downview Farm

Dukes Copse

B2138

A29

Bignor Park House

Hammond's Copse

BURY RD

3

15

Courthill Wood

Grevatt Wood

Bury Mill Farm

Bignor Mill

BIGNOR ROMAN VILLA (remains of)

2

Bignor

Manor Farm

Hadworth Farm

Hale Hill Farm

COUTES COTTS

MALTHOUSE COTTS

Jay's Farm

A29

1

Upper House

14

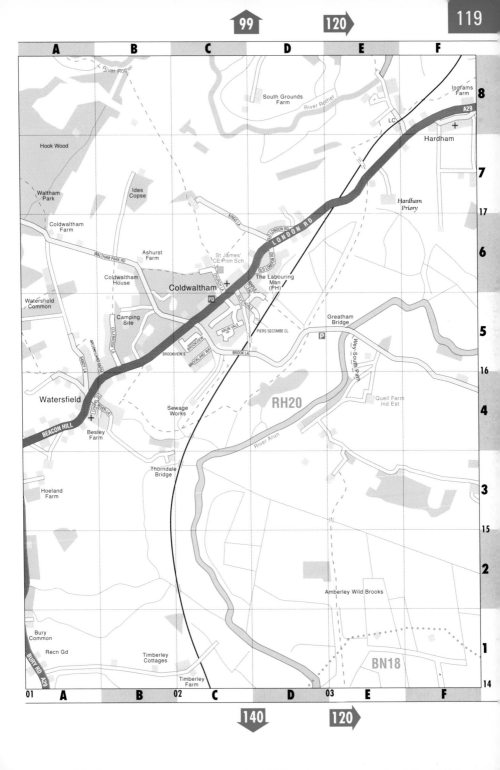

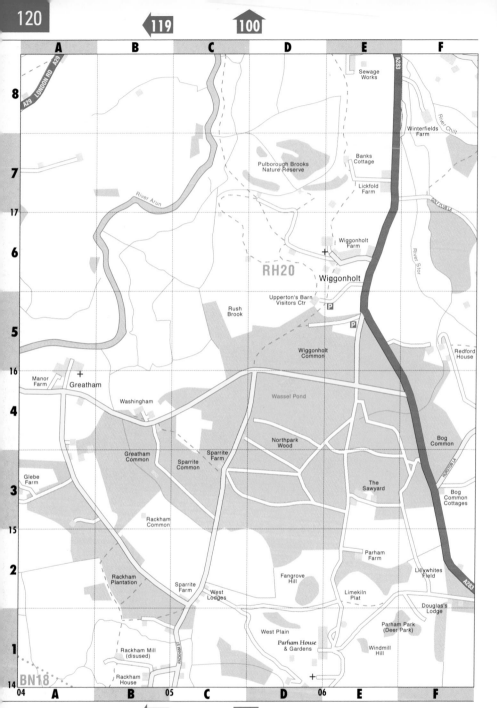

A   **B**   **C**   **D**   **E**   **F**

A29 LONDON RD A29

8

Sewage Works

A283

Winterfields Farm

River Chilt

7

Pulborough Brooks Nature Reserve

Banks Cottage

Lickfold Farm

River Arun

17

GOLF CLUB LA

6

Wiggonholt Farm

RH20

Wiggonholt

River Stor

Rush Brook

Upperton's Barn Visitors Ctr

5

P

P

Wiggonholt Common

Redford House

16

Manor Farm

Greatham

Wassel Pond

Washingham

Bog Common

4

Northpark Wood

Greatham Common

Sparrite Common

Sparrite Farm

The Sawyard

Bog Common Cottages

Glebe Farm

3

TUCKOLLS LA

Rackham Common

15

Parham Farm

Rackham Plantation

2

Fangrove Hill

Lillywhites Field

A283

Sparrite Farm

Limekiln Plat

West Lodges

Douglas's Lodge

West Plain

Parham Park (Deer Park)

1

Rackham Mill (disused)

Parham House & Gardens

Windmill Hill

BN18

Rackham House

14

04   **A**   **B**   05   **C**   **D**   06   **E**   **F**

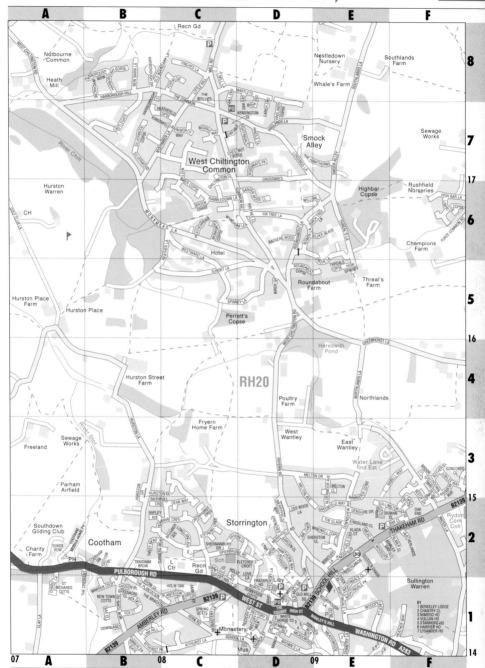

D1
1 RECTORY COTTS
2 WHITE HORSE CT
3 HAMMOND PL
4 MALDEN PL
5 LANGTON PL
6 LINDALE PL
7 MANOR CT
8 CHANCTONBURY WLK

E1
1 BERKELEY LODGE
2 CHANTRY CL
3 NIMROD HO
4 VULCAN HO
5 STANMORE HO
6 HARRIER HO
7 LYSANDER HO

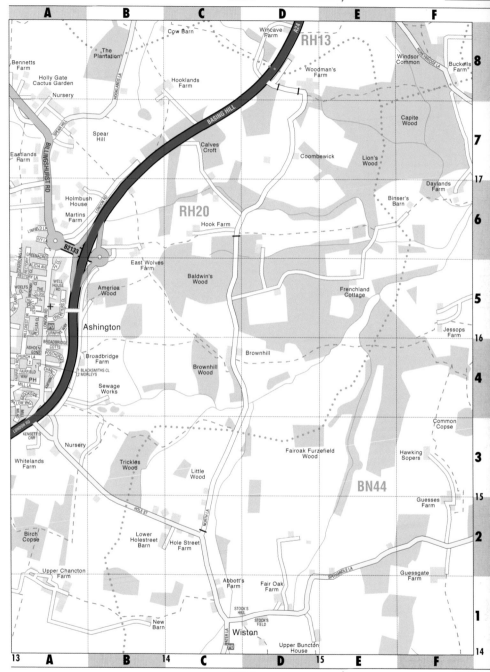

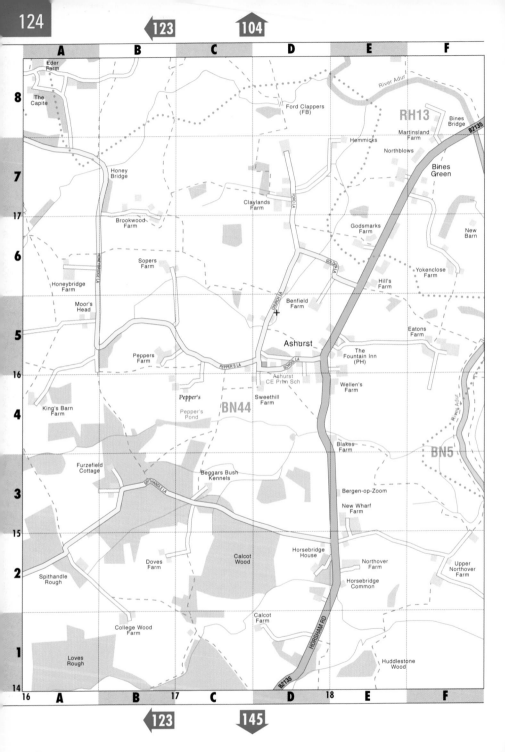

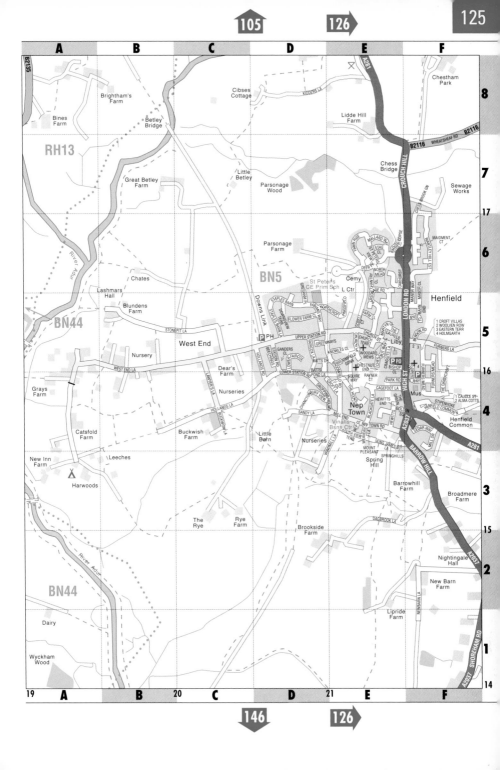

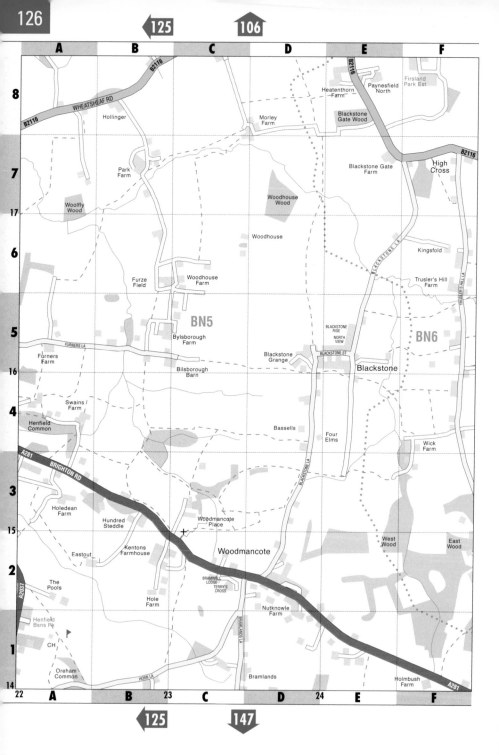

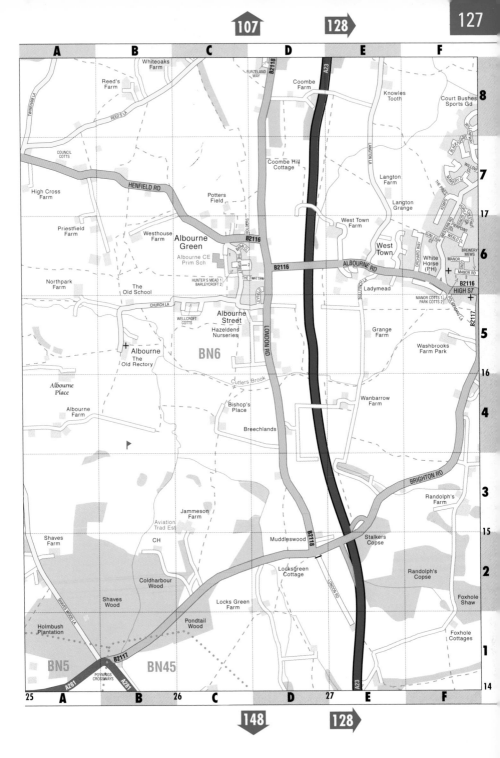

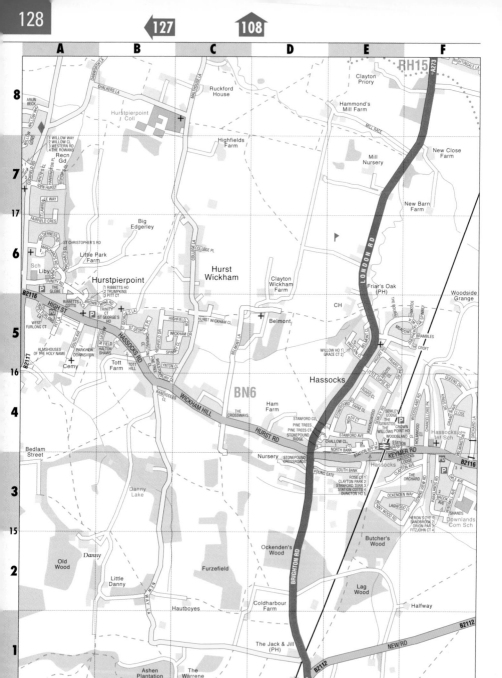

RH15

A B C D E F

8

ARUN BECK

1 WILLOW WAY
2 WILLOW CL
3 WESTERN RD
4 THE ROWANS

Recn Gd

Clayton Priory

Hammond's Mill Farm

Mill Race

Mill Nursery

New Close Farm

7

New Barn Farm

17

St CHRISTOPHER'S RD

Big Edgerley

Highfields Farm

6

Little Park Farm

Sch
Liby

Hurstpierpoint

College Pl

Hurst Wickham

Clayton Wickham Farm

Friar's Oak (PH)

Woodside Grange

B2116

HIGH ST

1 RIBBETTS HO
2 TRUMPKINS
3 PITT CT

BROWN TWIST LA

ST GEORGE'S HO

HIGHFIELD

WICKHAM DR

HURST WICKHAM CL

Belmont

CH

MEADOWS

BRAMBLES

THE CROFT

5

WEST FURLONG CT

HASSOCKS RD

BELMONT LA

WILLOW HO 1
GRACE CT 2

Hassocks

16

B2117

ALMSHOUSES OF THE HOLY NAME

PARKVIEW
DOWNSVIEW

Cemy

Tott Farm

TOTT HILL

LYNTON RD

WICKHAM HILL

BN6

Ham Farm

THE CROSSWAYS

STANFORD CL
PINE TREES
PINE TREES CT
STONEPOUND RIDGE

STONEPOUND FARM CL

SEMLEY LODGE
THE GENISTORS
CROWN
THE WILLOWS POINT HO
WOODSLAND CL

Hassocks Inf Sch

4

HURST RD

STANFORD AVE

CHALLOW CL

NORTH BANK

STATION APP W

STATION
APP E

KEYMER RD

HASSOCKS BRIDGE

CLAYTON AVE

Hassocks

Bedlam Street

Nursery

STONEPOUND CROSSROADS

POUND GATE

SOUTH BANK

Hassocks

THE ORCHARD

OCKENDEN WAY

B2116

Downlands Com Sch

3

Danny Lake

ROSE CT 1
CLAYTON PARK 2
STANFORD TERR 3
STATION COTTS 4
DUNCTON HO 5

LAGWOOD

HERON'S TYE 1
SANDBROOK 2
ORION PAR 3
FITZJOHN CT 4

SHANDS

15

Old Wood

Danny

Little Danny

Furzefield

BRIGHTON RD

Ockenden's Wood

Butcher's Wood

2

Lag Wood

Coldharbour Farm

Hautboyes

Halfway

B2112

1

The Jack & Jill (PH)

B2112

NEW RD

14

Ashen Plantation

The Warrene

B2112

28 A B 29 C D 30 E F

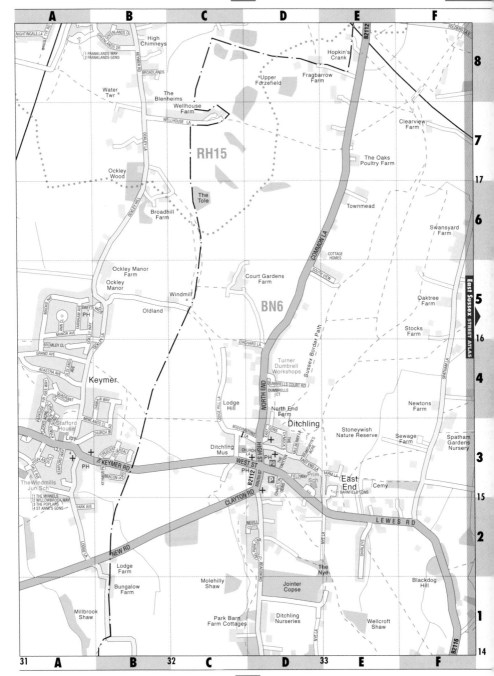

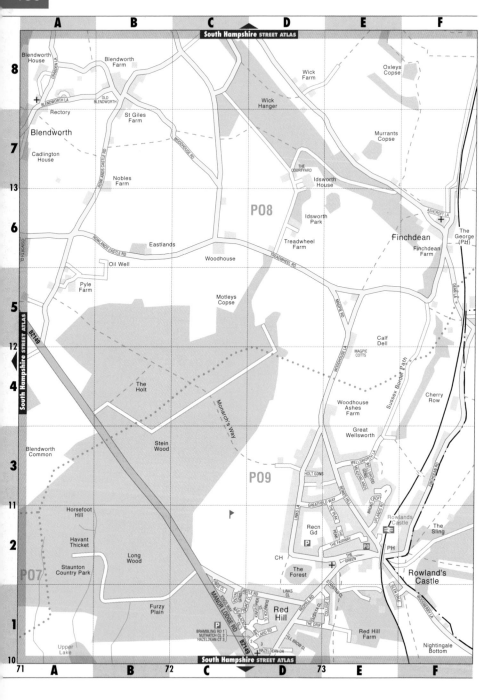

A B C D E F

8

Old Idsworth
Garden

PO8

Markwells
Wood

Manor
Copse

PO18

Lostlabour
Copse

Horsley
Farm

West Marden
Hall

7

High
Copse

Grub
Copse

13

South Holt
Farm

OLDHOUSE LA

Shortleys
Copse

6

LODGE LA

Adam's
Copse

Bottom
Copse

Northwood
Farm

Forestside

Lodge
Farm

Woods
Copse

Forestside
Farm

5

Deanlane
End

Warren
Down

12

Drews
Farm

PO9

Firtree
Piece

Batty's
Park

Wythy
Piece

4

Rosamond's
Hill

Stansted
Forest

Long
Copse

3

Forest
Hanger

Lumley
Seat

11

Hare
Warren

Lumley
Wood

2

North
Coopers
Wood

Orange
Grove

Stansted
Park

PO18

Horsepasture
Farm

The Avenue   Monarch's Way

Lyels
Wood

The
Slip

South
Coopers
Wood

Stansted
House

PO10

Sussex Border Path

Saw
Mill

1

10

A   **B**   **C**   **D**   **E**   **F**

B2146

DOWN COTTS

8

PH

West Marden

Sewage Works

7

Wheatcroft

13

Nore Down

6

OLDHOUSE LA

Cabragh House

5

Busto Copse

12

PO9

Watergate Hanger

4

Broadreed Farm

3

Oak Copse

11

WOODLANDS LA

2

Woodlands Cottages

Park Slip

1

10

Locksash Farm

Malthouse Copse

LOCKSASH LA

Fanny's Row

Birchin Copse

Watergate Farm

Watergate Park

Monarch's Way

Lordington Copse

B2146

River Ems

Dolly's Hanger

Grevitts Copse

Lyecommon

Warren Copse

Woodbarn

Piglegged Row

Manor Farm

COOKS LA
The Barley Mow (PH)

Walderton

Hill Farm

Blinkard Copse

Lower Farm

Lowerfarm Copse

Haslett Copse

Pitlands Farm

Holmes Row

Inholmes Wood

Dundarroch

Mitchmere Farm

MITCHMERE COTTS

BROOKLANDS COTTS

Walderton Down

Walderton Hill Plantation

PO18

77   **A**   **B**   78   **C**   **D**   79   **E**   **F**

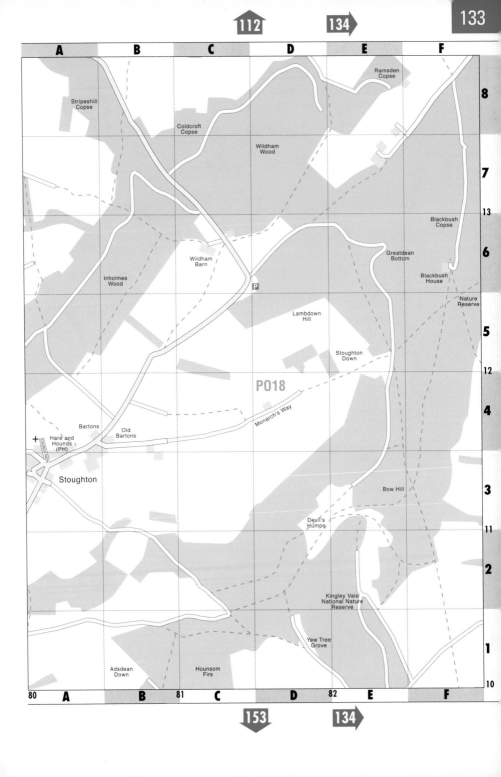

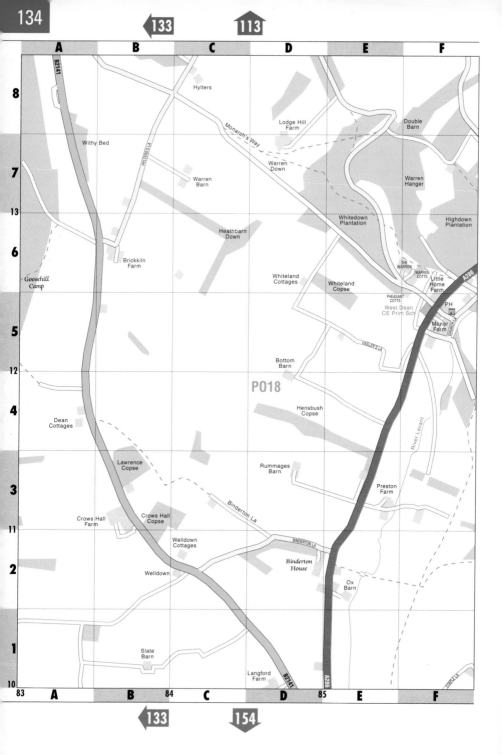

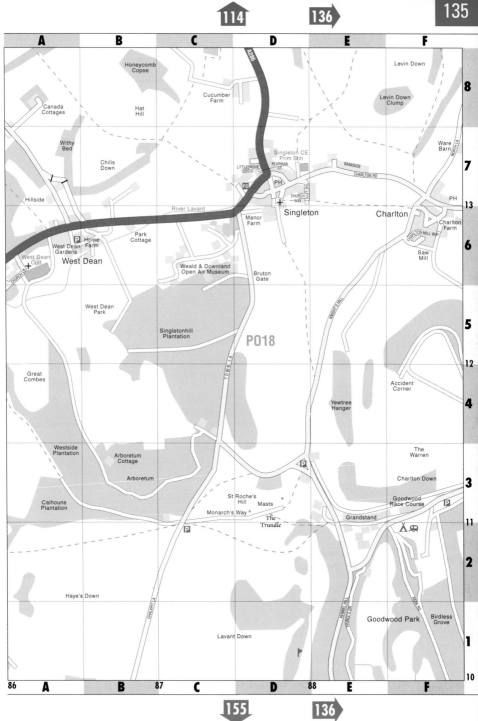

A **B** **C** **D** **E** **F**

8

Court Hill

Halfmoon
Piece

New Barn

Highdown
Croft

High Down

7

Green Hill

COURTYARD LA

13

CHARLTON RD

Manor Farm

PO

BUTCHERS LA

CHAPEL ROW

DROKE LA

Ide's
Barn

6

East Dean

Wallerdean
Hill

5

EASTDEAN HILL

Bubholts

Shotter's Ground

Chiseldown

Potcomb

12

Charlton
Park

Park
Hill

Eastdean
Park

PO18

Eastdean
Hill

Monarch's Way

4

Goodwood
Country Park

CHALK RD

Pilleygreen
Lodges

SELHURSTPARK RD

3

P ✕

Open
Winkins

Red
Copse

11

Appletree
Bottom

The
Plantation

MOLECOMB BROADWALK

Molecomb
Peak

Little
Copse

Halnaker Gallop

2

Hat Hill

Ladys
Winkins

Halnaker
Park

1

Denge
Bottom

10

Molecomb

89   **A**   **B**   90   **C**   **D**   91   **E**   **F**

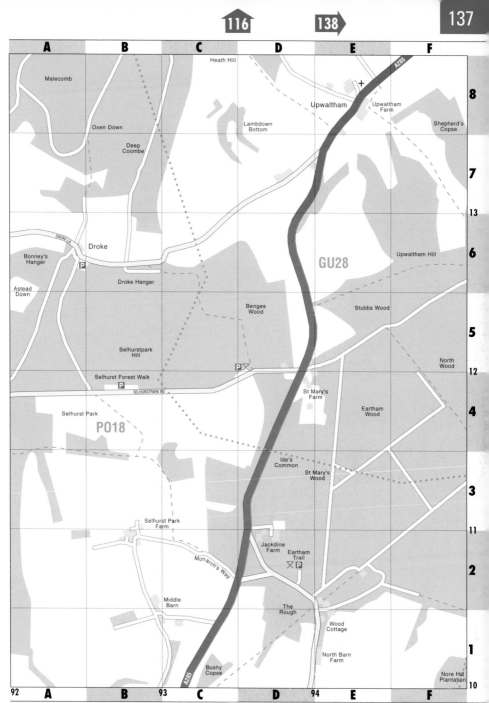

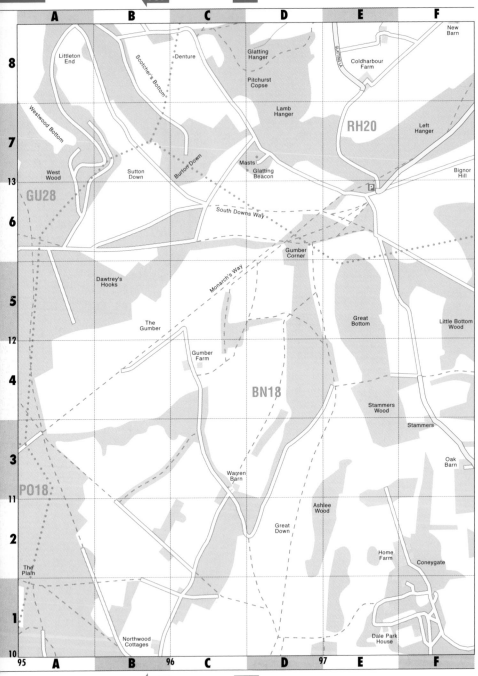

A B C D E F

8

Littleton
End

Scotcher's Bottom

Denture

Glatting
Hanger

Pitchurst
Copse

New
Barn

Coldharbour
Farm

Westwood Bottom

Lamb
Hanger

RH20

7

Left
Hanger

West
Wood

Sutton
Down

Burton Down

Masts

Glatting
Beacon

Bignor
Hill

13

GU28

6

South Downs Way

Gumber
Corner

Dawtrey's
Hooks

Monarch's Way

5

The
Gumber

Great
Bottom

Little Bottom
Wood

12

Gumber
Farm

4

BN18

Stammers
Wood

Stammers

3

Warren
Barn

Oak
Barn

PO18

11

Ashlee
Wood

2

Great
Down

Home
Farm

Coneygate

The
Plain

1

Northwood
Cottages

Dale Park
House

10

95 A B 96 C D 97 E F

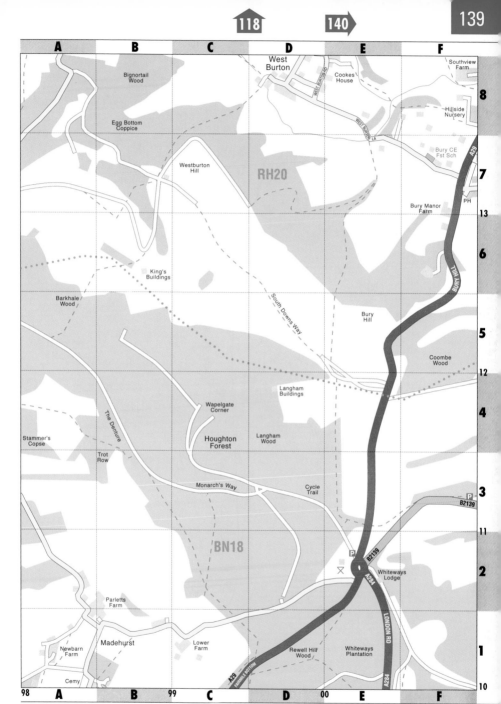

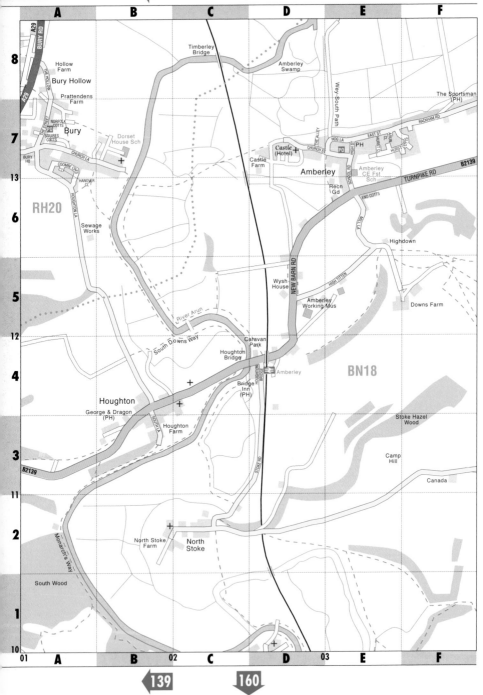

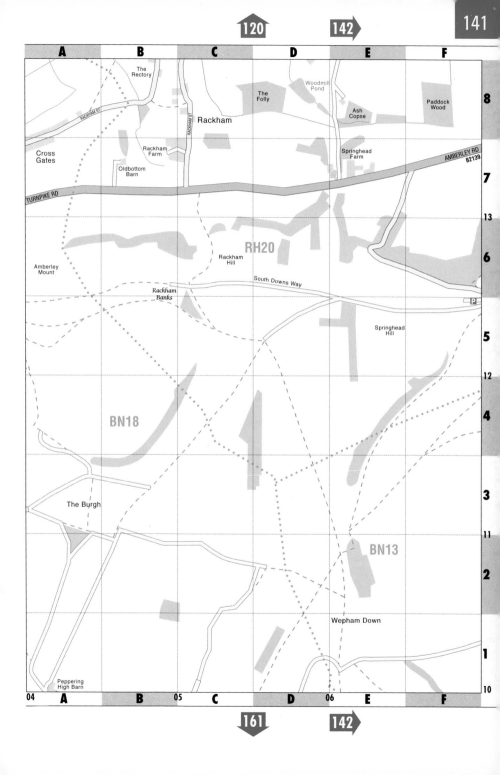

120
142

The Rectory

Rackham St

The Folly

Woodmill Pond

Rackham

Ash Copse

Paddock Wood

8

Cross Gates

Rackham Farm

Springhead Farm

AMBERLEY RD

B2139

Oldbottom Barn

TURNPIKE RD

7

13

RH20

Rackham Hill

6

Amberley Mount

South Downs Way

Rackham Banks

Springhead Hill

P

5

12

BN18

4

The Burgh

3

11

BN13

2

Wepham Down

1

10

Peppering High Barn

161
142

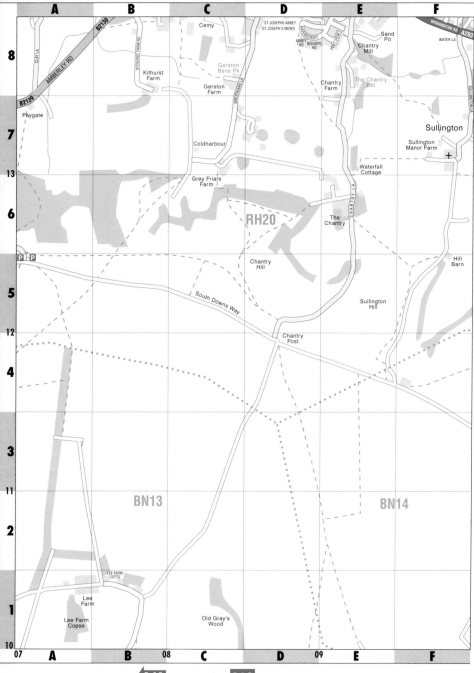

141
121

A   **B**   **C**   **D**   **E**   **F**

8

B2139

AMBERLEY RD

B2139

CLAY LA

KITHURST FARM RD

WASHINGTON RD

A283

WATER LA

SULLINGTON LA

Cemy

St Josephs Abbey
St Joseph's Mews

ABBEY
HO

BISHOPS
HO

BRANSCROFT

POST HSE

Sand
Pit

Chantry
Mill

Kithurst
Farm

Gerston
Bsns Pk

Chantry
Farm

The Chantry
Est

Gerston
Farm

GERSTON LA

7

Paygate

Coldharbour

Sullington
Manor Farm

Sullington

+

13

Grey Friars
Farm

Waterfall
Cottage

CHANTRY LA

6

RH20

The
Chantry

Hill
Barn

Chantry
Hill

5

South Downs Way

Sullington
Hill

12

Chantry
Post

4

3

11

BN13

BN14

2

1

Lee Farm
Cotts

Lee
Farm

Old Gray's
Wood

10

Lee Farm
Copse

A   **B**   08   **C**   **D**   09   **E**   **F**

07

141
162

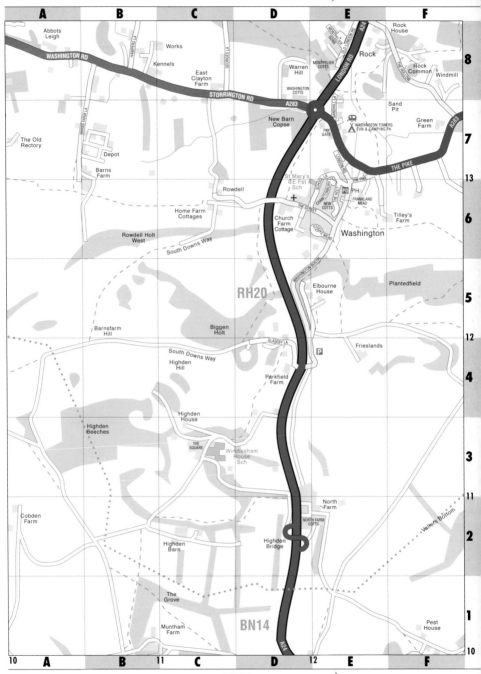

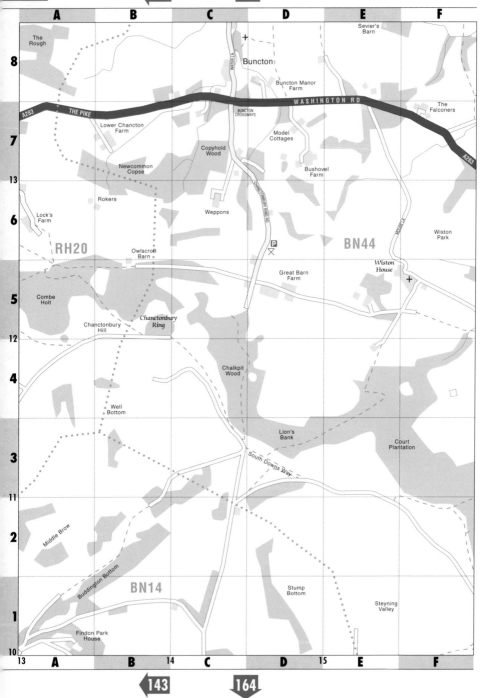

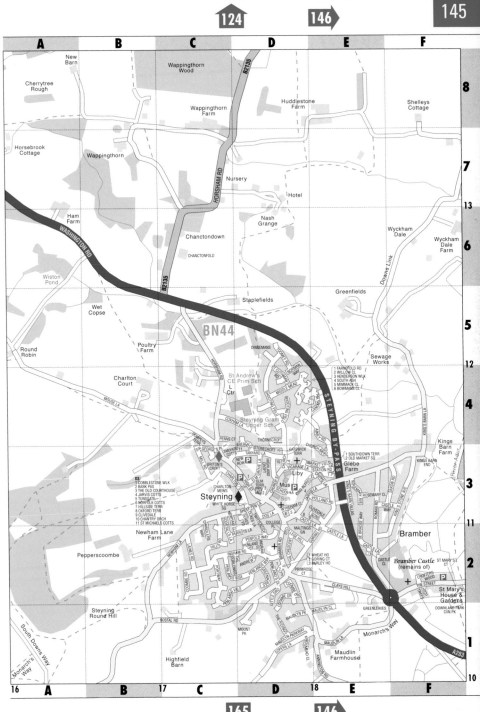

A B C D E F

8
7
13
6
5
12
4
3
11
2
1
10

New Barn
Cherrytree Rough
Horsebrook Cottage
Wappingthorn
Ham Farm
WASHINGTON RD
Wiston Pond
Round Robin
Charlton Court
MOYSE LA
Pepperscoombe
Newham Lane Farm
South Downs Way
Monarch's Way
Steyning Round Hill
BOSTAL RD
Highfield Barn
MOUNT PK

Wappingthorn Wood
B2135
Wappingthorn Farm
HORSHAM RD
Nursery
Chanctondown
CHANCTONFOLD
B2135
Wet Copse
Poultry Farm
BN44
DINGEMANS

Huddlestone Farm
Shelleys Cottage
Hotel
Nash Grange
Wyckham Dale
Wyckham Dale Farm
Greenfields
Downs Link
Staplefields
Sewage Works

St Andrew's CE Prim Sch
L Ctr
Steyning Gram Upper Sch
CONHAM LA
THORNCROFT
PENNS CT
BREHAM
TANYARD COTTS
NEW ROW
BRITON'S CROFT
CHARLTON MEWS
WHITE HORSE
STONECROFT
GATEWICK TERR
CHURCH ST
MARKET FIELD
STATION RD
Libv
Mus
Sch
Steyning
ELM TERR
HOLLAND RD
CLIVEDALE
SHEEP PEN LA
DOG LA
COLLEGE
PERROTS LA
PENFOLD WAY
PENLANDS
COOMBE RD
NEWHAM LA
HILLS
INGRAM RD
ST ANDREW'S
PENLANDS
THE CRESCENT
CASTLE LA
MALTINGS
GORING
PRIMROSE CT
FIELDS VALE
COOMBE DR
MAUDLYN PK
MAUDLYN PARKWAY
SOPERS LA
MAUDLYN RD
MAUDLYN CL
Highfield Barn
Maudlin Farmhouse

STEYNING BY-PASS
1 SOUTHDOWN TERR
2 OLD MARKET SQ
Glebe Farm
KING'S BARN LA
Kings Barn Farm
KINGS BARN END
RIVER ADUR
SAXON RD
CASTLE RD
ROMAN RD
ROSEMARY LA
CASTLE WAY
Bramber
CASTLE CL
Bramber Castle (remains of)
ST MARY'S
Monarch's Way
St Mary's House & Gardens
DOWNLANDS PARK CVN PK
GREENLEAVES
A283

1 FARNEFOLD RD
2 WILLOW CL
3 HENDERSON WLK
4 SOUTH ASH
5 MIMMACK CL
6 BOWMANS CL

D3
1 COBBLESTONE WLK
2 BANK PAS
3 THE OLD COURTHOUSE
4 JARVIS COTTS
5 TUNSGATE
6 NORFOLK COTTS
7 HILLSIDE TERR
8 OXFORD TERR
9 CLIVEDALE
10 CHANTRY ORCH
11 ST MICHAELS COTTS

1 WHEAT HO
2 GORING CT
3 FARLEY HO

16   17   18

145 125

8

A B C D E F

West Mill Farm

Stretham Farm

Stretham Manor

Stretham Farm House

NEWBERRY LA

SHOREHAM RD

HORN LA

A2037

Wood's Mill Countryside Ctr

STRETHAM LA

7

Downs Link

BN5

Hoe Wood

SILVER
BIRCHES

PINEWOOD

BEECH

NEW HALL LA

13

BN44

Wyckham Farm

New Hall

DOWNVIEW

NEW WOOD DR

MILL VIEW

TOTTINGTON DR

ORCHARD

6

Wyckham Dale Farm

Horton Wood

The Gamekeeper (PH)

LANDS LA

PO

3

1 SOUTHVIEW
2 THE OAKS
3 WOODSMILL CL

Small Dole

Mackley's Ind Est

River Adur

Landfill Site

BN5

Tottington Wood

HILLSIDE SCOUT CAMP

5

HILLSIDE LA

HILLSIDE PK

Longlands Wood

12

Nightingales

4

Freeland Cottages

Mannings Farm

Tottington Cottages

Hotel

Horton Hall

Burrells

HENFIELD RD

Tottington Manor Farm

3

Sele Priory

Works

Upper Horton

Riding Sch

THE PADDOCKS

THE DRIFTWAY

11

CHURCH

ST PETER'S GN

PEPPERSCOMBE LA

DEACONS WAY

SMUGGLERS LA

DOWNLANDS CLOSE AND CL

Golding Barn

2

RIVERSIDE CARAVAN PK

SALTINGS WAY

WINDMILL

ADUR VALLEY CT

SOUTHDOWN CVN PK

Golding Barn Farm (Works)

Room Bottom

BN43

Upper Beeding Prim Sch

P

HIGH ST

PYLE GDNS

HYDE LA

STANDEN CT

MAUDE RD

ADUR VALLEY CT

Windmill Hill

Beeding Bridge

ADUR VIEW

DAWN DRES

HOBS ACRE

COLLEGE DR

1

Upper Beeding

PH

SHOREHAM RD

A283

The Towers Convent Sch

Castle Town

Monarch's Way

South Downs Way

Tottington Barn

10

A283

STEYNING BY-PASS

Beeding Court Farm

A283

A B C D E F

19 **20** **21**

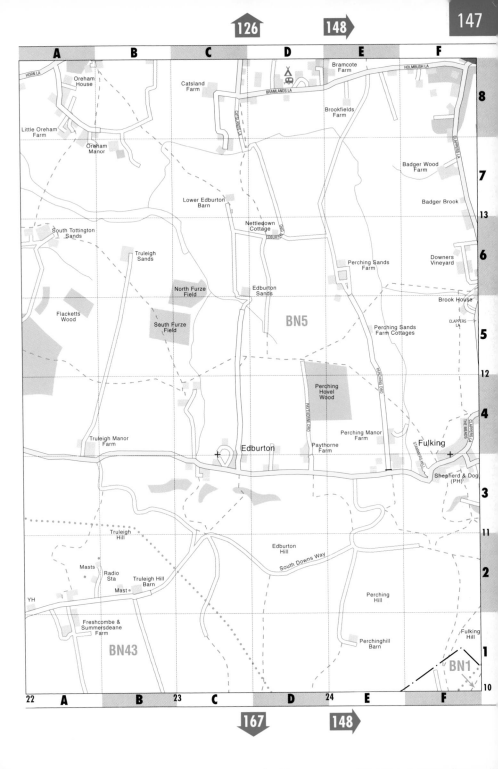

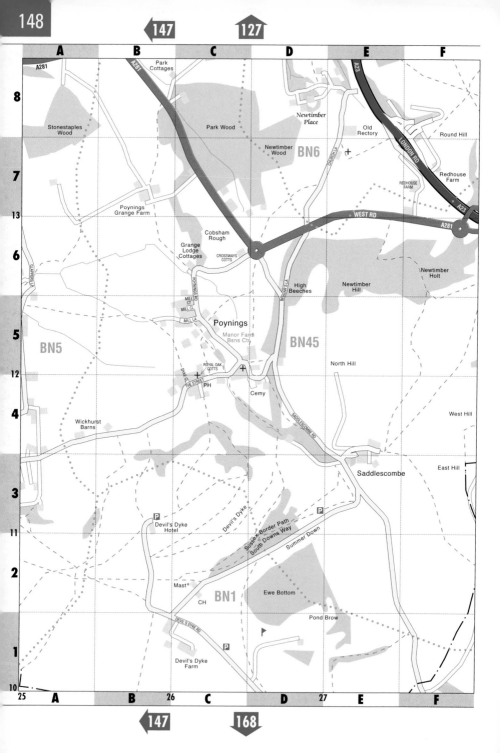

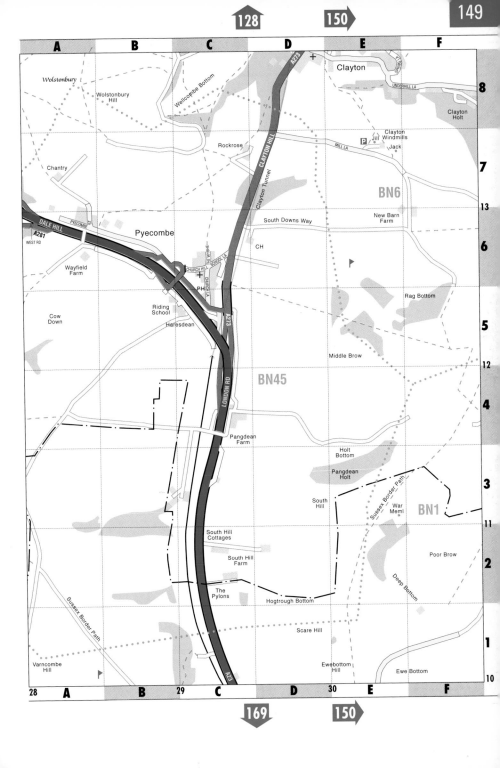

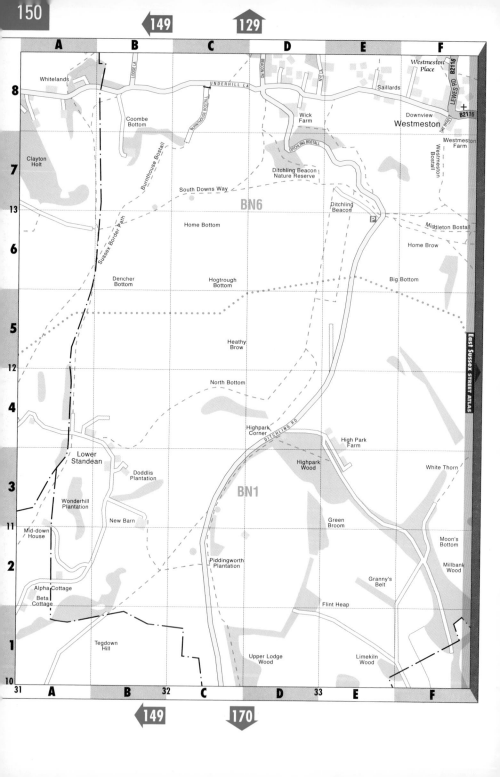

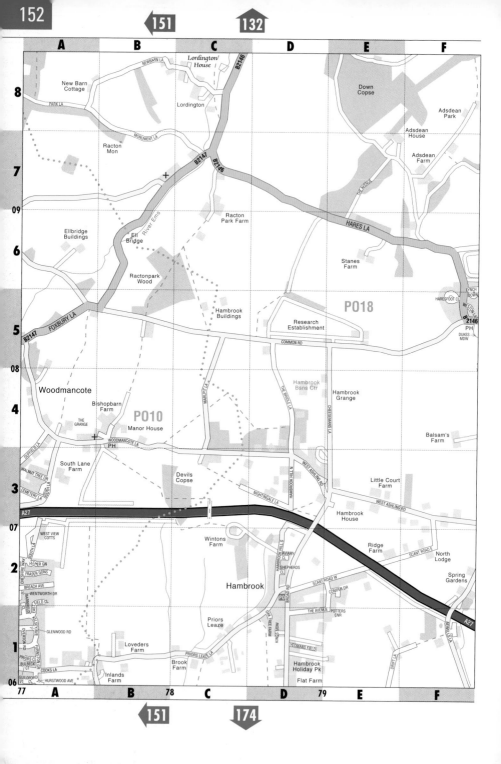

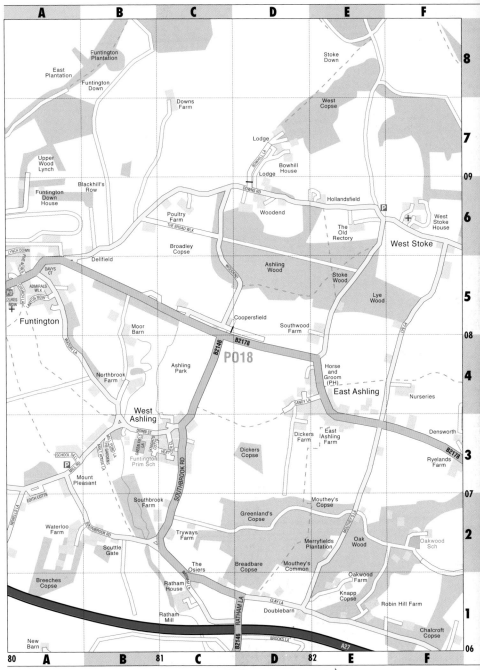

133
154
175
154

A   B   C   D   E   F

8
7
09
6
5
08
4
3
07
2
1
06

East Plantation

Funtington Plantation

Funtington Down

Downs Farm

Stoke Down

West Copse

Upper Wood Lynch

Blackhill's Row

Lodge

Bowhill House

Lodge

Funtington Down House

THE BROAD WLK

Poultry Farm

DOWNS RD

Woodend

Hollandsfield

West Stoke House

West Stoke

LYNCH DOWN

PINE ACRE

DAVYS CT

Dellfield

Broadley Copse

Ashling Wood

The Old Rectory

Stoke Wood

Lye Wood

ADMIRALS WLK

LANTON MDW

CHURCH LA

DUKES MDW

PO

Funtington

WATER LA

Moor Barn

Coopersfield

B2178

Southwood Farm

Horse and Groom (PH)

East Ashling

Nurseries

WOODEND

B2146

PO18

Ashling Park

Northbrook Farm

West Ashling

SANDY LA

Densworth

LYE LA

B2178

Ryelands Farm

SCHOOL DR

MILL RD

PO

DOWN ST

THE GARDENS

MALT HOUSE CT

HEBRIDES LA

J K NIGHTS COTTS

HEATH LA

Funtington Prim Sch

Dickers Copse

Dickers Farm

East Ashling Farm

Mount Pleasant

EDITH COTTS

BREWELLS LA

SOUTHBROOK RD

Southbrook Farm

Mouthey's Copse

Waterloo Farm

SOUTHBROOK RD

Tryways Farm

Greenland's Copse

Merryfields Plantation

Oak Wood

Oakwood Sch

Scuttle Gate

The Osiers

Breadbare Copse

Mouthey's Common

Oakwood Farm

WOTHEY LA

Breeches Copse

Ratham House

RATHAM LA

CLAY LA

Doublebarn

Knapp Copse

Robin Hill Farm

Ratham Mill

B2146

BROOKS LA

A27

Chalcroft Copse

New Barn

80   81   82

A   B   C   D   E   F

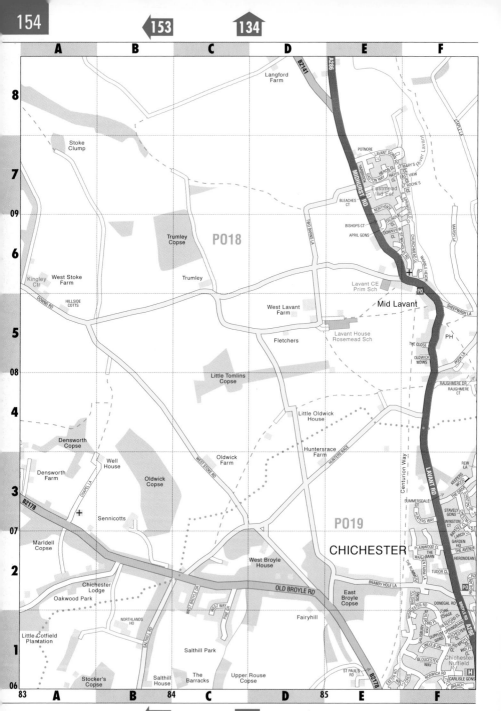

153
134

	A	B	C	D	E	F

8

Langford Farm

B2141

A286

7

Stoke Clump

MIDHURST LA

POTNORE

LAVANT DOWN

HERON CL

'ON WAY

HAYES CL

ST MARY'S CL

EAST VIEW

ST ROCHE'S

JARVELA

09

Eustmead

Old Far

BLEACHES CT

NORTHCOTE

ST ROCHES CL

MARSH LA

6

Trumley Copse

PO18

TWO BARNS LA

BISHOPS CT

DOWNVIEW

APRIL GDNS

CL

ST THOMAS'S CL

WARBLE HEATH

West Stoke Farm

Trumley

Lavant CE Prim Sch

PO

Mid Lavant

SHEEPWASH LA

Kingley Ctr

HILLSIDE COTTS

West Lavant Farm

PH

5

DOWNS RD

Fletchers

Lavant House Rosemead Sch

THE CLOSE

OLDWICK MDWS

ROOK LA

08

Little Tomlins Copse

RAUGHMERE DR.

RAUGHMERE CT

4

Little Oldwick House

Densworth Copse

Huntersrace Farm

WEST STOKE RD

Oldwick Farm

HUNTERS RACE

REW LA

KEEPERS WD CL

Well House

Centurion Way

LAVANT RD

THE DRIVE

Densworth Farm

DRUELLA

Oldwick Copse

3

B2178

SUMMERSDALE

HUNTERS WAY

STAVELY GDNS

MALTERS WAY

WINSTON CT

BARTON

CL

LARCH

GARDEN

HO

THE AVENUE

Sennicotts

PO19

Marldell Copse

07

Chichester Lodge

PLAINWOOD CL

THE BARN

WAR

FARM LA

HERONDEAN

Oakwood Park

West Broyle House

CHICHESTER

THE RUNNERS

TUDOR CL

BRANDY HOLE LA

2

WEST BROYLE LA

WEST WAY

PINE TREE RD

OLD BROYLE RD

East Broyle Copse

PO

Little Cotfield Plantation

NORTHLANDS HO

SALTHILL RD

Fairyhill

DONEGAL RD

YORK RD

HEREFORD RD

ROCHESTER

SPRINGFIELD

B1256

1

Salthill Park

LINCOLN GDNS

WOLLI

CL

GLOUCESTER WAY

Chichester Nuffield

H

06

Stocker's Copse

Salthill House

The Barracks

Upper Rouse Copse

ST PAUL'S RD

B2178

WORWICH RD

CARLISLE GDNS

BREACH

| 83 | A | B | 84 | C | D | 85 | E | F |

153
176

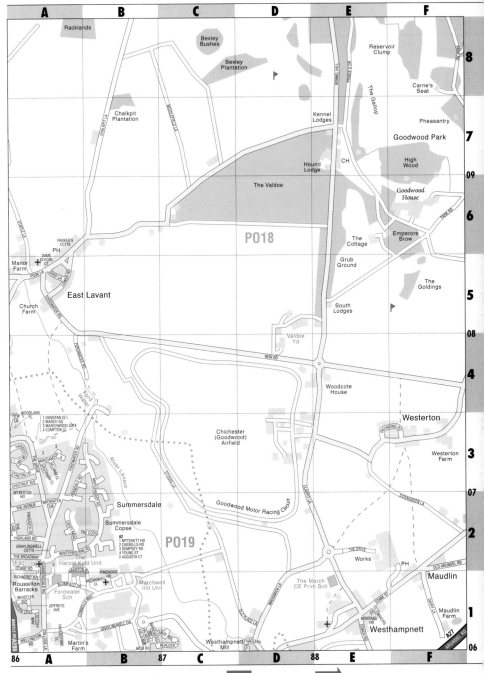

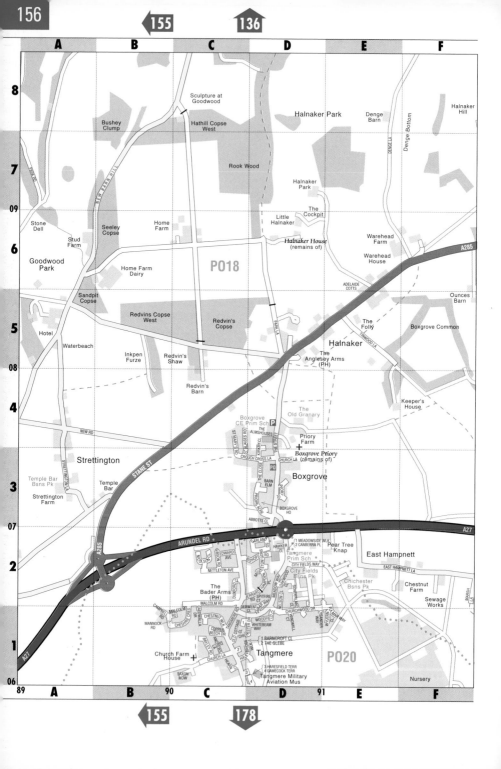

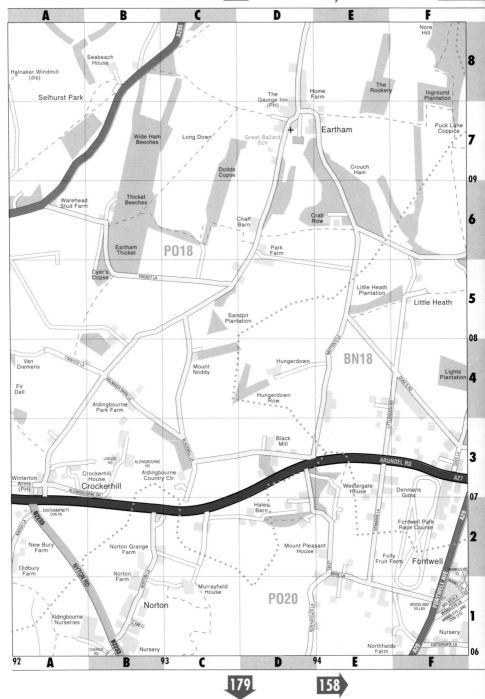

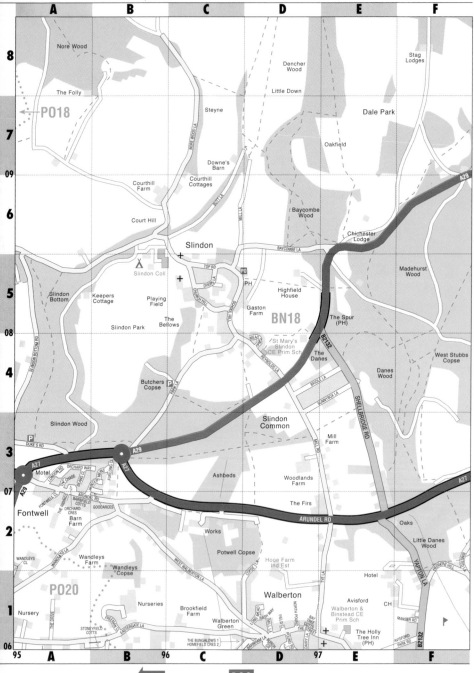

139
160
181
160

A B C D E F

8 7 6 5 4 3 2 1

09 08 07 06

98 99 00

Lonebeech Plantation
Madehurst Cottage
Black Barn Farm
Duchess Lodge
Fairmile Bottom Nature Trail
Dalesdown Wood
Horse Shoe Plantation
Rewell Hill
Yewtree Gate
Park Rough
Arundel Park
Punchbowl
Sherwood Rough
Training Gallops
The Rough
Rewell Wood
Green Doors Lodge
Screens Wood
Rewell House
BN18
Cricket Hill Farm
Rough Copse
Goblestubb's Copse
Park Farm
Park Farm Cotts
The Arundel Lodge
The Waterwoods
ARUNDEL RD
Havenwood Pk
Scotland Barn
Paine's Wood
CHICHESTER RD
A27
CANADA RD
ELLIS CL
Brickkiln Copse
Winchers Copse
Singer's Piece
Scotland
HERINGTON RD
Arundel CE Prim Sch
Barn's Copse
Stewards Copse
Pedler's Croft
Binsted Wood
Ash Piece
Tortington Common
OAK END
The Black Horse (PH)
Church Farm
ARUNDEL
Binsted
Priory Farm

A29
FAIRMILE BOTTOM
LONDON RD
A284
LONG LA
BINSTED LA
HILL TERR
JARVIS RD
PEARSON RD
DUKE CL
TORTON HILL RD
MAXWELL
STEWARDS RISE
HIGH RIDGE
BIRCH CL
DALLOWAY RD
HAZEL GR
MANDYKE RD
FERNANT RD

159
140

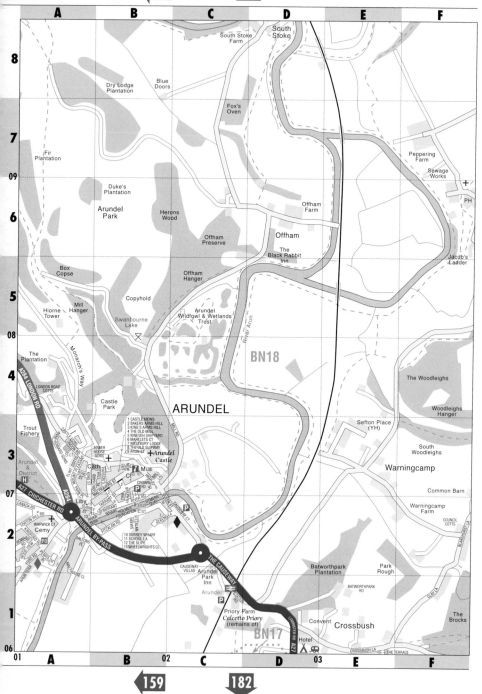

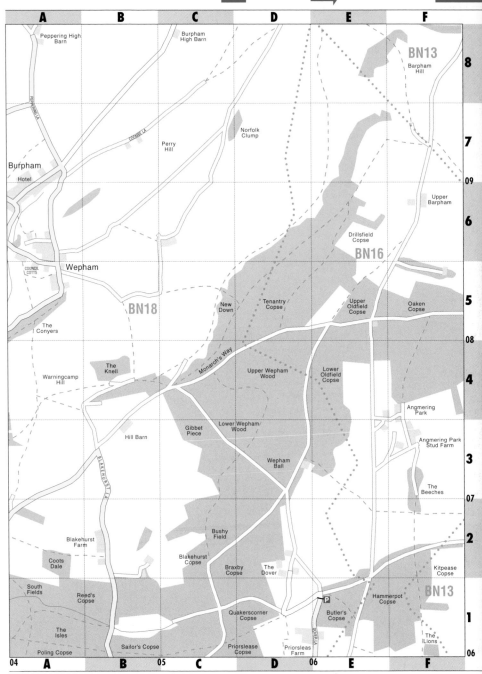

161
142

BN14

A B C D E F

8 Harrow Hill

Blackpatch Hill

7 Lower Barpham

09

6 Myrtle Grove Farm

Beech Copse

Michelgrove House

Monarch's Way

MICHELGROVE COTTS

BN16

5 BN13

08

Michelgrove Park

MYRTLE GR

LONGFURLONG LA

4 Michelgrove Park Lodges

Stables

Longfurlong Barn

A280

The Buckmans

Barnstake Copse

Patching Rough

Patching Hill

LONG FURLONG

3

Stonyland Copse

07

Selden Fields

Surgeon's Fields

Grub Ride

Church Copse

2 Olivers Copse

Patching Copse

Patching Farm

Patching

Clapham Farm

Parham Fields

Patching Farm

THE STREET

HILLSIDE COTTS

COUNCIL COTTS

CHURCH CL

ORLANDS CL

Norfolk House

Selden Farm

COLD HARBOUR LA

COUNCIL COTTS

THE STREET

CLAPHAM CL

1 Jewshead Wood

Clapham & Patching CE Prim Sch

PO

Clapham

FRANCIS LA

Gosling Croft Bsns Ctr

The Harehams

A280

Wyatt's Copse

06

07 A B 08 C D 09 E F

SWILLAGE LA

THE STREET

161
184

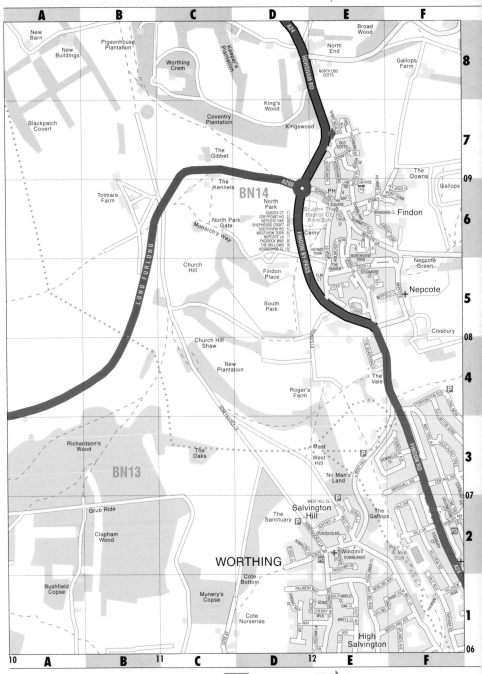

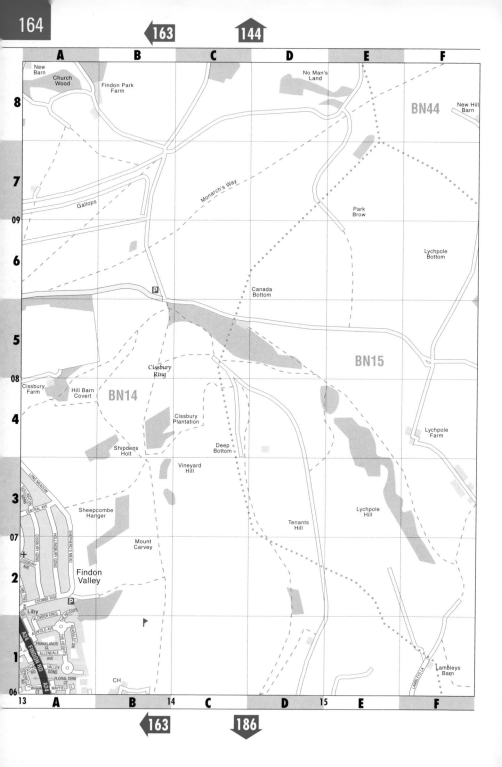

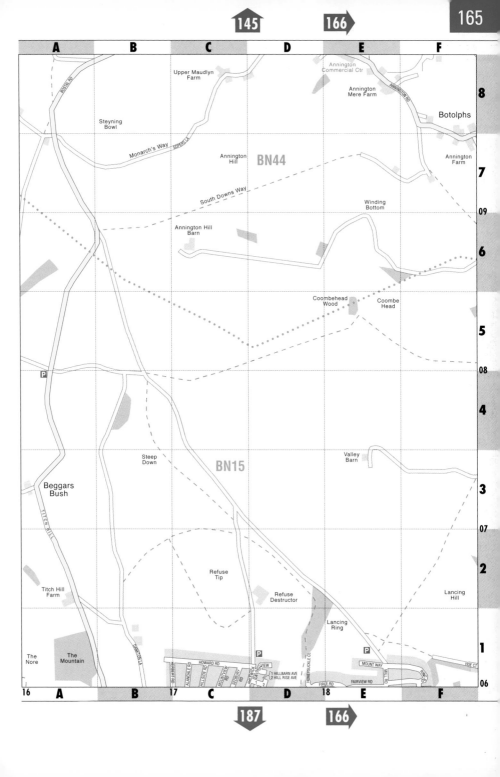

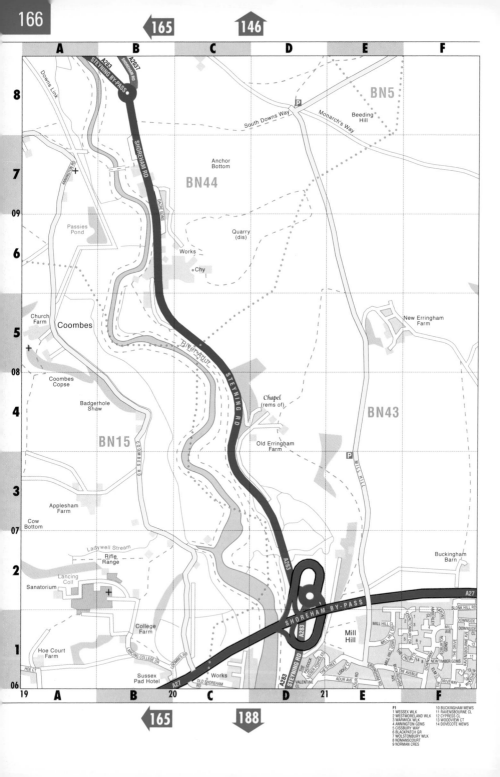

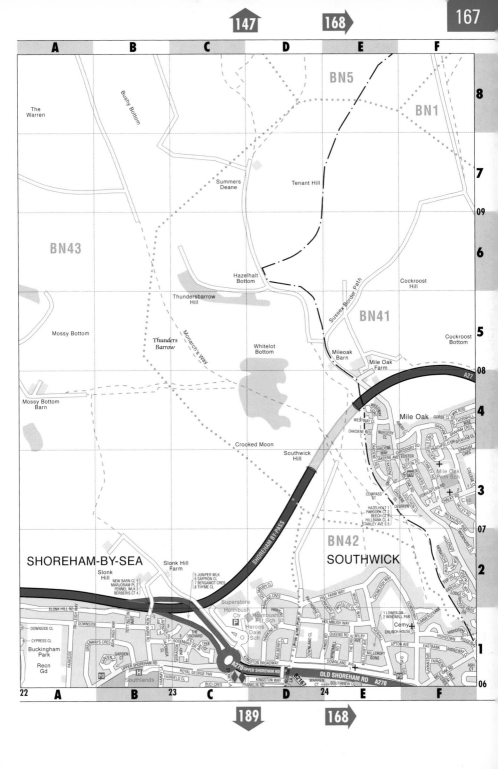

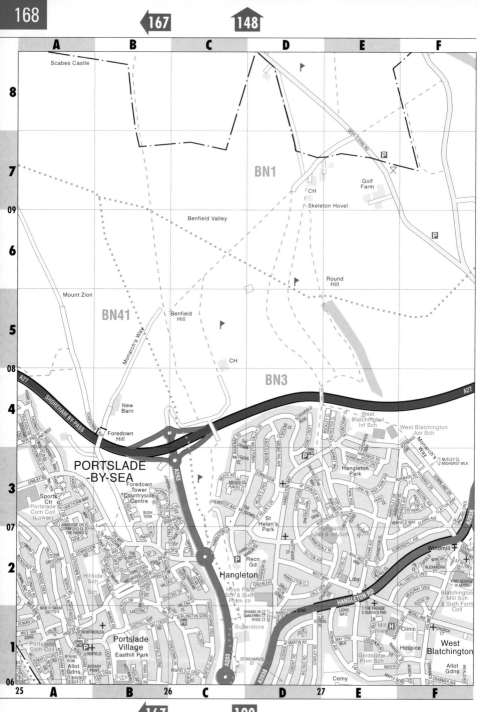

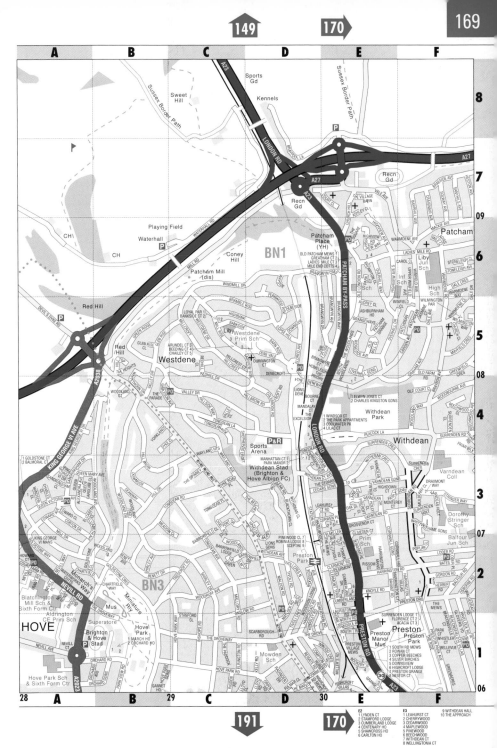

A | **B** | **C** | **D** | **E** | **F**

8

UPPER LODGES

Brighton & Hove City Coll

Stanmer

Pudding Bag

Stanmer Park

Stanmer House

Nurseries

COLDEAN RD

DITCHLING RD

OLD BOAT CNR

7

A27

Mast

LADIES MILE

Superstore

Hollingbury Ind Est

CROWHURST WLK

Enterprise Est

CROWHURST CNR

Stanmer House

Great Wood

09

Recn Gd

Carden Prim Sch

Coldean

Coldean Sch

Liby

SELHAM CL

ROTARY LODGE

FRAMFIELD

Coldean Wood

Marquee Brow

6

WALDRON PL 1
HAWKHURST PL 2
SELHAM PL 3
RUSPER RD 4
SELHAM CL 5
NEW LARCHWOOD 6

A27

Liby

Fernhurst Cres

1 CHEPSTOW CT
2 BARCOMBE PL
3 ANGMERING PL
4 FERRING CT
5 GORING CT
6 KINGSCOTE LODGE

A270

5

BN1

Wild Park Nature Trail

Sports Gd

EGGINTON RD

WOBURN PL

08

Hollingbury

Hollingbury Castle Fort

North Moulsecoomb

Mon

4

CH

Moulsecoomb Wild Park

Westergate Bsns Ctr 1
Fairway Bsns Ctr 2

Fairway Trad Est

1 OAKENDENE
2 HAWTHORN BANK

LARKFIELD WAY

SURRENDEN RD

BRIGHTON

UPPER ROEDALE COTTS

1 THE DIGGERS
2 LOWER ROEDALE COTTS
3 MIMOSA CT
4 LABURNUM GR
5 BRENTWOOD CL

WILD PARK CL

Kennels

THE ORCHARDS

L Ctr

East Moulsecoomb

LEWES RD

3

Varndean Sch

Recn Gd

30

Balfour Schs

STRINGER WAY

Allot Gdns

Hollingdean

Alternative Ctr for Ed

Home Farm Bsns Ctr

Moulsecoomb Prim Sch

BN2

07

BEACON RD

HUTTON RD

Hertford Jun Sch

FRAMROZE

Moulsecoomb

Bevendean

Norwich Cres

2

Stanmer

DOVER RD

ASHFORD RD

SANDGATE RD

KINGS PMR

HYTHE RD

Sch

The Cedar Ctr

Liby

40

Bevendean Prim Sch

1

PRESTON DRO

Hollingdean St

1 CRESTWAY PARADE
2 LINDFIELD CT

MARTHA GUNN RD

Racehill Valley

St Andrew's CE

Sch

GRANTHAM RD

RUGBY RD

1 RICHARD ALLEN CT

DUDENEY LODGE (NETTLETON)

FLORENCE

1 DENNIS HOBDEN CL
2 ROBIN DAVIS CT

DARTMOUTH

THE HYDE

06

31 | 32 | 33

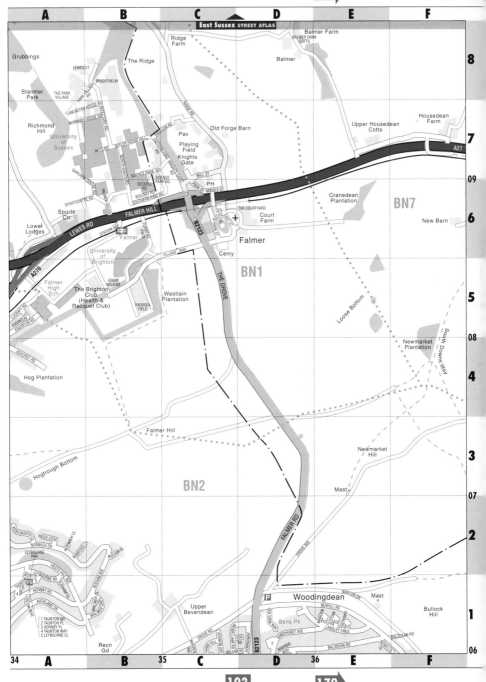

East Sussex STREET ATLAS

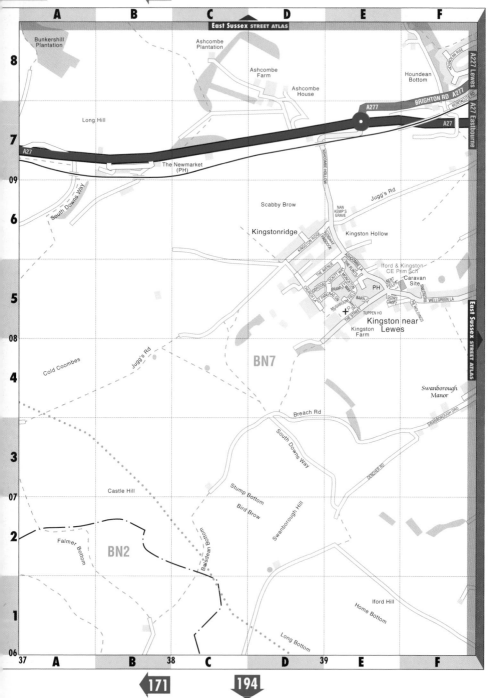

East Sussex STREET ATLAS

East Sussex STREET ATLAS

Bunkershill
Plantation

Ashcombe
Plantation

Ashcombe
Farm

Ashcombe
House

Houndean
Bottom

HOUNDEAN RISE

A277 Lewes

Long Hill

BRIGHTON RD

A277

MONTACUTE RD

A277

A27 Eastbourne

A277

A27

A27

The Newmarket
(PH)

South Downs Way

Scabby Brow

NAN
KEMP'S
GRAVE

Jugg's Rd

Kingstonridge

Kingston Hollow

KINGSTON RIDGE

GREENWAY
PARKBROOK

Iford & Kingston
CE Prim Sch

Caravan
Site

THE AVENUE

SOCKETT WAY

ASHCOMBE LA
THE ISHELDS

KENT
FIELDS

SPRINGETT AV
NEWTON RD

PH

CHURCHILL LA

ST STANISLAS LA

BRAMLEY RD

MUSHROOM FIELD

BARN CL

WELLGREEN LA

THE HOLLINGS

LOGANS
CROFT

THE STREET

TUPPEN HO

Kingston near
Lewes

Kingston
Farm

SWANBOROUGH

BN7

Swanborough
Manor

Cold Coombes

Jugg's Rd

Breach Rd

SWANBOROUGH DRO

South Downs Way

Castle Hill

Stump Bottom

Bird Brow

Swanborough Hill

DENCHER RD

Falmer Bottom

BN2

Balsdean Bottom

Iford Hill

Home Bottom

Long Bottom

37   A   38   B   C   38   D   39   E   F

8   7   09   6   5   08   4   3   07   2   1   06

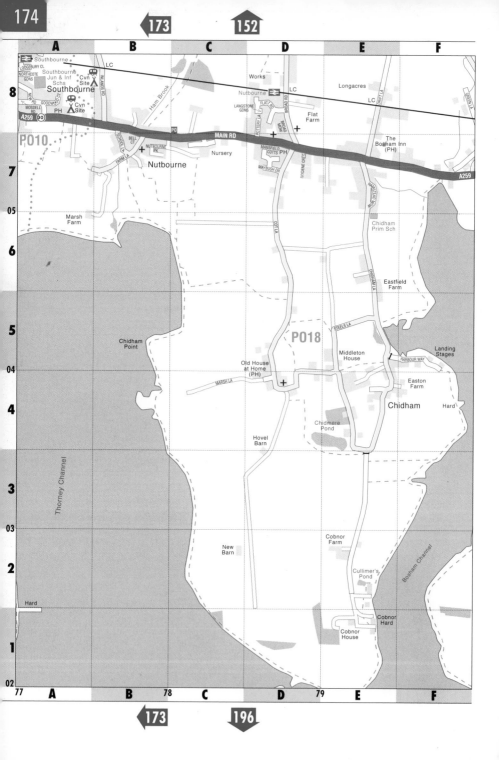

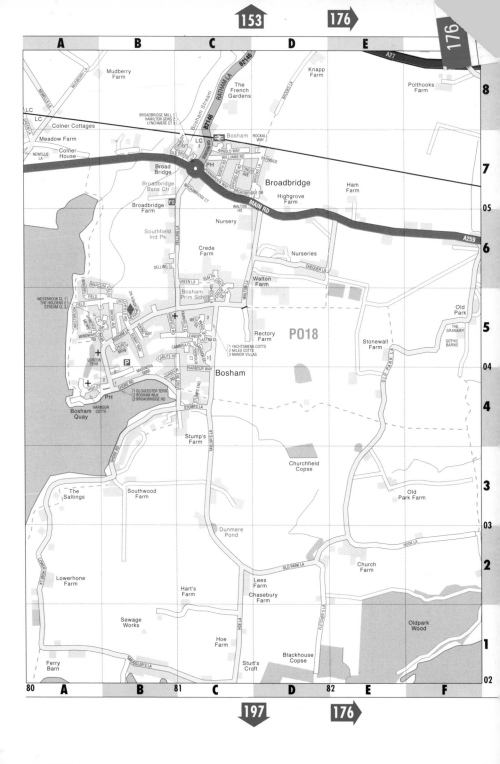

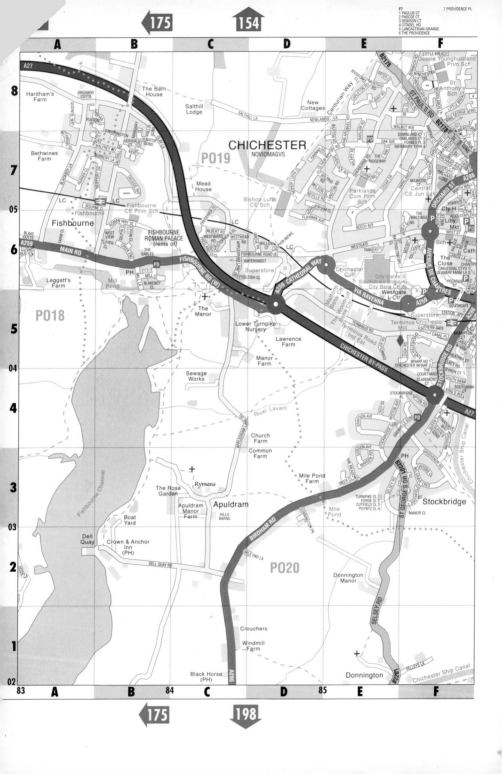

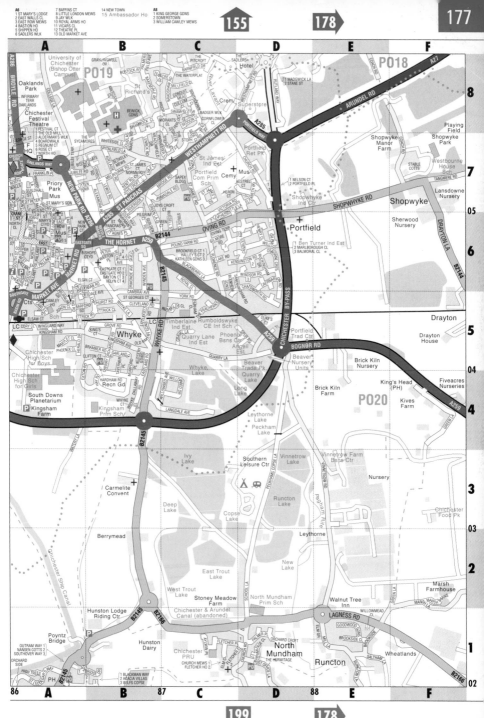

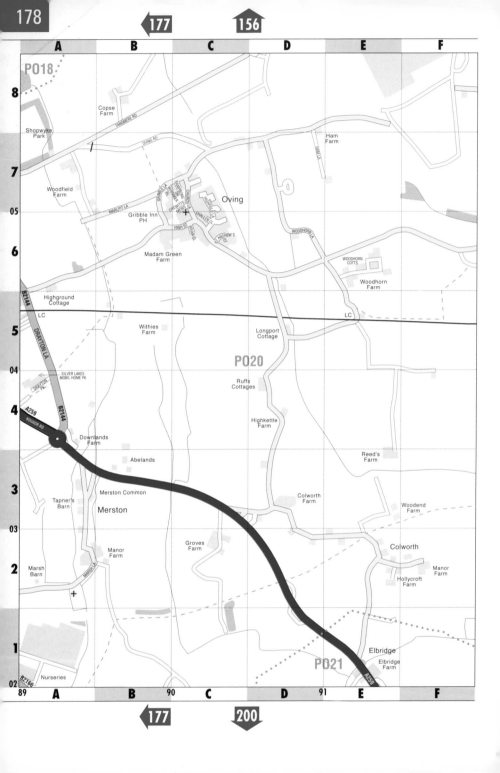

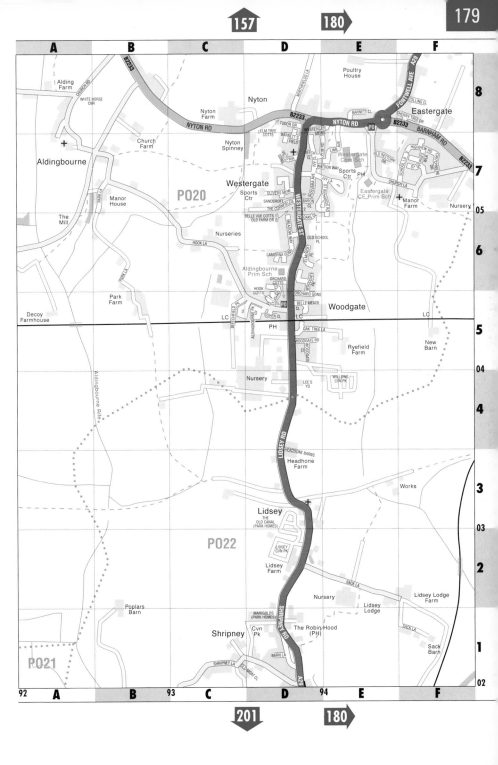

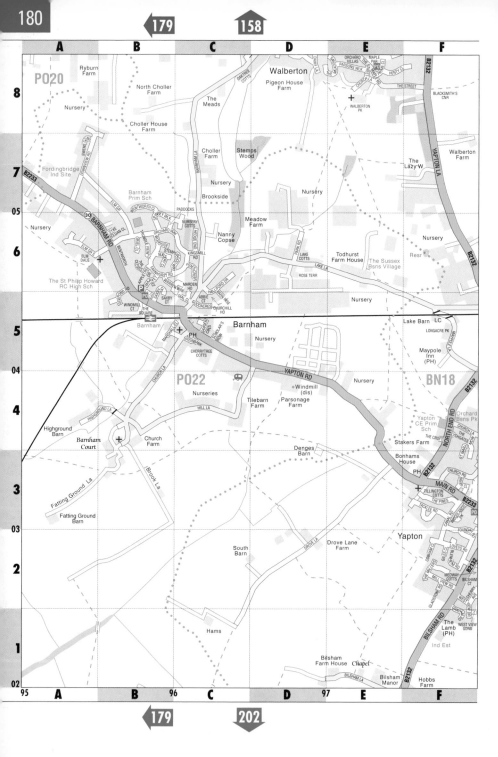

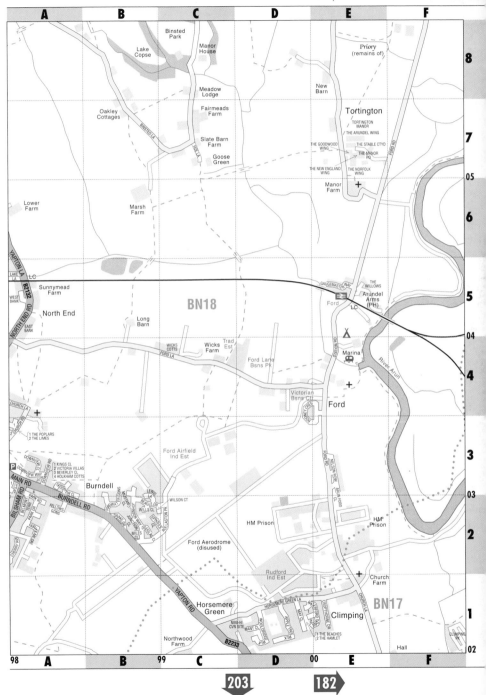

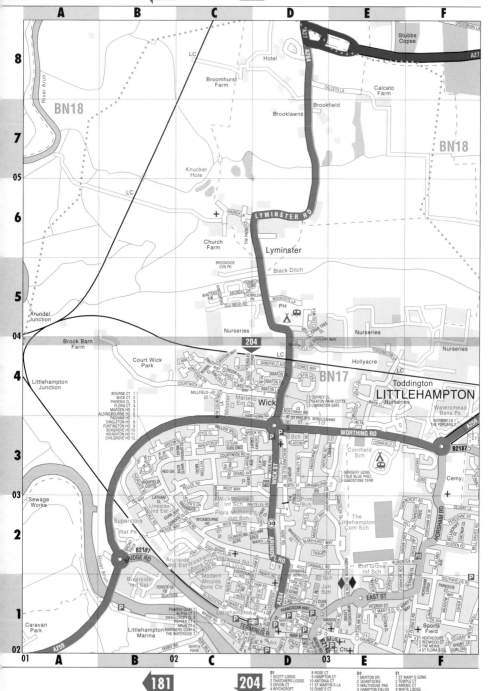

D1
1 SCOTT LODGE
2 THATCHERS LODGE
3 DEVON CT
4 WYCHCROFT
5 HOWARD PL
6 MADEHURST CT
7 DRUMMOND CT

8 ROSE CT
9 HAMPTON CT
10 ANTONIA CT
11 ST MARTIN'S LA
12 DUKE'S CT
13 ANCHOR SPRINGS
14 THE ARCADE
15 EVANS GDNS

D2
1 MERTON DR
2 QUANTOCKS
3 MALTHOUSE PAS
4 HAMPTON FIELDS

E1
1 ST MARY'S GDNS
2 TEMPLE CT
3 AMENIC CT
4 WHITE LODGE
5 SUMMERLEA GDNS
6 ST MARY'S CT

1 HEATHCOURT
2 REDWOOD CT
3 THE MEWS
4 ST FLORA'S CT

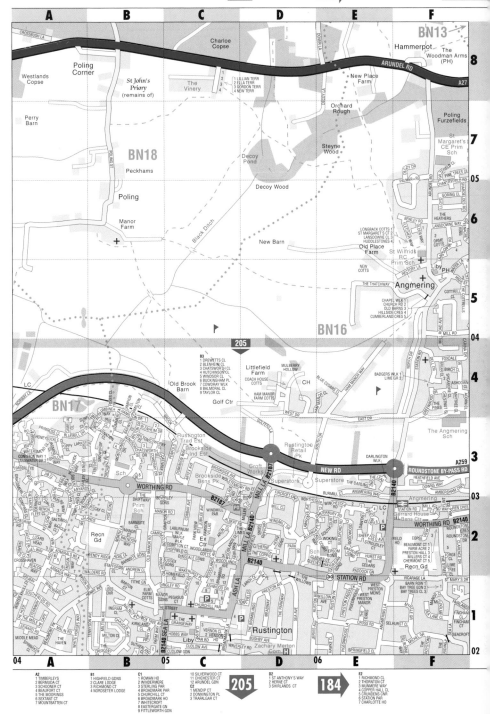

A2
1 TIMBERLEYS
2 BERMUDA CT
3 SCHOONER CT
4 BEAUFORT CT
5 THE MOORINGS
6 SEXTANT CT
7 MOUNTBATTEN CT

B1
1 HIGHFIELD GDNS

B2
1 CLARE LODGE
2 RICHMOND CT
3 NORDSETER LODGE

C1
1 ROWAN HO
2 WINDERMERE
3 STERLING PAR
4 BROADMARK RD
5 CHURCHILL CT
6 BROADMARK HO
7 WHITECROFT
8 EASTERGATE GN
9 FITTLEWORTH GDN

10 SILVERWOOD CT
11 CHICHESTER CT
12 ARUNDEL GDN

C2
1 MENDIP CT
2 DONNINGTON PL
3 TRAFALGAR CT

D2
1 ST ANTHONY'S WAY
2 HERNE CT
3 SHIRLANDS CT

E2
1 RICHMOND CL
2 THORNTON CT
3 MUNMERE WAY
4 COPPER HALL CL
5 CRUNDENS CNR
6 STATION PAR
7 CHARLOTTE HO

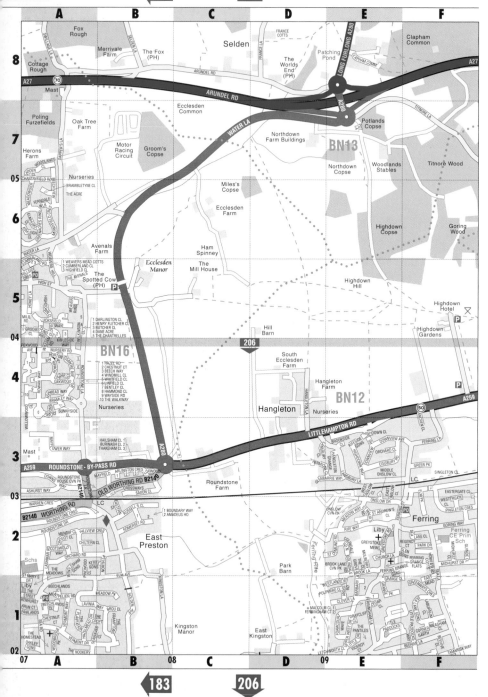

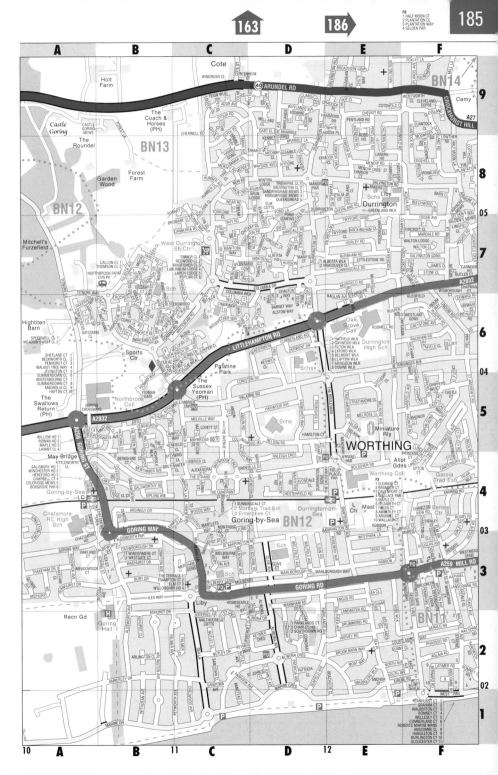

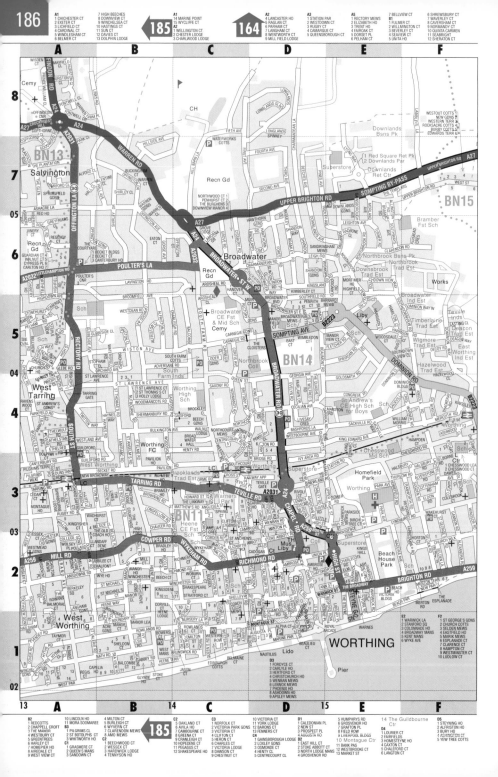

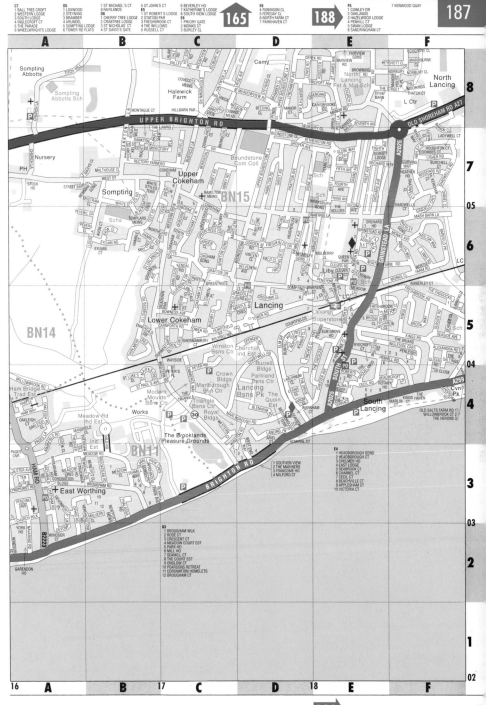

C7
1 BALL TREE CROFT
2 WESTERN LODGE
3 SOUTH LODGE
4 INGLECROFT CT
5 THE PARADE
6 WHEELWRIGHTS LODGE

D5
1 LOXWOOD
2 STEYNING
3 BRAMBER
4 ARUNDEL
5 SOMPTING LODGE
6 TOWER RD FLATS

7 ST MICHAEL'S CT
8 FAIRLANDS
D6
1 CHERRY TREE LODGE
2 CRABTREE LODGE
3 ST NICHOLAS CT
4 ST DAVID'S GATE

5 ST JOHN'S CT
E5
1 ST ROBERT'S LODGE
2 STATION PAR
3 FRESHBROOK CT
4 THE WILLOWS
5 RUSSELL CT

6 BEVERLEY HO
7 KATHERINE'S LODGE
8 SOUTH VIEW LODGE
E6
1 PRIORY GATE
2 MONKS CT
3 BURLEY CT

165

E6
4 ROBINSON CL
5 FEREDAY CL
6 NORTH FARM CT
7 PARKHAVEN CT

188

F5
1 COWLEY DR
2 OAKLANDS
3 HAZELWOOD LODGE
4 PENHILL CT
5 SWAN LODGE
6 SANDRINGHAM CT

7 KENWOOD QUAY

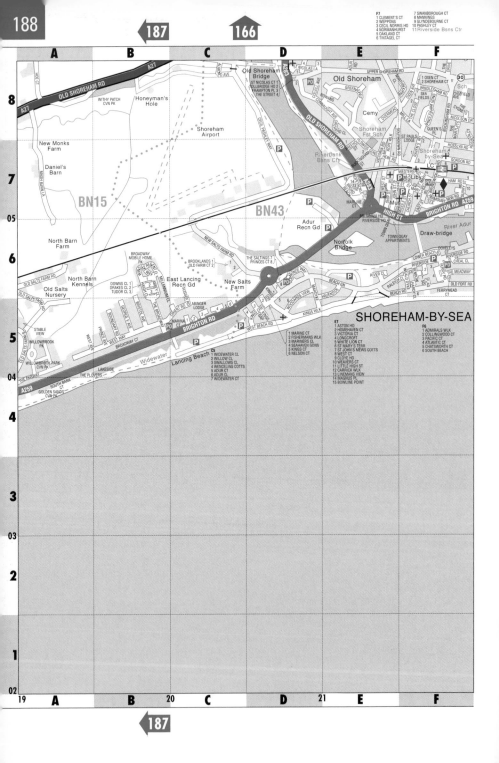

187
166
187

F7
1 CLEMENT'S CT
2 WEPPONS
3 CECIL NORRIS HO
4 NORMANHURST
5 OAKLAND CT
6 TINTAGEL CT

7 SWANBOROUGH CT
8 MANNINGS
9 GLYNDEBOURNE CT
10 PASHLEY CT
11 Riverside Bsns Ctr

OLD SHOREHAM RD
A27
A27
WITHY PATCH CVN PK
Honeyman's Hole
Old Shoreham Bridge
ST NICHOLAS LA
Old Shoreham
UPPER SHOREHAM RD
OXEN CT
SHOREHAM RD

New Monks Farm
Shoreham Airport
Cemy
Shoreham Fst Sch

Daniel's Barn

BN15
North Barn Farm

BN43
Adur Recn Gd

Shoreham by-Sea

North Barn Kennels
BROADWAY MOBILE HOME PK
East Lancing Recn Gd
New Salts Farm
THE SALTINGS 7 PRINCES CT 8
Norfolk Bridge
River Adur
Draw-bridge

Old Salts Nursery

BROOKLANDS 1 OLD FARM CT 2
ABINGER LODGE
BRIGHTON RD
BRIGHTON RD
WEST BEACH RD
KINGS WLK

STABLE VIEW
WILLOWBROOK PK

SHOREHAM-BY-SEA

1 MARINE CT
2 FISHERMANS WLK
3 MARINERS CL
4 SEAHAVEN GDNS
5 KINGS CT
6 NELSON CT

E7
1 ASTON HO
2 HOMEHAVEN CT
3 VICTORIA CT
4 LONGCROFT
5 WHITE LION CT
6 ST MARY'S TERR
7 ST JOHN'S MEWS COTTS
8 WEST CT
9 CLOVE HO
10 WEAVERS CT
11 LITTLE HIGH ST
12 CARRICK WLK
13 LINEMANS VIEW
14 MAGNUS PL
15 BOWLINE POINT

F6
1 ADMIRALS WLK
2 COLLINGWOOD CT
3 PACIFIC CT
4 ATLANTIC CT
5 CHATSWORTH CT
6 SOUTH BEACH

Lancing Beach
Widewater

C5
1 WIDEWATER CL
2 WILLOW CL
3 SWALLOWS CL
4 WENCELING COTTS
5 ADUR CL
6 ADUR PL
7 WIDEWATER CT

WILLOWBROOK PARK CVN PK
LAKESIDE
THE PLOVERS
GOLDEN SANDS CVN PK
A259
SOUTH BANK
THE FAIRWAY

19   A   20   C   D   21   E   F

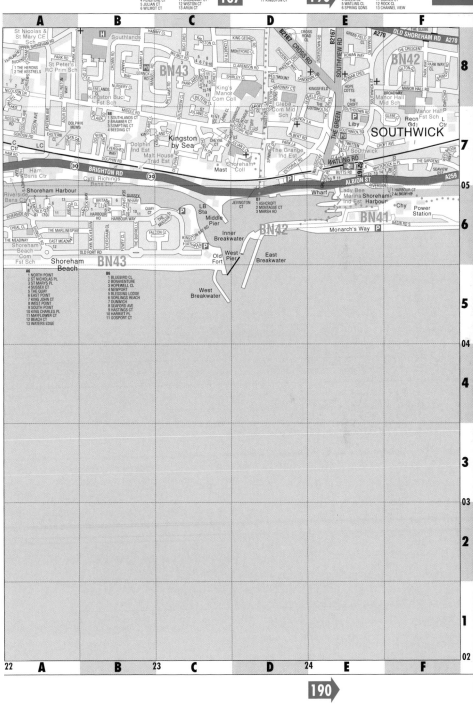

C8
1 LONEY CT
2 FRASER CT
3 MILWARD CT
4 PENSTONE CT
5 JULIAN CT
6 WILMOT CT

167

C8
7 OSBORNE CT
8 HOLMBUSH CT
9 DOWNES CT
10 ADUR CT
11 BROADWAY CT
12 WISTON CT
13 ARUN CT

C8
14 ARUNDEL CT
15 RECTORY CT
16 CAIUS CT
17 KINGSTON CT

190

E7
1 SCHOOL CL
2 TWITTEN CL
3 GREEN CT
4 GREEN CL
5 WATLING CL
6 SPRING GDNS

7 STATION RD
8 WATLING CT
9 GRANGE CT
10 LOCKS CT
11 COATES CT
12 ROCK CL
13 CHANNEL VIEW

14 SEA HO

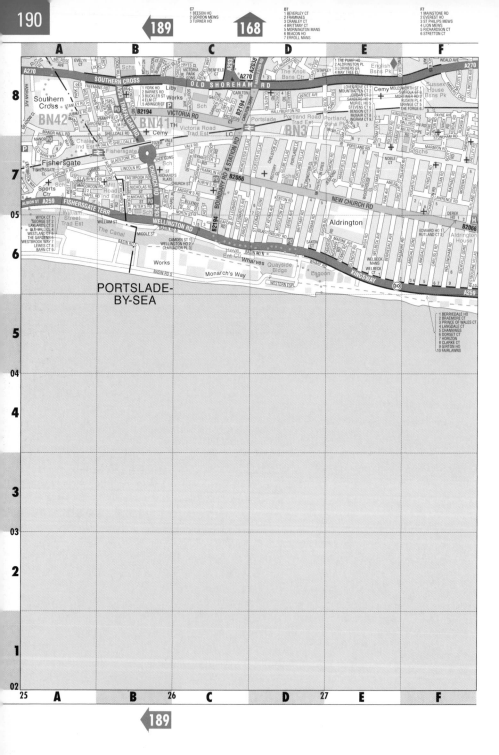

189
168
189

C7
1 BEESON HO
2 GORDON MEWS
3 TURNER HO

D7
1 BEVERLEY CT
2 FRAMNAES
3 CRANLEY CT
4 BRITTANY CT
5 MORNINGTON MANS
6 BEACON HO
7 ERROLL MANS

F7
1 MAINSTONE RD
2 EVEREST HO
3 ST PHILIPS MEWS
4 LION MEWS
5 RICHARDSON CT
6 STRETTON CT

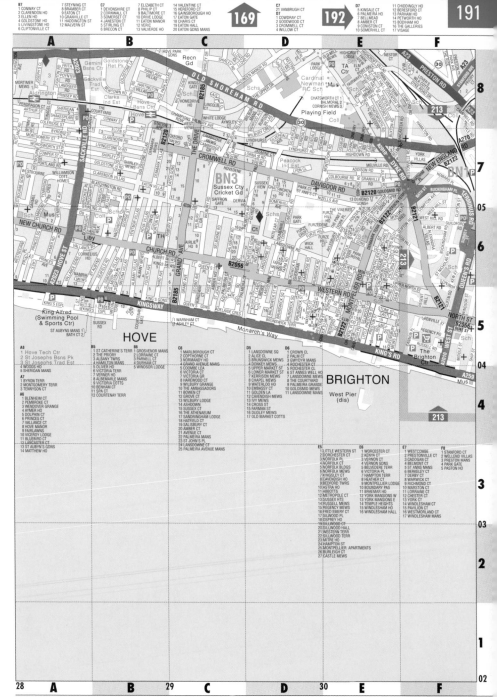

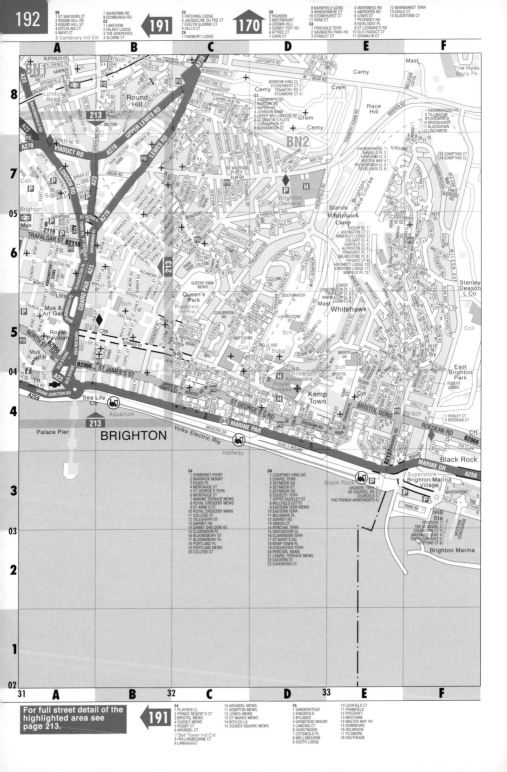

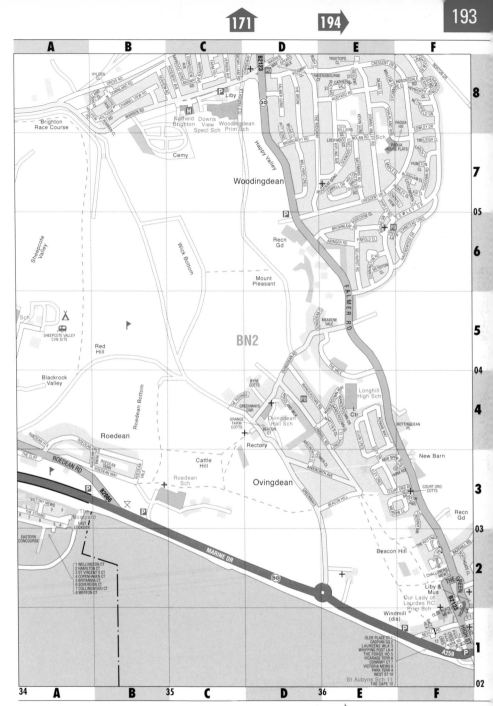

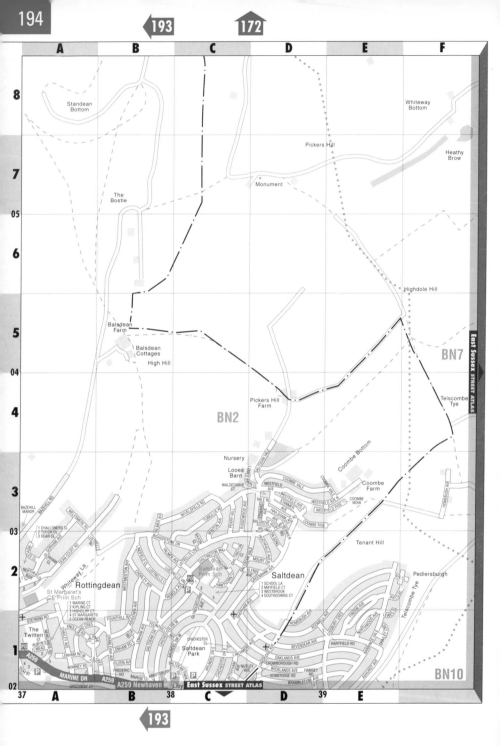

A B C D E F

8

7

05

6

05

5

04

4

03

3

2

1

02

37 A B 38 C D 39 E

Standean
Bottom

Whiteway
Bottom

Pickers Hill

Heathy
Brow

The
Bostle

Monument

Highdole Hill

East Sussex STREET ATLAS

BN7

Balsdean
Farm

Balsdean
Cottages

High Hill

BN2

Pickers Hill
Farm

Telscombe
Tye

Nursery

Looes
Barn

Coombe Bottom

Coombe
Farm

WALDEGRAVE
CT

WESTFIELD
AVE

COOMBE VALE

COOMBE
MDW

WESTFIELD RISE

COOMBE RISE

BAZEHILL
MANOR

1 CHALLONERS CL
2 TUDOR CL
3 DEAN CL

VALE RD

Tenant Hill

Pedlersburgh

Saltdean
Prim Sch

Saltdean

1 SCHOOL LA
2 MAYFIELD CT
3 WESTBROOK
4 SOUTHDOWNS CT

Rottingdean

St Margaret's
CE Prim Sch

1 MARINE CT
2 KIPLING CT
3 HIGHCLIFF CT
4 ST MARGARETS
5 OCEAN REACH

ORCHESTER
CL

Saltdean
Park

CROWBOROUGH RD

Hartfield RD

BEVENDEAN AVE

OAKLANDS AVE

WICKLANDS AVE

HAMSEY
RD

HOMERIDGE RD

BRAMBLE CHE

The
Twitten

A259

MARINE DR

A259

Newhaven

A259 Newhaven

East Sussex STREET ATLAS

BN10

8

PO10

7

01

Longmere
Point

6

Pilsey Island

5

00

Chichester Harbour

4

Stocker's Lake

3

East
Head

Black
Point

99

Marina

The
Spit

2

HAYLING ISLAND

THE
HOLLIES
CVN PK

THE
WILLOWS
CVN PK

EASTOKE RD

EARNLEY RD

SIDLESHAM
CL

SELSEY CL

Caravan
Pk

MILL RYTHE LN

HILLING RD

BRACKLESHAM RD

Lifeboat
Station

BIRDHAM RD

HAVEN RD

HAVEN RD

SANDY POINT RD

THE LOAM RD

PO20

South Hayling
PO11

WHEATLANDS AVE

WHEATLANDS
CRES

CONYMBROOM
RD

SANDY BEACH
EST

1

SOUTHWOOD RD

Eastoke Point

98

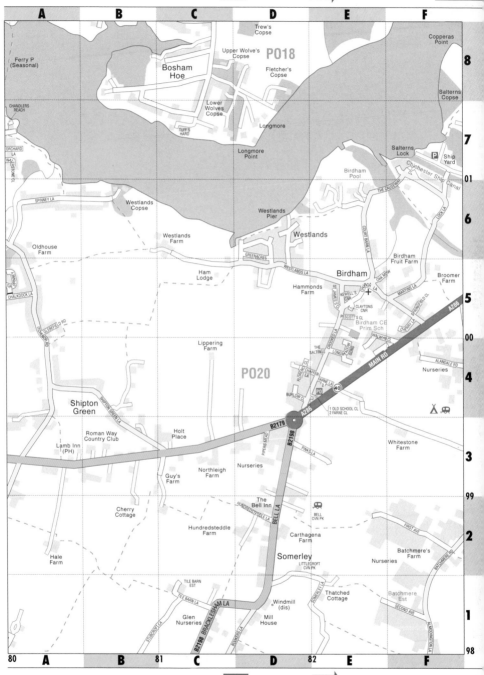

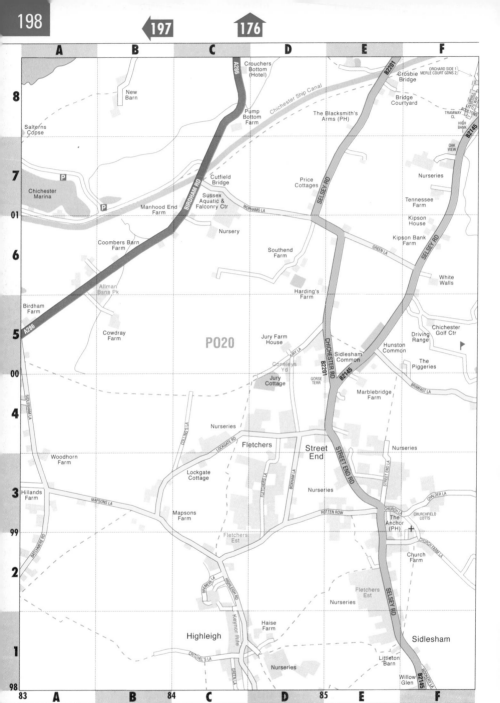

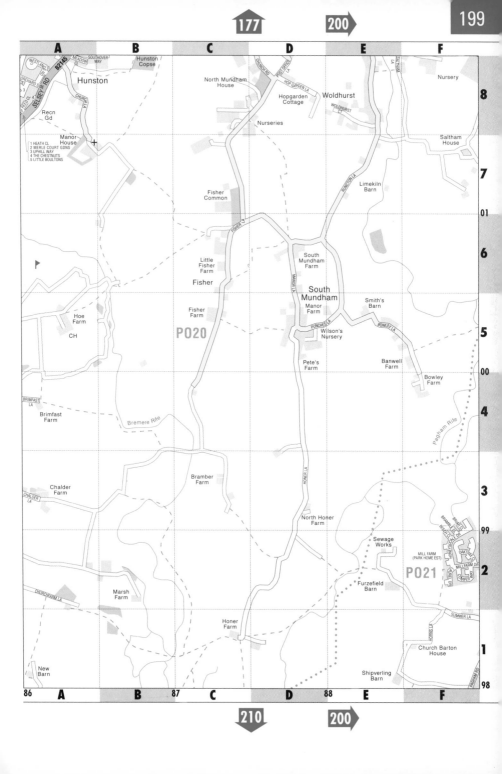

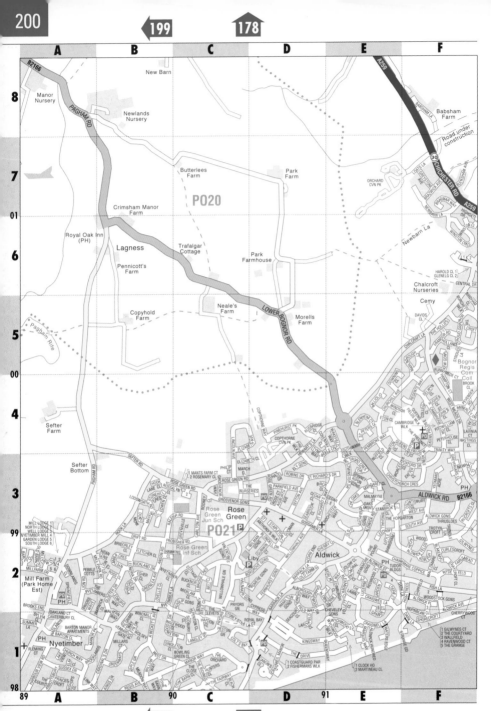

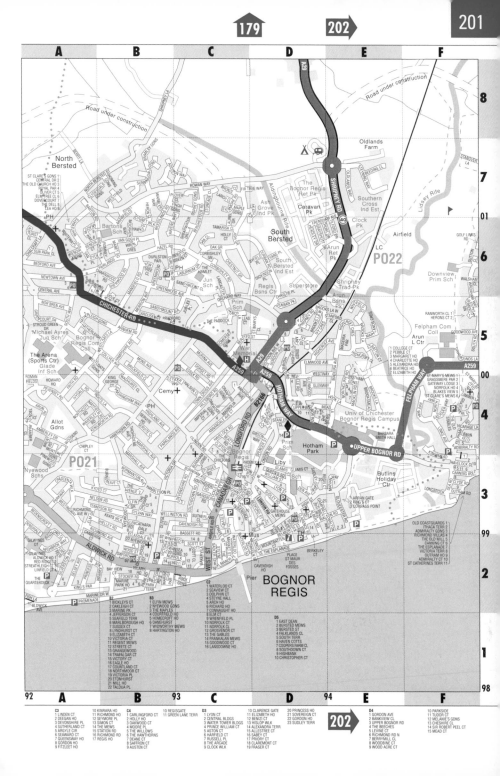

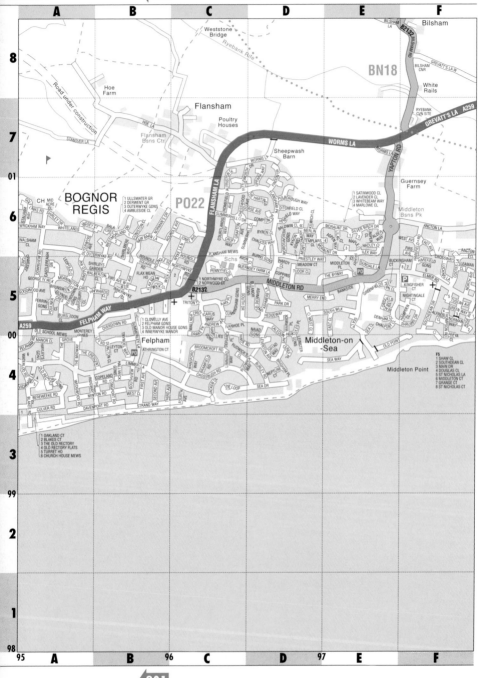

201
180

Weststone
Bridge

Ryebank Rife

BILSHAM
LA

B2132

Bilsham

BN18

GREVATT'S LA W

BILSHAM
CNR

White
Rails

Hoe
Farm

Road under construction

HOE LA

STANOVER LA

Flansham

Poultry
Houses

RYEBANK
CVN SITE

GREVATT'S LA A259

WORMS LA

Flansham
Bsns Ctr

Sheepwash
Barn

WORMS

YAPTON RD

Guernsey
Farm

**BOGNOR
REGIS**

CH MID
ACRE
INKS RD SHIRLEY RD
WROXHAM WAY

1 ULLSWATER GR
2 DERWENT GR
3 OUTERWYKE GDNS
4 AMBLESIDE CL

PO22

FLANSHAM LA

SUMMERHIELD
SUMMERLEA

ALRESFORD

THORNEFIELD

COURTLANDS

Flansham Mews

CHURCH
HARTING
LAVENDER

PULBROUGH WAY

DITCHFIELD CL
HEIGLD WAY

1 SATINWOOD CL
2 LAVENDER CL
3 WHITEBEAM WAY
4 MARLOWE CL

Middleton
Bsns Pk

ANCTON LA

WALSHAM
CL

BALA
HIGHLANDS

OLD RUNDWAY
CONSTITUTION

SUMMERLEA

GORSE AVE
COMPTON

BYRON CL

CHAUCER WAY

BALDWIN CL

MGRAUNT DR

ASH CL
TEMPLARS
CHESTNUT DR

MAPLE
SILVER BIRCH DR

HADLEY
ILEX CL

WEST AVE
FIRS
AVE

ANCTON
LA

CROSSWAYS

LEAMAN
CL

OUTERWYKE
GDNS

WHITELANDS

SHIRLEY'S
GARDEN
HALBERTON

FIRS
AVE

SCH4
1 NORTHWYKE CL
2 NORWOOD CT

BURNS GDNS

HARDY

PRIESTLEY WAY

MEADOW CT
TUDOR CL

MIDDLETON
PL
THE BYWAY

BUCKINGHAM

ELMER RD

SHEFFIELD
GDNS

GEORGE IV RD

BRUNSWICK

GOODWOOD AVE
FERRING
GDNS
BURSLEDON

WAYFARDS

FLAX MEAN
NICK CL
LOREL

ROUNDLE
SQUARE

NORTHWYKE
RD

PENNYTHE

MIDDLETON RD

ROPPINS
CT

ASHMERE

PARK DR

MERRY END
BANKSIDE

PO

KINGFISHER
CT

NIGHTINGALE
CT

LUSCAN AVE
GREEN WAY
NORTHMAN
WAY

A259

FELPHAM WAY

MONTEREY
PINES
GROVE

OVERDOWN RD

OLD SCHOOL MEWS

TRITON CL

B2132

1 CLOVELLY AVE
2 FELPHAM GDNS
3 OLD MANOR HOUSE GDNS
4 INNERWYKE MANOR

CARUS
NAMHOE CL

ANDREW

HEDGEWAY

CALCOT

SOUTH WLK

EAST CL

DENHAM
CHALFONT

OLD POINT

GREENFIELDS

GREENFIELDS RD
OLD
FIELD
CL

ALFRED RD

Felpham

ATHRINGTON CT

LIMMER LA

SLEYTON

DIRAC

NAIAD
GDNS

BROOMCROFT RD

Middleton-on
-Sea

SEA WAY

P5
1 SHAW CL
2 SOUTHDEAN CL
3 MAIN DR
4 DOUGLAS CL
5 ST NICHOLAS LA
6 MIDDLETON CT
7 GRANGE CT
8 ST NICHOLAS CT

FELPHAM RD
MANLEYS
PRIORY

WATERLOO RD
VICARAGE
BEREWEEKE RD
BLAKES RD

COPELAND
MINTON RD
MEGROOVND RD
FREEDOWN
HALLIWICK

FIRST AVE
SECOND AVE
THIRD AVE
FOURTH
AVE

CROSSBUSH RD

THE LOOP
SEA DR

Middleton Point

DAVENPORT RD
WEST CL
STRAND WAY

CULVER RD

1 OAKLAND CT
2 BLAKES CT
3 THE OLD RECTORY
4 OLD RECTORY FLATS
5 TURRET HO
6 CHURCH HOUSE MEWS

201

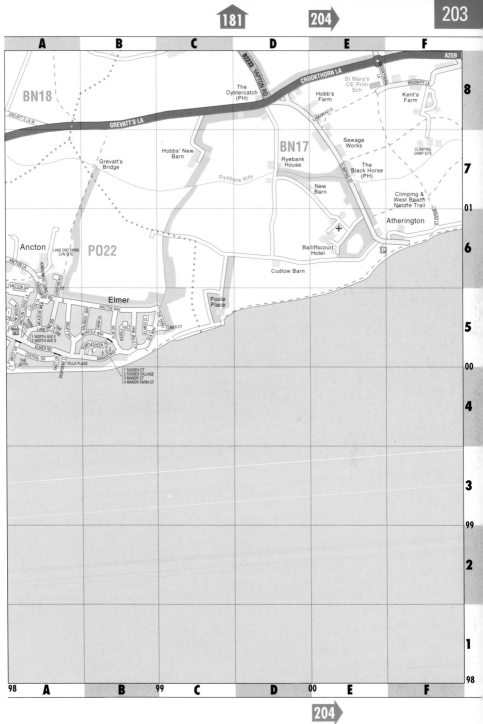

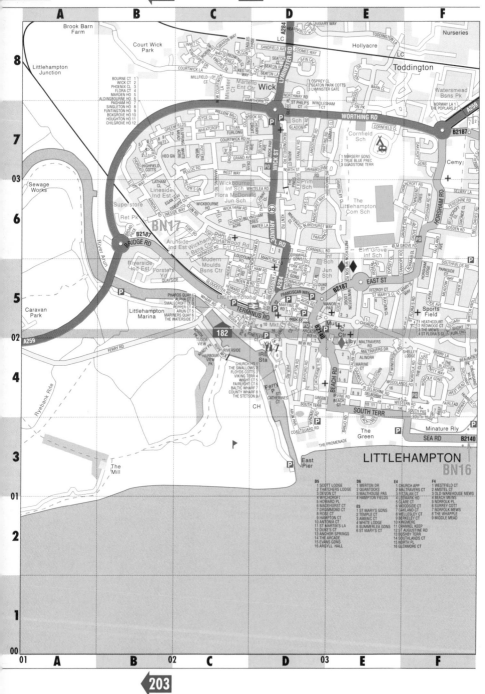

A **B** **C** **D** **E** **F**

Hangleton

South
Ecclesden
Farm

Hangleton
Farm

Nurseries

LITTLEHAMPTON RD

ROUNDSTONE · BY-PASS RD

A259

OLD WORTHING RD B2140

Roundstone
Farm

BN12

Ferring

WORTHING RD

B2140

East
Preston

BN16

Park Barn

Kingston
Manor

East
Kingston

184

Kingston
Gorse

West Kingston

COASTAL RD

A4
1 WENTWORTH CT
2 CROWN PL
3 CROWN CT
4 WILLOWHAYNE CL
5 WILLOWHAYNE CRES
6 SOUTH STRAND PAR
7 THE PARADE
8 PARADE MANS
9 WILLOWHAYNE CL
10 COASTGUARD COTTS
11 STRAND CT
12 PALM COURT COTTS
13 THE RAMBLERS

F4
1 ST AUBINS CT
2 ST HELIER CT
3 ST AUBINS RD
4 ST MALO CT
5 ELVERLANDS CL
6 DOONE END
7 MILBURY CL
8 FLORIDA GDNS

B8
1 HAZEL RD
2 CHESTNUT CT
3 BEECH WAY
4 WINDMILL CL
5 WHITFIELD CL
6 LINFIELD CL
7 BENTLEY CL
8 HAMMOND CL
9 WAYSIDE RD
10 THE WALKWAY

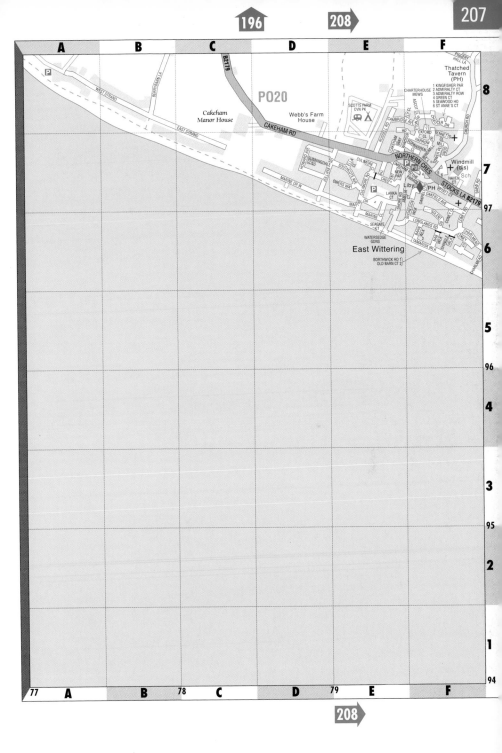

PO20

Cakeham
Manor House

Webb's Farm
House

CAKEHAM RD

EAST STRAND

WEST STRAND

Scotts Farm
CVN PK

Thatched
Tavern
(PH)

1 KINGFISHER PAR
2 ADMIRALTY CT
3 ADMIRALTY ROW
4 GREEN CT
5 SEAWOOD HO
6 ST ANNE S CT

CHARTERHOUSE
MEWS

NORTHERN CRES

Windmill
(dis)

Sch

STOCKS LA B2179

HAVEN

Lib

PH

East Wittering

SEAGATE
CT

WATERSEDGE
GDNS

BORTHWICK HO 1
OLD BARN CT 2

MARINE DR W

SUNNINGDALE
GDNS

OWERS WAY

LANKA
CT

LONGLANDS RD

TAMARISK WLK

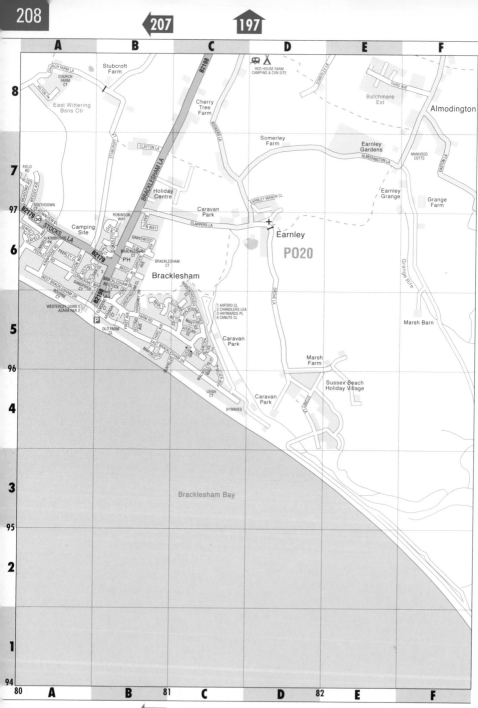

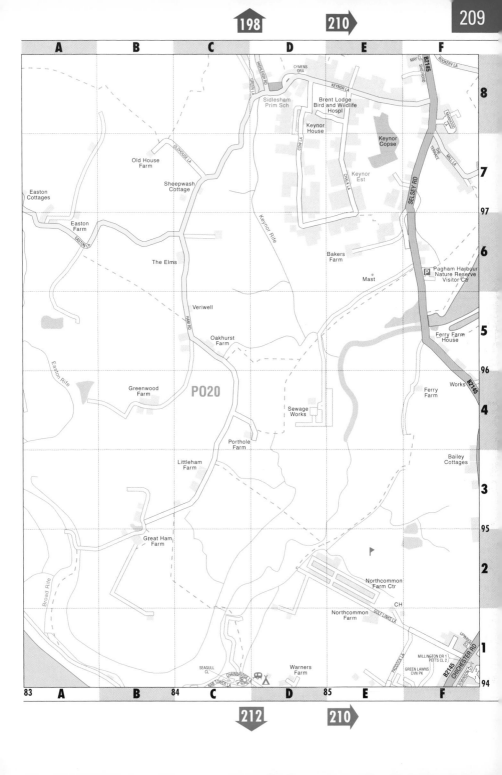

209
199

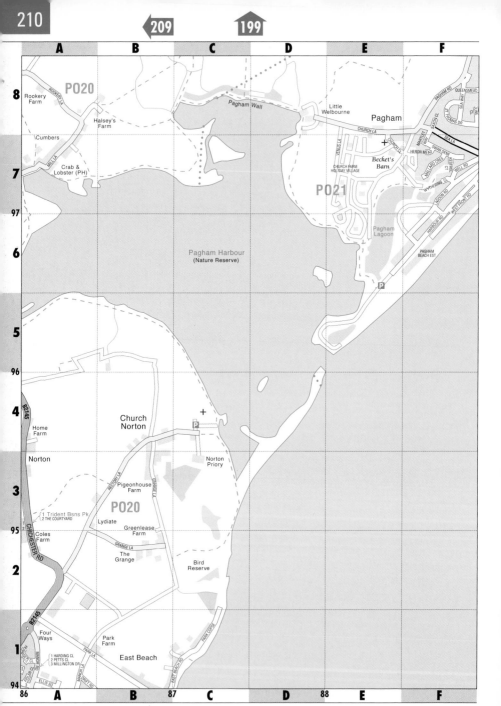

A **B** **C** **D** **E** **F**

8

PO21

TITHE BARN CT 1
BAY CT 2

BOGNOR
REGIS

7

1 ST THOMAS CT
2 CHURCHILL WLK
3 MULBERRY CT

97

6

5

96

4

3

95

2

1

94

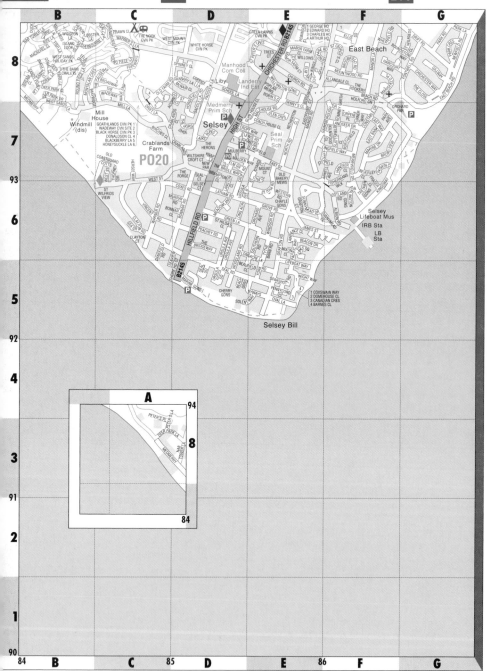

East Beach

Mill House

Windmill (dis)

Crablands Farm

PO20

ST WILFRIDS VIEW

GOATHLANDS CVN PK 1
WADEWAY CVN SITE 2
BLACK HORSE CVN PK 3
DONALDSON CL 4
BLACKBERRY LA 5
HONEYSUCKLE LA 6

Selsey

Medmerry Prim Sch

Manhood Com Coll

Landerry Ind Est

Seal Prim Sch

Selsey Lifeboat Mus

IRB Sta
LB Sta

Selsey Bill

1 COXSWAIN WAY
2 DOMEHOUSE CL
3 CANADIAN CRES
4 BARNES CL

A
94
PETER'S PL
DEER PARK LA
MEDMERRY
8
84

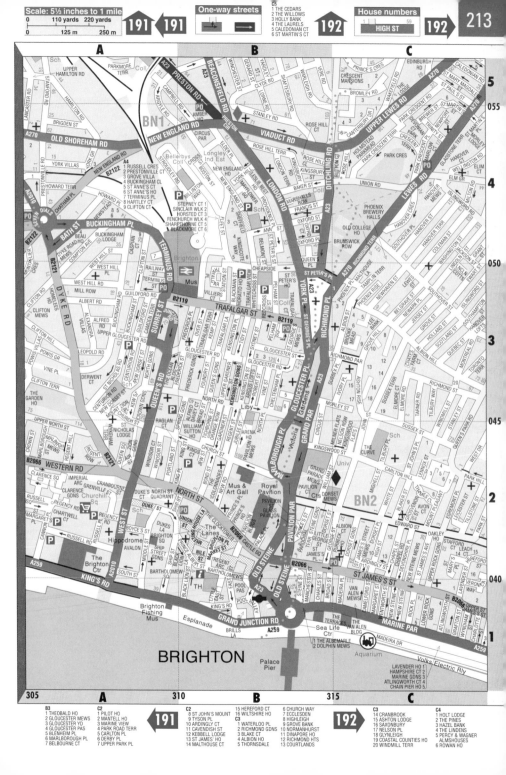

Index

Place name May be abbreviated on the map

Location number Present when a number indicates the place's position in a crowded area of mapping

Locality, town or village Shown when more than one place has the same name

Postcode district District for the indexed place

Page and grid square Page number and grid reference for the standard mapping

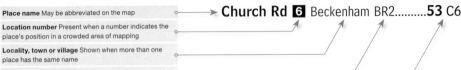

Church Rd **6** Beckenham BR2.........**53** C6

Cities, towns and villages are listed in CAPITAL LETTERS   Public and commercial buildings are highlighted in magenta
Places of interest are highlighted in blue with a star★

Abbreviations used in the index

Acad	Academy	Comm	Common	Gd	Ground	L	Leisure	Prom	Promenade
App	Approach	Cott	Cottage	Gdn	Garden	La	Lane	Rd	Road
Arc	Arcade	Cres	Crescent	Gn	Green	Liby	Library	Recn	Recreation
Ave	Avenue	Cswy	Causeway	Gr	Grove	Mdw	Meadow	Ret	Retail
Bglw	Bungalow	Ct	Court	H	Hall	Meml	Memorial	Sh	Shopping
Bldg	Building	Ctr	Centre	Ho	House	Mkt	Market	Sq	Square
Bsns, Bus	Business	Ctry	Country	Hospl	Hospital	Mus	Museum	St	Street
Bvd	Boulevard	Cty	County	HQ	Headquarters	Orch	Orchard	Sta	Station
Cath	Cathedral	Dr	Drive	Hts	Heights	Pal	Palace	Terr	Terrace
Cir	Circus	Dro	Drove	Ind	Industrial	Par	Parade	TH	Town Hall
Cl	Close	Ed	Education	Inst	Institute	Pas	Passage	Univ	University
Cnr	Corner	Emb	Embankment	Int	International	Pk	Park	Wk, Wlk	Walk
Coll	College	Est	Estate	Intc	Interchange	Pl	Place	Wr	Water
Com	Community	Ex	Exhibition	Junc	Junction	Prec	Precinct	Yd	Yard

Index of towns, villages, streets, hospitals, industrial estates, railway stations, schools, shopping centres, universities and places of interest

214 Abb–Ale

A

Abberton Field BN6......128 B5
Abbey Cl BN15..........188 B6
Abbey Ho RH20..........142 D8
Abbey Rd
  Brighton BN2............192 D4
  Lancing BN15...........187 C7
  Steyning BN44.........145 E4
  Worthing BN11.........186 B1
Abbie Ct PO22...........180 C5
Abbotsbury Cl BN2....194 B1
Abbotsbury Ct RH13....36 E3
Abbots Cl BN41.........128 E4
Abbotsfield Rd RH11....17 D4
ABBOTSFORD...........108 E6
Abbotsleigh RH13......82 A8
Abbots Way BN15......187 F6
Abbotswood Wlk
  BN16...................205 C4
Abbotts **11** BN1.......191 E5
Abbottsbury PO21....211 A8
Abbotts Cl
  Boxgrove PO18........156 D3
  Worthing BN11........186 D2
Abbotts View BN15....187 C8
A'becket Gdns BN13...185 F7
A'becket's Ave PO21...200 B1
Aberdare Cl PO19......177 B8
Aberdeen Rd **5** BN2...192 C8
Abergavenny Gdns
  RH10.....................7 D3
Abigail Ho **10** RH16....87 E4
Abingdon Wlk BN13...185 D6
Abinger Ct BN41........190 B8
Abinger Keep RH6........2 C4
Abinger Lo BN15......188 C5
Abinger Rd
  Portslade-by-S BN41...190 B8
  Woodingdean BN2.....193 E6
ABINGWORTH...........122 A6
Abrahams Rd RH11.....18 A1
Acacia Ave
  Hove BN3.................168 F1
  Worthing BN13.........185 F8
Acacia Ct BN1..........169 F2
Acacia Villas PO20.....177 B3
Acorn Ave RH13.........83 F1

Acorn Cl
  Angmering BN16......205 F8
  East Grinstead RH19....22 E8
  Horley RH6................2 C4
  Selsey PO20............212 D8
Acorn End PO21.........200 D2
Acorns RH13..............37 A4
Acorns The
  Burgess Hill RH15.....108 D4
  Crawley RH11...........18 B1
  Sayers Common BN6...107 D2
Acre Cl
  Haywards Heath RH16....87 D2
  Rustington BN16......205 B6
Acre Cl The BN11........186 B1
Acre Gdns BN11.........186 B1
Acre St PO20.............196 F2
Acre The BN16...........184 A6
Adams Cl BN1...........170 B2
Adams Mews GU30......25 C2
Adamson Ct **6** RH11...18 B1
Adastra Ave BN6........129 A4
Adderbury Ave PO10...151 B3
Addison Cl BN15........187 E6
Addison Rd BN3.........191 E7
Addison Way PO22.....201 C7
Adelaide Cl
  Crawley RH11............5 D1
  Horsham RH12..........36 F4
  Worthing BN13........185 C8
Adelaide Cotts PO18...156 E6
Adelaide Cres BN3.....191 C5
Adelaide Ho GU29......94 E6
Adelaide Rd PO19......177 B7
Adelaide Sq BN43.....189 B7
Adelphi Cl RH10........19 D4
Admers Cres GU30......25 C2
Admiral Ct BN15.......187 D4
Admiral Rd RH11........18 A3
Admiral's Bridge La
  RH19...................22 C2
Admirals Wlk
  Funtington PO18......153 A5
  Littlehampton BN17...205 A6
  1 Shoreham-by-S
  BN43....................188 F6
Admiralty Ct
  Bognor Regis PO22...201 F3
  East Wittering PO20..207 F7
Admiralty Gdns PO22..201 F3
Admiralty Row PO20...207 F7
Adrian Ct RH11..........18 B1

Adur Ave
  Shoreham-by-S BN43....166 E1
  Worthing BN13.........185 C9
Adur Cl **6** BN15......188 C5
Adur Ct
  5 Lancing BN15....188 C5
  10 Shoreham-by-S
  BN43....................189 C8
Adur Dr BN43............189 A7
Adur Rd
  Burgess Hill RH15....109 C4
  Shoreham-by-S BN43...188 E8
Adur Valley Ct BN44...146 B2
Adur View BN44.........146 A2
Adversane Ct RH12......36 D4
Adversane Cvn Pk
  RH14.....................79 A2
Adversane La RH14.....79 D2
Adversane Rd BN14....186 B5
Aegean Ho **3** BN16...205 A4
Agate Ho RH6............36 F5
Aglaia Rd BN11..........185 F2
Agnes St BN2............192 C7
Aigburth Ave PO21....200 D3
Ailsa Cl RH11............18 B3
Ainsdale Cl BN13......185 D7
Ainsdale Rd BN13.....185 D7
Ainsworth Ave BN2....193 D3
Ainsworth Ho **1** BN2...192 C7
Aintree Rd RH10........19 A4
Airedale Ct **8** BN11..186 B2
Airlie Ho BN3............191 C6
Airport Way RH6.........6 B8
Airport Way Rdbt E RH6....6 C8
Airport Way Rdbt W
  RH6......................5 F8
Air St BN1................213 A2
Aitken Ho GU27..........27 C7
Ajax Pl PO22............202 C5
Akehurst Cl RH10........7 B3
Alandale Rd
  Birdham PO20........197 F4
  Lancing BN15..........165 C1
Alan Way BN2...........192 F5
Albany Ct BN11..........186 A6
Albany Mews BN3......191 B6
Albany Rd RH11.........18 C6
Albany Twrs **3** BN3...191 B5
Albany Villas
  Cuckfield RH17.........87 A6
  Hove BN3...............191 B6

Albemarle Mans **8**
  BN3.....................191 B5
Albemarle The BN2....213 B1
Alberta Rd BN13........185 D7
Alberta Wlk BN13......185 D7
Albert Cl RH16...........88 A4
Albert Crane Ct RH11...18 A8
Albert Dr RH15..........108 E2
Albert Mews BN3......191 C6
Albert Rd
  Bognor Regis PO21...201 D3
  Brighton BN1...........213 A3
  Fishbourne PO19......176 C6
  Horley RH6...............2 A3
  Littlehampton BN17...204 D5
  Rustington BN16......205 C6
  Southwick BN42......189 D7
Albery Cl RH12..........36 B4
Albion Cl RH10...........19 D5
Albion Ct
  Brighton BN2..........213 C2
  Burgess Hill RH15....108 F2
  Horley RH6..............2 A3
Albion Hill BN2.........213 C3
Albion Ho
  4 Brighton BN2....213 C3
  Southwick BN42......189 F7
Albion Rd PO20.........212 F6
Albion St
  Brighton BN2..........213 C2
  Portslade-by-S BN41...190 B7
  Southwick BN42......189 E7
Albion Way RH12........36 C2
Alborough Way PO21..200 D2
Albourne CE Prim Sch
  BN6.....................127 C6
Albourne Cl BN3........190 F7
Albourne Rd BN6......127 E6
ALBOURNE STREET....127 C5
Albury Keep RH6........2 B4
Aldbourne Dr PO21...200 D2
Aldeburgh Ho RH6......2 A2
Alder Cl
  Crawley Down RH10....21 B8
  Worthing BN13........185 C6
Alder Copse RH12......57 F8
Alderfield GU32..........68 A3
Alderman's Wlk PO19...177 B7
Aldermoor Ave RH20...121 E3
Alderney Rd BN12......206 F4
Alders Ave RH19..........9 E3
Alders Gdns PO21......200 E3
Alders View RH19........9 E3
Alder Way PO22.........202 E6
Aldingbourne Cl RH11...17 F7

Aldingbourne Ctry Ctr★
  PO18....................157 C3
Aldingbourne Dr
  PO18....................157 B3
Aldingbourne Ho
  Crockerhill PO18......157 B3
  Littlehampton BN17...204 B7
Aldingbourne Pk
  PO20....................179 D5
Aldingbourne Prim Sch
  PO20....................179 D6
Aldrich Cl BN2...........192 F6
ALDRINGTON............190 E6
Aldrington Ave BN3....191 B8
Aldrington CE Prim Sch
  BN3.....................169 A2
Aldrington Cl BN3......190 F6
Aldrington House Hospl
  BN3.....................190 D8
Aldrington Sta BN3....191 A8
ALDSWORTH............151 F6
Aldsworth Ave BN12...185 B2
Aldsworth Common Rd
  PO10....................151 E5
Aldsworth Ct BN12....185 B3
Aldsworth Par BN12...185 B3
Aldsworth Manor Barns
  PO10....................151 F6
Aldsworth Par BN12...185 B3
ALDWICK................200 E2
Aldwick Ave PO21......200 E2
Aldwick Bay Est PO21..211 C8
Aldwick Cl **1** BN16...205 B3
Aldwick Cres BN14....164 A1
Aldwick Felds PO21....200 F2
Aldwick Gdns PO21...200 F3
Aldwick Ho PO21......201 A2
Aldwick Hundred
  PO21....................200 E1
Aldwick Pl PO21........200 F2
Aldwick Rd PO21......201 B2
Aldwick St PO21........200 E2
Aldwych Cl RH10........19 D4
Alexander Ct PO21....200 E2
Alexandra Ct
  6 Crawley RH10....18 D5
  Hove BN3................168 F2
  Worthing BN12........185 F4
Alexandra Ho PO22...201 E4
Alexandra Rd
  Burgess Hill RH15....109 C2
  Chichester PO19......177 B7
  Lancing BN15..........187 F5

Alexandra Rd *continued*
Worthing BN11 . . . . 186 F2
Alexandra Terr 14
PO21 . . . . 201 D3
Alexandra Villas BN1 . . . . 213 A3
ALFOLD BARS 31 E7
Alfold By-Pass GU6 . . . . 11 A5
Alfold Craft Ctr GU6 . . . . . . 11 A1
Alfold Crossways GU6 . . . . . 11 A3
Alfold Rd GU6 . . . . 11 B7
Alford Cl BN14 . . . . 186 A7
Alfred Cl
Crawley RH10 . . . . 19 E5
Middleton-on-S PO22 . . . . . 202 F5
Alfred Davey Ct BN1 . . . . 213 B3
Alfred Pl BN11 . . . . 186 F2
Alfred Rd BN1 . . . . 213 A3
Alfrey Cl PO10 . . . . 173 E8
Alfriston Cl
Bognor Regis PO22 . . . . . . 202 C6
Brighton BN2 . . . . 192 F6
Worthing BN14 . . . . 186 B5
Alfriston Ho 2 BN14 . . . . 186 D5
Alfriston Rd BN14 . . . . 186 B5
Alice Cl 2 BN3 . . . . 191 D5
Alice St BN3 . . . . 191 D5
Alicia Ave
Ashington RH20 . . . . 123 A5
Crawley RH10 . . . . 19 C6
Alicks Hill RH14 . . . . 79 D8
Alinora BN17 . . . . 204 E4
Alinora Ave BN12 . . . . 185 D2
Alinora Cl BN12 . . . . 185 D2
Alinora Cres BN12 . . . . . . 185 D2
Alinora Dr BN12 . . . . 185 D2
Allandale Cl PO20 . . . . 212 F8
Allangate Dr BN16 . . . . . . 205 D6
Allcard Cl RH12 . . . . 36 D4
Allcot Cl RH11 . . . . 17 E3
Allee Dr GU30 . . . . 25 B5
Allendale RH13 . . . . 57 F3
Allendale Ave
New Brighton PO10 . . . . . . 151 A3
Worthing BN14 . . . . 164 A1
Allen Rd RH16 . . . . 88 A4
Allen's Cl RH19 . . . . 23 D6
Allestree Ct 15 PO21 . . . . 201 D3
Alley Groves RH13 . . . . 83 F2
Alleyne Way PO22 . . . . 203 B5
Alley The
Amberley BN18 . . . . 140 D7
Stedham GU29 . . . . 72 A1
Allfrey Plat RH20 . . . . 100 D2
Allfreys Wharf RH20 . . . . . 100 B2
Allingham Gdns RH12 . . . . . 37 B5
Allington Rd BN14 . . . . . . 186 E7
Allman Bsns Pk PO20 . . . . 198 B6
All Saints CE Prim Sch
RH12 . . . . 36 F6
Allyington Way RH10 . . . . . 19 D5
Alma Cotts BN5 . . . . 125 F4
Alma Rd RH16 . . . . 88 B8
Alma St BN15 . . . . 187 E4
Almodington La PO20 . . . . 208 E7
Almond Ave BN43 . . . . 188 C8
Almond Cl RH11 . . . . 18 A5
Almshouses GU28 . . . . 116 B7
Almshouses of The Holy
Name BN6 . . . . 128 A5
Almshouses The
PO18 . . . . 156 D4
Alperton Cl PO21 . . . . 200 C1
Alpha Cotts RH20 . . . . 100 D2
Alpha Ct
Littlehampton BN17 . . . . . 204 C5
Worthing BN11 . . . . 186 D1
Alpha Rd RH11 . . . . 18 C6
Alpine Rd BN3 . . . . 190 F8
Alston Way BN13 . . . . 185 D6
Alternative Ctr for Ed
BN1 . . . . 170 C3
Alverstone Rd BN11 . . . . . 186 F3
Amadeus Ho BN16 . . . . . . 206 B6
Ambassador Ho 15
PO19 . . . . 177 A6
Ambassadors The 10
BN3 . . . . 191 C6
Amber Ct
20 Hove BN3 . . . . 191 C6
8 Hove BN3 . . . . 191 D7
Amber Glade RH13 . . . . 57 F1
Amber Ho
Brighton BN1 . . . . 213 B4
Hove BN3 . . . . 191 C6
Amberley CE Fst Sch
BN18 . . . . 140 E7
Amberley Cl
Burgess Hill RH15 . . . . 109 A4
Crawley RH10 . . . . 19 C6
Haywards Heath RH16 . . . . . 87 D4
Horsham RH12 . . . . 37 A6
Hove BN3 . . . . 168 E3
Littlehampton BN17 . . . . . 204 E6
Shoreham-by-S BN43 . . . . . 166 F1
Storrington RH20 . . . . 121 C1
Amberley Ct
Billingshurst RH14 . . . . 79 E7
Lancing BN15 . . . . 187 F6
8 Worthing BN11 . . . . 185 F3
Amberley Dr
Bognor Regis PO21 . . . . . . 201 A4
Hove BN3 . . . . 168 E3
Worthing BN12 . . . . 185 B2
Amberley Fields Cvn Pk
RH11 . . . . 5 B4
Amberley Gate RH20 . . . . . 121 B1
Amberley Ho 6 RH13 . . . . . 36 D1
Amberley Lo BN2 . . . . 192 F6
Amberley Rd
Horsham RH12 . . . . 37 A6
Littlehampton BN16 . . . . . 205 C4
Storrington RH20 . . . . 142 A8
Amberley Sta BN18 . . . . . . 140 D4
Amberley Working Mus*
BN18 . . . . 140 D5
Ambersham Cres
BN16 . . . . 205 F7
Amblefield Ct GU28 . . . . . . 51 A7
Ambleside Cl
Bognor Regis PO22 . . . . . . 202 B6
Crawley RH11 . . . . 17 D5
Ambleside Rd BN15 . . . . . 187 C6
Ambrose Ho BN11 . . . . 186 D2
Ambrose Pl BN11 . . . . 186 D2
Ambrose's Hill RH17 . . . . . 107 B7
Amelia Cres BN11 . . . . 186 C2
Amelia Ct PO20 . . . . 207 E7
Amelia Rd BN11 . . . . 186 C2
Amenic Ct 3 BN17 . . . . . . 204 E5
America La RH16 . . . . 88 A5
Amesbury Cres BN3 . . . . . 190 E7
Amey Ind Est GU32 . . . . 68 A3
Amherst Cres BN3 . . . . 190 F8
Amo Mews 8 BN11 . . . . . 186 C1
Amstel Ct 2 BN17 . . . . . . 204 F4
Amundsen Rd RH12 . . . . . . 36 D6
Anchor Cl BN43 . . . . 189 A6
Anchor Ct BN12 . . . . 185 E2
Anchor Hill RH17 . . . . 88 F3
Anchorhold The RH16 . . . . . 87 D5
Anchor Springs 13
BN17 . . . . 204 D5
Ancren Cl BN12 . . . . 206 F7
Ancton Cl PO22 . . . . 202 F5
Ancton Dr PO22 . . . . 203 A6
Ancton La PO22 . . . . 202 F6
Ancton Lodge La
PO22 . . . . 203 A5
Ancton Way PO22 . . . . 203 B5
Anderson Ct GU27 . . . . 27 C6
Andlers Ash Rd GU33 . . . . . 45 A3
Andrew Ave PO22 . . . . 202 C5
Andrew Cl
Rustington BN16 . . . . 205 B6
Steyning BN44 . . . . 145 D2
Andrews Cotts RH13 . . . . . . 81 F7
Andrews La GU29 . . . . 93 F7
Andrew's La RH13 . . . . 57 F1
Andrews Rd RH13 . . . . 81 F7
Andromeda Cl RH11 . . . . . . 17 E4
Angell Cl RH10 . . . . 19 C5
Angell Est PO19 . . . . 177 D5
Angel St GU28 . . . . 97 F8
Anglesea St BN11 . . . . 186 C3
Anglesey Cl RH11 . . . . 18 C2
Angmering Ct BN1 . . . . . . 170 F5
Angmering La BN16 . . . . . 205 E5
Angmering Sch The
BN16 . . . . 205 F7
Angmering Sta BN16 . . . . . 205 F6
Angmering Way BN16 . . . . 205 E7
Angola Rd BN14 . . . . 186 F4
Angus Cl RH12 . . . . 36 D4
Angus Rd BN12 . . . . 185 E3
Annandale Ave PO21 . . . . . 201 C4
Ann Cl BN6 . . . . 129 A5
Anne Howard Gdns
BN18 . . . . 160 A3
Annington Commercial Ctr
BN44 . . . . 165 E8
Annington Gdns 4
BN43 . . . . 166 F1
Annington Rd BN44,
BN15 . . . . 165 F8
Ann St
Brighton BN1 . . . . 213 B4
Worthing BN11 . . . . 186 E2
Annweir Ave BN15 . . . . . . 187 E6
Anscombe Cl BN11 . . . . . . 185 F2
Anscombe Rd BN11 . . . . . . 185 F2
Anscome 5 RH16 . . . . 87 D6
Ansisters Rd BN12 . . . . 206 E5
Anson Ct BN12 . . . . 185 C5
Anson Rd
Bognor Regis PO21 . . . . . . 200 B2
Worthing BN12 . . . . 185 C5
Ansty Cl BN2 . . . . 192 E5
Answorth Cl PO19 . . . . . . 155 B1
Anthony Way PO10 . . . . . . 151 B3
Antlands La RH6 . . . . 6 E5
Antlands La E RH6 . . . . 6 F5
Antlands La W RH6 . . . . 6 E6
Antonia Ct 10 BN17 . . . . . 204 D5
Anvil Cl
Billingshurst RH14 . . . . 79 C8
Portslade-by-S BN41 . . . . . 168 B2
Southwater RH13 . . . . 57 F1
Apperlie Dr RH6 . . . . 2 C1
Appledore Ct RH16 . . . . 88 A7
Appledore Gdns RH16 . . . . . 88 A6
Appledore Rd BN2 . . . . . . 170 F4
Appledram La (N)
PO19 . . . . 176 C6
Appledram La (S)
PO20 . . . . 176 C4
Applefield RH10 . . . . 18 E7
Apple Gr
Bognor Regis PO21 . . . . . . 200 B1
Hermitage PO10 . . . . 173 D8
Applesham Ave BN3 . . . . . 168 E2
Applesham Ct 9
BN15 . . . . 187 E4
Applesham Way
BN41 . . . . 168 A1
Appletree Dr PO22 . . . . . . 180 B6
Appletrees BN16 . . . . 206 B4
Apple Tree Wlk BN17 . . . . 181 D1
Approach The
10 Brighton BN1 . . . . 169 E3
Dormansland RH19 . . . . 9 F6
April Cl
Ferring BN12 . . . . 206 E4
Horsham RH12 . . . . 36 C4
April Gdns PO18 . . . . 154 E6
Apsley Ct RH11 . . . . 17 F4
Apsley Mews 9
BN11 . . . . 186 D3
Apsley Way BN13 . . . . 185 B6
Aquarium Sta* BN2 . . . . . 213 C1
Aquarius Ct RH11 . . . . 17 E4
Arbor Ct RH16 . . . . 87 E5
Arcade Rd BN17 . . . . 204 D5
Arcade The
8 Bognor Regis
PO21 . . . . 201 D3
Liss GU33 . . . . 45 A5
14 Littlehampton BN17 . . . 204 D5
Archer Ct RH15 . . . . 109 A3
Archers Ct 3 RH10 . . . . 18 D8
Arch Ho 5 PO21 . . . . 201 C2
Archibald Rd BN11 . . . . . . 187 A3
Arcturus Rd RH11 . . . . 17 E3
Ardale Cl BN11 . . . . 185 F3
Arden Rd RH10 . . . . 18 F4
Ardingly Cl RH11 . . . . 18 B8
Ardingly Coll Prep Sch
RH17 . . . . 64 A6
Ardingly Ct 10 BN2 . . . . . 213 C2
Ardingly Dr BN12 . . . . 185 B4
Ardingly Rd
Ardingly RH16 . . . . 64 C2
Cuckfield RH17 . . . . 86 F7
Ardingly St BN2 . . . . 213 C2
Ardings Cl RH17 . . . . 64 B7
Ardsheal Cl BN14 . . . . 186 C5
Ardsheal Rd BN14 . . . . 186 C6
Arena Ho BN1 . . . . 213 B2
Argus Lofts BN1 . . . . 213 B3
Argus Wlk RH11 . . . . 18 A3
Argyle Cir 5 PO21 . . . . . . 201 C3
Argyle Rd
Bognor Regis PO21 . . . . . . 201 C3
Brighton BN1 . . . . 213 A5
Argyll Hall 16 BN17 . . . . . 204 D5
Ariadne Rd BN11 . . . . 186 B1
Ariel Ct BN15 . . . . 187 D4
Arkendale RH19 . . . . 9 A4
Arlington Ave BN12 . . . . . 185 B2
Arlington Cl BN12 . . . . 185 B2
Arlington Cres
Brighton BN1 . . . . 170 E5
East Preston BN16 . . . . 206 B7
Arlington Ct RH16 . . . . 87 E5
Arlington Gdns BN2 . . . . . 194 D2
Armada Ct PO20 . . . . 208 B5
Armadale Rd PO19 . . . . . . 177 C7
Armada Way BN17 . . . . . . 205 A6
Arndale Rd BN17 . . . . 204 B6
Arne Cl RH11 . . . . 17 F3
Arne Gr RH6 . . . . 1 E5
Arnell Ave PO20 . . . . 212 E7
Arnfield Cl RH11 . . . . 17 E5
Arnhem Rd PO21 . . . . 201 B5
Arnold St BN2 . . . . 192 C7
Arnold Way PO18 . . . . 175 C7
Arnside Cl BN15 . . . . 187 C5
Arran Cl RH11 . . . . 18 B3
Arrancourt 1 RH12 . . . . 36 B2
Arran Gate PO21 . . . . 201 E3
Arrivals Rd RH6 . . . . 5 F8
Artel Croft RH10 . . . . 19 A6
Artex Ave BN16 . . . . 205 C7
Arthur Bliss Ho RH16 . . . . . 88 A8
Arthur Ho PO20 . . . . 212 E8
Arthur Rd
Crawley RH11 . . . . 17 E6
Horsham RH13 . . . . 36 D1
Arthur St BN3 . . . . 191 A8
Arts Rd BN1 . . . . 171 B7
Arun Beck BN6 . . . . 128 A8
Arun Bsns Pk PO22 . . . . . . 201 E5
Arun Cl
Amberley BN18 . . . . 140 E7
Lancing BN15 . . . . 187 C7
Petersfield GU31 . . . . 68 A2
Rustington BN16 . . . . 205 C6
Worthing BN13 . . . . 185 D8
Arun Cres BN13 . . . . 185 C8
Arun Ct
East Preston BN16 . . . . 206 A5
Littlehampton BN17 . . . . . 204 C5
Littlehampton, Wick
BN17 . . . . 204 D7
1 Pulborough RH20 . . . . . 100 C2
13 Shoreham-by-S
BN43 . . . . 189 C8
Arundale Sch RH20 . . . . . . 100 D2
Arundel 4 BN15 . . . . 187 D5
Arundel By-Pass
BN18 . . . . 160 B2
Arundel Castle &
Grounds* BN18 . . . . 160 B3
Arundel CE Prim Sch
BN18 . . . . 159 F2
Arundel Cl
Bognor Regis PO21 . . . . . . 201 A4
Conford GU30 . . . . 24 D8
Crawley RH10 . . . . 19 C6
Shoreham-by-S BN43 . . . . . 189 C8
Southwater RH13 . . . . 58 A1
Arundel Ct
Billingshurst RH14 . . . . 79 D7
6 Brighton, Black Rock
BN2 . . . . 192 E4
Arundel Ct *continued*
Brighton, Westdene
BN1 . . . . 169 C5
Burgess Hill RH15 . . . . 108 F4
Ferring BN12 . . . . 206 F4
14 Shoreham-by-S
BN43 . . . . 189 C8
9 Worthing BN11 . . . . 185 F3
Arundel & District Hospl
BN18 . . . . 160 A3
Arundel Dr BN17 . . . . 182 C5
Arundel Dr E BN2 . . . . 194 C1
Arundel Dr W BN2 . . . . . . 194 C1
Arundel Gdn 12 BN16 . . . . 205 C5
Arundel Ho 4 RH13 . . . . . . 36 E1
Arundel Mews
10 Brighton BN2 . . . . 192 E4
Haywards Heath RH16 . . . . . 87 F2
Arundel Mus & Heritage
Ctr* BN18 . . . . 160 B3
Arundel Pl BN2 . . . . 192 E3
Arundel RC Cathedral*
BN18 . . . . 160 B3
Arundel Rd
Angmering BN16 . . . . 183 F6
Brighton BN2 . . . . 192 E4
Chichester PO18, PO19,
PO20 . . . . 177 E8
Fontwell BN18 . . . . 157 F3
Littlehampton BN17 . . . . . 204 D6
Selden BN16, BN13 . . . . . . 184 C8
Tangmere PO18, PO21 . . . 156 C2
Walberton BN18 . . . . 158 D2
Worthing BN13 . . . . 185 D9
Arundel St BN2 . . . . 192 E3
Arundel Sta BN18 . . . . 160 C1
Arundel Terr BN2 . . . . 192 E3
Arundel Villas GU30 . . . . . . 24 D8
Arundel Way PO22 . . . . . . 203 B5
Arundel Wildfowl &
Wetlands Trust*
BN18 . . . . 160 C5
Arun Ford Cl BN18 . . . . . . 181 E3
Arun Lo BN13 . . . . 185 D8
Arun Par BN17 . . . . 204 D3
Arun Prospect RH20 . . . . . 100 A1
Arun Rd
Billingshurst RH14 . . . . 55 C1
Bognor Regis PO21 . . . . . . 201 A4
Arun Ret Pk PO22 . . . . 201 E6
Arunside RH12 . . . . 36 A1
Arunside Ind Est
BN17 . . . . 204 C6
Arunside Sch RH12 . . . . 36 A2
Arun St BN18 . . . . 160 B2
Arun Terr BN18 . . . . 160 A2
Arun Vale RH20 . . . . 119 C5
Arun Vale Inf Sch
BN17 . . . . 204 D5
Arun Way
Bognor Regis PO21 . . . . . . 211 B8
Horsham RH13 . . . . 36 E1
Ascot Cl PO20 . . . . 207 F8
Ascot Way BN16 . . . . 205 E6
Ashacre La BN13 . . . . 186 A7
Ashacre Mews BN13 . . . . . 185 F8
Ashacre Way BN13 . . . . . . 186 A6
Ashburnham Cl
Brighton BN1 . . . . 170 E5
Chichester PO19 . . . . 176 D7
Worthing BN13 . . . . 185 B6
Ashburnham Dr
Brighton BN1 . . . . 170 E5
Cuckfield RH17 . . . . 86 E6
Ashburnham Ho BN1 . . . . 169 E5
Ashburnham Mews
RH17 . . . . 86 E6
Ashburnham Rd RH10 . . . . . 19 A4
Ashby Ct 6 RH13 . . . . 36 E1
Ash Cl
Crawley Down RH10 . . . . . . 21 C8
Findon BN14 . . . . 163 E6
Hove BN3 . . . . 169 C3
Ashcombe Hollow
BN7 . . . . 172 D7
Ashcombe La BN7 . . . . 172 E5
Ashcroft 1 BN43 . . . . 189 D7
Ashcroft Cl BN43 . . . . 189 D8
Ashcroft Ct 5 GU32 . . . . . . 68 B4
Ashcroft La PO8 . . . . 130 F6
Ashcroft Way PO21 . . . . . 211 A8
Ash Ct
East Grinstead RH19 . . . . 9 E3
Southwick BN42 . . . . 167 F1
Ashdene Gdns RH20 . . . . . 123 A4
Ashdown 14 BN3 . . . . 191 C6
Ashdown Ave BN2 . . . . 194 B1
Ashdown Cl
Angmering BN16 . . . . 205 F8
Haywards Heath RH16 . . . . . 88 B4
Ashdown Ct
Crawley RH10 . . . . 18 F3
Horsham RH13 . . . . 36 F4
Ashdown Dr RH10 . . . . 18 E3
Ashdown Forest Llama
Pk* RH18 . . . . 44 E4
Ashdown Gate RH19 . . . . 9 D2
Ashdown Ho 8 BN11 . . . . . 186 D3
Ashdown Nuffield Hospl
RH16 . . . . 87 D6
Ashdown Pl RH18 . . . . 44 E8
Ashdown Rd
7 Brighton BN2 . . . . 192 B8
Forest Row RH18 . . . . 23 F2
Worthing BN11 . . . . 186 D3
Ashdown View RH19 . . . . . . 22 E7
Ashenground Cl 6
RH16 . . . . 87 E3
Ashenground Rd RH16 . . . . 87 E3
Ashfield RH14 . . . . 30 E2
Ashfield Cl GU29 . . . . 94 E8
Ashfield Rd GU29 . . . . 94 E7
Ashfold Ave BN14 . . . . 164 A1
Ashfold Crossways
RH13 . . . . 60 E6
Ashford Rd BN1 . . . . 170 A2
Ash Gr
Bognor Regis PO22 . . . . . . 201 C6
Fernhurst GU27 . . . . 49 A6
Haywards Heath RH16 . . . . . 87 D2
Liphook GU30 . . . . 25 D3
Worthing BN11 . . . . 186 E2
Ashgrove Cotts RH17 . . . . . 65 D5
Ash Grove Ind Pk
PO22 . . . . 201 D7
Ashington CE Fst Sch
RH20 . . . . 122 F5
Ashington Ct
Brighton BN2 . . . . 192 F6
3 Horsham RH12 . . . . 36 D5
4 Worthing BN14 . . . . 186 D5
Ash Keys RH10 . . . . 18 E5
Ash La BN16 . . . . 205 C5
Ashleigh Cl
Angmering BN16 . . . . 184 A6
Horley RH6 . . . . 1 F3
Ashleigh Rd RH12 . . . . 36 C4
Ashley Cl BN1 . . . . 169 E7
Ashley Ct BN3 . . . . 191 C5
Ashlings Way
Hove BN3 . . . . 168 E2
Shoreham-by-S BN43 . . . . . 167 B1
Ashmead Way BN16 . . . . . 206 A8
Ashmere Gdns PO22 . . . . . 202 D5
Ashmere La PO22 . . . . 202 D5
Ashmore Ave BN16 . . . . . . 206 A8
Ashmore Ho RH11 . . . . 5 D1
Ashmore La RH12 . . . . 16 C6
Ash Rd
Crawley RH10 . . . . 19 A8
Southwater RH13 . . . . 57 E1
Ashton Gdns BN16 . . . . . . 205 C4
Ashton Lo 15 BN2 . . . . 213 C3
Ashton Park Sch RH14 . . . . . 79 A1
Ashton Rise BN2 . . . . 213 C3
Ashurst Ave BN2 . . . . 194 E1
Ashurst CE Prim Sch
BN44 . . . . 124 D5
Ashurst Cl
Bognor Regis PO21 . . . . . . 201 A6
Horsham RH12 . . . . 37 A5
Worthing BN12 . . . . 185 B2
Ashurst Cotts RH19 . . . . 42 F4
Ashurst Dr
Crawley RH10 . . . . 19 D6
Worthing BN12 . . . . 185 B2
Ashurst Pl RH16 . . . . 87 E5
Ashurst Rd BN2 . . . . 170 F5
Ashurst Way BN16 . . . . 206 A7
Ashurstwood Abbey
RH19 . . . . 23 F6
Ashurst Wood Prim Sch
RH19 . . . . 23 E6
Ashway RH15 . . . . 109 A2
Ashwood 5 RH11 . . . . 18 D5
Ashwood Cl BN11 . . . . 186 F4
Ashwood Ct RH18 . . . . 23 F1
Ashwood Dr BN16 . . . . 205 C5
Ashwyn Bsns Ctr
RH15 . . . . 108 F5
Aspen Cl RH16 . . . . 88 B4
Aspen Ct RH19 . . . . 23 A8
Aspen Way
Horsham RH12 . . . . 36 E4
Middleton-on-S PO22 . . . . . 202 E6
Aspen Wlk RH16 . . . . 88 B4
Assissi Ct RH16 . . . . 87 F2
Assissi Hts RH16 . . . . 87 F2
Aston Ct
5 Bognor Regis
PO21 . . . . 201 D3
Crawley RH11 . . . . 18 B1
Aston Ho 1 BN43 . . . . 188 E7
Aston Rise RH20 . . . . 100 C3
Astra Bsns Ctr RH1 . . . . 2 A7
Astra Cl PO18 . . . . 175 C5
Astra Ho 10 BN1 . . . . 191 E5
Athelstan Cl RH10 . . . . 19 E6
Athelstan Rd BN14 . . . . . . 186 A4
Athelstan Way RH13 . . . . . . 58 E8
Athenaeum The 16
BN3 . . . . 191 C6
ATHERINGTON 203 F6
Athrington Ct PO22 . . . . . 202 B4
Atkinson Ct RH6 . . . . 2 B2
Atkinson Rd RH10 . . . . 19 C4
Atlantic Ct 4 BN43 . . . . . . 188 F6
Atlantic Ho 12 BN16 . . . . . 205 B4
Atlingworth Ct BN2 . . . . . 213 C1
Atlingworth St BN2 . . . . . . 213 C1
Attlee Ho 5 RH11 . . . . 18 B2
Attree Ct 6 BN2 . . . . 192 C6
Attree Dr BN2 . . . . 192 C6
Auchinleck Ct RH10 . . . . . . 21 B7
Auckland Cl RH11 . . . . 5 D1
Auckland Dr BN2 . . . . 170 F1
Audrey Cl BN1 . . . . 169 E5
Augusta Ct 5 PO19 . . . . . . 155 A2
Augusta Ho 4 BN11 . . . . . 186 D1
Augusta Pl BN11 . . . . 186 D1
Augustines Way RH16 . . . . . 87 F4
Aurum Cl RH6 . . . . 2 B2
Austen Cl RH19 . . . . 9 B1

Austen Ct [9] PO21 .... 201 C4
Austens GU29 .... 115 C8
Autumn Cl RH11 .... 18 C5
Avalon BN1 .... 213 A2
Avalon Ct PO10 .... 151 B2
Avalon Way BN13 .... 185 D7
Avebury Cl
　Bracklesham PO20 .... 208 C5
　Horsham RH12 .... 197 J7
Aveling Cl RH10 .... 19 C4
Avenals The RH6 .... 184 A5
Avenue App PO19 .... 176 F7
Avenue Cl GU30 .... 25 B4
Avenue Ct [21] BN3 .... 191 C6
Avenue De Chartres
　PO19 .... 176 F6
Avenue Gdns RH6 .... 2 C2
Avenue The
　Bognor Regis PO21 .... 201 B3
　Brighton BN2 .... 170 E1
　Chichester PO19 .... 155 A2
　Funtington PO18 .... 152 E7
　Hambrook PO18 .... 152 D1
　Haslemere GU27 .... 26 F7
　Horley RH6 .... 1 F2
　Horsham RH13 .... 57 D5
　Kingston near Lewes
　　BN7 .... 172 D5
　Liphook GU30 .... 25 B4
　Petersfield GU31 .... 68 B3
　Shoreham-by-S BN43 .... 166 F1
　Worthing BN12 .... 185 C5
Avery Cl BN41 .... 167 F4
Avian Gdns PO21 .... 200 B2
Aviary Cl PO18 .... 152 D2
Aviary Way RH10 .... 8 C1
Aviation Trad Est
　BN6 .... 127 B3
Avila Ho [6] BN11 .... 186 C2
Avisford Park Rd
　BN18 .... 158 F1
Avocet Quay PO10 .... 173 C7
Avocet Trad Est RH15 .... 108 F2
Avon Cl
　Bognor Regis PO22 .... 202 D5
　Lancing BN15 .... 187 B6
　Petersfield GU31 .... 68 A4
Avon Ct
　Brighton BN2 .... 213 C2
　Lancing BN15 .... 187 B6
Avondale Cl
　Horley RH6 .... 2 A5
　Worthing BN12 .... 185 D4
Avondale Rd BN3 .... 191 D7
Avonhurst RH15 .... 109 B3
Avon Rd BN47 .... 204 D5
Awbrook Cl RH17 .... 88 F3
Axford Cl PO20 .... 208 C5
Aylesbury BN3 .... 191 E6
Aylward Cl [8] RH12 .... 36 A1
Aylwin Pl PO19 .... 177 C1
Aymer Ho [4] BN2 .... 191 A6
Aymer Rd BN3 .... 191 A6
Aynsley Ct BN3 .... 191 C8
Ayshe Court Dr RH13 .... 36 C3
Azalea Cl RH20 .... 122 B2
Azalea Dr GU27 .... 26 F8
Azara Par PO20 .... 208 B6

B

Babsham La PO21 .... 200 F8
Back La
　Balcombe Lane RH10,
　　RH17 .... 41 C7
　Crawley RH10 .... 20 D1
　Plaistow RH14 .... 30 E2
Backwoods Cl RH16 .... 88 B6
Backwoods La RH16 .... 88 B6
Baden Dr RH6 .... 1 E4
Baden Rd BN2 .... 170 D1
Bader Ct [6] RH11 .... 18 D8
Badger Cl BN41 .... 168 B2
Badger Copse BN5 .... 126 F5
Badger Dr RH16 .... 87 C5
Badgers Cl RH12 .... 36 F8
Badgers Holt RH20 .... 122 B1
Badgers Way
　East Grinstead RH19 .... 9 F2
　Loxwood RH14 .... 32 A4
Badgers Wlk
　Angmering BN16 .... 205 F8
　Burgess Hill RH15 .... 109 D2
Badgers Wood RH20 .... 121 D6
Badger Way BN1 .... 170 E6
Badger Wlk PO19 .... 177 C8
Baffins Ct [7] PO21 .... 177 A6
Baffin's La PO19 .... 177 A6
Bailey Cl
　Horsham RH12 .... 35 A7
　Littlehampton BN17 .... 205 A4
Bailing Hill RH12 .... 35 E7
Baird Cl RH10 .... 6 A1
Bakehouse Barn Cl
　RH12 .... 36 E7
Bakehouse Cotts RH14 .... 53 A3
Bakehouse Rd RH6 .... 2 A5
Baker Cl RH10 .... 18 D4
Bakerfield GU29 .... 115 C8
Bakers Arms Hill
　BN18 .... 160 B3
Bakers Cl BN13 .... 57 F1
Bakers Ct BN13 .... 185 E8

Baker's La RH13 .... 81 B4
Bakers Mews RH13 .... 60 A3
Baker St BN1 .... 213 B4
Bakery La PO21 .... 201 C2
Bakery Mews BN1 .... 170 C1
Bala Cres PO22 .... 202 B6
Balchins Ct RH14 .... 78 B8
Balcombe Ave BN14 .... 186 C5
Balcombe CE Prim Sch
　RH17 .... 40 F2
Balcombe Ct
　Crawley RH10 .... 19 D7
　Worthing BN11 .... 186 B1
Balcombe Gdns RH6 .... 2 C2
Balcombe La
　Ardingly RH17 .... 63 F8
　Sharpthorne RH17, RH19 .... 43 E2
Balcombe Rd
　Balcombe Lane RH17 .... 40 F8
　Crawley, Tinsley Green RH6,
　　RH10 .... 3 D2
　Crawley, Worth RH10 .... 19 D5
　Haywards Heath RH16 .... 87 D7
　Horley RH6 .... 2 B2
　Balcombe Sta RH17 .... 40 F1
Baldwin Cl
　Crawley RH10 .... 19 C3
　Middleton-on-S PO22 .... 202 D6
Baldwins Field RH19 .... 9 D4
BALDWINS HILL 9 D4
Baldwins Hill Prim Sch
　RH19 .... 9 D3
Balfour Dr GU33 .... 45 B4
Balfour Gdns RH18 .... 23 E1
Balfour Inf Sch BN1 .... 170 A3
Balfour Jun Sch BN1 .... 170 A3
Balfour Rd BN1 .... 170 A2
Ballindune GU27 .... 27 C8
Balliol Cl
　Bognor Regis PO21 .... 200 E4
　Crawley RH10 .... 6 D1
Ball Tree Croft [1]
　BN15 .... 187 C7
Balmer Farm Cotts
　BN7 .... 171 D8
Balmoral
　Brighton BN1 .... 191 E8
　East Grinstead RH19 .... 23 A8
Balmoral Cl
　Bognor Regis PO21 .... 200 E2
　Chichester PO19 .... 177 D6
　[8] Rustington BN16 .... 205 B7
Balmoral Ct
　[6] Crawley RH11 .... 18 B2
　Hove BN3 .... 169 A3
　Worthing BN11 .... 186 A2
Balmoral Way GU32 .... 68 B4
Balsdean Rd BN2 .... 171 F1
Baltic Wharf BN1 .... 204 D4
Baltimore Ct [9] BN3 .... 191 C7
Bamborough Cl RH15 .... 58 A1
Bamford Cl RH11 .... 18 A1
Bampfield St BN41 .... 190 B8
Bancroft Rd RH10 .... 19 D5
Banjo Rd BN17 .... 204 E3
Bank La RH10 .... 17 B8
Bank Pas
　[2] Steyning BN44 .... 145 D3
　[1] Worthing BN11 .... 186 D2
Banks Croft RH20 .... 121 E2
Bankside
　Burgess Hill RH17 .... 85 C2
　Brighton BN1 .... 169 C5
　Hassocks BN6 .... 128 F5
　Middleton-on-S PO22 .... 202 E5
　Singleton PO18 .... 135 E7
Banks Rd BN13 .... 169 C5
Banks Rd
　Crawley RH10 .... 19 C5
　Scaynes Hill BN8 .... 89 F1
Bankview Cl [2] PO22 .... 201 D4
Bannerman Rd GU32 .... 68 A4
Bannings Vale BN2 .... 194 E1
Bannister Gdns RH10 .... 121 E3
Bannister Way RH16 .... 87 D6
Banstead Cl BN12 .... 185 C1
Baranscraig Ave BN1 .... 170 A7
Barbara Smith Hall
　PO21 .... 201 E4
Barbary La BN12 .... 206 E5
Barber Cl RH10 .... 19 C2
Barclay Ho [2] BN2 .... 192 C7
Barclays Ct [2] RH20 .... 100 C2
Barcombe Pl BN1 .... 170 F5
Barcombe Rd BN1 .... 170 E4
Barentin Way GU31 .... 168 C5
Barfield Pk BN15 .... 187 F6
Barford Rd PO19 .... 177 A5
Barham Rd GU32 .... 68 B3
Barkdale BN15 .... 109 D5
Barker Cl PO18 .... 176 A7
Barkworth Way RH20 .... 121 C7
Bar La RH13 .... 82 B5
BARLAVINGTON 117 E5
Barlavington Way
　GU29 .... 94 E5
Barley Cl
　Bognor Regis PO21 .... 200 D3
　Worthing BN13 .... 186 A5
Barleycroft
　Albourne Green BN6 .... 127 C6
　Cowfold RH13 .... 83 E1
Barley Dr RH15 .... 108 D4
Barley Ho BN44 .... 145 D2
Barleymead RH10 .... 7 B4
Barlow Rd
　Chichester PO19 .... 176 E8
　Crawley RH11 .... 17 E3

Barnard Gate RH16 .... 87 E7
Barnard Mews BN14 .... 186 E5
Barn Cl
　Albourne Green BN6 .... 127 C6
　Kingston near Lewes
　　BN7 .... 172 E5
　Littlehampton BN17 .... 204 E8
　Pease Pottage RH11 .... 39 B7
　Worthing BN13 .... 185 F8
Barn Cottage La RH16 .... 88 A5
Barncroft Cl PO20 .... 156 C1
Barn Ct BN42 .... 190 A7
Barn Elm PO18 .... 156 D3
Barn End BN5 .... 125 F5
Barnes Cl PO20 .... 212 E5
Barnes Mews [9] RH12 .... 36 B2
Barnes Rd BN41 .... 190 B8
Barnes Wallis Ave
　BN13 .... 57 D6
Barnett Cl PO20 .... 179 E8
Barnett Rd BN1 .... 170 B2
Barnett's Field PO20 .... 179 D7
Barnet Way
　Hove BN3 .... 168 E3
　Worthing BN13 .... 185 D6
Barn Feld PO22 .... 201 F4
Barnfield Cl PO10 .... 152 A1
Barnfield Cotts BN18 .... 158 A2
Barnfield Dr PO18,
　PO19 .... 177 C8
Barnfield Gdns
　[8] Brighton BN2 .... 192 C6
　Ditchling BN6 .... 129 E3
Barn Field Pl RH19 .... 10 A3
Barnfield Rd
　Crawley RH10 .... 18 E7
　Petersfield GU31 .... 68 E3
Barnham La BN18,
　PO22 .... 180 C7
Barnham Prim Sch
　PO22 .... 180 B6
Barnham Rd PO20,
　PO22 .... 180 A6
Barnham Sta PO22 .... 180 B5
Barnhouse Cl [8]
　RH20 .... 100 C2
Barn House La RH20 .... 100 C2
Barn La PO22 .... 179 D1
Barn Mdw RH17 .... 41 A1
Barnmead RH16 .... 87 D7
Barn Plat Cotts GU29 .... 94 D8
Barn Rd PO20 .... 207 F7
Barn Rise
　Barnham PO22 .... 180 C5
　Brighton BN1 .... 169 D5
Barn Row BN16 .... 205 F5
Barns Farm La RH20 .... 143 B7
Barnsfold La RH12 .... 32 E6
Barnside Ave RH15 .... 109 D1
Barnside Way GU33 .... 45 B3
Barnsite Cl BN16 .... 205 B6
Barnsite Gdns BN16 .... 205 B6
Barnsnap Cl RH12 .... 36 D6
Barn Stables Bsns Units
　RH10 .... 7 E6
Barn The PO19 .... 154 F2
Barn Wlk PO20 .... 207 F6
Barnwood RH10 .... 19 C7
Baron Cl PO20 .... 179 D7
Barons Ct
　Burgess Hill RH15 .... 109 B2
　[12] Worthing BN11 .... 186 C3
Barons Mead PO21 .... 211 A8
Barque Cl BN17 .... 205 A6
Barrack La PO21 .... 200 D2
Barrhill Ave BN1 .... 169 F7
Barrington Cl
　Haywards Heath RH16 .... 87 F8
　Worthing BN12 .... 185 C3
Barrington Gate RH12 .... 36 C2
Barrington Rd
　Crawley RH10 .... 18 D3
　Horsham RH13 .... 36 E2
　Lindfield RH16 .... 88 A8
　Worthing BN12 .... 185 C3
　Worthing, Goring-by-Sea
　　BN12 .... 185 C3
Barrington Wood RH16 .... 87 F8
Barrow Cl
　Billingshurst RH14 .... 79 C7
　Brighton BN1 .... 170 C2
Barrowfield Cl
　Brighton BN3 .... 169 C3
　Barrowfield Dr BN3 .... 169 D2
　Barrowfield Lo BN3 .... 169 C2
Barrow Hill
　Brighton BN1 .... 170 C2
　Henfield BN5 .... 125 F3
Barry Cl RH10 .... 18 E3
Barry Wlk BN2 .... 192 C6
Bartholomew Cl GU27 .... 27 D8
Bartholomew St BN1 .... 213 B2
Bartholomew Sq BN1 .... 213 B2
Bartholomew Way
　RH12 .... 37 A7
Barton Cl
　Bognor Regis PO21 .... 200 A1
　Worthing BN13 .... 186 A5
Barton Cres RH19 .... 23 A8
Barton La BN16 .... 205 B5
Barton La GU28 .... 97 F8
Barton Manor Apartments
　PO21 .... 200 A1
Barton Rd
　Bognor Regis PO21 .... 201 A7
　Chichester PO19 .... 176 E7
Bartons Inf Sch PO22 .... 201 B6

Barton Way PO20 .... 208 B6
Barton Wlk [4] RH10 .... 19 B4
Barttelot Rd RH12 .... 36 D2
Barwell Gr PO10 .... 151 A3
Barwick Cl BN16 .... 205 B7
Basepoint Bsns Ctr
　RH11 .... 5 D2
Bashfords La BN14 .... 186 D6
Bashford Way RH10 .... 19 D8
Bashurst Copse RH13 .... 56 F8
Bashurst Hill RH13 .... 56 E6
Basildon Way RH11 .... 17 E2
Basing Hill RH20,
　RH13 .... 123 C7
Basin Rd PO19 .... 177 A5
Basin Rd N BN41 .... 190 B6
Basin Rd S BN3, BN41 .... 190 B6
Bassels La RH13 .... 104 B5
Basset Rd
　Bognor Regis PO21 .... 201 C3
　Crawley RH10 .... 19 D3
Bastion Ho [4] PO19 .... 177 A6
Batchmere Est
　Almodington PO20 .... 197 F1
　Bracklesham PO20 .... 208 B5
Batchmere Rd PO20 .... 198 A2
Batemans Cl BN13 .... 185 B6
Batemans Ct RH10 .... 19 A3
Batemans Rd BN13 .... 193 E7
Bates Rd BN1 .... 169 F2
Bath Ct BN3 .... 191 A5
Bath Pl BN11 .... 186 D1
Bath Rd
　Emsworth PO10 .... 173 B8
　Worthing BN11 .... 186 B1
Bath St BN1 .... 213 A4
Batts Dr BN5 .... 125 D5
Batts La RH20 .... 100 F1
Batts Pond La BN5 .... 125 D4
Batworthpark Ho
　BN18 .... 160 L1
Bavant Rd BN1 .... 169 E2
Bax Cl RH10 .... 18 A1
Baxendale Rd PO19 .... 177 B8
Baxter Cl RH10 .... 19 B4
Baxters La RH17 .... 66 C6
Baxter St BN2 .... 192 C7
Bay Cl RH11 .... 1 E6
Baycombe La BN18 .... 158 D6
Bay Ct PO21 .... 211 B8
Bayfield Rd RH6 .... 1 C1
Bayford Rd BN2 .... 204 D4
Bayhams Field RH19 .... 42 F6
Bayhorne La RH6 .... 2 C1
Bayley Rd PO20 .... 156 C1
Baylis Cres RH15 .... 108 D4
Baylis Wlk RH11 .... 18 B1
Baynards Rd RH12 .... 12 A2
Bayton Ct PO19 .... 177 B6
Baytree Cl PO19 .... 154 D3
Bay Tree Cl RH10 .... 167 C1
Bay Tree Cotts BN18 .... 158 D1
Bay Tree Gdn BN16 .... 205 F5
Bay Trees Cl BN16 .... 205 F5
Bay View Ct PO21 .... 201 B2
Bay Wlk PO21 .... 211 C8
Baywood Gdns BN2 .... 193 C8
Bazehill Manor BN2 .... 193 B4
Bazehill Rd BN2 .... 193 B4
Beach Cl PO21 .... 200 C1
Beach Cres BN17 .... 204 E3
Beachcroft Pl BN15 .... 187 F4
Beach Ct
　Littlehampton BN17 .... 204 E4
　[6] Rustington BN16 .... 204 B3
　[12] Shoreham-by-S
　　BN3 .... 189 A6
Beaches The BN17 .... 181 D1
Beach Gdns PO22 .... 212 D5
Beach Gn BN43 .... 188 E6
Beach Ho BN11 .... 186 E2
Beach Mews [4] BN17 .... 204 F4
Beach Par BN11 .... 186 F2
Beach Rd
　Emsworth PO10 .... 173 A8
　Littlehampton BN17 .... 204 E4
　Pagham PO21 .... 211 A7
　Selsey PO20 .... 212 F8
　Shoreham-by-S BN43 .... 188 E6
Beachside Cl BN12 .... 185 E2
Beachville Ct [8] BN15 .... 187 E4
Beachy Rd BN11 .... 18 A1
Beacon Cl BN1 .... 170 A2
Beacon Ct
　Crawley RH13 .... 37 A4
　Ovingdean BN2 .... 193 D4
Beacon Dr PO20 .... 232 E6
Beacon Hill
　Dormansland RH7 .... 10 B8
　Ovingdean BN2 .... 193 E3
　Watersfield RH20 .... 119 A4
Beacon Ho [6] BN3 .... 190 D7
Beacon Hurst BN6 .... 129 B3
Beaconsfield Cl PO22 .... 202 E5
Beaconsfield Cotts
　RH17 .... 88 F3
Beaconsfield Rd
　Brighton BN1 .... 192 A8
　Chelwood Gate RH17 .... 66 D8
　Littlehampton BN17 .... 204 F4
　Portslade-by-S BN41 .... 190 B8
Beaconsfield Villas
　BN1 .... 169 F1
Beacon Sq PO10 .... 173 A7
Beaconsville Ct BN1 .... 169 F1
Beacon The RH19 .... 42 E7
Beacon Way BN17 .... 205 A6

Beagle Dr BN18 .... 181 B2
Beal Cres BN1 .... 170 B2
Beale Ct RH11 .... 18 A3
Beale St RH15 .... 108 F1
Bear Rd BN2 .... 192 D8
Bearsden Way RH12 .... 35 D3
Beatrice Ho PO22 .... 201 E4
Beatty Ave BN1 .... 170 D6
Beatty Rd PO21 .... 201 C4
Beaufield Cl PO20 .... 212 D5
Beaufield Gate GU27 .... 27 D7
Beaufort Ct [4] BN17 .... 205 A6
Beaufort Terr BN2 .... 192 C6
Beau Ho BN1 .... 213 A4
Beaulieu Ct BN11 .... 186 D1
Beaumont Cl [3] RH11 .... 17 E5
Beaumont Ct
　East Preston BN16 .... 205 F6
　[6] Pulborough RH20 .... 100 C2
Beaumont Pk BN17 .... 205 A6
Beaumont Rd BN14 .... 186 D5
Beaver Cl
　Fishbourne PO19 .... 176 B6
　Horsham RH12 .... 36 F6
Beaver Ind Est GU30 .... 25 C3
Beaver Nursery Units
　PO19 .... 177 D5
Beaver Trade Pk
　PO19 .... 177 D5
Beccles Rd BN11 .... 186 B2
Beckenham Terr
　PO10 .... 151 D4
Becket Bldgs BN14 .... 186 A6
Becket Ct BN41 .... 186 A6
Becket Rd BN14 .... 186 B3
Beckett La RH11 .... 5 D1
Beckett Way [11] RH19 .... 22 F8
Beckford Way RH10 .... 19 B2
Beckham La GU32 .... 67 F4
Beckley Ct BN2 .... 192 E5
Beckworth Cl
　Lindfield RH16 .... 88 A4
　Worthing BN13 .... 185 B6
Beckworth La RH16 .... 88 A6
Bedale Cl RH11 .... 18 C4
Bedales RH17 .... 88 D4
Bedales Cnr RH17 .... 88 D4
Bedales Hill RH16,
　RH17 .... 88 D4
Bedales Sch GU32 .... 68 A7
Bedelands Cl RH15 .... 109 B5
Bedenscroft PO21 .... 201 A3
Bedford Ave PO21 .... 201 A3
Bedford Pl BN1 .... 191 E5
Bedford Rd
　Horsham RH13 .... 36 D1
　Petersfield GU32 .... 67 F3
Bedford Row BN11 .... 186 E2
Bedford Sq
　Brighton BN1 .... 191 E5
　Partridge Green RH13 .... 114 F7
Bedford St
　Bognor Regis PO21 .... 201 D3
　Brighton BN2 .... 192 C7
Bedford Twrs [9] BN1 .... 191 E5
Bedham La RH20 .... 99 B5
Beech Ave
　Bracklesham PO20 .... 208 B6
　Chichester PO19 .... 176 E6
Beech Cl
　Bognor Regis PO21 .... 199 F2
　[2] East Grinstead RH19 .... 9 D2
　Findon BN14 .... 163 E7
　Portslade-by-S BN41 .... 167 F3
　Westergate PO20 .... 179 D7
Beechcroft Cl GU30 .... 24 D3
Beech Ct
　East Grinstead RH19 .... 9 D2
　Haslemere GU27 .... 27 D7
　Worthing BN11 .... 186 B2
Beechers Rd BN41 .... 167 F3
Beeches Ave BN14 .... 186 D7
Beeches Cres RH19 .... 18 E4
Beeches La RH19 .... 23 C6
Beeches Mead RH19 .... 10 F5
Beeches The
　[4] Bognor Regis
　　PO22 .... 201 D4
　Brighton BN1 .... 169 D3
　Brighton BN1 .... 170 E3
　Midhurst GU29 .... 94 E6
　Storrington RH20 .... 121 F3
Beech Hill RH16 .... 88 B4
Beech Holme RH12 .... 21 B8
Beech Hurst Cl RH16 .... 87 C4
Beech Hurst Cotts
　RH16 .... 87 C4
Beechings BN5 .... 125 D5
Beeching Way RH19 .... 9 E1
Beechlands Cl RH16 .... 206 A5
Beechlands Ct BN16 .... 206 A5
Beech Rd
　Findon BN14 .... 163 E7
　Haslemere GU27 .... 27 D8
　Horsham RH13 .... 37 B5
Beechside RH10 .... 18 E4
Beech Tree Cl RH10 .... 18 D7
Beech View RH16 .... 184 A6
Beech Way BN16 .... 206 A8

Beechwood
6 Brighton BN1 169 E3
Southwater RH13 81 F8
Beech Wood BN5 146 F7
Beechwood Ave
Brighton BN1 169 F4
Worthing BN13 185 F8
Beechwood Cl BN1 169 F4
Beechwood Ct
Liss GU33 45 C6
1 Worthing BN11 186 C2
Beechwood La GU28 117 B5
Beechwoods RH15 109 A1
Beechwood Villas RH1 2 A7
Beeding Ave BN3 168 F3
Beeding Cl
Bognor Regis PO22 201 E7
Horsham RH12 37 A5
Lancing BN15 187 D8
Beeding Ct
Brighton BN1 169 C5
4 Shoreham-by-S BN43 189 B8
Beedingwood Dr RH12 37 E6
Beehive Cl BN12 206 F5
Beehive La BN12 206 F5
Beehive Ring Rd RH6 6 B4
Beehive The RH6 6 B4
Beeson Ho 1 BN41 190 C7
Beggarshouse La RH6 4 C8
Beggar's La BN45 148 D6
Behenna Cl RH11 17 E5
Belbourne Ct 7 BN1 213 B3
Belfast St BN3 191 B7
Belgrave Cres PO19 176 F3
Belgrave Ct 3 RH20 100 C2
Belgrave Pl 11 BN2 192 D4
Belgrave St BN2 213 C3
Belgravia Ct 1 RH6 2 B3
Belinus Dr RH14 79 C8
Bellagio Pl RH19 9 D3
Bellamy Rd RH10 19 C2
Bell Cl
Chichester PO19 176 F8
Pulborough RH20 100 B2
Bell Ct
Bognor Regis PO21 200 C2
Nutbourne PO18 174 B7
Bell Ctr RH10 5 F2
Bell Cvn Pk PO20 197 E2
Bell Davies Rd BN17 204 F6
Belle Meade Cl PO20 179 D5
Bellerbys Coll BN1 213 B4
Bellevue Cotts BN2 192 F8
Belle Vue Cotts PO20 179 D7
Bellevue Ct BN1 169 F1
Belle Vue Ct BN2 192 D5
Belle Vue Gdns BN2 192 D4
Bellevue La PO10 151 B2
Bell Hammer RH19 22 E8
BELL HILL 68 A5
Bell Hill GU32 68 A5
Bell Hill Ridge GU32 68 A5
Bellingham Cres BN3 190 D8
Bell La
Cocking GU29 114 C8
Somerley PO20 197 D2
Bellmead 7 BN3 191 D7
Belloc Cl RH10 19 C7
Belloc Ct RH13 37 A3
Belloc Rd BN17 204 C7
Bell Rd
Kingsley Green GU27 27 B3
Warnham RH12 36 A8
Bellscroft Cl BN17 204 F6
Bell Tower Ind Est 7 BN2 192 E4
Bell Vale La GU27 27 C4
Bellview Ct 7 BN13 186 A5
Bellview Rd BN13 186 A5
Belmaine Ct BN11 186 C1
Belmer Ct 6 BN11 186 A1
Belmont BN1, BN3 191 E7
Belmont Cl BN6 128 E5
Belmont Ct 4 BN1 191 E7
Belmont La BN6 128 C5
Belmont St
Bognor Regis PO21 201 D3
Brighton BN1 213 B3
Belmont Terr BN18 181 A2
Belmont Wlk BN13 185 D6
Belsize Cl BN11 186 B3
Belsize Rd BN11 186 B2
Belton Cl BN2 192 B8
Belton Rd BN2 192 B8
Belvedere BN1 191 E8
Belvedere Ave BN15 187 D6
Belvedere Ct RH10 19 B7
Belvedere Terr 5 BN1 191 E6
Belvedere Wlk RH16 87 C3
Belverdere Cl GU32 68 B4
Belyngham Cres BN17 204 D6
Bembridge St BN2 192 C8
Benbow Cl BN43 188 F6
Benchfield Cl RH19 10 B1
Benedict Cl BN11 187 B3
Benedict Dr BN11 187 A3
Benett Ave BN3 169 B2
Benett Dr BN3 169 B2
Benfield Cl BN41 168 C1
Benfield Cres BN41 168 C1
Benfield Ct BN41 190 C8
Benfield Jun Sch BN41 190 C8
Benfield Way BN41 168 C1
Bengairn Ave BN1 170 A7
Benham Ct 10 BN3 191 B5
Benhams Cl RH6 2 A5
Benhams Dr RH6 2 A5
Benizi Ct 12 PO21 201 D3
Benjamin Lo RH15 109 D3
Benjamin Rd RH10 19 D4
Bennett Cl RH10 19 B2
Bennett Rd BN2 192 E4
Bennetts RH17 85 C3
Bennetts Cl PO20 207 F7
Bennetts Rd RH13 36 E1
Bennett's Terr 6 GU29 94 E7
Bens Acre RH13 37 A2
Benson Ct BN3 190 E7
Benson Rd BN5 125 F5
Benson's La RH12 16 C1
Bentham Rd BN2 192 C7
Bentley Cl BN16 206 A8
Bentons La RH13 103 E3
Bentswood Cres RH16 88 A5
Bentswood Rd RH16 87 F5
Ben Turner Ind Est PO19 177 D6
Bentworth PO22 180 B6
BEPTON 94 A1
Bepton Cl GU29 94 D6
Bepton Down GU31 68 C3
Bepton Rd GU29 94 B4
Berberis Ct BN43 167 B1
Beresford Ct 12 BN3 191 D7
Beresford Rd BN2 192 D5
Bereweeke Rd PO22 202 A4
Bergamot Cres BN43 167 C1
Berghestede Rd PO22 201 C6
Berkeley Cl RH11 17 E2
Berkeley Ct
Bognor Regis PO21 201 D2
6 Hove BN3 191 E7
9 Littlehampton BN17 204 E4
Berkeley Lo 1 RH20 121 E1
Berkeley Mews PO19 177 B7
Berkeley Sq BN11 186 A2
Berkshire Ct BN12 185 B4
Bermuda Ct 2 BN17 205 A6
Bernard Pl BN2 192 C7
Bernard Rd
Arundel BN18 159 F2
Brighton BN2 192 C7
Worthing BN11 185 F2
Berrall Way RH14 79 C7
Berriedale Ave BN3 190 E6
Berriedale Cl BN15 187 C7
Berriedale Dr BN15 187 C7
Berriedale Ho BN3 190 E6
Berrybarn La PO20 207 B8
Berry Cl RH15 109 A5
Berry La
Ardingly RH17 64 C7
Bognor Regis PO22 201 A7
Littlehampton BN17 204 F4
Berrylands GU33 45 C7
Berrylands Farm BN6 107 D1
Berrymeade Wlk 6 RH11 17 E5
Berrymill Cl 7 PO21 201 D4
Berstead Wlk 1 RH11 17 F3
Bersted Green Ct PO22 201 C6
Bersted Mews 2 PO22 201 D5
Bersted St
Bognor Regis PO22 201 C5
3 Bognor Regis PO22 201 D5
Berwick Rd BN2 194 D3
Bessborough Terr BN15 187 D4
Betchley Cl RH19 9 E3
Betchworth Works RH6 4 D6
Bethune Cl RH10 19 D5
Bethune Rd RH13 36 E1
Bethwines Cl PO18 176 A7
Betts Way RH10 5 D2
Bevan Ct RH11 18 B1
BEVENDEAN 170 F2
Bevendean Ave BN2 194 D1
Bevendean Cres BN2 170 E2
Bevendean Prim Sch BN2 170 F1
Bevendean Rd BN2 170 D1
Beverley Cl
Selsey PO20 212 F7
Yapton BN18 181 A3
Beverley Ct
1 Hove BN3 190 D7
5 Pulborough RH20 100 C2
3 Worthing BN11 186 B1
Beverley Gdns BN16 205 C7
Beverley Ho 6 BN15 187 E5
Beverley Mews RH10 19 A5
BEWBUSH 17 F3
Bewbush Com Prim Sch RH11 17 F3
Bewbush Dr RH11 17 F3
Bewbush Manor RH11 17 E2
Bewick Gdns PO19 177 B8
Bewley Rd BN16 183 F6
Bexhill Rd BN2 171 E1
Bex La GU29 94 E2
BEXLEYHILL 73 E7
Bickley Ct RH11 18 A3
Bickleys Ct 1 PO21 201 B2
Biddulph Mews GU28 117 D8
Biggin Cl RH11 18 C4
Bignor Cl
Horsham RH12 37 A7
Rustington BN16 205 D6
Bignor Park Rd RH20 118 E5
Bignor Roman Villa (remains of)* RH20 118 B2
Bigwood Ave BN3 191 D8
Bilberry Cl RH11 18 B3
Bilbets RH12 36 C3
Billingshurst Inf Sch RH14 79 B7
Billingshurst Jun Sch RH14 79 D7
Billingshurst Rd
Ashington RH20 122 F8
Broadbridge Heath RH12 35 D3
Wisborough Green RH14 78 C8
Billingshurst Sta RH14 79 D7
Billington Ct RH19 9 E2
Billinton Dr RH10 19 B5
Billinton Way BN1 213 B4
BILSHAM 202 F8
Bilsham Cnr BN18 202 F8
Bilsham Ct BN18 180 F2
Bilsham La BN18 180 E1
Bilsham Rd BN18 180 F1
Binderton La PO18 134 D2
BINES GREEN 124 F7
Bines Rd RH13 104 F2
Binney Ct RH10 6 E1
Binstead Cl RH11 18 B8
Binsted Ave PO22 202 A5
Binsted Cl BN16 205 B4
Binsted La BN18 181 B7
Biology Rd BN1 171 B6
Birch Ave RH17 88 A3
Birch Cl
Angmering BN16 205 F8
Arundel BN18 159 E1
Bognor Regis PO21 200 D3
Crawley Down RH10 21 C8
Haywards Heath RH17 88 B3
Lancing BN15 187 D4
Liss GU33 45 C4
Birch Ct BN42 168 A1
Birch Dr RH14 79 D7
Birch End RH20 121 D7
Birchen La RH16 87 F8
Birches Cl
Selsey PO20 212 C7
Worthing BN13 185 C6
Birches Ind Est RH19 9 A3
Birches Rd RH12 37 B5
Birches The
Crawley RH10 19 A7
Mannings Heath RH13 59 C7
West Chiltington Common RH20 121 C8
Birch Gr RH20 121 D5
Birch Grove Cres BN1 170 A5
Birchgrove La RH17 44 A1
Birchgrove Rd RH17 65 E7
Birch Lea RH10 6 A1
Bircholt Rd GU30 24 D4
Birch Tree Cl PO10 151 B4
Birch Tree Ct BN11 186 E3
Birch Tree Dr PO10 151 B4
Birch Tree Gdns RH19 9 B3
Birch Tree La RH20 121 E6
Birch Way
Haywards Heath RH17 88 A2
Heath Common RH20 122 B3
Birchwood Cl
Crawley RH10 19 C3
Horley RH6 2 B4
Ifold RH14 31 D3
Birchwood Grove Com Prim Sch RH15 109 C1
Birchwood Grove Rd RH15 109 C1
Birdham CE Prim Sch PO20 197 E5
Birdham Cl
Bognor Regis PO21 200 F5
Crawley RH11 18 B8
Birdham Pl BN2 170 E3
Birdham Rd
Apuldram PO19, PO20 176 D2
Brighton BN2 170 F3
South Hayling PO11 195 A2
Birkdale Cl BN13 185 D7
Birkdale Dr RH11 17 D5
Birkdale Rd BN13 185 D7
Birling Cl BN2 170 D1
Birthday Ho GU29 73 B2
Biscay Cl BN16 205 B6
Bisham Cl RH10 19 D3
Bishearne Gdns GU33 45 A5
Bishop Cl BN5 125 E5
Bishop Luffa CE Sch PO19 176 D7
Bishop Luffa Cl PO19 176 D7
Bishopric RH12 36 B2
Bishopric Ct 8 RH12 36 B2
Bishops Cl
Bognor Regis PO21 211 A8
Fernhurst GU27 49 A6
Worthing BN13 186 A4
Bishop's Cl BN6 128 A7
Bishops Ct
Horsham RH12 36 C1
Mid Lavant PO18 154 E6
Bishops Ctyd PO19 177 B6
Bishopsfield RH14 55 F5
Bishopsgate Wlk PO19 177 B7
Bishops Ho RH20 142 D8
Bishops Rd
Hove BN3 169 C1
Tangmere PO20 156 D2
Bishopstone Dr BN2 194 B2
Bishopstone La
Goddards' Green BN6 108 A5
Goddards' Green BN6, RH17 108 A7
Bishopstone Wlk RH11 18 C1
Bishop Tufnell CE Inf Sch PO22 202 C5
Bishop Tufnell CE Jun Sch PO22 202 C5
Bitmead Cl RH11 17 E5
Bittern Cl RH11 17 D5
Blackberry La
Chichester PO19 177 C6
Felcourt RH7 9 E8
Selsey PO20 212 C7
Blackberry Rd RH19, RH7 9 D8
Blackbird Cl RH15 108 D3
Blackbird Hill RH10 21 C5
Blackboy La PO18 176 A7
Blackbridge Ct RH12 36 A2
Blackbridge La RH12 36 A1
Blackbrook La BN8, RH17 89 E2
Blackcap Cl
Crawley RH11 18 C4
Red Hill PO9 130 C1
Black Cnr RH10 6 D4
Black Dog Wlk RH10 18 E8
Blackdown BN2 192 F7
Blackdown Rd BN13 185 F8
Black Down Wlks* GU27 28 A2
Blackett Rd RH10 19 C5
Blackfold Rd RH10 19 A5
Blackgate La BN5 125 E4
Black Gate La RH20 100 D7
Blackheath RH10 19 D8
Black Hill RH16 88 A7
Black Horse Cvn Pk PO20 212 C8
Black Horse Way RH12 36 C2
Blackhouse La
Burgess Hill RH15 109 B4
Foxhill GU28 76 D5
Blackhouse Rd RH13 38 D5
Blacklands Cres RH18 23 F2
Black Lion La BN1 213 A2
Black Lion St BN1 213 B1
Blackman St BN1 213 B3
Blackman Way PO20 177 B1
Blackmill La PO18 157 C3
Blackmore Ct BN1 213 B4
Blackpatch Gr 6 BN43 166 F1
BLACK ROCK 192 F3
Black Rock (for Marina) Sta* BN2 192 E3
Blacksmiths Cl RH20 123 A4
Blacksmith's Cnr BN18 180 F8
Blacksmiths Cres BN15 187 B6
Blackstone La
Blackstone BN5, BN6 126 E6
Woodmancote BN5 126 D3
Blackstone Rise BN5 126 E5
Blackstone St BN5 126 E5
Blackstone Way RH15 109 A5
Black Swan Cl RH11 39 B7
Blackthorn Cl
Brighton BN1 169 D3
Crawley RH11 5 C1
Horsham RH13 37 A2
Portslade-by-S BN41 168 B2
Blackthorns
Hurstpierpoint BN6 127 F7
Lindfield RH16 88 A7
Blackthorns Cl RH16 88 A6
Blackthorns Com Prim Sch RH16 88 A6
Blackthorns The RH15 109 B5
Blackwater La RH10 19 D6
BLACKWELL 9 E3
Blackwell Farm Rd RH19 9 F3
Blackwell Hollow RH19 9 F2
Blackwell Prim Sch RH19 9 E3
Blackwell Rd RH19 9 F2
Blake Cl RH10 18 F2
Blake Cotts PO18 176 A6
Blake Ct 3 BN2 213 C3
Blakehurst La BN18 161 B3
Blakehurst Way BN17 204 D6
Blakemyle PO21 200 F2
Blakeney Cl PO19 176 B6
Blaker St BN2 213 C2
Blakes Ct PO22 202 A4
Blakes Farm Rd RH13 58 A4
Blakes Rd PO22 202 A4
Blakes View PO22 201 F4
Blanches Rd RH13 105 A3
Blanches Wlk RH13 105 A3
Blatchen The BN17 204 F4
Blatchford Cl RH13 36 F3
Blatchford Rd RH13 36 F3
Blatchington Mill Sch & Sixth Form Coll BN3 169 A2
Blatchington Rd BN3 191 B7
Bleaches Ct PO18 154 E7
Bleach's Yard Ind Est GU30 25 B2
Blendworth La PO8 130 A8
Blenheim Ave BN13 185 E6
Blenheim Cl
Crawley RH10 6 D1
East Grinstead RH19 10 A3
2 Rustington BN16 205 B7
Blenheim Ct
Bognor Regis PO21 200 E4
1 Hove BN3 191 A6
Worthing BN13 185 C9
Blenheim Dr BN16 205 B7
Blenheim Fields RH18 23 E3
Blenheim Gdns PO19 177 C6
Blenheim Mews RH16 87 F2
Blenheim Pl 5 BN1 213 B3
Blenheim Rd
Horsham RH12 36 D4
Lancing BN15 187 D4
Yapton BN18 180 F2
Blessing Lo 5 BN43 189 B6
Bletchley Ct BN1 192 A8
Bligh Cl RH10 18 F4
Blindley Rd RH10 6 D1
Blomfield Dr PO19 155 A1
Blondell Dr PO21 200 D2
Bloomsbury Pl 17 BN2 192 C4
Bloomsbury St 16 BN2 192 C4
Bloor Cl RH12 36 D7
Blount Ave RH19 9 C1
Bluebell Cl
Crawley RH11 18 B3
East Grinstead RH19 9 B1
Haywards Heath RH16 87 F4
Horsham RH12 36 E5
Bluebell Dr BN17 205 A7
Bluebell Rly* RH17, RH19, TN22 43 A5
Bluebell Way RH15 108 D4
Blueberry Hill RH20 122 B1
Bluebird Cl 1 BN43 189 B6
Bluebird Ct 11 BN3 191 A6
Bluebird Ho RH6 1 D1
Blue Cedars Cl BN16 205 E8
Bluecoat Pond RH13 57 D6
Blue Idol The* RH13 80 B3
Blundell Ave RH6 1 F4
Blunden Dr RH17 86 F8
Blunts Way RH12 36 C3
Blunts Wood Cres RH16 87 B6
Blunts Wood Rd RH16 87 C6
Blytons The RH19 9 B1
Boardwalk PO19 177 A7
Boatyard The BN2 193 A3
Bob La BN5, RH17 106 E6
Boddingtons La BN6 129 D3
Boderton Mews GU28 117 D7
Bodiam Ave
Brighton BN2 171 B1
Worthing BN12 185 B3
Bodiam Cl
Brighton BN2 171 B2
Crawley RH10 19 C6
Southwater RH13 58 A2
Bodiam Ct RH16 87 E5
Bodiham Ho 15 BN3 191 D7
Bodmin Cl BN13 185 D9
Bodmin Rd BN13 185 D9
Bognor Rd
Chichester PO19, PO20 177 D5
Warnham RH12, RH5 14 D4
Bognor Regis Com Coll
Bognor Regis PO21 200 F4
Bognor Regis PO21 201 A5
Bognor Regis Mus* PO21 201 D2
Bognor Regis Ret Pk The PO22 201 D7
Bognor Regis Sta PO21 201 C3
Bohunt Sch GU30 25 B4
Boiler House Hill BN1 171 B7
Bolding Way RH16 87 E2
Boleyn Cl RH10 19 D3
Boleyn Dr PO21 200 B1
Bolney CE Prim Sch RH17 85 C2
Bolney Chapel Rd RH17 107 B7
Bolney Crossways RH17 85 D1
Bolney Ct RH11 17 F3
Bolney Grange Bsns Pk RH17 107 F6
Bolney Rd
Ansty RH17 86 A2
Bolney RH17 85 E2
Brighton BN2 170 F4
Bolnore RH16 87 B4
Bolnore Rd RH16 87 C4
BOLNORE VILLAGE 87 C2
Bolsover Rd
Hove BN3 190 E8
Worthing BN13 185 E4
Bolters Rd RH6 2 A5
Bolters Rd S RH6 1 F6
Bolton Rd RH10 19 C2
Boltro Rd RH16 87 D5
Bonaventure 2 BN43 189 B6
Bonchurch Rd BN2 192 C7
Bond St
Arundel BN18 160 A3

Bond St *continued*
Brighton BN1 . . . . .213 B2
Bonehurst Rd RH1, RH6 . . . .2 A7
Bonfire Hill RH13 . . . . .57 D1
Bonfire La RH17 . . . . .65 D5
Bonnar Cl PO20 . . . . .212 D6
Bonnar Rd PO20 . . . . .212 D6
Bonnetts La RH11 . . . . .5 A3
Bonny Wood Rd BN6 . . . . . .128 E3
Bookers La PO20 . . . . .208 C8
Bookers Vineyard∗
RH17 . . . . .85 B3
Booth Mus of Natural
History∗ BN1 . . . . .191 E8
Booth Rd RH11 . . . . .17 E3
Booth Way RH13 . . . . .36 E3
Borage Cl █ RH11 . . . . .1 A4
Borde Hill Gdn∗ RH16 . . . .63 C2
Bordehill La RH16,
RH17 . . . . .63 D3
Borden La GU30 . . . . .71 A6
Border Chase RH10 . . . . .7 A2
Border Cl GU33 . . . . .45 D1
Border Ct RH19 . . . . .9 F4
Border End GU27 . . . . .26 D6
Border Rd GU27 . . . . .26 D6
Borers Arms Rd RH10 . . . . . .7 C3
Borers Cl RH10 . . . . .7 C4
Borers Yard Cotts RH10 . . . .7 C3
Borers Yard Ind Est
RH10 . . . . .7 D3
Borers Yd RH10 . . . . .7 D3
Borough Gr GU32 . . . . .68 A2
BOROUGH HILL 68 A3
Borough Hill GU32 . . . . .68 A3
Borough Ho GU29 . . . . .94 F8
Borough Rd GU32 . . . . .68 A3
Borough St BN1 . . . . .191 E6
Borrowdale Cl RH11 . . . . . . .18 B4
Borrow King Cl PO20 . . . . .192 D8
Borthwick Ho PO20 . . . . . .207 F6
Bosham La PO18 . . . . .175 B5
Bosham Prim Sch
PO18 . . . . .175 C5
Bosham Rd PO20 . . . . .19 C3
Bosham Sta PO18 . . . . .175 C7
Bosham Wlk PO20 . . . . .19 C3
Bosmere Gdns PO10 . . . . . .151 B1
Bosmere Rd PO11 . . . . .195 A2
Bostal Rd BN44 . . . . .145 C1
Bostal The BN44 . . . . .146 C1
Bost Hill BN13, BN14 . . . . . .163 E3
Bostock Ave RH12 . . . . .37 A5
Bostock Rd PO19 . . . . .177 B8
Boston Ct RH16 . . . . .88 A5
Boston Rd RH16 . . . . .88 A5
Boswell Rd RH10 . . . . .18 E3
Botany Cl BN16 . . . . .205 E4
Bough Beeches RH15 . . . . . .109 C1
Boulevard The
Crawley RH10 . . . . .18 E6
Worthing BN12, BN13 . . . .185 E5
Boundary Cl
Crawley RH10 . . . . .18 E7
Worthing BN11 . . . . .186 B1
Boundary Pas █ BN3 . . . .191 E6
Boundary Rd
Balcombe Lane RH17 . . . . .41 B4
Brighton BN2 . . . . .192 F4
Crawley RH10 . . . . .18 E7
Lancing BN15 . . . . .188 B5
Portslade-by-Sea BN3,
BN41 . . . . .190 C7
Worthing BN11 . . . . .186 B1
Boundary Way BN16 . . . . . .206 B6
Boundstone Cl BN15 . . . . . .187 D7
Boundstone Com Coll
BN15 . . . . .187 D7
Boundstone La BN15 . . . . . .187 D6
Bourg-de-Peage Ave
RH19 . . . . .10 A1
Bourne Cl
Fishbourne PO19 . . . . . . .176 A7
Worthing BN13 . . . . .185 B7
Bourne Com Coll
PO21 . . . . .151 F1
Bourne Ct
Bracklesham PO20 . . . . . .208 A5
Brighton BN1 . . . . .169 D4
Littlehampton BN17 . . . . . .204 B7
Bourne The BN6 . . . . .128 E5
Bourne View Cl PO10 . . . . .151 F2
Bourne Way GU29 . . . . .94 E6
Bourns Ct RH13 . . . . .36 E3
Bowater Rd RH10 . . . . .19 C3
Bowen Ct █ BN1 . . . . .191 C6
Bowen La GU31 . . . . .68 B3
Bowerhill Cotts RH19 . . . . . .43 F6
Bower La RH20 . . . . .121 D6
Bowers Ct BN11 . . . . .186 B1
Bowers Pl RH10 . . . . .21 B8
Bower The
Crawley RH10 . . . . .19 C5
Haywards Heath RH16 . . . . .87 D5
Bowes Cl RH13 . . . . .36 E3
Bowes Hill PO9 . . . . .130 E3
Bowhill La PO18 . . . . .153 D7
Bowley La PO20 . . . . .199 E5
Bowline Point █
BN43 . . . . .188 E7
Bowling Green Cl
PO21 . . . . .200 D3
Bowling Green La
RH12 . . . . .36 D3

Bowman Ct RH10 . . . . .18 D7
Bowmans Cl BN44 . . . . .145 D4
Bowness Ave BN15 . . . . . . .187 C5
Bowness Cl █ RH11 . . . . . . .17 D5
Bowring Way RH20 . . . . . . .192 D4
Boxall Wlk RH13 . . . . .36 D1
Box Cl RH11 . . . . .18 C1
Boxes La RH17 . . . . .65 C5
Boxgrove BN12 . . . . .185 B5
Boxgrove CE Prim Sch
PO18 . . . . .156 D4
Boxgrove Gr BN15 . . . . .187 F8
Boxgrove Gdns PO21 . . . . .200 D2
Boxgrove Ho
Boxgrove PO18 . . . . .156 D3
Littlehampton BN17 . . . . . .204 B7
Boxgrove Par BN12 . . . . . .185 B4
Boxgrove Priory∗
PO18 . . . . .156 D3
Boxham La PO20 . . . . .198 O3
Box La RH15 . . . . .23 A6
Box's La RH17 . . . . .66 C6
Box Tree Ave BN16 . . . . . . .205 B5
Boyce's St █ BN1 . . . . .213 A2
Boyles La █ BN2 . . . . .192 E4
Brackenbury Cl BN41 . . . . .168 B2
Bracken Cl
Copthorne RH10 . . . . .7 B2
Crawley RH10 . . . . .18 F8
Heath Common RH20 . . . .122 B2
Bracken Gr RH12 . . . . .37 B5
Bracken La RH20 . . . . .122 B2
Bracken Rd GU31 . . . . .68 C2
Brackenside RH6 . . . . .2 B4
Brackens The RH20 . . . . . . .121 B1
Bracklesham Cl PO20 . . . . .208 B6
Bracklesham Ct PO20 . . . . .208 B6
Bracklesham La PO20 . . . . .208 B7
Bracklesham Rd
PO11 . . . . .195 B2
Bracknell Wlk RH11 . . . . . . .17 E3
Bradbury Rd RH10 . . . . .19 C3
Brading Rd BN2 . . . . .192 C7
Bradley Ho BN11 . . . . .186 B2
Bradlord Cl PO21 . . . . .201 A3
Bradshaw Rd PO19 . . . . . . .177 C8
Braemar Ho █ BN1 . . . . . . .191 E6
Braemar Way PO21 . . . . . . .200 F7
Braemore Ct BN3 . . . . .190 E6
Braemore Rd BN3 . . . . .190 E6
Braeside
RH6 . . . . .2 A3
Braeside Ave RH16 . . . . . . .170 A7
Braeside Cl
Findon BN14 . . . . .163 E6
Haslemere GU27 . . . . .26 F8
Brainsmead RH17 . . . . .86 F7
Brainsmead Ct RH17 . . . . . .86 E7
Bramber █ BN15 . . . . .187 D5
Bramber Ave
Hove BN3 . . . . .168 F3
Storrington BN20 . . . . .121 C2
Bramber Cl
Bognor Regis PO21 . . . . . .201 A4
Crawley RH10 . . . . .18 E8
Haywards Heath RH16 . . . . .87 D4
Horsham RH12 . . . . .37 B5
Lancing BN15 . . . . .187 D8
Bramber Ct
█ Hove BN3 . . . . .191 B7
█ Shoreham-by-S
BN43 . . . . .189 B8
█ Worthing BN11 . . . . . . .185 F3
Bramber Fst Sch
BN14 . . . . .186 F6
Bramber Ho █ RH13 . . . . . .36 E1
Bramber Rd
Chichester PO19 . . . . .177 B5
Steyning BN44 . . . . .145 D2
Worthing BN13 . . . . .186 E6
Bramber Sq BN16 . . . . .205 C6
Bramber Way RH11 . . . . . . .109 A4
Bramble Cl
Bognor Regis PO21 . . . . . .199 F2
Copthorne RH10 . . . . .7 B3
Worthing BN13 . . . . .185 D8
Bramble Cres BN13 . . . . . . .185 D9
Bramble Ct GU31 . . . . .68 E3
Brambledean Rd
BN1 . . . . .190 B7
Bramble Gdns RH15 . . . . . .108 C4
Bramble Hill RH12 . . . . .40 F2
Bramble La BN13 . . . . .185 D8
Bramble Mead RH11 . . . . . . .40 F1
Bramble Rd GU31 . . . . .68 E3
Bramble Rise BN1 . . . . .169 C5
Brambles BN6 . . . . .128 F5
Brambles The RH17 . . . . .82 A5
Bramble Twitten RH19 . . . . . .10 A1
Brambletye La RH18 . . . . . . .23 D4
Brambletye Prep Sch
RH19 . . . . .23 C5
Brambletye Rd RH10 . . . . . .19 A5
Brambletye Ave
BN2 . . . . .194 D1
Bramblewick La RH16 . . . . .184 A6
Bramble Way BN1 . . . . .170 C6
Brambling Cl RH13 . . . . .37 A1
Brambling La GU29 . . . . .72 C3
Brambling Rd
Horsham RH13 . . . . .37 A1
Red Hill PO9 . . . . .130 D1
Bramblings The
BN16 . . . . .205 D5
Bramfield Rd PO22 . . . . . . .202 C4
Bramlands La BN5 . . . . .147 D8

Bramley Cl
Crawley RH10 . . . . .18 F6
Kirdford RH14 . . . . .53 B3
Worthing BN14 . . . . .186 D6
Bramley Ct RH6 . . . . .1 F4
Bramley Gdns
Bognor Regis PO22 . . . . . .201 B7
Hermitage PO10 . . . . .173 D8
Bramley Ho BN11 . . . . .186 B3
Bramley Rd BN14 . . . . .186 D6
Bramleys BN7 . . . . .172 E5
Bramley Way BN16 . . . . . . .206 A8
Bramley Wlk RH6 . . . . .2 C3
Brampton Cl PO22 . . . . . . .212 D7
Brampton Ct PO19 . . . . . . .176 F5
Bramwell Lo BN5 . . . . .126 C2
Brandon Cl RH10 . . . . .19 D4
Brandy Hole La PO19 . . . . .154 E2
Brangwyn Ave BN1 . . . . . . .169 E5
Brangwyn Cres BN1 . . . . . .169 E6
Brangwyn Ct BN1 . . . . .169 E5
Brangwyn Dr BN1 . . . . .169 E6
Brangwyn's Acre BN6 . . . . .129 D3
Brangwyn Way BN1 . . . . . . .169 E5
BRANTRIDGE 40 B1
Brantridge La RH17 . . . . .62 B6
Brantridge Rd RH10 . . . . . . .18 F4
Brantridge Sch
Staplefield, Brantridge
RH17 . . . . .62 A8
Staplefield RH17 . . . . .61 E5
Brasslands Dr BN41 . . . . . . .167 F1
Braybon Ave BN1 . . . . .169 F4
Braybon Bsns Pk
RH15 . . . . .108 C2
Bray Cl RH10 . . . . .19 D4
Braypool La BN1 . . . . .169 D7
Brazwick Ave PO21 . . . . . . .200 F7
Breach Ave PO10 . . . . .152 A2
Breach Cl BN44 . . . . .145 D4
Bread La BN17 . . . . .203 F6
Bream Cl PO20 . . . . .212 B8
Brecon Cl BN13 . . . . .185 F8
Brecon Ct █ BN3 . . . . .191 C7
Brecon Hts RH11 . . . . .18 C5
Brede Cl BN2 . . . . .192 F5
Breezehurst Dr RH11 . . . . . .17 F3
Bremere La PO20 . . . . .198 C2
Bremner Ave RH6 . . . . .1 F4
Brendon Rd BN13 . . . . .185 E8
Brendon Way BN16 . . . . . . .205 B6
Brent Cl PO10 . . . . .173 A8
Brent Lodge Bird &
Wildlife Hospl∗
PO20 . . . . .209 E8
Brent Rd PO21 . . . . .201 A4
Brentwood Cl BN1 . . . . .170 B3
Brentwood Cres BN1 . . . . . .170 B3
Brentwood Rd BN1 . . . . . . .170 B3
Brettingham Cl RH11 . . . . . .17 E3
Bretton RH15 . . . . .108 E5
Bretts Orch RH17 . . . . .41 A1
Brewells La GU33 . . . . .46 A5
Brewer Rd BN1 . . . . .18 E4
Brewer St BN2 . . . . .213 C4
Brewers Yd RH20 . . . . .121 D1
Brewery Hill BN18 . . . . .160 B2
Brewery Mews BN6 . . . . . . .127 F6
Brewhurst La RH14 . . . . .32 A2
Breydon Wlk RH10 . . . . .19 B4
Briar Ave PO20 . . . . .196 F1
Briar Cl
Angmering BN16 . . . . .205 F8
Bognor Regis PO21 . . . . . .199 F3
Crawley RH11 . . . . .5 C1
Oving PO20 . . . . .178 C6
Woodingdean BN2 . . . . . . .193 D7
Yapton BN18 . . . . .202 B7
Briarcroft Rd BN2 . . . . .193 D7
Briars The BN15 . . . . .187 F5
Briars Wood RH6 . . . . .2 C4
Briarswood Cl RH10 . . . . . . .19 D8
Briar Wood GU33 . . . . .45 C7
Brickfield Cl PO21 . . . . .201 B5
Brickfield La RH6 . . . . .1 D1
Brick Kiln Cl RH13 . . . . .60 A3
Bricklands RH10 . . . . .21 B7
Brickyard La RH10 . . . . .21 B8
Brideake Cl RH11 . . . . .18 A3
Brideoake Cl PO19 . . . . . . .176 E8
Bridge Cl
Burgess Hill RH15 . . . . . . .108 F4
Lancing BN15 . . . . .187 E5
Worthing BN13 . . . . .185 C5
Bridge Cotts GU33 . . . . .45 A7
Bridge Ct
Bridgefield Cl GU29 . . . . . .94 E6
Bridgefoot Cotts GU29 . . .72 A2
Bridgefoot Path PO10 . . . .173 B8
Bridge Ind Est RH6 . . . . .2 B3
Bridgelands RH10 . . . . .7 A3
Bridge Mdws GU33 . . . . . . .45 A4
Bridge Rd
Chichester PO19 . . . . .177 C7
Emsworth PO10 . . . . .151 B1
Haslemere GU27 . . . . .27 C7
Haywards Heath RH16 . . . . .87 F6
Littlehampton BN17 . . . . . .204 B6
Rudgwick RH12 . . . . .33 D7
Worthing BN14 . . . . .186 D3
Bridge Road Bsns Pk
RH16 . . . . .87 F7
Bridgers Ho RH16 . . . . .87 E6
Bridgersmill RH16 . . . . .87 D6
Bridges Cl RH6 . . . . .2 D3
Bridges Ct RH12 . . . . .37 A5
Bridges Pl RH12 . . . . .36 C1
Bridgewater Cl RH14 . . . . . .79 C6

Bridgeway The PO20 . . . . . .212 D6
Bridgnorth Cl BN13 . . . . . . .185 B6
Bridle La BN18 . . . . .158 D4
Bridle La The PO18 . . . . . . .152 D4
Bridle Way RH10 . . . . .19 D7
Bridle Way The PO20 . . . . .212 D6
Bridorley Cl PO21 . . . . .200 B2
Brierley Gdns BN15 . . . . . . .187 F6
Brigden St █ BN1 . . . . .213 A4
Brigham Pl PO22 . . . . .202 D4
Brighthelm BN1 . . . . .171 B8
Brighton & Hove High
Sch Jun Dept BN3 . . . . .191 D8
Brighton Coll BN2 . . . . .192 D7
Brighton College Prep Sch
BN2 . . . . .192 D7
Brighton Fishing Mus∗
BN1 . . . . .213 A1
Brighton General Hospl
BN2 . . . . .192 D7
Brighton & Hove City Coll
BN1 . . . . .170 F8
Brighton & Hove High Sch
BN1 . . . . .191 E6
Brighton & Hove Stad
BN3 . . . . .169 B1
Brighton, Hove & Sussex
Sixth Form Coll BN1 . . .191 E8
Brighton Marina BN2 . . . .192 F2
Brighton Marina Village
BN2 . . . . .192 F3
Brighton Mus & Art Gall∗
BN1 . . . . .213 B2
Brighton Race Course
BN2 . . . . .193 A8
Brighton Rd
Crawley RH11 . . . . .18 D4
Handcross RH17 . . . . .61 C8
Hassocks BN6 . . . . .128 D3
Horley RH6 . . . . .1 C2
Horsham RH13 . . . . .36 E1
Horsham RH13 . . . . .58 F8
Hurstpierpoint BN6 . . . . . .127 F3
Kingston near Lewes
BN7 . . . . .172 B4
Mannings Heath RH13 . . . . .59 C6
Partridge Green RH13 . . . .105 D4
Pease Pottage RH11 . . . . . .39 B5
Shoreham-by-S BN43 . . . .189 B7
Woodmancote BN5 . . . . . .126 A3
Worthing BN11, BN15,
BN43 . . . . .187 C3
Brighton Sea Life Ctr∗
BN1 . . . . .213 B1
Brighton Sq █ BN1 . . . . . . .213 B2
Brighton Sta BN1 . . . . .213 B3
Brighton Steiner Sch Ltd
BN2 . . . . .192 F4
Brighton Toy & Model Mus∗
The∗ BN1 . . . . .213 B3
Brills La BN1 . . . . .213 B1
Brimfast La PO20 . . . . .198 F4
Brisbane Cl
Crawley RH11 . . . . .5 D1
Worthing BN13 . . . . .185 C7
Brisbane Ho GU29 . . . . .94 E6
Bristol Ave BN15 . . . . .188 B5
Bristol Cl RH10 . . . . .6 D1
Bristol Gate BN2 . . . . .192 D4
Bristol Gdns
Brighton BN2 . . . . .192 E4
Chichester PO19 . . . . .154 F2
Bristol Mews █ BN2 . . . . . .192 E4
Bristol Pl BN2 . . . . .192 E4
Bristol Rd BN2 . . . . .192 E4
Bristol Rise BN2 . . . . .192 D4
Bristol St BN2 . . . . .192 E4
Britannia Ave BN43 . . . . . . .189 B6
Britannia Ct BN2 . . . . .193 A3
Britannia Ho BN43 . . . . .188 E7
Britannia St GU31 . . . . .68 C5
British Engineerium Mus∗
BN3 . . . . .169 B2
Britnell Ho █ GU31 . . . . .68 B4
Briton's Croft BN44 . . . . . . .145 C3
Brittany Ct █ BN3 . . . . .190 D7
Brittany Rd
Hove BN3 . . . . .190 D6
Worthing BN14 . . . . .186 C4
Britten Cl
Crawley RH11 . . . . .17 F3
Horsham RH13 . . . . .37 B4
Britten's La BN18 . . . . .157 E4
Brittingham Ho RH11 . . . . . .17 E3
Broadbridge Bsns Ctr
PO18 . . . . .175 B7
Broadbridge Cotts
RH20 . . . . .123 A4
Broadbridge Dr PO18 . . . . .175 C7
Broadbridge Heath Rd
RH12 . . . . .35 D4
Broadbridge Ho RH10 . . . . .175 B4
Broadbridge La RH6 . . . . . . .7 B8
Broadbridge Mill
PO18 . . . . .175 C7
Broadbridge Ret Pk
RH12 . . . . .35 C4
Broad Croft PO9 . . . . .130 C3
BROADFIELD 18 C1
Broadfield RH19 . . . . .42 E7
Broadfield Barton █
RH11 . . . . .18 B2
Broadfield Dr RH11 . . . . . . .18 B3
Broadfield East Jun & Inf
Schs RH11 . . . . .18 C1
Broadfield Pl RH11 . . . . .18 B2

Broadfields BN2 . . . . .170 E3
Broadfields Rd BN2 . . . . . . .170 E3
Broadford Bridge Rd RH20,
RH14 . . . . .101 E4
Broad Gn BN2 . . . . .193 E6
Broad Green Ave
RH15 . . . . .109 C2
Broadland Cotts GU32 . . . . .68 D6
Broadlands
Burgess Hill RH15 . . . . . . .129 B8
Horley RH6 . . . . .2 C4
Broadlands Bsns Campus
RH12 . . . . .15 C4
Broadmark Ave BN16 . . . . .205 C4
Broadmark Beach
BN16 . . . . .205 C3
Broadmark Ho █ 205 C5
Broadmark La BN16 . . . . . .205 C4
Broadmark Par █
BN16 . . . . .205 C4
Broadmark Way
BN16 . . . . .205 C4
Broad Mdw PO18 . . . . .174 D8
Broadmead RH6 . . . . .2 C4
Broad Piece RH17 . . . . .204 B6
Broad Rd PO18 . . . . .152 D2
Broad Reach BN43 . . . . . . .188 E7
Broad Rig Ave BN3 . . . . . . .168 D3
Broad St
Brighton BN2 . . . . .213 B1
Cuckfield RH17 . . . . .87 A6
Broad Strand BN16 . . . . . . .205 D3
Broad View PO20 . . . . .212 F7
Broadview Gdns
BN13 . . . . .185 E9
BROADWATER 186 C6
Broadwater Bvd
BN14 . . . . .186 D5
Broadwater CE Fst & Mid
Sch BN14 . . . . .186 C5
Broadwater Hall
BN14 . . . . .186 C4
Broadwater Ind Est
BN14 . . . . .186 F6
Broadwater La RH13 . . . . . . .58 D2
Broadwater Manor Sch
BN14 . . . . .186 D6
Broadwater Mews
BN14 . . . . .186 C4
Broadwater Rd BN11,
BN14 . . . . .186 D4
Broadwater St E
BN14 . . . . .186 D6
Broadwater St W
BN14 . . . . .186 C6
Broadwater Way
BN14 . . . . .186 D6
Broadway
Selsey PO20 . . . . .212 C8
Southwick BN42 . . . . .189 F8
Broad Way GU32 . . . . .67 B8
Broadway Ct
Lancing BN15 . . . . .188 B5
█ Shoreham-by-S
BN43 . . . . .189 C8
Broadway Mans █
BN11 . . . . .186 C2
Broadway Mobile Home
Pk BN15 . . . . .188 B6
Broadway The
Balcombe RH17 . . . . .40 F2
Brighton BN2 . . . . .192 F4
Chichester PO19 . . . . .155 A4
Crawley RH10 . . . . .18 D6
Haywards Heath RH16 . . . . .87 E5
Lancing BN15 . . . . .188 B5
Worthing BN11 . . . . .186 E2
Broad Wlk
Crawley RH10 . . . . .18 D6
Heyshott GU28, GU29,
PO18 . . . . .115 D5
Broad Wlk The PO18 . . . . . .153 C6
Broadwood Cl RH12 . . . . . . .37 A5
Broadwood Rise RH11 . . . . .18 A2
Brock End RH17 . . . . .86 E8
Brockenden Keep RH6 . . . . .2 C4
Brockhurst BN2 . . . . .192 F7
Brockhurst Cl █ RH12 . . . . .35 F1
Brockhurst Farm
RH20 . . . . .119 B5
Brockley Cl BN14 . . . . .186 C6
Brock Rd RH11 . . . . .5 B1
Bromley Cl BN6 . . . . .129 A4
Bromley Rd BN2 . . . . .213 C5
Brompton Cl BN1 . . . . .169 E6
Brontes The RH19 . . . . .9 D1
Bronze Cl PO22 . . . . .201 C7
Brook Ave
Bosham PO18 . . . . .175 B5
Hassocks BN6 . . . . .128 F3
Brook Barn Way
BN15 . . . . .185 E2
Brook Chase PO20 . . . . . . .121 C6
Brook Cl
Bognor Regis PO21 . . . . . .200 F4
East Grinstead RH19 . . . . .10 B1
Storrington BN20 . . . . .121 D3
Worthing BN11 . . . . .187 A4
Brook Cotts PO10 . . . . .151 D3
Brook Ct RH12 . . . . .36 B5
Brookdean Rd RH11 . . . . . .187 B3
Brooke Mead BN2 . . . . .213 C3
Brookenbee Cl BN16 . . . . . .205 B7
Brooker Pl BN3 . . . . .191 A7
Brooker's Rd RH14 . . . . .79 D7
Brooker St BN3 . . . . .191 A7
Brookfield █ GU32 . . . . .68 A3

Brookfield Ct PO19 ...... 177 C6
Brookfield Way RH14 ...... 79 D6
Brook Gdns PO10 ...... 173 A8
Brook Gn RH17 ...... 62 E1
Brookham Sch GU30 ...... 25 E2
Brook Hill RH13 ...... 83 E3
Brookhill Cl RH10 ...... 7 A3
Brookhill Rd RH10 ...... 7 A3
Brook Ho **7** RH20 ...... 100 C2
Brookhouse Bottom
TN22 ...... 66 D4
Brook La
Coldwaltham RH20 ...... 119 C5
Faygate RH12 ...... 37 C8
Ferring BN12 ...... 206 E6
Haywards Heath RH16 ...... 87 F8
Rustington BN16 ...... 205 C7
Brookland Ho **5** RH19 ...... 9 E1
Brooklands
Bognor Regis PO22 ...... 200 A1
Haywards Heath RH16 ...... 87 C1
Shoreham-by-S BN43 ...... 188 C6
Brooklands Cotts
PO18 ...... 132 E2
Brooklands Rd RH11 ...... 18 C1
Brooklands Trad Est
BN14 ...... 186 C3
Brooklands Way RH20 ...... 22 D8
Brookland Way RH20 ...... 119 C5
Brook Lane Cvn Pk
BN12 ...... 206 E6
Brooklyn Ave BN11 ...... 185 F3
Brooklyn Ct BN11 ...... 185 F3
Brook Manor RH19 ...... 22 D7
Brookpit La BN17 ...... 203 F8
Brook Rd RH12 ...... 36 E6
Brook Sch The RH10 ...... 19 C3
Brooks End PO21 ...... 200 A2
Brooks Green Pk (Cvn Pk)
RH13 ...... 80 F7
Brookside
Ashington RH20 ...... 123 A4
Copthorne RH10 ...... 7 A3
Crawley Down RH10 ...... 21 B8
Crawley RH10 ...... 18 F7
Runcton PO20 ...... 177 E1
Brookside Ave BN16 ...... 205 C7
Brookside Bsns Pk
BN16 ...... 205 C7
Brookside Cl
Ferring BN12 ...... 206 E7
Runcton PO20 ...... 177 E1
Brookside Cvn Pk
BN17 ...... 182 C5
Brookside Ind Est
BN16 ...... 205 C7
Brookside Rd BN16 ...... 206 D4
Brooks La
Bognor Regis PO22 ...... 201 E4
Bognor Regis PO21 ...... 201 E5
Broadbridge PO18 ...... 175 D7
Brooks La W PO22 ...... 62 F2
Brooksmead PO22 ...... 201 E4
Brook St RH17 ...... 62 F2
Brooks The RH15 ...... 108 E5
Brooks Way RH20 ...... 100 C5
Brook The
Crawley RH10 ...... 18 D7
Southwater RH13 ...... 58 A2
Brookview
Coldwaltham RH20 ...... 119 C5
Copthorne RH10 ...... 7 A3
Brookview S RH20 ...... 119 C5
Brookway
Burgess Hill RH15 ...... 109 C3
Lindfield RH16 ...... 88 A8
Brook Way BN15 ...... 187 F5
Brookwood Ho 2 84
Brookwood Ho RH6 ...... 2 B6
Brookwood Rd PO22 ...... 202 C4
Broomdashers Rd
RH10 ...... 18 F7
Broome Cl RH12 ...... 36 D5
BROOMERSHILL 100 E4
Broomers Hill La
RH20 ...... 100 D5
Broomers Hill Pk
RH20 ...... 100 D5
Broomfield Ave BN14 ...... 186 B5
Broomfield Dr
Billingshurst RH14 ...... 79 E8
Portslade-by-S BN41 ...... 168 A3
Broomfield Gdns BN5 ...... 125 E5
Broomfield Rd
Henfield BN5 ...... 125 E5
Seaford PO10 ...... 212 F8
Broom Rd GU31 ...... 68 E2
Broomwicks Pl RH12 ...... 35 E3
Brou Cl BN16 ...... 206 B5
Brougham Ct **12**
BN11 ...... 187 B3
Brougham Ho BN11 ...... 187 A3
Brougham Rd BN11 ...... 187 B3
Brougham Wlk **1**
BN11 ...... 187 B3
Brow Cl RH20 ...... 121 B1
Brownfield Ho **4**
GU31 ...... 68 B3
Browning Cl RH10 ...... 19 C7
Browning Rd
Lancing BN15 ...... 187 E8
Worthing BN11 ...... 186 B3
Browning's Hill RH13 ...... 83 C2
Brownings The **3** RH19 ...... 7 C4
Browning Ct RH10 ...... 19 A7
Brownleaf Rd BN2 ...... 193 E6
Brown's La RH20 ...... 121 D1

Browns Wood RH19 ...... 9 E4
Brown Twins Rd BN6 ...... 128 B5
Brow The
Burgess Hill RH15 ...... 109 A2
Woodmancote BN2 ...... 193 D8
Broxmead La
Bolney RH17 ...... 85 D4
Cuckfield RH17 ...... 86 A5
Broyle Cl PO19 ...... 154 F1
Broyle Rd PO19 ...... 177 A8
Bruce Ave BN11 ...... 185 F4
Bruce Cl RH16 ...... 87 E3
Bruce Way BN11 ...... 185 F4
Brunel Ctr RH20 ...... 5 F2
Brunel Ho GU27 ...... 27 A6
Brunel Pl RH10 ...... 18 E5
Brunswick Cl
Bognor Regis PO22 ...... 202 A5
Crawley RH10 ...... 19 A4
Brunswick Ct **6** RH10 ...... 19 A4
Brunswick Mews **9**
BN3 ...... 191 D5
Brunswick Pl BN3 ...... 191 D5
Brunswick Rd
Hove BN3 ...... 191 D6
Shoreham-by-S BN43 ...... 188 F7
Worthing BN11 ...... 186 C1
Brunswick Row BN1 ...... 213 B4
Brunswick St E BN3 ...... 191 D5
Brunswick St W BN3 ...... 191 D5
Brunswick Sq BN1 ...... 191 D5
Brunswick Terr BN1,
BN3 ...... 191 D5
Brushes La RH16 ...... 88 B8
Brushwood Rd RH12 ...... 37 B6
Bryce Cl RH12 ...... 37 A5
Buchan Ctry Pk*
RH11 ...... 17 E1
Buchans Lawn RH11 ...... 18 B2
Buci Cres BN43 ...... 167 C1
Buck Barn Bglws RH13 ...... 82 A2
Buckbarn Crossroads
RH13 ...... 82 B2
Buckhurst Cl RH16 ...... 18 A5
Buckhurst Cotts RH12 ...... 33 D8
Buckhurst Mead RH19 ...... 9 C4
Buckhurst Way RH19 ...... 9 C3
Buckingham Ave
BN43 ...... 166 E1
Buckingham Cl
4 Brighton BN1 ...... 213 A4
Shoreham-by-S BN43 ...... 189 A8
Buckingham Com Mid Sch
BN43 ...... 188 F8
Buckingham Ct
Crawley RH11 ...... 18 B2
Middleton-on-S PO20 ...... 202 E5
Worthing BN14 ...... 186 B7
Buckingham Dr
Chichester PO19 ...... 177 D6
East Grinstead RH19 ...... 23 A8
Buckingham Gate RH6 ...... 6 C7
Buckingham Lo BN1 ...... 213 A4
Buckingham Mews **10**
BN43 ...... 166 F1
Buckingham Pl
6 Brighton BN1 ...... 213 A4
6 Rustington BN16 ...... 205 B7
Buckingham Rd
Brighton BN1 ...... 213 A3
Petersfield GU32 ...... 67 F3
Shoreham-by-S BN43 ...... 188 F8
Worthing BN11 ...... 186 D2
Buckingham Sq
Brighton BN1 ...... 213 A3
Shoreham-by-S BN43 ...... 188 E7
Buckland Dr PO21 ...... 200 B2
Buckler St BN41 ...... 190 B8
Buckley Cl BN3 ...... 168 E4
Buckley Pl RH10 ...... 21 A8
Buckmans Rd RH11 ...... 18 D6
Buckmore Ave GU32 ...... 67 F4
Bucknor Cl PO21 ...... 200 C2
BUCKS GREEN 33 B6
Bucksham Ave PO21 ...... 201 F7
Buckshead Hill RH13 ...... 59 F7
Buckswood Dr RH11 ...... 18 A4
Buckwish La BN5 ...... 125 C4
Buddington La GU29 ...... 72 F3
Budgen Cl RH10 ...... 6 D1
Budgenor Lo GU29 ...... 73 A3
Buffbeards La GU27 ...... 26 E6
Bugshill La GU29 ...... 93 D1
Bulbeck Cl RH10 ...... 108 E1
Bulbeck Ct PO10 ...... 152 A1
Bulkington Ave BN14 ...... 186 B4
Bulldogs Bank RH19 ...... 42 F5
Buller Rd BN2 ...... 170 D1
Bullfinch Cl
Horley RH6 ...... 1 E4
Horsham RH12 ...... 36 C7
Bullfinch La BN6 ...... 127 E6
Bull Hill GU33 ...... 46 A4
Bull's La RH13, RH17 ...... 84 D4
Bulrushes Bsns Pk
RH19 ...... 2 C1
Bunbury Cl RH20 ...... 122 B2
Bunch La GU27 ...... 27 B8
Bunch Way GU27 ...... 27 A6
Buncton Crossways
BN44 ...... 144 C2
Buncton La RH17 ...... 85 E3
Bungalows The BN18 ...... 158 D1
Bunting Cl RH13 ...... 36 F3
Bunyan Cl RH11 ...... 17 E3
Burbeach Cl RH11 ...... 18 B3
Burchell Ct BN15 ...... 187 F7
Burchens The BN14 ...... 186 D6

Burchetts Cl RH16 ...... 87 E2
Burchett Wlk PO21 ...... 200 F5
Burch Gr BN18 ...... 158 D1
Burdett Cl RH10 ...... 19 D5
Burdett Cl RH11 ...... 18 A2
Burdocks Dr RH15 ...... 18 D1
Burford Cl BN14 ...... 186 A7
Burford Rd RH13 ...... 36 E2
Burgesmede Ho **6**
GU32 ...... 68 B3
Burgess Ct BN41 ...... 190 B8
Burgess Hill Sch
RH15 ...... 109 B2
Burgess Hill Sta
RH15 ...... 109 B2
Burgh Cl RH10 ...... 6 D1
Burgh Hill Rd GU30 ...... 25 A7
Burlands RH15 ...... 5 A1
Burleigh Cl RH10 ...... 21 B8
Burleigh Ct
28 Brighton BN1 ...... 191 E5
5 Worthing BN11 ...... 186 C1
Burleigh La RH10 ...... 21 C7
Burleigh Way RH10 ...... 21 B8
Burley Cl
3 Lancing BN15 ...... 187 E6
Loxwood RH14 ...... 32 A4
Burley Rd PO22 ...... 202 D4
Burleys Rd RH10 ...... 19 C6
BURLEYS WOOD 19 E7
Burlington Ct BN11 ...... 185 F2
Burlington Gdns
Portslade-by-S BN41 ...... 168 C1
Selsey PO20 ...... 212 F6
Burlington Rd BN21 ...... 185 D4
Burlington St BN2 ...... 192 C4
Burlow
Birdham PO20 ...... 197 D4
Brighton BN2 ...... 192 E5
Burma Cl RH16 ...... 88 C4
Burmill Ct RH16 ...... 205 E7
BURNDELL 181 B3
Burndell Rd BN18 ...... 181 A2
Burners Cl RH15 ...... 109 D1
Burngreave Ct PO21 ...... 201 B3
Burnham Ave PO21 ...... 201 C3
Burnham Cl BN2 ...... 193 F7
Burnham Gdns PO21 ...... 201 C3
Burnham Pl **1** BN1 ...... 36 D1
Burnham Rd BN13 ...... 185 E7
Burns Cl RH12 ...... 36 E7
Burnside Cres BN15 ...... 187 C5
Burns Rd RH10 ...... 19 C8
Burns Way
Crawley RH10 ...... 17 C1
East Grinstead RH19 ...... 9 C1
Burnthouse Bostall
BN6 ...... 150 C8
Burnthouse La RH13 ...... 83 C4
Burnt House La RH12 ...... 17 A7
Burnt Oak La RH5 ...... 3 F1
Burrell Ave BN15 ...... 187 D5
Burrell Bldgs BN15 ...... 187 D5
Burrell Cl RH13 ...... 105 A3
Burrell Cotts RH17 ...... 86 E8
Burrell Rd BN17 ...... 17 F4
Burrell Gn RH17 ...... 86 F8
Burrell Rd RH10 ...... 87 D6
Burrells The BN43 ...... 189 B6
Burry Cotts BN15 ...... 187 C5
Bursledon Cl PO22 ...... 202 A5
Burstead Cl BN1 ...... 170 B3
Burston Gdns RH11 ...... 9 D4
Burstow Ct RH6 ...... 1 F1
Burstow Ho RH6 ...... 2 B6
Burton Cl RH6 ...... 2 A2
Burton Ho GU28 ...... 117 D7
Burton Park Rd GU28 ...... 117 D7
Burton Villas BN3 ...... 191 D8
Burton St RH17 ...... 36 C2
Burwash Cl BN1 ...... 170 C1
Burwash La BN1 ...... 170 C1
Burwash Rd
Crawley RH10 ...... 19 A5
Hove BN3 ...... 168 F3
Bury CE Fst Sch RH20 ...... 139 F7
Bury Dr BN12 ...... 185 B3
Bury Hill BN18, RH20 ...... 139 F6
Bury Ho
Bury RH20 ...... 140 A7
3 Worthing BN14 ...... 186 D5
BURY HOLLOW 140 A8
Bury Rd RH20 ...... 118 F3
Bushby Ave BN16 ...... 205 D5
Bushby Cl BN15 ...... 187 C5
Bushby Terr **1** BN17 ...... 204 E4
Bush Cl RH11 ...... 18 B3
Bush Cottage Cl
BN41 ...... 168 C2
Bush Farm Dr BN41 ...... 168 C3
Bushfield RH14 ...... 30 F2
Bush Terr BN41 ...... 168 B3
Busticle La BN15 ...... 187 B6
Butcher Cl BN16 ...... 184 A5
Butchers La PO18 ...... 136 C6
Bute St BN2 ...... 192 D5
Butler Ct BN13 ...... 185 F4
Butler's Green Ho
RH16 ...... 87 B5
Butler's Green Rd
RH16 ...... 87 C4
Butlers Rd RH13 ...... 37 B4
Butlins Holiday Ctr*
PO21 ...... 201 E3

Butser Wlk GU31 ...... 68 D4
Butterbox La RH17 ...... 89 D4
Buttercup Way RH13 ...... 58 A2
Buttercup Wlk BN1 ...... 170 B7
Butterfield RH19 ...... 9 B3
Buttermer Cl RH12 ...... 37 B6
Buttermere Way
BN17 ...... 205 A7
Butt La BN18 ...... 158 C6
Button Ct BN2 ...... 213 C4
Butts Cl RH11 ...... 18 B7
Butts Mdw RH14 ...... 54 B1
Butted Rise BN1 ...... 170 B5
Buxton Rd BN1 ...... 191 E7
Bycroft Way RH10 ...... 19 B8
Byerley Cl RH10 ...... 151 D5
Byerley Way RH10 ...... 19 E7
Byeway The
Bognor Regis PO21 ...... 211 C8
West Wittering PO20 ...... 196 C1
Byfield Pl PO22 ...... 201 D6
Byfleets La RH12 ...... 35 D6
Bylands **3** BN2 ...... 192 F5
Bylanes Cl RH17 ...... 86 F7
Bylanes Cres RH17 ...... 86 F8
Byne Cl RH20 ...... 121 E1
Byrd Rd RH11 ...... 17 F3
Byre Cotts BN3 ...... 193 D4
Byron Cl
Bognor Regis PO22 ...... 202 D6
Crawley RH10 ...... 19 B7
Horsham RH12 ...... 36 E6
Byron Ct
1 Haywards Heath
RH16 ...... 87 D5
Stockbridge PO19 ...... 176 F4
Byron Gr **2** RH19 ...... 9 C1
Byron Rd
Littlehampton BN16 ...... 205 A5
Worthing BN11 ...... 186 C1
Byron St BN3 ...... 191 A7
Byron Terr **1** BN3 ...... 191 A7
By Sunte RH16 ...... 87 F8
Bywater Way PO19 ...... 176 F4
Bywaves PO20 ...... 208 C4
Byways PO20 ...... 212 E5
Byway The
Brighton BN1 ...... 170 E5
Middleton-on-S PO22 ...... 202 E5
BYWORTH 98 B6
Byworth Cl BN2 ...... 192 F6

C

Caburn Ct RH11 ...... 18 C4
Caburn Hts RH11 ...... 18 C4
Caburn Rd BN3 ...... 191 E7
Cackstones The RH10 ...... 19 D7
Cadogan Ct
3 Brighton BN2 ...... 191 E7
Worthing BN11 ...... 186 D2
Caedwalla Dr PO20 ...... 156 C1
Caernarvon Rd PO19 ...... 177 D6
Caffins Cl RH10 ...... 18 E8
Caffyns Rise RH14 ...... 55 D1
Cagefoot La BN5 ...... 125 E4
Caister's Cl BN3 ...... 191 C8
Caius Ct **16** BN43 ...... 189 C8
Cakeham Rd PO20 ...... 207 B8
Cakeham Way PO20 ...... 207 E7
Calbourne RH16 ...... 87 D5
Calceto La BN17 ...... 182 E8
Caldbeck Ho **7** RH11 ...... 17 F3
Calderdale Cl RH11 ...... 18 B4
Caledon Ave PO22 ...... 202 D5
Caledonian Ct **5**
BN2 ...... 213 C5
Caledonian Ho **4**
RH10 ...... 18 D8
Caledonian Pl **1**
BN11 ...... 186 D1
Caledonian Rd
Brighton BN2 ...... 213 C5
Chichester PO19 ...... 177 B6
Caledonian Way RH6 ...... 6 B7
Callender Wlk RH17 ...... 86 F8
Callisto Cl RH11 ...... 17 E3
Callon Cl BN13 ...... 185 A7
Calluna Dr RH11 ...... 18 C4
Calvecroft GU30 ...... 25 C4
Calvin Wlk RH11 ...... 17 E3
Camargue Ct **4** BN11 ...... 186 A3
Camber Cl
Brighton BN2 ...... 192 F5
Crawley RH10 ...... 19 C6
Cambrai Ave PO19 ...... 177 B5
Cambria Cl PO18 ...... 175 C5
Cambridge Ave PO20 ...... 207 E8
Cambridge Dr PO21 ...... 200 F4
Cambridge Gr BN3 ...... 191 C7
Cambridge Mews
BN3 ...... 191 C7
Cambridge Rd
Horsham RH13 ...... 36 D2
Hove BN3 ...... 191 D6
Worthing BN11 ...... 186 D3
Cambridge Wlk PO21 ...... 200 F4
Camden St BN1 ...... 190 C6
Camden Terr BN1 ...... 213 A3
Camelford St BN2 ...... 213 C1
Camelia Cl BN17 ...... 205 A7
Camelot Cl RH13 ...... 58 A1
Camelot Ct RH11 ...... 17 E6
CAMELSDALE 26 F4

Camelsdale Fst Sch
GU27 ...... 26 F5
Camelsdale Rd GU27 ...... 26 F5
Camino Pk RH10 ...... 6 A4
Campbell Cres RH19 ...... 9 B1
Campbell Ct BN12 ...... 185 A4
Campbell Dr BN16 ...... 205 B6
Campbell Rd
Bognor Regis PO21 ...... 201 D3
Brighton BN1 ...... 213 A5
Crawley RH10 ...... 19 C5
Tangmere PO20 ...... 156 B1
Campion Cl BN16 ...... 205 B8
Campion Rd RH12 ...... 36 E5
Canada Cnr GU31 ...... 91 B6
Canada Cotts GU29 ...... 73 A3
Canada Gr
Bognor Regis PO21 ...... 201 C6
Midhurst GU29 ...... 73 A2
Canada Rd BN18 ...... 159 F3
Canada Way GU30 ...... 25 C3
Canadian Cres PO20 ...... 212 E5
Canal Pl PO19 ...... 176 F5
Canal Pl BN18 ...... 180 F3
Canal Wharf PO19 ...... 176 F5
Canberra Cl RH11 ...... 5 C1
Canberra Ct PO21 ...... 201 A2
Canberra Pl
Horsham RH12 ...... 36 F4
Tangmere PO20 ...... 156 D2
Canberra Rd
Thorney Island PO10 ...... 173 C3
Worthing BN13 ...... 185 C7
Candleford Gate GU30 ...... 25 B4
Canfield Cl BN2 ...... 170 D1
Canfield Rd BN2 ...... 170 D1
Canhouse La GU31,
GU33 ...... 46 C3
Canning Ct PO22 ...... 201 F3
Canning Rd PO22 ...... 201 F3
Canning St BN2 ...... 192 D5
Cannon Pl BN1 ...... 213 A2
Canonbury Cotts RH12 ...... 16 F6
Canon La PO19 ...... 176 F6
Canon's Cl PO21 ...... 200 D1
Canons Way BN44 ...... 145 E4
Cansiron La RH19 ...... 23 F6
Cantelupe Ho **1** RH19 ...... 9 F1
Cantelupe Mews **7**
RH19 ...... 9 E1
Cantelupe Rd RH19 ...... 9 F1
Canterbury Cl
Bognor Regis PO21 ...... 200 A1
Chichester PO19 ...... 176 F8
Canterbury Ct
Southwater RH13 ...... 58 A2
Worthing BN13 ...... 185 F4
Canterbury Dr **5**
BN2 ...... 213 C4
Canterbury Ho BN14 ...... 186 A6
Canterbury Rd
Crawley RH10 ...... 18 E2
Rustington BN16 ...... 205 E6
Worthing BN13 ...... 186 A3
Canter The RH10 ...... 19 E7
Canton **3** RH16 ...... 87 D6
Cants Cl RH15 ...... 109 C3
Cants La RH15 ...... 109 C3
Canute Cl PO20 ...... 208 C5
Canute Rd PO18 ...... 175 B5
Canvas Ct GU27 ...... 27 B6
Canvey Cl RH11 ...... 18 C3
Cape Copse RH12 ...... 33 D7
Capella Ho RH11 ...... 186 A1
Capel La RH11 ...... 17 F5
Capel Rd RH12 ...... 16 A8
Capenors RH15 ...... 108 F1
Cape The
Littlehampton BN17 ...... 205 A5
Rottingdean BN2 ...... 193 F1
Capricorn Cl RH17 ...... 17 E4
Capsey Rd RH11 ...... 17 E5
Capstan Dr BN17 ...... 205 A7
Capua Ct RH10 ...... 6 C2
Caraway Cl RH11 ...... 18 B2
Carden Ave
Brighton BN1 ...... 169 F5
Brighton BN1 ...... 170 B6
Carden Cl BN1 ...... 170 A6
Carden Cres BN1 ...... 170 A6
Carden Hill BN1 ...... 170 A6
Carden Prim Sch BN1 ...... 170 B6
Cardew Rd GU33 ...... 45 C3
Card Hill RH18 ...... 23 F1
Cardinal Cl **1** BN43 ...... 189 C8
Cardinal Newman RC Sch
RH6 ...... 1 C5
Cardinal's Dr PO21 ...... 200 B1
Carey Ho RH11 ...... 18 C6
Carfax RH12 ...... 36 C2
Cargo Forecourt Rd
RH6 ...... 5 D7
Cargo Rd RH6 ...... 5 D7
Carina Dr BN16 ...... 205 F8
Carisbrooke Cl RH11 ...... 187 E8
Carisbrooke Dr BN13 ...... 185 B6
Carisbrooke Rd BN12 ...... 192 E3
Carleton Rd PO19 ...... 176 E8
Carlingford Ct **1**
PO21 ...... 201 C4
Carlisle Gdns PO19 ...... 154 F1
Carlisle Rd BN3 ...... 190 F6
Carlton Ave PO21 ...... 200 C3
Carlton Cl RH10 ...... 18 E5

Carlton Ct
　Horley RH6 .... 2 A5
　Portslade-by-S BN41 ... 190 C8
Carlton Hill BN2 .... 213 C2
Carlton Hill Prim Sch
　BN2 .... 213 C2
Carlton Ho
　6 Brighton BN1 .... 169 E2
　Worthing BN13 .... 186 A6
Carlton Mews BN11 ..... 186 A2
Carlton Pl 5 BN2 .... 213 C2
Carlton Terr BN3,
　BN41 .... 190 C8
Carlton Tye RH6 .... 2 C3
Carlyle Ave BN2 .... 170 D1
Carlyle Ho 2 BN14 ..... 186 D3
Carlyle St BN2 .... 192 C7
Carman Wlk RH11 .... 18 B1
Carmel Ho
　Hove BN3 .... 191 A7
　Worthing BN11 .... 186 D3
Carmelstead Cl RH16 .... 88 A3
Carnation Cl BN17 ...... 205 B7
Carn Ct 7 BN2 .... 192 C6
Carnegie Cl BN14 .... 186 C5
Carnegie Gdns BN14 ... 186 D5
Carnegie Ho BN13 ...... 185 F7
Carnegie Rd BN14 ...... 186 C5
Carnforth Rd BN15 ..... 187 C5
Carnoustie Ct 18 RH16 .. 87 E4
Carol Cl BN1 .... 169 F6
Caroline Ct RH11 .... 18 D4
Carolyn Ho BN13 .... 185 E6
Caron Cl BN15 .... 187 E5
Carousel Ct PO21,
　PO22 .... 201 B5
Carpenters RH14 .... 79 D8
Carpenters Mdw
　RH20 .... 100 C2
Carrick Wlk 2 BN43 .... 188 E7
Carron La GU29 .... 94 E7
Carse Rd PO19 .... 155 C1
Carter Rd RH10 .... 19 D3
Cartersland Cnr GU30 ... 47 B3
Carterslodge La RH17 ... 60 E7
Cartersmead Cl RH11 .... 2 B4
Carters Way RH14 .... 78 B8
Carvel Way BN17 .... 205 A6
Caryll's Cotts RH12 ..... 16 F1
Carylls Mdw RH13 ...... 104 D7
Casher Rd RH10 .... 19 C3
Cashman Lo BN1 .... 170 A5
Caspian Cl PO19 .... 176 B8
Caspian Ct BN1 .... 213 A4
Caspian Ho 4 BN16 .... 205 A4
Caspian Sq BN2 .... 193 F1
Cassells Rd 2 PO19 .... 155 A2
Cassidy Pl RH20 .... 121 B1
Castle Cl
　Bramber BN44 .... 145 E2
　Worthing BN13 .... 185 F5
Castle Ct BN13 .... 185 F5
Castle Dr RH6 .... 2 C2
Castlegate RH20 .... 121 B7
Castle Gdns
　Arundel BN18 .... 160 A3
　Petersfield GU32 ...... 68 A3
Castle Goring Mews
　BN13 .... 185 A9
Castle La
　Bramber BN44 .... 145 E2
　West Grinstead RH13 ... 103 F7
Castle Mews
　Arundel BN18 .... 160 B3
　27 Brighton BN1 .... 191 E5
Castle Of Mey Ho
　GU27 .... 26 F6
Castle Rd
　Broadbridge Heath
　　RH12 .... 35 D3
　Red Hill PO9 .... 130 D1
　Worthing BN13 .... 185 F5
Castlereagh Gn PO22 ... 202 A5
Castle Sq BN1 .... 213 B2
Castle St BN1 .... 191 E5
Castle The RH12 .... 36 E7
CASTLE TOWN 146 C1
Castle Way
　Bramber BN44 .... 145 E3
　Worthing BN13 .... 185 F5
Castlewood Prim Sch
　RH13 .... 58 A2
Castlewood Rd RH13 .... 58 A2
Caterways RH12 .... 36 A3
Cathedral Ctyd PO19 ... 176 F6
Cathedral Way PO19 ... 176 D6
Catherine Vale BN2 .... 193 E8
Catherine Villas GU27 .. 27 B6
Catkin Way RH10 .... 88 B4
Catslands La BN5 ...... 147 C8
Cattswood La RH16 ..... 87 C2
Caudle St BN5 .... 125 F4
CAUSEWAY 68 A1
Causeway RH12 .... 36 C1
Causeway The BN18 .... 160 C2
Causewayside GU27 .... 27 D6
Causeway The
　Arundel BN18 .... 160 C2
　Birdham PO20 .... 197 F6
　Bognor Regis PO21 .... 211 A8
　Brighton BN2 .... 192 D6
　Partridge Green RH13 .. 105 A3
　Petersfield GU31 ...... 68 A1
　Selsey PO20 .... 212 C8
　Worthing BN12 .... 185 E4

Causeway Villas
　BN18 .... 160 C2
Cavalier Cl GU29 .... 94 E7
Cavalier Way RH19 ...... 22 F7
Cavell Way RH10 .... 19 C5
Cavendish Cl
　Horsham RH12 .... 36 D7
　Worthing BN13 .... 185 D4
Cavendish Ct 22 BN2 ... 192 D4
Cavendish Ho
　Bognor Regis PO21 .... 201 D2
　8 Brighton BN1 .... 191 E5
　Haywards Heath RH16 ... 87 F2
Cavendish Mews 12
　BN1 .... 191 D5
Cavendish Pl BN1 ...... 191 E5
Cavendish Rd PO21 .... 201 C3
Cavendish St
　11 Brighton BN2 ...... 213 C2
　Chichester PO19 ...... 176 F7
Caversham Ct 6
　BN11 .... 186 B1
Cawley Ho PO19 .... 177 A5
Cawley Rd PO19 .... 177 A5
Caxton Cl RH10 .... 18 E3
Caxton Ct 4 BN14 ..... 186 D4
Caxton Way 15 RH16 .... 87 E4
Cecil Ct 7 BN15 .... 187 E4
Cecilian Ave BN14 ..... 186 D4
Cecil Norris Ho 3
　BN43 .... 188 F7
Cecil Pashley Way
　BN43 .... 188 D8
Cedar Ave BN13 .... 185 F7
Cedar Cl
　Angmering BN16 .... 206 A8
　Bognor Regis PO21 .... 200 D3
　Burgess Hill RH15 .... 109 B5
　Crawley RH11 .... 5 C1
　Ferring BN12 .... 206 E5
　Horsham RH12 .... 36 D5
　Lancing BN15 .... 187 D4
　Worthing BN13 .... 185 F7
Cedar Cl E PO21 .... 200 E3
Cedar Ct
　Haslemere GU27 .... 27 A6
　Petworth GU28 .... 97 E7
　Worthing BN11 .... 186 A3
Cedar Ctr The BN1 ..... 170 C2
Cedar Dr
　Chichester PO19 ...... 176 E7
　Southwater RH13 ..... 58 A1
Cedar Lo RH11 .... 18 D4
Cedars Farm Cl BN14 ... 79 C8
Cedars Gdns BN1 ...... 169 E3
Cedars The
　Barnham PO22 .... 180 B6
　1 Brighton BN2 ...... 213 C5
　Brighton, Withdean
　　BN1 .... 169 E3
　Haywards Heath RH16 .. 87 D7
　Rustington BN16 ..... 205 E6
Cedar Way
　Haywards Heath RH16 .. 88 B4
　Henfield BN5 .... 125 F4
Cedarwood 8 BN1 ...... 169 E3
Cedric Ct 2 RH12 ..... 36 A1
Celandine Cl 1 RH11 ... 18 B2
Cello Ct 8 BN2 .... 192 C5
Cemetery La
　Tillington GU28 ...... 75 C1
　Westbourne PO10 ..... 151 F3
Centenary Ho 4 BN1 ... 169 E2
Centenary Ind Est 6
　BN2 .... 192 B8
Central Ave
　Bognor Regis PO21 .... 201 A6
　Littlehampton BN16 ... 205 C4
　Worthing BN14 .... 163 F3
Central Bldgs 2
　PO21 .... 201 D3
Central CE Jun Sch
　PO19 .... 176 F7
Central Dr
　Bognor Regis PO21 .... 201 A6
　Middleton-on-S PO22 .. 203 A5
Central Sussex Coll
　RH12 .... 36 D3
Central Sussex Coll
　(Haywards Heath
　Campus) RH16 .... 87 D6
Centrecourt Cl 8
　BN14 .... 186 C4
Centrecourt Rd BN14 ... 186 C4
Centurion Rd BN1 ...... 213 A3
Ceres Pl PO22 .... 202 D4
Chadborn Cl BN2 ...... 192 D5
Chadwick Cl RH11 ...... 18 B1
Chaffer La PO22 .... 197 D4
Chaffinch Cl
　Burgess Hill RH15 .... 108 D4
　Crawley RH11 .... 18 D8
　Horsham RH12 .... 36 D7
　Worthing BN13 ...... 185 C6
Chaffinch Way RH6 ..... 1 E4
Chailey Ave BN2 .... 194 A1
Chailey Cl 2 RH11 ..... 18 A3
Chailey Cres BN2 ...... 194 E1
Chailey Ct
　Brighton BN1 .... 169 C5
　2 Haywards Heath
　　RH16 .... 87 F3
Chailey Rd BN1 .... 170 E4
Chainbridge La PO20 ... 209 C1
Chain Pier Ho BN2 ..... 213 C1
Chaicraft La PO21 ..... 200 F5
Chalcraft Cl GU30 ..... 25 A4

Chalder La PO20 .... 198 F3
Chaldon Rd RH11 .... 18 C1
Chaleford Ct 5 BN14 ... 186 D4
Chalet Cl BN12 .... 206 E4
Chalet Gdns BN12 ...... 206 F4
Chalet Rd BN12 .... 206 E4
Chalex Ind Est BN42 ... 190 A7
Chalfont Cl PO22 ...... 202 E5
Chalfont Ct BN11 ...... 186 B2
Chalfont Dr BN3 .... 169 C3
Chalfont Way BN13 ..... 185 D7
Chalkdock La PO20 ..... 197 A5
Chalkers La BN6 .... 128 B8
Chalk La PO20 .... 209 E7
Chalkland Rise BN2 .... 193 E8
Chalkpit La PO18 ...... 155 B7
Chalk Rd
　Goodwood Park PO18 ... 136 A4
　Ifold RH14 .... 31 C3
Chalky Rd BN41 .... 168 A3
Challen Cl PO20 ...... 178 C6
Challen Ct RH12 ...... 36 B3
Challoners RH17 ...... 65 C4
Challoners Cl BN2 .... 194 A2
Challoners Mews
　BN2 .... 193 F2
Challow Cl BN6 .... 128 E4
Chalmers Cl RH6 ...... 4 E6
Chaloner Cl RH16 .... 88 B7
Chaloner Rd RH16 .... 88 B7
Chalvington Cl BN1 ... 170 E6
Champion's Gate RH13 .. 83 A2
Champions Row BN3 ... 191 C8
Chancellors Pk BN6 ... 128 F4
Chanctonbury RH20 .... 123 A4
Chanctonbury Cl
　Rustington BN16 ...... 205 B4
　Washington RH20 ..... 143 E6
Chanctonbury Dr
　BN43 .... 166 F1
Chanctonbury Rd
　Burgess Hill RH15 .... 109 A1
　Hove BN3 .... 191 E7
　Rustington BN16 ..... 205 B4
Chanctonbury Ring Rd
　BN44 .... 144 D6
Chanctonbury View
　BN5 .... 125 D4
Chanctonbury Way
　RH20 .... 18 C4
Chanctonbury Wlk 8
　RH20 .... 121 D1
Chancton Cl BN11 ..... 185 F4
Chancton Copse
　BN20 .... 122 B3
Chanctonfold BN44 .... 145 C6
Chancton View Rd
　BN11 .... 185 F4
Chandler Cl RH10 ...... 18 D4
Chandler Ct 4 BN2 .... 2 B3
Chandler Rd PO19 ..... 176 E5
Chandlers Lea PO20 ... 208 C5
Chandlers Reach
　PO20 .... 197 A7
Chandlers Way BN44 ... 145 C7
Chandos Rd BN11 ...... 186 A6
Channel Ct 6 BN15 .... 187 E4
Channel Keep 1
　BN17 .... 204 D4
Channel View
　Bognor Regis PO21 .... 211 A8
　13 Southwick BN42 ... 189 F7
Channel View Rd BN2 ... 193 B8
Chantlers Cl RH19 ..... 9 C2
Chantrelles The BN16 .. 184 A5
Chantrey Rd RH10 ..... 18 E3
Chantry Cl
　Henfield BN5 .... 125 E6
　Horley RH6 .... 1 F4
　2 Storrington BN20 .. 121 E1
Chantry Est The RH20 .. 142 E8
Chantryfield Rd BN16 .. 183 F6
Chantry La RH20 ...... 142 E6
Chantry Orch 10
　BN44 .... 145 D3
Chantry Rd BN13 ...... 186 A6
Chantry The PO19 ..... 176 F6
Chapel Cl
　Burgess Hill RH15 .... 108 F4
　Littlehampton BN17 ... 204 C6
　Watersfield RH20 .... 119 A4
Chapelfields RH17 ...... 86 F8
Chapel Ho BN2 .... 213 C2
Chapel La
　Ashurst Wood RH19 ... 23 D6
　Cootham RH20 .... 121 A1
　Copthorne RH10 ..... 7 F4
　East Ashling PO18 ... 154 A3
　Forest Row RH18 .... 23 F2
　Horsted Keynes RH17 . 65 C5
　West Wittering PO20 . 196 F2
Chapel Mews 8 BN1 .. 191 D5
Chapel Pl BN41 ...... 190 B7
Chapel Rd
　Barns Green RH13 .... 56 F2
　Charlwood RH6 ...... 4 F7
　Portslade-by-S BN41 . 190 A7
　Worthing BN11 ...... 186 D3
Chapel Row
　East Dean PO18 ...... 136 C6
　West Hoathly RH19 .. 42 E7
Chapel St
　Bognor Regis PO21 ... 201 C2
　Brighton BN2 .... 213 C2
　Chichester PO19 .... 176 F6
　Petersfield GU32 ... 68 B3
Chapel Terr 3 BN2 .. 192 D4

Chapel Terrace Mews 21
　BN2 .... 192 D4
Chapel Wlk BN6 ...... 183 F5
Chapman Ct BN13 .... 185 F7
Chapman Rd RH10 .... 19 C2
Chapman's La
　East Grinstead RH19 .. 9 B1
　East Grinstead RH19 .. 9 D1
Chappell Cl GU30 .... 25 C4
Chappell Croft 2
　BN11 .... 186 B2
Charis Ct 18 BN3 .... 191 C7
Charlecote Rd BN11 ... 186 E2
Charles Ave
　Burgess Hill RH15 .... 108 D2
　Chichester BN17 .... 177 D6
Charles Bennett Ct
　RH16 .... 88 A4
Charles Cl BN3 ...... 169 A3
Charles Ct 6 BN11 ... 186 C3
Charlesfield Rd RH6 .. 1 F4
Charles Ho
　Selsey PO20 .... 212 C8
　Worthing BN12 ...... 185 D3
Charles Kingston Gdns
　BN1 .... 169 E4
Charles St
　Brighton BN2 .... 213 B1
　Petersfield GU32 .... 68 A3
Charleston St RH10 ... 19 B3
Charlesworth Pk RH16 .. 88 C4
Charlmead PO20 ...... 207 F6
Charlock Cl 8 RH11 ... 18 A2
Charlock Way RH13 ... 58 A3
Charlotte Ct RH11 .... 18 C6
Charlotte Ho
　Bognor Regis PO22 ... 201 E4
　7 Rustington BN16 .. 205 E6
Charlotte St BN2 ..... 213 C1
Charlton Dr GU31 .... 68 C5
Charlton Gdns BN6 ... 129 D3
Charlton Mews BN44 .. 145 D3
Charlton Mill Way
　PO18 .... 135 F6
Charlton Rd PO18 .... 136 B6
Charlton St BN44 .... 145 C3
Charltons The BN1 ... 170 D6
Charlwood Cl RH10 .. 7 B4
Charlwood Ct RH11 .. 5 A2
Charlwood Gdns
　RH15 .... 109 C5
Charlwood La RH5 ... 4 A3
Charlwood Lo 3
　BN11 .... 186 A2
Charlwood Pl RH6 .... 4 E8
Charlwood Rd
　Burgess Hill RH15 ... 109 D6
　Crawley RH6, RH11 .. 5 C8
　Hookwood RH6, RH11 . 4 E2
Charlwoods Bsns Ctr
　RH19 .... 9 D2
Charlwoods Pl RH19 .. 9 E3
Charlwoods Rd RH19 .. 9 E3
Charlwood St PO21 .. 201 B2
Charlwood Wlk RH11 .. 5 A2
Charmandean La
　BN14 .... 186 D6
Charmandean Rd
　BN14 .... 186 D6
Charmans Cl RH12 .... 37 B5
Charm Cl RH6 .... 1 E4
Charnwood Rd PO22 .. 201 B6
Charrington Way RH12 .. 35 C3
Charter Gate RH16 ... 87 D5
Chartergrove Ho 14
　GU31 .... 68 B3
Charterhouse Mews
　PO20 .... 207 F8
Charter Wlk GU27 ... 27 C6
Chartfield BN3 ...... 169 A2
Chartfield Way BN3 .. 169 B2
Chartwell Bldg PO10 . 151 F1
Chartwell Ct BN1 .... 213 A2
Chartwell Mews GU27 .. 27 C6
Chartwell Rd BN15 ... 187 D5
Chase Cl GU33 ...... 45 C4
Chase La GU27 ...... 27 E3
Chase Rd GU33 ..... 45 C4
Chase The
　Crawley RH10 .... 19 A5
　Fontwell BN18 ...... 158 A3
　Negcote BN14 ...... 163 E5
Chatelet Cl RH6 ..... 2 B8
Chates Farm Ct BN2 . 213 C3
Chatfield Rd RH17 ... 87 A6
Chatfields RH11 ..... 18 B4
Chatham Pl BN1 ..... 213 A4
Chatham Rd BN11 .... 187 A3
Chatsmore Cres BN12 . 185 B4
Chatsmore Ho BN12 . 185 A3
Chatsmore RC High Sch
　BN12 .... 185 A4
Chatsworth Ave GU27 . 27 C8
Chatsworth Cl 3
　BN16 .... 205 B7
Chatsworth Ct
　Brighton BN1 .... 191 E8
　5 Shoreham-by-S
　　BN43 .... 188 F6
Chatsworth Rd
　Brighton BN1 .... 191 E8
　Chichester PO19 ... 177 D6
　Worthing BN11 ..... 186 D2
Chatsworth Row RH11 .. 18 C4

Chatsworth Sq BN3 ... 191 D7
Chaucer Ave
　3 East Grinstead RH19 .. 9 C1
　Rustington BN16 .... 205 B5
Chaucer Ct 2 RH16 .. 87 D5
Chaucer Dr PO20 .... 207 F8
Chaucer Rd
　Crawley RH10 .... 19 C8
　Worthing BN11 ..... 186 B3
Chaucer Way PO22 .. 202 D6
Chawkware Coppice
　PO21 .... 200 F2
Chayle Gdns PO20 ... 212 C6
Cheal Cl BN43 ...... 188 F6
Cheam Rd BN16 ..... 205 D4
Cheapside BN1 ...... 213 B3
Cheeleys RH17 ...... 65 C5
Cheesemans La PO18 . 152 E4
Chelmer Ho 3 BN15 .. 187 E4
Chelston Ave BN3 ... 190 D7
Cheltenham Pl BN1 .. 213 B3
Chelwood Ave BN12 . 185 C1
Chelwood Cl
　Brighton BN1 .... 170 C6
　Crawley RH10 ...... 18 F4
Chelwood Ct RH15 .. 109 A4
Chelwood Gate Rd RH17,
　TN22 .... 66 F7
Chene Collins Chase 11
　RH12 .... 36 F7
Chennells Way RH12 .. 36 E5
Chepstow Cl RH10 ... 19 E6
Chepstow St BN1 .... 170 F5
Chequer Grange RH18 . 23 E1
Chequer La PO18 .... 175 D6
Chequer Rd RH19 ... 9 F1
Chequers Ct
　Horsham RH13 ...... 36 E2
　Petworth GU28 ..... 97 F7
Chequers Dr RH6 ... 2 A4
Chequers Quay PO10 . 173 C8
Cherington Cl BN6 ... 128 B5
Chermont Ct BN16 .. 205 F6
Cherrimans Orch RH12 .. 26 F6
Cherry Ave BN18 ... 181 A2
Cherry Cl
　Bognor Regis PO21 .. 200 E2
　Burgess Hill RH15 .. 108 E3
Cherry Croft BN17 .. 204 D3
Cherry Ct 3 RH13 .. 36 D1
Cherry Gdns
　Selsey PO20 .... 212 D5
　Worthing BN13 .... 163 D1
Cherry La
　Birdham PO20 ...... 197 F5
　Bolney RH17 .... 85 C3
　Brook Street RH17 . 62 F5
　Crawley RH11 ...... 5 C1
Cherrylands Cl GU27 .. 49 B6
Cherry Lo RH6 ..... 2 B2
Cherry Mdws RH11 .. 18 C5
Cherry Orchard Rd
　PO19 .... 177 B5
Cherry Pl 10 RH16 .. 87 C2
Cherry Tree Ave GU27 .. 26 F7
Cherry Tree Cl
　Billingshurst RH14 .. 55 C1
　Crawley RH10 ...... 19 D8
　Worthing BN13 .... 163 D1
Cherrytree Cotts
　PO22 .... 180 C5
Cherry Tree Dr PO20 .. 179 F8
Cherry Tree Lo 1
　BN15 .... 187 D6
Cherry Trees RH17 .. 86 E8
Cherry Tree Wlk
　Horsham RH12 ..... 37 B6
　Petworth GU28 .... 97 E7
Cherry Wlk BN13 ... 163 E1
Cherrywood 2 BN1 .. 169 E3
Cherrywood Ct PO21 . 200 F2
Cherwell Rd BN13 ... 185 C9
Cherwell Ct BN1 .... 17 F5
Chesham Cl RH12 .. 185 E3
Chesham Pl BN2 .... 192 D4
Chesham Rd BN2 ... 192 D4
Chesham St BN2 ... 192 D4
Cheshire Cl 1 PO21 . 201 D4
Cheshire Cres PO20 . 156 C1
Chesholt Cl GU27 .. 49 B6
Chesley Cl BN13 ... 185 C7
Chess Brook Gn BN5 . 125 F7
Chesswood Ave PO22 . 202 C6
Chesswood Cl BN11 . 186 F4
Chesswood Jun Sch
　BN11 .... 186 F4
Chesswood Lea BN11 . 186 F4
Chesswood Mid Sch
　BN11 .... 186 E4
Chesswood Rd BN11 . 186 F4
Chester Ave
　Lancing BN15 ...... 187 E4
　Worthing BN11 .... 187 A3
Chester Ct 12 BN3 . 191 E7
Chesterfield Cl RH19 . 8 C4
Chesterfield Rd BN12 . 185 D4
Chester Lo 2 BN11 . 186 A2
Chesters RH6 ...... 1 E5
Chester Terr BN1 .. 170 A1
Chesterton Cl RH19 . 22 F7
Chesterton Ct RH13 . 37 A4
Chestnut Ave
　Chichester PO19 ... 154 F3
　Haslemere GU27 ... 27 C7

Chestnut Cl
Angmering BN16 . . . . 205 F8
Burgess Hill RH15 . . . . . . 109 B5
East Grinstead RH19 . . . . . 10 A1
Heath Common RH20 . . . 122 B3
Liphook GU30 . . . . 25 D3
Midhurst GU29 . . . . 94 E5

Chestnut Ct
Angmering BN16 . . . . 206 A8
East Preston BN16 . . . . . . 206 A5
Horsham RH13 . . . . 36 E2
■9 Worthing BN11 . . . . . 186 C3
Chestnut Dr GU31 . . . . . . 68 B1
Chestnut End BN5 . . . . . 125 E5
Chestnut Gdns RH12 . . . . 36 C5

Chestnut Gr
Bognor Regis PO22 . . . . . 201 C6
Hurstpierpoint BN6 . . . . . 127 F7

Chestnut Rd
Billingshurst RH14 . . . . . . 79 D7
Horley RH6 . . . . 2 B5
Chestnut Ridge RH20 . . . 121 C7
Chestnuts Cl RH16 . . . . . 88 A7

Chestnuts The
Haywards Heath RH16 . . . 87 F7
Horley RH6 . . . . 2 A3
Hunston PO20 . . . . 199 A8
Sayers Common BN6 . . . 107 D1
Chestnut Way BN5 . . . . . 125 E5

Chestnut Wlk
Crawley RH11 . . . . 5 C1
Felcourt RH19 . . . . 9 C8
Pulborough RH20 . . . . . . 100 B2
Tangmere PO20 . . . . 156 C1
Worthing BN13 . . . . 185 C6

Chesworth Cl
■7 Horsham RH13 . . . . . . 36 C1
Tower Hill RH13 . . . . 58 C8
Chesworth Cres RH13 . . . 36 C1
Chesworth Gdns RH13 . . . 36 C1

Chesworth La RH12,
RH13 . . . . 36 C1
Chetwood Rd RH11 . . . . . 17 D2
Cheveley Gdns PO21 . . . 200 E2
Chevening Cl RH11 . . . . . 18 C1

Cheviot Cl
East Preston BN16 . . . . . 206 A6
Worthing BN13 . . . . 185 E9
Cheviot Ct ■3 RH12 . . . . 36 F4
Cheviot Rd BN13 . . . . . . 185 E9
Cheviot Wlk RH11 . . . . . . 18 B6
Cheyne Ct BN43 . . . . . . 189 C7
Cheynell Wlk RH11 . . . . . 17 F4
Cheyne Wlk RH6 . . . . 2 A1

Chichester Bsns Pk
PO20 . . . . 156 E2

Chichester By-Pass
Chichester PO20 . . . . . . 177 D5
Stockbridge PO19 . . . . . 176 F4
Chichester Cath PO19 . . 176 F6

Chichester Cl
■18 Brighton BN2 . . . . . 192 D4
Crawley RH10 . . . . 18 E2
Hove BN3 . . . . 168 E4
Saltdean BN2 . . . . 194 C1
Chichester Coll PO19 . . 176 E6

Chichester Coll Brinsbury
Campus RH20 . . . . 78 F1

Chichester Ct
■11 Rustington BN16 . . 205 C5
■1 Worthing BN11 . . . . 186 A1
Chichester District Mus*
PO19 . . . . 177 A6
Chichester Dr PO20 . . . . 156 D1
Chichester Dr E BN2 . . . 194 C1
Chichester Dr W BN2 . . 194 B1

Chichester Festival
Theatre PO19 . . . . 177 A8
Chichester Food Pk
PO20 . . . . 177 F3
Chichester Gate PO19 . . 176 F5
Chichester High Sch for
Boys PO19 . . . . 177 A5
Chichester High Sch for
Girls PO19 . . . . 177 A4
Chichester Nuffield Hospl
PO19 . . . . 154 F1
Chichester Pl BN2 . . . . . 192 D4
Chichester PRU PO19 . . 177 C1

Chichester Rd
Arundel BN18 . . . . 159 E3
Bognor Regis PO21,
PO22 . . . . 201 B5
Midhurst GU29 . . . . 94 F5
Selsey PO20 . . . . 212 E8
Street End PO20 . . . . . . 198 E5
Chichester Sta PO19 . . . 176 F5

Chichester Terr
■18 Brighton BN2 . . . . . 192 D4
Horsham RH12 . . . . 36 D2

Chichester Way
Burgess Hill RH15 . . . . . 109 C5
Selsey PO20 . . . . 212 G8

Chichester Wharf
PO19 . . . . 176 F5

Chiddingly Cl
Brighton BN2 . . . . 192 F5
Crawley RH10 . . . . 19 B5
Chiddingly Ho ■11
BN3 . . . . 191 D7
Chidham La PO18 . . . . . 174 E6
Chidham Prim Sch
PO18 . . . . 174 E6

CHILGROVE 112 F1
Chilgrove Cl BN12 . . . . . 185 B4
Chilgrove Ho BN17 . . . . . 204 B7
Chilling St RH19 . . . . 43 D3
Chillis Wood Rd RH16 . . . 87 C5
Chilmark Ct GU33 . . . . . . 45 B4

Chiltern Cl
Crawley RH11 . . . . 18 B6
East Preston BN16 . . . . . 206 A6
Haslemere GU27 . . . . 27 B5
Shoreham-by-S BN43 . . . 189 C8
Chiltern Cotts RH6 . . . . . . 1 D2
Chiltern Cres BN13 . . . . 185 E8
Chiltern Ct ■2 RH12 . . . . 36 F4

Chiltington Cl
Burgess Hill RH15 . . . . . 108 F5
Saltdean BN2 . . . . 194 C2
West Chiltington Common
RH20 . . . . 121 C7
Chiltington Ct RH12 . . . . 36 D4
Chiltington Way BN2 . . . 194 C2
Chiltlee Cl GU30 . . . . 25 C4
Chiltlee Manor GU30 . . . 25 C3
Chiltley La GU30 . . . . 25 C3
Chiltley Way GU30 . . . . . . 25 C2
Chilton Cl GU30 . . . . 11 A2
Chiltons The PO21 . . . . . 201 C3
Chine The BN17 . . . . 205 A4
Chipley St PO21 . . . . 201 A4
Chippendale Rd RH11 . . . 18 B1
Chippers Cl BN13 . . . . . . 185 F5
Chippers Rd BN13 . . . . . 185 F5
Chippers Wlk BN13 . . . . 185 F5

Chithurst La GU31,
GU30 . . . . 71 C4
Chodds Cotts RH17 . . . . . 39 C1
Chorley Ave BN2 . . . . . . 194 B2
Chownes Mead La
RH16 . . . . 87 B4
Chrisdory Rd RH41 . . . . . 167 F3

Christchurch Cres
PO21 . . . . 200 E3

Christchurch Ho ■4
BN11 . . . . 186 D3

Christchurch Rd
BN11 . . . . 186 D3
Christie Pl PO22 . . . . . . 201 D6
Christies RH19 . . . . 22 D8
Christopher Ct ■10
PO21 . . . . 201 D5
Christopher Rd RH19 . . . . 9 E1

Christopher Way
PO10 . . . . 151 B2

Christ's Hospital Rd
Horsham RH13 . . . . 57 E6
Itchingfield RH13 . . . . . . 57 C6
Christ's Hospital Sta
RH13 . . . . 57 D5

Church App ■1 BN17 . . . 204 E4
Church Ave RH16 . . . . . . 87 C6

Church Cl
Ashington RH20 . . . . 122 F4
Brighton BN1 . . . . 169 F5
Burgess Hill RH15 . . . . . 109 A3
Clapham BN13 . . . . 162 F1
Lancing BN15 . . . . 187 E8
Lower Beeding RH13 . . . . 60 A3
Pagham PO21 . . . . 210 E7
Shipley RH13 . . . . 103 D8
Upper Beeding BN44 . . . 146 A3
Church Cotts ■2 BN11 . . 186 F2

Church Ct
■3 Haywards Heath
RH16 . . . . 87 E4
Hove BN3 . . . . 168 F1
Churcher Rd PO10 . . . . . 151 D4
Churcher's Coll GU31 . . . 68 C4
Churcher's Coll Jnr Sch
GU30 . . . . 25 D2

Church Farm Cotts
RH13 . . . . 59 F3
Church Farm Cl PO20 . . 208 A8

Church Farm Holiday
Village PO21 . . . . 210 E7

Church Farm La
East Wittering PO20 . . . 208 A8
Street End PO20 . . . . . . 198 F2

Church Farm Wlk
BN44 . . . . 146 A3
Churchfield RH20 . . . . . . 99 A3

Churchfield Cotts
PO20 . . . . 156 B2
Churchfield Ct GU30 . . . . 25 B3
Churchfield Rd GU31 . . . . 68 E4
Church Gn BN43 . . . . . . 189 C7
Church Gr RH20 . . . . 101 D1

Church Hill
Brighton BN1 . . . . 169 E7
Midhurst GU29 . . . . 94 F8
Pulborough RH20 . . . . . . 100 B2
Pyecombe BN45 . . . . . . 149 C6
Slindon BN18 . . . . 158 C5
West Hoathly RH19 . . . . . 42 F6

Church Ho
Littlehampton BN17 . . . . 204 D4
Worthing BN14 . . . . 186 A5

Church House Cl
BN42 . . . . 167 F1

Church House Mews
PO22 . . . . 202 A4

Churchill Ave
Bognor Regis PO20 . . . . 200 E4
Horsham RH12 . . . . 36 B3

Churchill Ct
Crawley RH10 . . . . 6 A1
■5 Rustington BN16 . . . 205 C5

Churchill Dr PO10 . . . . . 151 B4
Churchill Ho
Barnham PO22 . . . . 180 C5
Hove BN3 . . . . 168 E2
Churchill Ind Est
BN15 . . . . 187 D5
Churchill Par BN16 . . . . 205 C5
Churchill Sq BN1 . . . . . . 213 A2
Churchill Way RH15 . . . . 109 C2
Churchill Wlk PO21 . . . . 211 A8

Church La
Albourne Green BN6 . . . 127 B5
Ardingly RH17 . . . . 63 F8
Ashington RH20 . . . . 123 A4
Ashurst BN44 . . . . 124 D5
Barnham PO22 . . . . 180 B4
Birdham PO20 . . . . 197 E5
Bognor Regis PO22 . . . . 201 C5
Boxgrove PO18 . . . . 156 D3
Bramshott GU30 . . . . 25 C6
Broadbridge Heath RH12 . . 35 D3
Burgess Hill RH17 . . . . . 109 F6
Burstow RH6 . . . . 4 A7
Bury RH20 . . . . 140 A7
Climping BN17, BN18 . . 181 E1
Cocking GU29 . . . . 114 D7
Coldwaltham RH20 . . . . 119 C6
Compton PO18 . . . . 111 B2
Copthorne RH10 . . . . 7 B3
Crawley RH10 . . . . 18 F6
Danehill RH17 . . . . 66 A3
Ditchling BN6 . . . . 129 D3
Eastergate PO20 . . . . . . 179 E8
East Grinstead RH19 . . . . 9 F1
Ferring BN12 . . . . 206 E6
Funtington PO18 . . . . . . 153 A5
Haslemere GU27 . . . . 27 D7
Henfield BN5 . . . . 125 E5
Horsted Keynes RH17 . . . 65 C5
Hunston PO20 . . . . 199 A8
Kingston near Lewes

BN7 . . . . 172 D5
Lancing BN15 . . . . 187 A8
Littlehampton BN17 . . . . 182 C6
Lodsworth GU28 . . . . 74 C2
Oving PO20 . . . . 178 C7
Pagham PO21 . . . . 210 D8
Partridge Green RH13 . . 104 F3
Poynings BN45, BN6 . . . 148 E7
Pyecombe BN45 . . . . . . 149 C6
Southwater RH13 . . . . . . 57 E1
Southwick BN42 . . . . . . 189 D7
Steyning BN44 . . . . 145 D3
Street End PO20 . . . . . . 198 E3
Tangmere PO20 . . . . . . 156 C1
Upper Beeding BN44 . . . 146 A2
Walberton BN18 . . . . . . 180 E8
West Dean PO18 . . . . . . 134 F5
Yapton BN18 . . . . 180 F4

Church Mdw PO18 . . . . . 175 B5

Church Mead
Keymer BN6 . . . . 129 B3
Steyning BN44 . . . . 145 E3
Churchmead Cl PO18 . . 154 E6
Church Mews PO20 . . . . 177 D1

Church Path
■3 Emsworth PO10 . . . 173 B8
Stoughton PO18 . . . . . . 133 A4
Church Pk RH11 . . . . 5 E5

Church Pl
Brighton BN2 . . . . 192 E4
Pulborough RH20 . . . . . 100 B2
Church Platt RH17 . . . . . . 86 E5

Church Rd
Aldingbourne PO20 . . . . 179 A8
Angmering BN16 . . . . . . 183 F5
Bramshott GU30 . . . . 35 D3
Broadbridge Heath RH12 . . 35 D3
Burgess Hill RH15 . . . . . 109 A3
Burstow RH6 . . . . 4 A7
Copthorne RH10 . . . . 7 B3
Crawley, Lowfield Heath

RH11 . . . . 5 E5
Crawley, Worth RH10 . . . 19 E6
East Wittering PO20 . . . 207 F8
Fernhurst GU27 . . . . 49 B5
Haslemere, Shottermill

GU27 . . . . 26 F6
Haywards Heath RH16 . . . 87 E4
Horley RH6 . . . . 1 F2
Horley RH6 . . . . 2 A1
Horsham RH12 . . . . 37 B5
Hove BN3 . . . . 191 B6
Mannings Heath RH13 . . . 59 C6
North Mundham PO20 . . 177 D1
Partridge Green RH13 . . 104 F3
Portslade-by-S BN42 . . . 190 B7
Rustington BN16 . . . . . . 205 C5
Scaynes Hill RH17 . . . . . . 88 F3
Selsey PO20 . . . . 212 E6
Southbourne PO10 . . . . 173 F8
Steep GU32 . . . . 68 B7
Turners Hill RH10 . . . . . . 21 A3
West Chiltington RH20 . . 151 D3
West Thorney PO10 . . . . 173 F1
Worthing BN13 . . . . 186 A4
Yapton BN18 . . . . 180 F3
Churchside PO19 . . . . . . 177 A7

Church St
Amberley RH20 . . . . 140 D7
Brighton BN1 . . . . 213 B2
Crawley RH11 . . . . 18 C6
Cuckfield RH17 . . . . 86 E6

Church St *continued*
Liss GU33 . . . . 45 A6
Littlehampton BN17 . . . . 204 E5
Petworth GU28 . . . . 97 F8
Rudgwick, Cox Green

RH12 . . . . 12 E1
Rudgwick RH12 . . . . 33 E8
Shoreham-by-S BN43 . . . 188 F7
Steyning BN44 . . . . 145 D3
Storrington RH20 . . . . . . 121 D1
Warnham RH12 . . . . 35 F8
West Chiltington RH20 . . 101 C1
Church Terr
Cowfold RH13 . . . . 83 E2
Henfield BN5 . . . . 125 E5
Church View PO10 . . . . . 151 D3
Church View Cl RH6 . . . . . 1 F2
Church Walk Mews
RH15 . . . . 109 A3
Church Way
Bognor Regis PO21 . . . . 200 A1
■6 Brighton BN2 . . . . . 213 C3
Singleton PO18 . . . . 135 D7
Worthing BN13 . . . . 186 A5
Church Way Cl BN13 . . . 186 A5
Church Wlk
Burgess Hill RH15 . . . . . 109 A3
Crawley RH10 . . . . 18 D6
Horley RH6 . . . . 1 A6
Worthing BN11 . . . . 186 F2
CHURCHWOOD 99 B4
Church Wood PO20 . . . . . 99 B4
Churchwood Dr PO20 . . 156 D1
Churt Dr PO22 . . . . 201 D6
Chute Ave BN13 . . . . . . 163 E1
Chute Way BN13 . . . . . . 185 E9
Cidermill Hatch RH5 . . . . 3 F6
Cinder Hill RH19 . . . . 43 B1
Circle The BN10 . . . . . . 206 A4
Circus Par BN1 . . . . 213 B4
Circus St BN2 . . . . 213 B2
Cissbury Ave BN14 . . . . 163 F2
Cissbury Cl RH12 . . . . . . 37 A6
Cissbury Cres BN2 . . . . 194 E1
Cissbury Ct BN14 . . . . . 163 F2
Cissbury Dr BN14 . . . . . 163 F3
Cissbury Gdns BN14 . . . 164 A2
Cissbury Hill RH11 . . . . . 18 C4
Cissbury Rd
Burgess Hill RH15 . . . . . 108 E4
Ferring BN12 . . . . 206 F2
Hove BN3 . . . . 191 E7
Worthing BN14 . . . . 186 C6
Cissbury Ring ■5 BN14 . 164 B5
Cissbury Way ■5
BN43 . . . . 166 F1
Citadel Ho ■4 PO19 . . . 176 F7
City Bsns Ctr
Horsham RH13 . . . . 36 D1
City Bsns Ctr The RH11 . . 5 D2
City Coll Brighton & Hove
Brighton BN1 . . . . 213 A5
Brighton BN1 . . . . 213 B3
Brighton, Whitehawk

BN2 . . . . 192 F5
Hove BN3 . . . . 191 A6
City Fields Bsns Pk
PO20 . . . . 156 D2
City Fields Way PO20 . . 156 D2
City Gates PO19 . . . . . . 176 F5
Civic Way RH15 . . . . 109 B3
Claigmar Rd BN16 . . . . . 205 C5
Clair Ct RH16 . . . . 87 E5
Clair Rd RH16 . . . . 87 E5
Clammer Hill GU27 . . . . . 27 B8
Clapgate La RH13 . . . . . . 34 D4
Clapham Cl BN13 . . . . . 162 F1
Clapham Comm BN13 . . 184 E8
Clapham & Patching CE
Prim Sch BN13 . . . . . . 162 E1
Clappers Gate RH10 . . . . 18 D7
Clappers La
Bracklesham PO20 . . . . 208 C6
Fulking BN5 . . . . 147 F5
Clappers Mdw GU6 . . . . 11 A3
Clare Cl RH10 . . . . 6 C1
Clare Ct ■5 BN17 . . . . . 204 E4
Clare Gdns GU31 . . . . . . 68 E3
Clare Lo ■8 BN16 . . . . . 205 B5
Clarement Ct
PO21 . . . . 201 D3
Chichester PO19 . . . . . . 176 F4
Claremont Way GU27 . . 94 E7
Clarence Ave BN17 . . . . 204 C7
Clarence Ct
Horley RH6 . . . . 2 D4
■7 Worthing BN11 . . . . 186 F2
Clarence Dr
■2 East Grinstead

RH19 . . . . 22 F7
East Preston BN16 . . . . . 205 F6
Clarence Gate ■10
PO21 . . . . 201 D3
Clarence Gdns BN1 . . . . 213 A2
Clarence Rd
Bognor Regis PO21 . . . . 201 D3
Horsham RH11 . . . . 36 E1
Clarence Sq BN1 . . . . . . 213 A2
Clarence Way RH6 . . . . . . 2 D4
Clarendon Ho ■2 BN3 . . 191 B7
Clarendon Mews ■7
BN11 . . . . 186 C1
Clarendon Pl
■1 Brighton BN1 . . . . . 192 C4
Portslade-by-S BN41 . . . 190 C6

Clarendon Rd
Hove BN3 . . . . 191 B7
Shoreham-by-S BN42,
BN43 . . . . 189 D8
Worthing BN14 . . . . 186 E6

Clarendon Terr ■18
BN2 . . . . 192 D4
Clarendon Villas BN3 . . 191 B7
Clare Wlk BN2 . . . . 192 D5
Clarke Ave BN3 . . . . 168 F3
Clark Ct RH11 . . . . 18 A1
Clarks Ind Est BN3 . . . . 191 B8
Clay Hall La RH16 . . . . . . 49 E2
Clay Hill Ho GU27 . . . . . . 27 A6

Clay La
Cootham RH20 . . . . 121 A1
Crossbush BN18 . . . . . . 160 F1
Fishbourne PO18, PO19 . . 176 B7
West Ashling PO18 . . . . 153 D1
Claypit La PO19 . . . . . . 176 F6
Clays Cl RH19 . . . . 22 E8
Clays Hill BN44 . . . . 145 E2
Clayton Ave BN6 . . . . . . 128 F3
Clayton Ct PO20 . . . . . . 212 C6
Clayton Dr RH15 . . . . . . 108 F1

Clayton Hill
Clayton BN6, BN45 . . . . 149 D7
Crawley RH11 . . . . 18 C4
Clayton La PO20 . . . . . . 208 B7
Clayton Pk BN6 . . . . 128 E4

Clayton Rd
Brighton BN2 . . . . 192 E3
Ditchling BN6 . . . . 129 C3
Selsey PO20 . . . . 212 C6
Claytons Cnr PO20 . . . . 197 E5
Clayton Way BN3 . . . . . . 168 F3
Clayton Windmills*
BN6 . . . . 149 E7
Clayton Wlk RH11 . . . . . 185 D6
Clearwater La RH17 . . . . . 89 A3
Clearwaters La RH16 . . . 109 D8
Cleaver's La RH17 . . . . . . 62 B2
Cleeves Ct BN16 . . . . . . 205 E6
Cleeve Way RH14 . . . . . . 79 B8
Clement's Ct ■1 BN43 . . 188 F7
Clerks Acre BN6 . . . . . . 129 A4
Clermont Ct BN1 . . . . . . 169 E2
Clermont Rd BN1 . . . . . . 169 E2
Clermont Terr BN1 . . . . . 169 E2
Cleveland Cl BN13 . . . . . 185 F9

Cleveland Copse
BN13 . . . . 185 F9
Cleveland Gdns RH15 . . 109 B2

Cleveland Rd
Brighton BN1 . . . . 170 A1
Chichester PO19 . . . . . . 177 B5
Worthing BN13 . . . . 185 F9

Clevelands
Billingshurst RH14 . . . . . . 79 D8
Haywards Heath RH16 . . . 87 E6
Clevets The PO21 . . . . . 200 C1
Cleve Way RH14 . . . . 79 B8
Cliff App BN2 . . . . 192 F4
Cliff The BN2 . . . . 192 F4

Clifton Cl
■9 Brighton BN1 . . . . . 213 A4
Chichester PO19 . . . . . . 177 B5
Clifton Gdns BN11 . . . . . 186 C3
Clifton Hill BN1 . . . . 213 A3
Clifton Mews BN1 . . . . . 213 A3
Clifton Pl BN1 . . . . 191 E6
Clifton Rd
Bognor Regis PO21 . . . . 201 C4
Brighton BN1 . . . . 213 A3
Burgess Hill RH15 . . . . . 108 D5
Crawley RH10 . . . . 19 C5
Littlehampton BN17 . . . . 204 D4
Worthing BN11 . . . . 186 C3
Clifton St BN1 . . . . 213 A3
Clifton Terr BN1 . . . . . . 213 A3
Cliftonville ■6 BN3 . . . . 191 B7

Climping Camp Site
BN17 . . . . 203 F7
Climping Cl ■2
BN12,BN16 . . . . 205 B3
Climping Pk BN17 . . . . . 181 F1
Climping Rd BN11 . . . . . 181 B8
Climping St BN17 . . . . . 203 F7
Climping & West Beach
Nature Trail* BN17 . . . 203 F7
Clinton Hill RH7 . . . . 10 A8
Clitherow Gdns RH10 . . . 18 E5
Clive Ave BN12 . . . . 185 D3

Clive Ct
Haywards Heath RH16 . . . 87 E6
Worthing BN12 . . . . 185 D3
Clivedale ■9 BN44 . . . . 145 D3
Clivedale Gdns BN44 . . . 145 C4
Cliveden Ct RH15 . . . . . 169 E3
Clive Way RH10 . . . . 18 E5
Clock Ho PO22 . . . . 200 E1
Clock Ho The GU29 . . . . . 94 F8
Clock Pk PO20 . . . . 156 D2
Clocktower The BN1 . . . 213 B2
Clock Wlk PO21 . . . . 201 D3

Cloisters The
Littlehampton BN17 . . . . 204 F4
Worthing BN14 . . . . 186 D5

Close The
Ardingly RH17 . . . . 64 B7
Ashington RH20 . . . . 123 A5

Close The *continued*
Bognor Regis PO21 . . . . **200** C1
Boxgrove PO18 . . . . **156** D3
Brighton BN1 . . . . **169** E5
Burgess Hill RH15 . . . . . . **109** C4
East Grinstead RH19 . . . . .**22** D8
Hassocks BN6 . . . . **128** F4
Horley RH6 . . . . **2** C1
Ifold RH14 . . . .**31** D3
Lancing BN15 . . . . **187** F4
Liphook GU30 . . . .**25** C2
Middleton-on-S PO22 . . .**203** A5
Mid Lavant PO18 . . . . . . **154** F5
Rustington BN16 . . . . . . **205** D4
Selsey PO20 . . . . **212** G8
Shoreham-by-S BN43 . . .**188** F8
Closewalks GU29 . . . .**94** F7
Clothalls La RH13 . . . . . . **104** B5
Clovelly Ave PO22 . . . . . . **202** B5
Clovelly Rd
Breach PO10 . . . . **151** F1
Emsworth PO10 . . . . **173** A8
Clover Ct 8 RH14 . . . .**87** E4
Clover Field RH13 . . . .**34** D3
Cloverfields RH6 . . . . **2** B4
Clover La BN12 . . . . **206** E5
Cloverlands RH10 . . . .**18** F8
Clovers Cotts RH12 . . . . . .**16** F1
Clovers End
Brighton BN1 . . . . **170** B7
Horsham RH12 . . . .**37** A5
Clovers Way RH12 . . . .**37** D7
Clover Way BN41 . . . . . . **168** B2
Cloye Ho 9 BN43 . . . . . . **188** E7
Club Wlk BN16 . . . . **206** A4
Clun Rd BN17 . . . . **204** C6
Clyde Cl BN13 . . . . **185** C9
Clyde Rd
Bognor Regis PO22 . . . . **201** F3
Brighton BN1 . . . . **213** B5
Worthing BN13 . . . . **185** C9
Clydesdale Ave PO19 . . .**177** B5
Clydesdale Gdns
PO22 . . . . **201** A7
Coach & Horses La
RH17 . . . .**66** C6
Coach House Cl PO20 . . **212** E7
Coach House Cotts
BN16 . . . . **205** D8
Coach House Mews
BN11 . . . . **186** C2
Coach La RH17 . . . .**66** C6
Coachmans Dr RH11 . . . . .**18** B2
Coach Rd
Crawley, Gatwick Airport
RH6 . . . . **5** F8
Crawley, Gatwick Airport
RH6 . . . . **6** B7
Shopwyke PO20 . . . . **177** F7
Westhampnett PO18 . . . **155** E1
Coalbrook Ho BN2 . . . . . **192** C5
Coast 13 BN16 . . . . **205** B4
Coastal Counties Ho 10
BN2 . . . . **213** C3
Coastal Rd BN16 . . . . . . **206** C4
Coastguard Cotts 10
BN16 . . . . **206** A4
Coastguard La PO20 . . . **196** A1
Coastguard Par PO21 . . **200** D1
Coastguard Rd BN17 . . **204** D3
Coastguards Cotts
PO20 . . . . **196** A2
COATES **118** D8
Coates Castle RH20 . . . . **118** C8
Coates Ct 11 BN42 . . . . . **189** E7
Coates La RH20 . . . . **118** D8
Cobbett Cl RH10 . . . .**19** C8
Cobbetts Mead RH16 . . . .**88** B3
Cobbetts Mews RH20 . . **100** A2
Cobblers The RH13 . . . . . .**34** D3
Cobbles Cres RH10 . . . . . .**18** E7
Cobblestone Wlk 4
BN44 . . . . **145** D3
Cobblewood PO10 . . . . . **151** B3
Cob Cl RH10 . . . .**21** C8
Cobden Ho GU29 . . . .**94** E6
Cobden La GU27 . . . .**27** D7
Cobden Rd
Brighton BN2 . . . . **192** C7
Midhurst GU29 . . . .**94** E7
Worthing BN11 . . . . **186** C2
Cobham Cl BN18 . . . . **180** F2
Cobham Way RH10 . . . .**6** B4
Cob La RH17 . . . .**42** B1
Cobnor Cl RH11 . . . .**17** F4
Cobton Dr BN3 . . . . **169** A3
Coburn Ho 3 RH10 . . . . . .**19** B7
Cob Wlk RH11 . . . .**18** A6
Cockhaise Cotts RH16 . . .**89** A8
COCKING CAUSEWAY . . .**94** E4
Cocking Hill GU29 . . . .
PO18 . . . . **114** C5
Cohen Cl PO20 . . . . **179** D5
Cokeham Ct BN15 . . . . . . **187** C7
Cokeham Gdns BN15 . . . **187** C6
Cokeham La BN15 . . . . . . **187** C5
Cokeham Rd BN15 . . . . . . **187** C6
Colbourne Ave BN2 . . . . **170** D2
Colbourne Rd BN3 . . . . . **191** E7
Colchester Vale RH18 . . . .**23** E2
Colchins RH15 . . . . **108** F1
COLDEAN **170** D6
Coldean La BN1 . . . . **170** E6
Coldean Prim Sch
BN1 . . . . **170** D6

Coldean Rd BN1 . . . . **170** C8
Coldharbour Farm Rd
PO10 . . . . **151** B2
Coldharbour La BN13 . . . **162** D1
Coldwaltham La
RH15 . . . . **109** D2
Colebrook Cl BN11 . . . . . **186** F3
Colebrook Ct BN11 . . . . . **186** F3
Colebrook La RH20 . . . . . **119** B5
Colebrook Rd
Brighton BN1 . . . . **169** D4
Littlehampton BN17 . . . . **204** C7
Southwick BN42 . . . . **189** F7
Cole Cl RH11 . . . .**18** B1
Coleman Ave BN3 . . . . . . **190** E7
Colemans Hatch Rd
RH18 . . . .**44** E5
Coleman St BN2 . . . . **213** C4
Coleridge Cl
Horsham RH12 . . . .**36** E6
Worthing BN12 . . . . **185** B4
Coleridge Cres BN12 . . . **185** A4
Coleridge Mews
BN12 . . . . **185** B4
Coleridge Rd BN12 . . . . . **185** B4
Coleridge St BN3 . . . . . . **191** A8
Colet Rd RH10 . . . .**18** D3
Colgate Cl
Brighton BN2 . . . . **192** F6
Crawley RH11 . . . .**18** B8
Colgate Prim Sch
RH13 . . . .**38** C6
Colhook Ind Pk GU28 . . . .**51** D1
Colindale Rd BN12 . . . . . **206** E6
Colindale Rd N BN12 . . . **206** E6
Collards Gate GU27 . . . . . .**27** D6
Collards La GU27 . . . .**27** D6
Collard Way GU33 . . . .**45** B4
College Ct
Bognor Regis PO21 . . . . **201** E5
Brighton BN2 . . . . **192** C4
College Gdns
Brighton BN2 . . . . **192** C4
Worthing BN11 . . . . **186** A2
College Hill
Haslemere GU27 . . . .**27** C6
Steyning BN44 . . . . **145** D2
College Hill Terr GU27 . . .**27** C6
College La
Chichester PO19 . . . . . . **177** A8
East Grinstead RH19 . . . . .**9** F1
Hurst Wickham BN6 . . . . **128** C6
College Pl
Brighton BN2 . . . . **192** C4
Hurst Wickham BN6 . . . . **128** C6
Steyning BN44 . . . . **145** D2
College Rd
Ardingly RH16, RH17 . . . . .**64** A6
Brighton BN2 . . . . **192** C4
Haywards Heath RH16 . . .**87** E7
Southwater RH13 . . . .**57** E1
Upper Beeding BN44 . . . **146** C1
College St
11 Brighton BN2 . . . . . **192** C4
Petersfield GU31, GU31 . . .**68** B3
College Terr BN2 . . . . . . **192** D5
Collendean La RH6 . . . .**1** A5
Collier Row RH10 . . . .**18** D4
Collingford La RH17 . . . . .**66** B4
Collingwood RH20 . . . . . **100** C3
Collingwood Cl
4 East Grinstead
RH19 . . . .**22** F7
Horley RH6 . . . . **2** B4
Horsham RH12 . . . .**36** C4
Collingwood Ct
Brighton BN2 . . . . **193** A3
2 Shoreham-by-S
BN43 . . . . **188** F6
Collingwood Rd
Crawley RH10 . . . .**19** D5
Horsham RH12 . . . .**36** B4
Worthing BN12 . . . . **185** C5
Collingwood Way
GU31 . . . .**68** C5
Collins Cl PO20 . . . . **179** F8
Collins La GU31 . . . .**91** C7
Collins Rd RH11 . . . .**17** E4
Collins's La PO20 . . . . . . **198** C4
Coll of Richard Collyer
The RH12 . . . .**36** D4
Coll of St Barnabas RH7 . . . **9** F8
Collyer Ave PO21 . . . . . . **201** B5
Collyers Cotts GU28 . . . . .**74** B7
Collyers Cres GU28 . . . . . .**25** E4
Colmer Ct RH15 . . . . **108** E3
Colmer Pl RH15 . . . . **108** E3
Colne Cl BN13 . . . . **185** C9
Colne Wlk RH11 . . . .**17** F4
Colonades Ho RH20 . . . . **100** B3
Colonnade Ho 3
BN11 . . . . **186** E2
Colonnades The BN11 . . . **213** B2
Colonsay Rd RH11 . . . .**18** B3
Coltash Rd RH10 . . . .**19** A5
Colt's Bay PO21 . . . . **200** C1
Coltsfoot Dr RH12 . . . .**36** E5
Colt St PO20 . . . . **212** D8
Coltstaple La RH13 . . . . . .**58** C4
Columbia Dr BN13 . . . . . **185** D7
Columbia Wlk BN13 . . . . **185** C7

Columbine Way BN17 . . **205** B8
Colvill Ave BN43 . . . . **188** D8
Colwell Cl RH16 . . . .**87** F3
Colwell Gdns RH16 . . . . . .**87** F3
Colwell La
Haywards Heath, Fox Hill
RH17 . . . .**87** F1
Haywards Heath, Franklands
Village RH17 . . . .**88** B3
Colwell Rd RH16 . . . .**87** F3
Colwood La RH17 . . . .**85** B6
COLWORTH **178** E2
Colwyn Cl RH11 . . . .**17** F4
Commerce Way BN15 . . **187** C4
Commercial Rd RH15 . . . **108** F3
Commercial Sq RH16 . . . .**87** E6
Common Hill PO20 . . . . . **121** D6
Common La BN6 . . . . **129** D6
Common Rd PO10,
PO18 . . . . **152** D5
Commonside PO10 . . . . . **151** D5
COMMON THE **36** A4
Common The RH20 . . . . . **121** C8
Common View GU29 . . . . .**71** F1
Compass Cl RH17 . . . . . . **205** A6
Compass La BN41 . . . . . . **167** E3
Compassion Cl RH17 . . . .**17** E5
Compass Point PO21 . . . **201** E3
Comper Cl RH11 . . . .**17** F4
Compton Ave
Brighton BN1 . . . . **213** A4
Worthing BN12 . . . . **185** B3
Compton Cl PO19 . . . . . . **155** A3
Compton Dr BN1 . . . . . . **205** C6
Compton Dr PO22 . . . . . . **202** D6
Compton Rd
Brighton BN1 . . . . **169** D1
Lindfield RH16 . . . .**73** C2
Comptons Brow La
RH13 . . . .**37** A3
Comptons Ct 4 RH13 . . . .**36** F3
Comptons La RH13 . . . . . .**36** F3
Comptons The RH13 . . . . .**37** A3
Compton & Up Marden CE
Prim Sch PO18 . . . . **111** B2
Conbar Ave BN16 . . . . . . **205** C6
Concorde Cl RH10 . . . . . . **121** F3
Concorde Ho RH6 . . . .**6** B7
Condor Way RH15 . . . . . . **108** E3
Conduit Mead PO19 . . . . **177** C8
Coneleys Yd PO20 . . . . . **198** D5
Coney Cl
Crawley RH11 . . . .**18** B8
East Wittering PO20 . . . . **207** F6
Coney Croft RH12 . . . .**37** B5
Coneyhurst Rd RH14 . . . . .**79** F8
Coney Rd PO20 . . . . **207** F6
Coney Six PO20 . . . . **207** F6
Congreve Rd RH14 . . . . . **186** E4
Conifer Dr PO18 . . . . **152** E2
Conifers Cl RH12 . . . .**36** F4
Conifers Cl GU29 . . . .**73** A1
Conifer Way PO21 . . . . . . **199** F2
Conigar Rd PO10 . . . . **151** B3
Coniston Cl
Bognor Regis PO22 . . . . **202** B6
Crawley RH11 . . . .**17** D4
Horsham RH12 . . . .**36** B2
Lancing BN15 . . . . **187** C6
Coniston Ct 9 BN3 . . . . . **191** D7
Coniston Rd PO20 . . . . . . **185** C5
Coniston Way BN17 . . . . **205** A7
Connaught Ave BN43 . . **188** C8
Connaught Gdns 1
RH10 . . . .**18** D8
Connaught Ho 7
PO21 . . . . **201** C2
Connaught Jun Sch
BN17 . . . . **204** D5
Connaught Rd
Hove BN3 . . . . **191** A6
Littlehampton BN17 . . . . **204** D5
Connaught Terr BN3 . . . . **191** B7
Connell Dr BN2 . . . . **193** E7
Connolly Way PO19 . . . . **155** A1
Consort Way
Burgess Hill RH15 . . . . . . **108** E2
Horley RH6 . . . . **2** B2
Consort Way E RH6 . . . . **2** B2
Constable Ct RH10 . . . . . **212** F7
Constable Rd RH10 . . . . . .**18** F2
Control Tower Rd RH6 . . . . .**5** D6
Convent Ct PO10 . . . . **173** A8
Convent Gdns BN14 . . . . **163** F6
Convent La PO10 . . . . **173** A8
Conway Cl 1 BN3 . . . . . . **191** B7
Conway Dr PO21 . . . . **211** A8
Conway Pl BN3 . . . . **191** A8
Conway St BN3 . . . . **191** B8
Cook Rd
Crawley RH11 . . . .**18** F4
Horsham RH12 . . . .**36** D6
Cooksbridge Rd BN2 . . . **192** E6
Cooks Hill RH12 . . . .**33** A8
Cooks La
Breach PO10 . . . . **152** A1
Walderton PO18 . . . . **132** D2
Cooks Mdw RH12 . . . .**16** D7
Cooks Mead RH12 . . . .**16** F1
Cook's Pond Rd GU30 . . .**71** A7
Coolham Ct RH11 . . . .**17** F6
Coolham Dr BN2 . . . . **192** E7
Coolham Rd
Brooks Green RH13 . . . . . .**80** E4
Goose Green RH13,
RH20 . . . . **102** C5
Coolhurst La RH13 . . . .**37** A1

Coolwater Pk BN1 . . . . . **169** D4
Coombe Cl
Billingshurst RH14 . . . .**55** D1
Crawley RH11 . . . . **5** D1
Coombe Cotts RH19 . . . . .**42** F6
Coombe Cres RH20 . . . . . **140** A7
Coombe Dr BN44 . . . . **145** D2
Coombe Dro BN44 . . . . . . **145** D2
Coombe Hall Pk RH19 . . . .**22** D6
Coombe Hill RH14 . . . .**55** D1
Coombe Hill Rd RH19 . . . .**22** D6
Coombe La BN18 . . . . **161** B7
Coombelands La
Codmore Hill RH20 . . . . . **100** A5
Pulborough RH20 . . . . . . **100** A3
Coombe Lea 6 BN3 . . . . **191** C6
Coombe Mdw BN2 . . . . . **194** E3
Coombe Rd
Brighton BN2 . . . . **170** D1
Hill Brow GU33 . . . .**45** E1
Steyning BN44 . . . . **145** C2
Coombe Rise
Saltdean BN2 . . . . **194** D3
Worthing BN14 . . . . **164** A2
Coombe Road Prim Sch
BN2 . . . . **170** D1
Coombers La RH16 . . . .**88** B5
COOMBES **166** A5
Coombes Ct BN15 . . . . . . **187** F7
Coombes Rd BN15 . . . . . . **166** B3
Coombe Terr BN2 . . . . . . **170** C1
Coombe Vale BN2 . . . . . . **194** D3
Coomes Way BN17 . . . . . **204** D8
Cooper La RH6 . . . . **1** F2
Cooper Row RH10 . . . .**18** D3
Coopers Cl RH15 . . . . **109** B5
Coopers Farm Cl 7
PO22 . . . . **201** D5
Cooper St PO19 . . . . **177** A6
Coopers The RH13 . . . .**56** D4
Coopers Way BN5 . . . . . . **125** F4
Coopers Wood RH17 . . . . .**39** C3
Coos La RH17 . . . .**61** A6
Cootes Ave RH12 . . . .**36** A3
Cootes Cotts RH20 . . . . . **118** B2
Cootes La PO22 . . . . **202** F5
Cotham Brow RH20 . . . . **121** B1
Cotham Mobile Home Pk
RH20 . . . . **121** A2
Copeland Rd PO22 . . . . . **202** B4
Copenhagen Ct BN2 . . . . **193** A3
Copestake Dr RH15 . . . . . **109** D3
Copnall Way 17 RH12 . . . .**36** C2
Copper Beech Dr
PO20 . . . . **156** C1
Copper Beeches BN15 . . **169** E1
Copper Cl RH15 . . . . **108** C4
Copperfield Pl RH12 . . . . .**36** B4
Copperfields RH13 . . . .**59** B8
Copperfields Manor
RH13 . . . .**59** B8
Copper Hall Cl 4
BN16 . . . . **205** E6
Coppets Wood 8
BN16 . . . . **205** E4
Coppice La PO20 . . . . **212** D8
Coppice Rd RH12 . . . .**37** A5
Coppice The
Crawley Down RH10 . . . . .**21** B8
East Grinstead RH19 . . . . .**10** A3
Horsham RH12 . . . .**36** F6
Liss GU33 . . . .**45** D2
Southwater RH13 . . . .**57** F2
Copse Cl
Crawley Down RH10 . . . . .**21** B8
Haywards Heath RH16 . . .**88** B5
Southwater RH13 . . . .**57** F2
Worthing BN13 . . . . **185** D6
Copse Hill BN1 . . . . **169** D5
Copse La
Horley RH6 . . . . **2** C4
Walberton BN18 . . . . **158** D2
Copse Rd GU27 . . . .**26** D5
Copse The
Chichester PO19 . . . . . . **155** B2
Crawley RH11 . . . .**19** A6
Haywards Heath RH16 . . .**88** B5
Southwater RH13 . . . .**57** F2
Copse View RH16 . . . . . . **205** F6
Copthorne Bank RH10,
RH10 . . . . **7** C4
Copthorne CE Jun Sch
RH10 . . . . **7** C3
Copthorne Cl BN13 . . . . . **186** A8
Copthorne Common Rd
RH10 . . . . **7** C3
Copthorne Ct
1 Crawley RH10 . . . . **6** A1
2 Hove BN3 . . . . **191** C6
Copthorne Cvn Pk
PO21 . . . . **200** D4
Copthorne Hill RH13 . . . **185** F8
Copthorne Prep Sch
RH10 . . . . **7** C4
Copthorne Rd
Copthorne RH10 . . . . **6** F1
Crawley RH10 . . . .**19** E8
Domewood RH19 . . . . **8** D4
Copthorne Way
Bognor Regis PO21 . . . . **200** D4
Copthorne RH10 . . . . **6** F1
Copyhold Hill GU27 . . . . . .**49** C8

Copyhold La
Cuckfield RH17 . . . .**87** A4
Haywards Heath RH16 . . .**63** E2
Copyhold Rd RH19 . . . .**22** D8
Copythorne Ho 1
RH16 . . . .**87** E6
Coral Cl PO20 . . . . **212** B8
Coral La PO20 . . . . **212** B8
Corbishley Gn PO22 . . . . **201** C6
Corbishley Rd PO22 . . . . **201** C6
Corby Cl RH11 . . . .**17** E3
Corby Cres BN43 . . . . **189** A7
Cordal Cl BN16 . . . . **205** B4
Cordons BN7 . . . . **172** D5
Corfe Cl
Southwater RH13 . . . .**58** A1
Worthing BN13 . . . . **185** B6
Cormorant Way PO20 . . **208** A6
Cornelius Ho BN3 . . . . . . **191** A6
Corner Garth BN12 . . . . . **206** F5
Cornfield Cl BN17 . . . . . . **204** E7
Cornfield Sch BN17 . . . . **204** E7
Cornfields The PO20 . . . . **179** D7
Cornflower Cl PO19 . . . . **177** C8
Cornflower Way RH13 . . . .**58** A3
Cornford Cl
Burgess Hill RH15 . . . . . . **108** E5
Portslade-by-S BN41 . . . **168** B2
Cornish Mews BN1 . . . . . **191** E8
Cornwall Ct 8 BN3 . . . . . **191** C7
Cornwall Gdns
Brighton BN1 . . . . **169** E2
6 East Grinstead RH19 . . .**22** F8
Littlehampton BN17 . . . . **204** D6
Cornwall Ho BN1 . . . . . . **169** E2
Cornwall Rd BN17 . . . . . . **204** D6
Coronation Bldgs
BN11 . . . . **187** A3
Coronation Homelets 1
BN11 . . . . **187** B3
Coronation Rd
East Grinstead RH19 . . . . .**22** E7
South Hayling PO11 . . . . **195** A1
Coronation St 7 BN2 . . . **192** C7
Coronet Cl RH10 . . . .**19** E7
Coronet The RH6 . . . . **2** C1
Corsletts Ave RH12 . . . . . .**35** D3
Cortis Ave BN14 . . . . **186** C5
Corunna Dr RH13 . . . .**36** F2
Corvill Ct BN11 . . . . **186** B2
Cory Cl PO19 . . . . **177** A5
Costells Edge RH17 . . . . . .**88** F3
COTE **185** C9
Cote St BN13 . . . . **163** C1
Cot La PO18 . . . . **174** D6
Cotland Rd PO20 . . . . **212** F6
Cotsford RH12 . . . .**39** B7
Cotswold Cl
Crawley RH11 . . . .**18** B6
Worthing BN13 . . . . **185** E9
Cotswold Ct RH13 . . . .**36** E2
Cotswold Pl 7 BN2 . . . . . **192** F5
Cotswold Rd BN13 . . . . . **185** E8
Cotswolds The BN42 . . . **189** E7
Cotswold Way BN16 . . . . **206** A6
Cottage Cl
Bognor Regis PO21 . . . . **200** C2
Horsham RH12 . . . .**37** B6
Cottage Homes BN6 . . . . **129** E6
Cottage Pl RH13 . . . . **7** E3
Cottenham Rd BN11 . . . . **186** F3
Cottesmore St Mary's RC
Prim Sch BN3 . . . . **191** D8
Cottesmore Sch RH11 . . . .**39** A8
Cottingham Ave RH12 . . .**36** D7
Cotton Dr PO10 . . . . **151** A3
Cotton Wlk RH11 . . . .**18** A1
Cottrell Cl RH16 . . . . **183** F5
Cottrells The BN16 . . . . . **183** F5
Coulstock Rd RH15 . . . . . **108** C3
Council Cotts
Albourne Green BN6 . . . **127** A7
Clapham BN13 . . . . **162** E1
Crosspost RH17 . . . .**85** B1
Loxwood RH14 . . . .**32** A2
Plaistow RH14 . . . .**30** D3
Sayers Common BN6 . . . **107** E3
Southwater RH13 . . . .**81** F7
Sutton RH20 . . . . **117** E7
Twineham RH17 . . . . **107** B6
Warninglid BN18 . . . . . . **160** F2
Wepham BN18 . . . . **161** A5
Wisborough Green RH14 . . .**54** B2
Countisbury Cl PO21 . . . **200** F3
Countland Ct 17 PO21 . . **201** B2
Countryman La RH13 . . . **103** B7
County Mall RH10 . . . .**18** E5
COUNTY OAK **5** D2
County Oak Ave BN1 . . . **170** B6
County Oak Ind Est
RH10 . . . . **5** D2
County Oak La RH11 . . . . . . **5** D1
County Oak Ret Pk
RH11 . . . . **5** D2
County Oak Way RH10,
RH11 . . . . **5** D2
County Wharf BN17 . . . . **204** D4
Courcels BN2 . . . . **192** E3
Court Barn La PO20 . . . . **197** E6
Court Cl
Brighton BN1 . . . . **169** E7
East Grinstead RH19 . . . . . **9** F1
Liphook GU30 . . . .**25** B3
Court Cres RH11 . . . .**17** D4
Courtenay Gate BN3 . . . **191** B5
Courtenay Terr 12
BN3 . . . . **191** B5

Court Est The 8
BN11.......187 B3
Court Farm Rd
Hove BN3......169 A2
Rottingdean BN2...193 F3
Courtfield Ho 4
PO21......201 B3
Courtfields BN15...187 D5
Courtlands
15 Brighton BN2...213 C3
Haywards Heath RH16...87 E3
Courtlands Cl BN12...185 E2
Courtlands Way
Bognor Regis PO22...202 C6
Worthing BN11, BN12...185 F2
Court Lodge Rd RH6...1 F3
Court Meadow Sch
RH17......87 A8
Courtmead Rd RH17...86 F6
Courtney King Ho 1
BN2......192 D4
Court Ord Cotts BN2...193 F3
Court Ord Rd BN2...193 F3
Courts Hill Rd GU27...27 B6
Courts Mount Rd GU27...27 B6
Court The PO21......200 A1
Courtup Hill RH13...82 E5
Courtwick La BN17...204 C8
Courtwick Rd RH17...204 C7
Courtyard La PO18...136 C7
Courtyard The
Bognor Regis PO21...200 F2
Chichester PO19...176 F4
5 Crawley RH10...18 D5
East Grinstead RH19...10 B1
Falmer BN1......171 C6
Faygate RH12......37 E4
Finchdean PO8......130 D7
Haywards Heath RH16...87 F4
Hove BN3......191 B8
8 Hove BN3......191 D6
Lindfield RH16......64 C3
11 Petersfield GU31...68 B3
Selsey PO20......210 A3
West Grinstead RH13...82 A2
Worthing BN11......186 B3
Worthing, Salvington
BN14......186 A6
Cousins Copse Cvn Site
RH14 ....55 F8
Cousins Way RH20...100 C3
Coventry Cl PO21...200 D4
Coventry St BN1...191 E8
Cove Rd BN16......205 B4
Coverdale Ct RH19...9 C3
Covers La GU27...26 C6
Covert Cl RH10...18 E7
Covert Mead
Ashington RH20...122 F5
Handcross RH17...61 B7
Covey The RH10...19 E8
Covington Rd PO10...151 D5
Cowdens Cl BN3...168 D4
Cowdown La PO18...110 F4
Cowdray* GU29......95 A8
Cowdray Cl
Crawley RH10......19 C5
Rustington BN16...205 B7
Worthing BN12...185 D2
Cowdray Ct
1 Hove BN3......191 D7
Midhurst GU29...94 F8
Cowdray Dr
Rustington BN16...205 B7
Worthing BN12...185 D2
Cowdray Ho GU29...95 C8
Cowdray Rd GU29...73 A2
Cowdray Wlk 7 BN16...205 B7
Cowfold Cl RH11...17 F3
Cowfold Rd
Brighton BN2......192 E5
Cowfold RH13...82 D2
Crosspost RH13, RH17...84 C2
Cow La
Sidlesham PO20...209 D7
South Harting GU31...91 C4
Cowley Dr
1 Lancing BN15...187 F5
Woodingdean BN2...193 F7
Cownwy Ct BN2...193 F1
Cowper Rd BN11...186 B2
Cowper St BN1...191 A7
Cowslip Cl RH13...58 A2
Concomb Wlk RH11...18 A4
Coxes Mdw GU32...68 A5
Coxes Rd PO20...212 D6
Cox Gr RH15...108 E5
COX GREEN......12 E2
Cox Green Rd RH12...12 C2
Coxham La BN44...145 C4
Cox Ho RH12......36 B2
Crabbet PO20...212 D8
Crabbet Rd RH10...19 B7
Crabden La PO8...130 A8
Crablands PO20...212 D7
Crablands Cl PO20...212 C7
Crabtree Ave BN1...170 B5
Crab Tree Cl RH17...182 D5
Crabtree Cotts RH13...84 A7
Crabtree Gate RH13...83 F5
Crabtree La BN15...187 D6
Crabtree La 2 BN15...187 D6
Crabtree Rd RH11...18 C7
Cradock Pl BN13...185 E9
Crafts La GU31...68 C5
Craggits La BN5...125 E5
Craigans RH11...18 B2
Craignair Ave BN1...169 F7

Craigweil La PO21...200 E2
Craigweil Manor
PO21......200 D1
Cranborne Wlk RH10...18 F4
Cranbourne Cl RH6...2 B5
Cranbourne St BN1...213 A2
Cranbrook 14 BN2...213 C3
Crane St PO19......177 A6
Cranford Gdns PO21...201 C4
Cranford Rd GU31...68 A2
Cranham Ave RH14...79 C6
Cranleigh Ave BN2...194 B1
Cranleigh Cl 9 BN11...186 C2
Cranleigh Rd BN14...186 C5
Cranley Ct 3 BN3...190 D7
Cranmer Ave BN3...168 F1
Cranmer Rd BN13...186 A3
Cranmer Wlk RH10...19 C5
Cranston Rd RH19...9 F2
Cranston Way RH10...21 C8
Cranworth Rd BN11...186 F3
Craven Rd
Bognor Regis PO21...200 F5
Cocking GU29...114 D8
Crawley RH10...19 B5
Crawley Ave
Crawley, Ifield RH10,
RH11......18 A6
Crawley RH10......6 C1
Crawley Bsns Ctr RH10...5 E2
Crawley Coll RH10...18 E6
Crawley Coll (West Green
Annexe) RH11......18 C7
Crawley Down Rd RH10...8 F4
Crawley Down Village CE
Prim Sch RH10......21 B8
Crawley Foyer The
RH11......18 C6
Crawley Hospl RH11...18 C6
Crawley La
Balcombe RH17......40 E4
Crawley RH10......19 C7
Crawley Mus Ctr*
RH11......18 C5
Crawley Rd
Brighton BN1......170 D6
Crawley RH12......17 B1
Faygate RH12......37 D7
Horsham RH12......37 B5
Crawley Sta RH10...18 E5
Crawters Cl RH10...18 F7
Crawters La 8 GU31...68 B3
Crayford Rd BN2...170 D1
Cray La RH20......100 D5
Cray's Rd RH20...122 C8
Creamery Cotts RH14...53 B2
Creasys Dr RH11...18 A1
Crede Cl PO18...175 C5
Crede La PO18...175 C5
Creek End
Emsworth PO10...173 B7
Fishbourne PO19...176 B6
Cremorne Pl 8 GU32...68 B4
Crescenta Wlk PO21...201 A3
Crescent Cl
Burgess Hill RH15...109 B3
Woodingdean BN2...193 E8
Crescent Ct 3 BN11...187 B3
Crescent Dr N BN2...193 E8
Crescent Dr S BN2...193 E7
Crescent Mans BN2...213 C5
Crescent Pl BN2...192 C4
Crescent Rd
Bognor Regis PO21...201 C3
Brighton BN2......192 B8
Burgess Hill RH15...109 A3
East Grinstead RH19...9 D1
Worthing BN11...186 C2
Crescent Rise RH20...122 A3
Crescent The
Bognor Regis, Felpham
PO22......202 A4
Bognor Regis PO21...211 A8
Brighton BN2......192 B8
Cootham RH20...121 A2
East Wittering PO20...207 E7
Felcourt RH19......9 C8
Horley RH6......6 B8
Horsham RH12......36 A2
Keymer RH16......129 B3
Lancing BN15......187 E5
Rustington BN16...205 B5
Southbourne PO10...173 F8
Southwick BN42...189 F8
Steyning BN44...145 D2
West Kingston BN16...206 A4
Crescent Way
Burgess Hill RH15...109 A3
Horley RH6......2 A1
Crespin Way BN1...170 C2
Cressey Way PO19...155 A1
Crest Way BN41...168 B3
Crestway Par BN1...170 C2
Crestway The BN1...170 C2
Crewdson Rd RH6...2 B3
Cricket Ct RH19...9 E3
Cricketers Cl RH10...123 A5
Cricketers Par BN14...186 D6
Cricket Field Rd RH12...36 B1
Crimbourne La RH14...77 D3
Cripland Cl RH16...88 B6
Cripplecrutch Hill
GU27......28 F5
Cripplegate La RH13...82 A8
Cripps Ho RH11...18 B2
Cripps La BN44...145 E3
Critchel's La PO20...198 C1

Critchfield Rd PO18...175 B5
CRITCHMERE......26 E7
Critchmere Dr PO20...179 F7
Critchmere Hill GU27...26 E7
Critchmere La GU27...26 E6
Critchmere Vale GU27...26 E6
Crockford Rd PO10...151 D4
Crockhurst Hill BN13...185 F9
Crockhurst RH13......58 A2
Crockhurst Hill BN13...185 F9
Croft Ave BN42......189 F7
Croft Dr BN41......168 A3
Crofters Wood BN44...145 F2
Croft La BN5......125 E4
Croft Mead PO19...155 A2
Croft Rd GU27......26 F7
Crofton Manor GU27...27 C7
Croft Rd
Brighton BN2......169 D4
Selsey PO20......212 D7
Croft The
Bognor Regis PO21...200 F5
Cocking GU29...114 D8
Crawley RH11......18 A6
East Preston BN16...206 A5
Hassocks BN6......128 F5
Lodsworth GU28...74 B3
Southwick BN42...189 E8
Yapton BN18......180 F4
Croft Villas BN5...125 E5
Croft Way
Bognor Regis PO22...202 C6
Horsham RH12......36 A3
Selsey PO20......212 D7
Croft Works BN16...205 D7
Cromleigh Way BN42...167 E2
Crompton Fields RH10...5 E1
Crompton Way RH10...5 E1
Cromwell Ct 3 BN3...191 D7
Cromwell Mews RH15...108 F4
Cromwell Pl 1 RH19...22 F7
Cromwell Rd
Burgess Hill RH15...108 F3
Hove BN3......191 C7
Cromwell St BN2...192 C7
Crooked La PO20...197 E4
Crookhorn La RH13...81 B8
Crookthorn La BN17...203 E8
Cropthorne Dr BN17...181 E1
Crosbie Cl PO19...176 F3
Crosby Cl BN13......185 D7
Croshaw Cl BN15...187 D5
Crossbush La BN18...160 E1
Crossbush Rd
Bognor Regis PO22...202 C4
Brighton BN2......192 E6
Cross Colwood La
RH17......84 F5
Crossfield GU27......49 B5
Crossfield Lo RH13...57 F1
CROSS GATES...141 A7
Crosshaven BN17...205 A6
Cross Keys RH10...18 D6
Cross La
Barns Green RH13...57 A1
Burstow RH9......7 C8
Nepcote BN14...163 E5
Findon BN14......18 B1
Cross Oak La RH1......2 C7
Crosspath RH10...18 E7
Crosspost RH17...85 B1
Cross Rd
Rustington BN16...205 E5
Southwick BN42...189 D8
Cross Road Cl BN42...189 D8
Cross St
Brighton BN1......213 B4
14 Hove BN1, BN3...191 D5
Worthing BN11...186 C3
Crossway RH6......5 F8
Crossways
Bolney RH17......85 D2
Crawley RH10......19 A7
East Preston BN16...206 A4
Middleton-on-S PO22...202 F5
Midhurst GU29...73 A2
Navant Hill GU28...50 E4
West Chiltington Common
RH20......121 D7
Crossways Ave
East Grinstead RH19...9 C1
Crossways Cl BN15...187 F7
Crossways Cotts
Alfold Crossways GU6...11 A3
Poynings BN45...148 C6
Crossways Ct GU27...49 B6
Crossways Pk RH20...121 D7
Crossways The
Hassocks BN6......128 C4
Littlehampton BN17...204 C7
Crossway The
Brighton BN1......170 B2
Portslade-by-S BN41...168 A2
Crouch Cross La
PO18......156 D3
Crouch Hill BN5...125 F7
Crouchlands Farm
RH17......86 E8
Crowberry Cl 1 RH11...18 A2
Crowborough Dr
BN12......185 B3
Crowhurst Cl RH10...19 E6
Crowhurst Cnr BN1...170 C7
Crowhurst Cres RH20...121 C2
Crowhurst Keep RH10...19 E6

Crowhurst Rd BN1...170 C7
Crown Bldgs BN15...187 C4
Crown Cl 1 BN3...191 D6
Crown Cl 3 BN16...206 A4
Crown Gdns BN1...213 A2
Crown Hill 4 BN2...192 C6
Crown Pl 2 BN16...206 A4
Crown Point Ho BN6...128 F4
Crown Rd
Portslade-by-S BN41...190 A8
Shoreham-by-S BN43...189 B8
Crown St BN1......213 A2
Crown Yd BN18...160 B3
Crowsbury Cl PO10...151 A3
Croxton La RH16...88 B6
Croy Cl PO19......176 E4
Crundens Cnr 5
BN16......205 E6
Crundles GU31......68 D3
Crutchfield La RH6...1 B5
Crypt La GU29......114 C7
Cuckfield Cl RH11...17 F3
Cuckfield Cres BN13...185 F7
Cuckfield La RH17...61 B1
Cuckfield Mus* RH17...86 E6
Cuckfield Rd
Ansty RH17......86 C3
Burgess Hill RH15...108 E7
Goddards' Green BN6,
RH17......108 A8
Hurstpierpoint BN6...128 A7
Slough Green RH17...62 A2
Cuckmere Cres RH11...17 F5
Cuckmere Way BN1...170 C5
Cudlow Ave BN16...205 C5
Cudlow Gdn BN16...205 C4
Cudworth La RH5......3 E8
Cudworth Pk RH5......3 F8
Cuffs Hill RH10......19 E2
Culimore Cl PO20...207 E7
Culimore Rd PO20...207 E7
Culled La PO20......177 C8
Culpepper RH15...108 E4
Culpepper Cl BN2...170 D2
Culross Ave RH16...87 D5
Culver Cl BN15...187 E6
Culver Rd
Bognor Regis PO22...202 A4
Lancing BN15...187 E6
Culvers GU31......91 D3
Cumberland Ave
New Brighton PO10...151 B4
Worthing BN12...185 D6
Cumberland Cl BN16...184 A5
Cumberland Cres
BN16......183 F5
Cumberland Ct BN11...185 F2
Cumberland Dr BN1...169 C2
Cumberland Lo 3
BN1......169 C2
Cumberland Rd
Angmering BN16...184 A5
Brighton BN1......169 C2
Cumbernauld Wlk
RH11......17 E2
Cumbrian Cl BN13...185 E8
Cumnor House Sch
RH17......66 B5
Cunliffe Cl PO20...196 C2
Cunningham Gdns
PO22......202 C5
Curbey Cl RH20...101 D1
Curf Way RH15...109 C3
Curlescroft PO21...200 F2
Curlew Cl PO10...173 A7
Curlews The BN43...189 A8
Curteys Wlk BN13...18 A3
Curve The BN2......213 C2
Curvins Way BN15...187 F7
Curwen Pl BN1...169 E3
Curzon Ave RH12...36 B3
Curzon Cl BN13...185 F7
Curzon Ct RH19...155 A1
Cutfield Cl PO19...176 F3
Cuthbert Rd BN2...192 C5
Cuttinglye La RH10......8 C1
Cuttinglye Rd RH10......8 D2
Cygnets The BN43...188 F8
Cygnet Wlk PO22...201 B6
Cylinders The GU27...49 B5
Cymens Ora PO20...209 D8
Cypress Ave BN13...185 C6
Cypress Cl 12 BN43...166 F1
Cypress Pl BN14...186 A6
Cypress Rd PO22...200 D1
Cypress Mews RH15...109 B3
Cyprus Rd RH15...109 A3
Cyril Richings Bsns Ctr
BN43......189 B7

D

Dacre Gdns BN44...166 B7
Dagbrook La BN6...125 E3
Dagmar St BN11...186 B3
Dairy Farm BN2...185 A4
Dairyfields RH11...18 A5
Dairy La
Maudlin PO18...155 F1
Walberton BN18...158 D1
Diascroft The BN5...125 F4
Dakin Cl RH10......19 C2
Dakins The RH19...22 E8
Dale Ave
Brighton BN1......169 F5
Keymer BN6...129 A3
Dale Cl PO12......36 F5
Dale Copse GU27...49 B6

Dale Cres BN3...169 F6
Dale Ct PO21...201 B3
Daledene RH19...22 F8
Dale Dr BN1...170 A6
Dale Hill BN45...149 A6
Dale Rd
Forest Row RH18...23 F1
Worthing BN11...187 B4
Dale View
Haslemere GU27...26 F5
Hove BN3......168 D2
Dale View Gdns BN3...168 D2
Dalewood Gdns
Burgess Hill RH15...109 C2
Crawley RH10......18 F8
Dallaway Gdns RH19...9 E1
Dallaway Rd PO19...177 A4
Dalley Way GU33...45 B4
Dallington Rd BN3...190 F8
Dalloway Rd BN18...159 F1
Dalton Cl RH11...18 B1
Daltons Pl BN18...160 A2
Damer's Bridge GU28...97 F8
Dame School Ct
PO18......155 A5
Damian Way BN6...129 B4
Dampier Wlk RH11...18 B1
Danbury Ct PO10...151 C2
Danby Ct RH6......2 B5
Dane Acre BN16...184 A5
Danefield Rd PO20...212 C6
Danehill CE Prim Sch
RH17......66 B4
Danehill La RH17...65 E5
Danehill Rd BN2...192 F5
Daniel Cl BN15...187 F7
Daniels Ho 2 RH10...19 B7
Dankton Gdns BN15...187 B7
Dankton La BN15...187 B7
Danley La GU27......26 A3
Danny Sheldon Ho 14
BN2......192 C4
Danworth Farm BN6...108 A1
Danworth La BN6...108 B2
Dapper's La BN16...184 A7
Darcey Dr BN1...170 A6
Darenth Way RH6......1 F6
Dark La PO21......200 F1
Darleydale RH11......18 C3
Darlington Cl BN16...184 A5
Darlingtons The
BN16......205 E7
Darlington Wlk BN16...205 E7
Dart Cl BN13......185 D9
Dart Ct RH19......10 A3
Dartmouth Cl BN2...170 F1
Dartmouth Cres BN2...170 F1
Darwin Cl RH12......36 F4
D'aubigny Rd BN2...192 B8
Daux Ave RH14......79 D6
Daux Rd RH14......79 D6
Daux Way RH14......79 D6
Dauxwood Cl RH14...79 D7
Davenport Cl 3 BN11...185 F3
Davenport Rd PO22...202 B4
Davey Dr BN1......170 B1
Davids Cl PO21...200 F5
Davies Ct 12 BN11...186 A1
Davigdor Inf Sch BN3...191 D6
Davigdor Rd BN3...191 E7
Davison CE High Sch for
Girls BN11......186 F4
Davits Dr BN17...205 A6
Davys Ct PO18...153 A5
Dawes Ave BN11...186 F3
Dawes Cl BN11...186 F3
Dawlish Cl BN2...170 F1
Dawn Cl BN44...146 A1
Dawn Cres BN44...146 A1
Dawn Rise RH10......8 C1
Dawson Ct 8 BN11...186 C3
Dawson Terr BN2...192 C6
Dawtrey Rd GU28...97 F7
Daynes Way RH15...108 E1
Days La PO18......157 F3
Deacons Dr BN41...168 C2
Deacons Mead BN44...146 B2
Deacon Trad Est
BN14......186 F5
Deacon Way BN14...186 F5
Deak's La RH17...86 B4
Dean Cl
Littlehampton BN17...204 C7
Portslade-by-S BN41...168 C2
Dean Court Rd BN2...194 A2
Deane Ct 7 PO21...201 C4
Deanery Cl PO19...176 F6
Deanery Farm La
PO19......176 F6
Dean Gdns BN41...168 C2
Dean La
Finchdean PO8, PO9...130 F5
Gumber Rd GU28......75 A1
Deanland Rd RH17...41 A1
DEANLANE END...131 A5
Deans Cl
Brighton BN1......169 F5
Woodingdean BN2...193 E8
Dean St BN1......191 E5
Deanway BN3...169 B3

Dean Way RH20 .....121 C2
De Braose Way BN44 ....145 E2
Deco Bldg The **3**
  BN2 .....170 C1
De Courcel Rd BN2 ...192 E3
Decoy Dr BN16 .....183 F7
Decoy La BN18 .....183 E8
Decoy Rd RH14 .....186 F5
Dedisham Cl RH10 ....19 A5
Deegan Ho **2** PO21 ....201 C3
Deepdale RH6 .....2 B2
Deepdene GU27 .....26 E6
Deepdene Cl PO22 ....203 A5
Deepdene Sch BN3 ...190 D7
Deepfields RH6 .....1 E5
Deer Cl PO19 .....176 E3
Deer Park Cl PO20 ...212 B8
Deer Park Dr PO20 ...212 B8
Deer Park La PO20 ...212 B8
Deer Pk BN5 .....125 E6
Deers Leap RH6 .....87 C1
Deerswood Cl
  Crawley RH11 .....18 B7
  Worthing BN13 .....185 B6
Deerswood Ct RH11 ...18 A7
Deerswood Rd RH11 ...18 B7
Deer Way RH12 .....36 A1
Deeside Ave PO19 ...176 B7
Deeside The BN1 .....170 A7
Defiance Pl PO22 ...202 C4
Delancey Ct RH12 ....36 C4
De La Warr Rd RH19 ....9 F1
Delfont Cl RH10 .....19 D4
Delfryn BN41 .....167 F3
Delius Gdns RH12 ....37 B4
Dell Cl GU27 .....27 A7
Dell Dr BN16 .....205 F8
Delling Cl PO18 .....175 B6
Delling La PO18 .....175 C6
Dellney Ave RH16 ....87 F3
Dell Quay Rd PO20 ...176 B2
Dell The
  Bognor Regis PO22 ...201 A6
  East Grinstead RH19 ...10 B1
  Haywards Heath RH16 ...87 C5
  Horley RH6 .....2 B4
  Sidlow RH6 .....1 C5
Delrogue Rd RH11 .....5 A1
Delta Bglws RH6 .....2 A1
Delta Dr RH6 .....2 A1
Delta Ho RH6 .....2 A1
De Montfort Rd BN2 ...192 C7
Dempsey Rd **3** PO19 ...155 A2
Dempsey Wlk RH11 ...18 A8
Den Ave PO21 .....201 D3
Denbigh Rd GU27 ....27 D5
Dencher Rd BN7 .....172 E3
Denchers Plat RH11 ....5 D1
Dene Cl
  Haslemere GU27 .....27 C6
  Horley RH6 .....1 E5
Denecroft BN1 .....169 D5
Dene Ct BN11 .....186 B2
Dene Hospl The BN6 ...108 B5
Deneside BN1 .....169 D5
Dene The
  Hove BN3 .....168 D3
  Southwater RH13 .....58 A2
Dene Tye RH10 .....19 D7
Dene Vale BN1 .....169 D5
Deneway The
  Brighton BN1 .....169 D4
  Lancing BN15 .....187 C6
Denge La PO10 .....156 F7
Denham Cl PO22 .....202 E5
Denham Ct RH15 .....108 D3
Denham Rd RH15 .....108 D3
Denison Ct **3** PO19 ...176 F7
Denmans RH10 .....19 D7
Denman's Cl RH16 ....88 A8
Denmans Gdns*
  BN18 .....157 F3
Denmans La BN18,
  PO20 .....157 E2
Denman's La RH16 ....88 A7
Denmark Mews BN3 ...191 B7
Denmark Rd BN41 ...190 C7
Denmark Terr BN1 ...191 C6
Denmark Villas BN3 ...191 B7
Denne Par RH12, RH13 ...36 C1
Denne Pl RH12 .....36 C1
Denne Rd
  Crawley RH11 .....18 D5
  Horsham RH12 .....36 C1
Dennis Ct RH20 .....100 C2
Dennis Hobden Cl
  BN2 .....170 E1
Dennis Way GU33 ....45 C3
Denny's Cl PO22 .....212 E7
Denshare Rd PO20 ...212 E8
Denshire Dr RH20 ...121 E2
Denshiale PO21 .....201 A3
Denton Cl BN12 .....185 B4
Denton Dr BN1 .....170 A6
Denvale Trad Pk RH10 ...18 E5
Departures Rd RH6 .....5 F8
Depot Rd
  Crawley RH11 .....5 D1
  Horsham RH13 .....36 C1
Derby Ct **2** BN3 .....191 E7
Derby Pl **2** BN2 .....213 C2
Derby Rd GU27 .....27 B7
Derek Ave BN3 .....190 D6
Derek Ho BN3 .....190 F6

Derek Rd BN15 .....187 E8
Dervia Ho BN3 .....191 C7
Derwent Cl
  Crawley RH11 .....17 F5
  Horsham RH12 .....37 B6
  Lancing BN15 .....187 C5
  Littlehampton BN17 ...205 A7
Derwent Ct BN1 .....213 A3
Derwent Dr BN12,
  BN13 .....185 D6
Derwent Gr PO22 ...202 B6
Desmond Anderson Prim
  Sch RH10 .....18 D2
Desmond Way BN2 ...192 F6
Detling Rd RH11 .....18 C1
Devil's Dyke* BN1 ...148 C3
Devil's Dyke Rd BN1 ...168 E7
Devils La GU30 .....25 E3
Devon Ct **3** BN2 ...204 D5
Devonian Ct BN2 ...213 C4
Devonport Pl BN11 ...187 A3
Devonport Rd BN11 ...187 A2
Devonshire Ct **1**
  BN3 .....191 C7
Devonshire Lo BN11 ...185 F3
Devonshire Pl
  3 Bognor Regis
  PO21 .....201 C3
  Brighton BN2 .....213 C2
Devonshire Rd
  Bognor Regis PO21 ...201 C3
  Horsham RH13 .....36 D2
Devon Villas RH16 ....87 F4
Dew Cl **2** RH11 .....17 E5
Dew Rd BN2 .....213 C4
Dew Pond Cl RH13 ....36 F3
Dexter Dr RH19 .....22 E8
Dharma Sch The BN1 ...170 A6
Dial Cl PO22 .....180 C5
DIAL GREEN 50 B3
Diamond Cotts RH17 ....85 B1
Diana Cl PO10 .....151 A4
Dickens Cl RH19 .....9 C1
Dickens La GU31 .....68 C5
Dickens Rd RH10 .....18 E3
Dickinson Pl PO22 ...201 D6
Dickins Way RH13 ....58 F8
DIDLING 93 B2
Diggers The BN1 .....170 B3
Dinapore Ho **11** BN2 ...213 C3
Dingemans BN44 ....145 D5
Dingle Cl RH11 .....18 B7
Dingle The RH11 .....18 B6
Dingley Rd BN16 .....205 C5
Dinsdale Gdns BN16 ...205 C6
Dione Wlk RH11 .....17 E4
Dirty La RH19 .....23 E7
Discovery Mews RH10 ...7 C4
Discovery Ph RH10 .....6 A2
Ditcham Park Sch
  GU31 .....110 B8
Ditchfield Cl PO22 ...202 D6
Ditchling Beacon Nature
  Reserve* BN1 .....150 D7
Ditchling Bostall BN6 ...150 D7
Ditchling Cl BN12 ...185 B5
Ditchling Common Ctry
  Pk* BN6 .....109 F1
Ditchling Cres BN1 ...170 C5
Ditchling Ct **4** BN1 ...192 B8
Ditchling Gdns BN1 ...170 B1
Ditchling Hill RH11 ...18 C4
Ditchling Mus* BN6 ...129 C3
Ditchling Pl **1** BN1 ...170 A1
Ditchling Rd
  Brighton BN1, BN2 ...170 B4
  Westmeston BN1, BN6 ...150 D4
Ditchling Rise BN1 ...192 A8
Ditchling St Margaret's CE
  Prim Sch BN6 .....129 D3
Dobbins Pl RH11 .....17 E5
Dobson Rd RH11 .....5 D1
Dodsley Gr GU29 ....72 F2
Dodsley La GU29 .....73 A2
Dog Kennels GU28 ...117 B3
Dog La BN44 .....145 D3
Doity Terr RH6 .....4 E6
Dollis Cl RH10 .....19 C5
Dolphin Cl
  Fishbourne PO19 ...176 B6
  Haslemere GU27 .....26 E6
Dolphin Ct
  3 Bognor Regis
  PO21 .....201 C2
  5 Hove BN3 .....191 A6
  Rustington BN16 .....205 D4
  Worthing BN13 .....186 A3
Dolphin Ind Est BN43 ...189 B7
Dolphin Mews
  Brighton BN2 .....213 B1
  Chichester PO19 ...176 D6
  Shoreham-by-S BN43. ...189 A7
Dolphin Rd
  Haywards Heath RH16 ...87 D4
  Shoreham-by-S BN43 ...189 B7
Dolphin Way
  Rustington BN16 .....205 D4
  Shoreham-by-S BN43 ...189 B7
Domehouse Cl PO20 ...212 E5
Dominion Bldgs BN14 ...186 F4
Dominion Cl BN14 ...186 E5
Dominion Rd BN14 ...186 E5
Dominion Way
  Rustington BN16 .....205 C7
  Worthing BN14 .....186 F5

Dominion Way W
  BN14 .....186 F5
Donald Hall Rd BN2 ...192 D5
Donaldson Cl PO20 ...212 C8
Doncaster Wlk **1**
  RH10 .....19 A4
Donegal Rd PO19 ...154 F1
Donkey La RH6 .....6 D7
Donkey Mews **4** BN3 ...191 D5
Donne Cl RH10 .....19 B8
DONNINGTON 176 E1
Donnington Ct **2**
  RH11 .....17 F3
Donnington Pk PO20. ...176 D3
Donnington Pl **2**
  BN16 .....205 C6
Donnington Rd BN2 ...193 E6
Doomsday Gdn RH13 ...37 A1
Doomsday La RH13 ....59 A8
Doone End **3** BN12 ...206 F4
Dorchester Ct **2** BN1 ...191 E5
Dorchester Gdns
  BN11 .....186 A2
Dorking Rd
  Kingsfold RH12, RH5 ...15 B4
  Warnham RH12 .....36 B6
Dormans RH11 .....18 A5
Dormans Cl RH7 .....10 A8
Dormans Gdns RH19 ....9 E6
Dormans High St RH7 ...10 A8
Dormans Park Rd
  Dormans Park RH19 ....9 E6
  East Grinstead RH19 ....9 D3
Dormans Sta RH7 .....9 F8
Dormans Station Rd
  RH7 .....9 F7
Dorothy Rd BN3 .....190 D8
Dorothy Stringer High Sch
  BN1 .....169 F3
Dorset Ave RH19 .....9 C3
Dorset Cl BN17 .....204 E5
Dorset Ct
  3 Horsham RH12 .....36 D2
  Hove BN3 .....190 F6
Dorset Gdns
  Brighton BN2 .....213 C2
  East Grinstead RH19 ....9 C3
Dorset Ho RH13 .....80 D2
Dorset House Sch
  RH20 .....140 B7
Dorset Lo BN15 .....187 E7
Dorset Mews
  Brighton BN2 .....213 B2
  East Grinstead RH19 ....9 C3
Dorset Pl
  Brighton BN2 .....213 C2
  5 Worthing BN14 ...186 A5
Dorset Rd PO21 .....201 C5
Dorset St BN2 .....213 B2
Dorsten Sq RH11 .....17 F3
Doubledays RH15 ...109 B2
Douglas Ave BN11 ...185 F3
Douglas Cl
  4 Middleton-on-S
  PO22 .....202 F5
  Worthing BN11 .....185 F3
  Yapton BN18 .....181 B2
Douglas Martin Rd
  PO19 .....177 B7
Dove Cl RH11 .....18 D8
Dovecote Mews
  Lancing BN15 .....187 C8
  14 Shoreham-by-S
  BN43 .....166 F1
Dove Ct PO22 .....201 B5
Dovedale Cres RH11 ...18 A4
Doveleys Cl BN43 ...188 F6
Dover Cl RH13 .....57 F2
Dovercourt PO22 ...201 A6
Dover La BN16, BN18 ...183 E8
Dover Rd
  Brighton BN1 .....170 A2
  Worthing BN11 .....186 A1
Dower Cl BN2 .....193 D3
Dower Wlk RH11 .....18 A5
Dowlands La RH10, RH6 ...7 D7
Downash Cl BN2 .....192 E6
Down Cl GU28 .....115 C8
Down Cotts PO18 ...132 A8
Downe Cl RH6 .....1 E5
Downes Ct **9** BN43 ...189 C8
Downe Wlk BN13 ...185 D6
Downey Lo RH11 .....18 E4
Downford **18** BN2 ...192 F5
Downhill View BN2 ...193 E7
Downing Cl PO21 ...200 E4
Downland Ave BN42 ...167 E1
Downland Cl
  Findon BN14 .....163 E6
  Southwick BN42 .....167 D1
  Upper Beeding BN44 ...146 B2
  Woodingdean BN2 ...193 B8
Downland Dr
  Crawley RH11 .....18 C3
  Hove BN3 .....189 B3 — Downland Pl RH11 ...18 C4
Downland Rd
  Upper Beeding BN44 ...146 B2
  Woodingdean BN2 ...193 B8
Downlands
  Cootham RH20 .....121 B1

Downlands continued
  Partridge Green RH13 ...104 F3
Pulborough RH20 .....100 D2
Worthing BN13 .....163 E2
Downlands Ave BN14 ...186 D6
Downlands Bsns Pk
  BN14 .....186 E8
Downlands Cl
  Bognor Regis PO21 ...200 A2
  Lancing BN15 .....187 C7
Downlands Com Sch
  BN6 .....128 F3
Downlands Gdns
  BN14 .....186 E7
Downlands Par BN14 ...186 E7
Downlands Ret Ctr
  BN14 .....186 E7
Downsbrook Mid Sch
  BN14 .....186 E5
Downsbrook Trad Est
  BN14 .....186 E6
Downs Cl BN15 .....188 B6
Downscroft
  Burgess Hill RH15 ...109 D6
  Upper Beeding BN44 ...146 B1
Downside
  Brighton BN1 .....169 D5
  Hove BN3 .....169 B3
  Shoreham-by-S BN43 ...167 A1
Downside Ave BN14 ...163 F3
Downside Cl
  Shoreham-by-S BN43 ...166 F1
  Worthing BN14 .....163 F3
Downside Ct **6** BN16 ...205 B3
Downs Jun Sch BN1 ...192 B8
Downs Jun Sch BN1 ...170 A1
Downs Mead BN15 .....187 C8
Downs Park Sch
  BN41 .....168 B2
Downs Rd
  Burgess Hill RH15 ...108 E4
  West Stoke PO18 .....153 D6
Downs St PO18 .....153 B3
Downs Valley Rd BN2 ...193 E8
Downsview
  Brighton BN1 .....169 E1
  Hove BN3 .....168 D3
  Hurstpierpoint BN6 ...128 A5
  Small Dole BN5 .....146 F7
Downsview Ave
  Storrington RH20 .....121 E2
  Woodingdean BN2 .....193 C8
Downsview Cotts RH14 ...79 C8
Downsview Dr GU29 ...94 E5
Downsview Rd
  Horsham RH12 .....37 B6
  Kingston Gorse BN16 ...206 D4
  Portslade-by-S BN41 ...168 A2
Downs View Specl Sch
  BN1 .....192 A8
Downsview Terr BN5 ...125 D5
Downsway
  Shoreham-by-S BN43 ...166 F1
  Southwick BN42 .....167 F1
  Woodingdean BN2 .....171 D1
Downs Way BN16 .....205 F7
Down Terr BN2 .....192 C6
Down The BN3 .....168 D4
Downview Ave BN12 ...206 E7
Downview Cl
  East Wittering PO20 ...208 A6
  Mid Lavant PO18 .....154 E6
  Yapton BN18 .....181 A3
Downview Ct **8**
  BN11 .....186 A1
Downview Manor
  BN14 .....186 C6
Downview Prim Sch
  PO22 .....201 F6
Downview Rd
  Barnham PO22 .....180 A7
  Bognor Regis PO22 ...202 A5
  Ferring BN12 .....206 E7
  Findon BN14 .....163 E7
  Petworth GU28 .....97 E7
  Worthing BN11 .....186 A1
  Yapton BN18 .....181 A3
Downview Way BN18 ...181 A3
Doyle Ct GU27 .....27 A6
Dragons Green Council
  Cotts RH13 .....81 C5
Dragons Green Rd
  RH13 .....81 C5
Dragons La
  Dragons Green RH13 ...81 C5
  Partridge Green RH13 ...105 E7
Dragon St GU31, GU32 ...68 B3
Drake Ave PO18 .....185 D5
Drake Cl RH12 .....36 E6
Drake Gr BN18 .....181 B2
Drakeleys Field GU30 ...4 F2
Drake Pk PO22 .....202 C5
Drake Rd
  Crawley RH10 .....18 D5
  Horley RH6 .....1 E3
Drakes Cl BN15 .....188 B6
Draxmont Way BN1 ...169 F3
Draycliff Cl PO22 ...206 E5
Drayman's Mews
  PO19 .....177 B6
DRAYTON 180 A5
Drayton La PO20 .....178 A5
Drayton Pk PO22 .....178 A3
Drewetts Cl **1** BN14 ...205 B7
Drewitts Mews PO20 ...178 C7

Drift La
  Nutbourne PO18 .....174 E8
  Selsey PO20 .....212 C7
Drift Rd
  Bognor Regis PO21 ...200 B2
  Selsey PO20 .....212 G8
Drift The PO9 .....130 D1
Driftway The
  Littlehampton BN16 ...205 B7
  Upper Beeding BN44 ...146 B3
Drive Lo **10** BN3 .....191 C7
Drive Sch The
  BN3 .....191 C8
Drive The
  Bognor Regis PO21 ...200 D1
  Bosham PO18 .....175 C4
  Burgess Hill RH15 ...109 B4
  Chichester PO19 .....155 A3
  Ferring BN12 .....7 C3
  East Lavington GU28 ...116 E5
  Fontwell PO20 .....158 A1
  Horley RH6 .....2 B1
  Hove BN3 .....191 C7
  Ifold RH14 .....31 D2
  Lancing BN15 .....187 D4
  Shoreham-by-S BN43 ...166 F1
  Southbourne PO10 ...173 F8
  Southwick BN42 .....167 E1
  Westhampnett PO18 ...155 E2
  West Kingston BN16 ...206 B4
  Worthing BN11 .....185 F4
Driveway The BN43 ...166 F1
DROKE 137 B6
Droke La PO18 .....136 E6
Dropping Holms BN5 ...125 D4
Drove Ave BN2 .....171 D2
Drove Cres BN41 .....168 A2
Drove La
  Earnley PO20 .....208 D5
  Yapton BN18 .....180 D2
Drove Rd
  Portslade-by-S BN41 ...168 A1
  Woodingdean BN2 .....193 B8
Drovers RH17 .....85 C3
Drovers Cl BN41 .....168 C2
Drovers Way RH15 ...109 C1
Drove The
  Brighton BN1 .....169 D1
  Falmer BN1 .....171 C1
Droveway The
  Haywards Heath RH16 ...87 C6
  Hove BN3 .....169 B1
  Hove BN3 .....169 C1
Drum La GU32 .....68 B3
Drum Mead GU32 .....68 A3
Drummond Cl RH16 ...87 D4
Drummond Ct
  7 Littlehampton BN17 ...204 D5
Drummond Rd
  Crawley RH11 .....17 E5
  Worthing BN12 .....185 E2
Drungewick La RH14 ...32 D2
Drury Cl RH10 .....19 D4
Drury Lo **9** RH11 .....9 F2
Dryad Way PO22 .....202 D4
Dryden Way GU30 .....25 A5
Drygrounds La PO22 ...201 F5
Duck La
  Midhurst GU29 .....94 F7
  Selsey PO20 .....212 B8
Duckmead La GU32 ...45 D5
Duckyls Cotts RH19 ...42 D7
Dudeney Lo RH11 .....18 E4
Dudley Mews **16** BN3 ...191 D5
Dudley Rd BN1 .....170 B1
Dudley Terr GU33 .....45 C5
Dudwell Rd BN2 .....193 E7
Duffield La PO10 .....152 A3
Duke Cl RH10 .....19 C2
Dukes Barn Ct RH16 ...88 B7
Dukes Cl
  Arundel BN18 .....159 F2
  Petersfield GU32 .....67 F4
Dukes Ct
  Chichester PO19 .....177 D5
  12 Littlehampton BN17 ...204 D5
Duke's Hill RH20 .....122 A8
Dukes La
  Brighton BN1 .....213 A2
  Steyning BN44 .....145 D3
Dukes Mdw
  Bognor Regis PO21 ...200 B3
  Funtington PO18 .....152 F5
Duke's Mound BN2 ...192 D4
Dukes Rd RH16 .....88 B8
Duke's Rd
  Fontwell BN18 .....157 F4
  Newdigate RH5 .....3 D6
Dukes Row RH20 .....121 A2
Dukes Sq RH12 .....36 C1
Duke St
  Brighton BN1 .....213 A2
  Littlehampton BN17 ...204 D5
Dukes Yd BN44 .....145 D3
Dulcima Ho **13** RH12 ...36 C1
Dumbrells Court Rd
  BN6 .....129 D4
Dumbrells Ct BN6 ...129 D4
Dumbrells Ct RH15 ...109 A5
Dunbar Hill GU31 .....92 D8
Duncan Rd PO19 .....176 F8
Duncton CE Fst Sch
  GU28 .....117 B7
Duncton Cl
  Bognor Regis PO22 ...202 B4

Duncton Cl continued
Crawley RH11 . . . . .18 B8
Haywards Heath RH16 . . .87 D4
Duncton High St
GU28 . . . . .117 B6
Duncton Ho BN6 . . . . . . .128 E4
Duncton Rd BN16 . . . . . .205 C6
Dunes The PO21 . . . . . . .211 C8
Dunford Hollow GU29 . .94 F4
Dunhurst (Bedales Jun
Sch) GU32 . . . . .68 A6
Dunlop Cl BN6 . . . . .107 D1
Dunning's Rd RH19 . . . . .22 E7
Dunnock Cl PO9 . . . . . . .130 D1
Dunsfold Cl RH11 . . . . . .18 A5
Dunsfold Rd GU8, RH14 .30 C4
Dunstall Ave RH15 . . . .108 E4
Dunstall Farm Rd
RH15 . . . . .108 F4
Dunstan Cl PO19 . . . . . .155 A3
Dunster Cl BN1 . . . . . . .170 B1
Dunwich ⑦ BN43 . . . . . .189 B6
Durban Pk PO22 . . . . . .201 D5
Durban Rd PO22 . . . . . .201 D6
Durbans Rd RH14 . . . . . .54 C2
Durfold Rd RH12 . . . . . . .36 D7
Durfold Wood RH14 . . . .30 D5
Durfold Wood Woodlands
Wlks* GU8 . . . . .30 C6
Durford Rd GU31 . . . . . .68 E3
Durham Cl
Bognor Regis PO21 . . . .211 A8
Brighton BN2 . . . . .171 A1
Crawley RH10 . . . . .18 E2
Durham Ct ④ BN3 . . . . .191 B6
Durham Gdns PO19 . . . .154 F1
Durkins Rd RH19 . . . . . . .9 D3
Durlston Dr PO22 . . . . . .201 B6
Durlston Par PO22 . . . . .201 B6
Durnford Ct PO19 . . . . . .176 E7
DURRINGTON 185 E8
Durrington Ct
Brighton BN1 . . . . .169 C5
Worthing BN13 . . . . .185 E8
Durrington Fst Sch
BN13 . . . . .185 E8
Durrington Gdns
BN12 . . . . .185 D4
Durrington High Sch
BN13 . . . . .185 E6
Durrington Hill BN13 . . .185 D7
Durrington La BN13 . . . .185 D7
Durrington Mid Sch
BN13 . . . . .185 E8
Durrington-on-Sea Sta
BN12 . . . . .185 C5
Dutchells Copse RH12 . .36 E7
Duxford Cl PO20 . . . . . .156 C2
Duxhurst La RH2 . . . . . . .1 B7
Dyall Cl RH15 . . . . .108 E4
Dye House La GU28 . . . .117 C7
Dyers Almshouses
RH10 . . . . .18 D7
Dyers La BN18 . . . . . . .158 C5
Dyke Cl
Hove BN3 . . . . .169 B4
Poynings BN45 . . . . .148 C4
Dyke Rd BN1, BN3 . . . .191 E7
Dyke Road Ave BN1,
BN3 . . . . .169 C3
Dyke Road Dr BN1 . . . .191 F8
Dyke Road Mews
BN1 . . . . .213 A4
Dyke Road Pl BN1 . . . . .169 C3
Dymock's The BN6 . . . .129 D3
Dymoke St PO10 . . . . . .151 A4
Dyson Wlk RH11 . . . . . . .18 B1

E

Eady Cl RH13 . . . . .36 F2
Eagle Ct ⑮ BN2 . . . . . .192 C8
Eagle Est RH14 . . . . .79 D7
Eagle Ho PO21 . . . . .201 B2
Eagles Chase BN17 . . . .204 D8
Earle Ho ② RH19 . . . . . . .9 F2
Earles Mdw RH12 . . . . . .37 B6
Earlswood Cl RH13 . . . . .37 A4
Early Commons RH14 . . .18 F7
Earnley Gdns* PO20 . . .208 E7
Earnley Manor Cl
PO20 . . . . .208 D7
Earnley Rd PO22 . . . . . .206 D8
Eartham Trail* PO18 . .137 D2
Earwig La RH17 . . . . .84 E6
EASEBOURNE 73 B2
Easebourne CE Prim Sch
GU29 . . . . .73 B2
Easebourne La GU29 . . .73 A1
Easebourne St GU29,
GU29 . . . . .73 D5
East Ave
Middleton-on-S PO22 . . .202 F6
Worthing BN12 . . . . .185 F2
Eastbank BN42 . . . . .167 F1
East Bank
Selsey PO20 . . . . .212 F7
Yapton BN18 . . . . .181 A5
East Bank Wlk ②
BN17 . . . . .205 A4
EAST BEACH 212 F8
East Beach Rd PO20 . . .212 G8
Eastbourne Rd
Brighton BN2 . . . . .170 D1
Felbridge RH7 . . . . .8 E8
East Bracklesham Dr
PO20 . . . . .208 B5

Eastbrook Rd BN41 . . . .190 B7
Eastbrook Way BN42 . . .190 A7
East Cl PO22 . . . . .202 C5
Eastcourt Rd RH14 . . . . .36 C1
Eastcourt Villas ③ RH19 .9 F2
East Court Way RH15 . . .205 E6
Eastcroft Mews ②
RH12 . . . . .35 F1
East Ct BN14 . . . . .186 D5
Eastdale Rd RH15 . . . . . .109 D4
East Dean ① PO22 . . . .201 D5
Eastdean Hill PO18 . . . .136 C5
East Dr
Angmering BN16 . . . . . .205 E7
Brighton BN2 . . . . .192 C5
Middleton-on-S PO22 . . .203 A5
Easteds La RH13 . . . . . . .58 A2
EAST END 129 E3
East End La BN6 . . . . . .129 C3
Eastergate CE Prim Sch
PO20 . . . . .179 E7
Eastergate La ⑫ PO22 .206 F7
Eastergate Gn ⑧
BN16 . . . . .205 C5
Eastergate La BN18,
PO20 . . . . .158 B1
Eastergate Rd BN2 . . . .170 F4
Eastern Ave BN43 . . . . .189 A7
Eastern Cl
East Preston BN16 . . . . .206 B6
Shoreham-by-S BN43 . . .189 A7
Eastern Concourse
BN2 . . . . .193 A2
Eastern Cotts RH16 . . . .88 B7
Eastern Ring Rd BN2 . . .192 E4
Eastern Rd
Brighton BN2 . . . . .192 D4
Haywards Heath RH16 . .87 F3
Lindfield RH16 . . . . .88 C7
Eastern St BN2 . . . . .192 D4
Eastern Terr
⑩ Brighton BN2 . . . . . .192 D4
Henfield BN5 . . . . .129 F5
Eastern Terrace Mews ⑨
BN2 . . . . .192 D4
East Field Ct PO10 . . . . .152 A1
Eastfield Cres BN1 . . . . .170 A4
Eastfield Ho ④ BN1 . . . .186 F2
Eastfield La GU31 . . . . . .92 A4
East Front Rd PO21 . . . .211 A7
Eastgate Ct PO19 . . . . . .177 B6
Eastgate Ho PO19 . . . . .177 B6
Eastgate Mews ④
RH13 . . . . .36 D1
Eastgate Sq PO19 . . . . .177 A6
East Gdns BN6 . . . . .129 D3
East Grinstead Sta
RH19 . . . . .9 D1
East Grinstead Town
Mus* RH19 . . . . .9 F1
East Gun Copse RH13 . . .57 D5
EAST HAMPNETT 156 E2
Easthampnett Cvn Pk
PO18 . . . . .157 A2
East Hampnett La
PO18 . . . . .156 F2
East Ham Rd BN17 . . . . .204 D5
East Harting St GU31 . . .91 F3
East Hill RH19 . . . . .9 E6
East Hill Ct
Liss GU33 . . . . .45 C3
① Worthing BN11 . . . . . .186 D2
Easthill Dr BN41 . . . . . . .168 B2
East Hill Dr GU33 . . . . . . .45 C3
East Hill La RH10 . . . . . . .7 D5
Easthill Way BN41 . . . . .168 B1
Easting Cl BN14 . . . . . . .186 F5
East Lake PO21 . . . . .201 D4
Eastlake Cl GU31 . . . . . . .68 E3
East Lands PO10 . . . . . .177 B5
Eastleigh Ct BN13 . . . . .185 E8
EAST LISS 45 C4
East Lo
④ Haywards Heath BN15 .187 E4
Rogate GU31 . . . . .70 B4
East Lockside BN2 . . . . .193 A3
East Mascalls La RH16 . .88 E6
East Mead
Bognor Regis PO21 . . . .211 A8
Ferring BN12 . . . . .206 F5
Eastmead Ind Est
PO18 . . . . .154 E7
East Meadway BN43 . . . .189 A6
EAST MOULSECOOMB
Eastoke Ave PO11 . . . . .195 A2
Easton Cres RH14 . . . . . .79 E8
Easton La PO20 . . . . .209 A6
East Onslow Cl BN12 . . .206 E6
Eastover Way PO21 . . . .201 F4
East Pallant PO19 . . . . . .177 A6
East Park La RH7 . . . . . . .8 C8
East Pk RH10 . . . . .18 D5
East Preston Inf Sch
BN16 . . . . .206 A6
East Preston Jun Sch
BN16 . . . . .206 A6
East Row PO19 . . . . .177 A6
East Row Mews ③
BN17 . . . . .177 A6
East St
Amberley BN18 . . . . . . .140 E7
Billingshurst RH14 . . . . .79 D8
Brighton BN1 . . . . .213 B1

East St continued
Chichester PO19 . . . . . .177 A6
Falmer BN1 . . . . .171 C6
Horsham RH12 . . . . .36 C1
Lancing BN15 . . . . .187 E4
Littlehampton BN17 . . . .204 E5
Petworth GU28 . . . . .97 F8
Portslade-by-S BN41 . . .190 C7
Rogate GU31 . . . . .70 B4
Rusper RH12 . . . . .16 C7
Selsey PO20 . . . . .212 E7
Shoreham-by-S BN43 . . .188 F7
Turners Hill RH10, RH19 .21 C4
Westbourne PO10 . . . . . .151 D3
West Chiltington RH20 . .101 E1
East Strand PO20 . . . . . .207 C8
East Tyne BN13 . . . . .185 D7
East View PO18 . . . . .154 F7
East Walls PO19 . . . . . . .177 A6
East Walls Cl ② PO19 . .177 A6
Eastway BN6 . . . . .129 C3
East Way PO20 . . . . .212 F7
Eastway E RH6 . . . . .6 C7
East Wick BN16 . . . . .88 C7
Eastwick Cl BN1 . . . . . . .170 B7
East Wittering Bsns Ctr
PO20 . . . . .208 A8
East Wittering Com Prim
Sch PO20 . . . . .207 F7
Eastwood Ho 18 F6
EAST WORTHING 187 A3
East Worthing Ind Est
BN14 . . . . .186 F5
East Worthing Sta
BN14 . . . . .186 B6
Eaton Ct
Hove BN3 . . . . .191 B7
Worthing BN14 . . . . .186 B6
Eaton Gardens Mans ②
BN3 . . . . .191 C7
Eaton Gate ⑦ BN3 . . . . .191 C7
Eaton Gdns BN3 . . . . . . .191 C7
Eaton Gr BN3 . . . . .191 C7
Eaton Hall ⑱ BN3 . . . . .191 C7
Eaton Manor ① BN3 . . .191 C7
Eaton Pl BN2 . . . . .192 D4
Eaton Rd BN3 . . . . .191 C7
Eaton Villas BN3 . . . . . . .191 B7
Ebbisham Ct RH19 . . . . . .9 A4
Ecclesden ⑦ BN2 . . . . . .213 C3
Edburton Ave BN1 . . . . .170 A4
Edburton Dro BN5 . . . . .147 D6
Edburton Gdns BN43 . . .166 F1
Eddington Hill RH11 . . . .18 B1
Eden Rd RH11 . . . . .17 F4
Eden Vale
Dormans Park RH19 . . . .9 F5
East Grinstead RH19 . . . .9 D4
Edgar Ct RH10 . . . . .19 E5
Edgehill Cl BN13 . . . . . . .185 F8
Edgehill Way RH15 . . . . .167 F2
Edgell Rd PO21 . . . . .151 D4
Edgewood Ct GU33 . . . . .45 D2
Edith Cotts PO18 . . . . . . .153 A2
Edmonds Ho GU28 . . . . .97 F7
Edmonton Rd BN13 . . . .185 D7
Edrich Rd BN1 . . . . .170 B8
Edster Ct BN41 . . . . .167 F3
Edward Ave
Hove BN3 . . . . .169 A3
Saltdean BN2 . . . . .194 D3
Edward Bryant Prim Sch
PO21 . . . . .201 D4
Edward Cl BN3 . . . . .169 A3
Edward Ho
Hove BN3 . . . . .190 F6
Selsey PO20 . . . . .212 E6
Edward Rd RH16 . . . . . . .87 E2
Edwards Ave PO20 . . . . .156 C2
Edward St BN2 . . . . .213 C2
Edwards Terr BN15 . . . .186 F7
Edwards Way RH17 . . . .204 C8
Edward Way RH15 . . . . .108 D2
Edwen Cl PO21 . . . . .200 B3
Edwin Cl BN15 . . . . .187 C6
Eels Cross PO20 . . . . . . .212 B8
Effingham Cl BN2 . . . . . .194 C2
Effingham La RH11 . . . . . .7 E4
Effingham Rd RH10, RH6 .7 E4
Egan Way BN15 . . . . .204 C6
EGDEAN 98 D4
Egerton Cotts RH20 . . . . .98 F5
Egginton Cl BN1 . . . . . . .171 A5
Egginton Rd BN1 . . . . . . .170 F5
Egmont Ho GU29 . . . . . . .73 A1
Egmont Mews GU29 . . . .94 F8
Egmont Rd
Hove BN3 . . . . .168 D1
Midhurst GU29 . . . . .73 A1
Egremont Pl BN2 . . . . . .213 C2
Egremont Row GU28 . . . .97 F8
Eighth Ave BN15 . . . . . .187 E7
Eileen Ave BN2 . . . . .194 B1
Eirene Ave BN12 . . . . . . .194 A1
Eirene Rd BN12 . . . . .185 F2
Elbourne Ho ③ RH6 . . . .2 B3
ELBRIDGE 201 C4
Elbridge Cres PO21 . . . .200 C4
Elcombe Cl PO20 . . . . . .208 C5

Elder Cl BN41 . . . . .168 B2
Elderfield Cl PO10 . . . . . .151 C3
Elder Pl BN1 . . . . .213 B4
Eldon Rd BN11 . . . . .186 F3
Eldon Way BN17 . . . . . . .204 B6
Eldred Ave BN1 . . . . .169 D5
Eleanor Cl GU30 . . . . . . .24 D8
Eleanor Ct ① BN11 . . . .185 F3
Eleanor Gdns PO22 . . . .202 D5
Eley Cres BN2 . . . . .193 E3
Eley Dr BN2 . . . . .193 E3
Elfin Rd PO21 . . . . .201 B3
Elfin Mews ⑧ PO21 . . . .201 B3
Elgar Way RH13 . . . . .37 B4
Elgar Way RH10 . . . . .7 A4
Elgin Cl RH13 . . . . .36 F3
Elgin Ct PO19 . . . . .177 A5
Elgin Rd BN12 . . . . .185 D3
Eliot Ct BN2 . . . . .213 C4
Eliot Dr GU27 . . . . .26 E6
Eliotian Way RH10 . . . . .19 C5
Elizabeth Ave
Bognor Regis PO21 . . . .200 D4
Hove BN3 . . . . .169 A3
Elizabeth Cl
Bognor Regis PO21 . . . .200 C3
Hove BN3 . . . . .169 A3
Elizabeth Cres RH19 . . . .9 F3
Elizabeth Ct
Bognor Regis
PO21 . . . . .201 B2
Horley RH6 . . . . .2 A3
⑦ Hove BN3 . . . . .191 C7
⑥ Worthing BN11 . . . . . .185 F3
Elizabeth Ho
⑪ Bognor Regis
PO21 . . . . .201 D3
Elizabeth Pl BN15 . . . . . .187 C5
Elizabeth Rd
Chichester PO19 . . . . . .177 D7
Shoreham-by-S BN43 . . .189 C8
Worthing BN12 . . . . .186 C2
Elkham Cnr GU28 . . . . . . .52 C1
Ella Cl PO20 . . . . .207 E7
Ellanore La GU31 . . . . . . .92 B2
Ellasdale Rd PO21 . . . . .201 B2
Ella Terr BN18 . . . . .183 C8
Ellen Ho ③ BN3 . . . . . . .191 B7
Ellen St
Hove BN3 . . . . .191 B7
Portslade-by-S BN41 . . .190 C7
Elmesmere Orch PO10 . .151 D5
Elliot Cl RH10 . . . . .19 C4
Ellis Ave BN13 . . . . .163 E1
Ellis Cl BN18 . . . . .159 F2
Ellis Sq PO20 . . . . .212 F8
Ellis Way PO21 . . . . .211 A8
Ellman Rd RH11 . . . . .17 F4
Ellson Cl RH10 . . . . .19 C4
Elm Ave BN16 . . . . .206 B6
Elm Cl
Bognor Regis
PO21 . . . . .201 C2
Brighton BN1 . . . . .170 F6
③ East Grinstead RH19 . .9 D2
East Grinstead, Sunnyside
RH19 . . . . .22 E8
Nepcote BN14 . . . . .163 E5
Portslade-by-S BN41 . . .190 B8
Worthing BN12 . . . . .185 C3
Elm Cotts BN13 . . . . .185 D7
Elm Croft PO10 . . . . .18 E6
Elmcroft Pl PO20 . . . . . .179 D6
Elm Ct
Bognor Regis
PO21 . . . . .201 C2
Brighton BN1 . . . . .187 C3
③ East Grinstead RH19 . .9 D2
East Grinstead, Sunnyside
RH19 . . . . .22 E8
Elm Dale PO22 . . . . .180 A6
Elmdene Ct PO20 . . . . . .208 B5
Elm Dr
East Grinstead RH19 . . . .10 A1
Elmer PO22 . . . . .203 B5
Hove BN3 . . . . .168 E1
Petersfield GU31 . . . . . . .68 A1
Elmer Cl PO22 . . . . .203 B5
Elmer Ct PO22 . . . . .203 C5
Elmer Rd PO22 . . . . .202 F5
Elm Farm Cotts BN16 . .205 B5
Elm Gr
Barnham PO22 . . . . .180 B7
Bognor Regis PO21 . . . .201 A3
Brighton BN2 . . . . .192 C7
Cowfold RH13 . . . . .84 E2
Horsham RH13 . . . . .36 E1
Lancing BN15 . . . . .187 D5
Runcton PO20 . . . . .177 E1
Selsey PO20 . . . . .212 F4
Worthing BN11 . . . . .185 F3
Elm Grove Fst Sch
BN11 . . . . .185 F3
Elm Grove Ho BN15 . . . .187 E5
Elm Grove Inf Sch
BN17 . . . . .204 E6
Elm Grove La GU28 . . . .145 D3
Elm Grove Prim Sch
BN2 . . . . .192 C7
Elm Grove Rd BN17 . . . .204 F6
Elm Gr S PO22 . . . . .180 A6
Elmhurst Cl BN16 . . . . . .184 A6
Elmhurst La RH13 . . . . . .56 C6
Elmleigh GU29 . . . . .94 D8
Elmleigh Ct GU29 . . . . . .94 E8

Elm Mews BN13 . . . . . . .185 D7
Elmore Ct BN2 . . . . .213 C3
Elmore Rd BN2 . . . . .213 C3
Elm Pk
Bosham PO18 . . . . .175 C6
Ferring BN12 . . . . .206 F7
Elm Pl BN16 . . . . .205 D6
Elm Rd
Portslade-by-S BN41 . . .190 B8
Westergate PO20 . . . . . .179 E7
Worthing BN11 . . . . .186 E2
Elm Rise BN14 . . . . .163 E6
Elms Dr BN15 . . . . .187 D6
Elmsfield PO20 . . . . .212 E7
Elms La PO20 . . . . .196 C5
Elms Lea Ave BN1 . . . . .169 E3
Elms Ride PO20 . . . . . . .196 C1
Elmstead RH19 . . . . .22 E8
Elmstead Gdns PO20 . . .196 C2
Elmstead Park Rd
PO20 . . . . .196 C2
Elmstone Cl BN15 . . . . . .187 D6
Elms Way PO20 . . . . . . .196 C2
Elm Terr
Liss GU33 . . . . .45 A5
Steyning BN44 . . . . .145 D3
Elm Tree Cl
Bognor Regis PO21 . . . .201 A6
Worthing BN11 . . . . .212 E8
Elm Tree Cotts PO20 . . .179 D8
Elmwood Ave PO22 . . . .201 D5
Elrington Rd BN3 . . . . . .169 C1
Elsaw Ct PO19 . . . . .177 A5
Elsie Rd BN11 . . . . .186 B1
Elspring Mead BN17 . . .204 C2
Elsted Cl RH11 . . . . .18 B8
Elsted Cors BN1 . . . . . . .170 C6
Elsted Rd GU29 . . . . .93 C7
Elverlands Cl ⑤ BN12 . .206 F4
Elvin Cres BN2 . . . . .193 E4
Elwood Cl RH15 . . . . . . .108 F1
Elwyn Jones Ct BN15 . . .169 E4
Ely Cl
Crawley RH10 . . . . .18 F2
East Wittering PO20 . . . .207 F8
Worthing BN13 . . . . .185 F5
Ely Gdns PO21 . . . . .200 D3
Ely Rd BN13 . . . . .185 F5
Embassy Ct
⑩ Brighton BN1 . . . . . .191 D5
④ Haywards Heath
RH16 . . . . .87 E6
Emberwood RH11 . . . . . .18 D8
Emerald Quay BN43 . . . .189 A6
Emlyn Rd BN6 . . . . .1 E4
Emmabrook Ct BN16 . . .205 A3
Emms La RH13 . . . . .80 F7
Empire Villas RH1 . . . . . .2 A7
Emsbrook Dr PO10 . . . . .151 B2
Emsworth Ho RH10 . . . . .19 C3
Emsworth Common Rd
PO10, PO9 . . . . .151 C6
Emsworth House Cl
PO10 . . . . .151 A1
Emsworth Mus* 173 B8
Emsworth Prim Sch
PO10 . . . . .151 A1
Emsworth Rd PO10 . . . . .173 D2
Emsworth Sta PO10 . . . .151 B1
End Cotts BN18 . . . . .140 E6
Enfield Rd RH11 . . . . .18 C3
Engalee RH19 . . . . .9 C2
Englefield RH12 . . . . .35 F2
English Bsns Pk BN3 . . .190 E8
English Cl BN3 . . . . .190 E8
English Martyrs RC Prim
Sch BN12 . . . . .185 D6
Enmer Ct RH11 . . . . .66 A4
Ennerdale Cl BN11 . . . . .187 B5
Ennerdale Dr BN15 . . . .187 B5
Ensign Way BN17 . . . . . .205 A6
Enterprise Ct
Crawley RH10 . . . . .5 D2
Worthing BN12 . . . . .185 C4
Enterprise Ctr The RH10 .5 F2
Enterprise Pt BN2 . . . . . .132 C7
Enterprise Point BN2 . . .192 D8
Epping Wlk RH10 . . . . . .18 F4
Epsom Gdns PO20 . . . . .205 E6
Epsom Rd RH10 . . . . .19 A4
Erica Way
Copthorne RH10 . . . . . . .7 A2
Horsham RH12 . . . . .36 D5
Ericsson Way RH15 . . . .108 D2
Eridge Ct RH10 . . . . .19 C6
Eridge Rd BN3 . . . . .168 E1
Erin Way RH15 . . . . .108 E3
Eriskay Ct BN13 . . . . . . .185 B7
Eriswell Rd BN11 . . . . . . .186 C1
Erles Rd GU30 . . . . .25 C4
Ernest Cl PO10 . . . . .151 B1
Erringham Rd BN43 . . . .166 E1
Erroll Manor ⑦ BN3 . . . .190 D7
Erroll Rd BN3 . . . . .168 D1
Erskine Cl RH11 . . . . .17 E2
Esher Cl PO21 . . . . .200 B2
Esher Dr BN17 . . . . .204 F5
Eskbank Ave BN1 . . . . . .170 A7
Esmond Cl PO10 . . . . . . .173 B8
Esmonde Cl RH17 . . . . . .204 F6
Esplanade Ct ⑥ BN11 . .186 F2
Esplanade The
Bognor Regis, Felpham
PO22 . . . . .201 F3

Esplanade The continued
Bognor Regis PO21 . . . . . . .201 D2
Worthing BN11 . . . . .186 F2
Essenhigh Dr BN13 . . . . . . .185 B7
Essex Cl BN11 . . . . .186 A2
Essex Pl 3 BN2 . . . . .192 C4
Essex Rd PO21 . . . . .201 C5
Essex St BN2 . . . . .192 C4
Estates Rd BN1 . . . . .171 B7
Estcots Dr RH19 . . . . .10 A1
Estcots Prim Sch RH19 . . . . .10 A1
Estuary The BN17 . . . . .204 F5
Ethelred Rd BN14 . . . . .186 A4
Ethel St BN2 . . . . .191 B7
Ethelwulf Rd BN14 . . . . .186 A4
Eton Cl PO21 . . . . .200 E4
Eton Dr PO20 . . . . .207 F8
Etonhurst 20 PO21 . . . . .201 B2
Eton Rd BN11 . . . . .186 A3
Ettrick Cl PO19 . . . . .177 B5
Ettrick Rd PO19 . . . . .177 B5
Eurythmy Sch RH19 . . . . .22 E6
Evans Cl RH10 . . . . .19 D5
Evans Gdns 15 BN17 . . . . . .204 D5
Evans Pl PO22 . . . . .201 D6
Evelyn Ave BN16 . . . . .205 D4
Evelyn Cl RH19 . . . . .8 F4
Evelyn Clark Ho RH18 . . . . . .23 F2
Evelyn Ct BN41 . . . . .190 A8
Evelyn Glennie Ct 7
BN2 . . . . .192 C5
Evelyn Lancaster Ho
RH12 . . . . .36 E6
Evelyn Rd BN14 . . . . .186 D4
Evelyn Terr BN2 . . . . .192 C5
Evelyn Wlk RH10 . . . . .18 E3
Everest Ho 2 BN3 . . . . .190 F7
Eversfield RH13 . . . . .36 A4
Eversfield Rd RH13 . . . . .36 E1
Evershed Way BN43 . . . . . . .189 B7
Eversleigh Ct GU29 . . . . .73 A2
Ewart St BN2 . . . . .213 C3
Ewelands RH10 . . . . .2 C4
Ewens Gdns PO22 . . . . .180 A7
Ewhurst Cl RH11 . . . . .18 C6
Ewhurst Rd
Brighton BN2 . . . . .170 C1
Crawley RH11 . . . . .18 C7
Excalibur Cl RH11 . . . . .17 E5
Exceat Cl BN2 . . . . .192 E6
Excelsior The BN1 . . . . .169 D4
Exchange Rd RH10 . . . . .18 E6
Exeter Cl
Bognor Regis PO21 . . . . . .200 F3
Crawley RH10 . . . . .18 E2
New Brighton PO10 . . . . . .151 B2
Exeter Ct 2 BN1 . . . . .186 A1
Exeter Rd PO19 . . . . .154 E1
Exeter St BN1 . . . . .191 E8
Exford Wlk BN13 . . . . .185 D6
Exmoor Cl BN13 . . . . .185 E8
Exmoor Cres BN13 . . . . .185 E8
Exmoor Ct BN13 . . . . .185 E8
Exmoor Dr BN13 . . . . .185 E8
Exton Rd PO19 . . . . .177 A4
Eyles Cl BN7 . . . . .36 B4

F

Fabians Way BN5 . . . . .125 D5
Fairbank Rd RH13 . . . . .57 F1
Fairbanks RH16 . . . . .87 E4
Fairbridge Way RH15 . . . . . .108 F5
Faircox La BN5 . . . . .125 D5
Fairdene BN42 . . . . .167 F1
Fairfield Ave RH6 . . . . .2 A1
Fairfield Cl
Ardingly RH17 . . . . .64 A8
Bosham PO18 . . . . .175 C6
Burgess Hill RH15 . . . . . . .108 F4
New Brighton PO10 . . . . . .151 B2
Shoreham-by-S BN43 . . . . .167 C1
Fairfield Cotts RH13 . . . . . . .83 E2
Fairfield Cres BN16 . . . . . . .128 A6
Fairfield Ct RH13 . . . . .83 E2
Fairfield Gdns
Burgess Hill RH15 . . . . . . .108 F4
Portslade-by-S BN41 . . . . .168 B3
Fairfield Rd
Ashington RH20 . . . . .123 A4
Bosham PO18 . . . . .175 B5
Burgess Hill RH15 . . . . . . .108 F4
East Grinstead RH19 . . . . . .22 F8
Fairfield Rise GU28 . . . . .97 F7
Fairfields
2 Worthing BN14 . . . . . . .186 D4
Worthing, West Tarring
BN14 . . . . .186 A5
Fairfield Way
Ashington RH20 . . . . .123 A4
Haywards Heath RH16 . . . . .87 D8
Fairford Cl RH16 . . . . .87 E5
Fairholme Dr BN18 . . . . .181 A2
Fairlands
Bognor Regis PO22 . . . . . .201 B6
East Preston BN16 . . . . . . .206 A5
8 Lancing BN15 . . . . .187 D5
Fairlawn
1 Haywards Heath
RH16 . . . . .87 E4
Rustington BN16 . . . . .205 C4
Fairlawn Cres RH19 . . . . .9 B2
Fairlawn Dr
East Grinstead RH19 . . . . . . .9 B2
Worthing BN14 . . . . .186 D4
Fairlawn Ho RH10 . . . . .19 A6
Fairlawns
Horley RH6 . . . . .2 B2
9 Hove BN3 . . . . .191 A6
Shoreham-by-S BN43 . . . . .189 A8
Fairlea Cl RH15 . . . . .108 F4
Fairlead BN17 . . . . .204 F4
Fairlea Rd PO10 . . . . .151 B3
Fairlie Gdns BN1 . . . . .169 E3
Fairlight Cl BN17 . . . . .204 D4
Fairlight Pl 8 BN2 . . . . . . .192 C8
Fairlight Prim Sch
BN2 . . . . .192 C8
Fairmile Bottom
BN18 . . . . .159 B7
Fairmile Bottom Nature
Trail* BN18 . . . . .159 C8
Fairoak Ct 4 BN13 . . . . . . .186 A5
Fairstone Ct RH6 . . . . .2 B4
Fair View RH12 . . . . .36 A3
Fairview Ave BN12 . . . . .185 C2
Fairview Cotts BN13 . . . . . . .58 B3
Fairview Ct 15 RH19 . . . . . .22 F8
Fairview Gdns BN15 . . . . . . .187 E8
Fairview Rd BN15 . . . . .187 E8
Fairview Rise BN1 . . . . .169 D5
Fairway
Copthorne RH10 . . . . .7 B2
Crawley RH11 . . . . .17 D4
Littlehampton BN17 . . . . . .205 D4
Fairway Bsns Ctr BN2 . . . .170 E4
Fairway Cl
Copthorne RH10 . . . . .7 A2
Griggs Green GU30 . . . . . . .24 D3
Fairway Cres BN41 . . . . .168 C2
Fairway Inf Sch RH10 . . . . . . .7 B3
Fairways BN1 . . . . .191 E8
Fairway The
Bognor Regis PO21 . . . . . .211 B8
Lancing BN15 . . . . .188 A5
Midhurst GU29 . . . . .94 E6
Rowland's Castle PO9 . . . .130 E2
Fairway Trad Est BN2 . . . .170 E4
Faithfull Cres RH20 . . . . .121 B2
Falcon Cl
Crawley RH11 . . . . .18 D8
Shoreham-by-S BN43 . . . . .189 C6
Falcon Gdns BN17 . . . . .204 C8
Falkland Ave BN17 . . . . .204 F6
Falklands Cl 4 PO22 . . . . . .201 D5
Falklands Rd BN13 . . . . .37 B4
Fallow Deer Cl RH13 . . . . . . .37 B4
Fallowfield Cl BN3 . . . . .168 F2
Fallowfield Cres RH13 . . . . .168 F2
Fallowfield Way RH6 . . . . .2 B4
Falmer Ave
Rottingdean BN2 . . . . .194 B2
Worthing BN12 . . . . .185 B2
Falmer Cl
Crawley RH10 . . . . .18 D4
Worthing BN12 . . . . .185 C2
Falmer Gdns BN2 . . . . .193 D8
Falmer High Sch BN1 . . . . . .171 A5
Falmer Hill BN1 . . . . .171 B6
Falmer House Rd
BN1 . . . . .171 B6
Falmer Rd BN2 . . . . .193 E5
Falmer Sta BN1 . . . . .171 B6
Famet Ct RH19 . . . . .9 C3
Faraday Ave RH19 . . . . .22 F6
Faraday Cl BN13 . . . . .185 C6
Faraday Cl RH13 . . . . .5 F1
Faraday Ctr The RH10 . . . . . . .5 F1
Faraday Rd RH10 . . . . .5 F2
Farebrothers RH12 . . . . .35 F8
Faresmead PO21 . . . . .200 F2
Farhalls Cres RH12 . . . . .36 F6
Farlington Ave RH6 . . . . .87 F5
Farlington Cl RH16 . . . . .87 F5
Farlington Sch RH12 . . . . . . .35 B6
Farm Acre RH16 . . . . .205 F6
Farman St 15 BN3 . . . . .191 D5
Farm Ave RH12 . . . . .36 B3
Farm Cl
Barns Green RH13 . . . . .56 F2
Crawley RH10 . . . . .19 A7
East Grinstead RH19 . . . . . .23 B8
Elmer PO22 . . . . .203 B5
Fishbourne PO18 . . . . .176 A6
Hassocks BN6 . . . . .128 E4
Henfield BN5 . . . . .125 E5
Loxwood RH14 . . . . .32 A3
Portslade-by-S BN41 . . . . .168 A2
Warnham RH12 . . . . .35 F7
Farm Cnr PO22 . . . . .203 A5
Farm Cotts
Haywards Heath RH16 . . . . .87 C3
West Itchenor PO20 . . . . . .196 F6
Farmfield Dr RH6 . . . . .5 B8
Farmfield Hospl (private)
RH6 .1 B1
Farm Hill BN2 . . . . .193 C8
Farm La
Ditchling BN6 . . . . .129 C3
Nutbourne PO18 . . . . .174 B7
Farmleigh Cl RH10 . . . . .19 C8
Farm Mews BN3 . . . . .191 D6
Farm Rd
Bracklesham PO20 . . . . . . .208 B5
Hove BN3 . . . . .191 D6
Farm View PO10 . . . . .151 B3
Farm Way
Burgess Hill RH15 . . . . . . .109 D1
Rustington BN16 . . . . .205 B5
Southwick BN42 . . . . .190 A7
Farmway Cl BN3 . . . . .168 D2
Farncombe Rd BN11 . . . . . . .186 F2
Farndell Cl PO19 . . . . .177 C7
Farne Cl PO20 . . . . .197 E4
Farnefold Rd BN44 . . . . .145 D4
Farne La PO20 . . . . .197 E4
Farney Close Sch
RH17 . . . . .85 D2
Farnham Ave BN6 . . . . .129 A5
Farnham Cl RH11 . . . . .39 C8
Farnham La GU27 . . . . .27 A7
Farnham Rd
Liss GU33 . . . . .45 A4
Steep GU33 . . . . .68 D7
Farnhurst Rd PO22 . . . . .180 B6
Farnlea RH15 . . . . .109 D5
Faroes The BN17 . . . . .205 A6
Farr Cl RH17 . . . . .86 F8
Farriers Cl RH14 . . . . .79 C7
Farriers Ct RH12 . . . . .36 C2
FARTHER COMMONS 45 C1
Farthings Wlk RH12 . . . . .35 F3
Fastnet Way BN17 . . . . .205 A6
Faulkners Cl RH11 . . . . .39 C8
Faulkners Way RH15 . . . . . . .109 A5
Fawn Rise BN5 . . . . .125 E6
Faygate Bsns Ctr RH12 . . . . .16 F1
Faygate Ct BN2 . . . . .192 E6
Faygate La RH12 . . . . .16 F4
Faygate Sta RH12 . . . . .16 F1
Fay Rd RH12 . . . . .36 C5
Felbridge Ave RH10 . . . . .9 D7
Felbridge Cl RH19 . . . . .9 C3
Felbridge Ct RH19 . . . . .9 A4
Felbridge Ctr The RH19 . . . . . .9 A3
Felbridge Prim Sch
RH19 . . . . .8 F4
Felbridge Rd RH19 . . . . .8 D3
Felcot Rd RH19 . . . . .8 C4
Felcourt Cotts RH19 . . . . .9 C8
Felcourt La RH19 . . . . .9 C8
Felcourt Rd RH19, RH7 . . . . . .9 C7
Feld The RH19 . . . . .9 A4
Fellcott Way RH12 . . . . .35 F1
Fellows Gdns BN18 . . . . .181 A2
FELPHAM 202 B4
Felpham Com Coll
PO22 . . . . .201 F5
Felpham Gdns PO22 . . . . . . .202 B5
Felpham Rd PO22 . . . . .201 F4
Felpham Way PO22 . . . . .202 A5
Felride RH16 . . . . .87 E3
Felwater Ct RH19 . . . . .9 A3
Fenby Cl RH13 . . . . .37 C4
Fenchurch Rd RH10 . . . . .19 B4
Fenchurch Wlk BN1 . . . . . . .213 B4
Fender Ho RH12 . . . . .36 B2
Fenhurst Cl RH11 . . . . .35 F1
Fennel Cres RH11 . . . . .18 B2
Fennel Wlk BN43 . . . . .167 B1
Fenners Ct 15 BN11 . . . . . . .186 C3
Fereday Cl 5 BN15 . . . . .187 E6
Fermandy La RH10 . . . . .8 A1
Fern Cl GU31 . . . . .68 E3
Fern Cotts RH14 . . . . .55 F6
Ferndale Rd
Burgess Hill RH15 . . . . . . .109 C2
Chichester PO19 . . . . .155 A3
Hove BN3 . . . . .191 D7
Ferndale Wlk BN16 . . . . .184 A6
Fernden Hts GU27 . . . . .27 B2
Fernden La GU27 . . . . .27 C2
Ferndown
Crawley RH10 . . . . .6 D2
Horley RH6 . . . . .2 A5
Ferndown Gdns PO22 . . . . . .202 A5
FERNHILL 6 E7
Fernhill Cl RH10 . . . . .8 B1
Fernhill Rd RH6 . . . . .6 D7
Fernhurst Cl
Brighton BN1 . . . . .170 B6
Crawley RH11 . . . . .17 A8
Fernhurst Cres BN1 . . . . .170 B5
Fernhurst Ct BN11 . . . . .185 F2
Fernhurst Dr BN12 . . . . .185 A3
Fernhurst Gdns PO21 . . . . . .200 D2
Fernhurst Gn GU27 . . . . .49 B6
Fernhurst Prim Sch
GU27 . . . . .49 B6
Fernhurst Rd GU30 . . . . .47 C3
Fernleigh Cl PO19 . . . . .176 C6
Fern Rd RH20 . . . . .121 C1
Fernside RH19 . . . . .9 D2
Fern Way RH12 . . . . .36 D5
Fernwood Rise BN1 . . . . .169 D5
Feroners Cl RH10 . . . . .19 A4
Feroners Ct 4 RH10 . . . . . . .19 A4
Ferring CE Prim Sch
BN12 . . . . .206 F6
Ferring Cl
Crawley RH11 . . . . .18 B8
Ferring BN12 . . . . .206 E4
Ferring Ct BN1 . . . . .170 F5
Ferring Gdns PO22 . . . . .202 A5
Ferring Grange Flats
BN12 . . . . .206 E6
Ferring Grange Gdns
BN12 . . . . .206 E6
Ferringham La BN12 . . . . . . .206 E5
Ferringham La BN12 . . . . . . .206 E5
Ferringham Way
BN12 . . . . .206 E4
Ferring La BN12 . . . . .206 F7
Ferring Marine BN12 . . . . . . .206 F4
Ferring St BN12 . . . . .206 F6
Ferrymead Ct BN43 . . . . .188 F6
Ferry Rd
Littlehampton BN17 . . . . . .204 B4
Ferry Rd continued
Shoreham-by-S BN43 . . . . .188 F6
Festival Ct
Chichester PO19 . . . . .177 A7
Crawley RH10 . . . . .19 C4
Fetherston Rd BN15 . . . . . . .187 E7
Feversham Cl BN43 . . . . .189 B6
Fidler Cl PO20 . . . . .210 A1
Fidlers Copse GU27 . . . . .49 A6
Field Cl
Burgess Hill RH15 . . . . . . .108 E4
Lancing BN15 . . . . .187 D6
Walberton BN18 . . . . .153 D1
Fieldend RH12 . . . . .37 B5
Field End PO10 . . . . .121 E2
Fieldgate Cl RH13 . . . . .59 C4
Field Ho BN16 . . . . .205 F6
Fieldings Cotts RH14 . . . . . . .55 F5
Fieldings The
Horley RH6 . . . . .2 C4
Southwater RH13 . . . . .81 F7
Field Pl
Liphook GU30 . . . . .25 C3
Littlehampton BN17 . . . . . .204 D5
Field Place Fst Sch
BN12 . . . . .185 D5
Field Place Par BN12 . . . . .185 E4
Field Rd PO20 . . . . .208 A7
Field Row 8 BN11 . . . . . . .186 D2
Fields End Cl RH10 . . . . .87 F4
Fieldway RH6 . . . . .2 B4
Fieldway
Ditchling BN6 . . . . .129 D3
Haslemere GU27 . . . . .27 C7
Haywards Heath RH16 . . . . .87 F8
Fiennes Ct RH12 . . . . .36 D6
Fifth Ave
Lancing BN15 . . . . .187 E7
Worthing BN14 . . . . .186 C8
Filbert Cres RH11 . . . . .18 A6
Filey Cl RH11 . . . . .17 F4
Filton Wlk BN13 . . . . .185 D6
Fincham Cl BN16 . . . . .205 F5
Fincham Ct BN16 . . . . .205 F5
Finch Cres RH10 . . . . .21 C5
Finchdean Rd PO9 . . . . .130 E5
Finches Cl
Lancing BN15 . . . . .187 D5
Littlehampton BN17 . . . . . .204 C8
Partridge Green RH13 . . . .105 A3
Finches Ct RH16 . . . . .64 A1
Finches Gdns RH16 . . . . .88 A8
Finches La
Lindfield RH16 . . . . .88 A8
West Chiltington Common
PO20 . . . . .121 C8
Finches Park Rd RH16 . . . . .88 A8
Finches The BN43 . . . . .189 A8
Finch Gdns PO22 . . . . .201 B7
Finchmead La GU32 . . . . .67 D4
Findon Ave BN2 . . . . .194 E2
Findon By-Pass BN14 . . . . . .163 D6
Findon Cl BN3 . . . . .168 F3
Findon Dr PO22 . . . . .202 D6
Findon Rd
Brighton BN2 . . . . .192 F5
Crawley RH11 . . . . .18 B8
Worthing BN14 . . . . .163 F3
FINDON VALLEY 164 A2
Findon Way BN14 . . . . .35 D3
Finians Field RH15 . . . . .56 F2
Finisterre Way BN17 . . . . . . .205 A4
Finsbury La BN17 . . . . .204 E5
Finsbury Lo 1 BN2 . . . . . . .192 C6
Finsbury Rd BN2 . . . . .192 C6
Firbank Way RH19 . . . . .9 D1
Fir Cl BN2 . . . . .193 F7
Fircroft Ave BN15 . . . . .187 E8
Fircroft Cl
Brighton BN1 . . . . .169 E3
Worthing BN13 . . . . .185 F7
Fircroft Cres BN16 . . . . .205 D7
Firlands
Haywards Heath RH16 . . . . .87 F4
Horley RH6 . . . . .2 B4
Firle Cl RH10 . . . . .18 E8
Firle Rd
Brighton BN2 . . . . .192 D6
North Lancing BN15 . . . . . .165 E1
Worthing BN14 . . . . .163 E2
Firsdown Cl BN13 . . . . .163 E2
Firsdown Rd BN13 . . . . .163 E2
Firsland Park Ind Est
BN6 . . . . .126 F8
Firs Pk GU31 . . . . .68 E3
First Ave
Almodington PO20 . . . . . . .197 F2
Bognor Regis PO22 . . . . . .202 B4
Bracklesham PO20 . . . . . . .208 B5
Hove BN3 . . . . .191 C6
Lancing BN15 . . . . .187 E7
Middleton-on-S PO22 . . . . .202 F6
Southbourne PO10 . . . . . . .173 F8
Worthing BN14 . . . . .186 C7
Firs The GU30 . . . . .25 B3
Firtoft Cl RH15 . . . . .109 B3
Fir Tree Ave GU27 . . . . .26 D6
Fir Tree Cl
Crawley RH11 . . . . .5 B1
Lower Beeding RH13 . . . . . .60 D3
West Chiltington Common
RH20 . . . . .121 D6
Fir Tree Cotts GU33 . . . . .46 A4
Fir Tree La RH20 . . . . .121 D6
Fir Tree Way
Bognor Regis PO22 . . . . . .201 C7
Keymer BN6 . . . . .129 A4
Firview GU30 . . . . .25 B3
Fishbourne CE Prim Sch
PO19 . . . . .176 B6
Fishbourne Rd (E) 176 D6
Fishbourne Rd (W) PO19,
PO20 . . . . .176 C6
Fishbourne Roman Pal* . . . .
PO19 . . . . .176 B7
Fishbourne Sta PO19 . . . . . .176 B7
FISHER 199 C6
Fisher Cl RH10 . . . . .18 E4
Fisher La
Chiddingfold GU8 . . . . .29 E7
Dunsfold GU8 . . . . .30 B7
South Mundham PO20 . . . . .199 C6
Fishermans The
PO10 . . . . .173 C8
Fishermans Wlk
Bognor Regis PO21 . . . . . .200 D1
Selsey PO20 . . . . .212 F7
Shoreham-by-S BN43 . . . . .188 D5
South Hayling PO11 . . . . . .195 A2
Fishers Cl BN17 . . . . .205 A4
Fishers Ct RH12 . . . . .36 C4
Fishers Farm RH6 . . . . .2 B1
Fishers Farm Pk*
RH14 . . . . .54 D2
FISHERSGATE 190 A7
Fishersgate Cl BN41 . . . . . .190 A7
Fishersgate Fst Sch
BN41 . . . . .190 A7
Fishersgate Sta BN41 . . . . .190 B7
Fishersgate Terr
BN41 . . . . .190 A7
Fish La
Bognor Regis PO21 . . . . . .200 F2
Selsey PO20 . . . . .212 B8
Fitch Dr BN2 . . . . .170 F1
Fitchet Cl RH11 . . . . .18 B8
Fittleworth CE Fst Sch
RH20 . . . . .99 A3
Fittleworth Cl BN12 . . . . . . .185 B5
Fittleworth Dr 9 PO22 . . . .
BN16 . . . . .205 C5
Fittleworth Rd RH14 . . . . .77 F5
Fitzalan Cl
3 Littlehampton
BN17 . . . . .204 E4
4 Littlehampton BN16 . . . .205 B3
Fitzalan Mews BN18 . . . . . . .160 B2
Fitzalan Rd
Arundel BN18 . . . . .160 B2
Horsham RH12, RH13 . . . . .37 A4
Littlehampton BN17 . . . . . .204 E4
Fitzhamon Ho GU31 . . . . .68 C3
Fitzherbert Ct BN2 . . . . .192 D8
Fitzherbert Dr BN2 . . . . .192 D8
Fitzjohn Ct BN6 . . . . .128 F3
Fitzleet Ho 9 PO21 . . . . . . .201 C3
Fitzroy Ct BN17 . . . . .204 E5
Fitzwilliam Cl PO21 . . . . .200 F4
Five Acres
Crawley RH10 . . . . .18 E8
Funtington PO18 . . . . .153 A5
Five Oaks Rd
Broadbridge Heath RH12,
RH13 . . . . .35 A2
Itchingfield RH13 . . . . .56 D7
Fixcroft Cotts BN5 . . . . .106 D4
Flag Ct BN3 . . . . .191 B5
Flag Sq BN43 . . . . .188 F6
Flamsteed Hts RH11 . . . . .18 B1
Flansham Bsns Ctr
PO22 . . . . .202 B7
Flansham La PO22 . . . . .202 C6
Flansham Mews
PO22 . . . . .202 C6
Flansham Pk PO22 . . . . .202 D6
FLATHURST 76 A1
Flatt Rd PO18 . . . . .176 A6
Flaxman Ave PO19 . . . . .176 D6
Flax Mean PO22 . . . . .202 B5
Flax Mean Ho PO22 . . . . . . .202 B5
Fleet Cl BN17 . . . . .205 A6
Fleet St BN1 . . . . .213 B4
Fleet The RH20 . . . . .99 B3
Fleming Ct PO21 . . . . .200 F4
Fleming Ctr The RH10 . . . . . . .5 E2
Fleming Way RH10, RH11 . . . .5 F2
Fleming Wlk RH19 . . . . .22 F6
Fletcher Cl
Bognor Regis PO21 . . . . . .200 B2
Crawley RH10 . . . . .18 E4
North Mundham PO20 . . . .177 D1
Fletcher Ho
North Mundham
PO20 . . . . .177 C1
Southwater RH13 . . . . .57 E1
Fletcher Pl PO20 . . . . .177 C1
Fletcher Rd BN14 . . . . .186 E5
FLETCHERS 198 D4
Fletchers Cl RH13 . . . . .57 F3
Fletcher's Croft RH20 . . . . . .121 D2
Fletchers Est
Highleigh PO20 . . . . .198 C2
Sidlesham PO20 . . . . .198 E2
Fletchers Field GU30 . . . . . . .25 C3
Fletchers Ho PO22 . . . . .202 C6
Fletchers La PO18 . . . . .175 D1
Fletcher Way
Angmering BN16 . . . . .183 F6
Bognor Regis PO21 . . . . . .201 B4
4 Haywards Heath
RH16 . . . . .87 C2

Fletching Cl BN2 . . . . .192 F6
Flexfield Ho RH13 . . . . . .57 F1
Flimwell Cl BN2 . . . . .192 E5
Flint Cl
　Crawley RH10 . . . . .19 B3
　East Preston BN16 . . . . . .205 F6
　Portslade-by-S BN41 . . . .168 B2
Flint Cotts BN18 . . . . .160 A3
Flint Ho ◻ BN16 . . . . . . .205 C4
Flints The BN7 . . . . .172 E5
Flora Ct BN17 . . . . .204 B7
Floral Dene Ct BN14 . . . . .16 A4
Flora McDonald Jun Sch
　BN17 . . . . .204 C6
Florence Ave BN3 . . . . . . .190 D8
Florence Cl PO20 . . . . . . .197 D4
Florence Ct BN1 . . . . .169 F2
Florence Pl BN1 . . . . .170 B1
Florence Rd
　Brighton BN1 . . . . .192 A8
　Chichester PO19 . . . . . . .177 C6
Florets The BN44 . . . . .146 B1
Florida Cl BN12 . . . . .206 F4
Florida Gdns ◻ BN12 . . . .206 F4
Florida Rd BN12 . . . . .206 F4
Florlandia Cl BN15 . . . . . .187 B6
Flower Farm Cl BN5 . . . . .125 D5
Floyds Cotts BN17 . . . . . .204 D4
Foamcourt Waye
　BN12 . . . . .206 E5
Folders Cl RH15 . . . . .109 D1
Folders Gdns RH15 . . . . . .109 C1
Folders Grange RH15 . . . .109 C1
Folders La RH15 . . . . .109 D1
Folders La ◻ BN16 . . . . . .129 F8
Fold Sch The BN3 . . . . . . .190 D7
Follett Cl PO21 . . . . .200 E2
Follis Gdns PO19 . . . . . . .176 B8
Folly La
　Petersfield GU32 . . . . .68 B3
　Sutton GU28, RH20 . . . . .117 E3
Folly Market ◻ GU31 . . . . .68 B3
Fontana Ct RH10 . . . . .19 E5
Fonthill Lodge Sch
　RH19 . . . . .22 C6
Fonthill Rd BN3 . . . . .191 B8
Fontigarry Farm Bsns Pk
　RH6 . . . . .1 C8
Fontwell Ave BN18,
　PO20 . . . . .157 F1
Fontwell Cl
　Fontwell BN18 . . . . .158 A2
　Rustington BN16 . . . . . . .205 B4
　Worthing BN14 . . . . .186 A8
Fontwell Dr BN14 . . . . . . .186 A8
Fontwell Park Race
　Course* BN18 . . . . .157 F2
Fontwell Rd
　Crawley RH10 . . . . .19 A3
　Selsey PO20 . . . . .212 G8
Forbes Cl RH10 . . . . .19 B2
Forbes Pl PO19 . . . . .176 E8
Ford Airfield Ind Est
　BN18 . . . . .181 C3
Fordingbridge Cl RH12 . . .36 C1
Fordingbridge Ind Site
　PO22 . . . . .180 A7
Ford La
　Ashurst BN44 . . . . .124 D7
　Ford BN18 . . . . .181 C4
Ford Lane Bsns Pk
　BN18 . . . . .181 D6
Ford Rd
　Arundel BN18 . . . . .160 A2
　Ford BN18 . . . . .181 E3
　Tortington BN18 . . . . . . .181 F7
Ford Sta BN18 . . . . .181 E5
Fordwater Gdns
　BN18 . . . . .181 B2
Fordwater La PO19 . . . . . .155 A2
Fordwater Rd
　Chichester PO18,
　　PO19 . . . . .155 A3
　East Lavant PO18 . . . . . .155 A5
Fordwater Sch PO19 . . . . .155 A1
Fordyce Ct ◻ BN14 . . . . . .186 D3
Fore Bridge GU31 . . . . . . .68 B2
Foredown Cl BN41 . . . . . .168 B2
Foredown Dr BN41 . . . . . .168 B2
Foredown Rd
　Portslade-by-S BN41 . . . .168 B2
　Portslade Village BN41 . .168 B4
Foredown Tower
　Countryside Ctr*
　　BN41 . . . . .168 B3
　Portslade-by-S BN41 . . . .168 B3
Forest Cl
　Crawley Down RH10 . . . . .21 B8
　Horsham RH12 . . . . .37 B4
　Mannings Heath RH13 . . .59 C6
Forest Cnr GU33 . . . . .45 C7
Forester Rd BN18 . . . . . . .181 C4
Foresters The RH13 . . . . . .36 F1
Forestfield
　Crawley RH10 . . . . .19 B3
　Horsham RH12 . . . . .37 A3
Forest Gate RH11 . . . . .18 D1
Forest La BN18 . . . . .185 B9
Forest Lane Cl GU30 . . . . . .25 A4
Forest Lo
　◻ East Grinstead
　　RH19 . . . . .22 F8
　Horsham RH12 . . . . .37 B5
Forest Mews RH13 . . . . . . .37 B4
Forest Oaks RH13 . . . . . . .37 B4
Forest Pk RH13 . . . . .59 E6
Forest Rd
　Brighton BN1 . . . . .170 E6

Forest Rd *continued*
　Colgate RH11, RH12,
　　RH13 . . . . .38 C6
　Faygate RH12, RH13 . . . . .37 D5
　Liss GU33 . . . . .45 C7
　Midhurst GU29 . . . . .94 D6
　Worthing BN14 . . . . .186 D6
Forest Ridge RH19 . . . . . . .43 A6
Forest Rise GU33 . . . . .45 C6
Forest Row Bsns Pk
　RH18 . . . . .23 F3
Forest Row CE Prim Sch
　RH18 . . . . .23 F2
Forest Sch The RH13 . . . . .36 F1
FORESTSIDE 131 D6
Forestside PO9 . . . . .131 D6
Forest View RH10 . . . . .19 A3
Forest View Rd RH19 . . . . .22 E6
Forge Cl
　Broadbridge Heath
　　RH12 . . . . .35 D4
　East Preston BN16 . . . . . .205 F6
　Portslade-by-S BN41 . . . .168 B2
　Stockbridge PO19 . . . . . .176 F3
Forge Ho The BN2 . . . . . . .193 F1
Forge La
　Broadbridge Heath
　　RH12 . . . . .35 D4
　Crawley RH10 . . . . .19 A7
Forge Pl RH6 . . . . .1 E1
Forge Rd RH10 . . . . .19 A7
Forge The
　Handcross RH17 . . . . .61 C8
　Hove BN3 . . . . .190 F8
　Selsey PO20 . . . . .212 D7
　Southwater RH13 . . . . . . .57 F1
　Warnham RH12 . . . . .35 E7
Forge Way
　Billingshurst RH14 . . . . . .79 C8
　Burgess Hill RH15 . . . . . .109 A4
Forge Wood RH10 . . . . .6 D3
Forge Wood Ind Est
　RH10 . . . . .6 B2
Forrester Rd RH13 . . . . . .105 A3
Forsters Yd BN17 . . . . . . .204 B5
Forthaven BN43 . . . . .189 C6
Fort Ha BN17 . . . . .204 C6
Fort Rd E BN17 . . . . .204 C6
Forty Acre La GU31 . . . . . .90 E3
Forum The ◻ BN42 . . . . . . .36 C2
Foster La BN20 . . . . .122 F5
Fosters BN18 . . . . .205 E4
Fosters Cl BN16 . . . . .205 E4
Fotherby Ho RH10 . . . . . .173 F8
Foundry Ct RH13 . . . . .36 E4
Foundry Cotts GU29 . . . . . .95 C3
Foundry Ct RH15 . . . . .109 B3
Foundry Ct RH13 . . . . .36 E3
Foundry La
　Haslemere GU27 . . . . .27 A6
　Horsham RH13 . . . . .36 E3
Foundry Rd BN18 . . . . . . .180 F2
Foundry St BN1 . . . . .213 B3
Fountains Cl
　Brighton BN1 . . . . .170 B2
　Crawley RH11 . . . . .18 A4
Founthill Ave BN2 . . . . . . .194 B1
Founthill Rd BN2 . . . . .194 B1
Fourth Ave
　Bognor Regis PO22 . . . . .202 C4
　Hove BN3 . . . . .191 B6
　Lancing BN15 . . . . .187 E2
　Worthing BN14 . . . . .186 D3
Fowey Cl BN43 . . . . .189 B6
Fowler Cl RH10 . . . . .19 C4
Foxbridge Dr PO20 . . . . . .177 A1
Foxbridge La RH14 . . . . . . .31 C1
Foxbury La PO10 . . . . .151 E4
Fox Cl
　Burgess Hill RH15 . . . . . .108 F1
　Chichester PO19 . . . . . . .177 C8
　Crawley RH11 . . . . .5 E8
Fox Ct PO20 . . . . .121 B1
Foxdale Dr RH16 . . . . .205 F8
Fox Dell RH20 . . . . .121 B1
Foxdown Rd BN2 . . . . . . .193 F7
Foxes Cl
　Rustington BN16 . . . . . . .205 B8
　Southwater RH13 . . . . . . .81 F7
Foxes Croft PO22 . . . . . . .180 C6
Foxfield Cotts RH13 . . . . . .81 F7
Foxfields RH20 . . . . .121 C8
Foxglove Ave RH12 . . . . . .36 E6
Foxglove Cl RH15 . . . . . . .108 D4
Foxglove Wlk BN17 . . . . .205 A7
Foxglove Wlk
　Crawley RH11 . . . . .18 B3
　Worthing BN13 . . . . .185 C6
FOX HILL 87 E1
Fox Hill RH16 . . . . .87 E1
Fox Hill Cl RH16 . . . . .87 F1
Foxhill Ct ◻ RH16 . . . . . . .87 E3
Fox Hill Village RH16 . . . . .87 F1
Foxholes RH12 . . . . .33 D8
Foxhunters Rd BN41 . . . . .167 F3
Fox Lea BN14 . . . . .163 E5
Foxleigh Chase RH12 . . . . .36 F5
Foxley La BN13 . . . . .185 F9
Fox Rd
　Haslemere GU27 . . . . .26 C6
　Midhurst GU29 . . . . .73 A2
Foxwarren RH16 . . . . .87 C5
Foxwarren Cl PO20 . . . . . .207 F7
Fox Way BN41 . . . . .168 B2
Foxwells RH17 . . . . .41 A1
Foxwood Ave BN16 . . . . . .206 A8

Framfield ◻ BN2 . . . . .192 F5
Framfield Cl
　Brighton BN1 . . . . .170 E6
　Crawley RH11 . . . . .18 A8
Frampton ◻ BN5 . . . . .190 D7
Frampton Cl BN12 . . . . . .185 C3
Frampton Rd BN43 . . . . . .188 D8
Framptons The BN16 . . . . .206 B5
Framroze Ct BN1 . . . . . . .170 B2
France Cotts BN13 . . . . . .184 D8
France La BN13 . . . . .162 D1
Franciscan Way
　BN17 . . . . .204 D5
Frances Edwards Way
　RH11 . . . . .17 E2
Francislea RH16 . . . . .87 E2
Francis Rd RH16 . . . . .88 B8
Francis St BN1 . . . . .213 B4
Francome Ho BN15 . . . . . .187 D3
Frandor Rd PO21 . . . . . . .200 F5
Frankalan Mews ◻
　PO21 . . . . .201 C2
Frankland Mead
　RH20 . . . . .143 E6
Franklands Cl
　Burgess Hill RH15 . . . . . .109 B1
　Worthing BN14 . . . . .164 A1
Franklands Gdns
　RH15 . . . . .129 A8
FRANKLANDS VILLAGE
　. .88 A4
Franklands Way
　RH15 . . . . .129 A8
Frankland Terr ◻
　PO10 . . . . .173 C8
Franklin Pl PO19 . . . . .177 A7
Franklin Rd
　Brighton BN2 . . . . .192 C7
　Crawley RH10 . . . . .19 C2
　Portslade-by-S BN41 . . . .190 C7
　Shoreham-by-S BN43 . . .167 D1
　Worthing BN13 . . . . .185 C8
Franklin St BN2 . . . . .192 C8
Franklynn Ct RH16 . . . . . . .87 F3
Franklynn Rd RH16 . . . . . . .87 F3
Frankton Ave RH11 . . . . . . .88 A3
Frant Rd BN3 . . . . .169 A2
Frarydene PO10 . . . . .173 F8
Fraser Cl PO20 . . . . .212 F6
Fraser Ct
　◻ Bognor Regis
　　PO21 . . . . .201 D3
　◻ Shoreham-by-S
　　BN43 . . . . .189 C8
Fraser Gdns PO10 . . . . . . .152 A2
Frazier Ho RH20 . . . . .121 D1
Fred Emery Ct ◻
　BN1 . . . . .191 E5
Frederic Ho BN1 . . . . .194 B1
Frederick Cotts RH16 . . . . .88 B7
Frederick Gdns BN1 . . . . .213 B3
Frederick Pl BN1 . . . . .213 B3
Frederick St BN1 . . . . .213 B3
Freehold St BN43 . . . . . . .188 E7
Freehold Terr ◻ BN2 . . . . .192 E8
Freeks's La RH15 . . . . .109 A5
Freeland Cl PO19 . . . . . . .176 C6
Freeman Cl BN18 . . . . . . .158 B1
Freeman Rd RH12 . . . . .35 F8
Freemans Cl RH14 . . . . . . .79 C8
Freemans Rd BN41 . . . . . .190 A8
Freeways PO20 . . . . .212 C8
French Apartments The
　BN2 . . . . .192 E3
Frenches RH10 . . . . .121 D2
Frenches Mead RH14 . . . . .79 C8
Frenches Rdbt RH10 . . . . .121 D3
French Gdns RH16 . . . . . . .88 A6
Frenchmans Rd GU32 . . . . .68 A4
Frensham Ave PO22 . . . . .201 D6
Freshbrook Cl BN15 . . . . .187 E5
Freshbrook Ct ◻
　BN15 . . . . .187 E5
Freshbrook Rd BN15 . . . . .187 F5
Freshbrook Fst Sch
　BN15 . . . . .187 E6
Freshfield Bank RH18 . . . . .23 E2
Freshfield Cl RH10 . . . . . . .19 A5
Freshfield Crossway
　RH17 . . . . .89 C8
Freshfield Ind Est
　BN2 . . . . .192 C5
Freshfield La RH17 . . . . . . .65 E2
Freshfield Pl BN2 . . . . . . .192 C5
Freshfield Rd BN2 . . . . . . .192 D5
Freshfields Cl BN15 . . . . . .187 D6
Freshfields Dr BN15 . . . . .187 D6
Freshfield St BN2 . . . . . . .192 C6
Freshlands RH14 . . . . .79 C8
Freshwoods RH12 . . . . .33 D8
Freya Ct PO22 . . . . .202 F4
Friar Cl BN1 . . . . .170 A4
Friar Cres BN1 . . . . .170 A3
Friar Rd BN1 . . . . .170 A3
Friars Cl BN6 . . . . .128 E5
Friars Oak Rd BN6 . . . . . .128 E5
Friars Rookery RH10 . . . . .18 F6
Friar Wlk
　Brighton BN1 . . . . .169 F4
　Worthing BN13 . . . . .185 D4
Friary Cl PO22 . . . . .202 E5
Friary La PO19 . . . . .177 A6
Friary Way RH10 . . . . .18 E5
Friday St
　Faygate RH12 . . . . .15 E6
　Warnham RH12 . . . . .35 E7

Friends Cl RH11 . . . . .5 D1
Frimley Cl BN2 . . . . .193 F7
Friston Cl BN2 . . . . .170 F4
Friston Wlk RH11 . . . . .18 A7
Frith Pk RH19 . . . . .9 E3
Frith Rd
　Bognor Regis PO21 . . . . .201 A4
　Hove BN3 . . . . .191 A8
Frobisher Cl BN12 . . . . . .185 D5
Frobisher Gdns ◻
　PO10 . . . . .173 B8
Frobisher Rd PO21 . . . . . .200 C2
Frobisher Way
　Littlehampton BN16 . . . . .205 E4
　Worthing BN12 . . . . .185 D5
Fry Cl BN13 . . . . .18 B1
Fry Cres RH15 . . . . .108 E5
Fryern Ct RH20 . . . . .121 C2
Fryern Rd RH20 . . . . .121 D3
Fryland La BN5 . . . . .106 B4
Fuel Farm Rd
　Crawley RH6 . . . . .5 E8
Fulbeck Ave RH11 . . . . .1 E1
Fulbeck Ave BN13 . . . . . . .185 B7
Fulfords Hill RH13 . . . . .57 A7
Fulham Cl RH11 . . . . .18 B2
Fullers Wlk BN17 . . . . . . .182 D5
Fulmar Cl
　◻ Crawley RH11 . . . . .17 D5
　Hove BN3 . . . . .169 D1
Fulmar Dr RH19 . . . . .10 B3
Fulmer Ct ◻ RH11 . . . . . . .1 A1
Fulmer Ct ◻ BN1 . . . . . . .186 B1
Funtington Ho BN17 . . . . .204 B7
Funtington Prim Sch
　PO18 . . . . .153 B3
Furlong Cl BN18 . . . . .158 B3
Furlonge Ho PO10 . . . . . .151 A1
Furlongs The BN44 . . . . . .145 D2
Furlong Way RH6 . . . . .5 F8
Furnace Dr RH10 . . . . .18 F4
Furnace Farm Rd
　RH10 . . . . .19 A4
FURNACE GREEN 19 A5
Furnace Par RH10 . . . . . . .19 A4
Furnace Pl RH10 . . . . .19 A5
FURNACE WOOD 8 C4
Furnance Farm Rd
　RH19 . . . . .8 C3
Furners La BN5 . . . . .126 A5
Furners Mead BN5 . . . . . .125 F4
Furnston Gr PO10 . . . . . . .152 A1
Furse Feld PO21 . . . . .201 A2
Furze Cl
　Horley RH6 . . . . .2 D3
　Worthing BN13 . . . . .163 D2
Furze Common Rd
　RH20 . . . . .122 A6
Furze Croft BN3 . . . . .191 D6
Furzedene BN3 . . . . .191 D6
Furzedown BN17 . . . . . . .204 E4
Furzefield
　Crawley RH11 . . . . .18 C7
　East Wittering PO20 . . . .196 F1
Furzefield Chase RH19 . . . .9 E4
Furzefield Cl BN16 . . . . . .183 F7
Furzefield Ho RH13 . . . . . .57 F1
Furzefield Rd
　East Grinstead RH19 . . . . .9 D4
　Horsham RH12 . . . . .37 B5
Furze Hill BN3 . . . . .191 D6
Furze Hill Cl BN3 . . . . .191 E6
Furze Hill Ho BN3 . . . . . . .191 E6
Furzeholme BN13 . . . . .9 E4
Furze La RH19 . . . . .9 E4
Furzeland Way RH6 . . . . . .127 D8
Furze Mdw GU31 . . . . .92 A8
Furzen Cotts RH13 . . . . . . .13 A4
Furzen La RH12, RH5 . . . . .13 A4
Furze Rd
　Rudgwick RH12 . . . . .33 D8
　Worthing BN13 . . . . .163 E2
Furze View RH13 . . . . .56 B6
FYNING 70 C4
Fyning La GU31 . . . . .70 C5

G

Gableson Ave BN1 . . . . . . .169 B4
Gables The
　◻ Bognor Regis
　　PO21 . . . . .201 C2
　Copthorne RH10 . . . . .7 B3
　Cowfold RH13 . . . . .83 E1
　Fishbourne PO19 . . . . . . .176 B6
　Horsham RH12 . . . . .36 D4
　Southwater RH13 . . . . . . .81 F8
Gabriel Rd RH10 . . . . .19 C2
Gage Rd BN16 . . . . .183 C4
Gage Ridge RH18 . . . . .23 E2
Gaggle Wood RH13 . . . . . .59 C6
Gainsboro Rd PO21 . . . . . .201 C3
Gainsborough Ave
　BN14 . . . . .186 E7
Gainsborough Dr
　PO20 . . . . .212 F7
Gainsborough Ho
　◻ Hove BN3 . . . . .191 C7
Gainsborough Lo ◻
　BN14 . . . . .186 C6
Gainsborough Rd RH10 . . .18 F3
Gaisford Cl BN14 . . . . . . .186 C4
Gaisford Rd BN14 . . . . . . .186 B4
Galahad Rd BN15 . . . . . . .187 B2
Gales Cl GU27 . . . . .26 E5
Gales Dr RH10 . . . . .18 F6

Gales Pl RH10 . . . . .18 F6
Galleries The ◻ BN3 . . . . .191 D7
Galliers Cl BN1 . . . . .170 B6
Galsworthy Cl BN12 . . . . .185 B4
Galsworthy Rd BN12 . . . . .185 B4
Gamecock Terr PO20 . . . .156 D1
Gammon Cl GU31 . . . . .68 C5
Gander Cl RH15 . . . . .109 A5
Gander Gn RH16 . . . . .87 F7
Gander Hill RH16 . . . . .87 F7
Ganders Cl BN5 . . . . .125 D5
Gandersgate La RH14 . . . . .27 E7
Gannet Ho BN3 . . . . .169 B1
Gannon Rd BN11 . . . . .186 F3
Ganymede Ct RH11 . . . . . .17 E3
Garage Cotts ◻ GU32 . . . . .68 A4
Garbitts La GU31 . . . . .70 B4
Garcia Trad Est BN13 . . . .185 F4
Garden Ave PO20 . . . . . . .208 B6
Garden Cl
　Angmering BN16 . . . . . . .184 A7
　East Grinstead RH19 . . . . .22 F7
　Lancing BN15 . . . . .187 C6
　Portslade-by-S BN41 . . . .190 C8
　Shoreham-by-S BN43 . . .167 B1
　Storrington RH20 . . . . . . .121 D2
Garden Cres PO22 . . . . . . .180 C5
Garden Ct
　Bognor Regis PO21 . . . . .200 E2
　Shoreham-by-S BN43 . . .167 B1
Gardener Ho RH13 . . . . . . .57 C1
Gardeners Cl RH12 . . . . . . .35 E8
Gardeners Ct ◻ RH13 . . . . .36 D1
Gardeners Gn RH12 . . . . . .16 C6
Garden Ho The BN1 . . . . .190 B8
Garden House La RH19 . . .22 F7
Garden Lo PO21 . . . . .200 A2
Garden Mead RH19 . . . . . . .42 E6
Garden Mews
　Duncton GU28 . . . . .117 D8
　◻ Haywards Heath
　　RH16 . . . . .68 B3
Garden Pl ◻ RH12 . . . . . . .36 C4
Gardens The
　Fittleworth RH20 . . . . .99 A3
　Southwick BN42 . . . . . . .189 F7
　West Ashling RH14 . . . . .153 B3
Garden Wlk
　Crawley RH11 . . . . .18 C6
　◻ Horsham RH12 . . . . . . .36 C4
Garden Wood Cl
　RH20 . . . . .121 D6
Garden Wood Rd RH19 . . .22 C8
Gardner Centre Rd
　BN1 . . . . .171 B6
Gardner La RH10 . . . . .21 A8
Gardner Rd BN41 . . . . . . .190 A7
Gardner St BN1 . . . . .213 B2
Garendon Ho BN11 . . . . . .187 A2
Garland Ave PO10 . . . . . . .151 B3
Garland Ct PO19 . . . . .177 B5
Garland Rd RH19 . . . . .9 D2
Garland Sq PO20 . . . . . . .156 D2
Garmans RH14 . . . . .54 C1
Garnet Ho ◻ BN2 . . . . . . .192 C4
Garrett Ct RH11 . . . . .19 C4
Garrick Rd BN14 . . . . .186 E4
Garrick Wlk RH10 . . . . .18 E3
Garrones The RH10 . . . . . .19 E7
Garsons Rd PO20 . . . . . . .173 F8
Garton Cl RH11 . . . . .18 C1
Gaskyns Cl RH12 . . . . .33 D7
Gasson Wood Rd RH11 . . .17 E4
Gaston Way PO18 . . . . . . .154 E7
Gatcombe Cl BN13 . . . . . .185 B6
Gatefield Cotts RH13 . . . . .34 D2
Gateford Dr RH12 . . . . .36 F6
Gate No GU29 . . . . .92 F7
Gatehouse La
　Bolney ◻ Cocker BN6,
　　RH15 . . . . .108 C4
　Trotton GU31 . . . . .71 A4
Gatehouse Mews
　PO21 . . . . .201 D3
Gates Cl RH10 . . . . .19 C2
Gatesmead RH16 . . . . .87 F8
Gateway Lo PO22 . . . . . . .201 F4
Gatwick Terr BN44 . . . . . .145 D3
Gatwick Airport Beehive
　Area RH6 . . . . .6 B5
Gatwick Airport-London
　RH6 . . . . .5 F7
Gatwick Aviation Mus*
　RH6 . . . . .4 F6
Gatwick Gate Ind Est
　RH11 . . . . .5 E5
Gatwick Ho ◻ RH6 . . . . . . .6 E7
Gatwick Metro Ctr RH6 . . . .2 B3
Gatwick Park Hospl
　(private) RH6 . . . . .1 E2
Gatwick Rd RH6, RH10 . . . .6 A3
Gatwick Way RH6 . . . . .5 C4
Gaugemaster Way
　BN18 . . . . .181 C6
Gay St RH20 . . . . .101 C4
Gay Street La RH20 . . . . . .101 A6
Gaywood Wlk BN3 . . . . . .185 D6
Geddes Way GU31 . . . . . . .68 C4
Gemini Bsns Ctr BN3 . . . .191 B8

Gemini Cl RH11...........**17** E4
Genesis Bsns Ctr RH13....**36** F3
Genistos The BN6.........**128** E4
Genoa Cl BN17............**205** A6
Geoffrey's Lo 6 RH10 ......**6** A1
George Denyer Cl
GU27.....................**27** C7
George Ho PO20.........**212** E8
George IV Wlk PO22 ......**202** A5
George Pinion Ct RH12 ....**36** B3
Georges La RH20 ....**122** C1
George St
Brighton BN2............**213** B2
Chichester PO19 ....**177** A7
Hove BN3................**191** B6
Portslade-by-S, Aldrington
BN41....................**190** C7
Portslade-by-S, Fishersgate
BN41....................**190** A7
George V Ave
Lancing BN15............**188** B5
Worthing BN11 ....**185** F3
Georgia Ave BN14 ....**186** D4
Georgian Cl RH10.........**19** D5
Georgian Gardens Com
Prim Sch BN16.........**205** E6
Georgian Gdns BN16.....**205** E6
Gerald Cl RH15 ....**109** D3
Gerald Ct RH13..........**36** E2
Gerald Rd BN11..........**185** F2
Gerardes Lo GU27 ....**27** D8
Gerard St BN1...........**213** B5
Gerrard House Bsns Ctr
BN16 ....**205** F6
Gerston Bsns Pk
RH20 ....**142** C8
Ghyll Cres RH13 ....**58** F8
Ghyll Ct RH13 ....**57** F1
Ghyllside BN2............**170** E1
Gibbon Pl 8 RH11.........**18** D8
Gibbons Cl RH10 ....**19** C3
Giblets La RH12 ....**36** F7
Giblets Way RH12........**36** E7
Gibson Pl PO20 ....**156** C2
Gibson Way PO21........**201** D4
Giffards Cl RH19..........**9** F1
Gifford Rd PO18 ....**175** C7
Gifford St PO19 ....**176** E8
Gilberts The BN16 ....**205** B3
Giles Cl BN18............**180** F2
Gilham La RH18 ....**23** E2
Gillett Cl RH13............**37** B4
Gillett Ho RH13...........**37** B4
Gillham's La GU27 ....**26** A5
Gilligan Cl RH12..........**36** B2
Gilligans The RH15 ......**108** F5
Gilmans Ind Est RH14 ....**79** D6
Gillway PO20 ....**212** G8
Gilmore Rd PO19 ....**177** C6
Gilpin Cl PO19...........**176** B6
Gilwynes PO21..........**200** F2
Gilwynes Ct PO21........**200** F2
Ginhams Rd RH11 ....**18** B6
Girton Ho BN3............**190** F6
Glade Inf Sch PO21.......**201** A5
Gladepoint RH16 ....**87** E5
Glades The RH19 ....**10** B1
Glade The
Bognor Regis PO21 ......**211** A8
Crawley RH10 ....**19** A4
Horsham RH13 ....**37** A3
Storrington RH20........**121** E2
Gladonian Rd BN17.......**204** D7
Gladstone Ct 14 BN2......**192** C8
Gladstone Pl BN3.........**192** C8
Gladstone Rd
Burgess Hill RH15 ....**109** C4
Horsham RH12 ....**36** D3
Portslade-by-S BN41......**190** B7
Yapton BN18 ....**180** F2
Gladstone Terr
Brighton BN2............**213** C4
Littlehampton BN17......**204** D7
Gladys Rd BN1...........**190** D8
Glamis Ct PO21..........**201** D3
Glamis St PO21..........**201** D3
Glanville Wlk 7 RH11......**18** A3
Glaseby La RH20.........**143** D4
Glasshouse La GU28,
RH14 ....**76** F3
Glass Pavilion BN1.......**213** B2
Glastonbury Rd BN3......**190** D6
Glatting La RH20.........**117** E1
Glawood Ho BN14 ....**186** E6
Glaziers La GU29 ....**73** B2
Gleave Cl RH19............**10** A2
Glebe Cl
Crawley RH10............**18** E7
Lancing BN15............**187** E7
Norton PO20............**157** B1
Southwick BN42 ....**189** F7
Glebe Com Mid Sch
BN42 ....**189** D8
Glebefield Rd PO20......**197** A5
Glebelands
Crawley Down RH10 ......**21** A7
Loxwood RH14...........**31** F4
Pulborough RH20........**100** D2
Glebelands Ct BN43......**189** B8
Glebe Rd
Cuckfield RH17 ....**86** F6
Fernhurst GU27..........**49** B5
Worthing BN14 ....**186** A5
Glebeside Ave BN14 ......**186** A5
Glebeside Cl BN14........**186** B5

Glebe The
Copthorne RH10 ....**7** B3
Felbridge RH19 ....**9** A4
Horley RH6 ....**1** F3
Hurstpierpoint BN6 ....**128** A6
Lindfield RH16 ....**88** A8
Southwick BN42 ....**189** FB
Tangmere PO20.........**156** C1
Glebe Twitten RH17......**86** F6
Glebe View RH17 ....**41** A1
Glebe Villas
Hove BN3................**190** D7
Petworth GU28 ....**75** F1
Glebe Way
Lancing BN15............**187** E7
Wisborough Green RH14...**78** C8
Glenbarrie Way BN12 ....**206** F2
Glencathara Rd PO21 ....**201** B3
Glen Cres PO20..........**212** E7
Glen Dale PO9............**130** E1
Glendale Cl RH12..........**37** A6
Glendale Rd
Burgess Hill RH15........**109** B2
Hove BN3................**191** D7
Glendon Ho 10 RH10 .....**18** D5
Glendor Rd BN3.........**190** E6
Glendyne Cl RH19 ....**23** A8
Glendyne Way RH11......**23** A8
Glen Eagles RH6............**2** B2
Gleneagles Ct
Crawley RH10............**18** D5
13 Haywards Heath
RH16....................**87** E4
Glenelg Cl PO21..........**200** F6
Glenfalls Ave BN1........**170** A7
Glenfergus 3 RH16........**87** E6
Glenfield Cotts RH6........**4** D7
Glenfield Ct BN13........**185** F6
Glen Gdns BN12.........**206** F6
Glen Gordon RH16........**87** E6
Glenham Pl RH19..........**43** A5
Glenmore Ct 18 BN17 ....**204** E4
Glen Rise BN1...........**169** B5
Glen Rise Cl BN1.........**169** B5
Glenside 1 RH19..........**9** E1
Glen The
Southwater RH13 ....**58** A2
Worthing BN13 ....**186** A7
Glenview Cl RH10..........**18** F8
Glenville Rd BN16 ....**205** D4
Glen Vue RH19............**10** C1
Glenway PO22 ....**201** D4
Glenwood Ave PO22 .....**201** D4
Glenwood Rd PO10 ......**152** A1
Glenwood Sch PO10 .....**151** B1
Gleton Ave BN3.........**168** D2
Globe Pl BN17...........**204** D7
Gloster Dr PO21..........**200** B2
Gloucester Cl
East Grinstead RH19......**23** A8
Petersfield GU32..........**67** F3
Gloucester Ct
6 Petersfield GU32......**68** B4
Worthing BN12 ....**185** F2
Gloucester La BN17......**204** D5
Gloucester Mews 2
BN1....................**213** B3
Gloucester Pas 4
BN1....................**213** B3
Gloucester Pl
Brighton BN1............**213** B3
Littlehampton BN17......**204** D5
Gloucester Rd
Bognor Regis PO21......**201** E3
Brighton BN1............**213** B3
Burgess Hill RH15.......**108** F2
Crawley RH10 ....**18** E2
Littlehampton BN17......**204** C5
Gloucester St BN1........**213** B3
Gloucester Terr PO18 ....**175** B4
Gloucester Way PO19...**154** F1
Gloucester Yd 3 BN1.....**213** B3
Glovers Field GU27........**26** F6
Glovers Ho GU27 ....**26** F6
Glover's Rd RH6............**4** D7
Glovers Yd BN1..........**169** F1
Glynde Ave
Saltdean BN2.............**194** D2
Worthing BN11 ....**185** A3
Glyndebourne Ave
BN2....................**194** C2
Glyndebourne Ct 9
BN3....................**188** F7
Glynde Cl BN12..........**206** F6
Glynde Cres PO22 ....**202** A5
Glynde Ho
Crawley RH10............**18** E8
Hove BN3...............**191** D6
Worthing BN11 ....**186** B1
Glynde Pl 8 RH12.........**36** C2
Glynde Rd BN2..........**192** D6
Glyn House Cl PO20 .....**212** E7
Glynleigh 10 BN2.........**213** C3
Goathlands Cvn Pk
PO20 ....**212** C8
Gochers Ct BN2..........**192** C7
Goda Rd BN17...........**204** E5
Goddard Cl RH10..........**19** B3
Goddens The RH19.........**22** E7
Godman Cl PO21.........**200** D2
Godmans Ct RH13........**183** E1
Godolphin Ct RH10........**18** D5
Godstalls La BN44.......**145** C2
Godwin Cl PO10..........**151** A3
Godwin Ct 3 RH12........**36** A1
Godwin Rd BN3.........**168** D1
Godwin Way
Fishbourne PO18........**176** A8

Godwin Way *continued*
Horsham RH13 ....**37** A4
Goepel Ct RH10 ....**19** A7
Goffs Cl RH11............**18** C5
Goffs La RH11............**18** B6
Goffs Park Rd RH11.......**18** C4
Goldcrest Ave BN17......**204** C8
Goldcrest Cl RH6...........**1** E4
Golden Acre
Bognor Regis PO21 ......**211** A8
West Kingston BN16 .....**206** B4
Golden Ave BN16........**206** B5
Golden Avenue Cl
BN16 ....**206** B4
Goldenfields Cl GU30 ......**25** D3
Goldenfields Cl GU30 ......**25** D3
Golden Hill RH15 ....**109** D3
Golden La
Ashurst BN44 ....**124** E6
11 Brighton BN2..........**191** D5
Golden Sands Cvn Pk
BN15 ....**188** A4
Golden Sq
Henfield BN5 ....**125** E4
Petworth GU28 ....**97** F8
Goldfinch Cl
Crawley RH11 ....**18** D8
Horsham RH12 ....**36** C7
Golding Barn Farm
(Works) BN5...........**146** E2
Golding Cl RH10 ....**19** C5
Golding La RH11..........**59** D7
Goldsmid Mews 10
BN3....................**191** D6
Goldsmid Rd BN3........**191** E7
Goldsmith Rd BN14......**186** E4
Goldstone Cl BN3........**169** A2
Goldstone Cres BN3......**169** B2
Goldstone Ct BN3........**169** A3
Goldstone La 4 BN3......**191** B7
Goldstone Prim Sch
BN3....................**168** C1
Goldstone Rd BN3........**191** B7
Goldstone Ret Pk
BN3....................**191** B8
Goldstone St BN3........**191** B7
Goldstone Villas BN3.....**191** B7
Goldstone Way BN3......**169** A2
Golf Club La RH20.......**120** F7
Golf Dr BN1..............**170** B3
Golfers La BN16.........**205** D7
Golf Links La PO20 ......**209** E1
Golf Links Rd PO22 ......**202** A6
Goodacres
Barnham PO22..........**180** C5
Fontwell BN18 ....**158** B2
Goodhew Cl BN18 ....**181** A3
Goodwin Cl RH11..........**17** F3
Goodwins Ct RH19.........**9** D3
Goodwood Ave PO21 ....**201** F5
Goodwood Cl
Crawley RH10............**19** A3
Midhurst GU29 ....**94** E5
Rustington BN16 ....**205** E6
Goodwood Ct
15 Bognor Regis
PO22 ....**201** C2
2 Hove BN3..............**191** D7
Selsey PO20.............**212** E8
Southbourne PO10 ......**174** A8
Goodwood Ctry Pk*
PO18 ....**136** A4
Goodwood Gdns
PO20 ....**177** E1
Goodwood Ho* PO18 ....**155** F6
Goodwood Rd BN14.......**186** A7
Goodwood Way BN2 .....**170** F3
Goose Green Cl RH12 ......**36** D5
Goosegreen La RH20 .....**102** C2
Gooserye Ct GU30 ....**25** B3
Gordon Ave
1 Bognor Regis
PO22 ....**201** D4
Bognor Regis PO21 ......**201** D5
Shoreham-by-S BN43....**189** A7
Stockbridge PO19 ......**176** E3
Gordon Ave W PO22 .....**201** D5
Gordon Ct RH16 ....**87** E6
Gordon Ho
1 Bognor Regis
PO21 ....**201** C3
2 Bognor Regis PO21 ...**201** D3
Gordon Mews 2
BN41...................**190** C7
Gordon Rd
Brighton BN1............**169** F2
Burgess Hill RH15.......**109** C4
Haywards Heath RH16 ....**87** E6
Hermitage PO10 ....**173** D8
Horsham RH12 ....**36** D4
Lancing BN15............**187** D6
Portslade-by-S, Aldrington
BN41....................**190** A7
Portslade-by-S, Fishersgate
BN41....................**190** A7
Shoreham-by-S BN43....**189** A7
Worthing BN11 ....**186** D3
Gordon Terr
Arundel BN18 ....**183** C8
Bosham PO18 ....**175** A5
Goreside La RH17.........**86** F8
Gorham Ave BN2........**194** A2
Gorham Cl BN2..........**194** A2
GORING-BY-SEA **185** D4
Goring-by-Sea CE Fst Sch
BN12 ....**185** C3

Goring-by-Sea Sta
BN12 ....**185** A4
Goring Chase BN12.......**185** A5
Goring Crossways
BN12 ....**185** A5
Goring Ct
Brighton BN1............**170** F5
Steyning BN44 ....**145** D2
Goring Hall Hospl
(private) BN12 ....**185** B2
Goring Rd
Steyning BN44 ....**145** E2
Worthing BN12 ....**185** D3
Goring's Mead RH13 ......**36** D1
Goring St BN12..........**185** A4
Goring Way
Partridge Green
RH13 ....**105** A3
Worthing BN12 ....**185** A3
Worthing, Goring-by-Sea
BN12...................**185** B4
Gorling Cl RH11 ....**17** E5
Gorringe Cl RH14 ....**56** D6
Gorringes Brook RH12 ....**36** D6
Gorse Ave
Bognor Regis PO22 ......**202** D6
Kingston Gorse BN16 ....**206** D4
Worthing BN14 ....**186** A4
Gorse Bank Cl RH20 .....**122** C3
Gorse Cl
Copthorne RH10 ....**7** B2
Crawley RH11 ....**18** B1
Portslade-by-S BN41......**167** F4
Gorse Cotts GU26.........**26** C8
Gorse End RH12 ....**36** D5
Gorse La BN13 ....**163** E2
Gorselands RH14 ....**79** E8
Gorse Rd GU31............**68** E3
Gorse Terr PO20 ....**198** D4
Gosden Cl RH10 ....**19** A5
GOSDEN GREEN **173** E8
Gosden Rd BN17.........**204** F6
Gosling Croft Bsns Ctr
BN13 ....**162** E1
Gosling Croft BN13 ......**162** E1
GOSPEL GREEN **28** E4
Gospond Rd PO22 ....**180** B5
Gosport Cl 11 BN43......**189** B6
Gossamer La PO21.......**200** D3
Gossops Dr RH11 ....**18** A5
Gossops Green La
RH11 ....**18** A5
Gossops Green Prim Sch
RH11....................**18** A5
Gossops Par RH11 ....**17** F5
Gostrode La GU8 ....**29** A6
Gothic Barns PO18.......**175** F5
Goudhurst Cl RH10 ......**19** E6
Goudhurst Keep RH10 ....**19** E6
Gower Rd
Haywards Heath RH16 ....**87** E3
Horley RH6 ....**1** E3
Gowers Cl RH17 ....**64** B8
Gows Croft BN7 ....**172** E5
Grace Ct
Hassocks BN6 ....**128** E5
Horsham RH13 ....**37** A4
Grace Rd RH11 ....**18** A1
Graffham Cl
Brighton BN2............**192** E6
Chichester PO19 ....**155** A3
Crawley RH11 ....**18** B8
Graffham Fst Sch
GU28 ....**116** B6
Grafton Ave PO22.......**202** C6
Grafton Cl BN16 ....**205** C6
Grafton Ct PO20 ....**212** E6
Grafton Dr BN15.........**187** C6
Grafton Gdns BN15......**187** C6
Grafton Pl 7 BN11.......**186** D2
Grafton Rd
Selsey PO20.............**212** E6
Worthing BN11 ....**186** D2
Grafton St BN2..........**213** C1
Graham Ave
Brighton BN1............**169** F5
Portslade-by-S BN41......**167** F4
Graham Cl BN41.........**167** F4
Graham Cres BN41 ......**167** F4
Graham Ct
Lancing BN15............**187** C6
Worthing BN11 ....**185** F2
Graham Rd
Worthing BN12 ....**186** D2
Yapton BN18 ....**180** F1
Graham's Cotts RH16 ....**64** B1
Grailands Cl GU27........**49** C6
Granary Cl
Horley RH6 ....**2** A5
Horsham RH12 ....**35** F1
Granary La PO20........**212** D8
Granary The PO18 ......**175** F5
Granary Way
Horsham RH12 ....**36** A1
Littlehampton BN17......**204** D8
Grand Ave
Hassocks BN6 ....**128** F4
Hove BN3................**191** C6
Lancing BN15............**187** E7
Littlehampton BN17......**204** C7
Worthing BN11 ....**186** D3
Grand Avenue Mans 4
BN3....................**191** C6
Grand Cres BN2.........**194** A1
Grand Junction Rd
BN1....................**213** B1
Grand Par
Brighton BN2............**213** B2

Grand Par *continued*
Crawley RH10 ....**18** D6
Grand Parade Mews
BN2....................**213** B2
Grange Cl
Brighton BN1............**169** E1
Haywards Heath RH15 ....**109** C5
Crawley RH10 ....**19** A8
Ferring BN12............**206** E5
Grange Cres RH10 ....**21** B7
Grange Ct
Bognor Regis PO21......**200** E1
Hove BN3................**190** F8
7 Middleton-on-S
PO22 ....**202** F5
8 Southwick BN42......**189** E7
Grange Farm Cotts
BN6 ....**193** D4
Grange Field Way
PO21 ....**200** D2
Grange Ind Est The
BN42 ....**189** D7
Grange La PO20 ....**210** B2
Grange Mus & Art
Gallery* BN2 ....**193** F2
Grange Pk BN12.........**206** E5
Grange Rd
Crawley Down RH10 ......**21** A7
Hove BN3................**190** E8
Midhurst GU32 ....**94** F7
Petersfield GU32..........**68** A2
Southwick BN42 ....**189** E7
Grange The
Bognor Regis PO21 ......**200** E2
Felcourt RH19 ....**9** D7
Horley RH6 ....**2** A6
New Brighton PO10 ......**151** B2
Woodmancote PO10 .....**152** A4
Grange Way RH13 ....**57** F2
Grangeways BN1.........**169** E5
Grangeway The BN16.....**205** C5
Grangewood 6 PO21.....**201** B2
Grangewood Dr PO21.....**200** D2
Grant Cl PO20...........**212** D7
Grantham Rd BN1........**170** A1
Grantsmead BN15........**187** E8
Grant St BN2............**213** C4
Granville Ct 10 BN3.......**191** B7
Granville Rd
Hove BN3................**191** E7
Littlehampton BN17......**204** E4
Graperies The 3
BN2....................**192** C5
Grasmere Ave BN15......**187** B6
Grasmere Ct 1 BN11......**186** C1
Grasmere Gdns RH12......**37** B6
Grasmere Ho.............**2** C4
Grasmere Ct
Bognor Regis PO22 ......**201** F4
Littlehampton BN17......**205** A7
Grasmere Par PO22......**201** F4
Gratten La BN5, RH17....**106** D3
Grattons Dr RH10..........**6** C1
Grattons The RH13........**34** E3
Gratwicke Ct RH14........**79** D8
Gratwicke Rd BN11......**186** C2
Gravel La PO19 ....**177** C5
Gravelly Cres RH15 ......**187** F6
Gravelpit Cnr RH17........**39** C1
Gravelye Cl RH16..........**88** B5
Gravelye La
Haywards Heath RH16.....**88** A4
Walstead RH16 ....**88** B6
Graveney Rd RH10........**19** C5
Gravett Ct RH15.........**108** F2
Grayling Cl 3 RH10 ......**19** A4
Grayls La PO21...........**201** B4
Graydon Ave PO19 ......**176** E4
Graylingwell Cotts
PO19 ....**155** A2
Graylingwell Dr
Chichester PO19 ....**155** B1
Chichester PO19 ....**177** B8
Graylingwell Hospl
PO19 ....**155** B1
Grays Cl GU27............**27** E8
Grayshott Dr PO22.......**201** D6
Grays Wood RH6...........**2** C3
Grayswood Ave PO20 ....**208** B6
Grayswood Pl GU27.......**27** E8
Grayswood Rd GU27......**27** D8
Great Ballard Sch
PO18 ....**157** D7
Great College St BN2....**192** C4
Great Field Pl RH19.......**10** B3
Greatfield Way PO9......**130** D3
GREATHAM **120** A4
Greatham Ct BN1........**169** E6
Greatham Rd
Crawley RH10 ....**19** C3
Worthing BN14 ....**164** A1
Great Hanger GU31........**68** D3
Great Heathmead
RH16 ....**87** D6
Great House Ct 4
RH19 ....**22** F8
Greatlake Ct RH6..........**2** B4
Great Lime Kilns RH13.....**58** A1
Greatpin Croft PO20 ......**99** A3
Great Walstead Sch
RH16 ....**88** F6
Great Wilkins BN15......**171** B5
Grebe Cres RH13 ....**37** A1
Greenacre Cl RH20......**121** B1
Greenacres
Ashington RH20..........**123** A6
Birdham PO20 ....**197** D6

Greenacres continued
Brighton BN1 ....169 F1
Crawley RH10 ....19 A5
Horsham RH12 ....36 C4
Shoreham-by-S BN43...188 E8
Steyning BN44......... 145 D2
Greenacres Ring
BN16 ....184 A6
Greena Ct ⬛ BN11.....186 C2
Greenbank PO22.......180 C5
Greenbank Ave BN2 ..194 D2
Green Bushes Cl
BN16 ....205 B4
Green Cl
Southwater RH13 ....57 F3
⬛ Southwick BN42...189 E7
Greencourt Dr PO21 ..201 A5
Green Cross RH17......86 C3
Green Ct
Chichester PO19 ......177 C6
East Wittering PO20 ...207 F7
Littlehampton BN17...204 D4
⬛ Southwick BN42...189 E7
Greenfield RH20.......117 F2
Greenfield Cl
Brighton BN1 ....170 A5
Liphook GU30 ....25 C5
Green Field Cl BN42 ..189 E8
Greenfield Cres BN1..169 F5
Green Field La PO18...153 B3
Greenfield Rd RH13...34 D3
Greenfields
Liss GU33 ....45 C4
Littlehampton BN17...204 B7
Middleton-on-S PO22..202 E5
Nyewood GU31.........92 A7
Greenfields Cl
Horley RH6 ....1 E5
Horsham RH12 ....37 A6
Nyewood GU31.........92 A8
Greenfields Rd
Horley RH6 ....1 F5
Horsham RH12 ....37 A5
Greenfields Sch RH18 ..23 C1
Greenfield Way RH12 ..37 A6
Greenfinch Way RH12..36 D7
Greengates PO21.......50 D2
Green Hedges Ave
RH19 ....9 D2
Green Hedges Cl RH19...9 D2
Greenhill Pk RH17.....88 A2
Greenhill Way RH17....88 A2
Greenhurst La RH20...121 E4
Green La
Bosham PO18 ....175 C6
Broadbridge PO18.....175 A8
Burstow RH6 ....6 F6
Chichester PO19 ......177 B6
Copthorne RH10 ....7 F4
Crawley, Northgate
RH10.................18 E8
Crawley, Worth RH10...19 D6
Cudworth RH5 ....3 D8
Faygate RH12 ....15 F4
Kingsley Green GU27....27 B4
Merston PO20 ....177 F2
Runcton PO20 ....177 F2
Selsey PO20 ....212 D6
Sidlesham PO20.......209 C8
Street End PO20 .....198 E6
West Grinstead RH13 ..104 B8
Woodingdean BN2......193 D6
Greenland Cl BN13...185 E8
Greenland Rd BN13...185 E8
Greenlands Dr RH15..129 B8
Greenland Wlk BN13...185 E8
Green Lane Cl BN18...159 F2
Green Lane Terr ⓫
PO21 ....201 C4
Green Lawns Cvn Pk
PO20 ....212 E8
Greenlea Ave PO21 ...200 B2
Greenleas BN3........168 D2
Greenleaves BN44 ....145 E1
Green Mdws RH16......88 B8
Green Oaks BN15.....187 E8
Green Pk BN12 ....206 F7
Green Ridge BN1......169 B5
Greens La RH13 ....59 D7
Greenstede Ave RH19...9 F2
GREEN STREET 81 C2
Green The
Bognor Regis PO21 ...211 A8
Broadbridge Heath RH12 ..35 D4
Chichester PO19 .....177 C7
Copthorne RH10 ....7 B3
Crawley RH11 ....18 C7
Dial Post RH13 ......103 E3
East Lavington GU28...116 A5
Henfield BN5.........125 E4
Horsted Keynes RH17...65 C5
Hove BN3.............169 C2
Liss GU33 ....45 A5
Partridge Green RH13..105 A3
Pulborough RH20......100 C4
Rottingdean BN2......193 F2
Rowland's Castle PO9...130 E2
Southwick BN42.......189 E7
Shoreham-by-S.........121 F2
Greentree La RH13 ...105 C5
Greentrees
Lancing BN15.........187 C6
⬛ Worthing BN11....186 B2
Greentrees BN15.....187 C6
Greentrees Cres
BN15 ....187 C6

Green View RH15 .....108 E3
Greenview The RH11...39 C7
Greenway RH12.........36 B3
Green Way PO22.......202 F5
Greenway Ct BN2......194 A1
Greenways
Bognor Regis PO21 ...200 B1
Haywards Heath RH16...87 F6
Henfield BN5.........125 D5
Ovingdean BN2........193 D3
Portslade-by-S BN41..168 B1
Southwick BN42.......167 F1
Greenways Cnr BN2...193 D4
Greenways Cres
Ferring BN12.........206 F5
Shoreham-by-S BN43..167 A1
Greenways Wlk RH11...18 C1
Greenway The PO10...151 B4
Green Way The BN12..185 B5
Greenwich Cl RH11...18 C2
Guildbourne Ctr The ⓰
BN11 ....186 D2
Greenwood Ave PO22..201 B6
Greenwood Cl PO22...201 B6
Greenwood Ct ⬛ BN11..18 B1
Greenwood Dr BN16...85 F8
Greenwood Flats RH16..6 F6
Greet Rd BN15 ....187 D7
Gregory Cl RH10.......19 C2
Gregory Ct ⓶ RH19....9 E1
Gregsons RH12........35 E8
Grendon Cl RH6 ....1 F5
Grenehurst Way GU31..68 B4
Grenfield Ct PO10....151 B3
Grenville Ave BN12...185 D4
Grenville Cl
Liphook GU30 ....25 C4
Worthing BN12 ....185 D4
Grenville Gdns PO19..176 F4
Grenville St BN1.....213 A2
Gresham Pl BN5.......125 D5
Gresham Wlk RH10.....18 E3
Grevatt's La BN17,
BN18 ....203 B8
Grevatt's La W BN18..202 F8
Greville Gn PO10 ....151 A3
Grey Alders RH16......88 B6
Greyfriars BN3 ......191 D8
Greyfriars Cl
Bognor Regis PO21 ...200 F3
Worthing BN13 ....186 A6
Greyfriars La RH20...142 C8
Greyhound Slip RH10...19 D7
Greynville Cl PO21...200 C2
Greypoint Ho BN14 ..163 E6
Greystoke Mews
BN2 ....206 E6
Greystoke Rd BN12...206 E6
Greystone Ave
Bognor Regis PO21 ...200 F7
Worthing BN13 ....185 F6
Gribble La PO20 .....178 B7
Grier Cl RH11 ....17 E5
Griffin Cres BN17....204 D8
Griffith's Ave BN15..187 D8
Grinder's La RH13....103 E2
Grinstead Ave BN15..187 E6
Grinstead La
East Grinstead RH19...22 B1
Lancing BN15.........187 E6
Sharpthorne RH19....43 C7
Grinstead Mount ⬛
BN2 ....192 F5
Grisedale Cl RH11...18 C4
Groombridge Way ⬛
RH12 ....35 F1
Grooms Cl BN16......184 A5
Groomsland Dr RH14...79 C6
Grooms The RH10.....19 D8
Grosvenor Cl RH6 .....2 A1
Grosvenor Ct
⓶ Bognor Regis
PO21................201 C2
Grosvenor Gdns
PO21 ....200 C3
Grosvenor Ho ⬛ RH9...9 E3
Grosvenor Ho ⓰
BN11 ....186 D2
Grosvenor Mans ⬛
BN3 ....191 B6
Grosvenor Rd
East Grinstead RH19...9 D1
Stockbridge PO19 ...176 F3
⬛ Worthing BN11....186 D2
Grosvenor St BN2....213 C2
Grosvenor Way PO21..200 C3
Grouse Rd
Barnsnap RH11, RH13..38 D3
Mannings Heath RH13..59 F7
Grove Bank ⑨ BN2...213 C3
Grove Cres BN17.....204 F6
Grove Ct ⓲ BN2......191 C6
Grove Hill BN2.......213 C3
Grove La
Petworth GU28 ....98 A6
West Chiltington Common
RH20.................121 E5
Grovelands RH6.......2 B2
Grovelands Cl RH15..108 F1
Grovelands The BN15..187 E4
Grove La RH10 ....19 C4
Grove Pk PO19 ......176 D6
Grove Rd
Burgess Hill RH15....109 B3
Chichester PO19 .....177 B5
Horley RH6 ....1 F4

Grove Rd continued
Selsey PO20.........212 E6
Worthing BN14 ......186 C6
Grove St
Brighton BN2 ....213 C3
Petworth GU28 ....97 F7
Grove The
Bognor Regis PO22 ...202 A4
Crawley RH11.........18 C1
Ferring BN12.........206 E6
Haywards Heath RH16...88 B3
Horley RH6 ....1 F4
Liphook GU30 ....25 B4
Westbourne PO10 ....151 D3
Grove Villa ⬛ BN1...213 A4
Guardian Ct BN13 ...186 A6
Guernsey Cl RH11....18 A2
Guernsey Farm La
PO22 ....202 D5
Guernsey Rd BN12...206 F4
Guernsey
BN11 ....186 D2
Guilden Rd PO19 ....177 B6
Guildford Cl
Breach PO18 ....152 A1
Worthing BN14 ......186 A3
Guildford Pl PO19...154 F1
Guildford Rd
Brighton BN1 ....213 A3
Broadbridge Heath RH12...35 B6
Horsham RH12.........36 A2
Loxwood RH14........31 F4
Rowhook RH12, RH13...34 C7
Rudgwick RH12........33 C6
Rustington BN16.....205 E6
Worthing BN14 ......186 A3
Guildford St BN1 .....1 A3
Guildhall Mus* PO19..177 A7
Guildhall St PO19...177 A7
Guillards Oak GU29...94 E7
Guillemot Path ⑵
RH11 ....17 D5
Guillods Cotts GU28..116 A7
Guinevere Rd RH10...17 E6
Guinness Ct RH11....18 C2
Gunning Cl RH10.....18 A3
Gunns Farm GU30....25 C2
GUNTER'S BRIDGE 54 F4
Gunwin Ct PO21......200 D2
Guyhurst Spinney
RH20 ....122 A6
Gwydir Mans ⬛ BN3..191 D6
Gwynne Gdns RH19....9 C2

H

HABIN...............70 B2
Habin Hill GU31......70 B3
Hackenden Cl RH19....9 E3
Hackenden La RH19....9 E3
Haddington Cl BN3...191 B6
Haddington St ⓫
BN3 ....191 B7
Hadlands PO21.......200 A1
Hadley Ave BN14 ....186 D6
Hadley Cl PO22......202 E6
Hadlow Cl BN2 ......192 D6
Hadlow Way BN15....187 F6
Hadmans Cl RH12 ....36 C1
Hadrian Ave BN42 ...190 A8
Haglands Copse
RH20 ....121 D7
Haglands La RH20....121 D7
Haig Ave BN1 ....170 D6
Haigh Cl BN15.......188 B6
Hailsham Ave BN2....193 B6
Hailsham Cl RH16....206 B7
Hailsham Rd BN11...185 F2
Hale Cl PO20 ....208 B6
HALECOMMON..........70 A5
Hales Field GU27.....27 C6
Halewick Cl BN15....187 C8
Halewick La BN15....187 C8
Haleybridge Wlk
PO20 ....156 D1
Halfacres RH10 ......18 E7
Half Moon Ct ⓱ BN13..185 F8
Half Moon Hill GU27...27 C6
Half Moon La BN13...185 E8
Halfrey Cl PO18......176 A7
Halfrey Rd PO18, PO19..176 B7
HALFWAY BRIDGE 96 C8
Halfway Sta* BN2....192 C4
Halifax Cl RH10 ......6 E1
Halifax Dr BN13......185 C7
Halland Cl RH10 .....19 A7
Halland Rd BN2 .....170 D4
Hallands The RH15...109 C4
Hall Ave BN14 ....186 A7
Hall Cl BN14.........186 A7
Hallett Rd BN2 .....192 D7
Haley Cl RH11 ....18 B1
Halley's Cl RH11.....177 C6
Halliford Dr PO22....180 C6
Halliwick's Rd PO22..202 B4
Halls Dr RH12 ....16 F1
Hallsland RH10 ......22 A2
Hallyburton Rd BN3..190 D8
Halnaker Barn La
PO18 ....157 B4
Halnaker Gdns PO21..200 C2
Halnaker Wlk ⬛ RH11...17 F3
Halsbury Cl BN11....186 F3
Halsbury Rd BN11...186 F3
Halsford Croft RH19...9 B3
Halsford Gn RH19.....9 B3

Halsford La RH19......9 C3
Halsford Park Prim Sch
RH19 ....9 C2
Halsford Park Rd RH19...9 C2
Halson Cl PO21......201 C4
Halton Shaws BN6...128 B5
Hamble Cl BN15......187 B6
Hamble Gdns BN13...185 C8
Hamble Rd BN13.....185 C8
Hambleton Ct RH11...18 C4
Hambleton Mill RH11..18 C4
Hamble Way BN13....185 C8
Ham Rd
Shoreham-by-S BN43..188 F7
Sidlesham PO20......209 C5
Worthing BN11, BN14..187 A3
Hamsey Cl BN2.......192 F5
Hamsey Rd
Saltdean BN2.........194 D1
Sharpthorne RH19....43 A6
Hamshire Hill RH17...60 C5
Hamsland RH17......65 C4
Hamstead Mdw PO18..174 E7
Ham Way BN11 ......187 A4
Hanbury La RH16.....88 A5
Hanbury Rd RH11.....17 E5
Hanbury Sq GU31.....58 C5
Hancock Way BN43...189 B6
Handcross Park Prep Sch
RH17 ....39 C2
Handcross Prim Sch
RH17 ....39 C2
Handcross Rd
Balcombe RH17.......40 D3
Lower Beeding RH13,
RH17.................60 C5
Handford Way RH13...60 D6
Handsworth Ho ⓶
RH10 ....18 D5
Hangar Way GU31.....68 D3
Hangleton Cl BN3....168 D2
Hangleton Ct BN11...185 F2
Hangleton Gdns BN3..168 D1
Hangleton Grange
BN12 ....206 E7
Hangleton Jun & Inf Sch
BN3 ....168 E2
Hangleton La
Hangleton BN12......206 D8
Portslade-by-S BN41..168 B2
Hangleton Manor Cl
BN3 ....168 D2
Hangleton Rd BN3...168 D3
Hangleton Valley Dr
BN3 ....168 D4
Hangleton Way BN3..168 D3
Hanlye La RH17......87 B8
Hannah Sq PO19.....170 D7
Hannington Pl BN6...128 A7
Hanover Cl
Bury RH20 ....140 A7
Crawley RH10 ....18 F3
Selsey PO20.........212 F7
Hanover Cres BN2...213 C4
Hanover Ct
Brighton BN2 ....213 C4
Haywards Heath RH16...87 D4
⬛ Horsham RH13.....36 F3
Liphook GU30 ....25 B5
Midhurst GU29 ....73 E2
Worthing BN14 ......186 C6
Hanover Gdns RH13...83 E2
Hanover Lofts BN2...213 C3
Hanover Mews BN2...213 C4
Hanover St BN2......213 C4
Hanover Terr BN2...213 C4
Hanover Wlk RH10...121 D1
Harberton Cres PO19..155 A3
Harbelets Rd RH14,
RH20 ....102 A5
Harborough Cl RH20..121 B8
Harborough Dr RH20..121 B8
Harborough Gorse
RH20 ....121 B8
Harborough Hill
RH20 ....121 B8
Harborough Mdw
RH20 ....121 B8
Harbour Cotts PO18..175 A4
Harbour Ct
Bosham PO18 ....175 C5
⓰ Emsworth PO10...173 B8
Southwick BN42......189 F7
Harbour Ho BN43....189 B6
Harbour Rd
Bosham PO18 ....175 B4
Pagham PO21 ....210 F6
Harbour View Pk
BN17 ....204 C4
Harbour View Rd
PO21 ....211 A8
Harbour Way
Bosham PO18 ....175 C4
Chidham PO18 ....174 F5
Emsworth PO10 ......173 B8
Shoreham-by-S BN43..189 B6
Harcourt Way PO20..212 F8
Hardbarrow Woods
RH20 ....122 A6
HARDHAM.............119 F7
Hardham Cl
Crawley RH11 ....18 A8
Rustington BN16.....205 B4
Hardham Rd PO19....177 B5
Hard's Farm RH13....58 D5
Hard The PO22 ......203 C5
Hardwick Lo ⬛ BN11...186 C2

Hardwick Rd BN3........168 E3
Hardwick Way BN3........168 E3
Hardy Ave GU31 ....68 C5
Hardy Cl
  Bognor Regis PO22....202 D5
  Crawley RH10 ....1 E3
  Horley RH6 ....1 E3
  Horsham RH12 ....36 B4
  Shoreham-by-S BN43...188 F6
Harebell Cl BN17 ....205 B7
Harebell Dr BN41 ....168 A3
Harefield Ave BN13 .....185 F5
Harefield Gdns PO22....202 F5
Harefield Rd PO22......202 F6
Hare La
  Crawley RH11 ....18 B8
  Selsey PO20............212 B8
Haresfield Terr PO20....156 E3
Haresfoot Cl PO18......152 F5
Hares La PO18...........152 E6
Harewood Cl RH10........6 A1
Harewood Ct B BN3.....191 C6
Harfield Ct B PO21.....201 D3
Harlands Cl RH16.........87 C6
Harlands Ho RH16........87 D6
Harlands Prim Sch
  RH16 ....87 D7
Harlands Rd RH16........87 D6
Harlech Cl BN13 ....185 B6
Harley Ct B BN11 ......186 B2
Harmans Dr RH19 ....10 B1
Harmans Mead RH19 .....10 B1
Harmony Cl RH11.........17 E4
Harmony Dr PO20 ....208 B5
Harmsworth Cres
  BN3 ....168 E3
Harold Cl PO21.........200 F6
Harold Kidd Unit The
  PO19 ....155 A2
Harold Rd
  Crawley RH10 ....19 E5
  Westbourne PO10 ......151 D4
Haroldslea Ho..........2 E2
Haroldslea Cl RH6 ....2 C1
Haroldslea Dr RH6.......2 D1
Harold Terr PO10 ....151 B1
Harper Dr RH10 ....19 C2
Harrier Cl RH10..........6 D1
Harrier Ho B RH20....121 E1
Harrier Way GU31 ....68 E2
Harriet Pl B BN43......189 B6
Harrington Ct BN1......169 E2
Harrington Mans BN1....169 E2
Harrington Pl BN1......170 B2
Harrington Rd BN1......169 E2
Harrington Villas BN1...169 F2
Harriots Ct RH13.........59 A1
Harriot's Hill RH13......83 A8
Harris Cl RH11..........18 B3
Harris Ct GU30..........25 B2
Harris La PO8...........110 A5
Harrison Ct BN14.......186 E5
Harrison Rd BN14.......186 F5
Harris Path RH11........18 B3
Harrow Dr PO17.........207 F7
Harrow Ho RH6...........2 A3
Harrow La GU32..........68 B6
Harrow Rd BN11........186 B3
Harrowsley Ct RH6.......2 B4
Harrows The GU28.......97 B8
Harsfold Cl BN16.......205 B4
Harsfold Rd BN16.......205 B4
Hartfield Ave BN1......170 A5
Hartfield Rd
  Forest Row RH18........23 F2
  Saltdean BN2 ....194 D1
Harting Cl BN12 ....185 B5
Harting Ct RH11........17 F3
Harting Down GU31......68 D4
Harting Downs Nature
  Reserve* PO18 ....112 A7
Harting Rd BN17........204 D7
Hastings The PO22......202 D6
Hartington Ho B
  PO21 ....201 B3
Hartington Pl BN2......192 C8
Hartington Rd BN2......192 C8
Hartington Terr BN2....192 C8
Hartington Villas BN3...191 B8
Hartland Ct PO10.......151 F1
Hartley Ct B BN1......213 A4
Harvest Cl RH16.........88 B7
Harvester Ct PO19......177 C7
Harvesters
  Haywards Heath RH16 ...87 D2
  Horsham RH12 ....36 D5
Harvest Hill
  Ansty RH17 ....86 D1
  East Grinstead RH19 ...22 E8
Harvest Rd RH10........19 C4
Harvestside RH6.........2 C4
Harvey Cl
  Crawley RH11 ....18 A1
  Sayers Common BN6 ...107 D2
Harvey Rd BN12 ....185 E2
Harvey Villas GU30......24 D8
Harwarden Cl RH10.......21 C8
Harwood Ave BN12 .....185 D5
Harwood Pk RH1 ....2 A8
Harwood Rd
  Horsham RH12, RH13 ...37 A3
  Littlehampton BN17....204 C6
Harwood Road Ent Units
  BN17 ....204 C6
Harwoods Cl B RH19....22 F7

HARWOODS GREEN 99 E5
Harwoods La RH19 ....22 F7
Hascombe Ct RH11 ......18 A5
Hasle Dr GU27...........27 B6
Haslemere Educational
  Mus* GU27............27 D7
Haslemere Gdns
  PO11 ....195 B2
Haslemere Hospl
  GU27 ....27 D7
Haslemere Ind Est
  GU27 ....27 C7
Haslemere Prep Sch
  GU27 ....27 D5
Haslemere Rd
  Breach PO10 ....151 F2
  Fernhurst GU27.........49 B7
  Kingsley Green GU27....27 B1
  Liphook GU30 ....25 D4
Haslemere Sta GU27.....27 B6
Hasler's La PO18 ....134 E5
Haslett Ave E RH10 .....19 A6
Haslett Ave E RH10 .....18 D5
HASLINGBOURNE 98 A5
Haslingbourne La
  GU28 ....97 F5
Hassocks Ct B RH11....17 F3
Hassocks Inf Sch BN6..128 F4
Hassocks Lo BN6 ....128 F3
Hassocks Rd BN6.......128 B5
Hassocks Sta BN6......128 E4
Haste Hill GU27.........27 D5
Hastings Cl PO21.......200 F4
Hastings Ct
  B Shoreham-by-S
  BN43 ....189 B6
  B Worthing BN11......186 A1
Hastings Rd
  Brighton BN2...........192 C8
  Crawley RH10 ....19 C6
  Hayling Ct RH11 ....18 A5
  Hayling Ct RH11 ....18 A1
Hatch Cl GU6............41 A3
Hatch End RH18 ....23 F2
Hatches Cotts RH40....101 E1
Hatchetts Dr GU27......26 D7
Hatchgate RH6 ....1 F2
Hatchgate Cl RH17......87 A6
Hatchgate La RH17......87 A6
Hatch Hill GU27 ....27 B1
Hatch La
  Kingsley Green GU27....27 B2
  Liss GU33 ....45 E4
Hatchlands
  Cuckfield RH17 ....86 F6
  Horsham RH13 ....37 A7
Hatfield Ct B BN3.....191 C6
Hatfield Wlk
  Crawley RH11 ....17 E2
  Worthing BN13 ....185 D6
Hatherleigh Cl PO21....201 A5
Hatherleigh Gdns
  PO21 ....201 A5
Hathersham La RH1, RH6...2 F6
Haughton Ho GU27......27 B6
Havant Rd PO10 ....173 A8
Havelock Ct PO22......201 F3
Havelock Rd
  Bognor Regis PO21.....201 C4
  Brighton BN1..........169 F1
Haven Cotts B PO22...201 D5
Haven Ct PO20 ....207 F7
Havengate RH12.........36 F5
Haven Gdns RH10........8 B1
Haven Rd
  Rudgwick RH12, RH14....33 D3
  South Hayling PO11....195 A1
Havenside BN43 ....188 E6
Havenstoke Cl PO19....155 A1
HAVEN THE 33 D2
Haven The
  Lancing BN15...........187 F4
  Littlehampton BN17....205 A5
Havenwood Pk BN18....159 B3
Haversham Cl RH10......18 F6
Haversham Ho RH6.......2 B5
Hawker Cl PO20 ....156 D2
Hawkesbourne Rd
  RH12 ....36 B2
Hawkesmoor Rd RH11...17 E4
Hawkhurst Pl BN1......170 D6
Hawkhurst Rd BN1......170 D6
Hawkhurst Wlk B
  RH10 ....19 B4
Hawkins Cl
  Bognor Regis PO22....200 B2
  Shoreham-by-S BN43...167 D1
Hawkins Cres BN43.....167 D2
Hawkins Rd RH10........18 E4
Hawkley Rd GU33........45 A5
Hawkridge RH12..........12 E1
Hawksfold La E GU27....49 A6
Hawksfold La W GU27....49 A6
Hawkshaw GU30 ....25 D4
Hawks Mead GU33.......45 A5
Hawks Pl PO22 ....201 B6
Hawley Rd BN16........205 B4
Hawmead RH10..........21 C8
Hawth Ave BN10 ....68 A1
Hawth Ave RH10.........18 E4
Hawth Cl RH10 ....18 E4
Hawthorn Bank BN2....170 C4
Hawthorn Cl
  Burgess Hill RH15 ....109 D5
  Chichester PO19.......176 F7
  Crawley RH11 ....5 C1

Hawthorn Cl continued
  Horsham RH12 ....36 C4
  Midhurst GU29 ....94 D6
  B Rustington BN16 ...205 C4
  Saltdean BN2...........194 C2
Hawthorn Cres BN14....186 D6
Hawthorn Ct GU31......68 A8
Hawthorn Gdns BN14...186 D6
Hawthorn Pl B RH12...87 C2
Hawthorn Rd
  Bognor Regis PO21,
  PO22..................201 B4
  Littlehampton BN17....204 D7
  Worthing BN14 ....186 D6
Hawthorns Fst Sch
  BN13 ....185 C6
Hawthorns The
  B Bognor Regis
  PO21 ....201 C4
  Burgess Hill RH15 ....109 A5
  West Chiltington Common
  RH20..................121 E7
Hawthorn Trad Est
  RH13 ....36 E4
Hawthorn Way
  Portslade-by-S BN41...168 A3
  Storrington BN2........121 D2
Hayburn Dr RH12 ....36 E7
Haybourne Cl BN2......192 E7
Haybourne Rd BN2......192 E7
Haydon Cl PO21........200 C1
Hayes Cl
  Mid Lavant PO18.......154 E7
  Portslade-by-S BN41...190 C8
Hayes La RH13 ....34 D2
Hayes Wood Rd RH14....55 F5
Hayfields RH6.............2 C4
Hayley Rd BN15........187 F7
Hayley's Gdns PO22....202 A4
Hayling Cl RH16.........88 B5
Hayling Ct RH11 ....18 A5
Hayling Gdns BN13.....163 E1
Hayling Rise BN13......163 E1
Haynes Rd BN14........186 B4
Haynes Way BN14.......186 B4
Hay Rd PO19 ....177 B4
Hays Cotts GU32........67 F7
Haystacks GU29 ....115 C8
Hayton Ct BN13........185 B6
Haywards RH10...........6 D1
Haywards Cl PO22......202 B5
Haywards Heath Rd
  RH17 ....41 A1
Haywards Heath Sta
  RH16 ....87 E6
Haywards Pl PO20 .....208 C5
Haywards Rd
  Brighton BN1..........170 A6
  Haywards Heath RH16 ...87 E3
Haywards Rd RH16.......87 F3
Hazel Bank B BN2 ....213 C4
Hazelbank Cl
  Liphook GU30 ....25 D4
  Petersfield GU31.......68 D4
Hazelbank Mews GU30....25 D4
Hazel Cl
  Crawley Down RH10 ....21 C8
  Crawley RH11 ....5 C1
  Hove BN41.............168 C3
  Southwater RH13 ....58 A1
Hazel Ct B RH12 ....36 F4
Hazeldean Ct PO9......130 D1
Hazeldean Dr PO9......130 D1
Hazeldene Meads
  BN1 ....169 D3
Hazeldene Rd GU30......24 D4
Hazel Gr
  Arundel BN18 ....159 E2
  Bognor Regis PO21.....200 D3
  Burgess Hill RH15 ....109 B1
Hazelgrove Gdns B
  RH16 ....87 E4
Hazelgrove Rd RH16.....87 E4
Hazelholt BN1..........167 F3
Hazelhurst RH6...........2 C4
Hazelhurst Cres
  Horsham RH12 ....35 F1
  Worthing BN14 ....163 F3
Hazelhurst Dr RH10......19 E6
Hazelmead Dr BN16....206 A5
Hazel Rd
  Angmering BN16 ....206 A8
  Bognor Regis PO22....201 B6
Hazel Way RH10 ....21 C8
Hazelwick Ave RH10 .....19 B8
Hazelwick Mill La
  RH10 ....19 A8
Hazelwick Rd RH10 .....19 A7
Hazelwick Sch RH10....19 A8
Hazel Wlk GU30 ....68 B1
Hazelwood
  Billingshurst RH14 ....169 D3
  Crawley RH11 ....18 A5
Hazelwood Cl
  Crawley Down RH10 ....20 F8
  Heath Common RH20 ...122 B2
  Midhurst GU29 ....73 A3
  Worthing BN14 ....186 F4
Hazelwood Cotts GU6....11 D4
Hazelwood Lo B
  BN15 ....187 F5
Hazelwood Rd RH13 ...105 A3
Hazelwood Trad Est
  BN14 ....186 F5
Hazleden Cross RH19....22 B6
Headborough Ct B
  BN15 ....187 E4

Headborough Gdns B
  BN15 ....187 E4
Head Down BN2.........68 D3
Headhone Barns
  PO22 ....179 D4
Headley Cl PO22.........6 D1
Headley Dr PO22 ....201 D6
Headley Rd GU30 ....25 B5
Hearn Cl PO20..........156 C1
Hearnfield Rd BN17....204 D8
Heasewood RH16.........87 C3
Heath Bsns Ctr RH1......2 B8
Heath Cl
  Broadbridge Heath
  RH12..................35 E3
  B Haywards Heath
  RH16..................87 E4
  Hunston PO20 ....199 A8
  Mannings Heath RH13....59 D6
  Sayers Common BN6....107 D1
Heathcote Dr RH19 ....9 C2
Heathcotes RH10 ....19 D4
Heathcourt BN17.......204 D8
Heath Ct
  Haywards Heath RH16 ...87 E5
  Petersfield GU31.......68 B2
HEATH END 97 D2
Heath End GU28 ....97 D2
Heather Bank RH16.....87 C5
Heather Cl
  Copthorne RH10 ....7 B2
  Horsham RH12 ....36 D5
  West Ashling PO18 ....153 C3
Heather Ct
  B Brighton BN1 ....191 E6
  Chichester PO19.......176 F5
Heather Ho RH15........187 F7
Heather La
  West Chiltington Common
  RH20..................121 C6
  Worthing BN13 ....163 E2
Heatherlands
  Horley RH6 ....2 B4
  Storrington RH20......121 C7
Heatherlea Ho BN15....187 D6
Heatherleigh Ct RH12....36 C4
Heather Rd GU31........68 E3
Heathers The RH16.....183 F6
Heatherstone Rd
  BN11 ....187 B2
Heatherton Mews
  PO10 ....151 B3
Heatherway RH19........8 F7
Heather Way RH20......121 C7
Heather Wlk RH11........18 B3
Heatherwood GU29......94 D8
Heatherwood Rd GU29...94 D8
Heathfield RH10 ....19 D6
Heathfield Ave
  Angmering BN16 ....205 F7
  Saltdean BN2...........194 D2
Heathfield Cl
  B Midhurst GU29......94 E7
  Worthing BN13 ....185 F6
Heathfield Copse
  BN26 ....121 C7
Heathfield Cres BN41...167 F3
Heathfield Dr BN41.....167 F4
Heathfield Gate B
  GU29 ....94 E7
Heathfield Gdns GU29...94 E7
Heathfield Gn GU29.....94 E7
Heathfield Pk GU29.....94 E7
Heath Hill Ave BN2.....170 F1
Heath Lo GU33..........68 B2
Heath Pl PO22..........201 D7
Heath Rd
  Haslemere GU27........26 D5
  Haywards Heath RH16 ...87 E5
  Petersfield GU31.......68 C3
Heath Rd E GU31.......68 D2
Heath Rd W GU31.......68 C2
Heath Sq RH16..........87 D5
Heathtolt Cotts RH13....83 A6
Heath Way RH10 ....19 D6
Heaven Farm* RH17.....66 B1
Hebe Rd BN3...........188 E7
Hechle Wood PO21.....200 F2
Hectors La RH19........23 C7
Hedgecourt Pl RH19......8 E4
Hedge End PO22........180 C6
Hedgehog La GU27.......27 B5
Hedgerow Gdns PO10...151 B3
Hedgers Hill BN18.....158 F2
Hedgeside RH11..........18 C1
Hedgeway PO22........202 D5
Hedingham Cl RH10......2 C4
Heene CE Fst Sch
  BN11 ....186 C3
Heene Lo BN11.........186 B1
Heene Pl BN11.........186 C1
Heene Rd BN11.........186 B1
Heene Terr BN11.......186 B1
Heene Way BN11.......186 B1
Heghbrok Way PO21....201 A2
Heights The
  Brighton BN1..........169 B5
  B Haywards Heath
  RH16..................87 E4
  Worthing BN14 ....164 A1
Helena Cl BN3..........168 A3
Helena Rd BN2.........171 C1
Helen Ct B BN11.......185 F3
Helicon Rd RH10........18 C5
Hellingly Ct BN2.......192 C8
Helston Dr PO10.......151 B3
Helyer's Gn BN17......204 C6

Hempstead Rd BN2.....194 D3
Hemsby Wlk B RH10....19 B4
Hemsleys The BN11......39 B6
Henbane Ct B BN11.....18 B2
Henderson Rd RH11......18 B1
Henderson Way RH12....57 F8
Henderson Wlk BN44...145 D4
Hendon Ave BN16 ......205 A3
Hendon Ho BN16 ......205 C3
Hendon St BN2.........192 D5
Henfield Bsns Pk
  BN5 ....126 A1
Henfield Cl
  Brighton BN2..........192 F5
  Worthing BN11 ....185 B5
Henfield Common N
  BN5 ....125 F4
Henfield Mus* BN5....125 F4
Henfield Rd
  Albourne Green BN6...127 B7
  Upper Beeding BN44,
  BN5...................146 D3
Henfield Way
  Bognor Regis PO22....202 D6
  Hove BN3..............168 F3
Henge Way BN41 ......168 B2
Hengist Cl RH12 ....36 A1
HENLEY 73 B8
Henley Cl RH10.........19 D3
HENLEY COMMON 48 F1
Henley Ct
  Brighton BN2..........192 F4
  Worthing BN11 ....185 F4
Henley Rd BN2.........192 F4
Henry Ave RH16.........205 B5
Henry Burt Way RH15...108 E1
Henry Ho PO19.........177 D6
Henry Fletcher Cl
  BN16 ....184 A5
Henry St PO21..........201 D4
Henshaw Ct RH11........17 F4
Henson Rd RH10........19 B7
Henty Cl
  Crawley RH11 ....17 E3
  Walberton BN18 ....180 E8
  B Worthing BN14......186 C4
Henty Gdns PO19 ......176 F6
Henty Rd
  Ferring BN12 ....206 F4
  Worthing BN14 ....186 C4
Henwood Down GU31....68 C3
Heo Gn BN17...........204 B7
Hepplewhite Cl RH11....18 B1
Herald Dr PO19.........177 A5
Herbert Rd
  Brighton BN1..........169 F2
  North Lancing BN15...165 B1
Herbert Shiner Sch
  GU28 ....97 F7
Hercules Pl PO22 ......202 D5
Hereford Cl
  Chichester PO19.......154 F1
  Crawley RH10 ....18 E2
Hereford Ct
  B Brighton BN2........213 C2
  B Hove BN3...........191 C7
Hereford Ho BN12 .....185 A4
Hereford St BN2........192 C5
Herington Rd BN18.....159 F2
Heritage Lawn RH6.......2 C4
Heritage Pl B BN16....205 C4
Herm Cl RH11..........18 A2
Hermione Cl BN12......206 E7
Hermitage Cl PO20....177 D1
Hermitage La RH19......22 F8
Hermitage Rd RH19......9 D3
Hermitage The PO20....177 D1
Hermit Rd RH10.........18 F7
Hermit Terr BN14......163 E6
Hermonger La RH12.....12 F2
Hern Ct BN18..........206 F4
Herne Ct B BN16......205 D6
Herne Gdns BN16......205 D6
Herne Jun Sch GU31....68 C4
Herne La BN16.........205 D6
Herne St GU31..........68 C3
Heron Cl
  Bognor Regis PO22....201 B7
  Crawley RH11 ....18 C8
  B Horley RH6 ....154 E7
Heron Ct
  Chichester PO19.......177 D7
  B Worthing BN11......186 C3
Herondale GU27.........26 E6
Herondean PO19........154 F2
Heron La PO20 ....212 B8
Heron Mead PO21 ......210 F7
Heron Pl RH19..........22 F8
Heron Quay PO10.......173 C7
Herons Cl
  Domewood RH10 ....8 B5
  Kirdford RH14 ....53 B2
Heron's Court Cl B
  BN16 ....205 C4
Herons Ct PO22 ....201 F5
Herons Dale Sch
  BN43 ....167 C1
Herons Lea RH10........8 A4
Heron's Rye B PO20....100 C2
Herons The
  Lancing BN15...........187 F4
  Selsey PO20...........212 D7
  Shoreham-by-S BN43...189 A8
Heron's Tye BN6........128 F3
Heronswood Ct RH6......2 B4
Herontye Dr RH19 ....23 A8

Herontye Ho RH19 . . . . 22 F7
Heron Way RH13 . . . . 37 A1
Heron Way Prim Sch
  RH13 . . . . 37 A1
Herrick Cl RH10 . . . . 19 C8
Herschel Wlk 3 RH11 . . . . 18 E1
Hersee Way PO20 . . . . 212 C7
Hertford Cl PO21 . . . . 200 F3
Hertford Ct 3 BN11 . . . . . 186 D3
Hertford Inf Sch BN1 . . . . 170 B2
Hertford Jun Sch
  BN1 . . . . 170 C2
Hertford Rd
  Brighton BN1 . . . . 170 B2
  Worthing BN11 . . . . 186 D3
Heston Ave BN1 . . . . 169 F7
Heston Gr PO21 . . . . 200 C1
Hett Cl RH17 . . . . 64 B8
Hevers Ave RH6 . . . . 2 A4
Hevers Cnr RH6 . . . . 1 F4
Hewart's La PO21 . . . . 200 D4
Hewitts Cl 4 RH12 . . . . . . 36 C2
Hewitts BN5 . . . . 125 E4
Hewitts End BN5 . . . . 125 E4
Hewshott Gr GU30 . . . . . . 25 E5
Hewshott La
  Linchmere GU30 . . . . 26 A5
  Liphook GU30 . . . . 25 E5
Hexham Cl RH10 . . . . 19 E6
Heyshott La RH17 . . . . 187 F8
Heyworth Cl RH12 . . . . 193 F8
Heyworth Prim Sch
  RH16 . . . . 87 F4
Heyworth Ride RH16 . . . . . 87 C3
Hickling Wlk 3 RH10 . . . . 19 B4
Hickman's Cl RH16 . . . . . . 88 B8
Hickmans Ct RH16 . . . . 88 B8
Hickman's La RH16 . . . . . . 88 A8
Hickstead Int Arena*
  RH17 . . . . 107 D4
Hickstead La RH17 . . . . . . 107 C5
Hickstead Pk BN6 . . . . 107 D2
Hide Gdns BN16 . . . . 205 B6
Higgins La RH13 . . . . 36 E1
Highams Hill RH11 . . . . 17 F5
Highbank
  9 Bognor Regis
  PO22 . . . . 201 D5
  Brighton BN1 . . . . 169 C5
  Haywards Heath RH16 . . . 87 C1
High Bank PO20 . . . . 198 F8
High Bar La RH20 . . . . 122 A6
Highbarn BN14 . . . . 163 E7
High Beeches 7
  BN11 . . . . 186 A1
High Beeches Cotts
  RH17 . . . . 39 E2
High Beeches Gdns*
  RH17 . . . . 39 F2
High Beeches La RH17 . . . . 39 E2
High Beech La RH16 . . . . . . 63 F1
Highbirch Cl RH12 . . . . 37 B5
HIGHBROOK 42 E1
Highbrook Cl RH10 . . . . . . 170 D3
Highbrook La RH10 . . . . . . 42 F4
Highbury Cotts RH17 . . . . . 61 B8
Highbury Gr GU27 . . . . 27 C8
High Cl BN41 . . . . 168 A1
Highclere Way BN13 . . . . . 185 B6
Highcliff Ct BN2 . . . . 194 A1
Highcroft Ave PO22 . . . . . . 201 D5
Highcroft Cl PO22 . . . . 201 E5
Highcroft Cres PO22 . . . . . 201 E5
Highcroft Dr RH12 . . . . 12 E1
Highcroft Lo BN1 . . . . 191 E8
Highcroft Mews BN1 . . . . . 169 D1
Highcroft Rd RH19 . . . . 43 A6
Highcroft Villas BN1 . . . . . 191 E8
HIGH CROSS 126 F7
Highden 2 BN2 . . . . 192 C6
Highdown BN42 . . . . 167 F1
Highdown Ave BN13 . . . . . 186 A5
Highdown Cl
  Angmering BN16 . . . . 184 A5
  Ferring BN12 . . . . 206 E2
  Southwick BN42 . . . . 167 F1
Highdown Ct
  Brighton BN1 . . . . 169 E3
  Crawley RH10 . . . . 19 B8
Highdown Dr BN17 . . . . . . 204 D6
Highdown Gdns*
  RH12 . . . . 184 F5
Highdown Rd BN1,
  BN3 . . . . 191 E7
Highdown Way
  Ferring BN12 . . . . 206 E2
  Horsham RH12 . . . . 36 F6
Highercombe Rd GU27 . . . . 27 E8
Highfield BN17 . . . . 204 B7
Highfield Cl
  Angmering BN16 . . . . 184 A5
  Midhurst GU29 . . . . 73 A2
Highfield Cotts BN1 . . . . . 170 A5
Highfield Cres BN1 . . . . . . 170 A5
Highfield Ct
  7 Haywards Heath
  RH16 . . . . 87 E4
  Worthing BN14 . . . . 186 E6
Highfield Dr BN6 . . . . 128 C5
Highfield Gdns
  Bognor Regis PO22 . . . . . 201 D5
  Liss GU33 . . . . 45 D4
  1 Rustington BN16 . . . . . 205 B5
Highfield Ho RH11 . . . . 18 D7
Highfield La
  Liphook GU30 . . . . 25 E3
  Oving PO20 . . . . 178 C7

Highfield Rd
  Bognor Regis PO22 . . . . . 201 D5
  East Grinstead RH19 . . . . 9 D3
  Petersfield GU32 . . . . 68 B4
  Shoreham BN13 . . . . 186 A6
Highfields
  Brighton BN1 . . . . 170 E5
  Forest Row RH18 . . . . . . 23 F2
  Horsted Keynes RH17 . . . 65 C4
Highfield Sch GU30 . . . . . . 25 E2
HIGHGATE 23 F1
Highgate Cl RH11 . . . . 18 C2
Highgate Dr PO21 . . . . 200 F6
Highgate Rd RH18 . . . . 23 F1
Highground La PO22 . . . . . 180 B4
Highgrove Gdns
  BN11 . . . . 186 B2
High Hatch La BN6 . . . . . . 108 B4
High La GU27 . . . . 27 C8
Highland Ave PO21 . . . . . . 201 B4
Highland Cl RH10 . . . . 173 A8
Highland Croft BN44 . . . . 145 D3
Highland La RH17 . . . . 87 C4
Highland Rd
  Chichester PO19 . . . . 155 A2
  Emsworth PO10 . . . . 151 A1
  Haywards Heath RH16 . . . 87 F3
Highlands Ave RH13 . . . . . 36 E2
Highlands Cl
  Keymer BN6 . . . . 129 A3
  Worthing BN13 . . . . 163 E1
Highlands Cres RH13 . . . . . 36 E2
Highlands Dr RH15 . . . . . . 109 A4
Highlands Farm Bsns Pk
  RH17 . . . . 85 D3
Highlands Rd
  Horsham RH13 . . . . 36 F2
  Portslade-by-S BN41 . . . . 168 B1
Highlands The RH17 . . . . . 86 F8
Highleigh 3 BN2 . . . . 213 C3
Highleigh Rd PO20 . . . . . . 198 C2
High Mdw GU29 . . . . 114 D8
High Oaks RH11 . . . . 18 B4
High Park Ave BN3 . . . . . . 168 E3
High Path GU29 . . . . 73 A2
High Pines BN11 . . . . 186 B2
High Point RH16 . . . . 88 A3
High Ridge Cl BN41 . . . . . 159 F1
HIGH SALVINGTON 163 E1
High Salvington
  Windmill*
  BN13 . . . . 163 E2
High Seat Copse RH14 . . . . 55 D1
High Seat Gdns RH14 . . . . . 55 D1
High Spinney RH20 . . . . . . 121 E5
High St
  Amberley BN18 . . . . 140 E7
  Angmering BN16 . . . . 184 A5
  Ardingly RH17 . . . . 64 B8
  Arundel BN18 . . . . 160 B3
  Balcombe RH17 . . . . 40 C5
  Billingshurst RH14 . . . . . . 55 D1
  Bognor Regis PO21 . . . . . 201 D3
  Bosham PO18 . . . . 175 A4
  Brighton BN2 . . . . 213 C2
  Chichester PO19 . . . . 176 F7
  Crawley RH10 . . . . 18 B2
  Cuckfield RH17 . . . . 86 E6
  Ditchling BN6 . . . . 129 D3
  East Grinstead RH19 . . . . 22 F8
  Emsworth PO10 . . . . 173 B8
  Findon BN14 . . . . 163 E6
  Handcross RH17 . . . . 61 C8
  Henfield BN5 . . . . 125 C4
  Horley RH6 . . . . 2 E3
  Hurstpierpoint BN6 . . . . . 128 A5
  Lindfield RH16 . . . . 88 B8
  Littlehampton BN17 . . . . 204 D5
  Loxwood RH14 . . . . 31 F3
  Oving PO20 . . . . 178 C6
  Partridge Green RH13 . . . 105 A3
  Petersfield GU32 . . . . 68 B3
  Petworth GU28 . . . . 97 F8
  Portslade-by-S BN41 . . . . 168 A1
  Rottingdean BN2 . . . . . . 193 F1
  Rusper RH12 . . . . 16 D7
  Selsey PO20 . . . . 212 D7
  Shoreham-by-S BN43 . . . 188 E7
  Steyning BN44 . . . . 145 D3
  Storrington RH20 . . . . . . 121 D1
  Upper Beeding BN44 . . . . 146 A2
  Worthing BN11 . . . . 186 B2
  Worthing, West Tarring
  BN14 . . . . 186 A5
Highstanding La GU29 . . . . 95 A6
Highstead La GU28 . . . . . . 74 A8
High Titten BN44 . . . . 140 E5
High Trees
  Bognor Regis PO21 . . . . . 200 F2
  Bramber BN44 . . . . 145 F2
  Fittleworth RH20 . . . . 99 A3
  Haywards Heath RH16 . . . 87 F5
  Hunston PO20 . . . . 177 A1
High Trees Ct RH6 . . . . 1 A4
Highview BN15 . . . . 165 D1
High View RH13 . . . . 163 F1
Highview Ave N BN1 . . . . . 169 E6
Highview Ave S BN1 . . . . . 169 E6
Highview Rd
  Brighton BN1 . . . . 169 E6
  Eastergate PO20 . . . . 179 F7
Highview Way BN1 . . . . . . 169 E6
Highway Cl RH12 . . . . 170 D2
Highways BN41 . . . . 168 B2
Highway The BN2 . . . . 170 D3
Highwood Pk RH11 . . . . . . 18 C2
Highwoods Ct RH12 . . . . . . 35 D3

Hilary Ho PO21 . . . . 201 B2
Hilary Lo 2 BN2 . . . . 192 C5
Hilary Rd PO19 . . . . 176 E7
Hildon Cl BN13 . . . . 185 D6
Hildon Pk BN13 . . . . 185 D6
Hilgrove Rd BN2 . . . . 194 D3
Hilland Rdbt RH14 . . . . 55 D2
Hilary Cl RH10 . . . . 10 A3
Hillbank Cl BN41 . . . . 167 F3
Hillbarn Ave BN15 . . . . . . 165 D1
Hillbarn La GU29 . . . . 114 D6
Hill Barn La BN14 . . . . 186 C7
Hillbarn Par BN15 . . . . . . 187 C8
Hill Brow BN3 . . . . 169 B3
Hill Brow Cl PO9 . . . . 130 C5
Hillbrow Rd BN1 . . . . 169 D4
Hill Brow Rd GU33 . . . . 45 C3
Hill Cotts GU29 . . . . 115 C8
Hillcrest
  Brighton BN1 . . . . 169 C5
  Horsted Keynes RH17 . . . 65 C5
Hill Crest RH17 . . . . 9 E6
Hillcrest Cl
  Ashington RH20 . . . . 123 A5
  Crawley RH10 . . . . 19 D6
  Scaynes Hill RH17 . . . . . . 88 F3
Hillcrest Ct BN1 . . . . 169 C5
Hillcrest Dr RH20 . . . . 123 A5
Hillcrest La RH17 . . . . 88 F3
Hillcrest Pk RH20 . . . . 100 D2
Hillcroft
  Haslemere GU27 . . . . 27 C6
  Portslade-by-S BN41 . . . . 167 F2
Hill Ct GU27 . . . . 27 B6
Hill Dr BN3 . . . . 169 B3
Hill Farm Cl GU27 . . . . 26 F5
Hill Farm La RH20 . . . . . . 100 B5
Hill Farm Way BN42 . . . . . 167 E2
Hillfield Rd PO20 . . . . 212 D6
HILLGROVE 50 E6
Hill House Cl RH10 . . . . . . 21 A5
Hill House Hill GU30 . . . . . 35 A6
Hillhouse La RH12 . . . . 11 F1
Hillingdale RH11 . . . . 18 C1
Hill La
  Barnham PO22 . . . . 180 C4
  South Harting GU31 . . . . . 91 E2
Hillmead RH11 . . . . 17 F6
Hill Mead RH12 . . . . 36 B3
Hill Pl RH11 . . . . 18 C5
Hill Rd
  Haslemere GU27 . . . . 27 C6
  Littlehampton BN17 . . . . 204 F6
  Saltdean BN2 . . . . 194 B1
Hillrise Ave RH15 . . . . 187 D8
Hills Barns PO20 . . . . 176 C3
Hillsboro Rd PO21 . . . . 201 C4
Hills Farm La RH13 . . . . 35 F1
Hillside
  Brighton BN2 . . . . 170 E2
  Crawley Down RH10 . . . . 21 B8
  Forest Row RH18 . . . . . . 23 F3
  Horsham RH12 . . . . 36 A2
  Portslade-by-S BN41 . . . . 168 C1
  Southwick BN42 . . . . 167 F1
Hillside Ave BN14 . . . . . . 186 B7
Hillside Cl
  Crawley RH11 . . . . 18 B4
  East Grinstead RH19 . . . . 9 E3
Hillside Cotts
  Clapham BN13 . . . . 162 E1
  East Marden PO18 . . . . . 112 B1
  Hill Brow GU33 . . . . 45 D2
  West Stoke PO18 . . . . . . 154 A5
Hillside Cres BN16 . . . . . . 184 A5
Hillside La BN5 . . . . 146 E5
Hillside Pk BN5 . . . . 146 E5
Hillside Rd
  Haslemere GU27 . . . . 26 F5
  Heath Common RH20 . . . 122 A2
  Lancing BN15 . . . . 165 C1
  Storrington RH20 . . . . . . 121 D1
Hillside Scout Camp
  BN5 . . . . 146 E5
Hillside Terr 7 BN44 . . . . 145 D3
Hillside Way
  Brighton BN2 . . . . 170 E2
  Brighton, Westdene
  BN1 . . . . 169 C4
Hillside Wlk
  Haywards Heath RH16 . . . 87 C6
  Heath Common RH20 . . . 122 A2
Hills Manor RH12 . . . . 36 A2
Hills Pl RH12 . . . . 36 A2
Hills Rd
  East Grinstead RH19 . . . . 9 A3
  Steyning BN44 . . . . 145 C2
Hill Terr BN18 . . . . 159 F2
Hilltop BN14 . . . . 114 C6
Hill Top BN1 . . . . 169 B5
Hilltop Cotts RH6 . . . . 1 D2
Hilltop Prim Sch RH11 . . . . 18 C4
Hilltop Rd RH19 . . . . 42 E6
Hill View
  Elsted GU29 . . . . 92 D4
  Small Dole BN5 . . . . 146 F7
Hillview Cres BN16 . . . . . . 206 A6
Hillview Gdns RH11 . . . . . . 39 C8
Hillview Rd
  Woodingdean BN2 . . . . . 193 B8
  Worthing BN14 . . . . 163 F2
Hillview Rise BN41 . . . . . . 163 F1
Hillybarn Rd RH11 . . . . 4 C1
Hilton Ct
  11 Haywards Heath
  RH16 . . . . 87 E4
  Horley RH6 . . . . 2 C4
Hilton Pk PO20 . . . . 208 A8

Hinde Rd PO22 . . . . 202 C4
Hindhead Cl RH11 . . . . 18 C4
Hindhead Rd GU27 . . . . . . 26 E7
Hindleap La RH17,
  RH18 . . . . 44 C4
Hindleap Warren Outdoor
  Education Ctr RH18 . . . . . 44 D5
Hinds Cl PO21 . . . . 121 D7
Hinton Cl BN1 . . . . 170 C2
Hislop Wlk 3 PO21 . . . . . 201 D3
Hither Gn PO10 . . . . 152 A2
Hoad La RH16 . . . . 64 D4
Hoadlands GU31 . . . . 68 D4
Hoadlands Cotts RH17 . . . . 39 C2
Hoadley's Cnr RH15 . . . . . 109 B2
Hoathly Hill RH19 . . . . 42 F5
Hobart Cl BN13 . . . . 185 C8
Hobbs Ind Est RH7 . . . . 8 D7
Hobbs Rd RH11 . . . . 18 A2
Hobbs Sq GU31 . . . . 68 C5
Hobbs Way BN6 . . . . 205 C5
Hobdens La RH17 . . . . 64 B7
Hoblands RH16 . . . . 88 B4
Hockam Ave BN44 . . . . . . 146 B1
Hocken Mead RH10 . . . . . . 19 D8
Hodgkin Cl RH10 . . . . 19 C5
Hodshrove La BN2 . . . . . . 170 E3
Hodshrove Pl BN2 . . . . 170 E3
Hodshrove Rd BN2 . . . . . . 170 E3
Hoe Ct
  Lancing BN15 . . . . 188 A8
  North Lancing BN15 . . . . 165 F1
Hoefield La GU29 . . . . 114 C5
Hoe La
  Bosham PO18 . . . . 175 C1
  Flansham PO22 . . . . 202 B7
  Walberton BN18 . . . . 181 C7
Hoelands La GU29 . . . . . . 114 C6
Hoewood BN5 . . . . 146 F7
Hogarth Rd
  Crawley RH10 . . . . 18 F3
  Hove BN3 . . . . 190 F7
Hoggarth Cl GU32 . . . . 68 C4
Hog La BN18 . . . . 140 E7
Hogs Edge BN2 . . . . 171 A2
Hogwood Rd RH14 . . . . 31 C3
Holbein Rd RH10 . . . . 18 F3
HOLBROOK 36 E8
Holbrook 16 BN2 . . . . 192 F5
Holbrook Park Ho
  RH12 . . . . 36 E8
Holbrook Prim Sch
  RH12 . . . . 36 F7
Holbrook School La
  RH12 . . . . 36 E7
Holdens The PO18 . . . . . . 175 A5
Holder Rd RH10 . . . . 19 B3
Holders Cl BN6 . . . . 127 C6
Holders Ct RH14 . . . . 55 C1
Holdfast La GU27 . . . . 27 C8
Holdings The BN7 . . . . 172 F5
Hole St RH20 . . . . 123 B2
Holford Gn PO20 . . . . 212 F8
Holkham Cotts BN18 . . . . 181 A3
Holland Cl PO21 . . . . 200 F5
Holland Mews BN1 . . . . . . 191 D5
Holland Rd
  Hove BN3 . . . . 191 D6
  Steyning BN44 . . . . 145 E3
Hollands Ct RH19 . . . . 10 A4
Hollands Field RH13 . . . . . 36 F3
Hollands La BN5 . . . . 125 C4
Hollands Way
  East Grinstead RH19 . . . . 10 A4
  Warnham RH12 . . . . 35 F8
Hollies Cvn Pk The
  PO11 . . . . 195 A2
Hollies The
  Bognor Regis PO21 . . . . . 200 F5
  Lancing BN15 . . . . 187 C6
Hollin Ct RH10 . . . . 5 E1
Hollingbourne Cres
  RH11 . . . . 39 C8
Hollingbourne Ct 8
  BN2 . . . . 170 A4
HOLLINGBURY 170 B5
Hollingbury Copse
  BN1 . . . . 170 A4
Hollingbury Cres RH10 . . . 170 B2
Hollingbury Gdns
  BN14 . . . . 164 A2
Hollingbury Ind Est
  BN1 . . . . 170 C7
Hollingbury Park Ave
  BN1 . . . . 170 B4
Hollingbury Pl BN1 . . . . . . 170 B3
Hollingbury Rd BN1 . . . . . 170 B3
Hollingbury Rise BN1 . . . . 170 A3
Hollingbury Rise W
  BN1 . . . . 170 A3
Hollingbury Terr BN1 . . . . 170 B3
HOLLINGDEAN 170 B3
Hollingdean La BN1 . . . . . 192 B8
Hollingdean Rd BN2 . . . . . 192 B8
Hollingdean St BN1 . . . . . 170 B3
Hollingdean Terr
  BN1 . . . . 170 B3
Hollist La
  Midhurst GU29 . . . . 72 E2
  South Harting GU31 . . . . . 91 F4
Hollow La RH19, RH7 . . . . 10 D6
Hollow The
  Bury RH20 . . . . 140 A8
  Crawley RH11 . . . . 17 F5
  Haywards Heath RH16 . . . 88 B5
  Washington RH20 . . . . . . 143 F8

Hollow The continued
  West Chiltington RH20 . . . 101 D1
  West Hoathly RH19 . . . . . 42 F6
Hollyacres BN13 . . . . 185 D9
Holly Bank 3 BN2 . . . . . . 213 C5
Hollybank La PO10 . . . . . . 151 B4
Hollybush Bsns Ctr
  Copthorne RH10 . . . . 6 F4
  Crawley RH10 . . . . 6 F4
Hollybush Cl RH10 . . . . 18 E8
Hollybush Rd RH10 . . . . . . 18 E8
Holly Cl
  Brighton BN1 . . . . 169 E3
  Crawley RH10 . . . . 19 A8
  Horsham RH12 . . . . 37 B5
  Storrington RH20 . . . . . . 121 C1
  West Chiltington RH20 . . . 101 D1
  Worthing BN13 . . . . 185 C6
Hollycombe Cl GU30 . . . . . 25 C2
Hollycombe Prim Sch
  GU30 . . . . 47 D4
Hollycombe Steam
  Collection* GU30 . . . . 47 E7
Holly Ct
  Bognor Regis PO22 . . . . . 201 C6
  Storrington RH20 . . . . . . 121 C2
Holly Gate Cactus Gdn*
  RH20 . . . . 123 A8
Holly Ho 2 PO21 . . . . 201 C4
Hollyhock Way BN17 . . . . 205 A7
Holly Lo BN14 . . . . 186 B4
Holly Rd RH16 . . . . 88 A3
Hollyridge GU27 . . . . 27 B6
Hollywater Rd GU30,
  GU35 . . . . 24 C8
Hollywood Ct RH16 . . . . . . 87 E5
Holman Cl RH11 . . . . 39 B8
Holmans RH17 . . . . 64 A8
Holmbury Cl RH11 . . . . 18 C4
Holmbury Keep RH6 . . . . . . 2 C4
Holmbush Cl
  Haywards Heath RH16 . . . 87 E2
  Horsham RH12 . . . . 36 D6
  Shoreham-by-S BN43 . . . 167 D2
Holmbush Ct 8 BN43 . . . . 189 C8
Holmbush Farm World*
  RH12 . . . . 17 B1
Holmbush Fst Sch
  BN43 . . . . 167 D2
Holmbush Ind Est
  GU29 . . . . 94 E6
Holmbush La BN5 . . . . . . 147 F8
Holmbush Way
  Brighton BN1 . . . . 94 E6
  Southwick BN42 . . . . 167 E1
Holmcroft RH10 . . . . 18 E5
Holmcroft Gdns BN14 . . . 163 E6
Holmdale RH20 . . . . 157 F1
Holmes Ave BN3 . . . . 168 F1
Holmesdale Rd RH15 . . . . 109 A1
Holmes Foundation
  BN18 . . . . 160 B2
Holmes La BN16 . . . . 205 B4
Holmfield Cl BN16 . . . . . . 205 B6
Holmgarth BN5 . . . . 125 F5
Holm Ho RH15 . . . . 108 F3
Holming End RH12 . . . . 37 B5
Holm Oak RH20 . . . . 121 C1
Holm Oaks RH13 . . . . 83 F1
Holmstead BN2 . . . . 213 C4
Holmsted Hill RH17 . . . . . . 62 A1
Holmwood Cl PO20 . . . . . 196 C1
Holmwood Ct BN6 . . . . . . 128 F4
Holt Down GU31 . . . . 68 D3
Holt Gdns PO9 . . . . 130 D3
Holt Lo 1 BN2 . . . . 213 C4
Holton Hill BN2 . . . . 193 E7
Holt The
  Burgess Hill RH15 . . . . . 109 C2
  Washington RH20 . . . . . . 143 E6
Holtview Rd BN2 . . . . 193 B8
Holtye Ave RH19 . . . . 10 A3
Holtye Pl RH19 . . . . 10 B3
Holtye Rd RH19 . . . . 10 B3
Holtye Wlk RH10 . . . . 19 A4
Holy Cross Hospl GU27 . . . 26 F7
Holyrood RH19 . . . . 23 A8
Holy Trinity CE Prim Sch
  Cuckfield RH17 . . . . 86 F6
  Lower Beeding RH13 . . . . 60 A3
Holy Trinity CE Sec Sch
  The RH11 . . . . 18 A4
Homebush Ave
  Saltdean BN2 . . . . 194 D1
  Saltdean BN2 . . . . 194 F3
Home Cl RH10 . . . . 19 C8
Home Farm Ho 5
  PO21 . . . . 201 B3
Homedrive Ho BN3 . . . . . . 191 C8
Home Farm Bsns Ctr
  BN1 . . . . 170 D3
Home Farm Cl
  Chiddingfold GU8 . . . . 29 D5
  Horsted Keynes RH17 . . . 65 C5
Home Farm Ho 1
  RH12 . . . . 36 C2
Home Farm Rd BN1,
  BN2 . . . . 170 D3
Homefield Ave PO22 . . . . 202 C6
Homefield Cl RH6 . . . . 2 B4
Homefield Cotts GU33 . . . . 45 A5
Homefield Cres BN18 . . . . 158 D1

Homefield Rd
Westbourne PO10 . . . .**151** D4
Worthing BN11 . . . .**186** E3
Homegreen Ho GU27 . . . . .**27** A6
Homehaven Ct 2
BN43 . . . .**188** E7
Homelands GU27 . . . .**27** E1
Homelands Ave BN16 . . . .**206** A4
Homelands Copse
GU27 . . . .**49** D4
Homelees Ho BN1 . . . .**213** A3
Homeleigh BN1 . . . .**169** E5
Homepier Ho 7
BN11 . . . .**186** B2
Home Platt RH19 . . . .**43** A6
Home Rd BN1 . . . .**169** E1
Homeridge Ho BN12 . . . . .**194** D1
Homesacrie Ho BN12 . . . .**185** C3
Homestall Rd RH14 . . . .**23** E8
Homestead Cotts
BN12 . . . .**206** F6
Homestead La RH15 . . . . .**109** C6
Homestead The BN16 . . . .**206** A5
Homesteyne Ho 3
BN14 . . . .**186** D4
Homestream Ho RH12 . . . .**36** B1
Homethorne Ho RH11 . . . .**18** C5
Home Way GU31 . . . .**68** B3
Homewood RH14 . . . .**163** E7
Homing Gdns PO22 . . . . . .**201** B7
Honer La PO20 . . . .**199** D3
Honeybridge La
Ashurst BN44, RH13 . . . . .**124** A6
Dial Post RH13 . . . .**103** E1
**Honeybridge Pk Caravan
& Camping Site**
RH13 . . . .**103** E1
Honey Croft BN3 . . . .**168** D4
Honey La BN16 . . . .**184** A5
Honeysuckle Cl
Horley RH6 . . . .**2** C4
North Lancing BN15 . . . .**165** D1
Rustington BN17 . . . .**205** A7
Honeysuckle Dr PO21 . . . .**199** F2
Honeysuckle La
Crawley RH11 . . . .**5** C1
Selsey PO20 . . . .**212** C8
Worthing BN13, BN14 . . . .**163** C3
Honeysuckle Wlk
RH12 . . . .**37** A5
Honeywood La RH5 . . . .**13** F5
Honeywood Rd RH13 . . . . .**37** A4
Hooe Farm Ind Est
BN18 . . . .**158** D2
Hooe The BN17 . . . .**205** A5
Hook Cotts PO20 . . . .**199** E4
Hook La
Bognor Regis PO22 . . . . . .**201** E4
Bognor Regis, Rose Green
PO21 . . . .**200** B2
Bosham PO18 . . . .**175** F2
West Hoathly RH17,
RH19 . . . .**42** D4
Woodgate PO20 . . . .**179** C6
Hooklands La RH13 . . . . . .**103** B3
Hook Lane Cl PO21 . . . . . .**200** B3
Hooks The BN6 . . . .**125** E4
HOOKSWAY **112** D5
Hope Cotts BN42 . . . .**189** E8
Hope Ct RH11 . . . .**18** B1
Hopedene Ct 10 BN11 . . .**186** C2
Hopewell Cl 3 BN43 . . . . .**189** B6
Hop Garden La PO20 . . . . .**199** D8
Hopgarton The PO21 . . . . .**200** E3
Hop Gdn The GU31 . . . .**91** D3
Hophurst Cl RH10 . . . .**21** B8
Hophurst Dr RH10 . . . .**21** B8
Hophurst Hill RH19 . . . .**8** D2
Hophurst La RH10 . . . .**8** B1
Hopkins Ct RH11 . . . .**18** B1
Horatio Ho BN1 . . . .**213** B3
Horden Ct RH12 . . . .**36** A1
Hordens The RH13 . . . .**56** F2
Horizon BN3 . . . .**190** F6
Horizon Cl BN41 . . . .**190** B8
Horley Inf Sch RH6 . . . .**2** A3
Horley Lodge La RH1 . . . . . .**2** A8
Horley Pl BN2 . . . .**192** E6
Horley Rd RH6 . . . .**5** B7
Horley Row RH6 . . . .**2** A4
Horley Sta RH6 . . . .**2** B2
Hormare Cres RH20 . . . . . .**121** C2
Hornbeam Cl
Bognor Regis PO21 . . . . . .**200** F1
Horsham RH13 . . . .**36** F1
Hornbeams The
RH15 . . . .**108** D4
Hornbeam Way GU29 . . . . .**94** D5
Hornbrook Copse
RH13 . . . .**58** F8
Hornbrook Hill RH13 . . . . . .**58** F8
Hornby Pl BN2 . . . .**171** A1
Hornby Rd BN2 . . . .**171** A1
Horndean Cl RH10 . . . .**6** D2
Horndean Rd PO10 . . . . . .**151** A3
Hornet Rd PO10 . . . .**173** C3
Hornet The PO19 . . . .**177** B6
Horn La RH5 . . . .**126** B1
Hornshill La RH12 . . . .**32** F7
Horns La PO22 . . . .**199** F4
Horsebridge Hill RH14 . . . .**77** E2
Horsefield Rd PO20 . . . . . .**212** D8
Horse Hill RH6 . . . .**1** B4
HORSEMERE GREEN
. . . .**181** C1

Horsemere Green La
BN17 . . . .**181** D1
Horseshoe Cl
Crawley RH10 . . . .**19** D7
Findon BN14 . . . .**163** E6
Horse Shoe The
PO20 . . . .**212** D7
Horsgate Ho RH17 . . . .**87** A8
Horsgate La RH17 . . . .**87** A6
Horsham Cl BN2 . . . .**192** F6
Horsham Hospl RH12 . . . . .**36** C3
Horsham La RH17 . . . .**204** F5
Horsham Mus* RH17 . . . . .**36** C1
Horsham Rd
Alfold Crossways GU6,
RH12 . . . .**11** C1
Ashurst BN44 . . . .**145** C7
Cranleigh GU6 . . . .**12** B8
Crawley RH11 . . . .**18** B4
Findon BN14 . . . .**163** D8
Five Oaks RH13, RH14 . . . . .**56** A6
Handcross RH17 . . . .**61** B7
Kingsfold RH5 . . . .**15** C8
Littlehampton BN17 . . . . . .**204** F6
Pease Pottage RH11 . . . .**39** B6
Petworth GU28 . . . .**76** B2
Rowhook RH12, RH5 . . . . . .**13** D5
Rusper RH12 . . . .**14** B2
Steyning BN44 . . . .**145** C4
Wallis Wood RH5 . . . .**13** B8
Horsham Rd W BN17 . . . .**204** F6
Horsham Sta RH13 . . . .**36** D2
Horsham Trad Est
RH13 . . . .**36** E4
Horsted Ct BN1 . . . .**213** B4
Horsted Ct 1 RH16 . . . .**87** F3
Horsted Keynes Inf Pk
RH17 . . . .**65** B7
Horsted Keynes Sta
RH17 . . . .**65** A7
Horsted La
Danehill RH17 . . . .**66** A4
Sharpthorne RH19 . . . .**43** B3
Horton Cl RH11 . . . .**18** F2
Horton Pl RH10 . . . .**206** A8
Horton Rd BN41 . . . .**170** B1
Hoskins Pl RH19 . . . .**10** A4
Hotham Gdns PO22 . . . . . .**201** E4
Hotham Way PO21,
PO22 . . . .**201** D4
Houghton Bridge
BN18 . . . .**140** D4
Houghton Ct BN15 . . . .**187** F7
Houghton Ho BN17 . . . . . .**204** B7
Houghton La RH20 . . . .**140** A6
Houghton Rd RH10 . . . .**19** C3
Houndean Rise BN7 . . . . . .**172** F8
Housman Way RH19 . . . .**8** F4
Hova Villas BN3 . . . .**191** B6
Hove Bsns Ctr BN3 . . . .**191** B8
Hovedene BN3 . . . .**191** C7
Hove Ent Ctr BN41 . . . .**190** C6
Hove Manor 4 BN3 . . . . . .**191** A6
Hove Mus & Art Gall*
BN3 . . . .**191** A6
Hove Park Gdns
Hove BN3 . . . .**169** B1
Hove BN3 . . . .**191** B8
Hove Park Rd BN3 . . . .**169** C1
**Hove Park Sch & Sixth
Form Ctr**
Hove BN3 . . . .**168** D2
Hove BN3 . . . .**169** A1
Hove Park Villas BN3 . . . .**191** B8
Hove Park Way BN3 . . . . .**169** C1
Hove Pl BN3 . . . .**191** B5
Hove Sta BN3 . . . .**191** A6
Hove Sta BN3 . . . .**191** B8
Hove Tech Ctr 1
BN3 . . . .**191** A8
Howard Ave
Burgess Hill RH15 . . . .**108** E4
East Wittering PO20 . . . . . .**207** D7
Howard Cl BN3 . . . .**169** A2
Howard Ho PO21 . . . .**201** A4
Howard Pl
Brighton BN1 . . . .**213** A4
5 Littlehampton BN17 . . . .**204** D5
Howard Rd
Arundel BN18 . . . .**160** A2
Brighton BN2 . . . .**192** C7
Crawley RH11 . . . .**17** D2
Horsham RH13 . . . .**37** A4
Lancing BN15 . . . .**165** C1
Littlehampton BN17 . . . . . .**204** C5
Howards Way BN16 . . . . . .**205** B3
Howard Terr BN1 . . . .**213** A4
Howberry Chase GU27 . . . .**27** B6
Hoylake Cl RH11 . . . .**17** D5
HOYLE **95** D1
Hoyle La GU29 . . . .**95** D2
Huddlestones BN16 . . . . . .**183** F6
Hudson Cl
Liphook GU30 . . . .**25** C3
Worthing BN13 . . . .**185** D7
Hudson Dr BN16 . . . .**205** E4
Hudson Rd RH10 . . . .**18** E4
Huffwood Trad Est
Billingshurst RH14 . . . .**79** D7
Partridge Green RH13 . . . .**105** A3
Hughes Cl PO21 . . . .**200** F4
Hugo Platt GU31 . . . .**70** A4
Humber Ave BN13 . . . .**185** C8
Humber Cl
Littlehampton BN17 . . . . . .**204** F4
Worthing BN13 . . . .**185** C8

Humphrey Lo RH15 . . . . . .**109** D3
Humphrey's Gap
BN43 . . . .**189** A7
Humphrys Rd BN1 . . . .**186** D2
Hundredsteddle La
PO20 . . . .**197** D2
Hungers La GU28 . . . .**97** D6
Hunnisett Cl PO20 . . . .**210** A1
Hunstanton Cl 8
RH11 . . . .**17** D5
Hunston Cl BN2 . . . .**193** F7
Hunter Ho RH10 . . . .**18** D3
Hunter Rd
Crawley RH10 . . . .**18** D4
Thorney Island PO10 . . . . .**173** C3
Hunters Chase GU30 . . . . .**25** B5
Hunters Ct PO21 . . . .**200** C1
Hunters La RH11 . . . .**18** B4
Hunters Mead RH13 . . . . .**105** A3
Hunter's Mead BN6 . . . . . .**127** C6
Hunters Mews BN18 . . . . .**158** B3
Hunters Race PO19 . . . . . .**154** E3
Hunters Way PO19 . . . .**154** F3
Huntingdon Way
RH15 . . . .**109** D5
Huntsbottom La GU33 . . . .**45** D3
Huntscroft Gdns RH13 . . . .**83** E1
Hunt's Gate RH17 . . . .**89** E3
Hurley Rd RH13 . . . .**185** E2
Huron Dr GU30 . . . .**25** D3
Hurst Ave
Horsham RH12 . . . .**36** D3
Worthing BN13 . . . .**185** F3
Hurst Cl
Amberley BN18 . . . .**140** E7
Crawley RH11 . . . .**17** F4
Liphook GU30 . . . .**25** A5
Hurst Cotts BN18 . . . .**140** E7
Hurst Cres BN41 . . . .**190** B8
Hurst Ct
Brighton BN1 . . . .**169** D1
Horsham RH12 . . . .**36** D3
Hurst Farm Rd RH19 . . . . . .**22** D7
Hurstfield BN15 . . . .**187** C5
Hurstfield Cl RH17 . . . .**88** A2
Hurst Gdns BN6 . . . .**127** F7
Hurst Hill BN1 . . . .**170** C5
Hurstlands RH14 . . . .**79** C7
Hurston Cl
Cootham RH20 . . . .**121** B3
Worthing BN14 . . . .**186** A8
Hurston Gr RH20 . . . .**121** B3
Hurston La RH20 . . . .**121** B3
Hurstpierpoint Coll
BN6 . . . .**128** B8
Hurst Pk
Horsham RH12 . . . .**36** D3
Midhurst GU29 . . . .**72** D7
Hurst Rd
Hassocks BN6 . . . .**128** D4
Horley RH6 . . . .**1** E4
Horsham RH12 . . . .**36** D3
Rustington BN15 . . . .**205** E6
Hurst Wickham Cl
BN6 . . . .**128** C5
Hurstwood 6 BN2 . . . .**192** F5
Hurstwood Ave PO10 . . . .**152** A1
Hurstwood Cl GU29 . . . . . .**94** E5
Hurstwood La
Haywards Heath RH17 . . . . .**88** A2
Sharpthorne RH17,
RH19 . . . .**43** D1
Hurstwood Park Hospl
RH17 . . . .**88** A2
Hutchinson Cl 4
BN16 . . . .**205** B7
Hutchins Way RH6 . . . .**1** F5
Hutton Rd BN1 . . . .**170** B3
**Huxley's Experience Birds
of Prey Ctr*** RH13 . . . .**58** F8
Hyde Bsns Pk The
BN2 . . . .**192** F8
Hyde Cl BN2 . . . .**172** E5
Hyde Cotts RH17 . . . .**38** F1
Hyde Dr RH11 . . . .**17** E5
Hyde Heath Ct RH10 . . . . . .**19** D8
Hyde La BN44 . . . .**146** B2
Hyde Sq BN44 . . . .**146** B2
Hyde St BN44 . . . .**146** B1
Hyde The RH17 . . . .**38** F1
Hylands Cl RH10 . . . .**19** A5
Hylden Cl BN2 . . . .**193** B8
Hylters's La PO18 . . . .**134** B7
Hylton Rd GU32 . . . .**68** B3
Hyndman Cl RH11 . . . .**39** B8
Hyperion Cl RH11 . . . .**17** E5
Hyperion Wlk RH6 . . . .**2** B1
Hythe Cl BN17 . . . .**186** A1
Hythe Rd
Brighton BN1 . . . .**170** A2
Worthing BN11 . . . .**186** A1

Icarus Way PO22 . . . .**202** C5
Icklesham Ho 9 RH11 . . . .**17** F3
Iden Cl BN2 . . . .**192** E5
Iden Hurst BN6 . . . .**128** A7
Idsworth Cl RH10 . . . .**20** D8
Idsworth Down GU31 . . . . . .**68** C3
IFIELD **17** B1
Ifield Ave RH11 . . . .**18** C7
Ifield Dr BN12 . . . .**194** E2
Ifield Com Coll RH11 . . . .**18** A6
Ifield Dr RH11 . . . .**18** A7
Ifield Gn RH11 . . . .**5** A1

IFIELD GREEN **5** A1
Ifield Rd
Charlwood RH6 . . . .**4** E5
Crawley, West Green
RH11 . . . .**18** C6
Ifield St RH11 . . . .**17** F8
Ifield Sta RH11 . . . .**18** A6
Ifield Watermill*
RH11 . . . .**17** E5
IFIELDWOOD **4** E1
Ifield Wood RH11 . . . .**4** D1
Ifold Bridge La RH14 . . . . .**31** D4
Ifoldhurst RH14 . . . .**31** C2
Iford & Kingston CE Prim
Sch BN7 . . . .**172** F5
Ilex Cl RH16 . . . .**205** C4
Ilex Ct
Portslade-by-S BN42 . . . . .**168** A1
Worthing BN12 . . . .**185** B3
Ilex Ho 1 BN12 . . . .**185** B3
Ilex Way
Middleton-on-S PO22 . . . . .**202** E6
Worthing BN12 . . . .**185** B3
Image Cross RH19 . . . .**43** A5
Imberhorne Bsns Ctr
RH19 . . . .**9** B3
Imberhorne La 4 RH19 . . . . .**9** B2
Imberhorne Lower Sch
RH19 . . . .**9** D3
Imberhorne Sch RH19 . . . . . .**9** B3
Imberhorne Way RH19 . . . . .**9** B3
Imperial Arc BN1 . . . .**213** A2
Imperial Ct PO21 . . . .**201** C4
Imperial Coll RH10 . . . .**6** A3
Independent Bsns Pk The
RH19 . . . .**9** A3
Infirmary Dr RH13 . . . .**57** E6
Infirmary Terr PO19 . . . . . .**176** F8
Ingfield Manor Dr
RH14 . . . .**55** F6
Ingfield Manor Sch
RH14 . . . .**55** E6
Ingham Dr BN1 . . . .**170** D6
Inglecroft Cl 4 BN15 . . . . .**187** C7
Inglegreen Cl BN12 . . . . . .**186** C2
Inglenook RH13 . . . .**81** F7
Ingleside Cres BN15 . . . . .**187** F5
Ingleside Rd BN15 . . . .**187** E5
Inglewood Cl PO21 . . . . . .**200** C1
Inglewood Dr PO21 . . . . . .**200** B1
Ingram Cl
Horsham RH12 . . . .**36** A2
Rustington BN16 . . . .**205** B5
Steyning BN44 . . . .**145** D2
Ingram Cres E BN3 . . . . . .**190** E8
Ingram Cres W BN3 . . . . . .**190** E8
Ingram Ct BN3 . . . .**190** E8
Ingram Rd BN44 . . . .**145** D2
Ingram's Green La
GU29 . . . .**93** C4
Ingrams Ho 4 RH16 . . . . . .**87** E3
Inholmes Cl RH15 . . . .**109** C3
Inholmes Cotts RH17 . . . . .**36** B8
Inholmes Park Rd
RH15 . . . .**109** B3
Inkpen La RH18 . . . .**23** F1
Inlands Rd PO18 . . . .**174** B8
Inman La GU32 . . . .**68** D5
Innerwyke Cl PO22 . . . . . .**202** B5
Innerwyke Manor
PO22 . . . .**36** F4
Innes Rd RH12 . . . .**36** F4
Innovation Dr RH15 . . . . . .**108** D2
Institute Wlk 6 RH19 . . . . . .**9** E1
**International Coll of
Oriental Medicine The**
BN6 . . . .**128** B7
Inval Hill GU27 . . . .**27** C8
Inverness Rd 4 BN2 . . . . .**192** C8
Inwood Cres RH11 . . . .**169** E1
Inwood Rd GU33 . . . .**45** C3
Iona Cl RH11 . . . .**18** B3
Iona Way 12 RH16 . . . .**87** E4
IPING **71** E2
Iping La GU29 . . . .**71** E4
Iping Rd GU29, GU30 . . . . . .**47** C2
**Iping & Stedham
Commons Nature
Reserve*** GU29 . . . .**93** D8
Irene Ave BN15 . . . .**187** D7
Iris Cl BN17 . . . .**205** B7
Ironsbottom RH2, RH6 . . . . . .**1** A6
Irvine Rd BN17 . . . .**204** E4
Irving Wlk RH10 . . . .**18** E3
Ithaca Terr PO21 . . . .**201** B7
Ivanhoe Cl RH11 . . . .**5** D1
Ivanhoe Pl PO22 . . . .**202** C5
Iveagh Cl RH14 . . . .**79** D6
Ivor Rd BN2 . . . .**171** C1
Ivory Pl BN2 . . . .**213** C3

Ivory Wlk RH11 . . . .**17** E3
Ivy Arch Cl BN14 . . . .**163** F6
Ivy Arch Rd BN14 . . . .**186** D3
Ivy Cl
Ashington RH20 . . . .**123** A5
Southwater RH13 . . . .**57** F1
Westergate PO20 . . . .**179** D7
Ivy Cotts RH17 . . . .**86** E8
Ivy Cres PO22 . . . .**201** D5
Ivy Dene Rd PO21 . . . .**201** A4
Ivydene Cres PO18 . . . .**174** D7
Ivydene Ind Est RH19 . . . . .**23** D7
Ivy Dene La RH19 . . . .**23** D6
Ivydore Ave BN13 . . . .**185** D9
Ivydore Cl BN13 . . . .**185** D8
Ivy La
Ashington RH20 . . . .**123** A6
Bognor Regis PO22 . . . . . .**201** D5
Southwater PO20 . . . .**179** E7
Ivy Mews 3 BN3 . . . .**191** D5
Ivy Pl
Hove BN1, BN3 . . . .**191** D5
Worthing BN11 . . . .**186** B1

J

Jackdaw Cl RH11 . . . .**18** C8
Jackdaw La RH12 . . . .**36** E6
Jacken Cl PO22 . . . .**202** C4
Jacket's Hill RH20 . . . .**122** A5
Jackrells La RH13 . . . .**58** B2
Jackson Rd RH11 . . . .**39** B8
Jackson St BN2 . . . .**213** C4
Jack Vass Cotts RH16 . . . . .**63** C2
Jacobean Cl RH10 . . . .**19** C5
Jacobs Cl RH10 . . . .**19** C7
Jacqueline Du Pre Ct 6
BN2 . . . .**192** C5
**James Bradford
Almhouses** RH16 . . . .**87** C4
James Cl BN13 . . . .**185** F7
James Pl RH10 . . . .**18** D5
James Searle Ind Est
RH12 . . . .**36** E4
James St PO20 . . . .**212** E6
James Watt Way RH10 . . . . .**6** A4
Jane Murray Way BN6,
RH15 . . . .**108** C3
Janes Cl RH15 . . . .**109** C5
Janes La
Burgess Hill RH15 . . . .**109** D4
Rowe GU28 . . . .**74** E3
Janeston Ct 4 BN3 . . . . . .**191** C7
Japonica Cl BN43 . . . .**167** B1
Jarvis Cl RH11 . . . .**39** B8
Jarvis Cotts 4 BN44 . . . . .**145** D3
Jarvis Rd BN18 . . . .**159** F2
Jasmine Cl BN17 . . . .**205** A7
Jasmine Ct
Brighton BN1 . . . .**169** F5
Horsham RH12 . . . .**36** C2
Hove BN3 . . . .**191** D7
Jason Ct BN11 . . . .**186** C1
Javelin Ct RH10 . . . .**6** D1
Javelin Rd PO10 . . . .**173** C3
Jay Cl BN13 . . . .**58** A2
Jays Cl BN17 . . . .**204** D6
Jay's La GU27 . . . .**28** C3
Jay The RH15 . . . .**108** E4
Jay Wlk
9 Chichester PO19 . . . .**177** A6
Turners Hill RH10 . . . .**21** C5
Jeans Ct 10 RH11 . . . .**18** B1
Jefferies RH11 . . . .**65** C4
Jefferies La BN12 . . . .**185** C2
Jefferis Ho RH11 . . . .**5** A1
Jefferson Ct 2 PO21 . . . . .**201** B2
Jeffreys Ave PO19 . . . .**155** A1
Jengers Mead RH14 . . . . . .**55** D1
Jengers Pas RH14 . . . .**55** D1
Jenner Rd RH10 . . . .**5** F3
Jennings Way RH6 . . . .**2** D3
Jeremy's La RH17 . . . .**85** C6
Jerrard Rd PO20 . . . .**156** D2
Jersey Rd
Crawley RH11 . . . .**18** A2
Ferring BN12 . . . .**206** F4
Jersey St BN2 . . . .**213** C3
Jervis Ave BN16 . . . .**205** D5
Jesmond Cl BN3 . . . .**190** E7
Jesmond Rd BN3 . . . .**190** E7
**Jessie Younghusband
Prim Sch** PO19 . . . .**176** F8
Jessop Ho GU27 . . . .**27** A6
Jesters RH16 . . . .**109** C7
Jetty The PO22 . . . .**203** A5
Jevington Cl BN13 . . . .**185** B6
Jevington Ct
Shoreham-by-S BN43 . . . . .**189** D6
Worthing BN3 . . . .**185** B6
Jevington Dr BN2 . . . .**170** D1
Jewel Wlk RH11 . . . .**18** A3
Jew St BN1 . . . .**213** B2
Jib Cl BN17 . . . .**205** A7
Jikack Ind Est BN6 . . . .**108** B4
Jireh Ct RH16 . . . .**87** F5
Joan Nightingale Ho
RH16 . . . .**87** C4
Jobes RH11 . . . .**40** F1
Job's Cnr RH16 . . . .**107** C5
Job's La RH16 . . . .**107** F5
Jobson's La GU33 . . . .**28** D2
Jockey Mead RH12 . . . .**56** D5
John Arundel Rd
PO19 . . . .**176** E7

John King Shipyard
PO10 . . . . 173 C8
John Pounds Ho RH11 . . . .18 D4
Johnson Bank 4
BN2 . . . . 192 C7
Johnson Dr RH15 . . . . . 109 D3
Johnson Way BN18 . . . .181 B2
Johnson Wlk RH10 . . . . .18 E3
John St
Bognor Regis PO21 . . . . 201 D3
Brighton BN2 . . . . 213 C3
Shoreham-by-S BN43 . . .188 E7
John Whittle Lo BN2 . . . 170 C1
Jolesfield RH11 . . . . .18 D8
Jolesfield CE Prim Sch
RH13 . . . . 105 A4
Jolesfield Ct RH11 . . . . . .17 F3
Jolliffe Ct 15 GU32 . . . . .68 B3
Jolliffe Rd PO20 . . . . . . 207 D7
Jones Sq PO20 . . . . . . 212 E6
Jordan Ct BN3 . . . . 190 E8
Jordans Cres RH11 . . . . . .5 D1
Jordans The RH19 . . . . . .22 E8
Joyce Cl BN17 . . . . 204 C7
Joys Croft PO19 . . . . . . 177 B7
Joys Croft Cl PO19 . . . . 177 B7
Jubilee Ave RH16 . . . . . 205 C6
Jubilee Cl RH16 . . . . . . .88 A4
Jubilee Ct
Billingshurst RH14 . . . . . .79 D8
Brighton BN2 . . . . 170 E2
Worthing BN11 . . . . . . 186 B2
Jubilee Ho
Crockerhill PO18 . . . . . 157 B3
Emsworth PO10 . . . . . . 151 A1
Jubilee Mews PO10 . . . .173 E8
Jubilee Pl PO22 . . . . . . 201 C5
Jubilee Rd
Burgess Hill RH15 . . . . .108 E2
Chichester PO19 . . . . . 177 A7
Portslade-by-S BN41 . . .190 A8
Rudgwick RH12 . . . . . . .33 D8
Jubilee St BN1 . . . . 213 B2
Jubilee Terr
Chichester PO19 . . . . . 177 A7
Westbourne PO10 . . . . . 151 D3
Jubilee Way RH20 . . . . .121 F3
Jubilee Wlk
Crawley RH10 . . . . .19 A6
17 Horsham RH12 . . . . .36 C2
Judges Cl RH19 . . . . . . .22 E8
Judge's Terr RH19 . . . . .22 E8
Juggs La RH20 . . . . . . 101 E1
Juggs The PO20 . . . . . . 101 E1
Julian St 5 BN43 . . . . 189 C8
Julian Rd BN3 . . . . 191 E7
Junction Cl
Burgess Hill RH15 . . . . .109 C4
Yapton BN18 . . . . .181 B2
Junction Mews RH15 . . .109 B3
Junction Pl GU27 . . . . . .26 F6
Junction Rd
Brighton BN1 . . . . 213 A3
Burgess Hill RH15 . . . . .109 A3
June Cl PO21 . . . . 210 F8
June La GU29 . . . . .94 E8
June Mdws GU29 . . . . . .94 D8
June Rise GU29 . . . . . . .94 E8
Juniper Cl
Middleton-on-S PO22 . . .202 E6
Portslade-by-S BN41 . . .168 B3
Worthing BN13 . . . . . . 185 C6
Juniper Ct 11 RH16 . . . .87 C2
Juniper Rd RH11 . . . . . . .5 C1
Juniper Wlk BN43 . . . . 167 C1
Juno Ct BN12 . . . . 185 C4
Jupp's La BN12 . . . . . . 185 C4
Jura Cl RH11 . . . . .18 B3
Jury La PO20 . . . . 198 D5
Juxon Cl
Chichester PO19 . . . . . 177 A5
Crawley RH11 . . . . .17 F4

K

Kaithewood Ho RH12 . . . .37 B5
Kandy Pk BN17 . . . . . . 204 C4
Karenza Ct BN1 . . . . . . 192 A8
Katherine's Lo 2
BN15 . . . . 187 C6
Kathleen Gdns PO19 . . . 177 C6
Kearsley Dr RH14 . . . . . 164 A1
Keaton Ho 2 RH16 . . . . .87 E6
Keats Cl RH12 . . . . .36 F7
Keats Wlk PO21 . . . . . . 201 B3
Kebbell Lo 12 BN2 . . . . 213 C2
Keble Cl
Bognor Regis PO21 . . . . 200 F3
Crawley RH10 . . . . .6 D1
Keelson Way BN17 . . . . 205 A6
Keenans Cotts GU33 . . . .45 A5
KEEPER'S CORNER 7 C7
Keepers Wood PO19 . . . 154 F3
Keir Hardie Ho 7
RH11 . . . . .18 B1
Kelly Rd BN3 . . . . 169 D1
Kelmscott Rise RH11 . . . .39 B8
Kelsey Ave PO10 . . . . . 152 A1
Kelsey Cl
Horley RH6 . . . . .1 F3
Liss GU33 . . . . .20 E8
Kelsey Ct RH15 . . . . . . 109 D3
Kelso Cl
Crawley RH10 . . . . .19 E7
Lancing BN15 . . . . .187 B7

Kelsey Cl *continued*
Worthing BN13 . . . . . . .185 E5
Kelvin Bsns Ctr RH10 . . . .5 F1
Kelvin Ho 5 F2
Kelvin La RH10 . . . . .5 F2
Kelvin Way RH10 . . . . . . .5 F2
Kemnal Pk GU27 . . . . . .27 D7
Kemp Ct BN2 . . . . .192 E4
Kemps BN6 . . . . .127 F7
Kempshott Mews RH12 . . .36 B4
Kempshott Rd RH12 . . . .36 B4
Kemp St BN1 . . . . .213 B3
KEMP TOWN 192 D4
Kemptown Mews 1
BN2 . . . . .192 E4
Kemp Town Pl 10
BN2 . . . . .192 D4
Kendal Cl BN17 . . . . . . .205 A7
Kendale Ct RH10 . . . . . .19 C2
Kendall Ct RH16 . . . . . .87 F2
Kendal Rd
Hove BN3 . . . . .190 F8
Lancing BN15 . . . . .187 C6
Kenhurst BN16 . . . . . . .206 A5
Kenilworth Cl
Brighton BN2 . . . . .171 A2
Crawley RH11 . . . . .18 B2
Kenilworth Rd PO21 . . . .201 B4
Kenilworth Rd 1 . . . . . .79 C7
Kenmara Cl RH10 . . . . . . .6 A1
Kenmara Ct RH10 . . . . . . .6 A2
Kenmure Ave BN1 . . . . .170 A7
Kennard Ct RH18 . . . . . .23 C5
Kennedy Ave RH19 . . . . . .9 D3
Kennedy Rd RH13 . . . . . .36 D1
Kennel Hill PO18 . . . . . .135 E1
Kennel La
Hookwood RH6 . . . . .1 D2
Maplehurst RH13 . . . . . .82 E2
Kennet Cl
Crawley RH11 . . . . .17 F5
Worthing BN13 . . . . . . .185 D8
Kennet Rd GU31 . . . . . .68 A2
Kensett's Cnr RH20 . . . .123 A3
Kensington Cl RH20 . . . .121 C7
Kensington Gdns BN1 . . .213 B3
Kensington Pl BN1 . . . . .213 B3
Kensington Rd
Chichester PO19 . . . . . .177 D6
Crawley RH11 . . . . .18 C2
Kensington St BN1 . . . . .213 B3
Kent Cl 4 RH12 . . . . . .36 D2
Kent Cl BN43 . . . . .189 C7
Kent Fields BN7 . . . . . . .172 E5
Kent Mans 5 BN11 . . . .186 E2
Kenton Rd BN3 . . . . . . .190 D7
Kent Rd
Chichester PO19 . . . . . .177 B7
Littlehampton BN17 . . . .204 D6
Kents Rd RH16 . . . . . . .87 F3
Kent St BN5, BN13 . . . . .106 C6
Kentstreet La RH13 . . . . .84 C1
Kentwyns Dr RH13 . . . . .58 E8
Kentwyns Pl RH13 . . . . .58 E8
Kenton Rd BN3 . . . . . . .170 D7
Kenwood Quay 7
BN15 . . . . .187 F5
Kenya Ct
2 Brighton BN1 . . . . . .191 E6
Horley RH6 . . . . .1 F4
Kerrison Mews 7
BN3 . . . . .191 D5
Kerry Gdns BN16 . . . . . .206 A6
Kerves La RH13 . . . . . . .58 D6
Kestrel Cl
Bracklesham PO20 . . . . .208 A6
Crawley RH11 . . . . .18 C8
Horsham RH13 . . . . . . .36 E5
Hove BN3 . . . . .191 D8
Kestrel Ct
Chichester PO19 . . . . . .177 D7
Pagham PO21 . . . . .210 F7
Kestrels The BN43 . . . . .189 A8
Kestrel Way BN17 . . . . .204 C8
Kestrel Wlk RH10 . . . . . .21 C5
Keswick Cl
Crawley RH11 . . . . .17 D4
Worthing BN12 . . . . . . .185 D6
Ketche's La RH17, TN22 . . .89 E7
Ketch Rd BN17 . . . . . . .205 A8
Kew Gdns BN2 . . . . . . .193 E8
Kewell's Cnr PO20 . . . . .197 E5
Kew Gdns PO21 . . . . . . .200 F5
Kew St BN1 . . . . .213 A3
Keymer Cres BN12 . . . . .185 D2
Keymer Ct RH15 . . . . . .109 B2
Keymer End RH16 . . . . . .87 D3
Keymer Gdns RH15 . . . . .109 B1
Keymer Par RH15 . . . . . .109 B2
Keymer Pc BN6 . . . . . . .129 B3
Keymer Rd
Brighton BN1 . . . . .170 B4
Burgess Hill RH15 . . . . .129 B8
Hassocks BN6 . . . . .128 F3
Keymer Way BN12 . . . . .185 C2
Keynor Est PO20 . . . . . .209 E8
Keysford La RH16, RH17 . . .64 E3
Keystone Ct RH11 . . . . . .18 C3
Kidborough Rd RH11 . . . .17 F5
Kidbrook RH16 . . . . .87 F5
Kidbrooke Rise RH18 . . . .23 E2
Kidders La BN5 . . . . . . .106 D5
Kidd Rd PO19 . . . . .155 B1
Kidmans Cl RH12 . . . . . .36 F5

Kidworth Cl RH6 . . . . . . .1 F5
Killinghurst La GU27,
GU8 . . . . .28 D8
Kilmore Cl BN14 . . . . . .163 E6
Kiln Ave GU27 . . . . .27 C8
Kilnbarn Ct RH16 . . . . . .87 D2
Kilnbarn Way RH16 . . . . .87 D2
Kiln Cl RH10 . . . . .21 B7
Kilner Lo RH13 . . . . .57 F1
Kiln Field GU33 . . . . . . .45 A5
Kilnfield Rd RH12 . . . . . .33 D8
Kiln La
Haywards Heath RH16 . . . .88 B5
Horley RH6 . . . . .2 A5
Kilnmead RH10 . . . . . . .18 E7
Kilnmead Cl RH10 . . . . . .18 E7
Kiln Rd RH10 . . . . .21 B7
Kiln The RH15 . . . . .109 C3
Kilnwood Cl PO20 . . . . . .212 F7
Kilnwood La
Crawley RH12 . . . . .17 B3
Faygate RH12 . . . . .16 F3
Kilsham La GU28 . . . . . . .97 D4
Kilwich Ct PO22 . . . . . . .202 D6
Kimber Cl BN15 . . . . . . .187 D6
Kimberley Cl RH6 . . . . . . .1 E3
Kimberley Ct BN14 . . . . .186 D6
Kimberley Rd
Brighton BN2 . . . . .170 D1
Crawley RH10 . . . . .19 B7
Kimbers GU32 . . . . .68 A4
Kimbridge Pk PO20 . . . . .208 A6
Kimbridge Rd PO20 . . . . .208 A6
Kindersley Cl RH19 . . . . .10 B3
Kinfauns Dr BN13 . . . . . .163 D2
King Alfred Cl BN44 . . . .145 D3
King Charles Pl 10
BN43 . . . . .189 A6
King Edward Ave
BN14 . . . . .186 E4
King Edward Cl
Horsham RH13 . . . . . . .57 D6
Worthing BN14 . . . . . . .186 E4
King Edward Rd RH13 . . . .57 D6
Kingfisher Cl
Crawley RH11 . . . . .6 A1
Red Hill PO9 . . . . .130 D1
Worthing BN13 . . . . . . .185 C6
Kingfisher Ct
Middleton-on-S PO22 . . . .202 F5
10 Pulborough RH20 . . .100 C2
Worthing BN11 . . . . . . .186 A3
Kingfisher Dr
Haywards Heath RH16 . . . .87 C1
Haywards Heath RH16 . . . .87 C1
Littlehampton BN17 . . . .204 C8
Westbourne PO10 . . . . . .151 D4
Kingfisher La RH10 . . . . .21 C5
Kingfisher Par PO20 . . . .207 F7
Kingfisher Rise RH19 . . . .22 F8
Kingfisher Way RH14 . . . .36 C5
King George Ave
East Grinstead RH19 . . . . .9 C3
Petersfield GU32 . . . . . .68 B4
King George Gdns
PO19 . . . . .176 F8
King George Mews 7
GU32 . . . . .68 B4
King George Rd
BN43 . . . . .189 D8
King George VI Ave
BN3 . . . . .169 A3
King George VI Dr
BN3 . . . . .169 A4
King George VI Mans
BN3 . . . . .168 F2
King James's La BN5 . . . .125 E4
King John Ct 7 BN43 . . .189 A6
King La GU32 . . . . .67 B8
Kingley Ctr PO18 . . . . . .154 A6
**Kingley Vale National
Nature Reserve***
PO18 . . . . .133 E2
Kingmere 10 BN17 . . . . .204 E4
King Pl BN1 . . . . .213 A2
King's Arms Hill BN18 . . .160 B3
King's Ave PO19 . . . . . . .176 F4
Kings Barn End BN44 . . . .145 F3
King's Barn La BN44 . . . .145 F4
King's Barn Villas
BN44 . . . . .145 E3
Kingsbridge Mews
BN15 . . . . .185 D8
Kingsbury Rd BN1 . . . . .213 B4
Kingsbury St BN1 . . . . . .213 B4
Kings Cl
Lancing BN15 . . . . .187 F5
Red Hill PO9 . . . . .130 C1
Yapton BN18 . . . . .181 B2
Kings Copse 9 RH19 . . . .22 F8
Kingscote Hill RH11 . . . . .18 B4
Kingscote La RH11 . . . . .170 F5
Kingscote Way RH11 . . . .21 F4
Kings Cres BN43 . . . . . . .188 D5
Kings Ct
Brighton BN1 . . . . .213 B2
Hove BN3 . . . . .168 F2
Lancing BN15 . . . . .187 F4
Selsey PO20 . . . . .212 E8
Kings Ct PO19 . . . . .201 E3
King's Ct PO19 . . . . .177 B5
Kings Dr
Bognor Regis PO21 . . . . .211 B8

Kings Dr *continued*
Hassocks BN6 . . . . .128 F4
Midhurst GU29 . . . . . . .72 E7
Shoreham-by-S BN43 . . . .188 D5
King's Espl BN3 . . . . . . .191 A5
Kingsey Ave PO10 . . . . . .173 A8
Kingsfernsden La
GU32 . . . . .68 C5
Kingsfield
Henfield BN5 . . . . .125 E5
Storrington RH20 . . . . . .121 E2
Kingsfield Cl RH19 . . . . .189 E8
Kingsfold 2 BN2 . . . . . .192 F5
Kingsfold Cl RH12 . . . . . .79 D6
Kingsfold Ct RH12 . . . . . .15 B5
Kings Gate BN43 . . . . . .188 D5
Kings Gdns
Haywards Heath RH16 . . . .87 E6
Horsham RH12 . . . . . . .36 E3
Hove BN3 . . . . .191 C8
King's Gdns BN3 . . . . . .191 B5
Kings Hall BN11 . . . . . . .186 E2
Kingsham Ave PO19 . . . .177 B5
Kings La
Coldwaltham RH20 . . . . .119 C6
Marehill RH20 . . . . . . .100 F1
Southwater St RH13 . . . . .58 A4
King's La RH13 . . . . .106 B8
Kingsland Cl
Shoreham-by-S BN43 . . . .189 C7
Storrington RH20 . . . . . .121 C2
Kingsland Cotts BN6 . . . .107 C1
Kingsland Rd RH10 . . . . .19 A6
Kingsland Rd BN14 . . . . .186 D6
Kingslea RH13 . . . . .36 E3
Kingslea Prim Sch
RH13 . . . . .36 E3
Kingsley Cl
Horley RH6 . . . . .1 F5
Worthing BN14 . . . . . . .186 F4
Kingsley Ct 7 BN1 . . . . .191 E5
Kingsley Mews RH14 . . . .79 D7
Kingsley Rd
Brighton BN1 . . . . .169 D1
Crawley RH11 . . . . .18 A3
Horley RH6 . . . . .1 F5
King's Manor Com Coll
BN43 . . . . .189 D8
Kings Mdw PO18 . . . . . .152 D1
Kingsmead
Bognor Regis PO22 . . . . .201 F3
Littlehampton BN17 . . . .182 C5
Kingsmead Cl
Horsham RH12 . . . . . . .37 B6
Steyning BN44 . . . . . . .145 D1
Kingsmead Gdns
PO22 . . . . .203 A6
Kingsmead Pl RH12 . . . . .35 C3
Kingsmead Rd
Anston PO22 . . . . .203 A5
Broadbridge Heath RH12 . .35 D3
Kingsmere BN1 . . . . .169 C2
Kings Mews
Horsham RH12 . . . . . . .36 B2
Hove BN3 . . . . .191 B6
Kingsmill Rd PO22 . . . . .180 C6
Kings Par BN1 . . . . .170 A2
King's Par PO21 . . . . . . .201 A2
Kingspit La GU28 . . . . . . .98 D8
Kings Pl RH13 . . . . .103 D8
Kings Platt RH13 . . . . . . .103 D8
Kings Rd
Horley RH6 . . . . .2 A2
Lancing BN15 . . . . .187 F5
Petersfield GU32 . . . . . .67 F4
Rudgwick RH12 . . . . . . .33 D7
Southwick BN42 . . . . . .167 C1
King's Rd
Brighton BN1, BN3 . . . . .191 E5
Emsworth PO10 . . . . . . .173 A8
Haslemere GU27 . . . . . . .26 E2
Haywards Heath RH16 . . . .88 E3
Horsham RH13 . . . . . . .36 C1
Kings Rd Ind Est GU27 . . . .27 A6
Kings Ride RH15 . . . . . . .109 D1
King's Stone Ave
BN44 . . . . .145 F3
King St
Arundel BN18 . . . . .160 A3
Brighton BN1 . . . . .213 B2
East Grinstead RH19 . . . . .9 E1
Emsworth PO10 . . . . . . .173 C8
Worthing BN14 . . . . . . .186 D4
King's Terr 6 PO10 . . . .173 B8
Kingsthorpe Rd BN3 . . . .190 F8
Kingston Bay Rd
BN43 . . . . .189 C6
Kingston Broadway
BN43 . . . . .167 D1
Kingston Buci Fst Sch
BN43 . . . . .189 C7
KINGSTON BY SEA 189 C7
Kingston Cl
Brighton BN1 . . . . .170 E6
Hove BN3 . . . . .168 F2
Shoreham-by-S BN43 . . . .189 C8
Kingston Ct 8 BN43 . . . .189 C8
Kingston La
East Preston BN16 . . . . .206 B5
Southwick BN42, BN43 . . .189 D7
KINGSTONRIDGE 172 D6
Kingston Ridge BN7 . . . .172 D6
Kingston Way BN43 . . . . .167 D1

Kingsway
Bognor Regis PO21 . . . . .200 D1
Hove BN3 . . . . .191 B5
Selsey PO20 . . . . .212 F6
Worthing BN12 . . . . . . .185 F3
Kings Way
Burgess Hill RH15 . . . . .109 D2
Red Hill PO9 . . . . .130 C1
Kingsway Ct BN3 . . . . . .191 C5
Kings Wlk BN43 . . . . . . .188 D5
Kingswood PO20 . . . . . .121 C7
Kingswood Cl RH11 . . . . .39 C8
Kingswood Ct BN3 . . . . .191 C5
Kingswood St 5 BN3 . . .191 D7
King Williams Gate 11
GU32 . . . . .68 B3
Kinleside Way BN16 . . . .206 A8
Kinnell Cl PO10 . . . . . . .173 B8
Kinnara Ho 10 PO21 . . .201 C3
Kinsale 6 BN3 . . . . . . .191 D7
Kipling Ave
Woodingdean BN2 . . . . . .193 C7
Worthing BN12 . . . . . . .185 B4
Kipling Cl RH10 . . . . .19 C8
Kipling Ct
3 Haywards Heath
RH16 . . . . .87 C5
Horsham RH13 . . . . . . .37 A4
Rottingdean BN2 . . . . . .194 A1
Kipling Way RH19 . . . . . . .9 C1
Kippens La RH13 . . . . . . .82 B2
Kirdford Cl
Burgess Hill RH15 . . . . .109 C1
Crawley RH11 . . . . .18 A8
4 Rustington BN16 . . . .205 B4
Kirdford Rd BN18 . . . . . .160 A2
Kirkby Ct PO18 . . . . . . .156 D3
Kirkland Cl BN16 . . . . . .205 B5
Kites Cl RH11 . . . . .18 C6
Kithurst Cl
Crawley RH11 . . . . .18 D4
Littlehampton BN16 . . . .205 F4
Worthing BN12 . . . . . . .185 B5
Kithurst Cres BN12 . . . . .185 B5
Kithurst Farm Rd
RH20 . . . . .142 B8
Kithurst La PO20 . . . . . .207 D6
Kithurst Pk RH20 . . . . . .121 B1
Kitilear Ct BN3 . . . . .191 D6
Kitsbridge Ho RH10 . . . . .7 A2
Kittiwake Cl RH11 . . . . . .17 D4
Klada Ct RH20 . . . . .121 C2
Knap La PO20 . . . . .212 D7
Knepp Cl
Brighton BN2 . . . . .170 F2
Crawley RH10 . . . . .19 C6
Knepp Ho 7 RH13 . . . . .36 D1
Knighton Cl RH10 . . . . . . .6 D2
Knights Cotts PO18 . . . . .153 B3
Knightscroft Ave
BN16 . . . . .205 C4
Knightscroft Cl 5
BN16 . . . . .205 B4
Knightscroft Ho
BN16 . . . . .205 C4
Knightsfiled 4 GU32 . . . .68 A3
Knights Gate Rd BN1 . . . .171 C7
Knight's Hill PO18 . . . . . .135 C5
Knob Hill RH12 . . . . .15 A1
Knockhundred La
GU26 . . . . .26 C8
Knockhundred Row
GU29 . . . . .94 F9
Knole Cl RH10 . . . . .19 D7
Knole Gr RH19 . . . . .9 C3
Knole Rd BN2 . . . . .194 A1
Knoll Bsns Ctr The
BN3 . . . . .190 D8
Knoll Cl BN3 . . . . .168 D1
Knoll Pl RH16 . . . . .88 B5
Knowle Cl RH10 . . . . .7 C3
Knowle Dr RH10 . . . . .7 B3
Knowle La GU6, RH12 . . . .11 D4
Knowles Cl BN5 . . . . . . .125 C5
Knowles Mdw GU33 . . . . .45 D1
Knowle The RH17 . . . . . . .86 E7
Knoyle Rd BN1 . . . . .169 E2
Knyveton Ct RH15 . . . . . .109 B3
Kymer Gdns BN6 . . . . . .129 A3
Kynon Gdns PO22 . . . . .202 D6
Kyoto Ct PO21 . . . . .201 B3

L

Laburnum Ave BN3 . . . . .168 C1
Laburnum Cl
Ferring BN12 . . . . .206 F5
Lancing BN15 . . . . .187 D4
Laburnum Gr
Bognor Regis PO22 . . . . .201 C6
Brighton BN1 . . . . .170 B3
Chichester PO19 . . . . . .177 C4
Laburnum Grove Jun Sch
PO22 . . . . .201 C6
Laburnum Lo BN13 . . . . .185 C6
Laburnum Way RH16 . . . .88 B4
Laburnum Wlk BN16 . . . .205 C6
Lackenhurst La RH13 . . . .81 A6
Lacock Ct PO20 . . . . . . .208 C3
Lacy Ho PO19 . . . . .176 F5
Ladbroke Rd BN1 . . . . . .169 E2
Ladbrooke Cl BN16 . . . . .205 B4
Ladies Mile BN1 . . . . . . .170 B7

Ladies Mile Cl BN1 . . . . .169 F6
Ladies' Mile Ct BN1. . . . . . . .169 E6
Ladies' Mile Rd BN1. . . . . . . .169 F6
Lady Bee Marina Ind Est
BN42. . . . . .189 E6
Ladydell Rd BN11. . . . . .186 F3
Lady Margaret Rd
RH11. . . . . .18 A7
Lady Margaret Wlk
RH11. . . . . .18 A7
Ladymead RH15 . . . . .109 C5
Ladymead Cl RH10. . . . . . . .19 C3
Ladysmith Rd BN2 . . . . . . .192 D8
Ladywell Ct BN15. . . . . . . .187 F7
LAGNESS 200 B6
Lagness Rd PO20. . . . . .177 F1
Lagoon Rd PO21. . . . . .210 F7
Lagwood Cl BN6. . . . . .128 F3
Laine Cl BN1. . . . . .169 E3
Laines Rd BN44. . . . . .145 C2
Lake Cotts PO22 . . . . .180 D6
Lake La
Barnham BN18, PO22 . . . . .180 D6
Horley RH1, RH6 . . . . .2 C6
Laker Ct RH10. . . . . .19 A6
Lake Rd PO19 . . . . .177 C6
Lakers Lea RH14. . . . . .31 F1
Lakers Mdw RH14 . . . . . . .79 D8
Lakeside
Horsham RH12 . . . . .36 C5
Lancing BN15. . . . . .188 B5
Midhurst GU29 . . . . .94 E6
Lakeside Dr RH13. . . . . . . .58 A1
Lakeview
■ Brighton BN2 . . . . .192 C5
Littlehampton BN16. . . . . .205 A3
Lake View PO21. . . . . .200 A1
Lake View Rd
Copthorne RH19 . . . . .8 C4
Dormans Park RH19 . . . . . .9 F5
Lamberhurst Wlk
RH10 . . . . .19 A5
Lambert's La GU29 . . . . . . .94 F8
Lamberts Yd GU29 . . . . . .114 D8
Lambeth Cl RH11. . . . . . . .18 B2
Lambeth Wlk RH11 . . . . . .18 B2
Lambleys La BN14 . . . . . . .186 F8
Lambourn Ct RH19. . . . . . .9 E3
Lambourne Cl
Brighton BN1. . . . . .170 C2
Crawley RH10 . . . . .18 F4
Lambourne La GU29,
GU30 . . . . .47 E2
Lambourne Rd BN1 . . . . . .170 C2
Lambs Cres RH12. . . . . . . .36 F5
Lambs Farm Cl RH12 . . . . .37 A5
Lambs Farm Rd RH12. . . . .37 A6
Lambs Green Rd RH12 . . . .16 F6
Lambs Lease GU33. . . . . . .45 D3
Lambyn Croft RH6. . . . . . . .2 C4
Lammas Cl BN17 . . . . .204 E7
Lamorna Gdns
Ferring BN12. . . . . .206 F4
Westergate PO20 . . . . . . .179 D6
Lamorna Gr BN14. . . . . . .186 C6
Lampson Ct RH10. . . . . . . .7 B3
Lanark Cl RH13. . . . . .36 E2
Lanark Rd BN13. . . . . .185 E8
Landen Pk RH6. . . . . .1 E5
Landerry Ind Est The
PO20 . . . . .212 D8
Landseer Dr PO20 . . . . . . .212 F7
Landseer Rd BN3 . . . . . . .191 A8
Lane End Dr PO10 . . . . . . .173 B8
Lane End Farm Cvn Site
PO22. . . . . .203 A6
Lane End Rd PO22 . . . . . .203 A5
Lane Ho ■ RH13 . . . . .36 D2
Laneburst Gdns RH10. . . . .19 C8
Lanercost Rd RH11 . . . . . .18 C5
Lanes The* BN1. . . . . .213 B2
Lane The
Chichester PO19 . . . . .155 A2
Ifold RH14. . . . . .31 C4

Lanfranc Rd BN14 . . . . . . .186 B4
Langbury Cl BN12 . . . . . . .206 D7
Langbury La RH12 . . . . . . .206 E7
Langdale Ave PO19 . . . . . .177 C4
Langdale Cl BN15. . . . . . . .187 C5
Langdale Ct BN3 . . . . .190 F6
Langdale Gdns BN3. . . . . .190 F6
Langdale Rd
Crawley RH11 . . . . .17 D4
Hove BN3. . . . . .190 F6
Langham Ct ■ BN11. . . . . .186 A2
Langham Gdns BN11. . . . . .186 A2
Langhurst ■ BN2. . . . . . . .192 E4
Langhurst Cl RH12 . . . . . . .15 E4
Langhurst La RH12 . . . . . . .17 A8
Languhurstwood Rd
RH12. . . . . .15 D3
LANGLEY 46 B7
Langley Cres BN7 . . . . . . .171 E1
Langley Ct RH10. . . . . .19 A8
Langley Dr RH11. . . . . .18 D8
Langley Gr PO21. . . . . . . .200 C1
Langley Mount RH20 . . . . .100 C2
LANGLEY GREEN 5 C2
Langley Green Prim Sch
GU32 . . . . .67 C3
Langshott RH6 . . . . .2 C5
Langshott Inf Sch The
RH6 . . . . .2 C3
Langshott La RH6. . . . . .2 C4
Langstone Cl RH10 . . . . . . .19 C3
Langstone Gdns
PO18 . . . . .174 D8
Langton Cl PO20. . . . . . . .212 D6
Langton Ct ■ BN14. . . . . .186 D4
Langton Ho BN6 . . . . .127 E7
Langton Pl ■ RH20. . . . . .121 D1
Langton Rd
Chichester PO19 . . . . .176 E7
Worthing BN14 . . . . .186 D4
Lanka Ct PO20. . . . . .207 E7
Lansbury Rd RH11 . . . . . . .18 B1
Lansdown Ct RH12. . . . . . .37 B6
Lansdowne Cl
Angmering BN16 . . . . .183 F6
Worthing BN11 . . . . .186 A2
Lansdowne Ct ■
BN3 . . . . .191 C6
Lansdowne Ho ■
PO21 . . . . .201 C2
Lansdowne Mans ■
BN3 . . . . .191 D6
Lansdowne Mews ■
BN3 . . . . .191 D6
Lansdowne Pl
Hove BN3. . . . . .191 D6
Worthing BN11 . . . . .186 A2
Lansdowne Rd
Angmering BN16 . . . . .183 F6
Hove BN1, BN3 . . . . .191 D6
Littlehampton BN17. . . . . .204 D7
Worthing BN11 . . . . .186 A2
Lansdowne Sq ■
BN3 . . . . .191 D5
Lansdowne St BN3. . . . . . .191 D6
Lansdowne Way
BN16 . . . . .183 F6
Lansdown Terr PO10 . . . . .151 D5
Lanyards BN17 . . . . .205 A7
Lanyon Cl RH12. . . . . .37 A6
Lanyon Mews RH12. . . . . .37 A6
Lapwing Cl RH13 . . . . .36 F3
Larch Cl
Bognor Regis PO22 . . . . . .201 C2
Chichester PO19 . . . . .154 F2
Liphook GU30 . . . . .25 B3
Rustington BN16 . . . . .205 D5
Woodingdean BN2. . . . . . .193 F7
Larch End
Horsham RH12 . . . . .36 B4
West Chiltington Common
RH20. . . . . .121 D7
Larches Ho RH19 . . . . .10 B4
Larches The RH14. . . . . . . .37 C6
Larches Way RH10. . . . . . .21 C8
Larchfield Cl PO21. . . . . . .200 D1
Larch Lo RH13. . . . . .185 C6
Larch Way RH16. . . . . .88 B4
Larcombe Rd GU32. . . . . . .67 F2
Large Acres PO20. . . . . . . .212 D7
Larke Cl BN43 . . . . .189 C7
Larkfield Cl RH15. . . . . . . .187 F5
Larkfield Way BN1. . . . . . .170 A4
Lark Hill BN3. . . . . .168 E3
Larkins Rd RH6. . . . . .5 D7
Lark Rise
Crawley RH11 . . . . .18 C8
Liphook GU30 . . . . .25 A5
Turners Hill RH10 . . . . .11 A3
Lark Rise Cl RH16 . . . . . . .88 B5
Larksfield RH6. . . . . .2 B4
Larkspur Cl BN17 . . . . . . .205 A7
Larkspur Way RH13 . . . . . .58 A3
Lark Way PO10 . . . . .151 E4
Lashmar Rd BN2. . . . . . . .206 A6

Lashmere RH10. . . . . .7 D3
Laski Ct RH11 . . . . .18 B1
Latham Cl BN17. . . . . .204 B6
Latham Rd PO20. . . . . . . .212 D6
Latimer Cl RH11. . . . . .5 D1
Latimer Rd BN11 . . . . .185 F2
Laud Dr RH10 . . . . .19 D5
Lauder Cl PO10. . . . . .151 F2
Laughton Rd
Horsham RH12 . . . . .36 F5
Woodingdean BN2. . . . . . .193 F8
Laundry La RH17 . . . . .44 D1
Laureens Wlk BN2. . . . . . .193 F1
Laurel ■ RH16 . . . . .87 D6
Laurel Cl
Burgess Hill RH15 . . . . . . .109 D5
Horsham RH12 . . . . .19 A3
Laurel Dene RH19 . . . . . . .9 F1
Laurel Dr PO21. . . . . .199 F2
Laurel Gr PO22 . . . . .201 C6
Laurel Mount RH20 . . . . . .100 C2
Laurels Fst Sch The
BN13 . . . . .185 B7
Laurels The
■ Brighton BN2 . . . . .213 C5
Crawley RH10 . . . . .6 A1
Henfield BN5. . . . . .125 E5
Southwater RH13 . . . . .57 F2
Laurel Wlk RH13. . . . . .36 F1
Laurence Gn PO10. . . . . . .151 B4
Lauriston Rd BN1. . . . . . . .169 E2
Lavant CE Prim Sch
PO18 . . . . .154 E6
Lavant Cl
Crawley RH11 . . . . .17 F5
Worthing BN12 . . . . .185 A5
Lavant Ct ■ BN12. . . . . . . .68 A4
Lavant Down Rd
PO18 . . . . .154 E7
Lavant House Rosemead
Sch PO18. . . . . .154 E5
Lavant Rd PO18, PO19 . . .154 F3
Lavant St GU32 . . . . .68 A3
Lavender Cl PO22. . . . . . .202 E6
Lavender Hill BN43 . . . . . .167 B1
Lavender Ho BN2 . . . . . . .213 C1
Lavender Row GU29 . . . . . .72 A1
Lavender St BN2 . . . . .213 C1
Lavington Cl RH11. . . . . . . .18 A8
Lavington Rd BN14 . . . . . .186 B6
Lavinia Ct
Bognor Regis PO21 . . . . . .200 F4
Worthing BN12 . . . . .185 C4
Lavinia Way BN16. . . . . . .206 A5
Lawns Cotts RH12 . . . . . . .12 A3
Lawns Rd RH12. . . . . .12 A3
Lawns The
Lancing BN15. . . . . .187 C8
West Kingston BN16 . . . . .206 A4
Lawn The PO21 . . . . .200 E2
Lawrence Ave BN16 . . . . .205 D6
Lawrence Cl
Crawley RH10 . . . . .19 C4
Selsey PO20. . . . . .212 E6
Lawrence Rd BN3 . . . . . . .190 F7
Lawrie La RH16. . . . . .88 B5
Laws Ct RH11 . . . . .17 E5
Lawson-Hunt Ind Pk
RH12. . . . . .35 D4
Lawyer's La BN5. . . . . . . .125 C4
Laxton Mdw PO18 . . . . . .153 A5
Laylands Cl BN41. . . . . . . .190 A7
Laylands Rd BN41. . . . . . .190 A7
Layne The PO22 . . . . .203 A5
Lazy Acre PO10 . . . . .173 F8
Leach Ct BN2. . . . . .192 C5
Lea Cl RH11 . . . . .17 F5
Leacroft RH19 . . . . .9 D2
Lea Farm La RH20 . . . . . . .99 C2
Lea Ho PO22 . . . . .201 A6
Leahurst Court Rd
BN1. . . . . .169 E3
Leahurst Ct ■ BN1 . . . . . .169 E3
Leaman Cl PO22. . . . . . . .202 F5
Leander Rd PO18 . . . . . . .175 C5
Leas Ct PO22. . . . . .201 C5
Leas The
Angmering BN16. . . . . . . .205 E7
Burgess Hill RH15 . . . . . . .108 F4
Leatherbottle La
PO19 . . . . .177 C6
Lechford Rd RH6 . . . . .2 A1
Leconfield Rd BN15 . . . . . .187 C5
Ledbury Way PO21. . . . . .200 B2
Ledgers Mdw RH17 . . . . . .86 F6
Ledra Dr PO21. . . . . .211 B8
Lee Bank BN22 . . . . .23 F3
Leechpool Hill RH13 . . . . . .59 F2
Leechpool La RH12,
RH13. . . . . .37 A4
Leechpool & Owlbeech
Woods Nature Reserve*
RH13 . . . . .37 C4
Leechpool Prim Sch
RH13. . . . . .37 A4
Leecroft PO21. . . . . .200 E2
Leeds Cl
Southwater RH13 . . . . .58 A2
Worthing BN13 . . . . .185 B6
Lee Farm Cotts BN13. . . . .142 B1
Leemark Ho ■ BN17. . . . .204 E4
Lees Cnr BN16. . . . . .205 B5
Leeside RH12. . . . . .16 C6
Lee St RH6. . . . . .1 E4
Lee's Yd PO20 . . . . .179 D4
Leeward Cl RH10 . . . . . . .185 F6

Leeward Rd
Littlehampton BN17. . . . . .205 A5
Worthing BN13 . . . . .185 F6
LEGGATT HILL 74 B5
Leggs La GU29 . . . . .115 B8
Leggyfield Ct RH12 . . . . . .36 B5
Legion Way PO20. . . . . . .208 A6
Legsheath La
Forest Row RH19. . . . . . . .22 D1
Sharpthorne RH18, RH19 . .43 F8
Leicester Ct RH10 . . . . . . .19 D6
Leicester St BN2 . . . . .213 C2
Leicester Villas BN3. . . . . .190 D7
Leigh Ct PO20 . . . . .208 C4
Leigh Jenkins Way RH6. . . .6 B7
Leighlands RH10. . . . . .19 C8
Leigh Rd
Chichester PO19 . . . . .176 F5
Worthing BN14 . . . . .186 D6
Leighton Ave BN14 . . . . . .186 E6
Leighton Rd
Horsted Keynes RH17. . . . .65 C5
Hove BN3. . . . . .190 F8
Leighton Villas RH17. . . . . .65 C5
Leinster Gdns PO22. . . . . .202 D4
Leith View Cotts RH12 . . . .15 B6
Leith View Rd RH12. . . . . .37 A5
Le May Cl RH6. . . . . .2 A4
Lemmington Way
RH12. . . . . .37 A7
Lenham Ave BN2 . . . . . . .194 B1
Lenham Rd E BN2 . . . . . . .194 B1
Lenham Rd W BN2. . . . . . .194 A1
Lenhurst Way RH13. . . . . .185 F5
Lennox Mews ■
BN14 . . . . .186 D3
Lennox Rd
Chichester PO19 . . . . .177 B7
Hove BN3. . . . . .190 F8
Shoreham-by-S BN43. . . . .189 B8
Worthing BN11 . . . . .186 D3
Lennox St
Bognor Regis PO21 . . . . . .201 D2
Brighton BN2 . . . . .213 C2
Leonardslee Ct RH10. . . . . .19 B3
Leonardslee Gdns*
Crabtree RH13. . . . . .84 A8
Lower Beeding RH13. . . . . .60 A1
Leonard Way RH13. . . . . . .36 F2
Leonora Dr PO21. . . . . . . .200 B2
Leopold Cl PO22. . . . . . . .202 A5
Leopold Rd
Brighton BN1. . . . . .213 A3
Crawley RH11 . . . . .18 C6
Leslie Best Ho BN1 . . . . . .213 B4
Leslie Nation Ct ■
GU32 . . . . .67 E7
Lesser Foxholes
BN43 . . . . .166 D1
Letchworth Cl RH11 . . . . .206 E5
Letchworth Ct RH11. . . . . .17 E3
Level Mare La PO20. . . . . .157 E2
Leverett La RH11 . . . . .18 B8
Leverton Ave PO22. . . . . .202 D4
Levine Ct ■ PO22. . . . . . .201 D4
Lewes Cl
Bognor Regis PO21 . . . . . .200 F4
Brighton BN2 . . . . .19 C6
Saltdean BN2. . . . . .194 E1
Lewes Cres BN2 . . . . .192 E4
Lewes Ct
Falmer BN1 . . . . .171 A8
Southwick BN42 . . . . .190 A7
Lewes Mews ■ BN2. . . . . .192 E4
Lewes Rd
Ashurst Wood RH19 . . . . . .23 C6
Brighton BN2 . . . . .170 E3
Chelwood Gate RH17. . . . .44 C1
Danehill RH17 . . . . .66 B3
Ditchling BN6. . . . . .129 E2
Forest Row RH18. . . . . . . .23 E2
Horsted Keynes RH17. . . . .65 C5
Lindfield RH16. . . . . .88 B7
Scaynes Hill RH17. . . . . . .88 D4
Lewes St BN2 . . . . .213 C3
Lewin Cl RH15. . . . . .187 F7
Lewis Ct
■ Brighton BN2 . . . . .192 C8
Worthing BN13 . . . . .185 B6
Lewisham Cl RH11. . . . . . .18 C2
Lewis Rd
Chichester PO19 . . . . .177 B7
Lancing BN15. . . . . .187 D8
New Brighton PO10. . . . . .151 C3
Selsey PO20. . . . . .212 E7
Leybourne Cl
Brighton BN2. . . . . .171 A1
Crawley RH11 . . . . .18 C1
Leybourne Par BN2. . . . . .171 A1
Leybourne Pl RH19 . . . . . .9 F4
Leybourne Rd BN2 . . . . . .171 A1
Leyfield Ho ■ RH20. . . . . .123 C2
Leylands Pk RH15. . . . . . .109 B5
Leylands Rd RH15. . . . . . .109 A5
Ley Rd PO22. . . . . .202 B4
Leys The
Fernhurst GU27. . . . . .49 A5
Singleton PO18 . . . . .135 D7
Leyton Ct PO22. . . . . .202 B4
Leyton La RH17. . . . . .86 E6
Library Pl RH11. . . . . .186 E1
Lichfield Ct
■ Brighton BN2 . . . . .192 F5
■ Worthing BN11. . . . . . .186 A1
Lichfield Gdns PO22 . . . . .200 E3
Lidsey Cl RH10 . . . . .19 C4
Lidsey Cvn Pk PO22. . . . . .179 D2

Lidsey Rd PO20, PO22 . . . .179 D4
Lifeboat Way PO20 . . . . . .212 E5
Lilac Cl
Middleton-on-S PO22. . . . .202 E6
Rustington BN17 . . . . .205 A7
Worthing BN13 . . . . .185 B6
Lilac Ct BN1. . . . . .169 D4
Lilian Terr BN18. . . . . .183 C8
Lillywhite Cl RH15. . . . . . .108 F5
LIMBO 75 D5
Limbourne La RH20. . . . . . .99 B3
Limbrick Cl BN12 . . . . . . .185 C4
Limbrick Cnr BN12. . . . . . .185 C5
Limbrick La BN12. . . . . . . .185 C5
Limbrick Way BN12. . . . . .185 C5
Lime Ave
Horsham RH12 . . . . .37 A4
Woodgate PO20. . . . . . . .179 E7
Lime Chase RH20. . . . . . .121 D2
Lime Cl
Chichester PO19 . . . . .177 B7
Copthorne RH10 . . . . .7 B3
Crawley RH11 . . . . .5 C1
Lime Gr BN16 . . . . .205 F8
Lime Kiln Rd RH13. . . . . . .59 D6
Lime Rd BN14. . . . . .163 E6
Limes Ave BN2 . . . . .2 B1
Limes Cl
Bramshott GU30. . . . . . . .25 C3
Slindon GU33 . . . . .45 B4
Limes The
Dormans Park RH19 . . . . . .9 A5
Haslemere GU27 . . . . .27 A6
Rustington BN16 . . . . .205 C6
Worthing BN11 . . . . .186 B3
Yapton BN18 . . . . .181 A3
Lime Tree Ave BN14. . . . . .163 F2
Lime Tree Cl BN16 . . . . . .205 F6
Lime Tree Gr RH16 . . . . . .88 C7
Limmard Way PO22 . . . . .202 C4
Limmer La PO22. . . . . . . .202 B4
Limney Rd BN2 . . . . .192 E7
Linacre Dr GU6, RH12 . . . .12 C4
Lincett Ave BN13 . . . . . . .185 F5
Lincett Ct BN13. . . . . .185 F5
Lincett Dr BN13 . . . . .185 F4
Linchmere BN2. . . . . .192 F7
Linchmere Ave BN2. . . . . .194 C1
Linchmere Pl RH11 . . . . . .18 A7
Linchmere Rd
Haslemere GU27 . . . . .26 D5
Linchmere GU27 . . . . .26 C4
Linch Rd GU29 . . . . .72 B7
Lincoln Ave PO21. . . . . . .200 C4
Lincoln Cl
Crawley RH10 . . . . .18 E3
Horley RH6 . . . . .2 A2
Lincoln Cotts BN2 . . . . . . .213 C3
Lincoln Ct
Hove BN3. . . . . .191 C8
Liphook GU30 . . . . .25 C4
Lincoln Ho PO19. . . . . . . .154 F1
Lincoln Ho ■ BN12. . . . . .186 B2
Lincoln St BN2 . . . . .213 C4
Lincoln Wood RH16. . . . . .87 C5
Lindale Pl ■ RH20. . . . . . .121 D1
Linden Ave RH19 . . . . .9 C2
Linden Cl
■ Bognor Regis
PO21. . . . . .201 C3
Petworth GU28 . . . . .97 C7
Linden Dr GU33 . . . . .45 B4
Linden Gr RH16. . . . . .88 B7
Linden Pk BN17 . . . . .204 C5
Linden Rd
Bognor Regis PO21 . . . . . .201 C4
Littlehampton BN17. . . . . .204 C5
Lindens Cl PO10 . . . . .151 B2
Lindens The
■ Brighton BN2 . . . . .213 C4
Copthorne RH10 . . . . .7 B3
Lindfield BN41. . . . . .168 A1
Lindfield Cl BN1. . . . . .194 B2
Lindfield Cl BN1. . . . . .170 C2
Lindfield Ent Pk RH16. . . . .88 C6
Lindfield Prim Sch
RH16. . . . . .88 A7
Lindfield Rd RH17 . . . . . . .64 C6
Lindgren Wlk RH11 . . . . . .18 B1
Lindsey Ct PO22. . . . . . . .202 A6
Lindum Rd BN13. . . . . . . .185 F6
Lindum Way RH13 . . . . . .185 F6
Linemans View ■
BN43 . . . . .188 E7
Lineside Ind Est BN17. . . .204 B6
Lineside Rd BN17 . . . . . . .204 B6
Linfield Cl RH16 . . . . .206 A8
Linfield Copse RH20 . . . . .121 F6
Linfield Ct PO21 . . . . .201 A2
Linfield La RH20 . . . . .123 A6
Linfield Cl BN13 . . . . .185 F7
Lingfield Ave RH11 . . . . . .9 D3
Lingfield Rd RH19 . . . . . . .9 D3
Lingfield Way PO20 . . . . .100 C2
Link Dr RH10 . . . . .100 C2
Link Hill RH20 . . . . .121 B1
Link La RH20. . . . . .100 C2
Links Ave PO22 . . . . .201 F4
Links Cl
Portslade-by-S BN41. . . . .190 C8
Red Hill PO9 . . . . .130 D1
Links La PO9 . . . . .130 D2

Links Rd
Lancing BN15 . . . . . . .187 F6
Portslade-by-S BN41 . . . 190 C8
Worthing BN14 . . . . . . .186 A8
Link The RH11 . . . . .18 D6
Linkway RH6 . . . . .6 C7
Link Way PO21 . . . . .200 A1
Linkway The
Brighton BN1 . . . . .170 B1
Hove BN3 . . . . .186 C3
Linnell Cl RH11 . . . . .39 B8
Linnet Cl
Littlehampton BN17 . . . .204 C8
Petersfield GU31 . . . . . . .68 E2
Turners Hill RH10 . . . . . . .21 C6
Linton Ho GU28 . . . . .75 C1
Linton Rd BN3 . . . . .190 F8
Lintot Ct RH13 . . . . .57 F1
Lintot Sq NH13 . . . . .57 F1
Lintott Gdns RH13 . . . . . .36 E3
Lion Cl GU27 . . . . .26 F7
Lion Ct PO21 . . . . .200 B2
Lionel Ave PO22 . . . . . . .202 C6
Lion Gn GU27 . . . . .26 F7
Lion La
Haslemere GU27 . . . . . . .26 F7
Turners Hill RH10 . . . . . . .21 A4
Lion Mead GU27 . . . . . . .26 F6
Lion Mews [4] BN3 . . . . .190 F7
Lion Rd PO21 . . . . .200 A2
Lions Cl BN2 . . . . .192 E5
Lions Dene BN1 . . . . . . .169 D4
Lions Gate BN3 . . . . .168 E1
Lions Gdns BN1 . . . . . . .169 D2
Lion St PO19 . . . . .177 A6
Liphook CE Jun Sch
GU30 . . . . .25 B4
Liphook Cl BN11 . . . . . . .170 C1
Liphook Inf Sch GU33 . . .25 B4
Liphook Rd
Haslemere GU27 . . . . . . .26 F6
Hollywater GU35 . . . . . . .24 A8
Linchmere GU27 . . . . . . .26 B4
Liphook Sta GU30 . . . . . .25 C2
Lisher Rd BN15 . . . . .187 F7
Lisle Way PO10 . . . . .151 A3
Lismore Cres RH11 . . . . . .18 B3
Liss Inf Sch GU33 . . . . . . .45 C5
Liss Jun Sch GU33 . . . . . .45 C3
Liss Sta GU33 . . . . .45 C3
Lister Ave RH19 . . . . .22 F6
Listers RH17 . . . . .60 F1
Litten Terr RH17 . . . . .177 A7
Little Ashfield GU29 . . . . .94 E8
Little Babbsham
PO21 . . . . .200 E2
Little Barn Pl GU33 . . . . .45 D4
Little Bentswood RH16 . . .87 F5
Little Bentswood Cl
RH16 . . . . .87 F5
Little Black Hill RH16 . . . .88 B7
LITTLE BOGNOR 98 F5
Little Boultons PO20 . . . .198 F8
Little Breach PO19 . . . . . .176 F8
Little Bridges Ct RH13 . . .57 F1
Little Cl RH13 . . . . .81 F2
Little Comptons RH13 . . . .36 F2
Little Copse Rd RH14 . . . .128 E4
Littlecote GU28 . . . . .97 F7
Little Court Cl GU29 . . . . .94 D8
Little Crabtree RH11 . . . . .18 C7
Little Cres BN2 . . . . .194 B1
Littlecroft Cvn Pk
PO20 . . . . .197 D2
Little Dipper's RH20 . . . . .100 C2
Little Dr BN12 . . . . .206 C6
Little Dro RH14 . . . . .145 D2
Littlederove Cotts
PO18 . . . . .135 D7
Little East St
Billingshurst RH14 . . . . . .55 D1
Brighton BN2 . . . . .213 B1
Littlefield Cl PO20 . . . . . .212 E7
Littlefield Rd PO19 . . . . . .177 B5
Little Finches RH13 . . . . .105 A3
Little Gables BN13 . . . . . .185 F7
Little George St BN2 . . . .213 B1
Little Grebe RH12 . . . . . . .36 C5
Littlegreen Sch PO18 . . . .111 A4
Littlehampton Com Sch
The BN17 . . . . .204 E6
Littlehampton Information
Ctr* RH17 . . . . .204 D3
Littlehampton Mus*
BN17 . . . . .204 E5
Littlehampton Rd
Ferring BN12 . . . . .206 D7
Worthing BN12, BN13 . . .185 D6
Littlehampton Sta
BN17 . . . . .204 C5
Little Hatch RH12 . . . . . . .36 F5
LITTLE HAVEN 36 E5
Littlehaven Inf Sch
RH12 . . . . .36 F5
Littlehaven La RH12 . . . . .36 F5
Littlehaven Sta RH12 . . . .36 F5
Little Hayes Cotts
RH14 . . . . .55 F5
LITTLE HEATH RH14 . . . . .157 F5
Littleheath Rd BN18 . . . . .157 E4
Little High St
[1] Shoreham-by-S
BN43 . . . . .188 E7
Worthing BN11 . . . . . . .186 D3
Little Hill RH20 . . . . .121 C8
Little King St RH19 . . . . . . .9 E1
Little London PO19 . . . . .177 A6

Little London Mews [8]
PO19 . . . . .177 A6
Little Oak RH13 . . . . .105 A3
Little Paddocks BN12 . . . .206 E5
Little Paddocks Way
BN12 . . . . .206 F5
Little Park Enterprises
RH14 . . . . .4 E3
LITTLE PARKMINSTER
. . . . .105 E7
Little Pembrokes
BN11 . . . . .186 A3
Little Preston St BN1 . . . .191 E5
Littlestone Rd BN13 . . . . .185 E7
Little Western St [1]
BN1 . . . . .191 E5
Littleworth Cl BN2 . . . . . .193 F7
Littleworth La RH13 . . . . .105 A4
Liverpool Bldgs [9]
BN11 . . . . .186 D2
Liverpool Gdns BN11 . . . .186 D2
Liverpool Rd BN11 . . . . . .186 D2
Liverpool Terr BN11 . . . . .186 D2
Livesay Cres BN14 . . . . . .186 D4
Livingstone Ho [5]
BN3 . . . . .191 B7
Livingstone Rd
Burgess Hill RH15 . . . . . .108 F3
[1] Hove BN3 . . . . .186 C3
Horsham RH11 . . . . .36 D1
Hove BN3 . . . . .191 B7
Livingstone St BN2 . . . . .192 D5
Lizard Head BN11 . . . . . .205 A6
Llandaff Ct BN11 . . . . . . .186 A2
Lloyd Cl BN3 . . . . .191 C8
Lloyd Goring Cl BN16 . . . .183 F6
Lloyd Rd BN3 . . . . .191 C8
Lloyds Ct RH10 . . . . .5 E1
Loats La PO21 . . . . .200 F7
Lobster La PO20 . . . . . . .212 B8
Lobs Wood La RH20 . . . .121 D2
Locke Rd GU30 . . . . .25 D4
Lockgate Rd PO20 . . . . . .198 C4
Lockhart Ct RH16 . . . . . . .87 F2
Lockitt Way BN7 . . . . . . .172 E5
Lock La
Birdham PO20 . . . . .197 F6
Partridge Green RH13 . . .104 E2
Locksash Cl BN44 . . . . . .196 C2
Locksash La PO18 . . . . . .132 C7
Locks Cres BN41 . . . . . . .168 B1
Locks Ct [10] BN42 . . . . . .189 E7
Locks Hill BN41 . . . . .168 B1
Lockwood Cl
Horsham RH12 . . . . .37 A5
Woodingdean BN2 . . . . . .193 E7
Lockwood Cres BN2 . . . . .193 E7
Lockwood Ct RH10 . . . . . .10 F8
Lockyer Ct GU32 . . . . . . .68 D5
Loddon Cl BN13 . . . . . . .185 C9
Loder Gdns BN14 . . . . . .186 C5
Loder Pl BN1 . . . . .169 F2
Loder Rd BN1 . . . . .169 F2
Loders RH17 . . . . .64 B8
Lodgebury Cl PO10 . . . . .174 A8
Lodge Cl
Crawley RH10 . . . . .18 C6
East Grinstead RH19 . . . . .9 D1
Middleton-on-S PO22 . . . .203 A5
Portslade-by-S BN41 . . . .167 F2
Lodge Ct
Bognor Regis PO21 . . . .200 E2
Shoreham-by-S BN43 . . . .166 E1
Lodge Hill La BN6 . . . . . .129 C4
Lodge La
Bolney RH17 . . . . .85 B3
Keymer BN6 . . . . .129 A2
Salfords RH1 . . . . .11 F6
West Marden PO18 . . . . .131 F6
Lodgelands RH17 . . . . . . .64 B6
Lodge The BN2 . . . . .213 C5
Lodsworth Cl BN13 . . . . .192 F7
Lodsworth Rd BN13 . . . . .192 F7
LODSWORTH COMMON
. . . . .74 B6
Lodsworth Rd PO21 . . . . .200 B3
Lombard St GU28 . . . . . . .97 F8
Lomond Ave BN1 . . . . . .170 B7
Lond Meadow Villas
RH6 . . . . .4 E5
London Fields Ho
RH11 . . . . .18 C2
London La RH17 . . . . .86 F6
London Meed Com Prim
Sch RH15 . . . . .109 A1
London Rd
Albourne Green BN6 . . . . .127 D5
Arundel BN18 . . . . .159 E6
Ashington RH20 . . . . . . .123 A5
Balcombe RH17 . . . . .40 F2
Bognor Regis PO21 . . . .201 D3
Brighton BN1 . . . . .213 B4
Brighton, Withdean
BN1 . . . . .169 D4
Burgess Hill RH15 . . . . . .108 F3
Coldwaltham RH20 . . . . . .119 D6
Crawley RH10 . . . . .5 E3
Cuckfield RH17 . . . . .86 E7
Danehill RH17 . . . . .66 A4
East Grinstead RH19 . . . . .9 F4
Fontwell BN18 . . . . .158 A3
Forest Row RH18 . . . . . . .5 F2
Handcross RH11, RH17 . . .39 C2
Hassocks BN6, RH15 . . . .128 E6
Heath Common RH20 . . . .122 E2
Henfield BN5 . . . . .125 F6
Hill Side GU31, GU33 . . . .69 B8
Horsham RH12 . . . . .36 C2

London Rd continued
Hurstpierpoint BN6 . . . . .127 E2
Liphook GU30 . . . . .25 C5
Petersfield GU31 . . . . . . .68 D5
Petworth GU28 . . . . .75 D3
Poynings BN45, BN6 . . . .148 F7
Pyecombe BN1, BN45 . . .149 C4
Rake GU33 . . . . .46 A4
Washington RH20 . . . . . .143 E7
London Road (Brighton)
Sta BN1 . . . . .192 A8
London Road Cotts
BN18 . . . . .160 A4
London St BN11 . . . . .186 C3
London Terr BN1 . . . . . . .213 B4
Lonesome La RH2 . . . . . . .1 D8
Loney Ct [●] BN43 . . . . . . .189 C8
Long Acre
Crawley Down RH10 . . . . . .21 A8
Selsey PO20 . . . . .212 D6
Longacre Cl GU33 . . . . . .45 C4
Longacre Cres RH7 . . . . . .86 F8
Longacre Rd PO20 . . . . . .212 E6
Longacre Pk BN18 . . . . . .180 F5
Longback Cotts BN16 . . . .183 F6
Longbridge Gate RH6 . . . .5 E8
Longbridge Rd RH6 . . . . . .1 F1
Longbridge Rdbt RH6 . . . . .1 F2
Longbridge Way RH6 . . . . .5 F8
Longbridge Wlk RH6 . . . . .1 F1
Longbrook PO22 . . . . . . .201 F3
Longchamp Ct RH6 . . . . . .2 C3
Long Cl RH10 . . . . .19 D6
Long Copse Ct PO10 . . . .151 B4
Long Copse La PO10 . . . .151 C4
Longcroft [●] BN43 . . . . . .188 C7
Longdene Rd GU27 . . . . . .27 B6
Long Down GU31 . . . . . . .68 D4
Longfellow Cl RH12 . . . . . .36 E7
Longfellow Rd BN11 . . . . .186 B3
Longfield Rd
Haywards Heath RH16 . . . .87 F3
Slinfold RH13 . . . . .34 D3
Longfield Way RH6 . . . . . .5 E5
Long Furlong BN13,
BN14 . . . . .163 B5
Long Furlong La BN13 . . . .162 E4
Long Hill RH13 . . . . .83 F8
Longhill Cl BN2 . . . . .193 E4
Longhill High Sch
BN2 . . . . .193 E4
Longhill Rd BN2 . . . . .193 E4
Longhurst RH15 . . . . .109 D2
Longhurst Rd RH11 . . . . . .18 A1
Long La
Arundel BN18 . . . . .159 D4
East Marden PO18 . . . . . .112 B3
Longland Ave RH20 . . . . .121 C2
Longlands BN14 . . . . .186 D8
Longlands Glade
BN14 . . . . .186 D8
Longlands Rd
East Wittering PO20 . . . . .207 F6
Southbourne PO10 . . . . .173 F8
Longlands Spinney
BN14 . . . . .186 D8
Longley Ind Est BN1 . . . . .213 B4
Long Mdw BN14 . . . . . . .164 A3
Longmead GU33 . . . . .45 B4
Long Mead BN18 . . . . . . .158 D1
Longmeadow Gdns
PO20 . . . . .197 E4
Longmere Rd RH10 . . . . . .18 D8
Longmoor Dr GU30 . . . . . .24 D4
Longmoor Rd GU30 . . . . . .24 E4
Long Park Cnr BN6 . . . . . .129 D2
Longport Rd PO22 . . . . . .202 B4
Long Rd GU32 . . . . .68 C6
Longridge Ave BN2 . . . . .194 D1
Longships BN17 . . . . .205 A6
Longview RH10 . . . . .9 A4
Long Wlk RH16 . . . . .88 B4
Longwood View RH10 . . . .19 A3
Longyard Ho RH6 . . . . .2 B5
Looes Barn Cl BN2 . . . . .194 D3
Loop The PO22 . . . . .202 C4
Loose La BN15 . . . . .187 B6
Loppets Rd RH10 . . . . . . .18 A3
Lordings La RH20 . . . . . .121 D7
Lordings Rd RH14 . . . . . . .79 A6
Loriners RH10 . . . . .18 D3
Loriners Ct BN3 . . . . .190 D8
Lorne Rd BN1 . . . . .191 D7
Lorne Rd BN1 . . . . .213 B5
Lorraine Ct
[2] Hove BN3 . . . . .191 B6
[1] Hove BN3 . . . . .191 E7
Lotts La BN15 . . . . .187 C6
Loudoun Rd BN17 . . . . . .204 C5
Lourier Ct [1] BN14 . . . . . .186 D4
Lovegrove Ct BN3 . . . . . .190 E8
Love La
Petersfield GU31 . . . . . . .68 C4
[●] Petersfield GU31 . . . . . .68 D4
Storrington RH20 . . . . . . .121 D2
Lovelets RH11 . . . . .18 A5
Lovell Path [1] RH11 . . . . . .17 E5
Lovells Ct PO21 . . . . .200 B2
Lover's Wlk BN1 . . . . .191 F8
Lover's Wlk Cotts
BN1 . . . . .191 F8
Lovett Ct BN12 . . . . .185 C6
Loveys Rd BN18 . . . . . . .180 F2
Lowdells Cl RH19 . . . . .9 C4
Lowdells Dr RH19 . . . . .9 C4
Lowdells La RH19 . . . . .9 C4
Lowe Cl RH11 . . . . .39 B8
LOW HEATH 98 C7
Lowlands Rd RH15 . . . . . .109 B5
Lowther Rd
Brighton BN1 . . . . .170 A2
Worthing BN13 . . . . .185 F8
Loxdale (The Swedish
Folk High Sch)
BN41 . . . . .168 B1
Loxley Gdns [2] BN14 . . . .186 C4
Loxmeadows RH14 . . . . . .31 D3
Loxwood
East Preston BN16 . . . . . .206 B7
[1] Lancing BN15 . . . . . . .187 D5
Loxwood Ave BN14 . . . . .186 B5
Loxwood Farm Pl
RH14 . . . . .31 F3
Loxwood Prim Sch
RH14 . . . . .32 A4
Loxwood Rd
Alfold Crossways GU6 . . . .11 A3
Loxwood, Alfold Bars GU6,
RH14 . . . . .31 F8
Loxwood Rd, RH14 . . . . . .32 D4
Plaistow RH14 . . . . .31 A2
Rudgwick RH12 . . . . .33 A6
Loxwood Wlk RH11 . . . . .18 A8
Loyal Par BN1 . . . . .169 C5
Lucas Cl
Crawley RH10 . . . . .19 C3
East Grinstead RH19 . . . . .10 A1
Lucas Field GU27 . . . . . . .26 E6
Lucas Grange RH16 . . . . .87 D5
Lucas Rd GU31 . . . . .35 F8
Lucastes Ave RH16 . . . . . .87 D6
Lucastes La RH16 . . . . . . .87 D6
Lucastes Rd RH16 . . . . . .87 D5
Lucas Way RH16 . . . . . . .87 C5
Lucerne Cl BN41 . . . . . . .168 B1
Lucerne Ct PO21 . . . . . . .200 E2
Lucerne Dr RH10 . . . . . . .19 D4
Lucerne Rd BN1 . . . . .170 A4
Lucking La PO22 . . . . . . .202 F5
Lucksfield Way BN16 . . . .184 A6
Lucraft Rd BN2 . . . . .170 F5
Ludgate Cl PO21 . . . . . . .200 E2
Ludlow Cl [●] RH11 . . . . . .18 B1
Ludlow Rise BN2 . . . . . . .171 A1
Luffs Mdw GU28 . . . . .79 D8
Luggs Cl RH14 . . . . .79 D8
Luker Dr GU31 . . . . .68 D5
Lullington Ave BN3 . . . . . .190 F8
Lulworth Cl RH11 . . . . .18 B3
Lutener Cl RH6 . . . . .2 A4
Lumley Gdns PO10 . . . . . .173 C8
Lumley Path PO10 . . . . . . .173 C8
Lumley Rd
Horley RH6 . . . . .2 A3
Lumley PO10 . . . . .151 C1

Lumley Terr PO10 . . . . . . .151 C1
Lunce's Hill RH16,
RH17 . . . . .109 F8
Lund Ho GU28 . . . . .97 F7
Lundy Cl
Crawley RH11 . . . . .18 C3
Littlehampton BN17 . . . .205 A4
Lupin Cl BN17 . . . . .205 A7
Lurgashall RH15 . . . . .109 C1
Lustrells Cl BN2 . . . . .194 B2
Lustrells Cres BN2 . . . . . .194 C2
Lustrells Rd BN2 . . . . . . .194 A2
Lustrells Vale BN2 . . . . . .194 C2
Lutener Rd GU29 . . . . .73 A1
Luther Mews BN2 . . . . . .192 C7
Luther Ct BN2 . . . . .192 C7
Luth The
Wisborough Green
RH14 . . . . .54 B1
Wisborough Green RH14 . .78 A8
Lutman St PO10 . . . . .151 A4
Lutyens Cl RH11 . . . . .17 E4
Luxford Cl RH12 . . . . .36 F5
Luxford Rd RH16 . . . . .88 B7
Luxford Way RH14 . . . . . .79 C7
Lychgates The BN18 . . . . .180 F4
Lychpole Wlk BN12 . . . . .185 B4
Lydon Ho RH11 . . . . .5 D1
Lye La PO18 . . . . .153 F5
LYMINSTER 182 D6
Lyminster Ave BN1 . . . . . .170 A5
Lyminster Gate BN1 . . . . .204 D8
Lyminster Inf Sch
BN17 . . . . .204 D7
Lyminster Rd
Crossbush BN18 . . . . . . .160 D1
Littlehampton BN17,
BN18 . . . . .182 D6
Lynchborough Rd
GU30 . . . . .24 D8
Lynch Down PO18 . . . . . .153 A6
Lynchet Cl BN1 . . . . .170 C3
Lynchet Down BN1 . . . . . .170 C2
Lynchets Cres BN3 . . . . . .168 D3
Lynchette The BN43 . . . . .166 F1
Lynchet Wlk BN1 . . . . . . .170 C2
Lynchmere Ave BN15 . . . .187 D8
Lynchmere Ct PO18 . . . . .175 C7
Lynden Ct [●] BN3 . . . . . . .169 E2
Lyndhurst Cl RH11 . . . . . .18 D5
Lyndhurst Ct
[●] Bognor Regis
PO21 . . . . .201 B2
Hove BN3 . . . . .191 D7
Lyndhurst Farm Cl
RH19 . . . . .8 D4
Lyndhurst Fst Sch
BN11 . . . . .186 F3
Lyndhurst Rd
Chichester PO19 . . . . . . .177 B5
Hove BN3 . . . . .191 D7
Worthing BN11 . . . . .186 F3
Lyndons The GU32 . . . . . .24 D8
Lyndum Cl GU32 . . . . .68 B4
Lyne Ho RH5 . . . . .3 A1
Lyne Rd BN13 . . . . .185 C7
Lynton Cl
East Grinstead RH19 . . . . .10 A2
Hurstpierpoint BN6 . . . . .128 B5
Lynton Park Ave RH19 . . . .10 A2
Lynton Rd GU32 . . . . .68 A4
Lyntons RH20 . . . . .100 C2
Lynton St BN2 . . . . .192 C7
Lynwick St
Rudgwick, Cox Green
RH14 . . . . .12 D1
Rudgwick RH12 . . . . .33 C8
Lynwood Ct RH12 . . . . . . .36 C3
Lyon Cl
Crawley RH10 . . . . .19 C2
Hove BN3 . . . . .191 D7
Lyon Ct
[●] Bognor Regis
PO21 . . . . .201 D3
Horsham RH12 . . . . .36 E2
Lyon St W PO21 . . . . . . .201 D3
Lyons Cl RH13 . . . . .34 D3
Lyons Rd RH13 . . . . .34 D3
Lyon St PO21 . . . . .201 D3
Lyons Way BN14 . . . . . . .186 E7
Lyoth La RH16 . . . . .88 C4
Lyoth Ho RH16 . . . . .88 C4
Lyric Ct RH10 . . . . .19 D4
Lysander Ho [7] RH20 . . . .121 E1
Lysander Way PO20 . . . . .156 D1
Lyss Ct GU33 . . . . .45 B4
Lytham RH6 . . . . .9 D3
Lythe La GU32 . . . . .67 C5
Lytton Dr RH10 . . . . .19 D7

M

McGechie Ho RH19 . . . . . .9 D3
McIndoe Rd RH19 . . . . . . .9 D3
McIver Cl RH19 . . . . .8 F4
Mackenzie Ho RH19 . . . . . .9 A4
McKerchar Cl RH15 . . . . .187 F7
Mackerel Cl PO20 . . . . . .212 B8
Mackie Ave
Brighton BN1 . . . . .170 A7
Keymer BN6 . . . . .129 A5
Mackley's Ind Est
BN5 . . . . .146 F6

Macklin Rd PO22 . . . . .201 E4
Macleod Rd RH13 . . . . .36 F1
McNair Cl PO20 . . . . .212 D8
McNair Ct BN3 . . . . .190 E7
McRae Ct 2 RH20 . . . . . . .212 D7
McWilliam Rd BN2 . . . . . . .171 C1
Maddox Dr RH10 . . . . .19 E5
MADEHURST 139 B1
Madehurst Cl
　Brighton BN2 . . . . .192 D5
　Littlehampton BN16 . . . . .205 F4
Madehurst Ct
　Crawley RH11 . . . . .17 F3
　6 Littlehampton BN17 . .204 D5
Madehurst Way BN17 . . . .204 D6
Madeira Ave
　Bognor Regis PO22 . . . . .201 E5
　Horsham RH12 . . . . .36 C2
　Worthing BN11 . . . . . . .186 E2
Madeira Dr BN2 . . . . .192 C4
Madeira Par PO22 . . . . . . .201 E5
Madeira Pl BN2 . . . . .213 C1
Madeline Rd RH30 . . . . . . .68 B4
Madgwick La PO18 . . . . . .155 D1
Mafeking Rd BN2 . . . . . . .170 D1
Magdalene Cl RH10 . . . . . .6 C1
Magellan Terr RH10 . . . . . .6 A2
Magnolia Cl BN13 . . . . . .185 B6
Magnolia Ct
　Bognor Regis PO21 . . . . .201 C4
　Horley RH6 . . . . .2 A3
Magnus Pl 14 BN43 . . . . .188 E7
Magpie Cotts PO8 . . . . . . .130 E4
Magpie La PO20 . . . . .209 C1
Magpie Rd PO8 . . . . .130 E5
Magpie Wlk RH10 . . . . . . .18 E8
MAIDENBOWER 19 C4
Maidenbower Bsns Pk
　RH10 . . . . .19 C4
Maidenbower Dr RH10 . . . .19 D4
Maidenbower Jun & Inf
　Schs RH10 . . . . .19 C4
Maidenbower La RH10 . . . .19 C4
Maidenbower Pl RH10 . . . .19 C4
Maidenbower Sq RH10 . . . .19 C4
Maiden La RH11 . . . . .18 C8
Maidment Ct BN5 . . . . . . .125 F6
Main Dr 3 PO22 . . . . .202 F5
Maines Farm Rd
　BN44 . . . . .146 C1
Mainline Bsns Ctr
　GU33 . . . . .45 B4
Main Rd
　Birdham PO20 . . . . .197 E4
　Broadbridge PO18 . . . . .175 D7
　East Dean PO18 . . . . . .136 C6
　Hermitage PO10 . . . . . .173 E8
　Nutbourne PO10, PO18 . . .174 C7
　Yapton BN18 . . . . .180 F3
Mainstone Rd 1 BN3 . . . .190 F7
Maizecroft RH10 . . . . .2 C4
Major Cl RH11 . . . . .170 B1
Major's Hill RH10 . . . . . . .20 C5
Malcolm Cl BN2 . . . . .206 E5
Malcolm Gdns RH6 . . . . . .1 D1
Malcolm Rd PO20 . . . . . . .156 C2
Malden Pl 4 RH20 . . . . . .121 D1
Malden Way PO20 . . . . . . .212 D7
Maldon Rd BN1 . . . . .169 D2
Malham Cl RH10 . . . . .19 C3
Malin Rd BN17 . . . . .205 A5
Mallard Cl
　Haslemere GU27 . . . . . . .26 E6
　Horley RH6 . . . . .2 A5
　Horsham RH12 . . . . .36 C5
Mallard Cres PO21 . . . . . .210 F7
Mallard Pl RH19 . . . . .22 F8
Mallard Rd PO9 . . . . .130 D1
Mallards La PO20 . . . . . . .212 B8
Mallard Way
　Henfield BN5 . . . . .125 E6
　Westbourne PO10 . . . . . .151 E4
Mallion's La RH17 . . . . . . .61 E2
Mallon Dene RH16 . . . . . .205 D4
Mallory Rd BN3 . . . . .169 C2
Mallow Cl RH12 . . . . .36 E6
Malmayne Ct PO21 . . . . . .200 E3
Malthouse Cl
　Arundel BN18 . . . . .160 A2
　Lancing BN15 . . . . .187 B7
Malthouse Cotts
　Bignor RH20 . . . . .118 A1
　Cocking GU29 . . . . .114 D7
　West Wittering PO20 . . . .196 D3
　Worthing BN12 . . . . . . .185 C2
Malthouse Ct
　Brighton BN2 . . . . .213 C2
　Liphook GU30 . . . . .25 D4
Malthouse La
　Brighton BN2 . . . . .213 C3
　Burgess Hill BN6, RH15 . . .108 C2
　Burgess Hill RH15 . . . . .108 D4
　West Ashling PO18 . . . . .153 B3
Malthouse Mdws GU30 . . . .25 C4
Malthouse Pas 5
　BN17 . . . . .204 D6
Malthouse Rd
　Crawley RH10 . . . . .18 D4
Malt House Trad Est
　BN43 . . . . .189 B7
Maltings Gn BN44 . . . . . . .145 D2
Maltings The
　Billingshurst RH14 . . . . . .55 D1
　Burgess Hill RH15 . . . . .108 D4

Maltings The continued
　Chichester PO19 . . . . . . .176 F6
　Liphook GU30 . . . . .25 D4
　Petersfield GU31 . . . . . . .68 B3
Maltravers Ct 8
　BN17 . . . . .204 E4
Maltravers Dr BN17 . . . . . .204 E4
Maltravers Rd BN17 . . . . . .204 E4
Maltravers St BN18 . . . . . .160 B3
Malvern Cl BN11 . . . . .187 B3
Malvern Mews PO10 . . . . . .151 B1
Malvern Rd
　Crawley RH11 . . . . .18 C5
　Hill Brow GU33 . . . . .45 D2
Malvern St 12 BN3 . . . . . .191 B7
Malvern Way PO21 . . . . . .200 B1
Manaton Cl RH16 . . . . .87 F4
Manchester St BN2 . . . . . .213 B1
Manchester Terr
　PO10 . . . . .151 D4
Mandalay Ct BN1 . . . . . . .169 D4
Manet Sq PO22 . . . . .201 B6
Manhattan Ct BN1 . . . . . . .169 D3
Manhood Com Coll
　PO20 . . . . .212 D8
Manhood Cotts PO20 . . . . .208 F7
Manhood La PO20 . . . . . . .209 F8
Manitoba Way BN3 . . . . . .185 C7
Manley's Hill RH20 . . . . . .121 E1
Mann Cl RH11 . . . . .39 B8
Manning Cl RH19 . . . . .9 D2
Manning Rd BN17 . . . . . . .204 C6
Mannings 8 BN43 . . . . . .188 F7
Mannings Ct RH10 . . . . . . .6 D1
Mannock Rd PO20 . . . . . . .156 B1
Manor Ave BN6 . . . . .129 A5
Manor Cl
　Bognor Regis PO22 . . . . .202 A4
　Brighton BN2 . . . . .192 E5
　Burgess Hill RH15 . . . . .109 D4
　East Preston BN16 . . . . .205 F5
　Haslemere GU27 . . . . . . .26 E6
　Henfield BN5 . . . . .125 F5
　Horley RH6 . . . . .1 F3
　Lancing BN15 . . . . .187 F7
　Southwick BN42 . . . . . . .190 A8
　Stockbridge PO19 . . . . . .176 F3
　Storrington RH20 . . . . . .121 D1
　Worthing BN11 . . . . . . .186 B3
Manor Cotts BN6 . . . . . . .127 F6
Manor Cres
　Brighton BN2 . . . . .192 E5
　Haslemere GU27 . . . . . . .26 E6
Manor Ct
　Elmer PO22 . . . . .203 B5
　Horsham RH12 . . . . .37 A5
　Lancing BN15 . . . . .187 D8
　Rustington BN16 . . . . . .205 B6
　Southwick BN42 . . . . . . .190 A7
　7 Storrington RH20 . . . .121 D1
　Worthing BN11 . . . . . . .186 B1
Manor Dr
　Cuckfield RH17 . . . . .86 E7
　Horley RH6 . . . . .1 F3
Manor Farm Bsns Ctr
　BN45 . . . . .148 C5
Manor Farm Cl PO18 . . . . .212 E8
Manor Farm Ct
　Elmer PO22 . . . . .203 B5
　Selsey PO20 . . . . .212 E8
Manor Field Ind Est 186 D5
Manorfield Prim Sch
　RH6 . . . . .1 F3
Manor Field Prim Sch
　RH15 . . . . .109 C4
Manorfields RH11 . . . . .17 D2
Manor Fields
　Horsham RH12, RH13 . . . .37 A4
　Liphook GU30 . . . . .25 D4
Manor Gdns
　Breach PO10 . . . . .151 F1
　Brighton BN2 . . . . .192 E5
　Hurstpierpoint BN6 . . . . .127 F6
　Rustington BN16 . . . . . .205 B5
Manor Gn BN2 . . . . .192 E5
Manor Green Coll
　RH11 . . . . .18 A7
Manor Green Prim Sch
　RH11 . . . . .18 A7
Manor Hall Fst Sch
　BN42 . . . . .189 F7
Manor Hall Mid Sch
　BN42 . . . . .189 F8
Manor Hall Rd BN42 . . . . .189 F8
Manor Hill BN2 . . . . .192 E6
Manor Ho
　Horsham RH12 . . . . .36 C1
　Worthing BN11 . . . . . . .186 B2
Manor House Pl BN15 . . . .187 F8
Manor La
　Doomsday Green RH13 . . .59 B8
　Selsey PO20 . . . . .212 F8
　South Mundham PO20 . . .199 D6
Manor Lea
　Haslemere GU27 . . . . . . .26 E6
　Worthing BN11 . . . . . . .186 B1
Manor Lodge Rd PO9 . . . .130 C1
Manor Paddock BN2 . . . . .192 E4
Manor Par
　Littlehampton BN17 . . . . .204 D5
　Worthing BN13 . . . . . . .185 D8
Manor Pk PO21 . . . . .200 A1
Manor Pl
　Bognor Regis PO21 . . . . .201 C2
　Brighton BN2 . . . . .192 E4
Manor Rd
　Breach PO10 . . . . .151 F1
　Brighton BN2 . . . . .192 E5

Manor Rd continued
　Burgess Hill RH15 . . . . .109 D4
　East Grinstead RH19 . . . . .9 C2
　Horsham RH12 . . . . .37 A5
　Hurstpierpoint BN6 . . . . .127 F6
　Lancing BN15 . . . . .187 E8
　Portslade-by-S BN41 . . . .168 B3
　Rustington BN16 . . . . . .205 B6
　Selsey PO20 . . . . .212 F7
　Upper Beeding BN44 . . . .146 B2
　West Kingston BN16 . . . . .206 A4
　Worthing BN11 . . . . . . .186 B2
MANOR ROYAL 5 F2
Manor Royal BN3 . . . . .5 E1
Manor Royal Ind Est
　RH10 . . . . .5 E2
Manor The 3 BN11 . . . . . .109 D4
Manor View Ct BN14 . . . . .186 D5
Manor Villas PO18 . . . . . . .175 C5
Manor Way
　Bognor Regis PO22 . . . . .200 C1
　Breach PO10 . . . . .151 F1
　Brighton BN2 . . . . .192 E5
　Elmer PO22 . . . . .203 B5
　Henfield BN5 . . . . .125 F6
　Lancing BN15 . . . . .187 F7
Mansbergh Rd PO19 . . . . .155 B8
Mansell Cl RH15 . . . . .109 B8
Mansell Rd BN43 . . . . . . .189 B8
Manser Rd BN18 . . . . .158 F1
Mansfield Cl BN11 . . . . . . .187 A4
Mansfield Cotts PO18 . . . . .174 D7
Mansfield Rd
　Bognor Regis PO22 . . . . .201 B6
　Hove BN3 . . . . .190 D7
　Worthing BN11 . . . . . . .187 A4
Mansion Ct RH15 . . . . . . .109 D3
Mant Cl
　Climping BN17 . . . . .181 D1
　Storrington RH20 . . . . . .121 D1
Mantell Ho 2 BN2 . . . . . .213 C2
Mantelmas Cotts RH10 . . . .21 A4
Mantling Rd RH17 . . . . . . .204 D5
Manton Cl PO20 . . . . .208 C5
Manton Rd BN2 . . . . .170 E1
Mant Rd GU28 . . . . .97 F7
Mants Farm Ct PO21 . . . . .200 C3
Maple Cl
　Billingshurst RH14 . . . . . .55 C1
　Burgess Hill RH15 . . . . .109 B5
　Crawley RH11 . . . . .5 C1
　Haywards Heath RH16 . . . .88 B3
　Horsham RH12 . . . . .37 A5
　Middleton-on-S PO22 . . . .202 E6
　New Brighton RH10 . . . . .151 B2
　Woodingdean BN2 . . . . . .193 E7
　Worthing BN13 . . . . . . .163 E1
Maple Ct RH15 . . . . .108 D3
Mapledown Cl RH13 . . . . . .57 F2
Maple Dr
　East Grinstead RH19 . . . . .10 A1
Maple Gdns
　Bognor Regis PO22 . . . . .201 C7
　Hove BN3 . . . . .168 F1
Maplegreen RH11 . . . . . . .18 A5
Maple Ho BN12 . . . . .185 A5
Maplehurst Ct RH14 . . . . . .79 F7
Maplehurst Rd
　Chichester PO19 . . . . . . .155 B2
　Maplehurst RH13 . . . . . . .83 A3
　Portslade-by-S BN41 . . . .168 A1
Maple Leaf Ho PO20 . . . . .119 D6
Maple Par BN18 . . . . .180 E8
Maple Rd
　Billingshurst RH14 . . . . . .79 D7
　Walberton BN18 . . . . . . .180 E8
Maples The
　8 Bognor Regis
　　PO21 . . . . .201 B3
　Ferring BN12 . . . . .206 F4
Maple Wlk
　Lancing BN15 . . . . .187 B7
　Petersfield GU31 . . . . . . .68 B1
　Rustington BN16 . . . . . .205 C6
Maplewood 4 BN1 . . . . . .169 E3
Mapsons La PO20 . . . . . . .119 B6
Marama Gdns BN16 . . . . . .205 B3
Marchants Cl BN6 . . . . . . .128 A6
Marchants Rd BN6 . . . . . . .128 A6
Marchants Way RH15 . . . . .108 F5
March CE Prim Sch The
　PO18 . . . . .155 E1
March Cl PO21 . . . . .200 C3
Marches Rd RH12 . . . . . . .14 F4
Marches The
　Fernhurst GU27 . . . . .49 B5
　Kingsfold RH12 . . . . .13 B5
March Ho BN3 . . . . .169 B1
March Sq PO19 . . . . .155 A3
Marchwell Ind Unit
　PO19 . . . . .155 A3
Marchwood PO19 . . . . . . .155 A3
Marchwood Gate
　PO19 . . . . .155 A3
Marcuse Fields PO18 . . . . .175 B6
Mardale Rd BN13 . . . . . . .185 F7
Marden Ave PO19 . . . . . . .176 E3
Marden Cl BN2 . . . . .171 E1
Marden Ho
　Barnham PO22 . . . . .180 C6
　Littlehampton BN17 . . . . .204 B7
Marden The RH11 . . . . . . .18 B7
Marden Way GU31 . . . . . . .68 C3
Mardyke BN43 . . . . .188 D6
Mare Hill Rd RH20 . . . . . .100 E1
Maresfield Rd BN2 . . . . . . .192 E5

Margaret Cl PO21 . . . . . . .200 E3
Margaret Cotts RH13 . . . . . .83 E2
Margaret Ho PO22 . . . . . . .201 E4
Margaret St BN2 . . . . .213 C1
Margary Cl PO19 . . . . .176 B7
Margery Rd BN3 . . . . .190 D8
Marian Way PO21 . . . . . . .201 E3
Marigolds Lo 2 BN16 . . . .205 B4
Marigolds (Park Homes)
　PO22 . . . . .179 D1
Marik Mews 5 BN11 . . . . .186 F2
Marina Cl PO10 . . . . .173 C7
Marina Ct BN15 . . . . .188 C5
Marina Way BN2 . . . . .192 F3
Marine Ave BN3 . . . . .190 E6
Marine Cl
　East Wittering PO20 . . . . .207 E6
　Saltdean BN2 . . . . .194 B1
　Worthing BN11 . . . . . . .186 A1
Marine Cres BN12 . . . . . . .185 D2
Marine Ct
　Littlehampton BN17 . . . . .204 E4
　Rottingdean BN2 . . . . . .194 A1
　Shoreham-by-S BN43 . . . .188 D6
Marine Dr
　East Wittering PO20 . . . . .207 E7
　Rottingdean BN2 . . . . . .193 C2
　Saltdean PO20 . . . . . . .212 F7
　Worthing BN12 . . . . . . .185 B1
Marine Dr W
　Bognor Regis PO21 . . . . .201 A2
　East Wittering PO20 . . . . .207 D7
Marine Gdns
　Brighton BN2 . . . . .213 C5
　Selsey PO20 . . . . .212 D5
Marine Par
　Bognor Regis PO21 . . . . .201 B2
　Brighton BN2 . . . . .192 C4
　Worthing BN11 . . . . . . .186 D1
Marine Park Ho PO21 . . . . .201 B2
Marine Pk 3 PO21 . . . . . .201 B2
Marine Pl BN11 . . . . .186 D1
Marine Point 14
　BN11 . . . . .186 A1
Marine Rd BN43 . . . . .188 D5
Mariners Quay
　Brighton BN2 . . . . .192 F3
　Littlehampton BN17 . . . . .204 C5
Mariners Terr PO18 . . . . . .175 B4
Mariners The BN15 . . . . . .187 D3
Mariners Wlk BN16 . . . . . .205 D4
Marineside PO20 . . . . .208 B5
Marine Sq BN2 . . . . .192 C4
Marine Terrace Mews 7
　BN2 . . . . .192 C4
Marine View 3 BN2 . . . . .213 C2
Marion Rd RH10 . . . . .19 B3
Marisfield Pl PO20 . . . . . . .212 F8
Marjoram Pl BN43 . . . . . . .167 B1
Market Ave PO19 . . . . .177 A5
Market Cl PO22 . . . . .180 B6
Market Field BN14 . . . . . . .185 A8
Market Pl
　Haywards Heath RH16 . . . .87 D6
　Worthing BN13 . . . . . . .186 A4
Market Place Sh Ctr
　RH15 . . . . .109 A2
Market Rd PO19 . . . . .177 A6
Market Sq
　9 Horsham RH12 . . . . . .36 C2
　Petworth GU28 . . . . .97 F7
Market St
　Bognor Regis PO21 . . . . .201 C2
　Brighton BN1 . . . . .213 B2
　13 Worthing BN11 . . . . .186 D2
Markfield PO22 . . . . .201 B6
MARK STREET 66 F3
Markwick Mews
　BN11 . . . . .186 E3
Marlborough Bsns Ctr
　BN15 . . . . .187 C4
Marlborough Cl
　Chichester PO19 . . . . . . .177 D6
　Crawley RH11 . . . . .18 C2
　Horsham RH12 . . . . .36 D5
Marlborough Ct
　Bognor Regis PO22 . . . . .200 F5
　Burgess Hill RH15 . . . . .108 D3
　1 Hove BN3 . . . . .191 C6
Marlborough Dr
　RH15 . . . . .109 C2
Marlborough Ho 6
　PO21 . . . . .201 B2
Marlborough Mews
　BN1 . . . . .213 A2
Marlborough Pl
　8 Brighton BN1,
　　BN2 . . . . .213 B3
　Horsham RH12 . . . . .36 C3
Marlborough Rd
　Lancing BN15 . . . . .187 D4
　Worthing BN11 . . . . . . .186 D3
Marlborough St BN1 . . . . .213 A2
Marlborough Way
　BN12 . . . . .185 A5
Marle Ave RH14 . . . . .109 A4
Marles La
　Five Oaks RH14 . . . . .55 C8
　Rudgwick RH14 . . . . .33 C1
Marley Combe Rd
　GU27 . . . . .26 F4
Marley Hanger GU27 . . . . . .27 A3
Marley La GU27 . . . . .27 A3
Marley Way RH20 . . . . . . .121 E2
Marlin Ct BN15 . . . . .187 E4
Marline Ct BN43 . . . . .188 E7

Marlinespike The
　BN43 . . . . .189 A6
Marlings The RH16 . . . . . . .87 C3
Marlipins Mus*
　BN43 . . . . .188 E7
Marlow Ct
　Brighton BN2 . . . . .213 C4
　Crawley RH10 . . . . .18 D7
Marlow Dr RH16 . . . . .88 C4
Marlowe Rd BN14 . . . . . . .186 E5
Marlowe Rd BN2 . . . . .192 F4
Marlpit Cl RH19 . . . . .9 E4
Marlpit La
　Oving PO20 . . . . .178 B7
　Woodmancote PO10,
　　PO18 . . . . .152 C4
Marlpit Rd RH13 . . . . .43 A6
Marlpost Rd RH13 . . . . . . .57 C1
Marmion Rd BN3 . . . . .190 F7
Marquis Way PO21 . . . . . .200 E1
Marringdean Rd RH14 . . . . .79 C4
Marshall Ave
　Bognor Regis PO21 . . . . .201 B4
　Worthing BN14 . . . . . . .163 F3
Marshall Cl PO22 . . . . .180 B5
Marshall Rd BN14 . . . . . . .186 E5
Marshalls Row BN1 . . . . . .213 B4
Marshall Way BN3 . . . . . . .168 F1
Marsh Barns PO20 . . . . . . .177 F2
Marsh Ct RH11 . . . . .18 B1
Marsh Ho 3 BN42 . . . . . .189 D7
Marsh La
　Chidham PO18 . . . . .174 C4
　Crockerhill PO18 . . . . . .157 A2
　Merston PO20 . . . . .178 A2
　Mid Lavant PO18 . . . . . .154 F6
　Tangmere PO18 . . . . . . .156 F2
Marston Cl 10 RH12 . . . . .191 E7
Marston Rd BN14 . . . . . . .186 E4
Martello Ent Ctr
　BN17 . . . . .204 C8
Martha Gunn Rd BN2 . . . .170 E1
Martin Cl RH11 . . . . .18 D8
Martineau Cl PO22 . . . . . .200 E1
Martin Rd BN3 . . . . .168 D1
Martins La PO20 . . . . .197 F5
Martins The RH10 . . . . . . .21 C8
Martlet Cl PO19 . . . . .177 A5
Martlet Cnr RH12 . . . . .33 D7
Martlet Ct BN2 . . . . .192 C5
Martlet Ho BN1 . . . . .192 D8
Martlet Rd GU28 . . . . .97 F7
Martlets BN20 . . . . .121 D8
Martlets Cl RH12 . . . . .36 C5
Martlets Ct BN18 . . . . . . .160 E2
Martlets Sh Ctr The
　RH15 . . . . .109 A3
Martlets The
　Crawley RH10 . . . . .18 E6
　Lancing BN15 . . . . .187 C6
　Shoreham-by-S BN43 . . . .188 F8
Martlets Trad Est
　BN8 . . . . .185 C4
Martlets Way BN12 . . . . . .185 C4
Martlet The BN3 . . . . .169 D1
Martlet Way PO21 . . . . . . .210 F7
Marts The RH12 . . . . .33 D7
Martyn Cl BN5 . . . . .129 E1
Martyns Ct BN2 . . . . .193 E4
Martyns Pl RH19 . . . . .23 A8
Martyrs Ave
　Crawley RH11 . . . . .5 C1
　Crawley RH11 . . . . .5 D1
Marvell Cl RH10 . . . . .19 C8
Marylands RH16 . . . . .87 F5
Marylands Cres PO22 . . . . .61 A3
Masefield Rd RH11 . . . . . . .17 E3
Mash Barn La BN15 . . . . . .188 A7
Mason Cl RH19 . . . . .9 E2
Mason Rd RH10 . . . . .18 E4
Masons Field RH13 . . . . . . .59 C6
Masons Way RH20 . . . . . .100 D5
Massetts Rd RH6 . . . . .2 A2
Matform Bsns Ctr
　PO19 . . . . .176 E5
Matlock Rd BN1 . . . . .169 D2
Matthew Ho 14 BN3 . . . . .191 A6
Matthews Dr RH10 . . . . . . .19 C3
Matthey Pl RH10 . . . . .6 D1
Maudlin La BN44 . . . . .145 E1
Maudlin Cl BN44 . . . . .145 E1
Maudlyn Parkway
　BN44 . . . . .145 D1
Maudlyn Pk BN44 . . . . . . .145 D1
Maudslane Cl PO21 . . . . . .200 F2
Maunsell Pl RH16 . . . . .87 F3
Maunsell Rd RH10 . . . . . . .19 B6
Maxton Wlk RH11 . . . . . . .18 B2
Maxwell Rd
　Arundel BN18 . . . . .159 F1
　Littlehampton BN17 . . . . .204 C5
Maxwell Way RH10 . . . . . . .6 A1
Maybridge Cres BN12 . . . . .185 C4
Maybridge Sq BN12 . . . . . .185 C5
Maybush Dr PO18 . . . . . . .174 D7
May Cl
　Bognor Regis PO22 . . . . .201 D5
　Climping BN17 . . . . .181 D1
　Sidlesham PO20 . . . . . . .209 F8
　Worthing BN12 . . . . . . .185 C5
Maydwell Ave RH13 . . . . . .34 C2
Mayes Cl BN2 . . . . .193 D5
Mayes La RH12 . . . . .14 F3
Mayes Lane Cotts
　RH12 . . . . .14 F2
Mayfair Ct PO19 . . . . .176 F7

Mayfield
Crawley RH10 . . . . .19 D6
East Preston BN16 . . . . .206 B7
Mayfield Cl
Bognor Regis PO21 . . . . . .200 B3
Brighton BN1 . . . . .170 A5
Worthing BN14 . . . . .164 A1
Mayfield Cres BN1 . . . . . . .169 F5
Mayfield Ct
Burgess Hill RH15 . . . . .109 B3
Saltdean BN2 . . . . .194 C2
Mayfield Ho RH17 . . . . . . .86 F8
Mayfield Rd PO21 . . . . . . .201 A4
Mayfields RH17 . . . . .85 C4
Mayflower Cl RH10 . . . . .19 D5
Mayflower Ct
Haywards Heath RH16 . . . . .87 F4
B Shoreham-by-S
BN43 . . . . .189 A6
Mayflower Rd RH16 . . . . . .87 F4
Mayflower Sq BN41 . . . . . .213 B4
Mayflower Way BN16 . . . .206 A7
Mayhouse Rd RH15 . . . . . .108 F1
Maynard Cl RH10 . . . . .7 C4
Mayo Cl B BN2 . . . . .192 B8
Mayo Rd BN2 . . . . .192 B8
Maypole Rd
Ashurst Wood RH19 . . . . . . .23 E6
East Grinstead RH19 . . . . . . .9 D2
May Rd BN2 . . . . .192 D7
Mayridge PO20 . . . . .212 B8
May Tree Ave BN14 . . . . . .163 F3
Maytree Cl
Angmering BN16 . . . . .205 F8
Lancing BN15 . . . . .187 B6
May Tree Cl BN3 . . . . .190 D8
May Tree Wlk BN3 . . . . . . .168 E1
Mead Cotts GU31 . . . . .91 D4
Mead Ct B PO22 . . . . .201 D4
Mead Ho The RH13 . . . . . .57 F1
Mead La
Bognor Regis PO22 . . . . . . .201 E4
Storrington RH20 . . . . .121 E2
Meadow App RH10 . . . . .7 A3
Meadowbank RH14 . . . . . . .78 B8
Meadow Brook Ind Ctr
RH10 . . . . .6 A1
Meadow Cl
Balcombe RH17 . . . . .41 A1
Copthorne RH10 . . . . .7 A3
Horsham RH12 . . . . .37 A5
Hove BN3 . . . . .169 B3
Hunston PO20 . . . . .199 A8
Liphook GU30 . . . . .25 C4
Portslade-by-S BN41 . . . . .168 B2
Rottingdean BN2 . . . . .193 F3
Southwick BN42 . . . . .190 A8
Worthing BN11 . . . . .187 B3
Meadow Court Est B
BN11 . . . . .187 B3
Meadow Cres BN11 . . . . . .187 A3
Meadowcroft Cl
Crawley RH11 . . . . .17 F5
East Grinstead RH19 . . . . . . .9 C2
Meadow Croft Cl RH6 . . . . .6 C8
Meadow Ct
East Grinstead RH19 . . . . . . .9 E2
B Emsworth PO10 . . . . . . .173 B8
Middleton-on-S PO22 . . . . .202 D6
Meadow Dr RH16 . . . . .88 B6
Meadow End GU30 . . . . . . .25 C5
Meadow Farm La RH12 . . . .36 F7
Meadowfield Dr PO19 . . . .177 B7
Meadowgate RH12 . . . . . . .36 F7
Meadow La
Burgess Hill RH15 . . . . .108 F1
Lancing BN15 . . . . .187 E5
Lindfield RH16 . . . . .88 B6
West Wittering PO20 . . . . . .196 D1
Meadowland PO20 . . . . . . .212 D6
Meadowlands
Crawley RH11 . . . . .18 C6
Rowland's Castle PO9 . . . . .130 E3
Meadow Lands GU32 . . . . .68 A2
Meadow Par BN2 . . . . .193 F3
Meadow Pk BN16 . . . . .206 B5
Meadow Rd BN11 . . . . .187 B3
Meadow Road Ind Est
BN11 . . . . .187 B4
Meadows BN6 . . . . .128 F5
Meadowside
Angmering BN16 . . . . .184 A6
Horley RH6 . . . . .2 B4
Storrington RH20 . . . . .121 D1
Meadowside Ct BN12 . . . . .185 A3
Meadowside Wlk
PO20 . . . . .156 D2
Meadows Rd PO21 . . . . . . .208 A2
Meadows The
East Preston BN16 . . . . .206 A5
Hove BN3 . . . . .168 C3
Stockbridge PO19 . . . . .176 F3
Walberton BN18 . . . . .180 E8
Meadow Sweet Cl
BN13 . . . . .185 A6
Meadow Terr RH11 . . . . . . .41 A1
Meadow The RH10 . . . . .7 A3
Meadow Vale
Haslemere GU27 . . . . .27 A6
Ovingdean BN2 . . . . .193 E5
Meadowview BN2 . . . . .170 E1
Meadow View RH6 . . . . . . .107 C1
Meadowview Rd
BN15 . . . . .187 D8
Meadow Way
Bognor Regis, North Bersted
PO22 . . . . .201 A6
Bognor Regis PO21 . . . . . . .200 B1

Meadow Way continued
Ferring BN12 . . . . .206 E6
Liphook GU30 . . . . .25 C5
Littlehampton BN17 . . . . . .204 F5
Petworth GU28 . . . . .97 E7
Tangmere PO20 . . . . .156 D2
Westergate PO20 . . . . .179 D6
Meadow Wlk
Liss GU33 . . . . .45 B4
Middleton-on-S PO22 . . . . .203 A5
Mead Rd RH10 . . . . .18 F7
Meads Ave BN3 . . . . .168 C3
Meads Cl BN3 . . . . .168 C3
Meads Prim Sch RH14 . . . .22 E7
Meads The
Brighton BN1 . . . . .170 D5
Burgess Hill RH15 . . . . .108 F3
East Grinstead RH19 . . . . . .22 E7
Fulking BN5 . . . . .147 F4
Haslemere GU27 . . . . .26 F6
Meadsway BN18 . . . . .158 D4
Mead The
Liphook GU30 . . . . .25 B5
Liss GU33 . . . . .45 B4
Petersfield GU32 . . . . .67 F2
Meadvale RH12 . . . . .35 F2
Meadway
Haslemere GU27 . . . . .26 F6
Rustington BN16 . . . . .205 D5
Meadway Cres BN3 . . . . . .168 F2
Meadway Ct
Southwick BN42 . . . . .189 D8
Worthing BN13 . . . . .185 E5
Meadway The
Brighton BN2 . . . . .192 F5
Horley RH6 . . . . .2 C3
Shoreham-by-S BN43 . . . . .189 A1
Measham Cl BN12 . . . . . . .206 F5
MEATH GREEN 1 F5
Meath Green Ave RH6 . . . . .1 F5
Meath Green Inf Sch
RH6 . . . . .1 F5
Meath Green Jun Sch
RH6 . . . . .1 F5
Meath Green La
RH6 . . . . .1 E6
Mechanical Music & Doll
Mus* PO19 . . . . .177 D7
Medina Pl BN3 . . . . .191 B6
Medina Terr BN3 . . . . .191 B5
Medina Villas BN3 . . . . . . .191 B6
Medlar Cl RH11 . . . . .5 C1
Medmerry PO20 . . . . .212 A8
Medmerry Ct B
PO20 . . . . .212 D7
Medmerry Hill BN2 . . . . . .170 E2
Medmerry Prim Sch
PO20 . . . . .212 D7
Medway Ho RH10 . . . . .21 A5
Medway Cl BN13 . . . . .185 D8
Medway Cotts BN18 . . . . .180 F2
Medway Ct RH12 . . . . .37 B5
Medway Dr RH19 . . . . .22 D6
Medway Rd RH11 . . . . .35 A8
Medwin Wlk B RH12 . . . . .36 C2
Meeds Rd RH15 . . . . .109 A2
Meeting House La
BN1 . . . . .213 B2
Meiros Way RH20 . . . . . . .122 F5
Melanie's Gdns B
PO21 . . . . .201 D4
Melbourne Ave BN2 . . . . .185 C3
Melbourne Rd
Chichester PO19 . . . . .177 B7
Worthing BN10 . . . . .185 D3
Melbourne St BN2 . . . . . . .192 C8
Melbourne Way
Horsham RH12 . . . . .36 F5
Worthing BN12 . . . . .185 C3
Melchbourne Villas
RH19 . . . . .42 E6
Melksham Cl RH14 . . . . . . .36 E1
Melrose Ave
Portslade-by-S BN41 . . . . .168 A1
Worthing BN13 . . . . .185 E5
Melrose Cl
Brighton BN1 . . . . .170 C2
Worthing BN13 . . . . .185 E5
Melrose Rd RH13 . . . . .122 C3
Melton Ave RH20 . . . . .121 D3
Melton Cl RH20 . . . . .121 D3
Melton Dr RH20 . . . . .121 D3
Melville Rd BN3 . . . . .191 E7
Melville Way BN12 . . . . . . .185 C5
Mendip Cl BN16 . . . . .206 A6
Mendip Cres BN13 . . . . . . .185 D8
Mendip Rd BN13 . . . . .185 B8
Mendip Wlk RH11 . . . . .18 B6
Meon Cl GU32 . . . . .68 A4
Mercer Cl RH10 . . . . .19 C3
Mercer Rd RH12 . . . . .36 C8
Mercers Mead RH13 . . . . . .83 E1
Merchant St PO21 . . . . . . .201 C3
Mercury Cl RH11 . . . . .17 E3
Mere Cl PO20 . . . . .208 B5
Meredith Rd BN14 . . . . . . .186 F4
Merevale BN1 . . . . .170 B2
Mereworth Dr RH10 . . . . . .19 D8
Meridian Cl RH11 . . . . .17 F3
Meridian Gr RH6 . . . . .2 C4
Meridian Way RH19 . . . . . . .9 F3
Merle Court Gdns
PO20 . . . . .198 F8
Merle Way GU27 . . . . .49 A6
Merlin Cl
Crawley RH11 . . . . .17 E6

Merlin Cl continued
Hove BN3 . . . . .191 D8
Merlin Ct BN13 . . . . .185 F7
Merlin Ctr RH11 . . . . .5 D2
Merlin Way
East Grinstead RH19 . . . . . .10 A3
Middleton-on-S PO22 . . . . .202 D6
Merrion Ave PO21,
PO22 . . . . .201 B5
Merrivale Ct PO10 . . . . . . .151 F1
Merry End PO22 . . . . .202 D5
Merryfield Cres BN16 . . . .184 A6
Merryfield Dr
Horsham RH12 . . . . .36 A3
Selsey PO20 . . . . .212 F7
Merryfield Rd
Petersfield GU31 . . . . .68 D4
Storrington RH20 . . . . .121 D2
Merryfield Way RH20 . . . .121 D2
Merry Hills La RH14 . . . . . .32 A5
Merryweather Rd
PO18 . . . . .175 B5
Merrywood Ho RH20 . . . . .122 B3
Merrywood La RH20 . . . . .122 B4
Mersey Cl BN13 . . . . .185 C5
Mersey Rd BN13 . . . . .185 C8
Mersham Gdns BN12 . . . . .185 C3
Merston Cl BN2 . . . . .193 E6
Merton Ave BN16 . . . . .205 D4
Merton Cl PO21 . . . . .200 E4
Merton Dr B BN17 . . . . . . .204 D6
Merton Rd
Worthing BN11 . . . . .186 F2
Merton Terr BN11 . . . . . . .186 F2
Messenger Cl RH11 . . . . . . .18 A8
Metcalf Way RH11 . . . . .17 B4
Meteor Rd PO10 . . . . .173 C3
Metropole Ct B BN1 . . . . .191 E5
Mews Ct RH19 . . . . .22 F6
Mews The
B Bognor Regis
PO21 . . . . .201 C3
Bognor Regis PO22 . . . . . . .201 E4
Brighton, Preston BN1 . . . . .169 F2
Broadbridge Heath RH12 . . .35 D4
Littlehampton BN17 . . . . . .204 F5
Petersfield GU31 . . . . .68 B4
Petworth GU28 . . . . .97 F8
Pulborough RH20 . . . . .100 D2
Meyers Wood RH13 . . . . . .105 A2
Meyners Cl BN3 . . . . .168 C3
Michael Ayres Jun Sch
PO21 . . . . .201 A5
Michael Cres RH6 . . . . .2 A1
Michael Fields RH18 . . . . . .23 C2
Michael Hall Sch RH18 . . . .23 D1
Michelbourne Cl
RH15 . . . . .108 E1
Michel Gr BN13 . . . . .205 F5
Michelgrove Cotts
BN13 . . . . .162 C5
Michell Cl RH12 . . . . .36 A2
Micklam Cl PO21 . . . . .200 C2
Mid Acre PO22 . . . . .202 A6
Middlefield
Horley RH6 . . . . .2 C4
West Wittering PO20 . . . . . .196 C1
Middlefield La PO18 . . . . . .155 C7
Middle Mdw GU33 . . . . . . .45 C4
Middle Mead
Littlehampton BN17 . . . . . .205 A5
Steyning BN44 . . . . .145 D4
Middle Onslow Cl
BN12 . . . . .206 E7
Middle Rd
Brighton BN1 . . . . .169 E1
Lancing BN15 . . . . .187 D5
Partridge Green RH13 . . . . .105 A3
Shoreham-by-S BN43 . . . . .189 B7
Middle Row B RH19 . . . . . .22 F8
Middle St
Brighton BN1 . . . . .213 A2
Falmer BN1 . . . . .171 C6
B Horsham RH12 . . . . . . .36 C2
Petworth GU28 . . . . .97 F8
Shoreham-by-S BN43 . . . . .188 F7
Middle Street Prim Sch
BN1 . . . . .213 A2
Middleton Ave BN3 . . . . . .190 D6
Middleton Bsns Pk
PO22 . . . . .202 F6
Middleton Cl PO20 . . . . . . .208 B6
Middleton Ct B PO22 . . . . .202 F5
Middleton Gdns
PO20 . . . . .156 D2
Middleton Pl PO22 . . . . . . .202 E5
Middleton Rd
Horsham RH12 . . . . .36 A2
Middleton-on-S PO22 . . . . .202 D5
Middleton Rise BN1 . . . . . .170 E5
Middle Tyne BN13 . . . . .17 E5
Middle Tyne BN13 . . . . . . .185 D6
Middle Village RH16 . . . . . .87 C2
Middle Way
Burgess Hill RH15 . . . . .109 B3
Kingston Gorse BN16 . . . . .206 D4
Midfields RH15 . . . . .109 B3
Midfields Cl RH15 . . . . . . .109 B3
Midfields Dr RH15 . . . . . . .109 B3
Midfields Wlk RH15 . . . . . .109 B4
Midgley Rd RH10 . . . . .18 F8
Midholme BN16 . . . . .205 F5
Midhurst CE Prim Sch
GU29 . . . . .94 E7

Midhurst Cl
Crawley RH11 . . . . .18 A7
Ferring BN12 . . . . .206 F6
Midhurst Com Hospl
GU29 . . . . .72 F1
Midhurst Dr BN12 . . . . .185 A3
Midhurst Gram Sch
GU29 . . . . .94 F8
Midhurst Intermediate
Sch GU29 . . . . .73 A2
Midhurst Rd
Fernhurst GU27 . . . . .49 A4
Haslemere GU27 . . . . .27 B5
Liphook GU30 . . . . .25 C2
Mid Lavant PO18 . . . . .154 E7
Midhurst Rise BN1 . . . . . . .170 B6
Midhurst Wlk BN3 . . . . . . .168 F3
Midway Rd BN2 . . . . .193 C8
Midway The PO22 . . . . . . .202 A4
Mighell St BN2 . . . . .213 C2
Milborne Rd RH10 . . . . .19 C2
Milbury Cl B PO22 . . . . . . .206 F4
Milcote Ave BN3 . . . . .190 F8
Mile End Cotts BN1 . . . . . .169 E6
Mile End La PO20 . . . . .176 C2
MILE OAK 167 F4
Mile Oak Cres BN42 . . . . .167 F1
Mile Oak Gdns BN41 . . . . .168 A1
Mile Oak Prim Sch
BN41 . . . . .167 F3
Mile Oak Rd
Portslade-by-S BN41 . . . . .167 F3
Southwick BN42 . . . . .167 F1
Miles Cl BN18 . . . . .181 B2
Miles Cotts PO18 . . . . .175 C5
Miles Wlk BN3 . . . . .191 B6
Milford Ct BN15 . . . . .187 D3
Millais RH13 . . . . .37 A3
Millais Cl RH11 . . . . .17 D2
Millais Ct RH13 . . . . .37 A4
Millais Sch RH13 . . . . .36 F2
Milland La GU30 . . . . .47 A5
Millars Ct PO21 . . . . .200 B1
Mill Ave BN43 . . . . .166 F1
Millbank RH15 . . . . .109 B4
Millbrae The RH11 . . . . .17 F6
Mill Bay La RH12 . . . . .36 B1
Millbrook Cl GU33 . . . . .45 C4
Millbrook Ct GU29 . . . . .94 F8
Mill Cl
Burgess Hill RH15 . . . . .109 B4
Crabtree RH13 . . . . .84 A7
East Grinstead RH19 . . . . . .22 E7
Fishbourne PO19 . . . . .176 B6
Haslemere GU27 . . . . .26 E6
Horley RH6 . . . . .1 E4
Portslade-by-S BN41 . . . . .168 C1
Poynings BN45 . . . . .148 C5
Rustington BN16 . . . . .205 D6
Mill Copse Rd GU27 . . . . . .27 B4
Mill Cotts
East Grinstead RH19 . . . . . .22 E7
Rudgwick RH12 . . . . .33 D5
Millcroft Ave BN41 . . . . . . .167 E1
Millcroft Gdns BN42 . . . . .167 E1
Millcross Rd BN41 . . . . . . .168 B1
Mill Ct
Burgess Hill RH15 . . . . .109 B4
Poynings BN45 . . . . .148 C5
Worthing BN11 . . . . .186 B2
Mill End
Henfield BN5 . . . . .125 F4
Hermitage PO10 . . . . .173 D8
West Chiltington Common
RH20 . . . . .121 C8
Millennium Cl RH15 . . . . . .188 B6
Millennium Ho RH11 . . . . . .17 F3
Millennium Seedbank*
RH17 . . . . .41 F4
Miller Pl BN41 . . . . .168 A3
Millers Cl
Burgess Hill RH15 . . . . .109 A4
Rustington BN16 . . . . .205 D6
Millers Gate RH12 . . . . .36 D6
Miller's Rd BN1 . . . . .169 E1
Millers The BN18 . . . . .180 E2
Millers Way RH15 . . . . .109 B4
Millfarm Dr PO21 . . . . .200 A2
Mill Farm (Park Home Est)
PO21 . . . . .199 F2
Mill Farm Rd RH13 . . . . . . .37 A4
Millfield
Lancing BN15 . . . . .187 C7
Southwater RH13 . . . . .82 A7
Upper Beeding BN44 . . . . . .146 A2
Millfield Cl
Chichester PO19 . . . . .177 C8
Rustington BN16 . . . . .205 B3
Millfield Cotts B
BN2 . . . . .192 D4
Millfield Ct BN17 . . . . .204 C8
Millfield Lo B BN1 . . . . . . .186 A2
Millfields Cres RH6 . . . . . . .4 D6
Mill Gdns PO20 . . . . .207 F7
Mill Green Ind Est
RH16 . . . . .87 E6
Mill Green Rd RH16 . . . . . . .87 E6
Millhaven Ct RH15 . . . . . . .109 B3
MILL HILL 166 E1
Mill Hill BN43 . . . . .166 E2
Mill Hill Cl
Haywards Heath RH16 . . . . .87 E7
Shoreham-by-S BN43 . . . . .166 E1
Mill Hill Dr BN43 . . . . .166 E1

Mill Hill Gdns BN43 . . . . . .166 E1
Mill Ho
B Bognor Regis
PO21 . . . . .201 B2
B Worthing BN11 . . . . . . .187 B3
Mill House Gdns
BN11 . . . . .186 A2
Milliers Ct BN16 . . . . .205 F6
Millington Dr PO20 . . . . . .209 F1
Mill La
Amberley BN18 . . . . .140 E6
Arundel BN18 . . . . .160 B3
Ashington RH20 . . . . .122 F4
Balcombe RH17 . . . . .41 C1
Clayton BN6, BN45 . . . . . . .149 E5
Cocking GU29 . . . . .114 D8
Coolham RH13 . . . . .80 D3
Copthorne RH10 . . . . .7 E3
Crabtree RH13 . . . . .84 B7
Crawley RH11 . . . . .18 A8
Dormansland RH7 . . . . .9 F8
Dumpford GU31 . . . . .92 F8
Felbridge RH19 . . . . .9 D5
Fishbourne PO19 . . . . .176 B6
Goddards' Green BN6 . . . . .108 A3
Heyshott Green GU29 . . . . . .95 A2
Hookwood RH6 . . . . .1 D3
Kingsley Green GU27 . . . . . .27 C3
Littlehampton BN17 . . . . . .182 D5
Portslade-by-S BN41 . . . . .168 B1
Poynings BN45 . . . . .148 C5
Runcton PO20 . . . . .177 E1
Rustington BN16 . . . . .205 D4
Sayers Common BN6 . . . . . .107 E2
Selsey PO20 . . . . .212 C7
Shoreham-by-S BN43 . . . . .188 F8
Sidlesham PO20 . . . . .209 F7
Slindon BN18 . . . . .158 C6
South Harting GU31 . . . . . . .91 D4
Stedham GU31 . . . . .72 A2
Steep GU32 . . . . .68 A8
Storrington RH20 . . . . .121 D2
Trotton GU31 . . . . .71 A1
Walberton BN18 . . . . .158 D1
Westbourne PO10 . . . . .151 D2
West Chiltington Common
RH20 . . . . .121 C8
Worthing BN11 . . . . .186 A2
Mill Rd Ind Est BN41 . . . . .190 B7
Mill Rise BN16 . . . . .169 C5
Mill Row BN1 . . . . .213 A3
Mill Row BN1 . . . . .169 E3
Mill St BN1 . . . . .171 C7
Mill Straight RH13 . . . . .81 F8
Mill Stream Mdw
RH16 . . . . .87 D7
Millstream The GU27 . . . . . .26 E5
Millthorpe Rd RH12 . . . . . . .36 F4
Mill Vale Mdws GU30 . . . . .47 B3
Mill View Ho BN11 . . . . . . .168 E1
Mill View Rd BN18 . . . . . . .180 F2
Mill Way
Billingshurst RH14 . . . . .55 D1
East Grinstead RH19 . . . . . .22 E7
Millwood RH10 . . . . .21 E5
Mill Wood RH15 . . . . .109 B3
Milnard Cres BN2 . . . . .193 D7
Milne Cl RH11 . . . . .17 D1
Milner Flats BN2 . . . . .213 C2
Milner Rd BN2 . . . . .170 D1
Milnthorpe Rd BN3 . . . . . .190 F8
Milnwood Rd RH12 . . . . . . .36 C3
Milton Ave BN16 . . . . .205 B5
Milton Cl
Lancing BN15 . . . . .187 F5
Rustington BN16 . . . . .205 B5
Milton Cres RH19 . . . . .22 C6
Milton Ct
B Haywards Heath
RH16 . . . . .87 D5
B Worthing BN11 . . . . . . .186 C1
Milton Dr BN42 . . . . .189 F8
Milton Mount RH10 . . . . .6 D1
Milton Mount Ave
RH10 . . . . .19 D8

Milton Mount Prim Sch
RH10 ....19 C8
Milton Rd
Brighton BN2 ....213 C4
Crawley RH10 ....19 C7
Haywards Heath RH16 ....87 D6
Horsham RH12 ....36 C3
Worthing BN11 ....186 C1
Milton St BN11 ....186 C1
Milward Ct 3 BN43 .....189 C8
Milwood Ct PO19 ....176 F7
Mimmack Cl BN44 ......145 D4
Mimosa Ct BN1 ....170 B3
Mindelheim Ave RH19 ...10 B2
Minnels The BN6 ....129 A3
MINSTED 93 E6
Minsted Rd GU29 ....93 F7
Minster Ct BN17 ....204 C8
Minton Rd PO22 ....202 B4
Mint Rd GU33 ....45 D6
MINT THE 45 D6
Mint The GU1, GU32 ....68 B2
Miranda Wlk RH11 ....17 E4
Mistley Gdns RH6 ....1 D2
Mitchell Ct PO19 ......176 F7
Mitchell Gdns RH13 ....34 E3
Mitchells Rd RH10 .....18 F6
Mitchmere Cotts
PO18 ....132 F2
Mitford Wlk 10 RH11 ...18 A3
Mitre Ct 6 RH12 ....36 B2
Mitre Ho 12 BN11 .....191 E5
Mixon Cl PO20 ....212 E6
Moatfield La RH13 .....106 A8
Moat La RH20 ....100 D2
Moat Rd RH19 ....9 E2
Moat The RH20 ....100 C2
Moat Way BN12 ....185 E2
Moat Wlk RH10 ....19 C7
Mocatta Way RH15 .....108 D5
Modena Rd BN41 ....190 F7
Modern Moulds Bsns Ctr
Lancing BN15 ....167 C1
Littlehampton BN17 ....204 C6
Moggs Mead GU31 ......68 C3
Mole Cl RH11 ....18 B8
Molecombe Broadwalk
PO18 ....136 A2
Molesworth St BN3 ....190 F8
Mole The BN17 ....205 A5
Molineux Pl RH16 ......87 D5
Molins Ct 4 RH11 .....18 A3
Monarch Cl RH11 ....18 A3
Monarchs View BN41 ...167 C2
Monastery La RH20 ....121 C1
Monckton Way BN7 ....121 E5
Monk Cl BN1 ....170 E6
Monkmead Copse
RH20 ....121 B6
Monkmead La RH20 ....121 B6
Monks Ave BN15 ......187 F6
Monks Cl BN15 ....187 F6
Monks Ct 2 BN15 ....187 F6
Monksfield RH10 ....18 F7
Monk's Hill PO20 .....151 C5
Monks La RH5 ....13 F5
Monks Manor RH5 .....13 F5
Monks Orch GU32 .....146 B2
Monks Wlk BN44 ......146 B2
Monks Wood GU32 .....65 B5
Mons Ave PO21 ....201 B5
Montacute Rd BN7 ....172 F8
Montague Cl BN43 ....189 D7
Montague Ct
6 Brighton BN2 ......192 C4
Lancing BN15 ....187 B7
8 Shoreham-by-S
BN43 ....189 D7
Montague Ctr 10
BN11 ....186 D2
Montague Gdns GU31 ..68 D3
Montague Ho BN11 ...186 A3
Montague Pl
Brighton BN2 ....192 C4
Worthing BN11 ....186 D1
Montague St GU29 .....73 A2
Montague St
4 Brighton BN2 ......192 C4
Worthing BN11 ....186 D1
Montagu Ho PO18 .....155 E1
Montagu Rd PO19 ....176 E8
Montalan Cres PO22 ..201 E8
Montefiore Rd BN3 ...191 F7
Monterey Ct BN1 .....169 E3
Monterey Gdns PO21 ..201 A2
Monterey Pines PO22 ..202 A5
Montes Hill RH16 ......88 F8
Monteswood La RH16,
RH17 ....89 B8
Montford Cl BN43 ....189 D8
Montfort Rise RH11 .....1 F8
Montgomeri Dr RH10 ..205 B7
Montgomery Dr PO22 ..202 D6
Montgomery St BN3 ..191 A7
Montgomery Terr 2
BN3 ....191 A7
Montpelier Cotts
RH20 ....148 E8
Montpelier Cres BN1 .191 E6
Montpelier Gdns
RH20 ....143 E8
Montpelier Lo 9 BN1 .191 E6
Montpelier Pl BN1 ...191 E6
Montpelier Rd
Brighton BN1 ....191 E5

Montpelier Rd continued
East Preston BN16 .....206 A5
Montpelier St BN1 ....191 E6
Montpelier Terr BN1 .191 E6
Montpelier Villas
BN1 ....191 E6
Montpelier Apartments 23
BN1 ....191 E5
Montreal Rd BN2 .....213 C3
Montreal Way BN13 ...185 C7
Montreal Wlk GU30 ....25 C3
Montreux Ct RH11 .....18 B6
Montrose Cl BN12 ....185 C3
Montrose Ct BN12 ....185 C4
Monument La PO18 ...152 B7
Monument View BN2 ..192 D6
Moonhill Pl RH17 ......86 E1
Moonsgate 8 RH13 .....36 E1
Moons La RH13 ....36 E1
Moon's La RH7 ....10 E8
Moorcroft Ct RH11 .....18 B7
Moore Cl BN13 ....185 B7
Moore Ct RH12 ....36 A1
Moore Pl 4 PO21 .....201 D4
Moor Farm GU29 ....95 E7
Moorfield GU27 ....26 F5
Moorfoot Rd BN13 ....185 F8
Moorhead Rd RH12 ....37 B5
Moorhen Way PO22 ..201 B6
Moorhouse La GU29 ...71 D6
Moorings The
East Grinstead RH19 ....9 A3
Lancing BN15 ....187 F8
5 Littlehampton BN17 .205 A6
Shoreham-by-S BN43 ..189 C6
Moorland Rd RH10 .....19 C3
Moor Park Cres RH11 ..18 B7
Moor Pk RH6 ....2 B2
Moor Pl RH19 ....9 D2
Moor Rd GU27 ....26 C5
Morants Ct PO19 .....177 C8
Mora Soomaree 11
BN1 ....186 B2
Moraunt Dr PO22 .....202 E6
Morecambe Cl RH11 ...17 F4
Morecambe Rd BN1 ..170 A6
Moreton Rd PO18 ....175 B5
Morgan Ho 1 RH10 ....19 B6
Morland Ave BN14 ....186 E7
Morley Lo BN2 ....213 C4
Morleys RH10 ....18 F7
Morley St BN2 ....213 C3
Mornington Cres
Bognor Regis PO22 ...202 A5
Hove BN3 ....190 D7
Mornington Mans 5
BN3 ....190 D7
Morrell Ave RH12 .....36 F6
Morris Dr RH14 ....79 C7
Morrison Ct 1 RH11 ..18 B1
Morris Way RH20 ....121 C7
Morris Gdns BN14 ...186 E6
Morris Way RH20 .....121 C7
Mortimer Ho BN14 ...186 E6
Mortimer Mews BN1 ..191 A8
Mortimer Rd BN3 ....190 F8
Morton Cl RH11 ....39 B8
Morton Cl BN41 ......190 D8
Morton Rd RH19 ......22 E7
Mosdell Rd PO10 .....174 A8
Mosford Cl RH6 ....1 F5
Moss Cl GU33 ....45 C4
Mosse Gdns PO19 ....176 B7
MOULSECOOMB 170 E2
Moulsecoomb Prim Sch
BN2 ....170 D2
Moulsecoomb Sta
BN2 ....170 D2
Moulsecoomb Way
BN2 ....170 F4
Mountain Ash Cl 1
RH12 ....36 F4
Mountbatten Cl RH11 ..18 C2
Mountbatten Ct
Bognor Regis PO21 ...201 D2
Hove BN3 ....190 E8
1 Littlehampton BN17 .205 A6
Mount Cl RH10 ....19 D7
Mount Ct PO20 ....212 E7
Mount Dr BN2 ....194 D2
Mountfields BN1 .....170 C2
Mount La
Chichester PO19 .....176 F6
Turners Hill RH10 .....21 A4
Mount Noddy
Ansty RH17 ....86 C3
Crawley RH10 ....20 C2
Mount Pk BN44 ......145 D1
Mount Pleasant
Arundel BN18 ....160 A3
Brighton BN2 ....213 C2
Henfield BN5 ....125 E4
Mount The
Rusper RH1, RH12 .....4 B1
Worthing BN13 ....17 B8
Mountview Rd RH15 ..165 C1
Mount Way BN15 ....165 E1
Mountwood Rd
Breach PO10 ....151 F1
Selsey PO20 ....212 F8
Mount Zion Pl BN1 ...213 A3
Mouse La BN44 ......144 E6
Mouthey's La PO18 ..169 D1
Mowbray Dr RH11 .....17 F4
Mowden Sch BN1 ....169 D1
Moyne Cl BN3 ....168 E1
Moyne Rd RH11 ....18 C2
M'tongue Ave PO18 ..175 C7
Mudberry La PO18 ...175 A8

Muggeridge's Hill RH12,
RH5 ....15 E8
Muir Ct BN14 ....186 D5
Muirfield Cl
Crawley RH11 ....17 D5
Worthing BN13 ....185 E7
Muirfield Cl 16 RH16 ..87 E4
Muirfield Rd BN13 ...185 E7
Mulberry Cl
Brighton BN1 ....169 F3
Ferring BN12 ....206 E6
Horsham RH12 ....36 C5
Lancing BN15 ....187 E6
Shoreham-by-S BN43 ..167 D1
Worthing BN12 ....185 C4
Mulberry Ct
Bognor Regis PO21 ...211 A7
Petworth GU28 ....97 E7
Selsey PO20 ....212 D7
Worthing BN13 ....185 C3
Mulberry Gdns BN12 .185 C3
Mulberry Hollow
BN16 ....205 D8
Mulberry La
Ditchling BN6 ....129 D3
Bosham PO18 ....185 C3
Mulberry Rd RH11 .....5 B1
Mullein Wlk RH11 ......18 A2
Mumford Pl PO19 ....177 B4
Munmere Way 3
BN16 ....205 E6
Munnion Rd RH17 .....64 B7
Munns Dr RH15 ......109 B4
Muntham Dr RH13 .....56 F3
Muntham House Sch
RH13 ....56 E4
Muntham House School
Flats RH13 ....56 E4
Muriel Ho BN3 ....190 E8
Murina Ave PO21 ....201 C5
Murray Ct
Crawley RH11 ....18 A1
Worthing BN13 ....37 B4
Murray Rd PO20 .....212 D6
Museum Hill GU27 ....27 D6
Musgrave Ave RH19 ..22 E8
Mushroom Field BN7 .172 E5
Mustang Cl BN18 ....181 B2
Muster Ct RH16 ....87 D4
Muster Gn N RH16 ....87 D4
Muster Gn S RH16 ....87 D4
Mutton Hill RH7 ......10 B7
Mutton's La RH20 ...122 D3
Myrtle Cres BN15 ...187 D5
Myrtle Gr
Clapham BN13 ....162 E5
East Preston BN16 ...205 F5
Myrtle La BN14 ....79 D7
Myrtle Rd BN15 ....187 D5
Mytchett Ho 1 PO19 .155 A2
Mytten Bank RH17 ....86 F6
Mytten Cl RH17 ....86 F6

N

Nab Tower La PO20 ..212 B8
Nab Wlk PO20 ....207 F6
Nagels Cl PO20 ......208 A6
Naiad Gdns PO22 ....202 D5
Naldrett Cl RH12 ......36 F4
Naldretts La RH12 .....33 D5
Namrik Mews BN3 ...191 A6
Nan Kemp's Grave
BN7 ....172 E6
Nansen Cotts PO20 ..177 A1
Nanson Rd BN1 ......170 D6
Napier Ho 8 BN2 ....192 C7
Napier Way RH10 ......6 A1
Nappers Wood GU27 ..49 A6
Nash La RH17 ....89 B4
Nash Rd RH10 ....18 E3
Nash Way BN18 .....158 D1
Natal Rd BN2 ....170 D1
Natts La RH14 ....79 D6
Naunton Rd PO19 ....155 A2
Nautilus BN11 ....186 D1
Navarino Rd BN11 ...187 A2
Neale Cl RH19 ....9 B3
Needlemakers PO19 ..177 B6
Needles Cl RH12 ......36 B1
Need's Hill RH13 ....104 F6
Nell Ball RH14 ....30 E2
Nelson Cl
Crawley RH10 ....19 C5
Hermitage PO10 .....173 C8
Lancing BN15 ....187 D8
Tangmere PO20 .....156 D2
Nelson Ct
Chichester PO19 .....177 D7
Shoreham-by-S BN43 .188 D5
Nelson Dr BN2 ....65 C5
Nelson Pl 17 BN2 ...213 C3
Nelson Rd
Bognor Regis PO21 ..201 A3
Horsham RH12 ....36 C3
Worthing BN12 ....185 D5
Nelson Row
Brighton BN2 ....213 C2
Ford BN18 ....181 E3
Nep Ct BN13 ....185 C4
Nepcote BN14 ....163 F5
Nepcote La BN14 ...163 E5
Nepcote Par BN14 ..163 F5
Nepfield Cl BN14 ...163 F5
NEP TOWN 125 E4
Nep Town Rd BN5 ...125 E4
Neptune Cl RH11 .....17 E4

Neptune Ct
Bognor Regis PO22 ...202 D4
Brighton BN2 ....192 F3
Horsham RH12 ....36 B4
Neptune Way BN17 ..205 A4
Nesbit Ct RH11 ....17 E3
Nesbitt Rd BN2 ......170 D1
Nestor Ct BN1 ....191 E8
Nestor Ct BN1 ....191 E8
Netherfield Gn BN2 .193 F8
Netherton Cl
Selsey PO20 ....212 E7
Southwater RH13 ......57 F4
Netherwood RH11 .....18 B4
Netley Cl RH11 ....39 C8
Netley Ct BN17 ......204 B5
Nettleton Ave PO20 .156 C2
Nettleton Ct BN1 ...170 B1
Nevile Cl RH11 ....18 A3
Nevill Ave BN3 ....168 F1
Nevill Cl BN3 ....169 A2
Nevill Cotts BN6 ....129 D2
Nevill Ct BN3 ....169 A1
Neville Gdns PO10 ..151 A3
Neville Rd
Bognor Regis PO22 ..201 D4
Chichester PO19 .....176 D7
Nevill Gdns BN3 ....169 A2
Nevill Pl BN3 ....169 A2
Nevill Rd
Hove BN3 ....169 A2
Rottingdean BN2 .....193 F1
Nevill Way BN3 ......169 A2
Newark Pl BN2 ......213 C3
Newark Rd RH10 .....18 F8
New Barn RH14 ....53 A2
New Barn Cl
Portslade-by-S BN41 .168 B2
Shoreham-by-S BN43 .167 B1
New Barn Hill PO18 ..156 B7
Newbarn La
Henfield BN5 ....125 F2
Walderton PO18 .....152 B8
New Barn La
Bognor Regis, Felpham
PO22 ....202 B6
West Chiltington Common
RH20 ....121 B8
New Barn Rd
Amberley BN18 ......140 D5
Rottingdean BN2 .....167 B1
Shoreham-by-S BN43 ..167 B1
Newbridge Cl RH10 ...35 C3
Newbridge Rd E RH14 .79 B8
New Brighton Rd
PO10 ....151 B2
New Broadway BN14 .186 A3
Newbury La RH17 .....86 E5
Newbury Rd RH10 ....19 D6
New Church Rd BN3 ..190 E7
New Cotts
Angmering BN16 .....183 E5
Conford GU30 ....24 E8
Partridge Green RH13 .105 A3
Scaynes Hill RH17 ....88 F1
Turners Hill RH10 .....21 A4
Washington RH20 ...143 A5
New Courtwick La
BN17 ....204 C8
Newcroft Cotts RH17 ..42 A2
New Cut BN18 ....160 B3
Newdigate Rd RH12 ..16 C8
New Dorset St BN1 ..213 A3
Newells Cl RH21 .....171 E1
Newells La
Broadbridge PO18 ...175 A7
Monk's Gate RH13 ....59 D2
West Ashling PO18 ..152 F1
NEW ENGLAND 40 B2
New England Ho BN1 .213 B4
New England Rise
BN41 ....168 A4
New England St BN1 .213 B4
New Farthingdale RH7 .10 B8
Newfield Rd
Liss GU33 ....45 C6
Selsey PO20 ....212 G8
New Gdns BN15 .....186 F7
Newhall Cl PO21 ....200 F3
New Hall La BN5 .....146 E7
Newham Cl BN44 ....145 C3
Newham St BN2 .....213 C3
Newhaven Bsns Ctr
RH12 ....34 C7
Newhouse La
East Dean PO18 .....136 D8
Heath Common RH20 .122 C3
Newick House Sch
RH15 ....109 C1
Newick Rd BN1 ......186 A3
New La GU31 ....91 D2
Newland Rd
Upper Beeding BN44 .146 B2
Worthing BN11 ......186 B3
Newlands RH17 ....40 F1
Newlands Cl
Horley RH6 ....1 F5
Keymer BN6 ....129 D3
Newlands Cres RH19 ...9 D2
Newlands La PO19 ..176 D8
Newlands Pk RH10 ....7 E3
Newlands Pl RH18 ....23 F3

Newlands Rd
Crawley RH11 ....18 C5
Horsham RH12 ....36 C4
Rottingdean BN2 ....194 A1
Newland St BN11 ....186 B3
New Larchwood BN1 .170 D6
Newling Way BN13 ..163 E1
Newman Cl RH10 .....19 C4
Newman's Gdns BN15 .187 B7
Newmarket Rd
Brighton BN2 ....192 C8
Crawley RH10 ....19 A4
Newmarket Terr 12
BN2 ....192 C8
New Moorhead Dr
RH12 ....37 C6
New Par
East Wittering PO20 .207 F2
Selsey PO20 ....212 D7
Worthing BN11 ......186 F2
New Park Ct PO19 ...177 B6
New Park Rd PO19 ..177 A7
New Place Rd PO20 .200 C3
Newport BN43 ....189 B6
Newport Dr PO19 ...176 B7
Newport Mews BN11 ..187 A2
Newport Rd RH15 ...108 F3
Newport St BN2 .....213 C4
Newpound BN14 ......54 E3
NEWPOUND COMMON
......................54 E2
Newpound La RH14 ..54 D1
New Rd
Angmering BN16 ....205 E7
Billingshurst RH14 ...56 B2
Brighton BN1 ....213 B2
East Dean PO18 ....136 D8
Haslemere GU27 .....26 F5
Keymer BN6 ....129 D3
Littlehampton BN17 .204 D4
Midhurst GU29 ....94 E6
Shoreham-by-S BN43 .188 F7
South Ambersham GU29 .95 E4
Southbourne PO10 ..174 A8
Southwater RH13 .....57 F4
Upper Beeding BN44 .146 B1
Upperton GU28 ....75 A2
Westbourne PO10 ...151 D3
Westerton PO18 .....155 D4
Worthing BN13 ....185 C8
New Row BN44 ......145 C3
New Salts Farm Rd
BN43 ....188 C6
New St
Crawley RH10 ....19 A7
Horsham RH13 ....36 D2
2 Petworth GU28 ....97 F8
8 Worthing BN11 ...186 D1
Newstead RH1 ....213 A4
Newstead Hall RH6 ....2 D1
New Steine BN2 .....213 C1
New Steine Mews
BN2 ....213 C2
New Terr BN18 ......183 C8
Newtimber Ave BN12 .185 B4
Newtimber Dr BN1 ..168 A1
Newtimber Gdns
BN43 ....166 F1
Newton Ave RH19 ....22 F6
Newton Cl RH16 ......88 B7
Newton Ct RH16 .....87 C5
Newton Rd
Crawley RH10 ....5 F2
Lindfield RH16 ....88 C3
NEWTOWN 28 C7
NEW TOWN 58 E8
New Town
14 Chichester PO19 ..177 A3
Copthorne RH10 ......7 B3
Newtown Ave PO21 ..201 A6
New Town Cotts
RH20 ....121 B1
Newtown Rd
Hove BN3 ....191 B8
Liphook GU30 ....25 C3
New Town Rd RH20 .121 B1
New Way La BN6 ...128 B2
Nicholsfield RH14 .....31 F4
Nicolson Cl PO20 ...156 C2
Nicolson Dr BN43 ...189 A8
Nightingale Cl
Crawley RH11 ....18 C5
East Grinstead RH19 ..22 D7
Fernhurst GU27 ....49 A6
Haywards Heath RH16 .87 F4
Red Hill PO9 ....130 C1
Storrington RH20 ....121 C1
Nightingale Ct
Middleton-on-S PO22 .202 F5
Westbourne PO10 ...151 D4
Nightingale Ind Est
RH12 ....36 D3
Nightingale La
Burgess Hill RH15 ..128 F8
Hambrook PO18 .....152 D3
Storrington RH20 ...121 C1
Turners Hill RH10 .....21 C5
Nightingale Pk RH20 .121 E1
Nightingale Pl GU27 ..27 D7
Nightingale Rd
Horsham RH12 ....36 D3
Petersfield GU31 .....68 A2
Nightingales
Findon BN14 ....163 E7
West Chiltington Common
RH20 ....121 D7
Nightingales Cl RH13 .36 F2

Nightingale Wlk RH14 ....79 E8
Nile St
  Brighton BN1 ....213 B2
  Emsworth PO10.........173 B8
Nimbus CI RH11 ....205 A6
Nimrod Ct RH10 ....6 D1
Nimrod Ho 3 RH20 ...121 E1
Nine Acres GU29 ....94 D8
Nineveh Shipyard
  BN18 ....160 B3
Ninfield Ct RH11 ....17 F2
Ninfield PI
  Brighton BN2 ....192 E6
  Brighton BN2 ....192 E7
Nini-hi Cvn Site
  BN17 ....181 D1
Niven CI RH10 ....19 D5
Nizells Ave BN3 ....191 E7
Noahs Ark La RH16 ....88 C7
Noah's Ct RH10 ....21 A4
Noble Ct BN3 ....190 E7
Noel Gn RH15 ....109 B4
Noel Rise RH15 ....109 B4
Nolan Rd BN2 ....193 E7
Nonnington La GU28 ...96 B1
Nook Cvn Pk The
  PO20 ....212 C8
Nookery The BN16 ....206 A5
Nor'bren Ave PO21 ......201 A5
Norbury CI RH15 ....187 F8
Norbury Dr BN15 ....187 F8
Nordseter Lo 1 BN16...205 E6
Nore Down Way
  PO18 ....132 A8
Noreuil Rd GU32 ....67 F3
Nore Wood La BN18 ....158 C7
Norfolk Bldgs 5 BN1 ..191 E5
Norfolk CI
  11 Bognor Regis
  PO21 ....201 C2
  Crawley RH11 ....17 E2
  Horley RH6 ....2 A2
Norfolk Cotts
  Bury RH20 ....140 A7
  6 Steyning BN44 ......145 D3
Norfolk Ct
  1 Bognor Regis
  PO21 ....201 C2
  4 Brighton BN1 ....191 E5
  5 Rustington BN16 ...205 B4
  1 Worthing BN11 ....186 C3
Norfolk Gdns BN17......204 F4
Norfolk Ho PO22.........201 F4
Norfolk Mews
  6 Brighton BN1 ....191 E5
  7 Littlehampton BN17...204 F4
Norfolk PI
  5 Brighton BN1 ....191 E5
  5 Littlehampton BN17...204 F4
Norfolk Rd
  Brighton BN1 ....191 E6
  Horsham RH12 ....36 D2
  Littlehampton BN17....204 F4
Norfolk Sq
  Bognor Regis PO21 ....201 C2
  Brighton BN1 ....191 E5
Norfolk St
  Bognor Regis PO21 ....201 C2
  Brighton BN1 ....191 E5
  Worthing BN11 ....186 C3
Norfolk Terr
  Brighton BN1 ....191 E6
  7 Horsham RH12........36 D2
Norfolk Way PO22 ....203 B5
Norman CI
  Billingshurst RH14.......55 E1
  Littlehampton BN17....204 F4
Norman Cres 9 BN43...166 F1
Normandy RH12 ....36 C1
Normandy CI
  Crawley RH10 ....19 C4
  7 East Grinstead RH19 ...22 F8
Normandy Ct
  Chichester PO19 ....177 B7
  9 Worthing BN11 ....186 B1
Normandy Dr BN16......206 A4
Normandy Gdns 4
  RH12 ....36 C1
Normandy Ho 3 BN3 ..191 C6
Normandy La BN16 ......206 A4
Normandy Rd BN14 .....186 C4
Normanhurst
  1 Brighton BN2 ....213 C3
  4 Shoreham-by-S
  BN43 ....188 F7
Normanhurst CI
  Crawley RH10 ....18 F6
  Rustington BN16 ....205 C4
Norman Rd
  Burgess Hill RH15.......109 A3
  Hove BN3 ....190 E6
Normanscourt 8
  BN43 ....166 F1
Norman's Dr PO22.......202 B6
Normanton PO21 ....201 B3
Normanton St 8 BN2...192 D2
Norman Way
  Middleton-on-S PO22...202 F5
  Steyning BN44 ....145 D4
North Ash 1 RH12......36 C4
North Ave
  Middleton-on-S PO22...202 F5
  Worthing BN12 ....185 E2
North Ave E PO22.......203 A5
North Ave S PO22.......203 A5
North Bank BN6 ....128 E4
North Bay PO10 ....173 C3

NORTH BERSTED 201 A7
North Bersted St
  PO22 ....201 A7
Northbourne CI BN43 ...188 F8
Northbourne Bsns Pk
  BN14 ....186 E6
Northbourne Ct BN14 ...186 E6
Northbourne Coll
  Horsham RH12 ....36 C4
  Worthing, Goring-by-Sea
  BN12 ....185 B5
  Worthing, West Worthing
  BN11 ....186 D2
Northbrook Coll
  (Broadwater Campus)
  BN14 ....186 D5
Northbrook Farm Cvn Pk
  BN13 ....185 B7
Northbrook Rd BN14 ...186 E6
Northbrook Trad Est
  BN14 ....186 E6
Northchapel Com Prim
  Sch GU28 ....51 A7
North CI
  Chichester PO19 ....177 A7
  Crawley RH10 ....18 F7
  Portslade-by-S BN41 ...168 A2
Northcliffe Rd PO22 ....201 E4
Northcommon Farm Ctr*
  PO20 ....209 C2
Northcote Gdns PO10...174 A8
Northcote Rd PO21 .....201 A4
Northcourt CI BN16.....205 C6
Northcourt Mews
  BN14 ....186 C4
Northcourt Rd BN14 ....186 C4
Northcroft BN5 ....125 E5
North Ct BN6 ....128 E4
Northdown 1 RH12......36 F4
Northdown Terr RH19 ...9 D3
North Dr
  Angmering BN16 ....205 F8
  Brighton BN2 ....192 C6
  Dormansland RH19 ....10 B6
Northease CI BN3 ....168 D2
Northease Dr BN3 ....168 E3
Northease Gdns BN3....168 E3
North End BN6 ....129 D4
North End Cotts BN14...163 E8
Northend La BN6 ....107 F3
North End Rd BN18 .....180 F4
Northerlea BN41 ....168 A1
Northern Breach RH17...86 F6
Northern Cres PO20 ....207 F7
North Farm Cotts
  Findon RH20 ....143 D2
  Portslade-by-S BN41 ...168 A2
North Farm Ct 6
  BN15 ....187 E6
North Farm Rd BN15....187 F6
Northfield Rd BN13 .....186 A6
Northfield Rise
  Hove BN3 ....168 D4
  Rottingdean BN2 ....194 A2
Northfields La PO20 ....157 D1
Northfield Way BN1.....170 A4
NORTHGATE 18 F7
Northgate Ave RH10 ...18 F7
Northgate CI
  Lancing BN15 ....187 C6
  Rottingdean BN2 ....193 F2
Northgate PI RH10 ....18 E7
Northgate Prim Sch
  RH10 ....18 E7
Northgate Rd
  Crawley, Gatwick Airport
  ....5 F8
  Crawley RH10 ....18 D6
North Gdns BN1 ....213 A3
North Ham Rd BN17 ....204 D6
NORTH HEATH 100 F7
North Heath CI RH12...36 D5
North Heath Com Prim
  Sch RH12 ....36 D5
North Heath La RH12 ...36 E6
North Heath Lane Ind Est
  ....36 D6
North Ho PO19 ....177 A7
North Holmes CI RH12...37 B5
North La
  Buriton GU31 ....90 A5
  Charlton PO18 ....136 A8
  East Preston BN16 ......206 B6
  Littlehampton BN16.....205 B6
  Portslade-by-S BN41 ...168 A3
  South Harting GU31 ....91 D4
  West Hoathly RH19 ......42 E6
  Wiston BN44 ....123 C2
Northlands Ave RH16 ...88 B4
Northlands Bsns Pk
  RH12 ....14 C4
Northlands Cotts RH12...14 D4
Northlands La RH20 ....121 E4
Northlands Rd
  Horsham RH12 ....36 E7
  Warnham RH12 ....14 D2
Northlands Wood Com
  Prim Sch RH16...........88 B4
North Lo PO21.............200 A2
North Lodge Ind Pk
  GU30 ....25 D1

North Lodge Mans 3
  BN11 ....186 D2
NORTH MARDEN 112 B5
Northmead GU28 ....75 F1
North Mead
  Crawley RH10 ....18 B8
  Henfield BN5 ....125 E6
Northmoor Ct 18
  PO21 ....201 B2
NORTH MOULSECOMB
  ....170 E4
North Mundham Prim Sch
  PO20 ....177 D1
Northolmes Jun Sch
  RH12 ....37 A4
North Pallant PO19 .....177 A6
North Par RH12 ....36 C3
North Pk BN17 ....204 C5
North PI
  Brighton BN1 ....213 B2
  15 Littlehampton BN17...204 E4
North Point 1 BN43 ...189 A6
North Pound BN18 .....158 D1
North Rd
  Brighton BN1 ....213 B2
  Brighton, Preston BN1 ...169 E1
  Broadbridge RH18 ......175 C7
  Crawley RH10 ....19 A7
  Haywards Heath RH16 ...88 A4
  Lancing BN15 ....187 E6
  Petersfield GU32 ....68 B4
  Portslade-by-S BN41 ...168 A2
  Selsey PO20 ....212 E7
North St Quadrant
  BN1 ....213 A2
Northside RH18 ....154 E7
North-South Rd BN1 ...171 B7
North St
  Brighton BN1 ....213 B2
  Chichester PO19 ....177 A7
  Emsworth PO10 ....151 B1
  Horsham RH12, RH13 ...36 D3
  Littlehampton BN17 ....204 F2
  Midhurst GU29 ....94 F8
  Petworth GU28 ....75 F1
  Portslade-by-S BN41 ...190 C7
  Shoreham-by-S BN43 ...188 E7
  Storrington BN20 ....121 D1
  Turners Hill RH10 ....21 A4
  Westbourne PO10 ......151 D4
  Worthing BN11 ....186 D3
NORTH STOKE 140 C2
North Stroud La GU32 ...67 A3
North View BN5 ....126 E5
Northview Terr BN14 ....163 E6
North Walls PO19 ....176 F6
Northway
  Burgess Hill RH15 ....109 C4
  Crawley RH6 ....5 F4
North Way
  Bognor Regis PO22 ....201 F4
  Portwuild GU28 ....97 E7
Northway Rd BN17 ......204 D8
Northwood Ave BN2 ....194 E1
Northwood Ct BN14 ....186 C6
Northwood Pk RH10 ......4 E2
NORTH WYKE PO22 .....202 C5
Northwyke Rd PO22 ....202 C5
Norton CI BN3 ....191 B6
Norton Dr BN2 ....171 E1
Norton La PO20 ....157 B1
Norton Rd
  Hove BN3 ....190 D6
  Lancing BN15 ....187 D5
Norway La BN17 ....204 F7
Norway St BN41 ....190 C7
Norwich CI BN2 ....171 A2
Norwich Cres BN2 ....170 F2
Norwich Dr BN2 ....170 F2
Norwich House Rd
  BN1 ....171 B7
Norwich Rd
  Chichester PO19 ....154 F1
  Crawley RH10 ....18 F6
Norwood BN1 ....170 A4
Norwoodhill Rd RH6 ......4 E8
Norwood La GU28 ....116 E6
Norwood La S GU28 ....116 E5
Nowhurst La RH12 ....35 A5
Nuffield CI PO21 ....200 E3
Nuffield Hospl Brighton
  BN2 ....193 C8
Nunnington Farm Cvn Pk
  PO20 ....196 D2
Nurseries The
  Balcombe RH17 ....41 A1
  Bognor Regis PO22 ....200 C3
Nursery CI
  Barnham PO22. ....180 B6
  Haywards Heath RH16 ...87 F2
  Hurstpierpoint BN6 ....127 F7
  Lancing BN15 ....187 D7
  New Brighton PO21 ....151 B3
  Portslade-by-S BN41 ...167 E4
  Shoreham-by-S BN43 ...189 B8
  West Kingston BN16 ...206 A4
Nursery Cotts PO22 ....180 C6
Nursery Field GU33 ......45 A3
Nursery Gdns
  Chichester PO19 ....177 B5
  Littlehampton BN17 ....204 F7
Nursery La
  Fishbourne PO19........176 B7
  Hookwood RH6 ....1 D2
  Worthing BN11 ....186 C1
Nurserylands RH11 ....18 A6

Nursery Rd BN16 ....206 A8
Nursery The RH15 ....109 C4
NURSTED 90 E7
Nutbourne Ct 2 RH12...36 D5
Nutbourne Halt PO18 ...174 D8
Nutbourne La PO20 .....101 A4
Nutbourne Pk PO18....174 B7
Nutbourne Rd
  Nutbourne Common
  PO10. ....101 A1
  South Hayling PO11 ...195 A1
  Worthing BN14 ....186 B4
Nutbourne Vineyards*
  RH20 ....101 C2
Nutcombe La GU26,
  GU27 ....26 E8
Nutcroft RH20 ....100 C3
Nuthall La RH13 ....58 A1
Nuthatch CI PO9. ....130 D1
Nuthatch Way
  Horsham RH12 ....36 D7
  Turners Hill RH10 ....21 C5
Nuthurst CI
  Brighton BN2 ....192 E6
  Crawley RH11 ....18 A7
Nuthurst PI BN2 ....192 F5
Nuthurst Rd
  Maplehurst RH13 ....82 F6
  Monk's Gate RH13 ....59 B3
Nuthurst St RH13 ....59 A2
Nutley Ave
  Saltdean BN2 ....194 C1
  Worthing BN12 ....185 C2
Nutley CI
  Hove BN3. ....168 F3
  Worthing BN12 ....185 C2
Nutley Cres BN12 ....185 C2
Nutley Dr BN12 ....185 C2
Nye La
  Ditchling BN6. ....129 D1
  Westmeston BN6. ....150 D8
Nye Rd RH15 ....109 C3
Nyes CI BN5. ....125 F5
Nye's Hill RH17. ....84 E1
Nye's La RH13. ....57 F3
NYETIMBER 200 A1
Nyetimber CI PO21 .....200 B2
Nyetimber Copse
  RH20 ....121 C6
Nyetimber Cres PO21 ...200 B2
Nyetimber Hill BN2 .....170 E2
Nyetimber La
  Bognor Regis PO21 ....200 B2
  West Chiltington Common
  ....121 C7
Nyetimber Mill PO21 ...200 A2
Nyetimbers The PO21 ...200 A2
Nyewood CE Inf Sch
  PO21 ....201 A3
Nyewood CE Jun Sch
  PO21 ....201 A3
Nyewood Gdns 2
  PO21 ....201 B3
Nyewood La PO21 ....201 B3
Nyewood PI PO21 ....201 B3
Nymans CI RH12. ....37 A7
Nymans Cotts
  Handcross RH17. ....61 C7
  Henfield BN5. ....105 E1
Nymans Rd BN13 ....19 B3
NYTON 179 D8
Nyton Rd PO20 ....179 C8

O

Oakapple CI RH11 ....18 B1
Oak Apple CI RH13 ....83 E1
Oakapple Rd BN42 ......167 E1
Oak Ave
  Chichester PO19 ....176 E7
  Heath Common RH20 ...122 B3
Oak Bank RH16 ....87 F7
Oak CI
  Bognor Regis PO22 ....201 C6
  Brighton BN1 ....169 E3
  Chichester PO19 ....176 E7
  Copthorne RH10 ....7 A3
  Southwater RH13 ....81 F7
  Storrington RH20 ....121 F2
  Worthing BN13 ....163 E1
Oak Cotts GU27 ....26 E6
Oak Croft RH19 ....23 A8
Oakcroft Gdns BN17 ....204 F7
Oak CI RH10. ....19 C7
Oakdale Rd RH16 ....87 F3
Oak Dell RH10 ....19 C7
Oakdene RH16. ....87 D5
Oakdene Ave BN41 ......167 E3
Oakdene CI BN41 ....167 E3
Oakdene Cres BN41 .....167 E3
Oakdene Gdns BN41 ....167 E3
Oakdene Rise BN41 .....167 E4
Oak Dr GU31 ....68 A1
Oak End
  Arundel BN18 ....159 E2
  West Chiltington Common
  RH20. ....121 C7
Oakendene BN2 ....170 F4
Oakendene Ind Est
  RH13. ....84 B1
Oak Farm PI RH19 ....8 F3
Oakfield
  Lodsworth GU28 ....74 B3
  Plaistow RH14 ....30 E2
Oakfield Ave PO20 ....207 F7

Oakfield CI RH16 ....88 A7
Oakfield Cotts RH13 .....83 E1
Oakfield Mid Sch
  BN15 ....187 E7
Oakfield Rd
  Cowfold RH13 ....83 F1
  East Wittering PO20 ....207 F7
Oakfields
  Crawley RH10 ....19 D7
  Wallis Wood RH5. ....13 D8
Oakfield Way RH19 ....9 F3
Oak Gr
  Bognor Regis PO22 ....201 C6
  Loxwood RH14. ....32 A4
Oak Grove Coll BN13 ...185 E6
Oak Hall Pk RH15. ....109 B1
Oakhaven RH10 ....18 D4
OAKHILL 36 E1
Oakhill Chase RH10. .....19 D7
Oakhill Rd RH13 ....36 E2
Oakhurst
  Haywards Heath RH16 ...87 D8
  Henfield BN5 ....125 F6
  Midhurst GU29 ....94 D7
  Sayers Common BN6. ...107 D2
Oakhurst Bsns Pk
  BN14. ....58 A4
Oakhurst Gdns
  East Grinstead RH19 .....9 C2
  Rustington BN16 ....205 E6
Oakhurst La
  Haywards Heath RH16 ...87 D8
  Loxwood RH14. ....31 E7
Oakhurst Mews RH12 ...37 A4
Oak La RH12. ....35 E3
Oakland Ct
  Bognor Regis, Felpham
  PO22. ....202 A4
  Bognor Regis, Nyetimber
  PO21. ....200 A1
  2 Littlehampton BN17 ...204 E4
  5 Shoreham-by-S
  BN43. ....188 F7
  Worthing, Goring-by-Sea
  BN12. ....185 A3
  5 Worthing, West Worthing
  BN11. ....186 C2
Oaklands
  Ardingly RH17. ....64 88
  Billingshurst RH14. ....79 D7
  Haslemere GU27 ....27 C7
  Horley RH6. ....2 C3
  Horsham, Oakhill RH13. ...36 E2
  Horsham RH13. ....36 B5
  2 Lancing BN15. ....187 F5
Oaklands Ave BN2 ....194 D1
Oaklands Bsns Ctr
  BN11. ....185 F4
Oaklands CI RH13. ....58 E8
Oaklands Ct PO19 ....177 A8
Oaklands La GU29 ....94 F5
Oaklands Rd
  Haywards Heath RH16 ...87 D5
  Petersfield GU32. ....68 A4
Oaklands Way RH17 .....177 A7
Oakleigh CI BN11 ....187 A4
Oakleigh Ct
  2 Bognor Regis
  PO21. ....201 B2
  Worthing BN11. ....187 A4
Oakleigh Rd
  Horsham RH12 ....36 F4
  Worthing BN11. ....187 A4
Oakley CI RH19 ....23 B7
Oakley Cotts
  Handcross RH17. ....23 C7
  ....61 C8
Oakley Gdns BN16 ....206 A5
Oakley Ho BN2 ....213 C2
Oak Mdw PO20 ....197 E5
Oakmeadow CI PO10. ...151 C3
Oakmead Rd RH15. ......108 F1
Oak Rd
  Crawley RH11 ....18 C5
  Southwater RH13 ....57 E1
Oakroyd CI RH15 ....109 D5
Oaks CI
  Fernhurst GU27 ....49 A6
  Horsham RH12 ....37 B6
  Westergate PO20 ....179 D6
Oaks La RH6. ....2 C4
Oakside La RH6. ....2 C4
Oaks Mews PO21 ....200 E3
Oaks Prim Sch The
  RH10. ....18 F3
Oaks The
  Bognor Regis PO21 ....200 E3
  Burgess Hill RH15. ......108 D4
  East Grinstead RH19 ...23 B8
  Haywards Heath RH16 ...88 C4
  Haywards Heath RH16 ...88 A4
  Rustington BN16 ....205 E5
  Small Dole BN5 ....146 E6
  Southwater RH13 ....57 F2
Oaktree CI PO21 ....199 F2
Oak Tree CI RH19 ....9 C3
Oaktree Cotts BN18.....180 C8
Oak Tree Cotts
  Burgess Hill RH15. ......109 B3
  Danehill RH17. ....66 A4
Oak Tree CI GU29 ....94 E6
Oak Tree Dr
  Liss GU33 ....45 C4

Oak Tree Dr continued
  New Brighton PO10.....151 B4
Oak Tree Farm PO18 ... 152 D1
Oak Tree La
  Haslemere GU27........26 D6
  Woodgate PO20........179 D5
Oak Tree Way RH13......36 F4
Oakvale RH20..........121 C7
Oak View PO20..........198 F7
Oakwary RH13...........59 C6
Oak Way
  Crawley RH10...........18 E8
  Ifold RH14.............31 D2
Oakwood
  Haywards Heath RH16...87 D4
  Partridge Green RH13...105 A3
Oakwood Cl
  Bognor Regis PO21.....200 D2
  Bracklesham PO20......208 B5
  Haywards Heath RH17...88 A2
Old Farm Cl BN14......188 C6
Old Farm Dr PO20......179 D7
Old Farm La PO10......151 E3
Oakwood Ct
  3 Bognor Regis
    PO21...............201 C4
  Crawley RH11..........39 B8
  Petworth GU28.........97 E7
Oakwood Dr BN16......206 A8
Oakwood Gdns PO21....201 C4
OAKWOODHILL..........14 A7
Oakwood Ind Pk RH10 ... 6 A2
Oakwood Pk RH18......23 F2
Oakwood Rd
  Burgess Hill RH15.....109 B3
  Haywards Heath RH16...87 D4
  Horley RH6............2 B4
Oakwood Sch
  East Ashling PO18....153 F2
  Horley RH6............2 C3
Oates Wlk RH10........18 F3
Oathall Ave RH16......87 F6
Oathall Com Coll RH16...87 F6
Oathall Rd RH16.......87 E5
Oatlands
  Crawley RH11..........18 A5
  Horley RH6............2 C1
Oberon Way RH11......17 E3
Observer Ct RH12......36 C1
Ocean Bldg The BN1....213 A3
Ocean Cl BN12.........206 E4
Ocean Dr BN12.........206 E4
Ocean Par BN12........206 E4
Ocean Reach BN2......194 A1
Ockenden La RH17......86 E6
Ockenden Way BN6.....128 E3
Ockley Ct PO21........201 C3
Ockley Hill BN6, RH15...129 B6
Ockley La
  Burgess Hill RH15.....129 B7
  Keymer BN6............129 B4
Ockley Rd PO21........201 C3
Ockley Way BN6........129 A5
Octagon The BN2.......192 F3
OFFHAM...............160 D6
Offington Ave BN14....186 B6
Offington Cnr BN13,
  BN14................186 A8
Offington Ct BN14.....186 C6
Offington Dr BN14.....186 A7
Offington Gdns BN14...186 A6
Offington La BN13,
  BN14................186 A7
Ognells Flats GU29....94 F8
Okehurst La RH14......55 D4
Okehurst Rd
  Five Oaks RH14........55 A6
  Rudgwick RH14........33 C1
Old Arundel Rd PO18...155 F2
Old Bakery Gdns
  PO19................177 B5
Old Bakery Mews
  PO20................212 E7
Old Barn Cl PO21......200 A2
Old Barn Ct
  East Wittering PO20...207 F6
  Haywards Heath RH16...87 D2
Old Barns BN16........183 F5
Old Barn Sq GU31......69 C4
Old Barn Way BN42....190 A7
Old Blendworth PO8....130 B8
Old Boat Cnr BN1......170 D8
Old Boat Wlk BN1......170 B7
Old Boundary La
  RH20................121 B8
Old Bridge Rd PO18...175 C2
Old Brighton Rd N
  RH13................39 C7
Old Brighton Rd S
  Crawley RH11..........5 E5
  Pease Pottage RH19....39 B6
OLD BUDDINGTON.......72 E3
Old Buddington La
  GU29................72 E3
Oldbury Cl RH17.......37 A7
Old Canal (park homes)
  The PO21.............179 D3
Old Church Ho The
  PO21................201 A6
Old Coach Ho The
  BN11................186 B3
Old Coastguard Cotts
  PO20................212 C7
Old Coastguards
  PO22................201 F3
Old College Ho BN2....213 C4

Old Control Tower Rd
  RH6.................5 D6
Old Convent The RH19...9 E2
Old Cottage Cl PO20...156 C1
Old Cotts BN14........163 E7
Old Court Cl BN1......169 F4
Old Courthouse The 3
  BN44...............145 D3
Old Crawley Rd RH12...37 C7
Old Dairy Workshops
  PO10................151 D3
Old Denne Gdns 6
  RH12................36 C1
Olde Place Ct BN2.....193 F1
Olde Place Mews
  BN2.................193 F1
OLDER HILL...........48 B2
Older Way BN16........183 F6
Old Farm Cl
  Bognor Regis PO21.....200 D2
  Bracklesham PO20......208 B5
  Haywards Heath RH17...88 A2
Old Farm Ct BN14......188 C6
Old Farm Dr PO20......179 D7
Old Farm La PO10......151 E3
Old Farm Rd
  Brighton BN1..........169 F5
  Selsey PO20...........212 C8
Old Forge Cl RH11.....16 F1
Old Fort Rd BN43......189 B6
Old Glebe GU27........49 B6
Old Granary The
  PO18................156 D4
Old Guildford Rd RH12...35 E4
Old Haslemere Rd
  GU27................27 C5
Old Holbrook RH12.....15 F1
Old Hollow RH10.......18 D4
Old Horsham Rd RH11...18 B4
Old Hospital The RH17...86 F8
Oldhouse La
  Balls Green RH14,
    RH13...............80 B2
  Broadford Bridge RH14,
    RH20...............102 A7
  Sidlesham PO20........209 C7
  West Marden PO9,
    PO18................132 A6
Old House La RH13.....81 B6
Oldlands Ave
  Balcombe RH17.........41 A1
  Keymer BN6............129 A4
Oldlands Way PO22.....201 E7
Old London Rd
  Brighton BN1..........169 E6
  Coldwaltham RH20......119 D6
  Washington RH20.......143 E8
Old Manor Cl RH11.....18 A8
Old Manor Ct RH11.....18 A8
Old Manor House Gdns
  PO22................202 B5
Old Manor Rd BN16....205 B6
Old Market Ave 13
  BN3.................177 A6
Old Market Cotts 17
  BN3.................191 D5
Old Market Sq BN44...145 E3
Old Martyrs RH11......5 D1
Old Mead Rd BN17.....182 C5
Old Mill Cl
  Brighton BN1..........169 E5
  Portslade-by-S BN41....190 A7
Old Mill Dr RH10......121 D1
Old Mill La GU31......68 D5
Old Millmeads RH12...36 C5
Old Mill Mews BN1....191 E8
Old Mill Pl
  Haslemere GU27........26 F7
  Pulborough RH20.......100 D1
Old Mill Sq RH20......121 D1
Old Mill The
  Arundel BN18..........160 B3
  Bognor Regis PO22.....201 F3
  Chichester PO19.......177 C1
Old Moat Cl PO22.....179 C1
Old Mus Ct GU27.......27 D6
Old Orchards RH10.....19 E6
Old Parish La BN2.....193 C8
Old Park Cl RH17......87 A6
Old Park La
  Bosham PO18..........175 D2
  Fishbourne PO18.......175 E5
Old Patcham Mews
  BN1.................169 E6
Old Pl PO21...........200 E3
Old Place La PO18.....155 D1
Old Point PO22........202 E4
Old Quarry The GU27...26 F4
Old Rd RH19...........9 F1
Old Rectory Cl PO10...151 D3
Old Rectory Dr PO20...179 E7
Old Rectory Flats
  PO22................202 A4
Old Rectory Gdns
  Bognor Regis PO22.....202 A4
  Southwick BN42.......189 D8
Old Rectory The
  PO22................202 A4
Old Rowfant Cotts
  RH10................20 B8
Old Salts Farm Rd
  BN15...............188 A5
Old School Cl PO20....197 E4
Old School Ct RH16....88 B7

Old School Mews
  PO22................202 A5
Old School Pl
  Burgess Hill RH15.....108 F2
  Portslade-by-S BN3.....168 D1
  Woodgate PO20........179 D6
Old School Rd GU33....45 B4
Old School The
  Cocking GU29..........114 D8
  Fittleworth RH20......99 A2
OLD SHOREHAM........188 E8
Old Shoreham Rd
  Lancing BN15..........188 A8
  Portslade-by-S BN3,
    BN41...............190 C8
  Shoreham-by-S BN43....188 E8
  Southwick BN42.......167 E1
Old Slipway The
  BN18................160 B2
Old Stables The PO22...201 F4
Old Station Ct RH10....21 B7
Old Steine BN1........213 B2
Old Stocks Oak GU33....45 A5
Old Surgery The 4
  RH19................9 F2
Old Sussex Stud The
  RH13................82 B1
Old Viaduct Ct 10
  BN2.................192 C8
Old Warehouse Mews 8
  BN17................204 F4
Old Wickham La RH16...87 E7
Old Wickhurst La
  RH12................35 D2
Oldwick Mdws PO18....154 F5
Old Worthing Rd
  RH16................206 B7
Old Yard Cl RH13......105 A3
Olive Rd BN3..........190 D8
Oliver Ho 5 BN3......191 B5
Oliver Rd RH12........36 A1
Olivers Mdw PO20......179 D7
Oliver Whitby Rd
  PO19................176 E7
Olivia Ct PO21........201 B3
Olivier Cl BN2........192 C5
Olivier Ct PO21.......201 A6
Olivier Rd RH10.......19 D5
Onslow Ct
  2 Crawley RH10.......6 A1
  9 Worthing BN11.....187 B3
Onslow Cvn Pk BN12...206 E6
Onslow Dr BN12........206 E6
Onslow Rd BN1........169 C2
Ontario Ct BN13.......185 C7
Ontario Gdns BN13....185 C7
Ontario Way BN13......25 C3
Open Univ (South East)
  The RH19.............9 E1
Ophir Rd BN11.........187 A3
Orange Row
  Brighton BN1..........213 B2
  Emsworth PO10........173 B8
Orchard Ave
  Chichester PO19.......176 F7
  Hove BN3.............169 A1
  Lancing BN15..........187 E2
  Selsey PO20...........212 E6
  Worthing BN14........186 B5
Orchard Bsns Ctr The
  RH1.................2 A8
Orchard Bsns Pk
  BN18................180 F4
Orchard Cl
  East Harting GU31.....92 A4
  Elsted GU29...........92 D4
  Ferring BN12..........206 E7
  Haslemere GU27........26 F5
  Haywards Heath RH16...87 D8
  Horley RH6............2 A2
  Petworth GU28.........97 F7
  Scaynes Hill RH17.....88 F3
  Shoreham-by-S BN43....188 E8
  Small Dole BN5........146 F6
  Southwick BN42.......189 F8
  Worthing BN14........186 B5
Orchard Cl The PO21...201 B3
Orchard Cnr RH16......88 B5
Orchard Cott RH17.....86 F6
Orchard Cotts
  Charlwood RH6........4 F7
  Fishbourne PO18.......176 A8
  Woodgate PO20........179 D5
Orchard Cres BN18....158 A3
Orchard Croft PO20....179 D7
Orchard Ct BN11.......186 A3
Orchard Cvn Pk PO21...200 E7
Orchard Dell PO20.....101 E2
Orchard Farm Pk RH1...2 B8
Orchard Gdns
  Chichester PO19.......176 F7
  Hove BN3.............169 B1
  Rustington BN16.......205 D6
  Woodgate PO20........179 D5
Orchard Hill RH12.....33 C7
Orchard Ho
  Crawley RH10.........5 D1
  Hove BN3.............169 B1
  Lancing BN15..........187 E6
Orchard La
  Ditchling BN6.........129 D4
  Hassocks BN6.........109 D8
  Hermitage PO18.......173 D8
  West Itchenor PO20....197 A7
Orchard Par PO20......212 F8
Orchard Pk BN16.......205 B7
Orchard Pl BN18.......160 B3

Orchard Rd
  Burgess Hill RH15.....108 E3
  East Preston BN16.....206 A6
  Horsham RH13.........36 E2
  Hove BN3.............169 B1
Orchard Side PO20.....199 A8
Orchards Mid Sch The
  BN12................185 D5
Orchards Sh Ctr RH16...37 A4
Orchard St
  Chichester PO19.......176 F7
  Crawley RH10, RH11...18 D6
Orchards The
  Brighton BN2..........170 E3
  4 Crawley RH11......17 D5
  Horsham RH12.........37 B4
Orchard The
  Bognor Regis PO21.....200 C1
  Broadbridge Heath RH12...35 D3
  Hassocks BN6.........128 F3
  Horley RH6............2 A3
  Horsham RH12.........37 B4
  Shoreham-by-S BN43....167 C1
Orchard Villas BN18...180 E8
Orchard Way
  Barnham PO22.........180 B6
  Bognor Regis PO22.....201 C5
  Burgess Hill RH17.....85 D8
  Burgess Hill RH15.....108 F3
  East Grinstead RH19...9 E1
  Fontwell BN18.........158 A3
  Haywards Heath RH17...87 D8
  Hurstpierpoint BN6.....127 F6
  Lancing BN15..........187 E7
  Midhurst GU29.........94 F8
  Petersfield GU31......68 B1
  Pulborough RH20.......100 C3
Orchid Pk RH16........88 C4
Orchid View BN1.......170 C6
Orde Cl RH10..........6 D1
Oriel Cl
  Barnham PO22.........180 B6
  Crawley RH10.........6 C1
Oriel High Sch RH10...19 C2
Oriental Pl BN1.......191 E5
Orient Rd BN15........188 C5
Orion Ct
  Crawley RH11..........17 D4
  Horsham RH12.........36 B3
Orion Par BN6.........128 F3
Orkney Ct BN13........185 B6
Orlando Ho BN1.......192 A8
Orltons La RH12.......3 F2
Orme Cotts BN16......183 F6
Orme Rd BN11.........186 C3
Ormerod Ct RH16......87 E5
Ormesby Cres PO22....202 A5
Ormesby Wlk 6 RH10...19 B4
Ormonde Ave PO19.....177 B6
Ormonde Way BN43....188 D6
Orpen Pl PO20.........212 F7
Orpen Rd BN3.........169 D1
Orwell Rd GU31.......68 A2
Osborn Cl
  Littlehampton BN17....204 C6
  Sayers Common BN6....107 D1
Osborn Cres PO19.....155 A1
Osborne Cl BN15......187 C6
Osborne Cres PO19....177 D6
Osborne Ct
  6 Crawley RH11......18 B2
  7 Shoreham-by-S
    BN18................189 C8
Osborne Dr BN15......187 C6
Osborne Mews RH16....87 D4
Osborne Rd
  Brighton BN1..........170 A2
  Petersfield GU32......68 B4
Osborne Villas BN3....191 B6
Osier Rd GU31.........67 F2
Osmonde Cl BN14......186 C4
Osmonde Ct 3 BN14...186 C4
Osmond Gdns BN3.....191 E7
Osmond Rd BN3........191 E7
Osmunda Bank RH19....9 E6
Osmund Cl RH10.......19 E6
Osney Cl RH11........18 C5
Osprey Ct BN17.......204 D8
Osprey Gdns PO22.....201 C7
Osprey Ho 10 BN1.....191 E5
Osprey Quay PO10.....173 C7
Osterley Ho 6 RH12...36 F4
Ostlers View RH14.....79 C7
Otard Ct PO20.........212 E7
Otford Cl RH11........39 C8
Otmers Quay BN18.....160 B2
Ottafield Ct RH16.....87 F6
Ottawa Dr GU31.......25 C3
Otterbourne Pl RH19...9 B1
Otter Cl PO19.........176 E8
Otway Cl RH11........17 F4
Otway Rd PO19........176 E8
Oulton Wlk 9 RH10...19 B4
Our Lady of Lourdes RC
  Prim Sch BN2.........193 F1
Our Lady of Sion Sch
  (Juniors) BN11.......186 D2
Our Lady of Sion Sch
  (Seniors) BN11.......186 C2
Our Lady Queen of Heaven
  RC Sch RH11..........18 B8
Outerwyke Ave PO22...202 A6
Outerwyke Gdns
  PO22................202 A6
Outerwyke Rd PO22....202 B6
Outram Ho PO22.......201 F3
Outram Rd PO22.......201 F3
Outram Way PO20......177 A1

Oval La PO20..........212 E5
Oval The
  Findon BN14..........163 E7
  Liss GU33............45 B4
  Worthing BN13........186 A5
Oval Waye PO20.......206 E4
Overdene Dr RH11......18 A6
Overdown Rd PO22.....202 B5
Overdown Rise BN41....167 F4
Overhill BN42.........167 E1
Overhill Dr BN1.......169 E5
Overhill Gdns BN1.....169 E5
Overhill Way BN1......169 E6
Overmead BN43........188 E8
Over St BN1...........213 B3
Overstrand Ave RH16...205 C4
Overton Ct 4 RH19....9 E1
Overton Rd PO10......152 A1
Overton Shaw RH19....9 E4
Ovingdean Cl BN2.....193 D5
Ovingdean Hall Sch
  BN2.................193 D6
Ovingdean Rd BN2.....193 D5
Owen Cl RH15.........108 F1
Owers Ct RH13........36 E2
Owers Way PO20.......207 E7
Owlbeech Ct RH13.....37 B4
Owlbeech Lo RH13.....37 B4
Owlbeech Pl RH13.....37 B4
Owlbeech Way RH13....37 B4
Owletts RH10.........19 E7
Owlscastle Cl RH12....36 D5
Oxen Ave BN43........188 F8
Oxen Ct BN43.........188 F8
Oxford Cl PO20.......207 F7
Oxford Ct
  Brighton BN1..........213 B4
  7 Midhurst GU29.....94 E7
Oxford Dr PO21.......200 F3
Oxford Mews BN1......191 C7
Oxford Pl BN1........213 B4
Oxford Rd
  Crawley RH10.........18 F2
  Horsham RH13.........36 E2
  Worthing BN11........186 C3
Oxford St
  Bognor Regis PO21.....201 B2
  Brighton BN1..........213 B4
Oxford Terr 8 BN44...145 D3
Oyster Mews 7 PO10...173 B8

P

Pacific Cl 3 BN43....188 F6
Pacific Ho 11 BN16...205 B4
Pacific Way PO20.....212 E6
Packer Cl RH19........10 A3
Packham Way RH15....108 F4
Pack House Cotts
  RH14................53 B3
Paddock Cl GU27......49 A5
Paddock Cl BN41......167 F3
Paddock Field BN1....171 B5
Paddock Gdns RH19....22 E7
Paddock Gn BN16.....205 E6
Paddockhall Rd RH16...87 C5
Paddockhurst La RH17...41 D3
Paddockhurst Rd
  Crawley, Gossops Green
    RH11................18 A5
  Crawley RH10.........20 C2
Paddock La PO20.......212 D8
Paddocks PO22........180 B6
Paddocks The
  Haywards Heath RH16...87 C3
  Lancing BN15..........187 F5
  Upper Beeding BN44....146 B3
Paddock The
  Bognor Regis PO22.....201 C5
  Crawley RH10.........19 D7
  Haslemere GU27........27 A8
  Hove BN3.............169 C1
  Littlehampton BN17....182 C6
  Shoreham-by-S BN43....166 D1
Paddock Way
  Findon BN14..........163 E6
  Liphook GU30.........25 C5
  Petersfield GU32......67 F2
Padstow Wlk RH11.....17 F4
Padua Ho BN2.........193 F8
Padua House Flats
  BN2.................193 F8
Padwick Rd RH13......37 A2
Padwicks Field RH20...99 A3
Page Ct RH13.........36 D1
Pages Cl BN21........187 A3
Pages La BN11........187 A4
Paget Cl RH13........58 E8
PAGEWOOD............4 D7
Pagewood Cl RH10.....19 D4
Pagham Beach Est
  PO21................210 F6
Pagham Cl PO10......173 C8
Pagham Gdns RH11....195 B2
Pagham Harbour Nature
  Reserve* PO20.......210 C6
Pagham Harbour Nature
  Reserve Visitor Ctr*
  PO20................209 F6
Pagham Ho BN17......204 B7
Pagham Rd
  PO21................200 A3

Pain's Flat RH15,
RH17 . . . . 108 D8
Palace Pier* BN2 . . . . . 213 B1
Palace Pl BN1 . . . . 213 B2
Palace Yd PO19 . . . . . . 176 F6
Palatine Rd BN12 . . . . . 185 D5
Palatine Sch BN12 . . . . 185 D6
Palings Way GU27 . . . . . 49 A5
Pallant The BN12 . . . . . 185 B5
Pallingham Dr RH10 . . . 19 C3
Pallingham La RH14 . . . . 77 F2
Palm Court Cotts ⑫
BN16 . . . . 206 A4
Palm Ct
⑦ Hove BN3 . . . . 191 D6
Worthing BN13 . . . . . 185 E8
Palm Dr BN2 . . . . 192 F3
Palmeira Ave BN3 . . . . . 191 D6
Palmeira Avenue Mans ㉕
BN3 . . . . 191 C6
Palmeira Ct BN3 . . . . . . 191 C6
Palmeira Grande ⑨
BN3 . . . . 191 C6
Palmeira Ho ⑥ BN3 . . . 191 D7
Palmeira Mans ㉒
BN3 . . . . 191 D7
Palmeira Pl BN3 . . . . . . 191 D6
Palmeira Sq BN3 . . . . . 191 C6
Palmer Cl
Horley RH6 . . . . 1 F5
Storrington RH20 . . . . 121 F2
Palmer Pl PO20 . . . . . . 177 D1
Palmer Rd
Angmering BN16 . . . . 183 F7
Crawley RH10 . . . . . . 19 C3
Palmers Field Ave
PO19 . . . . 155 B1
Palmer's Rd PO10 . . . . 151 B1
Palmers Rd Ind Est
PO10 . . . . 151 B1
Palmerston Ave BN12 . . 185 C3
Palmers Way BN13 . . . . 163 D1
Pangdean La BN6,
RH15 . . . . 108 C4
Pangdene Cl RH15 . . . . 108 F1
Pankhurst Ave BN2 . . . . 192 D6
Pankhurst Ct ⑪ RH11 . . 18 B1
Pannell Cl RH19 . . . . 9 D5
Pannells Ash RH14 . . . . 31 C3
Pannett RH15 . . . . 108 E4
Pantiles The RH12 . . . . 206 E5
Panton Cl PO10 . . . . . . 151 A3
Parade Mans ⑧
BN16 . . . . 206 A4
Parade The
Bognor Regis PO21 . . . 211 A7
Brighton BN1 . . . . . . 169 B4
Crawley RH10 . . . . . . 18 E7
East Wittering PO20 . . 207 F7
Hove BN3 . . . . 168 E2
⑤ Lancing BN15 . . . . 187 C7
Loxwood RH14 . . . . . 31 F4
Nepcote BN14 . . . . . 163 E5
⑦ West Kingston
BN16 . . . . 206 A4
Paradise La PO10 . . . . 151 D4
PARBROOK 79 C7
Parchment St PO19 . . . 176 F7
Parham Cl
Brighton BN2 . . . . . . 192 D5
Chichester PO19 . . . . 177 C5
Littlehampton, Wick
BN17 . . . . 204 D6
Rustington BN16 . . . . 205 B4
Worthing BN14 . . . . . 163 F1
Parham Ct ⑤ BN1 . . . . 186 A2
Parham Ho ⑬ BN3 . . . 191 D7
Parham House & Gdns*
RH20 . . . . 120 D1
Parham Rd
Crawley RH11 . . . . . . 17 F7
Worthing BN14 . . . . . 163 F1
Parish Ho ⑧ RH11 . . . . 18 D5
Parish La RH10, RH11 . . 39 E6
Park Apartments The
BN1 . . . . 169 D4
Park Ave
Hove BN3 . . . . 190 E7
Keymer BN6 . . . . 129 A2
Selsey PO20 . . . . . . 212 F7
Shoreham-by-S BN43 . . 189 A8
Worthing BN11 . . . . . 186 E3
Park Cl
Brighton BN1 . . . . . . 170 E5
Burgess Hill RH15 . . . 108 F4
Hove BN3 . . . . 168 E3
Hurstpierpoint BN6 . . 128 A6
Portslade-by-S BN41 . . 168 B5
Worthing BN14 . . . . . 186 A7
Park Copse PO20 . . . . 210 C1
Park Cotts BN6 . . . . . . 127 F6
Park Cres
Brighton BN2 . . . . . . 213 C4
Emsworth PO10 . . . . 151 A1
Midhurst GU29 . . . . . 94 E8
Portslade-by-S BN41 . . 190 A8
Rottingdean BN2 . . . . 193 F1
Selsey PO20 . . . . . . 212 G8
Worthing BN11 . . . . . 186 E4
Park Crescent Pl BN2 . . 213 C4
Park Crescent Rd
BN2 . . . . 213 C4
Park Crescent Terr
BN2 . . . . 213 C4
Park Ct
⑪ Brighton BN2 . . . . 192 C6
Brighton, Patcham BN1 . 169 E6
Brighton, Preston BN1 . 169 F1

Park Ct continued
Burgess Hill RH15 . . . 109 A3
④ Haywards Heath
RH16 . . . . 87 E4
Hove BN3 . . . . 191 D7
⑧ Petersfield GU32 . . 68 B3
Park Dr
Bognor Regis PO22 . . . 202 D5
Ferring BN12 . . . . . . 206 F6
Rustington BN16 . . . . 205 D6
Yapton BN18 . . . . . . 181 A2
Park E RH16 . . . . 87 F2
Parker Cl RH10 . . . . . . 19 D5
Park Ct BN41 . . . . 168 B2
Parkers RH13 . . . . 186 A4
Parker's Cotts PO18 . . 155 A6
Park Farm Ct RH12 . . . 36 D7
Park Farm Cotts
BN18 . . . . 159 E3
Park Farm Rd RH12 . . . 36 D7
Parkfield RH12 . . . . . . 36 C3
Parkfield Ave PO21 . . . 200 D3
Parkfield Cl RH11 . . . . 17 F6
Parkfield Ct BN13 . . . . 186 A4
Parkfield Rd BN13 . . . . 186 A4
Parkfield Way RH16 . . . 87 C3
Park Gate
④ Brighton BN1 . . . . 191 F8
Hove BN3 . . . . 191 D6
Parkhaven Ct ⑦
BN15 . . . . 187 E6
Park Hill BN2 . . . . 213 C2
Park Ho
Burstow RH6 . . . . 6 F6
⑥ Worthing BN11 . . . 187 B3
Parkhurst Gr RH6 . . . . . 1 F4
Parkhurst Rd RH6 . . . . . 1 F4
Park La
Aldingbourne PO20 . . . 179 B7
Ashurst Wood RH19 . . . 23 D6
Henfield GU27 . . . . . . 49 B1
Halnaker PO18 . . . . . 156 D5
Heath Common RH20 . . 122 D5
Lindfield RH16 . . . . . . 64 D2
Maplehurst RH13 . . . . 83 B6
Selsey PO20 . . . . . . 210 A1
Slindon BN18 . . . . . . 158 C4
Southwick BN42 . . . . 189 D7
Westbourne PO10,
PO18 . . . . 151 E8
West Grinstead RH13 . . 104 D8
Parkland Bsns Ctr
BN15 . . . . 187 D4
Parklands BN43 . . . . . 189 C8
Parklands Ave
Bognor Regis PO21 . . . 201 B4
Worthing BN12 . . . . . 185 D3
Parklands Com Prim Sch
PO19 . . . . 176 E7
Parklands Ct BN12 . . . 185 D3
Parklands Rd
Chichester PO19 . . . . 176 F7
Hassocks BN6 . . . . . . 128 F3
Parklawn Ave RH6 . . . . . 1 F5
Park Lo BN3 . . . . 191 D8
Park Manor BN1 . . . . . 169 D3
Parkmead BN2 . . . . . . 213 C4
Parkmore Terr BN1 . . . 213 A5
Park Par RH16 . . . . 87 E4
Park Pl
Arundel BN18 . . . . . . 160 A3
⑦ Horsham RH12 . . . 36 C1
Park Rd
Barnham PO22 . . . . . 180 D6
Bognor Regis PO21 . . . 201 B2
Breach PO10 . . . . . . 151 F1
Brighton BN1 . . . . . . 170 E5
Burgess Hill RH15 . . . 109 A3
Burstow RH9 . . . . 7 C8
Dormans Park RH19 . . . 9 F6
East Grinstead RH19 . . . 9 D1
Faygate RH12 . . . . . . 16 F1
Forest Row RH18 . . . . 23 F2
Goodwood Park PO18 . 155 F8
Handcross RH17 . . . . 61 B6
Haslemere GU27 . . . . 27 C5
Haywards Heath RH16 . . 87 E4
Henfield BN5 . . . . . . 125 C4
③ Petersfield GU31 . . 68 B3
Petworth GU28 . . . . . 97 F8
Rottingdean BN2 . . . . 193 F1
Selsey PO20 . . . . . . 212 G8
Shoreham-by-S BN43 . . 189 B8
Slinfold RH13 . . . . . . 34 D3
Worthing BN11 . . . . . 186 E3
Yapton BN18 . . . . . . 181 A2
Park Rise
Horsham RH12 . . . . . 36 B4
Hove BN3 . . . . 168 E3
⑧ Petersfield GU32 . . 68 B3
Park Road Terr ④
BN2 . . . . 213 C2
Park Royal BN1 . . . . . 191 E6
Parkside
⑩ Bognor Regis
PO21 . . . . 201 D4
Burgess Hill RH15 . . . 108 F3
Crawley RH10 . . . . . . 18 E6
East Grinstead RH19 . . . 9 C1
Keymer BN6 . . . . 129 A2
Shoreham-by-S BN43 . . 167 A1
Worthing BN11 . . . . . 186 E3
Parkside Ave BN17 . . . 204 F5
Parkside Ct BN17 . . . . 204 F5
Parkside Mews RH12 . . 36 D2
Park Sq BN2 . . . . 192 F3
Park St
Brighton BN2 . . . . . . 213 C2

Park St continued
Falmer BN1 . . . . 171 C6
Horsham RH12 . . . . . 36 D2
Slinfold RH13 . . . . . . 34 C3
Parks The BN41 . . . . . 168 B3
PARK STREET 34 C4
Park Terr
Bognor Regis PO21 . . . 201 B2
Rottingdean BN2 . . . . 193 F1
Tillington GU28 . . . . . 75 C1
Park Terr E RH13 . . . . . 36 D1
Park Terr W RH13 . . . . . 36 D1
Park The BN2 . . . . 194 A1
Parkview BN6 . . . . 128 A5
Park View
Brighton BN2 . . . . . . 192 C6
Brighton, Preston BN1 . 191 E8
Crawley RH11 . . . . . . 18 C5
Haywards Heath RH16 . . 87 E6
Horley RH6 . . . . 2 A3
Park View Cl BN3 . . . . 169 B1
Park View La RH16 . . . 205 C6
Park View Terr BN1 . . . 191 E8
Park View Rd BN1 . . . . 169 B1
Park Village The BN1 . . 171 B8
Park W RH16 . . . . 87 F2
Parkway
Bognor Regis PO21 . . . 201 A3
Crawley RH10 . . . . . . 19 C7
Horley RH6 . . . . 2 A3
Park Way
Horsham RH12 . . . . . 36 C2
Midhurst GU29 . . . . . 73 B2
Southwick BN42 . . . . 189 F8
Park Way Cl BN42 . . . . 189 F8
Parkway Ho ② BN42 . . 36 C1
Parkway The BN1 . . . . 205 D5
Parnell Cl RH10 . . . . . 19 D4
Parnell Ct ③ BN3 . . . . 191 B6
Parochial Terr BN2 . . . 213 B2
Parry Cl RH13 . . . . 37 C4
Parry Dr BN16 . . . . . . 205 B5
Parsonage Bsns Pk
RH12 . . . . 36 E4
Parsonage Cl GU32 . . . 68 D5
Parsonage Est GU31 . . 70 B4
Parsonage Rd
Henfield BN5 . . . . . . 125 E6
Horsham RH12, RH13 . 36 E4
Worthing BN12 . . . . . 36 E1
Parsons Cl
Angmering BN16 . . . . 206 A8
Haslemere GU27 . . . . 27 C8
Horley RH6 . . . . 1 E4
Parsons Gn GU27 . . . . 27 C8
Parson's Hill BN18 . . . 160 B3
Parsons Wlk
Horsham RH12 . . . . . 57 F8
Walberton BN18 . . . . 180 E8
Parthings La RH12,
RH13 . . . . 57 F8
Partridge Green Rd
RH13 . . . . 105 C3
Partridge La RH5, RH12 . . 3 F3
Partridge Pl RH10 . . . . 21 C6
Pascoe Ct ② PO19 . . . 176 F7
Pashley Ct ⑩ BN43 . . 188 F7
Passfield Ent Ctr GU30 . 24 E8
Passfield Rd GU30 . . . . 24 E8
Paston Ho ⑤ BN1 . . . 191 F8
Paston Pl BN2 . . . . . . 192 D4
Pasture Hill Rd RH16 . . 87 D6
Pasture The RH10 . . . . 19 C6
Patcham By-Pass
BN1 . . . . 169 E6
Patcham Grange BN1 . . 169 E5
Patcham High Sch
BN1 . . . . 169 F6
Patcham House Special
Sch BN1 . . . . 169 E6
Patcham Inf Sch BN1 . . 169 E6
Patcham Jun Sch
BN1 . . . . 169 F6
Patcham Pl BN1 . . . . . 169 F5
Patching Cl
Crawley RH11 . . . . . . 17 F7
Worthing BN12 . . . . . 185 B5
Patchings RH13 . . . . . 36 F3
Paterson Wilson Rd
BN17 . . . . 204 E6
Pathfield Cl RH12 . . . . 33 D7
Pathfield Rd RH12 . . . . 33 D7
Pathfields GU27 . . . . . 27 D7
Pathfields Cl GU27 . . . 27 D7
Path Link RH10 . . . . . . 18 E7
Patricia Ave BN12 . . . . 185 D2
Patricia Cl BN12 . . . . . 185 D2
Patrick's Cl GU33 . . . . 45 C4
Patrick's Copse Rd
GU33 . . . . 45 C4
Patrington Cl RH11 . . . 18 A3
Patterdale Cl RH11 . . . 18 C4
Paulus Ct ① PO19 . . . 176 F7
Pavement The RH10 . . 18 E6
Pavilion Bldgs BN1 . . . 213 B2
Pavilion Cl BN6 . . . . . 128 E5
Pavilion Ct
⑱ Brighton BN1 . . . . 191 E7
⑧ Brighton BN2 . . . . 213 B2
Pavilion Mews BN1 . . . 213 B2
Pavilion Par BN2 . . . . 213 B2
Pavilion Rd
Falmer BN1 . . . . 171 C4
Worthing BN14 . . . . . 186 B3
Pavilion Ret Pk BN2 . . 170 C1
Pavilion St BN2 . . . . . 213 B2
Pavilion Way RH19 . . . 10 B8
Pavilions The RH11 . . . 39 C6

Pavilion Way RH19 . . . . 22 E8
Pax Cl RH11 . . . . 17 E4
Paxmead Cres BN14 . . 186 F6
Pay Gate RH20 . . . . . . 143 E7
Payne Ave BN3 . . . . . . 190 F8
Payne Cl
Bognor Regis PO21 . . . 211 A8
Crawley RH10 . . . . . . 19 D8
Paynesfield RH17 . . . . 85 C3
PAYNES GREEN 14 D8
Paynes Green Cotts
RH5 . . . . 14 C8
Payne Terr BN1 . . . . . . 170 B1
Paythorne Cl BN42 . . . 167 D1
Paythorne Dro BN5 . . . 147 D4
Payton Dr RH15 . . . . . 108 F2
Peace Cl BN1 . . . . 170 C1
Peacemaker Cl RH11 . . 17 E4
Peace Rd GU29 . . . . . . 95 A2
Peacheries The PO19 . . 177 C5
Peachey Ho GU29 . . . . 94 E7
Peachey Rd PO20 . . . . 212 D6
Peacock Cl PO19 . . . . 155 C1
Peacock Ind Est BN3 . . 191 D7
Peacock La RH11 . . . . 18 D7
Peacocks RH13 . . . . . 105 A3
Peacock's Hill RH13 . . 83 D6
Peacocks La RH20 . . . 102 C1
Peacock Wlk ⑥ RH11 . . 18 A3
Peak La BN16 . . . . . . 206 C4
Peak The PO9 . . . . . . 130 E2
Pearman Ct PO18 . . . . 135 D7
Pears Gr PO10 . . . . . . 173 F8
Pearson Rd
Arundel BN18 . . . . . . 159 F2
Crawley RH10 . . . . . . 19 C6
Pearsons Retreat ⑩
BN11 . . . . 187 B3
Peartree Cl RH15 . . . . 108 C3
Peartree Cnr RH13 . . . 83 C2
Pear Tree Hill RH1 . . . . 2 A8
Peary Cl RH12 . . . . . . 35 C6
Pease Croft GU31 . . . . 91 D3
Pease Pottage Hill
RH11 . . . . 18 D1
Pebble Cotts PO21 . . . 200 B3
Pebble Ct PO22 . . . . . 201 E5
Pebble Wlk BN17 . . . . 205 A7
Peckhams Copse La
PO20 . . . . 177 D3
Peeks Brook La
Crawley RH6 . . . . 6 E7
Horley RH6 . . . . 2 F2
Peel Cl BN17 . . . . 204 C6
Peel Rd BN2 . . . . 192 F4
Peerley Cl PO20 . . . . . 208 A6
Peerley Rd PO20 . . . . 208 A6
Pegasus Cl GU27 . . . . 26 D5
Pegasus Ct
Chichester PO19 . . . . 176 F6
Crawley RH11 . . . . . . 17 F8
Rustington BN16 . . . . 205 C5
Pegasus Rd RH10 . . . . . 6 A1
Pegasus Way RH19 . . . 10 B3
Pegler Way RH11 . . . . 18 D6
Pegwell Ct RH11 . . . . . 17 F4
Pelham Cl
② Brighton BN2 . . . . 170 C1
⑧ Horsham RH12 . . . 36 C1
⑥ Worthing BN13 . . . 186 A5
Pelham Ct Bsns Ctr
RH11 . . . . 18 B2
Pelham Dr RH11 . . . . . 18 A2
Pelham Pl RH11 . . . . . 18 A2
Pelham Place Cotts
RH16 . . . . 88 A7
Pelham Rd
Lindfield RH16 . . . . . . 88 A6
Worthing BN13 . . . . . 186 A5
Pelham Sq BN1 . . . . . 213 B3
Pelham St BN1 . . . . . . 213 B3
Pelham Terr
① Brighton BN2 . . . . 170 C1
Emsworth PO10 . . . . 173 C8
Pelleys La PO20 . . . . . 186 E2
Pemberton Cl BN15 . . . 187 E7
Pembley Gn RH10 . . . . . 7 E3
Pembroke Ave
Hove BN3 . . . . 191 A7
Worthing BN13 . . . . . 185 F3
Pembroke Cres BN3 . . 191 A7
Pembroke Ct ② BN3 . . 191 A6
Pembroke Gdns BN3 . . 191 A6
Pembroke Rd PO19 . . . 176 E1
Pembroke Way PO21 . . 200 E4
Pembury Cl
Haywards Heath RH16 . . 88 B3
Worthing BN14 . . . . . 186 D4
Pembury Rd BN14 . . . . 186 D4
Penarth Gdns BN17 . . 182 C5
Pendean Cl RH15 . . . . 109 C1
Pende Cl BN15 . . . . . . 187 D8
Pendine Ave BN11 . . . 187 A2
Pendragon Ct BN3 . . . 191 A8
Penfold La BN16 . . . . . 205 C7
Penfold Manor GU27 . . 27 D6
Penfold Rd
Crawley RH10 . . . . . . 19 D3
Penfolds Pl ⑨ BN1 . . . 160 A2
Penfold Way BN44 . . . 145 D2
Penhill Cl ④ BN15 . . . 187 E5
Penhill Rd BN15 . . . . . 187 E5
Penhurst Cl
Worthing BN13 . . . . . 185 B6

Penhurst Ct continued
Worthing, Broadwater
BN14 . . . . 186 C6
Penhurst Pl BN2 . . . . . 192 F6
Penland Cl RH16 . . . . . 87 D7
Penland Ct BN3 . . . . . 145 D2
Penland Rd RH16 . . . . 87 D7
Penland's Cl BN44 . . . 145 C2
Penlands Rise BN44 . . 145 C2
Penlands Vale BN44 . . 145 C2
Penlands Way BN44 . . 145 C2
Penleigh Cl BN15 . . . . 187 F5
Penn Cl
Crawley RH11 . . . . 5 D1
Middleton-on-S PO22 . 202 C5
Penn Cres RH14 . . . . . 88 A5
Pennells Cl GU30 . . . . 47 B2
Pennett Ho RH16 . . . . 87 D2
Penn Gdns RH20 . . . . 122 E5
Pennine Cl RH11 . . . . 18 B6
Pennington Ho RH16 . . 88 A3
Penns Cl BN44 . . . . . 145 C4
Penns Rd GU31 . . . . . 68 A5
Penns Rd GU32 . . . . . 68 A4
Pennthorpe Sch RH12 . 33 D7
Penny Cl ⑤ GU32 . . . 68 B3
Pennycord Cl PO20 . . 212 E5
Pennycress Ave BN13 . 185 A6
Pennyfields PO22 . . . . 202 C5
Penny La PO10 . . . . . 173 D8
Penny Rd BN14 . . . . . 186 D5
Pensford La RH14 . . . . 33 E5
Penshurst Cl RH10 . . . 19 D7
Penstone Cl BN15 . . . 187 E6
Penstone Ct ④ BN43 . . 189 C8
Penstone Pk BN15 . . . 187 E6
Pentland Rd BN13 . . . 185 E8
Penwarden Way
PO18 . . . . 175 C7
Penwith Dr GU27 . . . . 26 C5
Peperham Cotts GU27 . 27 C7
Peperham Ho GU27 . . 27 C7
Peppard Rd RH10 . . . . 19 D3
Pepper Ct BN17 . . . . . 204 C5
Pepper Dr RH15 . . . . . 108 F1
Peppering La BN18 . . . 161 A7
Pepperscoombe La
BN44 . . . . 146 B2
Peppersgate RH13 . . . 84 A7
Pepper's La BN44 . . . . 124 C5
Perche Cl GU29 . . . . . 94 D6
Perching Dro BN5 . . . . 147 E4
Percival Mans ㉐
BN2 . . . . 192 D4
Percival Terr ⑭ BN2 . . 192 D4
Percy Cotts RH17 . . . . 86 F8
Percy Rd BN2 . . . . 36 B3
Percy Terr GU28 . . . . . 97 F8
Percy & Wagner
Almshouses ⑤ BN2 . 213 C4
Peregrine Rd BN17 . . . 204 F6
Perimeter Rd E RH6 . . . 6 B6
Perimeter Rd N RH6 . . . 5 D8
Perimeter Rd S RH6,
RH11 . . . . 5 E5
Perkstead Ct ⑥ RH11 . . 18 A3
Perrots La BN44 . . . . . 145 C2
Perry Ave RH19 . . . . . . 9 E3
Perryfield Ho ⑦ RH10 . 18 D5
Perryfield Rd RH11 . . . 84 C6
Perryfield Rd RH11 . . . 18 D5
Perryfields RH15 . . . . 108 E4
Perry Hill BN2 . . . . . . 194 C3
Perrylands RH6 . . . . . . 4 F7
Perrylands La RH6 . . . . 2 F2
Perryman's La RH17 . . 66 D3
Perrymount Rd RH16 . . 87 E5
Perth Cl RH11 . . . . 5 D1
Perth Ho GU29 . . . . . . 94 E6
Perth Way RH12 . . . . . 36 F4
Pescott's Cl PO20 . . . 197 E5
Peskett Cl RH13 . . . . . 56 F2
Peterborough Rd RH10 . 18 E2
Peter Gladwin Prim Sch
BN41 . . . . 168 B2
Peterhouse Ct PO21 . . 200 F4
Peterhouse Par RH10 . . 6 C1
Peterlee Wlk RH10 . . . 17 E2
Peter Rd BN15 . . . . . . 187 F5
Peters Cl RH13 . . . . . . 82 A6
Petersfield Bsns Pk
GU32 . . . . 67 F3
Petersfield Hospl
GU32 . . . . 68 A3
Petersfield Inf Sch
GU32 . . . . 68 B3
Petersfield Mus*
GU32 . . . . 68 B3
Petersfield Sch The
GU32 . . . . 68 A2
Petersfield Sta GU32 . . 68 A4
Peter's La PO20 . . . . . 212 A8
Peter's Pl PO20 . . . . . 212 A8
Peter Weston Pl
PO19 . . . . 177 B6
Petland Ho RH16 . . . . 87 F3
Petlands Rd RH16 . . . . 87 E3
Pett Cl BN2 . . . . 192 F6
Petts Cl PO20 . . . . . . 209 F1
Petworth Ave BN12 . . 185 C1
Petworth CE Prim Sch
GU28 . . . . 97 F7

Petworth Cottage Mus★
GU28 . . . . .97 F8
Petworth Ct
Billingshurst RH14. . . . . . . .79 D7
Crawley RH11 . . . . .17 F3
Haslemere GU27 . . . . .27 D6
5 Rustington BN16 . . . . .205 B3
Petworth Dr
Burgess Hill RH15 . . . . .109 A4
Horsham RH12 . . . . .36 F7
Petworth Ho **14** BN2 . . . .191 D7
Petworth Ho★ GU28 . . . . .97 F7
Petworth Park★ GU28. . . . .75 D2
Pevensey Cl RH10 . . . . .19 C5
Pevensey Gdns BN11. . . . .186 A1
Pevensey Rd
Bognor Regis PO21 . . . . . .201 A4
7 Brighton BN2 . . . . . . .192 C8
Southwater RH13 . . . . .58 A2
Worthing BN11 . . . . .186 A1
Peverel Ct GU30 . . . . .25 B5
Peverel Rd
Crawley RH11 . . . . .17 C5
Worthing BN14 . . . . .186 A4
Peveril Cl BN15. . . . . .187 B6
Peveril Dr BN15. . . . . .187 B6
Pharos Quay BN17 . . . . . .204 C5
Pheasant Cotts PO18 . . .134 F6
Philip Ct
Bognor Regis PO21 . . . . . .200 C3
3 Hove BN3. . . . . .191 C7
Phillips Cl RH10 . . . . .19 C2
Philliswood La PO18. . . . .112 D3
PHILPOTS 42 C5
Philpots Manor Sch
RH19 .42 C5
Phoenix Brewery Halls
BN2 .213 C4
Phoenix Bsns Ctr
PO19 . . . . .177 C5
Phoenix Cl
Chichester PO19 . . . . .177 A5
Littlehampton BN17. . . . . .204 A5
Phoenix Cres BN42 . . . . . .189 D8
Phoenix Ct PO21. . . . . .201 C3
Phoenix Ho **7** BN14 . . . .186 D3
Phoenix La RH19 . . . . .23 E6
Phoenix Pl BN2 . . . . .213 C3
Phoenix Rise BN2 . . . . . . .213 C3
Phoenix Terr RH19. . . . . . .23 E6
Phoenix Way BN42 . . . . . .189 D8
Phrosso Rd BN11. . . . . . . .185 F2
Pickers Gn RH16. . . . . .88 A8
PICKETTS 2 C8
Picketts La RH11 . . . . .2 C8
PICKHURST 100 A6
Pickhurst La RH20. . . . . . .100 B6
Pickhurst Rd GU8. . . . . .26 D7
Pickwell La RH17. . . . . .85 F4
Picton St BN2 . . . . .192 C7
Picts Hill RH13 . . . . .58 A7
Picts La RH13 . . . . .84 A4
Pierces La **7** RH16 . . . . . .87 C2
Pier Five Rd **6** BN6 . . . . . .5 E8
Pier Four Rd N RH6 . . . . . . .5 F8
Pierpoint Cl BN6 . . . . .127 F6
Pier Rd BN17 . . . . .204 D4
Piers Secombe Cl
RH20 . . . . .119 D5
Pigbush La RH14 . . . . .32 A7
Pigeonhouse La BN16. . .205 E4
Pigeon Pass RH10 . . . . .21 C5
Piggery Hall La PO20 . . . .196 F1
Pike The RH20 . . . . .143 F7
Pilgrim Ct PO19 . . . . .177 B7
Pilgrims Cl **1** BN14. . . . . .186 B3
Pilgrims Terr BN13. . . . . . .186 A3
Pilgrims Way PO21 . . . . . .200 B1
Pilgrims Wlk BN13. . . . . . .186 A3
Pilot Ho **1** BN2 . . . . .213 C2
Piltdown Rd BN2 . . . . .192 F6
Pine Cl
Billingshurst RH14. . . . . . . .55 C1
Crawley RH11 . . . . .5 C1
Heath Common RH20 . . . .122 B2
Midhurst GU29 . . . . .94 F5
Pine Cotts GU33 . . . . .45 C7
Pine Ct PO10 . . . . .151 B4
Pine Gdns RH6 . . . . .2 A2
Pine Gr
Chichester PO19 . . . . .154 C1
East Grinstead RH19 . . . . . . .9 B3
Pineham Copse RH16 . . . .87 F4
Pinehurst
Burgess Hill RH15 . . . . . . .109 A4
Horsham RH12 . . . . .36 C4
Pinehurst Pk PO21. . . . . . .200 D4
Pine Shaw RH14. . . . . .186 D7
Pine Shaw RH10 . . . . .19 D7
Pines Rd GU30 . . . . .24 E4
Pines The
Angmering BN16 . . . . .205 F8
2 Brighton BN2 . . . . . . .213 C4
Crawley RH10 . . . . .19 D6
Haywards Heath RH16 . . . .98 B7
Horsham RH12 . . . . .37 C5
Hove BN3. . . . . .191 E6
Hurstpierpoint BN6 . . . . . .127 F7
Littlehampton BN17. . . . . .204 D6
Yapton BN18. . . . . .180 F3

Pine Tree Cl BN6 . . . . .128 B5
Pine Trees BN6 . . . . .128 D4
Pinetrees Cl RH10 . . . . .7 B3
Pine Trees Cl RH16 . . . . . .183 F7
Pine Trees Cl BN6 . . . . . . .128 D4
Pine View Cl GU27 . . . . . . .27 C8
Pine Way Cl RH19 . . . . .22 E7
Pine Wlk
Bognor Regis PO21 . . . . . .200 D4
Liss GU33 . . . . .45 C6
Pinewood **6** BN1. . . . . . .169 E3
Pinewood Cl
Brighton BN1. . . . . .169 D2
Broadbridge Heath RH12 . . .35 D3
East Preston BN16 . . . . . . .206 A6
Pinewood Ct
Haywards Heath RH16 . . . .87 D2
West Lavington GU29 . . . . . .95 A6
Pinewood Gdns PO21 . . .201 A3
Pinewood Ho PO19 . . . . . .155 B1
Pinewood Way
Haywards Heath RH16 . . . .87 D2
Midhurst GU29 . . . . .94 E5
Pinfold **4** RH16 . . . . .87 D6
Pinfold Cl BN2 . . . . .193 E6
Pinkhurst La RH13. . . . . . . .35 A2
Pinks La PO20 . . . . .197 D3
Pinland Rd RH13 . . . . .104 F1
Pipers Cl
Hove BN3. . . . . .168 C3
Southwater RH13 . . . . .57 F1
Pipers End RH13. . . . . .34 E3
Pipers La
Balls Cross GU28. . . . . .52 A4
Northchapel GU28 . . . . .51 A7
Pipers Mead PO20 . . . . . .197 D3
Piries Pl RH13 . . . . .36 C2
Pitcroft La GU31 . . . . .90 B5
Pitcroft The PO19. . . . . . . .177 C8
Pitfold Ave GU27 . . . . .26 D6
Pitfold Cl GU27 . . . . .26 E6
Pit La BN6 . . . . .128 A5
Pitsham La GU29 . . . . .94 D5
Pitsham Wood GU29. . . . . .94 D6
Pitt Ct BN6. . . . . .128 A5
Pitt Gdns BN2 . . . . .193 D7
Place St Maur Des Fosses
PO21 . . . . .201 D2
Plainfields Ave BN1. . . . . .170 A7
Plainwood Cl PO19 . . . . . .154 F2
Plaistow Dr BN2 . . . . .192 F6
Plaistow Rd
Chiddingfold GU8. . . . . .29 D6
Dunsfold GU8 . . . . .30 B7
Ifold RH14. . . . . .31 D1
Kirdford RH14 . . . . .53 B5
Plantain Cres RH11 . . . . . . .18 A2
Plantation E **2** BN13. . . . .185 F8
Plantation Rd GU33 . . . . . .45 D2
Plantation Rise BN13 . . . .186 A7
Plantation The
Cootham RH20. . . . . .121 B1
East Preston BN16 . . . . . . .206 A5
Horne RH7. . . . . .8 C7
Worthing BN13 . . . . .186 A7
Plantation Way
Storrington RH20 . . . . .121 C1
3 Worthing BN13. . . . . .185 F8
Plat The RH12 . . . . .36 A3
Platts Mdw RH14 . . . . .79 C8
Platts Rdbt RH14 . . . . .79 C8
Platt The
Dormansland RH7 . . . . .10 A8
Handcross RH17 . . . . .61 C8
Haywards Heath RH16 . . . .88 B5
Plaw Hatch La RH18,
RH19 .43 E5
Playden Ct **1** BN2 . . . . . .192 E4
Playden Ct **3** BN11. . . . . . .18 A3
Playing Field Cl GU27 . . . .27 C8
Plaza Ct BN11 . . . . .186 C1
Pleasant La PO10 . . . . .173 F1
Plough Cl RH11 . . . . .17 F8
Plough La RH12 . . . . .36 E5
Plover Cl
Bognor Regis PO22 . . . . . .201 C7
Bracklesham PO20 . . . . . .208 A6
Crawley RH11 . . . . .18 C8
Plovers Rd RH13 . . . . .36 F3
Plovers The BN15 . . . . . . .188 A5
Plummerden La RH16. . . . .64 F2
Plumpton Rd BN2 . . . . . . .192 D6
Plum Pudding Cnr
GU28 .98 D6
Plumtree Cross RH13 . . . . .57 A5
Plumtree Cross La
RH13 .57 A5
Plymouth Ave BN2. . . . . . .170 F1
Poels Ct RH19 . . . . .9 E2
Polecat La RH13. . . . . .82 C8
Poles La RH11. . . . . .5 C3
Polestub La RH17. . . . . .86 F7
Policemans La BN6 . . . . . .127 F5
POLING 183 B6
Poling Cl BN12 . . . . .185 B5
Poling St BN18 . . . . .183 B7
Pollard Ct BN11 . . . . .186 A2
Pollards RH11 . . . . .18 A5
Pollards Dr RH13 . . . . .36 F2
Pollards Hill RH13 . . . . .82 A6
POLLINGFOLD 12 F5
Polperro Cl BN12. . . . . . . .185 C6
Pomper La BN6 . . . . .108 A2
Pompeys Terr BN44 . . . . . .145 C4

Pond Cl
Billingshurst RH14. . . . . . . .79 C8
Loxwood RH14 . . . . .32 A4
Pond Copse La RH14. . . . . .31 F5
Pondcroft Rd RH16 . . . . . . .88 B7
Pond Farm RH13. . . . . .57 F3
Pondfield Rd RH12 . . . . . . .33 E8
Pond La BN13 . . . . .185 D8
Pond Mews BN13 . . . . . . .185 D8
Pond Rd
Bracklesham PO20 . . . . . .208 B6
Shoreham-by-S BN43. . . .188 F7
Pond Rise RH20 . . . . .101 E1
Pondside RH10 . . . . .87 C3
Pondtail Cl RH12 . . . . .36 D6
Pondtail Copse RH12 . . . . .36 D6
Pondtail Dr RH12 . . . . .36 D7
Pondtail Pk RH12 . . . . .36 D6
Pondtail Rd RH12 . . . . .36 D6
Pond Way RH19 . . . . .10 B1
Pond Wood Rd RH10. . . . . .19 A8
Pony Farm BN14. . . . . .163 F6
Pookbourne La BN6 . . . . .107 E4
Pook La PO18 . . . . .155 A5
Pool Pas BN1 . . . . .213 B1
Pool Valley BN2. . . . . .213 B1
Popes Ct BN2 . . . . .170 B1
Popes Mead GU27 . . . . . . .27 C7
Poplar Ave BN3. . . . . .168 E3
Poplar Cl
Brighton BN1. . . . . .169 F2
Crawley RH11 . . . . .5 C1
Hove BN3. . . . . .168 E3
Poplar Ct
Pulborough RH20. . . . . . . .100 A2
Worthing BN13 . . . . .185 C6
Poplar Mews
12 Haywards Heath
RH16. . . . . .87 C2
Selsey PO20. . . . . .212 E8
Poplar Rd BN13 . . . . .185 C6
Poplars Cl RH15 . . . . .108 E3
Poplars The
Cudworth RH5 . . . . .3 E8
Ferring BN12. . . . . .206 E4
Horsham RH13 . . . . .36 E3
Keymer BN6. . . . . .129 A3
Littlehampton BN17. . . . . .204 F7
Yapton BN18. . . . . .181 A3
Poplar Way GU29 . . . . .94 E5
Poplar Wlk GU31 . . . . .68 A1
Poppy Cl
Rustington BN17 . . . . .205 A7
Southwater Street RH13. . .58 A3
Porchester Cl RH13. . . . . . .58 A2
PORTFIELD 177 D6
Portfield Ave BN1 . . . . . . .170 A6
Portfield Com Prim Sch
PO19 . . . . .177 C7
Portfield Pl PO19 . . . . .177 C7
Portfield Ret Pk
PO19 . . . . .177 D7
Portfield Trad Ctr
PO19 . . . . .177 D5
Portfield Way PO19 . . . . . .177 D8
Port Hall Ave BN1. . . . . . . .191 E8
Port Hall Mews BN1 . . . . .191 E8
Port Hall Pl BN1. . . . . .191 E8
Port Hall Rd BN1 . . . . .191 E8
Port Hall St BN1. . . . . .191 E8
Portland Ave BN3. . . . . . . .190 E7
Portland Bsns Pk
BN3 .190 E8
Portland Cl RH17 . . . . .205 A6
Portland Ho **5** RH19. . . . .22 F8
Portland La BN3 . . . . .190 D7
Portland Mews **19**
BN2 .192 C4
Portland Pl **1** BN2 . . . . . .192 C4
Portland Rd
Burgess Hill RH15 . . . . . . .108 F3
East Grinstead RH19 . . . . . .22 F8
Hove BN3. . . . . .190 E7
Worthing BN11 . . . . .186 D2
Portland Road Trad Est
BN3 .190 D8
Portland's Cl GU32 . . . . . . .68 D5
Portland Sq
Liss GU33 . . . . .45 B4
Worthing BN11 . . . . .186 D2
Portland St BN1. . . . . .213 A2
Portland Villas BN3 . . . . . .190 D7
Portside BN2 . . . . .192 F3
Portslade Com Coll
BN41 . . . . .168 A1
Portslade Com Coll
(Lower) BN41 . . . . .168 A3
Portslade Inf Sch
BN41 . . . . .190 B8
Portslade Sta BN3 . . . . . . .190 C8
Portsmouth La RH16 . . . . .87 F8
Portsmouth Rd
Bramshott GU26, GU30. . . .25 E6
Liphook GU30 . . . . .25 B2
Portsmouth Wood
RH16. . . . . .87 F8
Portsmouth Wood Cl
RH16 .87 F8
Portsmouth Wood Dr
RH16. . . . . .87 F8
Portway BN44 . . . . .145 C2
Posthorses RH20 . . . . .123 A4
Post Office La PO20 . . . . . .177 D1
Post View RH20. . . . . .142 E8
Pot La BN13 . . . . .184 E7
Potnore PO18 . . . . .154 E7
Potters Cnr RH18 . . . . .152 E1
Potters Croft RH13 . . . . . . .36 E2

Pottersfield RH10. . . . . .18 D7
Potters Field GU33 . . . . . . .45 C4
Potters Gn RH13. . . . . .83 E2
Potters La RH15 . . . . .108 F1
Potters Mead RH21 . . . . . .204 C7
Potters Pl RH12 . . . . .36 C2
Pottery La PO18 . . . . .174 D8
Poulner Ct PO22. . . . . .202 A5
Poulter's Cnr BN14 . . . . . .186 A6
Poulter's La BN14 . . . . . . .186 B6
Pound Cl
Loxwood RH14 . . . . .31 F5
Petworth GU28 . . . . .97 F7
Pound Cnr
Shipley RH13 . . . . .103 D7
Warnham RH12 . . . . .14 E2
Pound Cotts GU29 . . . . . . .73 A1
Pound Farm Rd PO19 . . . .177 C6
Poundfield La RH14 . . . . . . .31 B3
Pound Gate BN6. . . . . .128 D3
POUND HILL 19 C8
Pound Hill Jun & Inf Schs
RH10 .19 C7
Pound Hill Par RH10. . . . . .19 C7
Pound Hill Pl RH10 . . . . . . .19 C8
Pound La
Mannings Heath RH13. . . . .59 C6
Shipley RH13 . . . . .81 D1
Upper Beeding BN44 . . . . .146 B2
Pound Rd
Walberton BN18 . . . . .158 D1
West Wittering PO20. . . . .196 B2
Pound St GU28 . . . . .97 F8
Pound The
Bognor Regis PO21 . . . . . .200 E2
Bognor Regis PO21 . . . . . .200 E2
Pound Way RH10 . . . . .19 C8
POVEY CROSS 1 D1
Povey Cross Rd RH6 . . . . . .1 E1
Poveys Cl RH15. . . . . .108 D3
Powell Cl RH6 . . . . .1 E4
Powis Gr BN1 . . . . .213 A3
Powis Rd BN1 . . . . .191 E6
Powis Sq BN1 . . . . .191 E6
Powis Villas BN1 . . . . .213 A3
Poynes Rd RH6 . . . . .1 E5
Poynings Crossways
BN6 .127 B1
Poynings Dr BN3 . . . . .168 F3
Poynings Rd
Crawley RH11 . . . . .17 E5
Poynings BN45 . . . . .148 C6
Poynter Rd BN3 . . . . .191 A8
Poynter Rd BN3 . . . . .191 A8
Poyntz Rd BN1 . . . . .191 F3
Pratton Ave RH15 . . . . . . .187 D7
Prawn Cl PO20 . . . . .212 C8
Prebendal Sch The
PO19 . . . . .176 F6
Precinct The PO21. . . . . . .200 F4
Prescott Gdns RH15 . . . . .109 A3
PRESTON 169 F1
Preston Ave BN16 . . . . . . .205 D5
Preston Cir BN1 . . . . .213 B4
Preston Dro BN1 . . . . .169 F2
Preston Grange BN1. . . . .169 E1
Preston Hall La RH15 . . . .205 F6
Preston Manor Mus★
BN1. . . . . .169 F1
Preston Mans **3** BN1. . .191 F8
Preston Paddock
BN15. . . . . .205 E5
Preston Park Ave
BN1. . . . . .169 F1
Preston Park Sta
BN1. . . . . .169 D2
Preston Rd BN1 . . . . .191 F8
Preston St BN1 . . . . .213 A1
Preston Village Mews
BN1. . . . . .169 E1
Prestonville Ct **2**
BN1. . . . . .191 E7
Prestonville Rd BN1 . . . . .213 A4
Prestwick Cl RH11 . . . . .17 D5
Prestwood Cl RH11 . . . . . . .5 B1
Prestwood La RH11 . . . . . . .4 C3
Pretoria Ave GU33 . . . . . . .45 F4
Pretoria Rd **4** GU29 . . . . .94 E7
Pricehome RH17. . . . . .64 B7
Price Way RH17 . . . . .64 B7
Priest Croft Cl RH11 . . . . . .18 A6
Priest House (Mus) The★
RH19 .42 E6
Priestlands Cl RH6. . . . . .1 A3
Priestley Way
Crawley RH10 . . . . .6 A3
Middleton-on-S PO22 . . . .201 A1
Primrose Ave RH6 . . . . .2 B1
Primrose Cl
Burgess Hill RH15 . . . . . . .108 D4
Crawley RH11 . . . . .18 B3
Rustington BN17 . . . . .205 A7
Primrose Copse RH12. . . . .36 A7
Primrose Ct BN44 . . . . . . .145 D2
Primrose La GU33 . . . . .45 F4
Prince Albert St **8**
BN1. . . . . .213 B2
Prince Ave BN15. . . . . .188 B5
Prince Charles Cl
BN42 . . . . .168 A2
Prince Of Wales Ct
BN3 .213 A2
Prince Regent's Cl
BN2 .192 E4
Prince Regent's Ct **2**
BN2 .192 E4
Princes Ave BN3 . . . . .191 A6
Princes Cres BN3. . . . . .191 A6
Prince's Cres BN2 . . . . . . .213 C5

Princes Croft PO21 . . . . . .200 A1
Princes Ct
6 Hove BN3. . . . . .191 A6
Shoreham-by-S BN43. . . .188 D6
Prince's Dr RH10 . . . . .135 E1
Princes Gate BN11. . . . . . .185 F3
Prince's Pl BN1 . . . . .213 B2
PRINCE'S MARSH 45 A2
Prince's Pl BN1 . . . . .213 B2
Princes Rd GU32 . . . . .67 F4
Prince's Rd BN2. . . . . .192 B8
Princess Anne Rd
RH12. . . . . .33 D7
Princess Ave
Bognor Regis PO21 . . . . . .201 A2
Worthing BN13 . . . . .185 F5
Princess Ct
Haywards Heath RH16 . . . .87 C5
Worthing BN13 . . . . .185 F4
Princess Ho **20** PO21. . . .201 D3
Princess Margaret Rd
RH12. . . . . .33 D7
Princes Sq BN3. . . . . .191 A6
Princess Rd RH11. . . . . .18 C6
Princess Royal Hospl RH16,
RH17 .88 A3
Prince's Terr BN2 . . . . .213 B2
Prince's Terr BN2 . . . . .192 E4
Prince William Cl
BN14 . . . . .186 A8
Prince William Ct **4**
PO21 . . . . .201 D3
Prings La RH13 . . . . .83 C8
Prinsep Rd BN3 . . . . .191 A8
Prinsted La PO10 . . . . .173 F7
Printers Mews PO19 . . . . .177 C8
Priors Acre PO18 . . . . .156 D3
Priors Cl
Breach PO10 . . . . .152 A1
Upper Beeding BN44 . . . . .146 A2
Priors Leaze La PO18 . . . .152 C1
Priors Waye PO21 . . . . . . .200 A2
Priors Wlk RH10 . . . . .18 F6
Priors Wood
Haslemere GU27 . . . . .26 F6
Kingsfold RH12 . . . . .15 B6
Priory Cl
Bognor Regis PO21 . . . . . .211 B8
Boxgrove PO18 . . . . .156 D3
Horley RH6 . . . . .1 F4
Lancing BN15. . . . . .187 B7
Worthing BN14 . . . . .186 A4
Priory Ct
7 Bognor Regis
PO21. . . . . .201 D3
Brighton BN1. . . . . .191 E8
7 Haywards Heath
RH16. . . . . .87 E3
Priory Field BN44 . . . . .146 A2
Priory Flats GU29. . . . . .73 B1
Priory Gate **1** BN15 . . . .187 E6
Priory Ho PO19 . . . . .177 A7
Priory Rd
Arundel BN18 . . . . .159 F2
Burgess Hill RH15 . . . . . . .109 A1
Chichester PO19 . . . . .177 A7
Forest Row RH18. . . . . .23 D2
Hassocks BN6 . . . . .128 E5
Littlehampton BN16. . . . . .205 B6
Priory The
Brighton BN1. . . . . .169 D5
2 Hove BN3. . . . . .191 B5
Priory Way RH16 . . . . .87 F4
Proctor Cl RH10 . . . . .19 C4
Promenade PO21 . . . . .201 A2
Promenade The
Emsworth PO10. . . . . .173 B7
Littlehampton BN17. . . . . .204 E3
Prospect Pl
Crawley RH11 . . . . .18 C6
3 Worthing BN11 . . . . .186 D1
Providence Pl
Brighton BN1. . . . . .213 B4
7 Chichester PO19 . . .176 F7
Providence Terr
BN11 . . . . .186 A6
Providence The **6**
PO19 . . . . .176 F7
Pruetts La GU31, GU33. . . .45 B1
Pryors Gn PO21 . . . . .200 C2
Pryors La PO21 . . . . .200 C1
Puckshott Way GU27. . . . .27 D8
Pudding La RH6. . . . . .4 E7
Puffin Hill RH10 . . . . .19 C5
Puffin Rd RH11 . . . . .17 D5
Pulborough Brooks Nature
Reserve★ RH20 . . . . .120 D7
Pulborough Cl BN2 . . . . . .192 F7
Pulborough Rd RH20 . . . .121 B2
Pulborough Sta RH20. . . .100 A2
Pulborough Way
PO22. . . . . .202 D6
Pulens Cess GU31 . . . . .68 C4
Pulens La GU31. . . . . .68 B8
Pump Ho The BN3 . . . . . . .190 D8
Punch Copse Rd RH10 . . .18 F7
Punches La PO20 . . . . .199 D5
Punnetts Ct RH11. . . . . .17 F2
Purbeck Ho BN2. . . . . .213 C4
Purbeck Pl BN17 . . . . .204 C5
Purcell Rd RH11 . . . . .17 F1
Purley Cl RH10 . . . . .19 D8
Purrocks The GU32 . . . . . . .68 B5
Purton Rd RH12 . . . . .36 B4
Putmans La GU31. . . . . .91 B7
Puttick Cl RH20. . . . . .121 C2
Puttocks Cl GU27 . . . . .26 D5

Pyecombe Ct [4] RH11 . . . . 17 F3
Pyecombe St BN45 . . . . 149 A6
Pyrford Cl PO21 . . . . 200 B2

Q

Quadrangle The
[2] Horley RH6 . . . . 2 B3
Nepcote BN14 . . . . 163 E4
Quadrant The
Keymer BN6 . . . . 129 A4
Worthing BN12 . . . . 185 C4
Quail Cl RH12 . . . . 36 D7
Quakers La RH16 . . . . 88 A5
QUAKER'S PLATT 10 A8
Quantock Cl
Crawley RH11 . . . . 18 B6
Worthing BN13 . . . . 185 F9
Quantock Rd BN13 . . . . 185 F8
Quantocks [2] BN17 . . . . 204 D6
Quarries The RH13 . . . . 59 D6
Quarry Bank Rd BN1 . . . . 170 B2
Quarry Cl
Burgess Hill RH15 . . . . 109 D3
Horsham RH12 . . . . 36 F6
Quarry Hill RH16 . . . . 87 C6
Quarry La PO19 . . . . 177 C5
Quarry Lane Ind Est
PO19 . . . . 177 C5
Quarry Rise RH19 . . . . 10 A3
Quarry Way RH13 . . . . 57 F2
Quarterbrass Farm Rd
RH12 . . . . 36 D7
Quarterdeck The
PO21 . . . . 201 A2
Quarter Mile The
RH13 . . . . 57 D5
Quashetts The
Worthing BN14 . . . . 186 D4
Worthing, Broadwater
BN14 . . . . 186 D5
Quay Ct BN43 . . . . 189 B6
Quayside BN17 . . . . 204 B5
Quayside Bldgs BN41 . . . . 190 D6
Quay The [5] BN43 . . . . 189 A6
Quebec GU31 . . . . 91 C7
Quebec Cl GU30 . . . . 25 C3
Quebec St BN2 . . . . 213 C3
Queen Alexandra Ave
BN3 . . . . 169 A3
Queen Caroline Cl
BN3 . . . . 169 A3
Queen Elizabeth Ave
RH15 . . . . 109 A2
Queen Elizabeth II Silver
Jubilee Sch RH13 . . . . 36 F1
Queen Elizabeth Rd
RH12 . . . . 33 D7
Queen Mary Ave BN3 . . . . 169 A3
Queen's Ave PO19 . . . . 176 F4
Queensborough Ct [5]
BN11 . . . . 186 A3
Queensbury Mews
BN1 . . . . 191 E5
QUEEN'S CORNER 71 E8
Queens Cres RH15 . . . . 109 A2
Queens Ct RH13 . . . . 36 D1
Queen's Ct
Haywards Heath RH16 . . . . 87 F6
Horley RH6 . . . . 2 A3
Queensdown School Rd
BN1, BN2 . . . . 170 D2
Queens Dr BN6 . . . . 128 F4
Queens Fields E PO21 . . . . 200 F4
Queens Fields W
PO21 . . . . 200 F4
Queens Fields Wlk
PO21 . . . . 200 F4
Queens Gate RH6 . . . . 6 A8
Queen's Gdns
Brighton BN1 . . . . 213 B3
Hove BN3 . . . . 191 C5
Stockbridge PO19 . . . . 176 F4
Queens La BN18 . . . . 160 B2
Queen's Mans [2]
BN11 . . . . 186 C1
Queensmead
Bognor Regis PO21 . . . . 210 F8
Worthing BN13 . . . . 185 E7
Queen's Par BN3 . . . . 168 E2
Queen's Par BN15 . . . . 187 E6
Queens Park Mews
BN2 . . . . 192 C6
Queen's Park Prim Sch
BN2 . . . . 192 C5
Queen's Park Rd BN2 . . . . 192 C6
Queen's Park Rise
BN2 . . . . 192 C6
Queen's Park Terr
BN2 . . . . 192 C6
Queen's Pl
Brighton BN1 . . . . 213 B4
Hove BN3 . . . . 191 C6
Shoreham-by-S BN43 . . . . 188 F7
Queen Sq BN1 . . . . 213 A2
Queens Rd
Griggs Green GU30 . . . . 24 C3
Haywards Heath RH16 . . . . 87 E6
Lancing BN15 . . . . 187 F5
Petersfield GU32 . . . . 67 F4
Southwick BN42 . . . . 167 E1
Queen's Rd
Brighton BN1 . . . . 213 A3
East Grinstead RH19 . . . . 9 E1
Horley RH6 . . . . 2 A3
Worthing BN11 . . . . 186 C1
Queens Sq RH10 . . . . 18 D6
Queen's Sq PO21 . . . . 201 D3
Queens St GU29 . . . . 72 A2
Queen St
Arundel BN18 . . . . 160 B2
Emsworth PO10 . . . . 173 C8
Horsham RH13 . . . . 36 D1
Littlehampton BN17 . . . . 204 D5
Worthing BN14 . . . . 186 C4
Queensway
Bognor Regis, Aldwick
PO21 . . . . 200 E1
Bognor Regis PO21 . . . . 201 C3
Brighton BN2 . . . . 192 D6
Crawley RH10 . . . . 18 E6
East Grinstead RH19 . . . . 9 E1
Horsham RH13 . . . . 36 C1
Lancing BN15 . . . . 187 E6
Queensway Ho [7]
PO21 . . . . 201 C3
Queen's Wlk RH19 . . . . 9 E1
Queen Victoria Ave
BN3 . . . . 169 A3
Queen Victoria Hospl The
RH19 . . . . 9 F3
Quell Farm Ind Est
RH20 . . . . 119 E4
Querneby Cl BN43 . . . . 189 D7
Quest Cl PO19 . . . . 177 B6
Quinta Carmen [10]
BN11 . . . . 186 B1
Quinton Fields PO10 . . . . 151 C3
Quoin Est The BN15 . . . . 187 D4

R

Racecourse Rd RH6 . . . . 6 A8
Racecourse Way RH6 . . . . 5 F8
Rackfield GU27 . . . . 26 D7
Rackham Cl
Crawley RH11 . . . . 18 D4
Worthing BN13 . . . . 185 F6
Rackham Rd
Amberley BN18 . . . . 140 F7
[3] Rustington BN16 . . . . 205 B3
Worthing BN13 . . . . 185 F6
Rackham St
Amberley BN18,
RH20 . . . . 141 A8
Rackham RH20 . . . . 141 C8
Racton Rd PO10 . . . . 151 C3
Radbone Cl BN14 . . . . 186 E6
Radford Rd
Bognor Regis PO21,
PO22 . . . . 201 B5
Crawley RH6, RH10 . . . . 6 C4
Radinden Dr BN3 . . . . 169 D1
Radinden Manor Rd
BN3 . . . . 191 D8
Radnor Cl BN13 . . . . 185 F5
Radnor Ho RH16 . . . . 87 D6
Radnor Rd BN13 . . . . 185 F5
Raglan Ave BN13 . . . . 185 E6
Raglan Ct
Brighton BN1 . . . . 213 A2
[5] Worthing BN11 . . . . 186 A2
Raglan Terr PO10 . . . . 151 C1
Railey Rd RH10 . . . . 18 E7
Railway App
East Grinstead RH19 . . . . 9 E1
Worthing BN11 . . . . 186 D3
Railway Cotts
East Grinstead RH19 . . . . 21 F3
Horsted Keynes RH17 . . . . 65 A8
Railway St BN1 . . . . 213 A3
Railway Terr GU29 . . . . 94 D7
Rainbow Way RH20 . . . . 121 F3
Rake Bsns Pk GU33 . . . . 46 B4
Rake CE Fst Sch GU33 . . . . 46 B5
RAKE HANGER 45 E2
Rake Rd
Liss GU33 . . . . 45 D4
Milland GU30 . . . . 47 A2
Rakers Ridge RH12 . . . . 36 D5
Raleigh Cl BN43 . . . . 188 F6
Raleigh Cres BN12 . . . . 185 D4
Raleigh Ct RH10 . . . . 6 A3
Raleigh Rd PO21 . . . . 200 C3
Raleigh Way BN12 . . . . 185 C4
Raleigh Wlk RH10 . . . . 18 E4
Rambledown La
RH20 . . . . 121 C6
Ramblers Ct RH12 . . . . 35 E3
Ramblers The [13]
BN16 . . . . 206 A4
Ramblers Way RH11 . . . . 39 B8
Ramillies Gdns PO22 . . . . 202 C5
Ramsdean Rd GU32 . . . . 67 B2
Ramsey Cl
Horley RH6 . . . . 1 F3
Horsham RH12 . . . . 36 D5
Ramsey Ct [18] RH11 . . . . 18 B1
Ramshill GU31 . . . . 68 C4
RAMSNEST COMMON
. . . . 29 A6
Rams Wlk GU32 . . . . 68 B3
Randall Scofield Ct
RH10 . . . . 19 A7
Randiddles Cl BN6 . . . . 128 B4
Ranelagh Villas BN3 . . . . 191 B8
Rangers Lo RH13 . . . . 36 E2
Ranmore Cl RH11 . . . . 39 C8
Ransome Cl RH11 . . . . 17 E3
Ranville Cl GU28 . . . . 97 E7
Ranworth Cl PO22 . . . . 201 F5
Rapeland Hill RH12 . . . . 15 F2
Raphael Rd BN3 . . . . 190 F7
Rapley Ave RH20 . . . . 121 B2
Rascals Cl RH13 . . . . 81 F7
Rastrick Cl RH15 . . . . 108 F1
Ratham La
Broadbridge PO18 . . . . 175 C8
West Ashling PO18 . . . . 153 C1
Rathbone Ho RH11 . . . . 18 B1
Rathlin Rd RH11 . . . . 18 B3
Raughmere Ct PO18 . . . . 154 F4
Raughmere Dr PO18 . . . . 154 F4
Raven Cl
Horsham RH12 . . . . 36 E6
Turners Hill RH10 . . . . 21 C5
Ravendene Ct [3] RH10 . . . . 18 D5
Raven La RH11 . . . . 18 C8
Ravensbourne Ave
BN43 . . . . 166 F1
Ravensbourne Cl [11]
BN43 . . . . 166 F1
Ravensbourne Ct
BN2 . . . . 193 D8
Ravenscroft RH20 . . . . 142 D8
Ravens Croft [7] BN16 . . . . 205 C4
Ravenscroft Ct RH12 . . . . 36 C3
Raven's Rd BN43 . . . . 188 F7
Ravens Way PO22 . . . . 201 B6
Ravenswood BN6 . . . . 128 E4
Ravenswood Ct BN13 . . . . 186 A4
Ravenswood Dr BN2 . . . . 193 F6
Ravenswood Rd RH15 . . . . 109 B3
Ravenwood Ct PO21 . . . . 200 E2
Rawlinson Rd RH10 . . . . 19 D4
Raworth Cl RH10 . . . . 19 C4
Rawson Ct [10] BN16 . . . . 205 B4
Rawson Villas BN16 . . . . 205 C6
Ray Cl GU31 . . . . 68 C5
Raycroft Cl PO21 . . . . 200 F2
Rayden Cl BN17 . . . . 204 E5
Raylands Park Cvn Site
RH13 . . . . 58 B2
Raymede Ho BN11 . . . . 186 B3
Raymer Wlk RH6 . . . . 2 C4
Rayner Ct BN5 . . . . 125 E4
Reading Rd BN2 . . . . 192 F4
Readon Cl GU31 . . . . 68 C4
Readon Ho GU31 . . . . 68 C4
Reapers Cl RH12 . . . . 36 D5
Record Rd PO10 . . . . 151 A1
Rectory Cl
Ashington RH20 . . . . 123 A5
Hove BN3 . . . . 190 D7
Pulborough RH20 . . . . 100 C2
Shoreham-by-S BN43 . . . . 189 D7
Storrington RH20 . . . . 121 D1
Rectory Cotts [1]
RH20 . . . . 121 D1
Rectory Ct [15] BN43 . . . . 189 C8
Rectory Farm Rd
BN15 . . . . 187 B7
Rectory Gdns BN14 . . . . 186 C5
Rectory La
Angmering BN16 . . . . 183 F5
Ashington RH20 . . . . 122 E6
Bramshott GU30 . . . . 25 D7
Charlwood RH6 . . . . 4 D7
Church Norton PO20 . . . . 210 B3
Crawley RH11 . . . . 17 F8
Pulborough RH20 . . . . 100 C2
Rusper RH11 . . . . 4 F1
Rectory Mews [1]
BN14 . . . . 186 A5
Rectory Pl RH20 . . . . 122 F5
Rectory Rd
Shoreham-by-S BN43 . . . . 189 D7
Storrington RH20 . . . . 121 D1
Worthing BN13, BN14 . . . . 186 A5
Rectory Wlk
Lancing BN15 . . . . 187 C7
Storrington RH20 . . . . 121 D1
Red Acre Ct PO21 . . . . 201 D4
Red Admiral St RH12 . . . . 36 E5
Redcotts [1] BN11 . . . . 186 B2
Redcross St BN1 . . . . 213 B3
Red Deer Cl RH13 . . . . 37 B4
Redditch Cl RH11 . . . . 17 E2
Redehall Ind Pk RH6 . . . . 7 C7
Redehall Rd RH6 . . . . 7 C8
REDFORD 48 A1
Redford Ave RH12 . . . . 36 B4
Redgarth Ct RH19 . . . . 9 B3
Redgrave Dr RH10 . . . . 19 D5
Redhill Cl BN1 . . . . 169 C5
Redhill Distribution Ctr
RH1 . . . . 2 A8
Redhill Dr BN1 . . . . 169 C5
Redhill Rd PO9 . . . . 130 D1
Red Ho BN13 . . . . 186 A7
Red House Ct GU31 . . . . 70 B4
Redhouse Farm BN6 . . . . 148 F7
Red House Farm Camping
& Cvn Site PO20 . . . . 208 D8
Redhouse Mews GU30 . . . . 25 C2
Redkiln Cl RH13 . . . . 36 F4
Redkiln Close Trad Est
RH13 . . . . 36 F3
Redkiln Way RH13 . . . . 36 F3
Red La RH13 . . . . 81 D1
Redlands La
New Brighton PO10 . . . . 151 B4
Shipton Green PO20 . . . . 196 F3
Red Lion St GU29 . . . . 94 F7
Red Oak Ct GU29 . . . . 73 A2
Red Ridges PO21 . . . . 201 A2
Red River Ct RH12 . . . . 36 B5
Redshank Ct [5] RH11 . . . . 17 D5
Red Square Ret Pk
BN14 . . . . 186 E7
Redvers Rd BN2 . . . . 170 D1
Redwing Cl
Horsham RH13 . . . . 36 F3
Littlehampton BN17 . . . . 204 C8
Redwood Cl
Crawley RH10 . . . . 18 E8
Worthing BN13 . . . . 185 C6
Redwood Ct BN17 . . . . 204 F5
Redwood Dr RH16 . . . . 87 D3
Redwood Manor GU27 . . . . 27 C7
Redwood Pl PO21 . . . . 200 E2
Reed Cl
Hunston PO20 . . . . 199 A8
Storrington RH20 . . . . 121 C1
Reedings RH11 . . . . 17 D4
Reed Pond Wlk RH16 . . . . 88 A4
Reeds La
Liss GU33 . . . . 45 F6
Southwater Street RH13 . . . . 58 B3
Reed's La BN6 . . . . 127 B8
Reef Cl BN17 . . . . 204 F4
Rees Cl BN13 . . . . 185 B7
Reeves Hill BN1 . . . . 170 D5
Reeves Ho [2] RH10 . . . . 19 B6
Refectory Rd BN1 . . . . 171 B7
Regal Dr [10] RH19 . . . . 22 F8
Regency Ct
Brighton BN1 . . . . 169 D3
Ferring BN12 . . . . 206 F6
Worthing BN13 . . . . 186 A6
Regency Mews [15]
BN1 . . . . 191 E5
Regency Rd BN1 . . . . 213 A2
Regency Sq BN1 . . . . 191 E5
Regent Arc BN1 . . . . 213 B2
Regent Bsns Pk RH15 . . . . 108 E2
Regent Cl BN15 . . . . 188 B6
Regent Hill BN1 . . . . 213 A2
Regent Mews
[11] Bognor Regis
PO21 . . . . 201 B2
Petersfield GU32 . . . . 67 F4
Regent Row BN1 . . . . 213 A2
Regents Cl RH11 . . . . 18 C2
Regents Mews RH6 . . . . 2 A3
Regent St BN1 . . . . 213 B2
Regents Way PO21 . . . . 200 F4
Regis Ave PO21 . . . . 211 B8
Regis Bsns Ctr PO22 . . . . 201 D6
Regis Ct
Bognor Regis PO21 . . . . 201 D3
Worthing BN11 . . . . 186 A1
Regisgate [10] PO21 . . . . 201 C4
Regis Ho [17] PO21 . . . . 201 C3
Regnum Ct PO19 . . . . 177 A7
Reigate Cl RH10 . . . . 6 D1
Reigate Ct BN11 . . . . 185 F3
Reigate Rd
Brighton BN1 . . . . 169 D1
Hookwood RH2, RH6 . . . . 1 C6
Worthing BN11 . . . . 185 F4
Renfields RH16 . . . . 87 C3
Renoir Ct PO22 . . . . 201 A6
Renoir Mews PO22 . . . . 201 A6
Renton Cl RH14 . . . . 79 D8
Reservoir La GU32 . . . . 68 B6
Retreat The RH14 . . . . 31 F5
REWELL HILL 159 A7
Rew La PO19 . . . . 154 F3
Rex Ct GU27 . . . . 26 F6
Reydon Ho BN11 . . . . 186 F3
Reynard Cl RH12 . . . . 37 B5
Reynolds La BN18 . . . . 158 D4
Reynolds Pl RH11 . . . . 18 C7
Reynolds Rd
Crawley RH11 . . . . 18 C7
Hove BN3 . . . . 190 F7
Rhodes Way RH10 . . . . 18 F3
Ribbetts Cotts BN6 . . . . 128 A5
Ribbetts Ho BN6 . . . . 128 A5
Rices Hill RH19 . . . . 9 E1
Richard Allen Ct BN2 . . . . 170 C1
Richard Ho [6] PO21 . . . . 201 C2
Richardson Ct
[17] Crawley RH11 . . . . 18 B1
[5] Hove BN3 . . . . 190 F7
Richardson Rd BN3 . . . . 190 F7
Richborough Ct RH11 . . . . 18 C6
Richmond Ave
Bognor Regis PO21 . . . . 201 B2
Chichester PO19 . . . . 155 A1
Richmond Ave W
PO21 . . . . 201 A3
Richmond Cl [1] BN16 . . . . 205 E6
Richmond Ct
Crawley RH10 . . . . 18 E5
[9] Hove BN3 . . . . 191 E7
[3] Rustington BN16 . . . . 205 B5
Worthing BN11 . . . . 186 C2
Richmond Gdns [2]
BN2 . . . . 213 C3
Richmond Ho [11]
PO21 . . . . 201 C3
Richmond Hts [12]
BN2 . . . . 213 C3
Richmond Par BN2 . . . . 213 C3
Richmond Pl BN2 . . . . 213 B3
Richmond Rd
[16] Bognor Regis
PO21 . . . . 201 C3
Brighton BN2 . . . . 192 B8
Horsham RH12 . . . . 36 D4
Westerton PO18 . . . . 155 F3
Worthing BN11 . . . . 186 D2
Richmond Rd N [6]
PO21 . . . . 201 D4
Richmond Sq RH19 . . . . 9 D2
Richmond St BN2 . . . . 213 C3
Richmond Terr BN2 . . . . 213 C4
Richmond Villas
PO22 . . . . 201 F3
Richmond Way RH19 . . . . 22 F8
Rickfield RH11 . . . . 18 A5
Rickman's La
Kirdford RH14 . . . . 53 B8
Plaistow RH14 . . . . 30 F2
Rickwood RH6 . . . . 2 B4
Riddens The RH12 . . . . 33 A6
Ride The
Brighton BN1 . . . . 169 F1
Ifold RH14 . . . . 31 C2
Ridge Cl BN41 . . . . 168 A4
Ridge Common La
GU32 . . . . 67 E6
Ridgedale RH10 . . . . 21 B8
Ridgehurst Dr RH12 . . . . 35 F1
Ridge Rd BN1 . . . . 171 C7
Ridgeside RH10 . . . . 18 F6
Ridgeside Ave BN1 . . . . 169 E5
Ridge The RH12 . . . . 33 E8
Ridge Top La
Froxfield Green GU32 . . . . 67 B7
Froxfield Green GU32 . . . . 67 C7
Ridge View BN1 . . . . 170 E5
Ridgeway
East Grinstead RH19 . . . . 22 E7
Southwick BN41, BN42 . . . . 167 F1
Ridge Way RH17 . . . . 88 B2
Ridgeway Cl BN42 . . . . 167 F1
Ridgeway Gdns BN2 . . . . 193 E7
Ridgeway Ho RH6 . . . . 2 A1
Ridgeway Office Pk
GU31 . . . . 67 F2
Ridgeway The
Burgess Hill RH15 . . . . 109 B4
Chichester PO19 . . . . 176 E7
Fernhurst GU27 . . . . 49 B6
Horley RH6 . . . . 2 A1
Horsham RH12 . . . . 36 B4
Ridgewood Ave BN2 . . . . 194 C3
Ridgway Cl BN2 . . . . 193 D8
Ridgway Paddock
BN7 . . . . 172 E6
Ridgway The
Bognor Regis PO22 . . . . 202 A4
Woodingdean BN2 . . . . 193 D8
Ridings The
Bognor Regis PO21 . . . . 200 C1
Burgess Hill RH15 . . . . 109 C2
Crawley RH10 . . . . 19 D7
Fontwell BN18 . . . . 158 A2
Liss GU33 . . . . 45 D4
Littlehampton BN16 . . . . 205 F4
Ovingdean BN2 . . . . 193 C4
Steyning BN44 . . . . 145 D1
Ridley Ct RH10 . . . . 19 D8
Ridleys RH19 . . . . 42 E6
Rife La PO20 . . . . 212 B8
Rifeside Gdns BN12 . . . . 206 E7
Rife Way
Bognor Regis PO22 . . . . 201 F4
Ferring BN12 . . . . 206 E6
Rigden Rd BN3 . . . . 169 C1
Rikkyo Sch-in-England
RH14 . . . . 32 D8
Riley Rd BN2 . . . . 170 C1
Rillside RH10 . . . . 19 A3
Rill Wlk RH19 . . . . 10 B1
Rimmer Cl RH11 . . . . 39 B8
Ringley Ave RH6 . . . . 2 A2
Ringley Oak RH12 . . . . 36 F4
Ringley Rd RH12 . . . . 36 E4
Ringmer Cl BN1 . . . . 170 E4
Ringmer Dr BN1 . . . . 170 F4
Ringmer Rd
Brighton BN1 . . . . 170 E4
Worthing BN13 . . . . 185 E6
Ring Rd BN15 . . . . 165 F1
Ring Rd N RH6 . . . . 6 C8
Ring Rd S RH6 . . . . 6 C7
Ringwood Cl RH10 . . . . 18 E4
Ripley Rd BN11 . . . . 185 F4
Ripon Gdns PO21 . . . . 200 E3
Rise The
Crawley RH10 . . . . 19 D6
East Grinstead RH19 . . . . 22 F8
Haywards Heath RH16 . . . . 88 B5
Partridge Green RH13 . . . . 105 A4
Portslade-by-S BN41 . . . . 167 F2
Rissom Ct BN1 . . . . 169 E2
Ritchie Cl RH10 . . . . 19 C2
Rival Moor Rd GU31 . . . . 68 E2
Riverbank Bsns Ctr
BN43 . . . . 188 E7
River Cl BN43 . . . . 188 E6
RIVERHILL 98 E7
Riverhill La GU28, RH20 . . . . 98 E7
River La
River GU28 . . . . 74 E3
Watersfield RH20 . . . . 119 B4
Rivermead RH20 . . . . 100 D1
River Mead
Crawley RH11 . . . . 5 A1
Horsham RH12 . . . . 36 B1
Rivermead Ct PO10 . . . . 151 C3
River Rd
Arundel BN18 . . . . 160 B2
Littlehampton BN17 . . . . 204 C5
Riverside
Chichester PO19 . . . . 177 B7
Forest Row RH18 . . . . 23 E3
Horley RH6 . . . . 2 A1
Horsham RH12 . . . . 36 A2
Littlehampton BN17 . . . . 204 C4

Riverside *continued*
Shoreham-by-S BN43....**188** F6
Southwick BN42 ....**189** E7
Storrington BN20.......**121** D2
Upper Beeding BN44......**146** A2
Riverside Bsns Ctr
BN43 ....**189** A7
Riverside Caravan Pk
BN44 ....**146** A2
Riverside Cl GU33 ....**45** B4
Riverside Cres RH20 ....**100** A1
Riverside Ho BN43........**188** E6
Riverside Ind Est
BN17 ....**204** B5
Riverside Rd BN43........**188** F6
Riverside Terr 🔢 **173** C8
Riverside Wlk GU31......**68** D3
River's Rd RH16 ....**63** D3
River St PO10 ....**151** D4
Rivoli Ct BN11 ....**186** D3
Rixons Ct RH17 ....**65** C5
Rixons Orch RH17 ....**65** C5
Robell Way RH20 ....**121** F3
Robert Lo BN2 ....**192** F4
Roberts Cl RH13 ....**57** F4
Roberts Marine Mans
BN11 ....**185** F2
Robertson Rd BN1 ....**169** D1
Roberts Rd BN15 ....**187** E4
Robert St BN1 ....**213** B3
Robert Way RH12 ....**36** F7
Robin Cl
Crawley RH11 ....**18** C8
🔢 East Grinstead RH19 .....**9** F2
Littlehampton BN17........**204** C8
Southwater RH13 ....**58** A2
Robin Davis Cl BN2......**170** E1
Robin Dene BN2..........**192** E4
Robin Hood La RH12......**35** F5
Robinia Lo BN1............**169** E2
Robin Rd RH15 ....**108** D2
Robin Rise RH16..........**87** F3
Robin Row RH10..........**21** C5
ROBINS **71** D7
Robin's Cl PO20 ....**212** E8
Robins Dr PO21 ....**200** D3
Robins La GU27 ....**71** D7
Robinson Cl
🔢 Lancing BN15...........**187** E6
Selsey PO20...............**212** E8
Robinson Ho RH10.......**18** D5
Robinson Way PO20 ....**208** B6
Robins Row BN41........**168** A1
Robinswood Ct RH12 ....**36** F4
Robson Cl BN2 ....**185** E4
Robson Rd BN2...........**185** E3
Rochester Cl
Chichester PO19 ....**154** F1
🔢 Hove BN3...............**191** D6
Worthing BN13 ....**185** B6
Rochester Ct 🔢 BN1....**191** D6
Rochester Gdns BN3.....**191** D6
Rochester St BN2.........**192** D5
Rochester Way PO21....**200** E3
ROCK **143** E8
Rockall Cl BN17 ....**205** A7
Rockall Way PO18 ......**175** D7
Rock Cl 🔢 BN42.........**189** E7
Rockdene Cl RH19.........**10** A1
Rockeries The 🔢 GU29...**94** E7
Rock Gdns PO21 ....**201** C2
Rock Gr BN2 ....**192** A2
Rockingham Cl BN13 ....**185** E7
Rockingham Ct BN13 ....**185** E7
Rock La RH20 ....**122** E1
Rockpit Cotts GU33.......**45** D4
Rock Pl BN2 ....**213** C1
Rock Rd RH20 ....**122** C2
Rocksacre Cotts
BN15 ....**186** F7
Rocks La RH17 ....**40** F1
Rock St BN2 ....**192** E4
Rocks The RH19 ....**23** D6
Rockwood Ct PO10 .....**151** B1
Rocky La RH16 ....**87** D1
Rodgate La GU27 ....**28** E5
Rodmell Ave BN2 ....**194** D1
Rodmell Pl BN1 ....**170** A6
Rodmell Rd BN13.........**185** E6
Rodney Cl PO21 ....**200** C3
Rodney Cres BN18.......**181** D4
Roebuck Cl RH13 ....**37** B4
Roedale Ct 🔢 BN1.......**170** B1
Roedale Rd BN1 ....**170** B1
ROEDEAN **193** B4
Roedean Cres BN2........**193** A4
Roedean Ct BN2..........**192** F4
Roedean Hts BN2.........**193** A4
Roedean Path BN2 ....**193** A3
Roedean Rd
Brighton BN2..............**192** F4
Worthing BN13 ....**185** E7
Roedean Sch BN2 ....**193** C3
Roedean Terr BN2.......**193** B3
Roedean Vale BN2........**193** B3
Roedean Way BN2........**193** B3
Roedeer Copse GU27 ....**26** B6
ROFFEY **37** A5
Roffey Cl RH6 ....**1** F3
Roffey Cnr RH12............**37** B4
Roffey's Cl RH10............**37** A4
Roffye Ct RH12 ....**37** A4

Rogate CE Prim Sch
GU31 ....**70** B4
Rogate Cl
Lancing BN15..............**187** B7
Worthing BN13 ....**186** A6
Rogate Rd BN13...........**186** A6
Roger's La BN14..........**163** E4
Rokewood Dr RH11 ....**5** A1
Rolfe Dr RH15 ....**109** D3
Rollaston Pk BN18........**181** C2
Rolston Ho GU27 ....**26** F6
Romaine Cl RH15.........**109** D5
Roman Acre BN17........**204** C6
Roman Ave BN16.........**206** A8
Roman Cres BN42........**189** E8
Roman Ct RH15...........**109** A3
Roman Fields PO21.......**201** A4
Roman Landing PO20 ....**196** B2
Roman Rd
Bramber BN44.............**145** E3
Hove BN3.................**190** D6
Southwick BN42 ....**189** E8
Roman Way
Billingshurst RH14..........**55** D1
Fishbourne PO19 ....**176** B6
Southwick BN42 ....**189** E8
Roman Wlk BN15.........**187** B7
Romany Cl BN41...........**190** B8
Romany Rd BN13.........**185** B6
Romney Broadwalk
PO22 ....**201** B6
Romney Ct BN11..........**185** F2
Romney Garth PO20 .....**212** F7
Romney Rd
Rottingdean BN2 ....**194** A1
Worthing BN11 ....**185** F2
Romsey Cl BN11 ....**170** C2
Rona Ct RH11 ....**18** B3
Rookcross La RH13 ....**104** A4
Rookery Cl BN15..........**169** E1
Rookery La PO20 ....**209** F8
Rookery The
Lumley PO10 ....**151** C1
Selsey PO20................**212** F8
Rookery Way RH16........**87** E1
Rookes Mews GU31.......**68** C4
Rook Way RH12 ....**36** F6
Rookwood La PO20 ......**196** D4
Rookwood Pk RH12........**35** F3
Rookwood Rd PO20 ......**196** C2
Ropeland Way RH12 ....**36** E7
Ropes La GU27 ....**49** C5
Ropetackle BN43 ....**188** E7
Rope Wlk
Littlehampton BN17.......**204** C4
Shoreham-by-S BN43......**188** E7
Rosamund Rd RH10 ....**19** B3
Rosary Cl BN15............**109** B2
Rosary The RH13 ....**104** F3
Rose Ave PO22 ....**202** F5
Rosebarn Cl RH15.........**109** B2
Rosebery Ave
Woodingdean BN2 ....**193** C8
Worthing BN13 ....**185** E3
Rose Cottage La RH17 ...**62** A5
Rose Cotts
Danehill RH17 ....**66** A4
Forest Row RH18...........**23** E3
Handcross RH17 ....**61** C8
Horsham RH12 ....**37** D7
Rosecroft Cl BN15.........**187** E5
Rose Ct
Bognor Regis PO21 ....**200** D3
Chichester PO19 ....**177** A7
Hassocks BN6 ....**128** E4
🔢 Littlehampton BN17....**204** D5
🔢 Worthing BN11.........**187** B3
Rosedale Cl RH11..........**18** A4
Rosedene Cl BN2 ....**193** E6
Rose Garden The*
PO20 ....**176** C3
ROSE GREEN **200** C3
Rose Green Inf Sch
PO21 ....**200** C2
Rose Green Jun Sch
PO21 ....**200** C3
Rose Green Rd
Bognor Regis PO21 ....**200** C3
Bognor Regis PO21 ....**200** D3
Rosehill RH14 ....**55** D1
Rose Hill BN2 ....**213** C4
Rose Hill Cl BN1..........**213** B4
Rose Hill Ct BN1..........**213** B4
Rose Hill Terr BN1........**213** C4
Roseleigh Gdns RH17......**88** F3
Rosemary Ave BN44 .....**145** E3
Rosemary Cl
Bognor Regis PO21 ....**200** C3
Bramber BN44.............**145** E3
Haywards Heath RH16......**87** B6
Petworth GU28 ....**97** F8
Storrington RH20.........**121** D1
Rosemary Ct
Haslemere GU27 ....**27** C7
Horley RH6 ....**1** E4
Rosemary Dr BN43.......**167** C1
Rosemary Ho 🔢 RH10 .....**6** A1
Rosemary La
Alfold GU6 ....**31** E8
Charlwood RH6 ....**4** E7
Horley RH6 ....**2** B3
Petworth GU28 ....**97** F8
Rosemarys Ctyd GU29....**94** F8
Rosemead BN17..........**204** E5
Rosemead Gdns RH10 ....**18** E5
Rose Pl BN17.............**205** B7
Rose Terr PO22 ....**180** D6

Rose Wlk
Burgess Hill RH15........**109** C7
Worthing BN13 ....**185** E2
Rosewood GU27 ....**27** C5
Rosier Commercial Ctr
RH14 ....**79** F7
Rosier Way RH14 ....**79** E6
Roslan Ct RH6...............**2** B2
Rossalyn Ct PO21........**200** B3
Ross Cl
Bognor Regis PO21........**200** B2
Crawley RH10 ....**18** F3
Ross Ct 🔢 RH6.............**2** B3
Rossiter Rd BN15.........**187** E8
Rosslyn Ave BN43........**189** A7
Rosslyn Ct BN43..........**188** F7
Rosslyn Rd BN43..........**188** F7
Rossmore Cl RH10..........**6** D2
Rostock Ct PO20.........**208** B6
Rosvara Ave PO20........**179** D7
Rotary No BN15...........**187** E4
Rotary Lo
Brighton BN1..............**170** C6
Worthing BN11 ....**186** B3
Rotary Point BN14.........**186** B1
Rothbury Rd BN3.........**190** D7
Rotherbank Farm La
GU33 ....**45** C6
Rotherbridge La GU28....**97** E5
Rotherbrook Ct GU31.....**67** F2
Rother Cl
Petersfield GU31............**68** E4
Storrington RH20.........**121** F3
Rothercombe La GU32....**67** C4
Rother Cres RH11..........**17** F5
Rotherfield Cl BN1 ....**170** B6
Rotherfield Cres BN1 ....**170** B5
Rother Ho RH10............**45** B3
Rother La GU31.............**71** A1
Rotherley 🔢 GU32.........**68** A4
Rothermead GU28 ....**97** E7
Rothervale RH6.............**1** F5
Rothesay Cl BN13.........**185** E5
Rothley Chase RH16.......**87** F4
Rotten Row PO20.........**198** E3
Rottingdean Pl BN2......**193** F4
Rotyngs The BN2.........**193** F2
Rough Field RH19...........**9** D4
Rough Way RH12 ....**36** F5
Roundabout Copse
BN16 ....**121** D5
Roundabout Cotts
RH12 ....**33** C5
Roundabout La RH20 ....**121** D6
Roundabouts The
GU33 ....**45** C5
ROUND HILL **192** B8
Round Hill Cres BN2......**192** B8
Round Hill Rd 🔢 BN2....**192** B8
Round Hill St 🔢 BN2.....**192** B8
Roundhouse Mdw
PO10 ....**173** C7
Roundle Ave PO22 ......**202** C5
Roundle Rd PO22 ....**202** C5
Roundle Sq PO22.........**202** B5
Roundle Square Rd
PO22 ....**202** B5
Round Piece La PO20 ....**212** B8
Roundstone By-Pass Rd
BN16 ....**206** A7
Roundstone Cres
BN16 ....**206** A6
Roundstone Dr BN16.....**206** A6
Roundstone House Cvn Pk
BN16 ....**206** A8
Roundstone Pk RH13.....**57** F3
Roundstone Way
PO20 ....**212** F8
ROUNDSTREET COMMON
..............................**54** C6
Roundway
Brighton BN1..............**170** E5
Haywards Heath RH16......**87** C1
Roundway The 🔢 RH10...**18** D8
Roundway The BN16.....**205** D4
Roundwood BN15.........**185** F9
Roundwood La RH16......**87** F8
Rowan Ave BN3 ....**168** A1
Rowan Cl
Crawley RH10 ....**18** F6
Haywards Heath RH16......**88** B4
Horsham RH12 ....**37** B5
Portslade-by-S BN41......**168** A1
Storrington RH20.........**121** F2
Rowan Ct
Billingshurst RH14..........**55** D1
Brighton BN1..............**169** E1
Rowan Dr RH14............**55** D1
Rowan Ho
🔢 Brighton BN2..........**213** C4
🔢 Rustington BN16 ......**205** C5
Worthing BN12 ....**185** A5
Rowans BN43 ....**188** E8
Rowans The
Burgess Hill RH15........**108** D4
Hurstpierpoint BN6 ....**128** A7
Worthing BN14 ....**186** A2
Rowan Tree Cl GU33......**45** C4
Rowan Way
Angmering BN16 ....**206** A8
Bognor Regis PO22 ....**201** C7
Horsham RH12 ....**37** C5
Ovingdean BN2 ....**193** E4
Rowan Wlk RH10..........**21** C8
Rowena Ct 🔢 RH12.......**36** A1
Rowfant Bsns Ctr
RH10 ....**20** E6

Rowfant Cl RH10 ....**19** E6
Row Hill La RH17..........**62** E7
Rowhook Cl RH12 ....**34** F8
Rowhook Rd
Rowhook RH12 ....**13** E1
Slinfold RH12 ....**35** A8
Rowland Cl RH10............**7** E5
Rowlands Castle Rd
Blendworth PO8 ....**130** B6
Blendworth PO8 ....**130** B7
Rowlands Castle Sta
PO9 ....**130** E2
Rowlands Ct BN11........**186** C1
Rowlands Rd
Horsham RH12 ....**37** A6
Worthing BN11 ....**186** B1
Rowner Rd RH14 ....**55** A2
Rowplatt Cl RH19...........**8** E4
Rowplatt La RH19...........**8** E4
Roxburgh Cl BN13........**185** F8
Royal Alexandra Children's
Hospl BN2 ....**192** D4
Royal Arc BN11............**186** D1
Royal Arms Ho 🔢
PO19 ....**177** A6
Royal Bay Ct PO21.......**200** D1
Royal Bldgs BN15.........**187** C4
Royal Cres BN2...........**192** C4
Royal Crescent Mans 🔢
BN2 ....**192** C4
Royal Crescent Mews 🔢
BN2 ....**192** C4
Royal Gdns PO9 ....**130** C1
Royal George Cl
RH15 ....**108** F3
Royal George Par
BN43 ....**167** C1
Royal George Rd
RH15 ....**108** E3
Royal Oak Cotts BN45...**148** C5
Royal Oak Ho RH10......**21** A7
Royal Par PO21 ....**201** A6
Royal Pavilion* BN1.....**213** B2
Royal Sussex Cty Hospl
BN2 ....**192** D4
Royce Cl PO20............**196** C1
Royce Rd RH10..............**6** A3
Royce Way PO20.........**196** C1
Royles Cl BN2 ....**194** A2
Royston Cl RH10............**6** A2
Roystons The BN16......**205** F4
Ruckmans La RH5 ....**14** B7
Rucrofts Cl PO21.........**200** F3
Rudd Ho BN13............**185** E8
Rudford Ind Est BN18....**181** D2
Rudge Ho 🔢 RH19..........**9** F1
Rudgwick Ave BN12.....**185** A3
Rudgwick Cl RH11........**18** B1
Rudgwick Keep RH6........**2** C4
Rudgwick Prim Sch
RH12 ....**33** D7
Rudgwick Rd RH11 ....**17** F7
Rudkin Pl PO20 ....**176** A8
Rudwick's Cl PO22.......**202** C4
Rudwick Way PO22 ......**202** C4
Rudyard Cl BN2 ....**193** E8
Rudyard Kipling Prim Sch
BN2 ....**193** E7
Rudyard Rd BN2..........**193** E8
Rufwood RH10 ....**21** A8
Rugby Ct
🔢 Brighton BN2..........**192** E4
🔢 Worthing BN11.........**186** A3
Rugby Pl BN2 ....**192** E4
Rugby Rd
Brighton BN1..............**170** A1
Worthing BN11 ....**186** A3
Ruislip Gdns PO21 ....**200** C2
Rumbolds Cl PO19 ....**177** C5
Rumbolds Hill GU29.......**94** F7
Rumbolds La RH14 ....**87** D2
Rumboldswyke CE Inf Sch
PO19 ....**177** C5
Rummers The PO19......**154** F2
Runcorn Cl RH11 ....**17** F7
Runcton La PO20 ....**199** E7
Runnymede Ct PO21....**200** F5
Runshooke Ct 🔢 RH11...**18** A3
Rusbridge Cl PO21........**200** D4
Rushams Rd RH12..........**36** B3
Rushes Ct GU32 ....**68** A4
Rushes Farm GU32 ....**68** A4
Rushes La GU32............**68** A4
Rushes The RH16..........**88** C4
Rushetts Pl RH11...........**5** C1
Rushetts Rd RH11...........**5** B1
Rushfield Rd GU33.........**45** B3
Rushlake Cl BN1..........**170** E5
Rushlake Rd BN1..........**170** E5
Rushwood Cl RH16........**88** B4

Ruspers RH15 ....**109** D2
Ruspers Keep RH11........**17** F7
Russell Cl BN14...........**186** E5
Russell Cres 🔢 BN1......**213** A4
Russell Ct
🔢 Lancing BN15...........**187** E5
🔢 Midhurst GU29 ....**94** E7
Russell Ho 🔢 GU29........**94** E7
Russell Mews BN1 ....**191** E5
Russell Pl
🔢 Bognor Regis
PO21 ....**201** D3
Brighton BN1..............**213** A2
Russell Rd
Brighton BN1..............**213** A2
East Wittering PO20 ......**207** E7
Russell's Cl RH16.........**206** B6
Russells Cres RH6...........**2** A2
Russells Dr BN15..........**187** E5
Russell Sq BN1 ....**213** A2
Russell St PO19 ....**177** C6
Russell Way
Crawley RH10 ....**19** A5
Petersfield GU31...........**68** C2
Russet Cl RH6..............**2** C3
Russet Gdns PO10........**173** D8
Russett Ct
Fernhurst GU27 ....**49** B5
Horsham RH12 ....**37** A4
Russett Pl RH14 ....**53** A3
Russ Hill RH6................**4** C5
Russ Hill Cotts RH6.........**4** C4
Russ Hill Rd RH6...........**4** D6
Rustington Comm Prim Sch
BN16 ....**205** B6
Rustington Rd BN1 ......**170** A5
Rustington Retail Pk
BN16 ....**205** D7
Rustington Trad Est
BN16 ....**205** D7
Rustlings Cl RH16 ....**88** B5
Ruston Ave BN16.........**205** D5
Ruston Cl RH10............**19** C3
Ruston Pk BN16...........**205** E5
Rutherford Way RH10......**6** A3
Rutherford Way Ind Est
RH10 ....**6** A3
Rutherwick Cl RH6 ....**1** F3
Ruthven Cl RH17..........**86** F7
Rutland Cl BN3............**186** F6
Rutland Gdns BN3........**190** F7
Rutland Rd BN3...........**191** A7
Rutland Way PO19 ......**177** D8
Rydal Cl
Crawley RH11 ....**17** D4
Littlehampton BN17.......**205** A4
Ryde Ct BN3...............**168** D1
Ryde Rd BN2 ....**192** D7
Rydex Way RH12 ....**36** F7
Rydon Com Coll
RH20 ....**122** A2
Rye Ash RH10 ....**19** A7
Ryebank Cvn Site
BN18 ....**202** F7
Rye Cl
Saltdean BN2..............**194** F2
Worthing BN11 ....**186** A1
Ryecroft
🔢 Brighton BN2..........**192** F5
Haywards Heath RH16......**87** E3
Ryecroft Ct BN15.........**187** E5
Ryecroft Ct RH11..........**36** A3
Ryecroft Gdns BN12.....**185** C3
Ryecroft La RH20.........**121** D1
Ryecroft Mdw RH13......**57** F9
Ryecroft Rd RH17..........**85** C3
Rye Farm La RH13 ....**57** A2
Ryefield Cl GU31...........**68** E3
Ryelands
Crawley RH11 ....**18** A5
Horley RH6 ....**2** C3
Ryelands Dr BN2 ....**170** D3

S

Sabey Ct 🔢 PO21........**201** D3
Sabre Rd PO10 ....**173** C3
Sack La PO22...............**179** E2
Sackville Cl RH19...........**9** C3
Sackville Coll* RH19.......**9** F1
Sackville Cres BN14......**186** E4
Sackville Ct 🔢 RH19......**22** F8
Sackville Gdns
East Grinstead RH19.........**9** C3
Hove BN3.................**190** F6
Sackville La RH19...........**9** C3
Sackville Rd
Hove BN3.................**191** A7
Worthing BN14 ....**186** E4
Sackville Sch RH19..........**10** A1
Sackville Trad Est
BN3 ....**191** B8
Sackville Way BN14......**186** E4
Saddle La PO20...........**212** D8
Saddler Row RH10..........**18** D3
Saddlers Cl
Billingshurst RH14..........**79** C8
Burgess Hill RH15........**109** D1
Saddler's Row GU28.......**97** F8
SADDLESCOMBE **148** E3
Saddlescombe Rd
BN45 ....**148** D4
Sadler St PO21 ....**201** C2
Sadlers The PO18.........**155** D1
Sadlers Wlk
🔢 Chichester PO19 ....**177** A6

Sadlers Wlk continued
Hermitage PO10 . . . . 173 C8
Sadler Way BN2 . . . . 192 F6
Saffron Cl
Crawley RH11 . . . . 18 A3
Shoreham-by-S BN43 . . . . 167 C1
Saffron Ct 2 PO21 . . . . . . 201 C4
Saffron Gate BN3 . . . . . . 191 C7
Saffrons Ct BN13 . . . . . . 186 A3
Saffrons The RH15 . . . . . 108 F5
Sage Ho 3 RH10 . . . . 6 A1
St Agnes Pl PO19 . . . . . . 177 B6
St Agnes Rd RH19 . . . . 9 E2
St Andrews RH6 . . . . 2 B2
St Andrew's CE High Sch
  for Boys BN14 . . . . 186 E4
St Andrew's CE Prim Sch
  Crawley RH10 . . . . 19 A4
  Hove BN3 . . . . 191 B7
  Nuthurst RH13 . . . . 59 A1
  Steyning BN44 . . . . 145 D4
St Andrew's Cl
  Ferring BN12 . . . . 206 E6
  Oving PO20 . . . . 178 C6
St Andrews Cl BN11 . . . . . 186 C2
St Andrew's Gdns
  BN13 . . . . 186 A4
St Andrews La PO20 . . . . . 156 C1
St Andrew's Rd
  Burgess Hill RH15 . . . . . 109 C4
  Crawley RH11 . . . . 17 D5
St Andrew's Rd
  Brighton BN1 . . . . 170 A1
  Portslade-by-S BN41 . . . . 190 C7
  Worthing BN13 . . . . 185 F5
St Anne's Ct
  5 Brighton BN1 . . . . . . 213 A4
  9 Brighton, Kemp Town
  BN2 . . . . 192 C4
  East Wittering PO20 . . . . 207 F7
St Anne's Gdns BN6 . . . . . 129 A3
St Anne's Ho 6 BN11 . . . . 213 A4
St Anne's Rd RH10 . . . . 6 C2
St Annes Well Ho 6
  BN3 . . . . 191 D6
St Ann's Ct BN3 . . . . 191 D7
St Ann's Hill GU29 . . . . . . 94 F7
St Ann's Ho GU29 . . . . 94 F8
St Anns Mans 2 BN1 . . . . . 191 E7
St Anselm's Rd BN14 . . . . 186 B4
St Anthony's Sch
  PO19 . . . . 176 F8
St Anthony's Way 1
  BN16 . . . . 205 D6
St Aubin's Wlk
  PO21 . . . . 200 D3
St Aubin Cl RH11 . . . . 17 F2
St Aubins Cl 1 BN2 . . . . . 206 F4
St Aubins Cl 3 BN12 . . . . 206 F4
St Aubyns BN3 . . . . 191 B6
St Aubin's Cres BN41 . . . . 190 B7
St Aubyn's Gdns 13
  BN3 . . . . 191 A6
St Aubyns Mans BN3 . . . . 191 A5
St Aubyn's Mead BN2 . . . . 194 A1
St Aubyn's Rd
  Portslade-by-S, Aldrington
  BN41 . . . . 190 C7
  Portslade-by-S, Fishersgate
  BN41 . . . . 190 A7
St Aubyns S BN3 . . . . 191 A5
St Augustine Rd 12
  BN17 . . . . 204 E4
St Augustine's CE Prim
  Sch BN17 . . . . 88 F3
St Augustines Cl RH17 . . . . 88 F3
St Barnabas Rd RH10 . . . . . 19 C7
St Bartholomew's CE Prim
  Sch
  Brighton BN1 . . . . 213 B4
  Haslemere GU27 . . . . 27 C7
St Bartholomews Cl
  PO19 . . . . 176 E6
St Bernadette's RC Prim
  Sch BN1 . . . . 169 E2
St Bernards Ct BN11 . . . . . 187 E5
St Blaises Rd PO18 . . . . . 156 C4
St Botolphs Ct 2
  BN11 . . . . 186 B3
St Botolph's Rd BN11 . . . . 186 B3
St Breladtes Rd RH11 . . . . . 17 F2
St Catherines Ct
  BN17 . . . . 204 D4
St Catherine's Ct RH19 . . . . . 9 D2
St Catherine's RC Prim
  Sch BN17 . . . . 204 D6
St Catherines Rd RH10 . . . . . 6 C1
St Catherine's Rd
  BN17 . . . . 204 D4
St Catherines Terr
  PO22 . . . . 201 F3
St Catherine's Terr 1
  BN3 . . . . 191 B5
St Christophers Cl 5
  RH12 . . . . 36 C4
St Christopher's Cl
  Chichester PO19 . . . . . . 176 C6
  Haslemere GU27 . . . . 27 A6
St Christopher's Gn
  GU27 . . . . 27 A6
St Christopher's Rd
  Haslemere GU27 . . . . 27 A6
  Hurstpierpoint BN6 . . . . . 128 A6
St Christopher's Sch
  BN3 . . . . 191 A6
St Clare's Gdns PO21 . . . . . 201 A6
St Clare's Mews PO22 . . . . 201 F4

St Clement Rd RH11 . . . . . . 17 F2
St Cuthmans Cl BN2 . . . . . 192 F6
St Cuthman's Rd
  BN44 . . . . 145 D4
St Cyriacs PO19 . . . . 177 A7
St David's Gate 4
  BN15 . . . . 187 D6
St Dunstan's Rd BN13 . . . . 186 A3
St Edmunds Cl RH11 . . . . . . 5 D1
St Edmund's Rd RH11 . . . . . 87 F3
St Edward's Cl RH19 . . . . . . 9 C1
St Elmo Rd BN14 . . . . 186 B4
St Flora's Cl BN17 . . . . . . 204 F5
St Flora's Rd BN17 . . . . . . 204 F5
St Francis Cl RH16 . . . . . . 87 F2
St Francis Gdns RH10 . . . . . . 7 C4
St Francis of Assisi RC
  Prim Sch RH10 . . . . 18 E4
St Francis Wlk RH11 . . . . . . 17 E4
St Gabriels Rd RH14 . . . . . 79 E8
St Georges RH6 . . . . 2 B2
St Georges Cl RH6 . . . . 2 B3
St George's Cl PO20 . . . . . 212 F8
St Georges Ct
  Chichester PO19 . . . . . . 177 B5
  Crawley RH10 . . . . 18 D8
  East Grinstead RH19 . . . . . 9 C3
St George's Dr PO19 . . . . . 176 F3
St George's Gdns
  Horsham RH13 . . . . 36 E4
  1 Worthing BN11 . . . . . . 186 E4
St George's La BN6 . . . . . . 128 B5
St George's Mews
  BN1 . . . . 213 B3
St George's Pl
  Brighton BN1 . . . . 213 B3
  Hurstpierpoint BN6 . . . . . 128 B5
St Georges Rd RH13 . . . . . 185 A3
St George's Rd
  Brighton BN2 . . . . 192 D4
  Worthing BN11 . . . . 186 F2
St George's Terr 5
  BN2 . . . . 192 C4
St Georges Wlk PO20 . . . . . 179 F7
St Georges Wood
  GU27 . . . . 27 D8
St Giles CE Prim Sch
  BN1 . . . . 65 C6
St Helen's Cres BN3 . . . . . 168 D3
St Helen's Dr RH11 . . . . . . 168 D3
St Helen's Rd BN2 . . . . . . 192 D7
St Helier Ct RH11 . . . . 18 A2
St Helier Ct 2 BN12 . . . . . 206 F4
St Helier Ct 2 BN12 . . . . . 206 F4
St Heliers Ave BN3 . . . . . . 190 E7
St Hilda's Ct
  Crawley RH10 . . . . 6 C1
  Horley RH6 . . . . 2 B3
  Selsey PO20 . . . . 212 D6
Saint Hill Gn RH19 . . . . . . 22 D4
Saint Hill Manor*
  RH19 . . . . 22 C4
Saint Hill Rd RH19 . . . . . . 22 C5
St Hugh's CE Prim Sch
  RH11 . . . . 6 C1
St Itha Cl PO20 . . . . 212 E7
St Itha Rd PO20 . . . . 212 E6
St Ives PO20 . . . . 19 C7
St Ives Sch GU27 . . . . 27 E8
St James Ave BN15 . . . . . . 187 E8
St James CE Prim Sch
  PO10 . . . . 151 B2
St James' CE Prim Sch
  RH20 . . . . 119 C6
St James Cotts RH17 . . . . . 41 A1
St James Ct
  Chichester PO19 . . . . . . 177 B7
  East Grinstead RH19 . . . . . 9 E1
St James' Ho 1 BN2 . . . . . 213 C2
St James' Ind Est
  PO19 . . . . 177 C7
St James Rd RH19 . . . . 9 D1
St James' Rd
  Chichester PO19 . . . . . . 177 B7
  Emsworth PO10 . . . . 151 B1
St James's Ave BN2 . . . . . 213 C2
St James's Cl PO20 . . . . . . 197 E5
St James's Pl BN2 . . . . . . 213 C2
St James's Sq PO19 . . . . . 177 C7
St James's Street Mews
  BN2 . . . . 213 C2
St James Wlk RH11 . . . . . . 18 C2
St Joan Cl RH11 . . . . 5 D1
St John Cl RH13 . . . . 105 A3
St John's Ave
  Burgess Hill RH15 . . . . . 108 F4
  Worthing BN12 . . . . 185 D2
St John's Cl
  Bognor Regis PO21 . . . . . 200 F4
  East Grinstead RH19 . . . . . 9 E2
  Midhurst GU29 . . . . 94 E7
  Worthing BN12 . . . . 185 D2
St John's Coll BN2 . . . . . . 192 D5
ST JOHN'S COMMON
  . . . . 108 E4
St John's Cres RH12 . . . . . 35 E3
St John's Ct RH11 . . . . . . 109 A3
St John's Ct 5 BN15 . . . . . 187 D6
St John's Mews Cotts 7
  BN43 . . . . 188 E7
St John's Mount 8
  BN2 . . . . 213 C2
St John's Pl
  Brighton BN2 . . . . 213 C2
  23 Hove BN3 . . . . 191 C6

St John's RC Prim Sch
  RH12 . . . . 36 A1
St Johns Rd RH15 . . . . 109 A3
St John's Rd
  Breach PO10 . . . . 151 F1
  Crawley RH11 . . . . 9 E2
  East Grinstead RH19 . . . . . 9 E2
  Haywards Heath RH16 . . . . 87 E2
  Hove BN3 . . . . 191 C5
St John's Sch BN2 . . . . . . 192 D5
St John's Sch PO19 . . . . . . 177 A6
St John The Baptist CE
  Prim Sch BN14 . . . . 163 E6
St John the Baptist RC
  Sch BN2 . . . . 192 D5
St Josephs Abbey
  RH20 . . . . 142 D8
St Josephs Bsns Pk 2
  BN3 . . . . 191 A3
St Joseph's Cl BN3 . . . . . . 191 A8
St Joseph's Mews
  RH20 . . . . 142 D8
St Joseph's RC Prim Sch
  Brighton BN2 . . . . 192 C5
  Haywards Heath RH16 . . . . 87 E4
St Joseph's Trad Est 3
  BN3 . . . . 191 A8
St Josephs Way RH16 . . . . . 87 E4
St Julian RH19 . . . . 9 F2
St Julians Cl BN43 . . . . . . 189 C7
St Julian's La BN43 . . . . . . 189 C7
St Keyna Ave BN3 . . . . 190 D6
St Lawrence Ave
  BN14 . . . . 186 B4
St Lawrence CE Prim Sch
  BN15 . . . . 128 A6
St Lawrence Ct BN14 . . . . . 186 A4
St Lawrence Way
  BN15 . . . . 128 A6
St Ledegar's Way
  PO20 . . . . 177 A1
St Leonards RH12 . . . . 36 F4
St Leonard's Ave BN3 . . . . 190 C7
St Leonards Dr RH10 . . . . . 19 A4
St Leonard's Gdns
  BN15 . . . . 187 E6
St Leonard's Park Ho
  RH13 . . . . 37 C3
St Leonards Pk RH19 . . . . . . 9 E1
St Leonards Rd RH19 . . . . . 37 A1
St Leonard's Rd
  6 Brighton BN2 . . . . . . 192 C8
  Hove BN3 . . . . 190 C7
St Louie Cl BN42 . . . . 190 A8
St Luke's Cl BN15 . . . . . . 187 B4
St Lukes Ct RH15 . . . . . . 109 A3
St Luke's Inf Sch BN2 . . . . 192 D5
St Luke's Jun Sch
  BN2 . . . . 192 C6
St Luke's Rd BN2 . . . . 192 C6
St Luke's Terr BN2 . . . . . . 192 C6
St Malo Cl BN2 . . . . 206 F4
St Malo Ct 4 BN12 . . . . . . 206 F4
St Margarets BN2 . . . . 194 A1
St Margaret's Ave RH19 . . . . 9 F1
St Margaret's CE Prim Sch
  Angmering BN16 . . . . . . 183 F7
  Crawley RH11 . . . . 18 B7
  Rottingdean BN2 . . . . . . 194 A2
St Margaret's Cotts
  GU29 . . . . 49 B6
St Margarets Ct RH12 . . . . . 35 F7
St Margaret's Ct
  BN16 . . . . 183 F6
St Margaret's Pl BN1 . . . . . 213 A2
St Margaret's Rd RH19 . . . . . 9 F1
St Margaret's Sch
  GU29 . . . . 94 E8
St Mark's CE Prim Sch
  Brighton BN2 . . . . 192 E5
  Staplefield RH17 . . . . . . 61 F5
St Mark's Cres BN15 . . . . . 187 B4
St Mark's La RH12 . . . . . . 36 E6
St Mark's Mews 13
  BN2 . . . . 192 E4
St Martin Cl RH17 . . . . 61 B7
St Martins CE Prim Sch
  BN2 . . . . 192 D5
St Martin's Ct 6 BN2 . . . . 213 C5
St Martin's Flats 4
  BN2 . . . . 192 C7
St Martin's La 11
  BN17 . . . . 204 D5
St Martin's Pl BN2 . . . . . . 192 C7
St Martins Rd BN17 . . . . . . 204 D5
St Martin's Sq PO19 . . . . . 177 A7
St Martin's St
  Brighton BN2 . . . . 213 C5
  Chichester PO19 . . . . . . 177 A7
St Mary Magdalene St
  BN2 . . . . 213 C5
St Mary Magdalen RC
  Prim Sch BN1 . . . . 191 E5
St Mary's 12 RH20 . . . . . . 142 D8
St Mary's Abbey GU27 . . . . 26 D7
St Mary & St Paul CE Fst
  Sch GU31 . . . . 91 D3
St Mary's CE Fst Sch
  RH20 . . . . 143 D6
St Mary's CE Prim Sch
  Climping RH11 . . . . 203 E8
  Horsham RH12 . . . . 36 C1
  Pulborough RH20 . . . . . . 100 C3
St Mary's CE RH19 . . . . 9 D2
St Marys Cl
  Bognor Regis PO22 . . . . . 201 D5
  Lancing BN15 . . . . 187 B1

St Mary's Cl
  Billingshurst RH14 . . . . . 79 D8
  Littlehampton BN17 . . . . 204 E5
  Mid Lavant PO18 . . . . . . 154 F7
  Pulborough RH20 . . . . . . 100 C2
  Shoreham-by-S BN43 . . . . 188 F7
St Mary's Ct
  Bramber BN44 . . . . 145 F2
  6 Littlehampton BN17 . . . 204 E5
  Worthing BN13 . . . . 185 D7
St Mary's Ctyd PO22 . . . . . 201 F4
St Mary's Ctyd PO19 . . . . . 177 A6
St Mary's Dr
  Crawley RH10 . . . . 19 B8
  Rustington BN16 . . . . . . 205 F5
St Mary's Gdn PO19 . . . . . 177 A6
St Mary's Gdns
  Horsham RH12 . . . . 36 C1
  1 Littlehampton BN17 . . . 204 E5
St Mary's Ho 5 RH12 . . . . . 36 C1
St Mary's Ho & Gdns*
  BN44 . . . . 145 F2
St Mary's Mdw BN18 . . . . . 180 F4
St Mary's Mews PO22 . . . . 201 F4
St Marys Pl 3 BN3 . . . . . . 189 A6
St Mary's Pl BN2 . . . . 213 C2
St Mary's RC Prim Sch
  Bognor regis PO21 . . . . . 201 C2
  Portslade-by-S BN41 . . . . 190 B7
  Worthing BN11 . . . . 186 C2
St Mary's Rd
  Boxgrove RH10 . . . . 156 C4
  Burgess Hill RH15 . . . . . 108 F4
  Liss GU33 . . . . 45 B4
  Shoreham-by-S BN43 . . . . 188 F7
St Mary's Slindon CE Prim
  Sch BN18 . . . . 158 D4
St Mary's Sq 17 BN2 . . . . . 192 D4
St Mary's Terr 6
  BN2 . . . . 188 E7
St Mary's Way BN17 . . . . . 204 E5
St Matthews Ct BN2 . . . . . 192 C5
St Matthew's Rd
  BN11 . . . . 186 C3
St Maur's Rd BN12 . . . . . . 206 E6
St Michaels Cl GU28 . . . . . 51 A7
St Michaels Cotts 11
  BN44 . . . . 145 D3
St Michael's Cl
  BN15 . . . . 187 D5
St Michael's Ct BN11 . . . . . 186 B2
St Michael's Pl BN1 . . . . . 191 E6
St Michaels Rd RH19 . . . . . . 9 E2
St Michael's Rd
  Portslade-by-S BN41 . . . . 190 B7
  Worthing BN11 . . . . 186 B2
St Michaels Way
  RH13 . . . . 105 A3
St Nicholas' CE Jun Sch
  BN11 . . . . 190 B8
St Nicholas Cl
  Crawley RH10 . . . . 19 C7
  Lindfield RH16 . . . . 88 A6
  8 Middleton-on-S
  . . . . 202 F5
St Nicholas' Ct 3
  BN15 . . . . 187 D6
St Nicholas Lo 5
  PO22 . . . . 202 F5
St Nicholas Lo BN11 . . . . . 213 A2
St Nicholas Pl 2
  BN3 . . . . 189 A6
St Nicholas Rd
  Brighton BN1 . . . . 213 A3
  Mid Lavant PO18 . . . . . . 154 E6
  Portslade-by-S BN41 . . . . 190 B7
St Nicolas Cl BN43 . . . . . . 188 D8
St Nicolas La BN43 . . . . . . 188 D8
St Nicolas & St Mary CE
  Fst & Mid Sch BN43 . . . . 189 A8
St Osmund Rd BN12 . . . . . 206 E6
St Pancras PO19 . . . . 177 B7
St Pancras Ct PO19 . . . . . 177 B6
St Pancras Gn BN7 . . . . . . 172 E5
St Patrick's La GU33 . . . . . 45 F5
St Patrick's Rd BN3 . . . . . . 191 A7
St Paul's Ave BN15 . . . . . . 187 B4
St Paul's CE Prim Sch
  BN1 . . . . 213 A3
St Paul's Cl RH16 . . . . 87 F5
St Paul's Gdns PO19 . . . . . 176 F7
St Pauls Lo BN43 . . . . 188 F7
St Paul's RC Coll
  RH15 . . . . 108 D5
St Paul's Rd PO19 . . . . . . 176 F8
St Paul's St BN2 . . . . 213 C5
St Peter's PO19 . . . . 177 A7
St Peter's CE Prim Sch
  Ardingly RH17 . . . . 64 A8
  Cowfold RH13 . . . . 83 E2
  Henfield BN5 . . . . 125 D5
St Peters Ct PO21 . . . . . . 200 E4
St Peter's Cl
  Cowfold RH13 . . . . 83 E1
  Hove BN3 . . . . 168 F2
St Peter's Com Inf Sch
  BN41 . . . . 190 B7
St Peter's Cres PO20 . . . . . 212 E6
St Peter's Ct 1 PO21 . . . . . 173 C8
St Peter's Gdn 6 GU32 . . . . 68 B3
St Peter's Gn BN44 . . . . . . 146 A2
St Peter's Ho BN44 . . . . . . 213 B3
St Peter's Pl
  Brighton BN1, BN2 . . . . . 213 B3
  Seaford BN25 . . . . 187 C4
St Peter's RC Prim Sch
  BN43 . . . . 189 A8

St Peter's RC Sch RH19 . . . . . 9 C1
St Peters Rd
  Crawley RH11 . . . . 18 C6
  Petersfield GU32 . . . . . . 68 B3
  Portslade-by-S BN41 . . . . 190 B7
St Peter's Sq 9 PO10 . . . . 173 B8
St Peter's St BN1 . . . . 213 B4
St Peters View BN5 . . . . . . 125 C6
St Philip Howard RC High
  Sch The PO22 . . . . 180 A6
St Philip's Ct BN17 . . . . . . 204 D7
St Philips Mews 3
  BN3 . . . . 190 F7
St Philip's RC Prim Sch
  BN18 . . . . 160 A3
St Raphael Rd BN11 . . . . . 185 F3
St Richards Cl BN12 . . . . . 185 C4
St Richards Cotts
  Codmore Hill RH20 . . . . . 100 D6
  Cootham RH20 . . . . 121 A1
  Fittleworth RH20 . . . . . . 99 A2
St Richard's Cotts
  GU31 . . . . 92 A4
St Richard's Ct BN3 . . . . . 168 D8
St Richard's Dr PO21 . . . . . 200 D3
St Richard's Flats GU29 . . . 94 D8
St Richard's Flats
  BN44 . . . . 190 B7
St Richard's Hospl
  PO19 . . . . 177 B8
St Richard's RC Prim Sch
  PO19 . . . . 177 A5
St Richards Rd PO20 . . . . . 179 E7
St Richard's Rd BN41 . . . . . 190 B7
St Richard's Way
  PO21 . . . . 200 D3
St Richard's Wlk
  PO19 . . . . 176 F6
St Robert's Lo 1
  BN15 . . . . 187 E5
St Robert Southwell RC
  Prim Sch RH12 . . . . 37 A6
St Roche's Cl PO18 . . . . . . 154 F7
St Sampson Rd RH11 . . . . . 17 F2
St Saviours Ct 8 BN1 . . . . 192 B8
St Stephen Cl RH11 . . . . . . 5 D1
St Stephen's Cl GU27 . . . . . 26 F6
St Swithun's Ct RH19 . . . . . . 9 F1
St Thomas Ct PO21 . . . . . . 211 A8
St Thomas Dr PO21 . . . . . . 210 F8
St Thomas's Rd BN14 . . . . . 186 B4
St Valerie Rd BN11 . . . . . . 186 A1
St Vincent Cl RH10 . . . . . . 19 D5
St Vincent's Ct BN2 . . . . . 193 A3
St Wilfred Ho BN15 . . . . . . 187 C5
St Wilfred's Cl PO20 . . . . . 212 G8
St Wilfred's Ct BN14 . . . . . 186 D4
St Wilfrid Rd PO19 . . . . . . 176 D7
St Wilfrid's CE Prim Sch
  BN17 . . . . 87 F3
St Wilfrids Cl RH15 . . . . . 109 B4
St Wilfrids Flat's BN2 . . . . 192 C7
St Wilfrids RC Comp Sch
  RH11 . . . . 18 B5
St Wilfrids RC Prim Sch
  BN16 . . . . 183 F6
St Wilfrids Rd RH15 . . . . . 108 F2
St Wilfrids Rd RH15 . . . . . 109 B4
St Wilfrids View
  PO20 . . . . 212 G8
St Wilfrid's Way RH16 . . . . 87 C4
St Winefride's Ct
  BN17 . . . . 204 E4
St Winifred's Cl PO21 . . . . 201 B2
Sake Ride La BN5 . . . . 106 C1
Salbrook Rd RH1 . . . . 2 A8
Salcombe Rd BN14 . . . . . . 19 E6
Salisbury Ct
  10 Hove BN3 . . . . 191 C6
  Southwater RH13 . . . . . . 58 A2
Salisbury Ho BN12 . . . . . . 185 A4
Salisbury Rd
  Crawley RH10 . . . . 18 F2
  Hove BN3 . . . . 191 C6
  Tower Hill RH13 . . . . 58 A8
  Worthing BN11 . . . . 186 D2
Salisbury Way PO19 . . . . . 154 F1
Salt Box Cl RH13 . . . . 56 F2
Saltdean Cl BN2 . . . . 194 B1
Saltdean Park Rd
  BN2 . . . . 194 C1
Saltdean Prim Sch
  BN2 . . . . 194 D2
Saltdean Vale BN2 . . . . . . 194 D2
Salterns Rd RH10 . . . . 19 C5
Saltham La PO20 . . . . 177 E1
Salthill La RH19 . . . . 176 E8
Salthill Rd PO19 . . . . 176 C8
Saltings The
  Birdham PO20 . . . . 197 E4
  Lancing BN15 . . . . 187 F5
  Littlehampton BN17 . . . . 205 A6
  Shoreham-by-S BN43 . . . . 188 E7
Saltings Way BN44 . . . . . . 146 A2
SALVATION 186 A7
Salvington Cl BN13 . . . . . 185 D8
Salvington Ct BN13 . . . . . 163 F2
Salvington Gdns
  BN13 . . . . 185 F2
SALVINGTON HILL 163 E2

Salvington Hill BN13 . . . . .163 E1
Salvington Rd
  Crawley RH11 . . . . .17 F3
  Worthing BN13 . . . . .185 E8
Samarian Ct RH11 . . . . . .17 E4
Samphire Cl RH11 . . . . . .18 A3
Samphire Dr BN3 . . . . . .185 A6
Sampsons Dr PO20 . . . . .178 C7
Sanctuary La PO20 . . . . .122 C1
Sandbrook BN6 . . . . .128 F3
Sandcroft PO20 . . . . .179 F7
Sandeman Way RH13 . . . . .58 F8
Sanders Ho BN3 . . . . . . .190 E8
Sanderstead BN2 . . . . . . .192 C8
Sandfield Ave BN17 . . . . .204 D8
Sandgate La RH20 . . . . . .122 A2
Sandgate Rd BN1 . . . . . . .170 A2
Sandhawes Hill RH19 . . . . .10 A4
Sandhill La
  Crawley Down RH10 . . . . .21 B7
  Washington RH20 . . . . . .143 E7
Sandhills Rd RH13 . . . . . . .56 F3
Sandhurst Ave BN2 . . . . .171 D1
  Sandhurst Sch BN11 . . . .186 F2
Sandown Ave BN12 . . . . .185 C2
Sandown Cl BN12 . . . . . .185 C2
Sandown Ct
  Crawley RH10 . . . . .19 D6
  Hove BN3 . . . . .168 D1
  ⑨ Worthing BN11 . . . . .186 C1
Sandown Rd
  Brighton BN2 . . . . .192 D7
  Southwick BN42 . . . . . . .189 E8
Sandpiper Cl RH11 . . . . . .17 D4
Sandpiper Ct PO20 . . . . .208 A6
Sandridge La RH16 . . . . . .63 F1
Sandringham Cl
  Bracklesham PO20 . . . . .208 B5
  East Grinstead RH19 . . . . .23 A8
  Hove BN3 . . . . .169 A3
Sandringham Ct ⑧
  BN15 . . . . .187 F5
Sandringham Dr BN3 . . . .169 A3
Sandringham Ho ⑰
  BN3 . . . . .191 C6
Sandringham Mews
  Worthing BN14 . . . . .186 D6
  Worthing, Durrington
  BN13 . . . . .185 D8
Sandringham Rd
  Chichester PO19 . . . . . . .177 C6
  Crawley RH11 . . . . .18 B2
  Petersfield GU32 . . . . .68 B4
Sandringham Way
  PO21 . . . . .201 B4
Sandrock
  Haslemere GU27 . . . . .27 C6
  Midhurst GU29 . . . . .94 D8
Sandrock Cotts GU28 . . . . .51 A7
Sandrocks Way RH16 . . . . .87 E2
Sandsbury La GU32 . . . . . .67 E5
Sands La BN5 . . . . .146 F6
Sands The RH20 . . . . .123 A5
Sandwich Rd BN11 . . . . . .185 F2
Sandy Beach Est
  PO11 . . . . .195 B1
Sandy Cl GU31 . . . . .68 E3
Sandy Cotts RH10 . . . . . . .21 A8
Sandygate La RH13 . . . . . .59 F3
Sandy La
  Chelwood Gate RH17 . . . . .66 C8
  Crawley Down RH10 . . . . .21 A8
  East Ashling PO18 . . . . .153 D4
  East Grinstead RH19 . . . . . .9 F1
  Fittleworth RH20 . . . . .99 A2
  Haslemere GU26, GU27 . . . .26 C7
  Heath Common RH20 . . . .122 C1
  Henfield BN5 . . . . .125 D4
  Midhurst GU29 . . . . .94 D8
  Rake GU33 . . . . .46 A4
  Steep GU32 . . . . .68 D8
  Watersfield RH20 . . . . . . .119 A5
  West Hoathly RH20 . . . . . .42 E6
Sandymount Ave
  PO22 . . . . .201 B5
Sandymount Cl PO22 . . . .201 C4
Sandy Point Cl PO20 . . . .212 B8
Sandy Point La PO20 . . . .212 B8
Sandy Point Rd PO11 . . . .195 A1
Sandy Way
  Fittleworth RH20 . . . . .99 A2
Sandy Vale RH10 . . . . .22 C2
San Feliu Ct RH19 . . . . . . .10 B2
Sangers Dr RH16 . . . . .1 F3
Sanyhils Ave BN1 . . . . . .169 F7
Sapex Bldgs PO19 . . . . . .177 C7
Sarel Way RH6 . . . . .2 B5
Sargent Cl RH10 . . . . .18 F2
Sarisbury Cl PO22 . . . . . .202 A5
Sark Cl RH11 . . . . .18 A8
Sark Gdns BN12 . . . . .206 F4
Satellite Bsns Village The
  RH10 . . . . .5 E2
Satinwood Cl PO22 . . . . .202 E6
Saturn Cl RH11 . . . . .17 E4
Saucelands La RH13 . . . . .102 E7
Saunders Cl RH10 . . . . . . .19 B7
Saunders Hill BN1 . . . . . .170 D7
Saunders Ho BN2 ❷
  BN2 . . . . .192 C8
Saunders Park Rise
  BN2 . . . . .170 C1
Saunders Park View
  BN2 . . . . .170 C1
Savernake Wlk RH10 . . . . .18 F3
Saville Ct RH14 . . . . .79 D7

Saville Gdns RH14 . . . . . . .79 D7
Savill Rd RH16 . . . . .88 A8
Sawyers Cl RH15 . . . . . . .109 D1
Saxby Cl PO22 . . . . .180 B5
Saxby Ct PO22 . . . . .180 B5
Saxby Rd RH15 . . . . .108 D4
Saxifrage Way BN13 . . . . .185 A6
Saxley RH6 . . . . .2 C4
Saxley Ct RH6 . . . . .2 C3
Saxonbury ⑩ BN2 . . . . . .213 C3
Saxon Cl
  Billingshurst RH14 . . . . . . .55 D1
  East Preston BN16 . . . . . .206 B7
  Pagham PO21 . . . . .210 F8
  Saltdean BN2 . . . . .194 C2
Saxon Cres RH12 . . . . .36 B4
Saxon Ct BN3 . . . . .190 D6
Saxon Mdw PO20 . . . . . .156 C1
Saxon Rd
  Bramber BN44 . . . . .145 F3
  Crawley RH10 . . . . .19 E5
  Hove BN3 . . . . .190 D6
Saxons BN43 . . . . .166 F1
Saxons Rd BN14 . . . . . . .186 C4
Saxony Rd BN14 . . . . . . .186 C4
Sayers The ⑤ RH19 . . . . . .9 C1
Scallows Cl RH10 . . . . .19 A7
Scallows Rd RH10 . . . . . . .19 A7
Scamps Hill RH16 . . . . . . .88 C6
Scant Rd E PO18 . . . . . . .152 F2
Scant Rd W PO18 . . . . . . .152 E2
Scarborough Rd BN1 . . . .169 D1
Sceptre BN1 . . . . .169 E2
Schaffer Ho RH10 . . . . . . .18 C6
Scholars Cl RH10 . . . . .21 A8
Scholar's Row PO22 . . . . .180 C5
School Cl
  Burgess Hill RH15 . . . . . .108 F2
  Fittleworth RH20 . . . . .99 A3
  Horsham RH12 . . . . .37 A6
  ① Southwick BN42 . . . . .189 E7
School Ct RH14 . . . . .53 B2
School Dell PO18 . . . . . . .153 A3
School Hill
  Findon BN14 . . . . .163 E6
  Slindon RH18 . . . . .158 C5
  Storrington RH20 . . . . . . .121 E1
  Warnham RH12 . . . . .35 F8
School La
  Arundel BN18 . . . . .160 A2
  Ashurst BN44 . . . . .124 D5
  Ashurst Wood RH19 . . . . .23 E6
  Billingshurst RH14 . . . . . . .79 E7
  Bosham PO18 . . . . .175 C5
  Compton PO18 . . . . .111 B2
  Danehill RH17 . . . . .66 B5
  Eastergate PO20 . . . . . . .179 F7
  Emsworth PO10 . . . . .173 B8
  Fittleworth RH20 . . . . .99 A3
  Forest Row RH18 . . . . . . .206 F6
  Lindfield RH16 . . . . .88 B7
  Liss GU33 . . . . .45 B4
  Lodsworth GU28 . . . . .74 B4
  North Mundham PO20 . . .177 D2
  Nutbourne PO18 . . . . . . .174 B7
  Petersfield GU32 . . . . .68 D6
  Pyecombe BN45 . . . . . . .149 C6
  Saltdean BN2 . . . . .194 C2
  Selsey PO20 . . . . .212 D8
  Shipley RH13 . . . . .81 C1
  Stedham GU29 . . . . .71 F1
  Steyning BN44 . . . . .145 D3
  Storrington RH20 . . . . . . .121 C1
  Sutton RH20 . . . . .117 F4
  Washington RH20 . . . . . .143 E6
  Westbourne PO10 . . . . . .151 D5
School Rd
  Amberley BN18 . . . . .140 E7
  Haslemere GU27 . . . . .26 F5
  Hove BN3 . . . . .190 F8
  Upper Beeding BN44 . . . .146 B2
  Wisborough Green RH14 . . .78 C8
School Rise BN2 . . . . . . .192 E6
Schooner Ct ⑨ BN21 . . . .205 A6
Science Park Rd BN1 . . . .171 B7
Science Park Sq BN1 . . . .171 B6
Scolliers Crossways
  RH13 . . . . .81 B3
Scory Cl RH11 . . . . .18 A3
Scotland La GU27 . . . . . . .27 C5
Scotlands Cl GU27 . . . . . .27 B5
Scotlands Dr GU27 . . . . . .27 C5
Scotland St BN2 . . . . .213 C3
Scotney Cl BN13 . . . . . . .185 B6
Scott Cl PO21 . . . . .201 C2
Scott Lo ① BN17
  BN17 . . . . .204 D5
Scott Rd
  Crawley RH10 . . . . .18 F3
  Hove BN3 . . . . .190 F7
Scotts Farm Cvn Pk
  PO20 . . . . .207 E8
Scott St PO21 . . . . .202 C6
Scrace Hill Terr RH16 . . . .109 F8
Scrase Lo RH15 . . . . .109 D3
Scratchings La GU28 . . . . .52 C5
Sculpture at Goodwood*
  PO18 . . . . .156 C8
Sea Ave BN16 . . . . .205 D5
Seabright ⑪ BN11 . . . . . .186 B1
Seabrook Cl PO21 . . . . . .200 D3
Seabrook Ct ⑤ RH15 . . . .187 E4
Sea Cl
  Middleton-on-S PO22 . . . .202 E5
  Worthing BN12 . . . . .185 E3
Seacourt Cl PO21 . . . . . . .200 D2
Seacroft BN16 . . . . .205 F5
Seadown Par BN15 . . . . . .187 C5

Sea Dr
  Bognor Regis PO22 . . . . .202 D4
  Ferring BN12 . . . . .206 F4
Seafarers Wlk PO11 . . . . .195 B1
Seafield Ave BN12 . . . . . .185 D2
Seafield Cl
  East Wittering PO20 . . . . .208 A6
  Littlehampton BN16 . . . . .205 C4
Seafield Rd
  Hove BN3 . . . . .191 B6
  Littlehampton BN16 . . . . .205 C4
  West Kingston BN16 . . . . .206 A4
Seafields
  Bracklesham PO20 . . . . .208 C5
  Emsworth PO10 . . . . .173 B8
  Shoreham-by-S BN43 . . . .188 F8
Seafield Terr ⑧ PO21 . . . .201 B2
Seafield Way PO20 . . . . . .208 A6
Seaford Ave BN43 . . . . . .189 B6
Seaford Rd
  Crawley RH11 . . . . .18 A2
  Hove BN3 . . . . .190 C6
Seagate Ct PO20 . . . . . . .207 E6
Seagate Wlk ❶ BN17 . . . .205 A4
Sea Gr PO20 . . . . .212 C6
Seagull Cl PO20 . . . . .209 C1
Seagull Cl PO10 . . . . .151 B1
Seagull La PO10 . . . . .151 B1
Seahaven Gdns BN43 . . . .188 D5
Sea Ho ⑭ BN42 . . . . .189 D7
Sea La
  Ferring BN12 . . . . .206 F6
  Kingston Gorse BN16 . . . .206 D4
  Littlehampton BN16 . . . . .205 F4
  Middleton-on-S PO22 . . . .202 E5
  Pagham PO21 . . . . .210 F7
  Rustington BN16 . . . . . . .205 B4
  Worthing BN12 . . . . .185 C2
Sea Lane Cl
  East Preston BN16 . . . . . .205 F5
  Ferring BN12 . . . . .206 F6
Sea Lane Gdns BN12 . . . .206 F5
Seal Ct PO20 . . . . .212 D8
Seal Prim Sch PO20 . . . . .212 E7
Seal Rd PO20 . . . . .212 D8
Seal Sq PO20 . . . . .212 D8
Seamill Cl ❶ BN1 . . . . . . .187 B3
Seamill Park Ave
  BN11 . . . . .187 B3
Seamill Park Cres
  BN11 . . . . .187 B3
Seamill Way BN11 . . . . . .187 B3
Sea Pl BN12 . . . . .185 E2
Sea Rd
  Bognor Regis PO22 . . . . .201 F3
  Littlehampton BN16,
  BN17 . . . . .205 A3
  Searle's View RH12 . . . . . .36 E5
  Sea-Saw Way BN12 . . . . .192 F7
  Seaside Ave BN15 . . . . . .187 F5
  Seaside Cl BN15 . . . . . . .187 F5
  Seaside Rd BN15 . . . . . . .187 F5
Sea Spray Ave BN43 . . . . .189 B6
Seaton Cl BN17 . . . . .204 D8
Seaton La BN17 . . . . .204 D8
Seaton Park Cotts
  BN17 . . . . .204 D8
Seaton Pk BN17 . . . . .204 D8
Seaton Rd BN17 . . . . .204 D8
Seaview Ave
  Kingston Gorse BN16 . . . .206 D4
  West Kingston BN16 . . . . .206 A4
Sea View Cotts PO10 . . . .173 B8
Seaview Ct
  ❷ Bognor Regis
  PO21 . . . . .201 C2
  Lancing BN15 . . . . .187 D4
  Selsey PO20 . . . . .212 D6
  ❹ Worthing BN11 . . . . .186 B1
Seaview St BN42 . . . . . . .189 F7
Seaview Gdns ⑤
  BN16 . . . . .205 C4
Seaview Rd
  West Kingston BN16 . . . . .206 A4
  Woodingdean BN2 . . . . . .193 B8
Sea View Rd BN11 . . . . . .186 B1
Sea View Way BN2 . . . . . .171 D1
Seaward Cl ⑥ PO21 . . . . .201 C3
Seaward Dr PO20 . . . . . . .196 C1
Seawaves Cl BN16 . . . . . .206 A5
Sea Way
  Bognor Regis PO21 . . . . .210 F8
  Elmer PO22 . . . . .203 B4
  Middleton-on-S PO22 . . . .202 E4
Seawood Ho PO20 . . . . . .207 F7
Second Ave
  Almodington PO20 . . . . . .197 F1
  Bognor Regis PO22 . . . . .202 B4
  Bracklesham PO20 . . . . .208 B5
  Hove BN3 . . . . .191 C6
  Lancing BN15 . . . . .187 C7
  Southbourne PO10 . . . . .173 B8
  Worthing BN14 . . . . .186 C8
Sedbury Rd BN15 . . . . . . .187 C8
Seddon Cl PO19 . . . . .177 C8
Seddon Rd RH11 . . . . .18 B1
Sedgefield Cl RH10 . . . . . .19 C6
Sedgewick Cl RH10 . . . . . .18 D2
Sedgewick La RH13 . . . . . .58 C1
Sefter Rd PO21 . . . . .210 E6
Sefton Ave PO21 . . . . . . .200 D3
Sefton Cl BN15 . . . . .185 D7
Sefton Rd BN41 . . . . .167 F3
Selba Dr BN2 . . . . .210 E3
Selborne BN12 GU32 . . . . .68 C5

Selborne Pl
  Hove BN3 . . . . .191 C7
  Littlehampton BN17 . . . . .204 E4
Selborne Rd
  Hove BN3 . . . . .191 C6
  Littlehampton BN17 . . . . .204 E4
  Worthing BN11 . . . . .186 F3
Selborne Way BN16 . . . . .205 F4
Selbourne Cl RH10 . . . . . . .6 D2
Selby Ct RH16 . . . . .87 E3
Selden La
  Selden BN13 . . . . .162 B1
  Worthing BN13 . . . . .186 F2
Selden Mews ❸
  BN11 . . . . .186 F2
Selden Par ❹ BN13 . . . . .185 F8
Selden Rd BN11 . . . . .186 F2
Selden's Mews BN13 . . . .185 F7
Selden's Way BN13 . . . . .185 F8
Sele Gdns BN44 . . . . .146 B2
Selham Cl
  Brighton BN1 . . . . .170 D6
  Chichester PO19 . . . . . . .155 A3
  Crawley RH11 . . . . .18 A7
Selham Dr BN1 . . . . .170 D6
Selham Pl BN1 . . . . .170 D6
Selham Rd GU29 . . . . .95 C6
Selhurst Cl BN16 . . . . . . .205 F5
Selhurstpark Rd
  PO18 . . . . .137 B4
Selhurst Rd BN2 . . . . .193 E6
Selkirk Cl BN13 . . . . .185 E5
Selmeston Pl BN2 . . . . . .192 F6
Selsey Ave PO21 . . . . . . .201 A2
Selsey Bsns Ctr ❸
  PO20 . . . . .212 D7
Selsey Cl
  Brighton BN1 . . . . .170 E6
  South Hayling PO11 . . . . .195 B2
  Worthing BN13 . . . . .185 F6
Selsey Ct
  ❸ Crawley RH11 . . . . . . .18 B2
  Littlehampton BN16 . . . . .205 B4
  Selsey PO20 . . . . .212 D6
Selsey Lifeboat Mus*
  PO20 . . . . .212 F6
Selsey Rd
  Crawley RH11 . . . . .18 A2
  Sidlesham PO20 . . . . . . .209 F7
  Stockbridge PO19 . . . . . .176 E3
  Street End PO20 . . . . . . .198 D2
  Street End PO20 . . . . . . .198 F6
SELSFIELD COMMON
  RH22 . . . . .BN31 D3
Selsfield Dr BN2 . . . . .170 D3
Selsfield Rd
  Little London RH17,
  RH19 . . . . .42 A4
  Turners Hill RH10, RH19 . . .21 A2
  West Hoathly RH19 . . . . . .42 C7
Selway La BN17 . . . . .204 F6
Selwyn Ave BN17 . . . . . . .204 D7
Selwyn Cl
  Bognor Regis PO21 . . . . .200 F4
  Crawley RH10 . . . . .6 C1
Semley Lo BN6 . . . . .128 E4
Semley Rd
  Brighton BN1 . . . . .170 A1
  Hassocks BN6 . . . . .128 E4
Senator Gdns PO19 . . . . .176 B7
Sequoia Pk RH11 . . . . .18 D4
Sergison Cl RH16 . . . . . . .87 C5
Sergison Rd RH16 . . . . . . .87 D5
Serrin Way RH12 . . . . .36 E5
Service Rd RH6 . . . . .5 F8
Service Ho PO21 . . . . .201 B4
Servite Ho PO21 . . . . .201 B4
Sett The BN41 . . . . .168 B2
Sevelands Cl RH12 . . . . . .192 F7
Seven Dials BN1 . . . . .213 A4
Sevenfields RH15 . . . . . . .108 D4
Seventh Ave BN15 . . . . . .187 E8
Severals Rd GU29 . . . . . . .94 C7
Severn Rd RH10 . . . . .19 C5
Seville St BN2 . . . . .192 C7
Sewill Cl RH6 . . . . .2 B6
Sextant Ct ❻ BN17
  BN17 . . . . .205 A6
Seymore Ho ❺ BN2 . . . . .192 D4
Seymour Ho ❺ BN2 . . . . .192 D4
Seymour Prim Sch
  RH11 . . . . .18 B2
Seymour Rd RH11 . . . . . . .18 B2
Seymour Sq BN2 . . . . . . .192 D4
Seymour St BN2 . . . . .192 D4
Shackleton Rd RH10 . . . . . .19 C5
Shadwells Cl BN15 . . . . . .187 F7
Shadwells Ct BN15 . . . . . .187 F7
Shadwells Rd BN15 . . . . . .187 F7
Shaftesbury Ave BN12,
  BN13 . . . . .185 E4
Shaftesbury Ct ❹
  BN16 . . . . .205 C4
Shaftesbury Pl
  Brighton BN1 . . . . .192 A8
  Rustington BN16 . . . . . . .205 C4
Shaftesbury Rd
  Brighton BN1 . . . . .213 B5
  Crawley RH10 . . . . .19 C6
  Littlehampton BN16 . . . . .205 C4
Shakespeare Ct RH11 . . . .186 C2
Shakespeare Ho ⑫
  BN1 . . . . .186 C3
Shakespeare Rd
  BN11 . . . . .186 C3
Shakespeare St BN3 . . . . .191 A8
Shalbourne Cres
  PO20 . . . . .208 C5
Shalesbrook La RH18 . . . . .23 F1

Shamrock Cl
  Bosham PO18 . . . . .175 C5
  Chichester PO19 . . . . . . .177 B8
Shandon Gdns BN14 . . . . .186 D6
Shandon Rd BN14 . . . . . .186 D6
Shandon Way BN14 . . . . .186 D6
Shandys BN3 . . . . .128 F3
Shandys Cl RH12 . . . . .36 C1
Shanklin Ct
  ❶ Brighton BN2 . . . . . . .192 C8
  Hove BN3 . . . . .168 D1
Shanklin Rd BN2 . . . . . . .192 C8
Shannon Cl BN17 . . . . . . .205 A4
Shardeloes Rd RH16 . . . . .183 F6
Sharon Cl ❷ RH10 . . . . . . .19 A4
Sharpthorne Cl RH11 . . . . .17 F6
Sharpthorne Cres
  BN41 . . . . .168 C4
Sharpthorne Ct BN1 . . . . .213 B4
Sharrow Cl RH16 . . . . .87 E5
Shaves Wood La BN6 . . . .127 A2
Shaw Cl ❶ RH10
  RH10 . . . . .202 F5
Shawcross Ho ❺ BN1 . . . .169 E2
Shaw's La RH11 . . . . .57 D1
Shaw Rd RH10 . . . . .18 F7
Shear Hill GU31 . . . . .68 D5
Shearwater Ct ❻
  RH11 . . . . .17 D5
Shearwater Dr PO22 . . . . .201 C6
Sheddingdean Bsns Ctr
  RH15 . . . . .108 F5
Sheddingdean Cl
  RH15 . . . . .109 A4
Sheddingdean Com Prim
  Sch RH15 . . . . .109 A5
Sheddingdean Ct
  RH15 . . . . .108 F4
Sheddingdean
  Neighbourhood Ctr
  RH15 . . . . .109 A5
Sheepbell Cl RH11 . . . . . . .17 D5
Sheepcote Valley Cvn Site
  BN2 . . . . .193 A5
Sheepdown Cl GU28 . . . . . .98 A7
Sheepdown Dr GU28 . . . . . .98 A7
Sheep Fold Ave BN16 . . . .205 E6
Sheep La GU29 . . . . .94 F8
Sheep Pen La BN44 . . . . .145 D3
Sheep St GU32 . . . . .68 B3
Sheepwash La
  East Lavant PO18 . . . . . .154 F5
  Shipton Green PO20 . . . . .196 E4
Sheep Wlk BN2 . . . . .193 F1
SHEET 68 D6
  Sheet Prim Sch GU32 . . . .68 D6
Sheffield Cl RH10 . . . . .19 B4
Sheffield Ct BN1 . . . . .213 B4
Sheffield Mews RH16 . . . . .87 D5
Shelby Rd BN13 . . . . .185 C7
Sheldon Cl RH10 . . . . .19 D5
Sheldon Ct BN11 . . . . . . .186 E1
Shelhurst Forest Wlk*
  PO18 . . . . .137 B4
Shellbridge Rd BN18 . . . . .158 E3
Shelldale Ave BN41 . . . . .190 B7
Shelldale Cres BN41 . . . . .190 B7
Shelldale Rd BN41 . . . . . .190 B8
Shelley Cl RH10 . . . . .19 C8
Shelley Ct ❹ RH16
  RH16 . . . . .37 D3
Shelley Dr RH13 . . . . .35 C3
Shelley Ho ❼ RH12 . . . . . .36 B2
Shelley Lo BN17 . . . . .204 F4
  Shelley Prim Sch RH12 . . .35 E3
Shelley Rd
  Bognor Regis PO21 . . . . .201 B3
  East Grinstead RH19 . . . . . .9 D1
  Horsham RH12 . . . . .36 B3
  Hove BN3 . . . . .190 F7
  Worthing BN11 . . . . .186 C2
Shelleys Cl RH13 . . . . .37 A3
Shelley Wood RH15 . . . . .108 D4
Shell La RH17 . . . . .41 C1
Shenfield Way BN1 . . . . . .170 B3
Shenstone RH16 . . . . .108 C4
Shepham Ave BN2 . . . . . .194 D2
Shepherd Cl RH10 . . . . . . .18 E3
Sherborne Cl BN13 . . . . . .168 D3
Sherbourne Cl PO20 . . . . .212 B8
Sherbourne La PO20 . . . . .186 A3
Sherbourne Rd BN3 . . . . .168 D3
Sherbourne Way BN3 . . . .168 D3
Sherbrooke BN13 . . . . . . .185 D7
Sheridan Ho BN3 . . . . . . .191 D6

Sheridan Mans BN3..... 191 A8
Sheridan Pl RH19........9 C1
Sheridan Rd BN14.....186 E5
Sheridan Terr BN3.....191 A8
Sherlock Ave PO19....176 E7
SHERMANBURY........105 D3
Shermanbury Ct
  Horsham RH12........36 D4
  Lancing BN15........187 C5
Shermanbury Dr
RH20................121 C2
Shermanbury Grange
RH13................105 C3
Shermanbury Rd
  Partridge Green
  RH13..............105 B3
  Worthing BN14......186 B4
Sherrington Mews 1
PO20................212 F8
Sherrington Rd BN2...193 F8
Sherston Cl RH20.....121 E2
Sherwood Cl
  Bognor Regis PO21...201 B6
  Liss GU33...........45 C7
Sherwood Dr RH16.....87 C5
Sherwood Rd PO22....201 B6
Sherwood Wlk RH10....18 F3
Shetland Cl RH10......19 E7
Shetland Ct BN13.....185 E6
Shillinglee Rd BN14...30 B4
Shimmings GU28.......98 B8
Shingle Rd BN43......189 A6
Shingle Wlk PO20.....207 F6
Shinwell Wlk 3 RH11...18 B1
Shipfield PO21........200 F2
SHIPLEY BRIDGE.......6 F6
Shipley Bridge La RH6,
RH10................6 F4
Shipley CE Prim Sch
RH13................81 B1
Shipley Cl GU30.......25 C3
Shipley Paygate RH13..81 E2
Shipley Rd
  Crawley RH11........18 A6
  Southwater RH13.....81 E5
  Woodingdean BN2....193 E7
Shipley Windmill*
RH13................103 C8
Shippen Ho 5 PO19...177 A6
Ship St
  Brighton BN1........213 A2
  East Grinstead RH19..22 E8
  Shoreham-by-S BN43..188 E7
Ship Street Gdns
BN1.................213 A2
Shipton Green La
PO20................197 B4
Shire Par RH10........19 D7
Shire Pl RH10.........19 D7
Shirlands Ct 3 BN16..205 D6
Shirley Ave BN3......169 B2
Shirley Cl
  Bognor Regis PO21...211 A8
  Crawley RH11........17 E2
  Rustington BN16.....205 D4
  Shoreham-by-S BN43..189 D8
  Worthing BN14......186 B7
Shirley Dr
  Bognor Regis PO22...202 A6
  Hove BN3...........169 C2
  Worthing BN14......186 B6
Shirley Mews BN3.....191 B7
Shirley Rd BN3.......191 C8
Shirley Sho..........129 E2
Shirleys Gdn PO22....202 B5
Shirley St BN3.......191 B7
Shooting Field BN44...145 D4
Shopfield Cl BN16....205 C6
Shop La PO18.........155 A5
Shopsdam Rd RH15....187 F4
Shopwhyke Ind Ctr
PO20................177 D7
Shopwhyke Rd PO20...177 E7
Shorecroft PO21......200 F1
Shoreham Airport Info
BN43................188 C8
SHOREHAM BEACH....189 A6
Shoreham Beach Com Fst
Sch BN43...........143 A2
Shoreham By-Pass BN41,
BN43................167 D2
Shoreham-by-Sea Sta
BN43................188 F7
Shoreham Coll BN43..189 D7
Shoreham Ct BN43....188 F8
Shoreham Fst Sch
BN43................188 E7
Shoreham Rd
  Crawley RH10........19 C3
  Small Dole BN5.....146 F8
  Upper Beeding BN44..166 B7
Shore Ho PO20.......212 D5
Shore Rd
  Bosham PO18........175 B3
  East Wittering PO20..207 E2
Shoreside Wlk PO20...207 F7
Short Cl RH11........18 D8
Short Furlong BN17...200 F4
Short Gallop RH10.....19 D7
Shortgate Rd BN2....170 F4
Shorts Cl RH16.......87 E3
Shortsfield Cl RH12...36 C5
Shotford PO20.......209 F8
Shotterfield Terr GU33..45 B4
SHOTTERMILL.........26 F6
Shottermill Rd RH12...37 A7
Shottermill Inf Sch
GU27................26 F7

Shottermill Jun sch
GU27................26 F7
Shottermill Pk GU27...26 E7
Shottermill Rd GU27...26 E7
Shotters RH15........108 E1
Shovelstrode La RH19..23 D8
Shrewsbury Ct 6
BN11................186 B1
Shripney La PO22.....179 C1
Shripney Rd
  Bognor Regis PO22...201 D5
  Bognor Regis PO22...201 E7
Shripney Trad Pk
PO21................201 E6
Shrubbs Dr PO22.....202 F5
Sickle Mill Cl GU27...26 F6
Sickle Rd GU27.......27 A5
Sidehill Dr BN41......167 F2
Sidengreen La PO18..155 F2
Sideways La RH6......1 J2
Sidings The RH12.....33 D7
Sidlesham Cl RH11...195 B2
Sidlesham La PO20...198 A4
Sidlesham Prim Sch
PO20................209 D8
Sidney Tidy Ho 5
BN2.................192 C6
Siena Dr RH10........6 C2
Silchester Dr RH11....18 B1
Silkin Wlk 8 RH11....18 B1
Sillwood Ct 18 BN1...191 E5
Sillwood Hall 20 BN1..191 E5
Sillwood Pl 17 BN1...191 E5
Sillwood Rd BN1.....191 E5
Sillwood St BN1......191 E5
Sillwood Terr 22 BN1..191 E5
Silver Birch Cl GU33...45 C4
Silver Birch Dr
  Middleton-on-S PO22..202 E6
  Worthing BN13......185 C6
Silver Birches
  Brighton BN1.......169 E1
  Haywards Heath RH16..88 A4
  Small Dole BN5.....146 F7
Silver Birch Ho RH11..18 C1
Silver Ct RH19........9 B2
Silverdale
  Coldwaltham RH20...119 C5
  Keymer BN6.........129 B3
Silverdale Ave BN3...191 D7
Silverdale Cl PO21...211 A8
Silverdale Dr BN15..187 C5
Silverdale Ind Est
BN11................187 B3
Silverdale Rd
  Burgess Hill RH15...109 B2
  Hove BN3...........191 D7
Silver Glade RH20....121 E6
Silver La RH14.......79 D8
Silver Lakes Mobil Home
Pk PO20............178 A4
Silverlea Gdns RH6....2 C2
Silverlock Cl PO19...177 C8
Silverlock Pl PO10...101 A3
Silverston Ave PO17..201 A2
Silvertrees PO10.....151 B2
Silver Way PO20.....208 C4
Silverwood RH20.....121 B7
Silverwood Copse
RH20................121 B7
Silverwood Ct 10
BN16................205 C5
Simon Ct 3 BN2.....201 C3
Sinclair Cl RH10.....19 C4
Sinclair Wlk BN1....213 B4
Sincox La RH13......102 D6
Singleton CE Prim Sch
PO18................135 D7
Singleton Cl
  Bognor Regis PO21...200 C1
  Ferring BN12.......206 F7
Singleton Cres BN12..206 F6
Singleton Ho BN17...204 B7
Singleton Rd
  Brighton BN1.......170 A6
  Broadbridge Heath RH12..35 D3
Singleton Way RH15..108 E1
Sinnocks RH20.......101 E1
Sir George's Pl BN44..145 C3
Sir Robert Peel Ct 14
PO21................201 D4
Siskin Ave RH10......21 C5
Siskin Cl RH12.......36 E5
Sissinghurst Cl RH10..19 D7
Siward Ho 1 GU32....68 A3
Six Acres RH13.......34 D2
Six Acres Cl RH13....56 F2
Skelmersdale Wlk
RH11................17 E2
Skeyne Dr 4 RH20..100 C2
Skiff La
  Kirdford RH14.......53 F5
  Loxwood RH14.......32 A1
Skipton Way RH6.....2 B5
Skylarks RH14........79 C7
Skylark View RH12....36 D7
Slade La GU31.......19 D4
Slattsfield Cl PO20...212 F7
SLAUGHAM...........61 B5
Slaugham Ct RH11....17 F3
Slaugham La RH17....61 A2
Sleets Rd RH12.......35 E3
Slider's La
  Furner's Green TN22...66 B1
  Scaynes Hill TN22....89 F6
Slimbridge Rd RH15..108 F3
Slindon Bottom Rd
BN18................158 A4

Slindon Cl BN14......186 D6
Slindon Coll BN18....158 B5
Slindon Rd BN14.....186 D6
Slinfold CE Prim Sch
RH13................34 D4
Slinfold Cl PO22.....192 D5
Slinfold Wlk RH11....18 A6
Slipe The BN18.......160 B2
Slipper Cvn Pk PO10..173 C8
Slipper Rd PO10.....173 C8
Sloane Ct 4 BN2.....192 C5
Sloe Ct PO19........177 C7
Slonk Hill Rd BN43...167 A1
Sloop La RH17........89 D5
Sloughbrook Cl RH12..36 F6
Sloughgreen La RH17..61 E1
Slugwash La RH17....88 D2
Small Cl GU31.......68 C5
Smallcroft Cl BN17..204 C5
Smallcutts Ave PO10..151 F1
Smallfield Rd RH6.....2 B3
Small's La RH11......18 C6
Small's Mead RH11...18 C6
Smeeds Cl RH19......10 A3
Smithbarn RH13......37 A2
Smithbarn RH6........2 B4
SMITHBROOK.........74 B4
Smith Cl RH10.......18 D2
Smithers Cotts RH12..33 F7
Smithers Hill La RH13..81 B2
Smithfields Ho RH13..57 F1
Smith La PO10......173 F1
Smith's Cross RH13...84 C3
Smithy The RH13.....83 E1
SMOCK ALLEY.......121 D7
Smock Alley RH20...121 C7
Smokejack Hill RH5....13 D7
Smokyhouse La GU28..96 B5
Smolletts RH19.......22 C8
Smugglers End RH17..61 C8
Smugglers' La
  Barns Green RH13....56 D3
  Barns Green RH13....57 A3
Smuggler's La PO18..175 B1
Smuggler's La RH5....14 E7
Smugglers Way RH11..56 F2
Smugglers Wlk BN12..185 E2
Snapes Rd RH11.....121 F3
Snednore BN7.......172 F5
Snell Hatch RH11.....18 B6
Snipe La GU27........27 A1
Snowdrop Cl
  Crawley RH11........18 A2
  Rustington BN17....205 B7
Snowdrop La RH16....88 C4
Snowflakes La RH16...88 D6
SNOW HILL..........8 A4
Snow Hill
  Copthorne RH10......7 F3
  Domewood RH10......7 F3
Snow Hill Bsns Ctr
RH10................8 A4
Snow Hill Cvn Site
PO20................196 B1
Snowhill La RH10......7 F5
Soalwood La GU32....67 A8
Soames Ct RH15.....108 F4
Soane Ct RH11........17 E4
Sobell Ct BN5.......125 E5
Soberton Dr GU31....68 C5
Solent Cl BN17.......205 D5
Solent Rd PO20......207 F6
Solent Way PO20....212 E5
Solway Ave RH11.....169 F7
Solway Cl BN17......205 A5
Somergate RH12......35 F2
Somerhill Ave BN3....191 D5
Somerhill Ct 16 BN3..191 D7
Somerhill Jun Sch
BN3.................191 D6
Somerhill Rd BN3....191 D6
Somerley La PO20....197 E1
Somersbury La GU6,
RH12................12 F7
Somerset Cl BN13....186 A5
Somerset Ct 3 BN3...191 C7
Somerset Gdns PO21..201 C5
Somerset Hospl GU28..97 F8
Somerset Point 1
BN2.................192 C4
Somerset Rd
  East Preston BN16...206 B6
  Ferring BN12.......206 F4
Somerset St BN2.....192 C5
Somerston Ho RH10...18 E5
Somerton Gn PO22...201 F5
Somerville Dr RH10....6 C1
SOMPTING..........187 B7
Sompting Abbotts Sch
BN15................187 A8
Sompting Ave BN14...186 D5
Sompting By-Pass
BN14................186 E7
Sompting Cl
  Brighton BN2.......192 F7
  3 Shoreham-by-S
  BN43................189 B8
Sompting Lo 5 BN15..187 D5
Sompting Rd
  Lancing BN15.......187 D5
  Worthing BN14......186 E6
Sopers La BN44......165 C7
Sorings Reach 6
BN43................189 B6

Sorrel Cl RH11........18 A2
Sorrel Rd RH12.......36 E5
South Acre GU31.....91 D3
Southall Ave BN2....170 D2
Southampton St BN2..213 C3
South Ash BN44.....145 D4
South Ave
  Bognor Regis PO21...200 F3
  Brighton BN2.......192 C5
  Hurstpierpoint BN6..128 A5
  Worthing BN12......185 E2
South Bank
  Hassocks BN6.......128 E3
  Stockbridge PO19...176 F4
Southbank Ct PO19...176 F4
South Bank BN15....188 A4
South Bay PO10......173 C3
South Beach 6 BN43..188 F6
SOUTH BERSTED....201 D6
South Bersted CE Prim
Sch PO22...........201 C5
South Bersted Ind Est
PO22................201 D6
Southbourne Ave
PO10................173 D8
Southbourne Halt
PO10................174 A8
Southbourne Jun & Inf
Schs PO10..........174 A8
Southbrook RH11.....18 C1
Southbrook Rd
  West Ashling PO18..153 B2
  West Ashling RH18..153 C3
South Cl
  Burgess Hill RH15..108 E3
  Crawley RH10.......18 F7
Southcote Ave PO20..207 F7
Southcourt Cl BN16...205 E6
Southcourt Rd BN14..186 C3
Southdean Cl 2
PO22................202 F5
Southdean Dr PO22..202 F5
Southdown Ave
  Brighton BN1.......170 A1
  Portslade-by-S BN41..190 C8
Southdown Bldgs
PO19................176 F5
Southdown Cl
  Chichester PO19....177 C8
  Haywards Heath RH16..87 D2
  Horsham RH12........37 A5
  Midhurst GU29.......94 D6
Southdown Ct
  Bognor Regis PO21...201 F5
  Brighton BN1.......170 A1
  Portslade-by-S BN41..168 A2
  3 Shoreham-by-S BN43..188 F7
  Southwick BN42.....189 E7
  Worthing BN14......186 C1
Southdown Rd
  Brighton BN2.......194 C2
South Downs
  Planetarium*
  PO19................177 A4
Southdown Terr
BN44................145 C3
Southdown View Cl
BN14................186 F5
Southdown View Rd
BN14................186 E6
Southdown View Way
BN14................186 E6
Southdown Way
RH20................121 F3
South Dr
  Angmering BN16....205 E2
  Bognor Regis PO22...202 C5
  Burgess Hill RH15..108 E3
Southease BN2......192 F5
SOUTHERN CROSS...190 A8
Southern Cross BN41..190 B8
Southern Cross Ind Est
PO22................201 E2
Southern Gate PO19..176 F5
Southern Rd PO20...212 E6
Southern Ring Rd
BN1.................171 B6
Southern Rd BN1....186 C1
South Farm Cotts
BN14................186 C5
South Farm Inds
BN14................186 C5
South Farm Rd BN14..186 C5
Southfield Ind Pk
PO18................175 B6
Southfield Rd BN14..186 D5
Southfields Cl PO19..176 F3
Southfields Rd BN17,
BN14................204 F5
Southgate BN14......204 E4
SOUTHGATE.........18 C4
Southgate Ave RH10..18 E4
Southgate Par RH10..18 D4
Southgate Prim Sch
RH10................18 D4
Southgate Rd
  Lancing BN15.......187 D5
  Worthing BN14......186 E6

South Gr continued
  Petworth GU28.......97 F7
South Holmes Rd
RH13................37 B4
South La
  Breach PO10........152 A2
  Houghton BN18.....140 B3
  Littlehampton BN16...96 F7
  Woodmancote PO10...152 A3
SOUTH LANCING....187 E4
Southlands
  East Grinstead RH19...22 E7
  Horley RH6..........1 F3
Southlands Ave RH6....2 A4
Southlands Cl
  5 Haywards Heath
  RH16................87 E6
  14 Littlehampton BN17..204 E4
  1 Shoreham-by-S
  BN43................189 B8
Southlands Hospl
BN43................167 B1
Southlands La RH20...121 E8
Southlands Pk GU29...94 E5
South Leas RH13......83 E1
Southleigh Rd PO10,
PO9.................151 B3
Southleys GU27.......49 A5
South Lo
  Bognor Regis PO21...200 A2
  9 Brighton BN2.....192 F5
  3 Lancing BN15.....187 C5
South Lodge Cl RH15..108 F4
Southmount BN1.....170 B1
Southon Cl BN41.....167 F3
Southon View BN15...187 C3
Southover Pl BN2....213 C4
Southover St BN2....213 C3
Southover Way PO20..177 A1
South Pallant PO19...177 A6
South Par RH6........1 F4
South Path BN17.....204 F5
South Perimeter Tk
RH11................5 B5
South Pier Rd RH6....6 B7
South Point 8 BN43..189 A6
South Rd
  Bognor Regis PO22...201 F5
  Brighton BN1.......169 E1
  Haywards Heath RH16..87 E4
  Liphook GU30.......25 D1
South Rd Mews BN11..169 F1
Southsea Ave BN12..185 E2
Southside RH20......100 D2
South St
  Brighton BN1.......213 A2
  Chichester PO19....177 A6
  Cuckfield RH17......86 F6
  Ditchling BN6......129 D3
  Emsworth PO10.....173 B8
  Falmer BN1.........171 C6
  Horsham RH12........36 C2
  Lancing BN15.......187 E4
  Midhurst GU29.......94 F7
  Partridge Green RH13..105 A3
  Portslade-by-S BN41..168 A1
  Worthing BN11......186 D1
South Terr
  6 Bognor Regis
  PO22................201 D5
  Littlehampton BN17..204 E4
Southview
  Scaynes Hill RH17....88 F3
  Small Dole BN5.....146 F6
South View
  Ditchling BN6......129 E5
  West Kingston BN16..168 E3
Southview Cl
  Shoreham-by-S BN43..189 C7
  Southwick BN42.....167 E1
South View Cl RH10...7 E3
Southview Dr BN11...186 A2
Southview Gdns
BN11................186 A2
South View Lo 8
BN15................187 E5
Southview Rd
  Bognor Regis PO22...202 B4
  Findon BN14........163 E6
  Southwick BN42.....189 E8
South View Terr BN5..125 C4
Southwark Cl RH11...18 B2
Southwark Wlk PO21..200 E4
Southwater Bsns Pk
RH13................57 F1
Southwater Cl
  Brighton BN2.......192 D6
  Crawley RH11........18 A6
  Worthing BN12......185 B4
Southwater Ctry Pk*
RH13................81 F8
Southwater Inf Sch
RH13................57 F2
Southwater Jun Sch
RH13................57 F2
Southwater St BN5...58 A4
Southway
  Burgess Hill RH15..108 D3

Southway continued
Littlehampton BN17......204 F4
South Way PO21........201 A5
Southway Jun Sch
RH15..................108 D3
Southways Ave BN14...186 E6
Southways Pk RH10......5 D3
Southwick Cl RH19.......9 D2
Southwick Ho RH10......7 D2
Southwick Sq BN42......189 E7
Southwick St BN42.......189 E8
South Wlk PO22.........202 E5
Southwold Cl BN13.......163 E1
South Woodlands
BN1...................169 E5
Southwood Rd PO11...195 A1
Sovereign Bsns Pk
RH15..................108 A2
Sovereign Ct
21 Bognor Regis
PO21..................201 D3
Brighton BN2............193 A3
Sovereign Ctr RH15.....108 E2
Spa Ct 11 BN3.........191 B5
Spain Bldgs **3** GU32....68 A3
Spain The GU32..........68 A3
Spanish Ct RH15.........109 B4
Sparks Ct BN17..........204 D5
Spark's La RH17.........62 E2
Sparrows La RH20.......123 A5
Sparrow Way RH15.......108 D3
Sparshott Rd PO20.......212 E5
Spartan Cl PO10.........173 C3
Spartan Way RH11........5 A1
Spatham La BN6.........129 F4
Spear Hill RH20..........123 A7
Spears Wlk BN2..........193 D8
Speedwell Cl BN13.......185 A6
Speedwell Way RH12.....36 E5
Spencer Ave BN3........168 D3
Spencer Rd
Lancing BN15............187 D5
New Brighton PO10.......151 A4
Spencers La RH6........1 A2
Spencers Pl RH12........36 B4
Spencers Rd BN13........18 D5
Spencer's Rd RH12........36 B3
Spencer St PO21........201 D4
Spey Cl BN13............185 C9
Spicers Cl RH15.........108 F5
Spierbridge Rd RH20....121 C2
Spiers Way RH6...........2 B3
Spindle Way RH10........18 F5
Spinnaker Cl RH17.......205 A5
Spinnals Gr BN42........189 D7
Spinney Cl
Crawley Down RH19......21 C8
Horsham RH12............37 B6
Hurstpierpoint BN6......128 C5
Selsey PO20............212 D8
Spinney La
West Chiltington Common
RH20..................121 D5
West Itchenor PO20.....197 A6
Spinney N RH20.........100 D2
Spinney The
Bognor Regis PO21......200 A8
Burgess Hill RH15.......109 B5
Crawley RH11............18 B4
Haslemere GU27.........27 C8
Hassocks BN6...........128 F5
Haywards Heath, Franklands
Village RH16.............87 F3
Haywards Heath RH16...87 D8
Horley RH6..............2 A5
Hove BN3...............169 C3
Pulborough RH20........100 D2
West Itchenor PO20.....197 A5
West Kingston BN16.....206 A4
Spinney Wlk PO22.......180 B6
Spinningfield Ho 1
GU32..................68 B4
Spiro Cl RH20............100 B2
Spitalfield La PO19......177 B7
Spitfire Ct PO20.........156 D2
Spithandle La BN44.....124 B3
Spooners Rd RH12.......37 A4
Sportcentre Rd BN1.....171 A6
Springate Rd BN42......189 F8
Springbank PO19........154 F1
Spring Cl 11 RH11.......18 D5
Spring Copse
Copthorne RH10..........7 C3
East Grinstead RH19.....9 B4
Spring Copse Bsns Pk
RH13..................34 C3
Spring Cotts RH20......121 C1
Spring Ct BN11..........186 C3
Springfarm Rd GU27....26 E5
Springfield
Bognor Regis PO21......200 A2
East Grinstead RH19.....9 D4
Liss GU33...............45 B4
Springfield Cl
Birdham PO20...........197 F5
Bolney RH17............85 C4
Mid Lavant PO18........154 F7
Rustington BN16.........185 D5
Springfield Cotts RH17...85 C4
Springfield Cres RH12...36 D3
Springfield Ct
Crawley RH11............18 D5
2 Horsham RH12......36 C2

Springfield Fst Sch
BN14..................186 E4
Springfield Gdns
BN13..................186 A7
Springfield La RH12.....38 B5
Springfield Park Ho
RH12..................36 C3
Springfield Park Rd
RH12..................36 B2
Springfield Rd
Brighton BN1............192 A8
Crawley RH11............18 D5
Horsham RH12...........36 C2
Springfields Farm Ind Est
RH17..................109 F5
Spring Gdns
Brighton BN1............213 B2
Copthorne RH10..........7 C3
Emsworth PO10.........173 C8
Heath Common RH20....122 E2
Horsham RH12...........36 C3
2 Southwick BN42......189 C7
SPRINGHEAD.............26 E5
Springhills BN5..........125 E4
Spring La
Clayton BN6............149 E8
Lindfield RH16...........64 B1
Slinfold RH13............34 C3
Spring Mdw RH18........23 F1
Spring Mdws GU29........6 A1
Springmead Ct GU27....26 D5
Spring Plat RH10........19 C6
Spring Plat Ct RH10.....19 C6
Spring St BN1............191 E5
Spring Way RH10........10 A4
Spronkett's La RH17.....84 E3
Sproule Cl BN18.........181 B2
Sproutes La RH13.......102 D8
Sprucefield Ct RH11......18 B8
Spruce Pl RH19...........10 A3
Spurgeon Cl RH11........18 C7
Spur Rd PO19...........177 D5
Spy La RH14..............32 A4
Squadron Dr BN13.......185 B7
Square Dr
Fernhurst GU27..........49 B7
Kingsley Green GU27.....27 B1
Square The
Barnham PO22...........180 B5
Brighton BN1............169 E6
Compton PO18...........111 B2
Crawley RH10............18 D6
Findon BN14............163 E6
Liphook GU30............25 B4
Petersfield GU32.........68 B3
Prinsted PO10...........173 F7
South Harting GU31......70 D6
Storrington RH20........121 D1
Washington RH20.......143 C3
Westbourne PO10.......151 D3
Squires Cl RH10.........21 A8
Squires Cotts RH20.....140 A7
Squires The RH11........39 B6
Squire Way BN5.........125 E4
Squirrel Cl RH11..........5 B1
Squirrels Copse
RH20..................122 C3
Stable Cl RH10...........19 D3
Stable Cotts
Crawley RH11............39 A8
Shopwyke RH20.........177 F7
Stable Field PO22......203 B5
Stable La
Findon BN14............163 E6
7 Petersfield GU31.....68 B3
Stable View BN15.......188 A5
Stace Way RH10.........19 E8
Stackfield Rd RH11......17 E5
Stafford Cl BN2..........213 C2
Stafford Ho BN6.........129 A3
Stafford Rd
Brighton BN1............191 E8
Crawley RH11............5 B1
Petersfield GU32.........68 B5
Staffords Cl BN16.......205 B6
Staffords Pl RH6..........2 B2
Stafford Way BN6.......129 A3
Stag Cl BN5.............125 E6
Stagelands RH11.........18 C8
Stagelands Ct RH11......18 C8
Stairbridge La RH17.....107 E7
Stakers La
Southwater RH13........58 A1
Southwater RH13........82 A8
Stalham Way PO22......202 A6
Stallard Cl PO10.........151 A1
Stallhouse La RH20.....101 A7
Stamford Cl RH10........87 D6
Stamford Ct **2** BN11...169 E2
Stammer Ind Est
RH12..................15 E8
Stammers Hill BN5......147 F3
Stanbridge Cl RH11......17 E6
Stanbridge Way RH17...64 B7
Stanbrok Cl PO21.......200 E3
Stanbury Cl PO18.......175 C7
Standean Cl BN1........170 D6
Standen Cl RH19..........9 A4
Standen Ct BN44........146 B2
Standen Ho* RH19......22 D4
Standen Pl RH17.........37 A7
Standgrove Rd RH17.....64 A6
Standinghall La RH10...20 A3
Stane St
Billingshurst RH14,
RH20..................79 A4
Codmore Hill RH20......100 D6
Five Oaks RH14..........55 E4

Stane St continued
Slinfold RH13............34 C4
Strettington PO18......156 B3
Westhampnett PO18....155 E1
Wisborough Green RH14,
RH20..................78 F1
Stane Street Cl RH20...100 C4
Stanford Ave
Brighton BN1............170 A1
Hassocks BN6...........128 E4
Stanford Cl
Bognor Regis PO22.....201 E5
Hassocks BN6...........128 E4
Hove BN3...............169 C1
Stanford Ct
1 Brighton BN1.......191 F8
Crawley RH10...........19 C4
Stanford Inf Sch RH12..191 E8
Stanford Jun Sch
BN1...................191 F8
Stanford Orch RH12......35 F8
Stanford Rd BN1.........191 F8
Stanford Sq **2** BN11...186 E2
Stanford Terr BN6.......128 E4
Stanford Way RH12......35 D3
Stan Hill RH6.............4 D8
Stanhope Rd
Littlehampton BN17.....204 E5
Worthing BN11...........186 D3
Stanley Cl
Crawley RH10...........19 B5
Stanley Ave BN41......167 F3
Stanley Ave S BN41....167 F3
Stanley Cl
Bognor Regis PO21.....201 D4
Crawley RH10...........18 E4
Stanley Ct **3** BN2......192 C8
Stanley Ctr RH10.........5 F2
Stanley Rd
Brighton BN1............213 B4
Emsworth PO10.........173 C8
Littlehampton BN17.....204 D7
Portslade-by-S BN41...190 A8
Worthing BN11...........186 D3
Stanley St BN2..........213 C3
Stanley Wlk **8** RH13....36 D2
Stanmer BN1............170 F8
Stanmer Ave BN2.......194 D3
Stanmer Ho BN1........170 A2
Stanmer Ho BN1........170 B2
Stanmer Park Rd
BN1...................170 B2
Stanmer St BN1........170 B2
Stanmer Villas BN1.....170 A2
Stanmore Gdns PO21...200 E2
Stanmore Ho
Billingshurst RH14......79 D8
3 Storrington RH20...121 C1
Stanover La PO22.......202 A7
Stansfield Ct BN16......205 D6
Stanstead Cres BN2....194 F3
Stansted Cl PO9.........130 E2
Stansted* PO9...........131 E1
Stan's Way 10 BN13....36 C2
Stanton Dr RH10........155 A3
Stanton Rd GU32.........68 A4
Stanwater La GU29......71 F3
Staplecross Cl **1**
RH11..................18 A3
Staplefield Ct RH17......61 F6
Staplefield Dr BN17.....170 F3
Staplefield Rd
Cuckfield RH17...........86 C8
Staplefield RH17..........61 E4
Staple La PO18..........154 F8
Staples Barn BN5.......125 D5
Staples Barn La BN5....125 D5
STAPLES HILL............52 F3
Staples Hill RH13.......104 F4
Stapleton Ct PO21......200 D2
Stapley Cl BN3..........190 D8
Stapley Rd BN3.........168 D1
Starborard Cl BN2.......213 B2
Starboard Wlk BN17....204 F4
Starborough Cotts RH7..9 F7
Star Cl RH13.............37 A4
Starling Cl RH15.........108 C3
Star Rd BN13...........105 A2
Star Road Trad Est
RH13..................105 A2
Station App
Chichester PO19.........176 F5
Falmer BN1............170 F2
Faygate RH12............16 F1
Haslemere GU27..........27 B6
Hassocks BN6...........128 F4
Horley RH6...............2 E2
Horsted Keynes RH17....65 A7
Hove BN3...............191 B8
Pulborough RH20........100 A2
Station App **6** BN6.....128 E4
Station Approach Ind Est
RH20..................100 A2
Station Approach Rd
RH6...................6 B7
Station App W BN6.....128 E4
Station App Ct RH13....36 D3
Station Cotts
Hassocks BN6...........128 F4
Horsham RH13...........57 D7
Station Hill RH14.........19 B7
Station Par
2 Lancing BN15......187 E5
6 Rustington BN16....205 E6
1 Worthing BN11.....186 A3
Station Rd
Angmering BN16........205 F8
Baynards RH12...........12 C3
Billingshurst RH14.......79 D7

Station Rd continued
15 Bognor Regis PO21...201 C3
Brighton BN1............169 D3
Broadbridge PO18.......175 C7
Burgess Hill RH15.......109 B2
Cowfold RH13............83 B2
Crawley Down RH10......21 B8
Crawley RH11............18 D5
Crossbush BN18.........160 C1
East Grinstead RH19......9 D1
East Preston BN16......205 F6
Ford BN18..............181 E4
Forest Row RH18.........23 F3
Henfield BN5............125 D5
Horley RH6..............2 B3
Horsham RH13...........36 D2
Horsted Keynes RH17....65 C5
Itchingfield RH13.........57 D7
Liphook GU30............25 C2
Liss GU33...............45 B4
Loxwood RH14...........32 A3
Midhurst GU29...........94 D7
Petersfield GU31, GU32...68 A4
Petworth GU28...........97 E5
Portslade-by-S BN3,
BN41..................190 C7
Pulborough RH20........100 A2
Rudgwick RH12...........33 D7
Sharpthorne RH19........43 A6
7 Southwick BN42....189 E7
Warnham RH12...........36 B8
Worthing BN11...........186 A3
Station Road N RH13....57 F1
Station Road S RH13....57 F1
Station St BN1..........213 B3
Station Villas RH20.....100 A2
Station Way RH10,
RH11..................18 D5
Staunton Cntry Pk*
PO9...................130 A2
Stavely Gdns PO19.....154 F3
Stean Furlong BN17.....204 C2
Stedham Hall GU29......72 A2
Stedham La GU29........72 A3
Stedham Prim Sch
GU29..................71 F1
Steeds Cnr RH13........82 D6
Steele Cl PO20..........101 E1
Steels La PO18..........174 E5
Steep CE Prim Sch
GU32..................68 B7
Steep Cl BN44..........163 E5
Steepdown Rd BN15....187 C8
Steep La BN14..........163 E5
Steeple View BN13......186 A5
Steeres Hill RH12........16 C6
Steers La RH10..........19 C6
Steine Gdns BN2........213 B2
Steine St BN2...........213 B1
Stein Rd PO10...........151 F2
Stemp Dr RH14...........79 C8
Stempswood Way
PO22..................180 C6
Stennings The RH19......9 C3
Stephens Cl PO19.......177 C7
Stephenson Dr RH19.....22 F7
Stephenson Pl RH10.....19 B6
Stephenson Way RH10...19 B6
Stephens Rd BN1.......170 B2
Stepney Cl RH10.........19 C4
Stepney Rd BN1.........213 B4
Sterling Bldgs **6** RH12...36 C2
Sterling Cl RH10.........205 C5
Sterling Pk RH10.........19 B6
Sternway BN17.........205 A5
Stetson The BN17.......204 D4
Stevenage Rd RH11......17 E3
Stevens Cl BN3..........190 E7
Stevenson Rd BN2.....192 C5
Stewards Rise BN18....159 F1
Steyne Gdns BN11.......186 E2
Steyne Hall **1** PO21....201 C2
Steyne St BN1..........201 C3
Steyne The
Bognor Regis PO21.....201 C2
Worthing BN11...........186 E2
Steyning 2 BN15......187 D5
Steyning By-Pass
BN44..................163 F3
Steyning Cl
Crawley RH10............18 E8
Lancing BN15............187 D8
Worthing BN12...........185 B4
Steyning Cres RH20....121 C2
Steyning Ct **7** BN3.....191 B7
Steyning Gram Lower Sch
BN44..................145 D3
Steyning Gram Upper Sch
BN44..................145 D4
Steyning Ho 1 BN14....186 D5
Steyning Mus **9** BN44..145 D3
Steyning Rd
Rottingdean BN2........194 A1
Shoreham-by-S BN43,
BN44..................145 D3
Shoreham-by-S, Mill Hill
BN43..................166 C1
West Grinstead RH14...104 C2
Stilde Gdns GU27........26 F6
Stile Gdns GU27.........26 F6
Stilton Mews RH19........9 C3
Stipenbeke BN5.........125 F4
Stirling Cl
Burgess Hill RH15.......109 C4
Crawley RH10............19 C5

Stirling Court Rd
RH15..................109 C4
Stirling Ct **5** BN3......191 C7
Stirling Pl **3** BN3.......191 A6
Stirling Pl PO19..........177 A5
Stirling Way
Bognor Regis PO21.....200 C3
East Grinstead RH19.....10 B3
Horsham RH13...........36 E3
Stirrup Way RH10.......19 D7
Stoatley Hollow GU27....27 A8
Stoatley Rise GU27......27 A8
Stockbridge Gdns
PO19..................176 E4
Stockbridge Pl PO19....176 F4
Stockbridge Rd PO19...176 F4
Stockcroft Rd RH17......41 A1
Stocker Rd PO21........201 B2
Stockfield RH6............2 B2
Stockham Ho BN15......187 A7
Stocklands Cl RH17......86 F8
Stocks Cl RH6............2 B2
Stock's Field BN44.....123 D1
Stock's Hill BN44........123 D1
Stocks La
Bracklesham PO20......208 A6
Chichester PO18, PO19...155 C3
Stocks Mead RH20......143 E6
Stockwell Ct
Burgess Hill RH15.......108 F3
1 Haywards Heath
RH16..................87 E3
Stockwell Ctr RH10......19 A6
Stockwell Rd RH19.......22 E6
Stodham La
Hill Side GU33...........45 C2
Liss GU33...............45 B1
Stoke Abbott Ct 2
BN11..................186 D2
Stoke Abbott Rd
BN11..................186 D2
Stoke Brunswick Sch
RH19..................23 F2
Stoke Cl BN11..........186 B1
Stoke Rd BN18..........140 D3
Stokers Cl RH6............5 E7
Stokes Cl RH10..........19 C4
Stoneage Cl PO22......201 C7
Stonebridge Ct
Crawley RH11............18 C2
Horsham RH12...........36 A2
Stonechat Cl GU31......68 E2
Stone Cl BN13...........185 F7
Stone Cotts RH10........20 B1
Stonecourt Cl RH6.......2 C3
Stonecourt Cotts RH17...62 A5
Stonecroft BN44........145 D3
Stonecroft Cl RH10.....168 E4
Stonecrop Cl RH11.......18 B3
Stone Cross RH14........64 D3
Stonecross Rd BN2.....170 F4
Stone Ct
Crawley RH10............19 D5
Midhurst GU29...........94 D8
Stonefield Cl RH10,
RH11..................18 D5
Stonefields RH16.......205 D5
Stonehall Way RH15....108 F5
Stonehall La RH17........63 C6
Stoneham Cl GU32.......67 F4
Stoneham Pk GU32......67 F4
Stoneham Rd BN3......190 F7
Stone Hatch GU6.........11 A3
Stonehill Cres PO21.....200 C8
Stonehouse La RH13.....83 B1
Stonehouse Rd GU30...25 D4
Stonehurst Ct **10** BN2..192 C6
Stonehurst Rd BN13...186 A5
Stone La BN13..........185 F7
Stoneleigh Ave BN1....169 F6
Stoneleigh Cl
Brighton BN1............169 F6
East Grinstead RH19.....9 F1
Stonepit La BN15........125 C5
Stonepound Crossroads
BN6...................128 D3
Stonepound Rd BN6....128 E4
Stonepound Ridge
BN6...................128 D4
STONEQUARRY...........10 A3
Stone Quarry Rd RH7....10 A4
Stonery Cl BN41.........168 A2
Stonery Rd BN41........168 A2
Stone St BN1............191 E5
Stonewall Cotts RH14....53 A3
Stoneybrook **1** RH12....35 F1
Stoneycroft Wlk **3**
RH11..................17 D5
Stoneyfield Cotts
PO20..................158 B1
Stoney La
Balcombe Lane RH17.....41 B5
Bracklesham PO20......208 D4
Shoreham-by-S BN43....189 C8
Stoney Stile Cl PO21....200 C3
Stoney Stile La PO21....200 C1
Stoneywish Nature
Reserve* BN6...........129 E3
STOPHAM...............99 D3
Stopham Cl BN14.......186 A5
Stopham Rd
Crawley RH10............19 C3
Pulborough RH20........100 B2
Stor Mdw RH20.........121 D2
Storrington Ct
Fishbourne PO19........176 B7
Hove BN3...............168 E2

Storrington Ct RH11 . . . . .18 A7
Storrington & District
  Mus ★ RH20 . . . . 121 D1
Storrington Fst Sch
  RH20 . . . . 121 C2
Storrington Rd
  Heath Common RH20 . . . . 122 A5
  Washington RH20 . . . . . . 143 C8
Storrington Rise
  BN14 . . . . .163 F4
Story Rd PO19 . . . . 177 C7
Stour Cl
  Petersfield GU31 . . . . .68 A2
  Worthing BN13 . . . . .185 C9
Stour Rd BN13 . . . . 185 C9
Strachey Ct ■ RH11 . . . . .18 B1
Strand Cl RH10 . . . . .19 D4
Strand Ct
  Rustington BN16 . . . . 205 B3
  ■ West Kingston
    BN16 . . . . 206 A4
Strand Par BN12 . . . . .185 E4
Strand The
  Brighton BN2 . . . . .193 A3
  Ferring BN12 . . . . .206 E4
  Worthing BN12 . . . . 185 C4
Strand Way PO22 . . . . .202 B4
Strange Gdn PO22 . . . . .200 E1
Stratford Ct BN11 . . . . 186 C2
Strathfield RH17 . . . . .87 F4
Strathmoor Gdns GU29 . . . .72 F1
Strathmore Cl BN13 . . . . . . 185 E1
Strathmore Rd
  Crawley RH11 . . . . .5 A1
  Worthing BN13 . . . . .185 E5
Stratton Ct PO22 . . . . .201 E5
Strawberry Field
  RH20 . . . . 100 D3
Strawberry La PO22 . . . . . . 122 B5
Strawson Ct RH10 . . . . .1 F4
Stream Cl PO18 . . . . .175 B5
Stream La RH20 . . . . .101 B1
Stream Pk RH19 . . . . .9 A3
Streatheigh Ct PO21 . . . . . .201 A2
Streel's La GU28 . . . . .51 F5
Street Barn BN15 . . . . .187 A7
Streete Ct ⓶ PO21 . . . . . . .201 B2
Street End La PO20 . . . . . . .198 E3
Street End Rd PO20 . . . . . . 198 E3
Streetfield Rd RH13 . . . . .34 E3
Street Hill RH10 . . . . .19 E5
Street La RH17 . . . . .64 A8
Street The
  Albourne Green BN6 . . . . . 127 C6
  Bolney RH17 . . . . .85 C3
  Boxgrove PO18 . . . . .156 D4
  Bramber BN44 . . . . 181 C7
  Bury RH20 . . . . .140 A7
  Charlwood RH6 . . . . .4 E7
  Clapham BN13 . . . . 162 E1
  Cowfold RH13 . . . . .83 E2
  East Preston BN16 . . . . . . 205 F6
  Kingston near Lewes
    BN7 . . . . 172 E5
  Lancing BN15 . . . . .187 F8
  Nutbourne RH20 . . . . 101 A2
  Patching BN13 . . . . 162 D2
  Plaistow RH14 . . . . .30 E2
  Rustington BN16 . . . . 205 C5
  Shoreham-by-S BN43 . . . . 166 E1
  Slinfold RH13 . . . . .34 D4
  South Harting GU31 . . . . . . .91 C3
  Stedham GU29 . . . . .72 A1
  Thakeham RH20 . . . . .122 B7
  Walberton BN18 . . . . .158 D1
  Warninglid RH17 . . . . .84 F8
  Washington RH20 . . . . . . 143 D6
  West Itchenor PO20 . . . . .196 F7
  Westmeston BN6 . . . . 150 F8
Stretch Hill RH20 . . . . .99 A5
Stretham Farm BN15 . . . . . 146 C8
Stretham La BN15 . . . . .146 C8
Strettington La PO18 . . . . . 156 A3
Stretton Ct ■ BN3 . . . . 190 F7
Strettons Copse GU30 . . . . . .47 B2
Strickland Cl ⓸ RH11 . . . . . .17 E5
Stride Cl PO19 . . . . .177 C6
Stringer Way BN1 . . . . .169 F3
Stronc Ct BN11 . . . . .185 F2
STROOD GREEN 35 A6
Strood La RH12 . . . . .35 C7
Stroud End GU32 . . . . .67 D4
Stroud Green Dr
  PO21 . . . . .200 F5
Stroudley Cl RH10 . . . . .19 B5
Stroudley Ct RH10 . . . . 205 E6
Stroudley Rd BN1 . . . . .213 B4
Strouds La PO21 . . . . .200 C1
Strudgate Cl ■ RH10 . . . . . .19 B4
Strudwick Rd BN1 . . . . 187 A3
Stuart Cl
  Crawley RH10 . . . . .19 D5
  Worthing BN11 . . . . 186 F4
Stuart Ho ⓹ RH13 . . . . .36 F3
Stuarts Mdw GU28 . . . . 116 C8
Stuart Way RH19 . . . . .22 F7
Stubbermere PO19 . . . . 151 B8
Stubcroft La PO20 . . . . .208 B7
Stubfield RH12 . . . . .36 A3
Stubpond La RH17 . . . . .8 C8
Stumblemead RH17 . . . . .41 A1
Stumblets RH10 . . . . .2 A6
Stumps End PO18 . . . . .175 C4
Stumps La RH18 . . . . .175 C4
Sturges Rd PO21 . . . . .201 C3
Sturt Ave GU27 . . . . .26 F5
Sturt Rd GU27 . . . . .26 F5
Sudbury Cl PO21 . . . . .200 C1

Sudeley Pl BN2 . . . . .192 D4
Sudeley St BN2 . . . . 192 D4
Sudeley Terr ⓺ BN2 . . . . . . .192 D4
Sudley Gdns PO21 . . . . .201 D3
Sudley Rd PO21 . . . . .201 D3
Sudley Terr ⓶ PO21 . . . . . . .201 D3
Suffolk Cl RH6 . . . . .2 A2
Suffolk St BN3 . . . . .190 F8
Sugar La RH17 . . . . .65 C4
Sugden Rd BN1 . . . . .186 F3
Sugworth Cl RH16 . . . . .87 D7
SULLINGTON 142 F7
Sullington Cl BN2 . . . . 170 F4
Sullington Copse
  RH20 . . . . .121 F2
Sullington Gdns BN14 . . . . 163 F3
Sullington Hill RH11 . . . . . . .18 D4
Sullington La RH20 . . . . 142 F7
Sullington Mead RH12 . . . . .35 E3
Sullington Way BN43 . . . . . 189 A8
Sullivan Dr RH11 . . . . .17 E3
Sultan Rd RH20 . . . . 151 B1
Summer Cl BN41 . . . . .190 A7
Summerdale Rd BN3 . . . . . . 168 D2
Summerdown Cl
  BN13 . . . . .185 B6
Summerdown Ct
  BN13 . . . . .185 B6
Summerfield Rd
  PO20 . . . . .196 C2
Summerfields BN14 . . . . . . .163 E6
Summerfold RH13 . . . . .33 E8
Summerhill Cl
  Bognor Regis PO22 . . . . . .202 D6
  Hayward Heath RH16 . . . . .87 F7
Summerhill Dr
  Bognor Regis PO22 . . . . . .202 C6
  Lindfield RH16 . . . . .88 A7
Summerhill Grange
  RH16 . . . . .87 F7
Summerhill La RH16 . . . . . . .87 F7
Summer Ho RH11 . . . . .18 C5
Summer La PO21 . . . . .199 F1
Summerlea BN16 . . . . .205 B8
Summerlea Com Prim Sch
  BN16 . . . . .205 B7
Summerlea Gdns ⓹
  BN17 . . . . .204 C5
Summerley La PO22 . . . . . . 202 B5
Summers Cl BN16 . . . . 205 C4
SUMMERSDALE 155 B2
Summersdale Ct
  PO19 . . . . .154 F3
Summersdale Rd
  PO19 . . . . .155 A1
Summersdeane BN42 . . . . . 167 F1
Summersfield GU33 . . . . .45 B4
Summers Ho GU29 . . . . .94 D6
Summersvere Cl RH10 . . . . . .6 A1
Sumners RH17 . . . . .64 B7
Sun Brow GU27 . . . . .27 A5
Sun Ct ⓶ BN1 . . . . .186 A1
Sundale La PO22 . . . . 202 E5
Sunderland Dr PO20 . . . . . . 156 D2
Sundew Cl RH17 . . . . .87 A3
Sunflower Cl BN17 . . . . 205 B7
Sunleigh Ct BN6 . . . . .127 F6
Sunningdale RH6 . . . . .2 B2
Sunningdale Ct
  Crawley RH10 . . . . .18 D4
  Worthing BN12 . . . . 185 C4
Sunningdale Gdns
  Bognor Regis PO22 . . . . . .201 B7
  East Wittering PO20 . . . . .207 D7
Sunninghill Ave BN13 . . . . 185 E7
Sunninghill Ave BN1 . . . . . 168 F2
Sunninghill Cl BN3 . . . . 168 E2
Sunnybox La BN18 . . . . .158 E4
Sunny La GU27 . . . . 185 E2
Sunnycroft Cl RH17 . . . . .88 E2
Sunnydale Ave BN1 . . . . . . 170 A6
Sunnydale Cl BN1 . . . . 170 A6
Sunnydown Cl BN16 . . . . . .205 A3
Sunnyhill Cl RH10 . . . . .21 A8
Sunnymead RH11 . . . . .18 D6
Sunnymead Cl
  Ancton PO22 . . . . .203 A6
  Selsey PO20 . . . . .212 E6
Sunnymead Dr PO20 . . . . . .212 E6
Sunnyside GU27 . . . . .22 E7
Sunnyside Cl BN16 . . . . 206 A8
Sunnyside Cotts
  RH20 . . . . .121 D1
Sunny Way PO18 . . . . .175 B5
Sunnywood Ct RH16 . . . . . . .87 D3
Sunnywood Dr RH16 . . . . . . .87 D3
Sun Park Cl PO21 . . . . .201 A6
Sunset La RH20 . . . . 121 C5
Sunte Ave RH16 . . . . .87 E7
Sunte Cl RH16 . . . . .87 E7
Sunvale Ave GU27 . . . . .26 D6
Sunvale Cl GU27 . . . . .26 D6
Surrenden Cl BN1 . . . . 169 F4
Surrenden Cres BN1 . . . . . . 169 E4
Surrenden Holt BN1 . . . . . . 169 F3
Surrenden Lo BN1 . . . . 169 F2
Surrenden Pk BN1 . . . . .170 A4
Surrenden Rd BN1 . . . . .169 F4
Surrenden Rise BN1 . . . . . . 169 C8
Surrey Cott ⓺ BN17 . . . . . .204 F4
Surrey Ho ⓹ RH12 . . . . .36 D2
Surrey Ho ⓵⓶ BN2 . . . . . . .192 D4
Surrey St
  Arundel BN18 . . . . 160 A2
  Brighton BN1 . . . . .213 A3
  Littlehampton BN17 . . . . .204 D5
  Worthing BN11 . . . . 186 C1

Surrey Wharf BN18 . . . . . . .160 B2
Surry St BN43 . . . . .188 F7
Sussex Aquatic & Falconry
  Ctr ★ PO20 . . . . .198 C7
Sussex Bsns Village The
  PO22 . . . . .180 E6
Sussex Cotts BN19 . . . . .43 A6
Sussex Ct
  Billingshurst RH14 . . . . .79 D7
  ⓻ Bognor Regis PO21 . . .201 B2
  Elmer PO22 . . . . .203 B5
  Findon BN14 . . . . .163 E6
  ⓶ Haywards Heath
    RH16 . . . . .87 E3
  ⓷ Horsham RH13 . . . . . . .36 E1
  ⓹ Hove BN3 . . . . 191 C6
  ⓸ Shoreham-by-S
    BN43 . . . . 189 A6
  Worthing BN11 . . . . 186 C2
Sussex Cty Cricket Gd
  BN3 . . . . .191 C7
Sussex Dr PO21 . . . . .200 A1
Sussex Eye Hospl
  BN2 . . . . .192 D4
Sussex Gdns
  Haywards Heath RH17 . . . . .88 B3
  Petersfield GU31 . . . . .68 B2
  Rustington BN16 . . . . 205 C6
Sussex Gr PO20 . . . . .208 C5
Sussex House Bsns Pk
  BN3 . . . . .190 F8
Sussex Lo BN11 . . . . 191 E5
Sussex Lo RH12 . . . . .88 E4
Sussex Manor Bsns Pk
  RH10 . . . . .6 A2
Sussex Mews ⓸ BN2 . . . . .192 E4
Sussex Pl BN2 . . . . 213 C3
Sussex Rd
  Haywards Heath RH16 . . . . .87 E3
  Hove BN3 . . . . .191 B5
  Lancing BN15 . . . . .188 C5
  Petersfield GU31 . . . . .68 D1
  Worthing BN11 . . . . 186 D3
Sussex Sq
  Brighton BN2 . . . . .192 E4
  RH16 . . . . .87 E4
Sussex Square Mews ⓶
  BN2 . . . . .192 E4
Sussex St
  Bognor Regis PO21 . . . . . .201 D3
  Brighton BN2 . . . . .213 C2
  Littlehampton BN17 . . . . .204 D6
Sussex Terr
  Brighton BN2 . . . . .213 C3
  ⓷ Midhurst GU29 . . . . . . .94 E7
  Sussex View BN3 . . . . 191 D7
Sussex Village PO22 . . . . . . 203 B5
Sussex Way RH15 . . . . 108 E5
Sussex Wharf BN43 . . . . . . 189 A6
Sutherland Cl
  Bognor Regis PO22 . . . . . .201 C3
  Rustington BN16 . . . . 205 B5
Sutherland Ct ⓸
  PO21 . . . . .201 C3
Sutherland Rd BN2 . . . . 192 C5
Sutton Ave BN16 . . . . 205 C4
Sutton Cl
  Bognor Regis PO22 . . . . . .201 F6
  Woodingdean BN2 . . . . . . .171 E1
SUTTON END 118 A5
Sutton Tye RH16 . . . . .87 F6
Suva Ct RH10 . . . . .9 C3
Swainsthorpe Cl RH16 . . . . .87 F1
Swaledale Cl RH13 . . . . .18 C3
Swallowfield Cl RH13 . . . . . .59 C5
Swallow Field Copse
  RH13 . . . . .58 A3
Swallow Rd RH11 . . . . .18 C8
Swallow Rest RH15 . . . . 108 C3
Swallows Cl ⓷ BN15 . . . . . 188 C5
Swallows Green Dr
  BN13 . . . . .185 C6
Swallows La RH13 . . . . 103 F6
Swallow St RH10 . . . . .21 C5
Swallows The BN17 . . . . 204 D4
Swallowtail Rd RH12 . . . . . . .36 E6
Swan Barn Rd GU27 . . . . . . .27 D6
Swanborough Ct ⓻
  BN43 . . . . .188 F7
Swanborough Dr BN2 . . . . .192 F7
Swanborough Dro
  BN7 . . . . .172 F4
Swanborough Pl BN2 . . . . . 192 F7
Swanbourne Cl BN15 . . . . .187 F8
Swanbourne Rd
  BN17 . . . . .204 D7
Swan Cl
  Emsworth PO10 . . . . .173 C8
  Southwater RH13 . . . . .58 A2
  Storrington RH20 . . . . 121 C2
Swan Cnr RH20 . . . . 100 B2
Swandean Cl BN13 . . . . 185 B6
Swan Dene PO21 . . . . .210 F7
Swanfield Dr PO19 . . . . .177 C8
Swan La RH6 . . . . .4 F7
Swan Lo ⓹ BN15 . . . . .188 C5
Swann Cl RH15 . . . . 109 D3
Swann Way RH12 . . . . .35 E3
Swansea Gdns PO21 . . . . . .201 B2
Swans Ghyll RH18 . . . . .23 E3
Swan Sq RH12 . . . . .36 C2
Swan St GU28 . . . . .63 A8
Swan View RH20 . . . . 100 C1
Swan Wlk RH12 . . . . .36 C2
Sweda Ct ⓵⓷ BN2 . . . . .192 D4
Sweetlands BN6 . . . . .129 B5

Swift Cl RH15 . . . . 108 D3
Swift La RH11 . . . . .18 C8
Swift Rd PO10 . . . . 173 C3
Swift Way BN17 . . . . .204 D8
Swillage La BN6 . . . .
  BN13 . . . . .184 A8
Swindon Rd RH12 . . . . .36 B4
Swiss Gdns BN43 . . . . 188 E7
Swissland Hill RH19, RH7 . . .9 E7
Sycamore Ave RH12 . . . . . . .37 C6
Sycamore Cl
  Angmering BN16 . . . . .205 F8
  Crawley RH11 . . . . .5 C1
  Horsham RH12 . . . . .36 B1
  Woodingdean BN2 . . . . . . .193 E8
Sycamore Ct
  Brighton BN2 . . . . .192 D8
  Nepcote BN14 . . . . .163 E5
Sycamore Dr RH19 . . . . .10 A1
Sycamore Rd PO22 . . . . 201 C7
Sycamores The
  Chichester PO19 . . . . .177 A7
  Sayers Common BN6 . . . . 107 D1
Sycamore Wlk GU31 . . . . . . .68 A3
Sydenham Terr PO10 . . . . . 151 D5
Sydney Rd RH16 . . . . .87 E6
Sydney St BN1 . . . . .213 B3
Syers Cl GU33 . . . . .45 B4
Syers Rd GU33 . . . . .45 B4
Syke Cluan Cl PO22 . . . . . . 180 B6
Sylvan Cl RH16 . . . . .88 B4
Sylvan Rd
  Crawley RH10 . . . . .19 A4
  Lancing BN15 . . . . .187 B6
Sylvan Way PO21 . . . . .201 B3
Sylvester Way BN3 . . . . 168 C3
Sylvia Cl PO21 . . . . 200 A1
Symbister Rd BN41 . . . . 190 C7
Syresham Gdns RH16 . . . . . .87 F4

T

Tabard Gate PO21 . . . . 200 B1
Tacklee Rd BN18 . . . . 180 F3
Talbot Cres BN13 . . . . 170 D6
Talbot La RH12 . . . . .36 C1
Talbot Rd BN17 . . . . 204 C5
Taldua Pl BN2 PO21 . . . . . . .201 B2
Tallis Cl RH11 . . . . .17 F3
Tall Oaks RH16 . . . . .88 B5
Talman Ct RH11 . . . . .18 E5
Tamar Ave BN13 . . . . 185 C6
Tamar Cl
  Crawley RH10 . . . . .19 C5
  Worthing BN13 . . . . 185 C8
Tamarisk Cl PO22 . . . . 201 C6
Tamarisk Way
  Ferring BN12 . . . . .206 F5
  Littlehampton BN16 . . . . .205 F4
Tamarisk Wlk PO20 . . . . . . 207 F6
Tamar Way PO21 . . . . .200 E3
Tamplin Terr BN2 . . . . 213 C3
Tamworth Rd BN3 . . . . .190 F7
Tanbridge Ho RH12 . . . . .36 B1
Tanbridge House Sch
  RH12 . . . . .35 F2
Tanbridge Pk RH12 . . . . .36 B1
Tanbridge Ret Pk
  RH12 . . . . .36 B1
Tanbridge Rd BN3 . . . . 190 E6
Tanfield Ct BN12 . . . . 185 C4
Tangle Oak RH19 . . . . .8 E4
Tangmere Gdns PO21 . . . . .205 C4
Tangmere Gdns PO21 . . . . .200 D2
Tangmere Military
  Aviation Mus ★
    PO20 . . . . 156 D1
Tangmere Prim Sch
  PO20 . . . . .156 D2
Tangmere Rd
  Brighton BN1 . . . . .170 A6
  Crawley RH11 . . . . .17 F6
  Oving PO20 . . . . .178 B4
Tankerdale La
  Liss GU33 . . . . .45 A1
  Steep GU33 . . . . .68 F8
Tanners Cross ■ RH16 . . . . .87 C2
Tanners La GU27 . . . . .27 C7
Tanners La GU27 . . . . .27 C7
Tanners Mead RH17 . . . . . . .61 E5
Tannery Cl
  Chichester PO19 . . . . .176 E6
  Slinfold RH13 . . . . .34 D3
Tannery Ct ■ RH13 . . . . .36 B1
Tansy Mead RH13 . . . . 121 B2
Tanyard Ave RH19 . . . . .23 A8
Tanyard Cl
  Crawley RH10 . . . . .19 C3
  Horsham RH13 . . . . .36 B4
Tanyard Cotts BN44 . . . . . . 145 C3
Tanyard La
  Chelwood Common RH17,
    TN22 . . . . .25 B3
  Steyning BN44 . . . . 145 D3
Tanyard Way RH6 . . . . .2 E2
Tarham Cl RH6 . . . . .2 E2
Tarmount La BN43 . . . . .188 F7
Tarner Rd BN2 . . . . 213 C3
Tarragon Way BN43 . . . . . . 167 C1
Tarrant St BN18 . . . . 160 D2
Tarrant Wharf BN18 . . . . . . 160 B2
Tarring Gate BN14 . . . . 186 A4
Tarring Rd BN14 . . . . .186 B3
Tasman Cl RH16 . . . . .87 B5
Tasman Way BN13 . . . . 185 C7
Tatchells GU29 . . . . .94 D6

Tate Cres RH15 . . . . .108 F5
Tate's Way RH12 . . . . .33 D7
Tatham Ct RH11 . . . . .18 B1
Taunton Cl RH10 . . . . .19 E5
Taunton Gr BN2 . . . . .171 A1
Taunton Pl BN2 . . . . 171 A1
Taunton Rd BN2 . . . . .170 F1
Taunton Way BN2 . . . . .171 A1
Tavern Ct GU27 . . . . .49 B6
Taverner Pl PO19 . . . . .177 B5
Tavistock Down BN1 . . . . . . .17 A2
Tavistock & Summerhill
  Sch RH16 . . . . .87 F7
Tavy Cl BN13 . . . . 185 C7
Tavy Rd BN13 . . . . .185 C7
Tawny Rd BN13 . . . . 185 D8
Taylor Cl ⓽ BN16 . . . . .205 B8
Taylors Field GU29 . . . . .94 E6
Taylor's La GU29 . . . . .175 C4
Taylors Rise GU29 . . . . .94 E6
Taylor Wlk RH11 . . . . .18 C6
Taymor Ct BN11 . . . . .186 A1
Teachers Terr GU33 . . . . .45 B4
Teal Cl RH12 . . . . .36 C5
Teal La RH20 . . . . .212 C8
Teazle Cl GU31 . . . . .68 E2
Teesdale RH11 . . . . .18 B3
Teg Cl BN41 . . . . 168 C2
Teg Down GU31 . . . . .68 D4
Teign Wlk BN13 . . . . 185 C9
Teknol Ho RH15 . . . . 108 E2
Telegraph La GU31 . . . . .92 A3
Telegraph St ⓵⓶ BN2 . . . . .192 C4
Telford Pl RH10 . . . . .18 E5
Telgarth Rd BN12 . . . . .206 F4
Telham Cl ⓹ RH11 . . . . .17 F3
Templars PO22 . . . . .202 D6
Templars Fst Sch
  BN15 . . . . .187 B6
Templars Mews BN15 . . . . .187 B6
Templars The BN14 . . . . . . .186 E7
Temple Bar Bsns Pk
  PO18 . . . . .156 A3
Temple Cl RH10 . . . . .19 D5
Temple Ct ⓶ BN17 . . . . . . .204 E5
Temple Gdns BN1 . . . . 191 E6
Temple Gr RH15 . . . . 108 D4
Temple Hts ⓵⓸ BN1 . . . . . .191 E6
Temple St BN11 . . . . .45 C6
Templesheen Rd
  PO22 . . . . .203 B5
Temple St BN1 . . . . .191 E6
Tenacre Cl PO19 . . . . .177 C8
Ten Acres BN11 . . . . 187 A3
Tenantry Down Rd
  BN2 . . . . .192 D8
Tennis Rd BN3 . . . . 190 E6
Tennyson Ave BN16 . . . . . . 205 B5
Tennyson Cl
  Crawley RH10 . . . . .19 B8
  Horsham RH12 . . . . .36 E6
Tennyson Ct
  ⓹ Haywards Heath
    RH16 . . . . .87 D5
  ⓷ Hove BN3 . . . . 191 A4
Tennyson Ho ⓸ BN1 . . . . . .186 C2
Tennyson Rd
  Bognor Regis PO21 . . . . . .201 B3
  Worthing BN11 . . . . 186 C2
Tennyson Rise RH19 . . . . . . .22 C8
Tennysons Mill PO19 . . . . . 176 F5
Tennysons Ridge GU27 . . . . .27 E5
Terminus Pl
  ⓻ Brighton BN1 . . . . .213 A4
  Littlehampton BN17 . . . . .204 D5
Terminus Rd
  Brighton BN1 . . . . .213 A4
  Chichester PO19 . . . . .176 E5
  Littlehampton BN17 . . . . .204 C5
Terminus Road Ind Est
  PO19 . . . . .176 E5
Terminus St BN1 . . . . 213 A3
Tern Rd RH11 . . . . .17 D5
Terraces The BN2 . . . . 213 C1
Terrace The
  Crossbush BN18 . . . . .160 E1
  Lancing BN15 . . . . .187 E4
  Sidlesham PO20 . . . . 209 F7
  Worthing BN12 . . . . 185 C3
Terringes Ave BN13 . . . . . . .185 F6
Terry Rd RH11 . . . . .18 B1
Terry's Cross BN5 . . . . 126 C2
TERWICK COMMON 70 D6
Terwick La GU27 . . . . .29 A5
Terwick Rise GU31 . . . . .70 D6
Test Cl GU31 . . . . .68 A2
Testers Cl RH13 . . . . .82 A7
Test Rd BN15 . . . . 187 B6
Teville Gate BN11 . . . . 186 D3
Teville Inds BN14 . . . . .186 F5
Teville Pl BN11 . . . . 186 D3
Thackeray Rd BN14 . . . . . . .186 B6
Thakeham Cl
  East Preston BN16 . . . . . . 206 A4
  Worthing BN13 . . . . 185 A3
Thakeham Copse
  RH20 . . . . .122 B3
Thakeham Dr BN12 . . . . . . .185 A3
Thakeham Fst Sch
  RH20 . . . . .122 B7
Thakeham Rd RH20 . . . . . . .121 F2

Thalassa Rd BN11 . . . .**187** B3
Thames Cl
  Brighton BN2 . . . .**213** C2
  Littlehampton BN12 . . . . . .**205** A4
Thames Way BN13 . . . .**185** D8
Thatch Ct BN15 . . . .**187** F8
Thatcher Cl RH10 . . . .**18** D3
Thatchers Cl
  Burgess Hill RH15 . . . .**109** D1
  Horley RH6 . . . .**2** B5
  Horsham RH12 . . . .**36** E4
Thatchers Lo ⏹2
  BN17 . . . .**204** D5
Thatchway Cl BN17 . . . . . .**204** D6
Thatchway The
  Angmering BN16 . . . .**183** E5
  Rustington BN16 . . . .**205** D4
Theatre La PO19 . . . .**177** A6
Theatre Pl ⏹12 PO19 . . . .**177** A6
Thelton Ave RH12 . . . .**35** D3
Theobald Ho ⏹1 BN1 . . . .**213** B3
Theobalds Rd RH15 . . . .**109** D6
Thesiger Cl BN11 . . . .**187** A4
Thesiger Rd BN11 . . . .**187** A4
Thetford Wlk RH11 . . . .**17** C2
Theydon Ct RH10 . . . .**19** A4
Thicket La PO18 . . . .**157** B5
Third Ave
  Almodington PO20 . . . .**208** E8
  Bognor Regis PO22 . . . . . .**202** B4
  Bracklesham PO20 . . . .**208** B5
  Hove BN3 . . . .**191** B6
  Lancing BN15 . . . .**187** E7
  Worthing BN14 . . . .**186** D7
Thirlmere Cres BN15 . . . . . .**187** B5
Thirlmere Rd RH11 . . . .**17** D4
Thirlmere Way PO22 . . . . . .**202** B6
Thistledowne Gdns
  PO10 . . . .**173** D8
Thistledown Vale
  RH14 . . . .**31** D3
Thistle Way RH13 . . . .**58** A3
Thomas A Becket Fst Sch
  BN13 . . . .**186** A5
Thomas A Becket Mid Sch
  BN14 . . . .**186** A5
Thomas Bennett Com Coll
  RH10 . . . .**18** D2
Thomas Rd GU31 . . . .**68** C5
Thompson Rd
  Brighton BN1 . . . .**170** C1
  Middleton-on-S PO22 . . . .**202** F5
Thompson's Hospl
  GU28 . . . .**75** F1
Thomson Cl BN13 . . . .**185** B7
Thomson Ct ⏹8 RH11 . . . . . .**18** B1
Thorgate Rd BN17 . . . .**204** B7
Thorlands GU27 . . . .**27** A7
Thornberry Middle Sch
  BN15 . . . .**187** F5
Thornbush Cres BN41 . . . . .**168** B3
Thorn Cl GU31 . . . .**68** B2
Thorncroft Rd BN17 . . . .**204** F6
Thorndean Dr RH17 . . . .**85** D7
Thorndean Rd BN2 . . . .**170** D3
Thornden RH13 . . . .**83** E2
Thorndene Ave PO21 . . . . . .**201** B4
Thorndyke Cl RH10 . . . .**19** D5
Thorney Dr PO20 . . . .**212** C2
Thorney Island Com Prim
  Sch PO10 . . . .**173** C3
Thorney Old Pk PO10 . . . .**173** F1
Thorney Rd PO10 . . . .**173** D6
Thornham La PO10 . . . .**173** E6
Thornham Marina
  PO10 . . . .**173** E6
Thornhill RH11 . . . .**18** B4
Thornhill Ave BN1 . . . .**170** A4
Thornhill Cl BN3 . . . .**168** E2
Thornhill Rise BN1 . . . .**168** A4
Thornhill Way BN41 . . . .**168** A3
Thornhurst RH15 . . . .**109** C1
Thornlea Pk BN17 . . . .**182** C5
Thorn Rd BN11 . . . .**186** C1
Thornscroft BN44 . . . .**145** D4
Thornsdale ⏹5 BN2 . . . . . .**213** C3
Thornton Cl RH6 . . . .**1** E3
Thornton Ct ⏹2 BN6 . . . .**70** D1
Thornton Mdw RH14 . . . .**78** B8
Thornton Pl RH6 . . . .**1** F3
Threals Copse RH20 . . . . . .**121** E5
Threal's La RH20 . . . .**121** E6
Three Acres RH12 . . . .**36** A1
THREE BRIDGES **19** A8
Three Bridges Inf Sch
  RH10 . . . .**19** A7
Three Bridges Jun Sch
  RH10 . . . .**18** F6
Three Bridges Rd
  RH10 . . . .**19** A6
Three Bridges Sta
  RH10 . . . .**19** B6
Three Gates La GU27 . . . . . .**27** C8
Threestile Cnr RH12 . . . .**14** E1
Threestile Rd RH12 . . . .**14** F1
Thrusloes PO21 . . . .**200** F3
Thurlow Rd BN11 . . . .**186** F3
Thurne Way RH12 . . . .**33** D7
Thyme Cl BN43 . . . .**167** C1
Thyme Ho ⏹5 RH10 . . . .**6** A1
Ticehurst Cl RH10 . . . .**19** E6
Ticehurst Rd BN2 . . . .**192** F5
Tichborne Cotts RH16 . . . . . .**88** C6
Tichborne St BN1 . . . .**213** B2
Tideway BN17 . . . .**205** A4

Tide Way PO20 . . . .**208** C5
Tideys Mill RH13 . . . .**104** F3
Tidy St BN1 . . . .**213** B3
Tilbury Pl BN2 . . . .**213** C2
Tilbury Way BN2 . . . .**213** C3
Tilebarn Ct RH16 . . . .**87** E2
Tile Barn Est PO20 . . . .**197** C1
Tile Barn La PO20 . . . .**197** C1
Tilemakers Cl PO18 . . . .**155** E1
Tilers Cl RH15 . . . .**109** D3
Tilford Dr PO22 . . . .**201** E6
TILGATE **18** E2
Tilgate Cl BN2 . . . .**192** D6
Tilgate Dr RH10 . . . .**18** E2
Tilgate Forest Bsns Ctr
  RH11 . . . .**18** D1
TILGATE FOREST ROW **39** C5
Tilgate Forest Row
  RH11 . . . .**39** C5
Tilgate Mans RH10 . . . .**18** F1
Tilgate Par RH10 . . . .**18** E3
Tilgate Pl RH10 . . . .**18** F1
Tilgate Way RH10 . . . .**18** E3
Tilletts La RH12 . . . .**35** E8
Tillinghurst La RH17 . . . .**42** A2
Tillington BN2 . . . .**192** F7
Tillington Cotts BN18 . . . . .**180** F3
Tillington Rd GU28 . . . .**97** E7
Tillstone Cl RH10 . . . .**19** D5
Tillstone Cl BN2 . . . .**170** D2
Tillstone St BN2 . . . .**213** C2
Tilmore Gdns GU32 . . . .**68** B5
Tilmore Rd GU32 . . . .**68** B5
Tilsmore ⏹7 BN2 . . . .**192** F5
Tiltwood Dr RH10 . . . .**21** C8
Timber Cl BN13 . . . .**185** C6
Timber Ct RH12 . . . .**36** C3
Timberham Farm Rd
  RH6 . . . .**5** D8
Timberham Ho RH6 . . . .**5** E8
Timberham Way RH6 . . . .**5** E8
Timberlaine Ind Est
  PO19 . . . .**177** C5
Timberlaine Trad Est
  BN14 . . . .**185** E1
Timberlands
  Crawley RH11 . . . .**18** B1
  Storrington RH20 . . . .**121** E2
Timberlea Cl RH20 . . . .**123** A5
Timberleys ⏹1 BN17 . . . . .**205** A6
Timber Mill RH13 . . . .**57** F2
Timbermill Ct GU27 . . . .**26** F6
Timbers The
  East Grinstead RH19 . . . .**9** C2
  Mannings Heath RH13 . . . . .**59** C6
Tindal Cl RH15 . . . .**109** D3
Tingall PO21 . . . .**200** E3
Tinsley Cl RH10 . . . .**6** A1
Tinsley La RH10 . . . .**6** A1
TINSLEY GREEN **6** B4
Tinsley La N RH10 . . . .**6** A1
Tinsley La S RH10 . . . .**19** A8
Tintagel Ct
  Horsham RH13 . . . .**36** D1
  Hove BN3 . . . .**191** A8
  ⏹6 Shoreham-by-S
Tintern Cl BN1 . . . .**170** B1
Tintern Rd RH11 . . . .**18** A4
Tinwood La
  Crockerhill PO18 . . . .**157** A4
  Halnaker PO18 . . . .**156** E5
Tipper La GU31 . . . .**91** D3
Tiree Path RH11 . . . .**18** B3
Tisbury Rd BN3 . . . .**191** C6
TISMAN'S COMMON **33** A6
Titchfield Cl RH15 . . . .**109** D1
Titch Hill BN15 . . . .**165** A3
The Barn BN15 . . . .**187** E8
The Barn Chalets
  PO20 . . . .**212** B8
The Barn Cl PO20 . . . .**200** C1
The Barn Ct PO20 . . . .**211** B8
The Barn Way PO21 . . . .**200** B1
Tithe Gn BN16 . . . .**205** B5
Tithe Orch RH19 . . . .**8** E4
Tithe The RH11 . . . .**5** A1
Titian Rd BN3 . . . .**190** F7
Titmus Dr RH10 . . . .**18** F2
Titmore La BN12, BN13 . . . .**185** A7
Titnore Way BN12,
  BN13 . . . .**185** A7
Tivoli BN1 . . . .**169** E2
Tivoli Cres BN1 . . . .**169** D1
Tivoli Cres N BN1 . . . .**169** D2
Tivoli Pl BN1 . . . .**169** D2
Tivoli Rd BN1 . . . .**169** D2
Toat Hill RH13 . . . .**56** E8
Toat La RH20 . . . .**100** A8
Tobias Sch of Art
  RH19 . . . .**22** E6
TODDINGTON **204** E8
Toddington La BN17 . . . .**204** E8
Toddington Pk BN17 . . . . . .**204** E7
Todds Cl RH6 . . . .**1** E5
Toftwood Cl RH10 . . . .**19** C5
Tollbridge Ho BN43 . . . .**188** D8
Tollgate Hill RH11 . . . .**18** C1
Tollgate La RH11 . . . .**17** E6
Tollgate Hill ⏹7 RH11 . . . . . .**86** E8
Tollgate Pl ⏹12 RH19 . . . . . .**22** F8
Tollhouse Cl PO19 . . . .**176** F6
Tompset's Bank RH18 . . . . . .**23** F1
Tomtit Cres RH10 . . . .**21** C5

Tomtits La RH18 . . . .**23** E1
Tongdean Ave BN3 . . . .**169** C3
Tongdean La BN1 . . . .**169** C4
Tongdean Pl BN3 . . . .**169** C3
Tongdean Rd BN3 . . . .**169** C3
Tongdean Rise BN1 . . . .**169** C4
Toomey Rd BN44 . . . .**145** D5
Top Hill Cl BN41 . . . .**167** F2
TOPLEIGH **95** F2
Top Rd
  Sharpthorne RH19 . . . .**43** B5
  Slindon BN18 . . . .**158** C5
Top St RH17 . . . .**85** C4
Torberry Dr GU31 . . . .**68** D2
Torcross Cl BN2 . . . .**170** E1
Toronto Cl BN13 . . . .**185** D7
Toronto Terr BN2 . . . .**192** C6
Torrance Cl BN3 . . . .**168** F1
Torridge Cl BN13 . . . .**185** C8
Tortington Manor,
  Arundel Wing The
  BN18 . . . .**181** E7
Tortington manor,
  Goodwood Wing The
  BN18 . . . .**181** E7
Tortington Manor, Manor
  Ho The BN18 . . . .**181** E7
Tortington ManorNew
  England Wing The
  BN18 . . . .**181** E7
Tortington Manor,
  Norfolk Wing The
  BN18 . . . .**181** E7
Tortington Manor, Stable
  Ctyd The BN18 . . . .**181** E7
Torton Hill Rd BN18 . . . .**159** F2
Tor Way GU31 . . . .**68** C3
TOTE HILL **72** A6
Tote La GU29 . . . .**72** A5
Totland Rd BN2 . . . .**192** D7
Tott Hill BN6 . . . .**128** B5
Tottington Dr BN5 . . . .**146** F6
Tottington Way BN43 . . . . .**167** B1
Tower Approach Rd
  RH6 . . . .**5** E6
Tower Cl
  Chichester PO19 . . . .**176** F7
  East Grinstead RH19 . . . .**9** E2
  Horley RH6 . . . .**1** F3
  Lipbook GU30 . . . .**25** B4
  Tower Hill RH13 . . . .**58** A8
Tower Ct RH19 . . . .**9** E2
Towergate BN1 . . . .**169** E2
Tower Hill RH13 . . . .**58** A8
Tower Ho
  Brighton BN1 . . . .**169** E2
  Burgess Hill RH15 . . . .**109** B2
Tower House Ct RH17 . . . . . .**86** E7
Tower House Gdns
  BN18 . . . .**160** B3
Tower Pl PO20 . . . .**207** F7
Tower Rd
  Brighton BN2 . . . .**192** C6
  Colgate RH12 . . . .**38** A7
  Faygate RH12 . . . .**37** F8
  Lancing BN15 . . . .**187** D5
  Lipbook GU30 . . . .**25** B4
  Worthing BN11 . . . .**186** E3
Tower Rd Flats ⏹6
  BN15 . . . .**187** D5
Towers Convent Sch The
  BN44 . . . .**146** B1
Towers Rd BN44 . . . .**146** B2
Tower St
  Chichester PO19 . . . .**176** F6
  Emsworth PO10 . . . .**173** C8
Town Barn Rd RH11 . . . .**18** C7
Town Cross Ave
  PO21 . . . .**201** C4
Townfield RH14 . . . .**53** B2
Town La
  Petersfield GU32 . . . .**68** D5
  Singleton PO18 . . . .**135** C4
Town Mead RH11 . . . .**18** D4
Town Place Farm Cotts
  RH17 . . . .**89** C7
Town Quay BN43 . . . .**188** E6
Town Quay Appartments
  BN43 . . . .**188** E6
Townsend Cres BN17 . . . . .**204** F6
Townsend Way RH10 . . . .**19** D4
Tozer Ct BN41 . . . .**190** B7
Trafalgar Cl RH10 . . . .**36** C4
Trafalgar Cl
  ⏹14 Bognor Regis
  PO21 . . . .**201** B2
  Brighton BN1 . . . .**213** B3
  ⏹8 Rustington BN16 . . . .**205** C6
Trafalgar Gate BN2 . . . .**192** F3
Trafalgar Gdns ⏹1
  RH10 . . . .**19** B7
Trafalgar La BN1 . . . .**213** B3
Trafalgar Pl BN1 . . . .**213** B3
Trafalgar Rd
  Horsham RH12 . . . .**36** C4
  Portslade-by-S BN41 . . . . .**190** B8
Trafalgar St BN1 . . . .**213** B3
Trafalgar Terr BN1 . . . .**213** B3
Trafalgar View BN1 . . . .**213** B3
Tramway Cl PO20 . . . .**198** F8
Treadcroft Dr RH12 . . . .**36** E5
Treadwheel Rd PO8 . . . .**130** D6
Tredcroft Rd BN1 . . . .**169** C2
Treemans Rd (Lewes Rd)
  RH17 . . . .**65** B2

Trees Ct PO20 . . . .**212** E8
Treetops RH13 . . . .**81** F7
Treetops Cl BN2 . . . .**193** E8
Treeview RH11 . . . .**18** C1
Trefoil Cl RH12 . . . .**36** E5
Trefoil Cres RH11 . . . .**18** A2
Tregarth Rd PO19 . . . .**155** A2
Tregenna Ho GU30 . . . .**25** B5
Treharne Ct BN13 . . . .**185** D8
Treloar Rd PO11 . . . .**195** B1
Tremola Ave BN2 . . . .**194** C2
Trendle Gn PO21 . . . .**200** F2
Trenear Cl RH13 . . . .**36** E2
Trent Cl
  Crawley RH11 . . . .**17** F4
  Lancing BN15 . . . .**187** C6
Trent Ho ⏹3 BN4 . . . .**186** A5
Trent Rd BN12 . . . .**185** E3
Tretawn Gdns PO20 . . . .**212** F6
Trevanne Plat RH10 . . . .**19** D7
Trevelyan Pl RH16 . . . .**87** E5
Treveor Cl BN11 . . . .**186** C2
TREYFORD **92** F2
Treyford Cl
  Crawley RH11 . . . .**17** F6
  Woodingdean BN2 . . . .**171** E1
Triangle Bsns Ctr
  BN15 . . . .**187** C4
Triangle Ho ⏹4 RH16 . . . . . .**87** F3
Triangle Rd RH16 . . . .**87** F3
Triangle The BN15 . . . .**187** C4
Triangle Way RH20 . . . .**123** A5
Trident Ct RH9 . . . .**1** C8
Trident Bsns Pk PO20 . . . . .**210** A3
Trinity Cl RH10 . . . .**19** C8
Trinity Ct
  Horsham RH12 . . . .**36** C3
  Hurstpierpoint BN6 . . . . . .**128** B5
Trinity Rd BN6 . . . .**128** A5
Trinity Sq RH12 . . . .**36** C3
Trinity St BN2 . . . .**213** C4
Trinity Way
  Bognor Regis PO21 . . . . . .**200** F4
  Littlehampton BN17 . . . . .**204** F4
Tripp Hill RH20 . . . .**118** F7
Tristar Bsns Ctr RH13 . . . .**105** A2
Tristram Ct BN15 . . . .**187** B7
Trist Way RH11 . . . .**18** A8
Triton Pl PO22 . . . .**202** C5
Tritton Pl RH20 . . . .**121** B2
Troon Ho BN1 . . . .**28** B2
Troon Cl RH11 . . . .**17** D5
Troon Ct RH16 . . . .**87** E4
TROTTEN MARSH **70** C7
Trotton Cl RH10 . . . .**19** C3
Trotton Rd GU29, GU31 . . . . . .**93** A7
Trotyn Croft PO21 . . . .**200** F2
Trout La RH13 . . . .**34** C4
Trout Rd GU27 . . . .**26** E6
Troymede RH12 . . . .**41** A1
True Blue Prec BN17 . . . . . .**204** D7
Truggers RH17 . . . .**61** C8
Truggers Ct RH17 . . . .**61** C8
Truleigh Cl BN2 . . . .**193** F7
Truleigh Dene BN44 . . . .**146** B2
Truleigh Dr BN41 . . . .**168** A4
Truleigh Hill YH
  BN43 . . . .**147** A2
Truleigh Rd BN44 . . . .**146** B2
Truleigh Way BN43 . . . .**167** A1
Trumpkins BN6 . . . .**128** A5
Trumps Alley GU28 . . . .**97** F8
Trundle Cl PO18 . . . .**154** E6
Trundle Mead RH12 . . . .**36** C5
Trundle View Cl PO22 . . . . .**180** B6
Truro Cl RH10 . . . .**19** C4
Truro Cres PO21 . . . .**200** E3
Trusler's Hill La BN6 . . . . . .**126** F6
Tryndel Way PO22 . . . .**202** B4
Tudor Ave PO10 . . . .**151** A4
Tudor Bldgs PO21 . . . .**200** E2
Tudor Cl
  Chichester PO19 . . . .**154** F2
  Crawley RH10 . . . .**19** D5
  East Grinstead RH17 . . . . . .**28** F8
  Findon BN14 . . . .**163** E6
  Hove BN3 . . . .**168** F2
  Lancing BN15 . . . .**188** B6
  Marehill RH20 . . . .**100** F1
  Middleton-on-S PO22 . . . .**202** C6
  Rottingdean BN2 . . . .**194** A2
Tudor Ct
  ⏹11 Bognor Regis
  PO21 . . . .**201** D4
  Haslemere GU27 . . . .**27** C7
Tudor Dr
  Upper Beeding BN44 . . . . .**146** A3
  Westergate PO20 . . . .**179** D8
Tudor Gdns RH15 . . . .**108** F4
Tudor Ho RH13 . . . .**36** B3
Tudor View BN17 . . . .**204** A6
Tudor Village RH20 . . . .**122** C3
Tuff's Hard PO18 . . . .**197** C7
Tufts Field PO19 . . . .**94** E6
Tufts Mdw GU29 . . . .**94** E6
Tuggles Plat RH12 . . . .**35** E7
Tulip Ct RH13 . . . .**36** B3
Tullett Rd RH10 . . . .**20** D4
Tulleys Farm* RH10 . . . .**20** D6
Tumulus Rd BN2 . . . .**192** C1
Tunbridge Cres GU30 . . . . . .**25** B5
Tunbridge La GU30 . . . .**25** B6
Tunnel Rd RH6 . . . .**1** F2
Tunnmeade ⏹7 RH11 . . . .**17** F5
Tunsgate BN45 . . . .**145** D3
Tuppen Ho BN7 . . . .**172** E5
Tuppenny La PO10 . . . .**173** D6
TURKEY ISLAND **91** F3
Turkey La RH15 . . . .**109** B3

Turnberry Ct ⏹14 RH16 . . . . . .**87** E4
Turnbull Rd PO19 . . . .**177** B7
Turner Ave RH14 . . . .**79** C6
Turner Ct RH19 . . . .**10** A3
Turner Dumbrell
  Workshops BN6 . . . .**129** D4
Turner Rd BN1 . . . .**190** C7
Turner Rd BN14 . . . .**186** E6
Turners Cl RH13 . . . .**82** A8
Turners Hill CE Sch
  RH10 . . . .**21** A3
TURNERS HILL PARK **21** C5
Turners Hill Rd
  Copthorne RH10 . . . .**7** F2
  Crawley Down RH10 . . . . . .**21** A7
  Crawley RH10 . . . .**20** C5
  Turners Hill RH10 . . . .**20** F5
Turner's Hill Rd RH19 . . . . . .**22** B6
Turners Mead RH20 . . . . . .**121** B2
Turners Mill Cl RH16 . . . .**87** D7
Turners Mill Rd RH16 . . . . . .**87** D6
Turners Way RH15 . . . .**108** F4
Turner Way PO20 . . . .**212** F7
Turner Wlk RH10 . . . .**182** F5
Turnpike Cl PO19 . . . .**176** F3
Turnpike Ct RH17 . . . .**64** B8
Turnpike Ho RH13 . . . .**57** F1
Turnpike Piece RH11 . . . . . .**171** B6
Turnpike Rd BN18 . . . .**140** F6
Turnpike Way RH20 . . . .**123** A5
Turret Ct RH19 . . . .**9** F4
Turtledove Ave RH10 . . . .**21** C5
Turton Cl BN2 . . . .**192** D5
Tuscan Ave PO22 . . . .**202** F5
Tuscany Gdns RH10 . . . .**18** E8
Tushmore Ave RH10 . . . .**5** E1
Tushmore Cres RH10 . . . .**5** E1
Tushmore Ct RH10 . . . .**18** E8
Tushmore La RH10 . . . .**18** E8
Tushmore Rdbt RH11 . . . .**18** D8
Tussock Cl RH11 . . . .**18** A4
Tuxford Cl RH10 . . . .**19** C4
Tweed La RH11 . . . .**4** F1
Twineham CE Prim Sch
  RH17 . . . .**107** A4
Twineham La BN2 . . . .**192** F7
TWINEHAM GREEN **107** B6
Twineham La BN6,
  RH17 . . . .**107** A4
Twitten Cl ⏹2 BN42 . . . . . .**189** E7
Twitten La RH19 . . . .**8** E4
Twittenside BN44 . . . .**145** D2
Twitten The
  Albourne Green BN6 . . . . .**127** C6
  Burgess Hill RH15 . . . .**109** B4
  Crawley RH11 . . . .**18** C6
  Ditchling BN6 . . . .**129** D3
  Southwick BN42 . . . .**189** E7
Twitten Way BN14 . . . .**186** A4
Two Barns La PO18 . . . .**154** D6
Two Mile Ash Rd
  Barns Green RH13 . . . .**56** F3
  Two Mile Ash RH13 . . . .**57** D3
Two Ways RH14 . . . .**32** A4
Twyford Cl BN13 . . . .**185** E7
Twyford Gdns BN13 . . . .**185** E7
Twyford Rd
  Brighton BN1 . . . .**170** G6
  Worthing BN13 . . . .**185** E7
Twyhurst Ct RH19 . . . .**9** D3
Twyne Cl RH11 . . . .**17** F4
Twyner Cl RH6 . . . .**2** D4
Tye La BN18 . . . .**158** E1
Tylden Way RH12 . . . .**36** F6
Tyler Rd RH10 . . . .**18** E3
Tyler's Grn RH16, RH17 . . . . .**87** B4
Tylston Mdw GU30 . . . .**25** B5
Tymperley Ct RH13 . . . .**36** E3
Tyne Cl
  Crawley RH10 . . . .**19** C5
  Worthing BN13 . . . .**185** C8
Tyne Way PO21 . . . .**200** D3
Tynings The BN15 . . . .**188** A4
Tyson Pl ⏹5 BN2 . . . .**213** C2
Tythe Barn RH17 . . . .**85** C3
Tythe Barn Rd PO20 . . . . . .**212** E6

U

Uckfield Cl BN2 . . . .**192** F6
Ullswater Dr BN17 . . . .**205** A7
Ullswater Gr PO22 . . . .**202** B6
Ullswater Rd BN15 . . . .**187** B5
Underdown Rd BN42 . . . . . .**189** E8
Underhill La
  Clayton BN6 . . . .**149** E8
  Westmeston BN6 . . . .**150** C8
Undermill Rd BN44 . . . .**146** B2
Underwood Cl RH10 . . . .**21** B8
Underwood Rd GU27 . . . .**26** F7
Unicorn Trad Est The
  GU27 . . . .**27** B3
Unifax BN12 . . . .**185** C4
Union Pl BN11 . . . .**186** D2
Union Rd BN2 . . . .**213** C4
Union St BN1 . . . .**213** B2
Unita Ho ⏹5 BN11 . . . .**186** B1
Univ of Brighton
  Brighton BN1 . . . .**213** B2
  Falmer BN1 . . . .**171** B6
Univ of Brighton
  (Cockcroft/Watts
  Annexes) BN2 . . . .**170** D2
Univ of Brighton (St
  Peter's Ho) BN2 . . . .**213** B3

Univ of Chichester
(Bishop Otter Campus)
PO19 .... **177** A8
Univ of Chichester Bognor
Regis Campus PO21...**201** E4
Univ of Sussex BN1.... **171** A7
Updown Hill RH16....... **87** C2
Upfield RH6................2 A1
Upfield Cl RH6.............2 A1
Upfield Villas RH14.... **54** C2
Uphill Way PO20....... **199** A8
Uplands Ave BN13..... **185** F9
Uplands Cl GU27.........**27** D8
Uplands Rd
Brighton BN1.......... **170** C2
Rowland's Castle PO9 .. **130** E2
UP MARDEN............. **111** F1
Uppark* GU31.......... **111** B8
Uppark Gdns RH12......**36** F6
Uppark Way PO22 ..... **202** D7
Upper Abbey Rd BN2 ... **192** C4
Upper Bedford St
BN2 .... **192** C4
Upper Beeding Prim Sch
BN44 .... **146** A2
Upper Bevendean Ave
BN2...................**170** C1
Upper Bognor Rd
 Bognor Regis
 PO21................. **201** D4
 Bognor Regis PO21...**201** E4
Upper Boundstone La
 Lancing, North Lancing
 BN15................. **187** D8
 Lancing, Upper Cokeham
 BN15................. **187** D7
Upper Brighton Rd
 Lancing BN15.......... **187** C8
 Worthing BN14 .... **186** D7
Upper Chalvington Pl
BN2...................**192** E5
Upper Cl RH18...........**23** F2
UPPER COKEHAM...... **187** C7
Upper Dr BN16........ **206** B4
Upper Dr The BN3 .... **191** D8
Upperfield GU29.........**72** F2
Upper Forecourt RH6.....6 B7
Upper Gardner St
BN1................... **213** B3
Upper Gloucester Rd
BN1 .... **213** A3
Upper Hamilton Rd
BN1 .... **213** A5
Upper Heyshott GU31....**68** C3
Upper High St BN1..... **186** E3
Upper Hollingdean Rd
BN1...................**170** B1
UPPER IFOLD............**30** F7
Upper Kingston La BN42,
BN43 .... **167** D1
Upper Lewes Rd BN2 .. **213** C4
Upper Lodges BN1..... **145** C8
Upper Market St
BN3 .... **191** D5
Upper Mount GU33 ......**45** A3
Upper North St BN1... **213** A2
UPPER NORWOOD...... **116** D8
Upper Park Pl BN2 .. **213** C2
Upper Rock Gdns
BN2 .... **213** C2
Upper Roedale Cotts
BN1...................**170** B4
Upper St James's St
BN2 .... **213** C1
Upper St Johns Rd
RH15................. **190** C5
Upper School Dr GU27...**26** F5
Upper Shoreham Rd
BN43 .... **167** B1
Upper Sq RH18..........**23** F3
Upper St RH20..........**99** A3
Upper Stables RH16.....**87** C3
Upper Station Rd
BN5 .... **125** D5
Upper Sudeley St
BN2 .... **192** D4
Upperton Rd GU28......**75** C1
Upperton's Barn Visitors
Ctr* RH20............. **120** D5
UPPER WARDLEY........**47** C6
Upper Wardown GU31...**68** A4
Upper Wellington Rd
BN2...................**192** C7
Upper West Dr PO20.. **206** E5
Upper West La BN15... **187** E8
Upper Winfield Ave
BN1...................**169** F6
Upper Wlk AveA* A1
Upton Ave RH6......... **167** A1
Upton Cl BN13......... **185** F4
Upton Gdns BN13..... **185** F5
Upton Rd
 Stockbridge PO19..... **176** F4
 Worthing BN13....... **185** F5
UPWALTHAM........... **137** E8
Upways Cl PO20....... **209** F1
Ursa Cl BN2....... **192** C8
Ursula Ave N PO20.... **212** D6
Ursula Ave N PO20.... **212** D6
Ursula Sq PO20....... **212** D5

V

Vachery La GU6..........**11** E7
Valdoe Yd PO18........ **155** D4
Vale Ave
 Brighton BN1......... **169** E7
 Worthing BN14....... **163** F2

Valebridge Cl RH15.... **109** C6
Valebridge Dr RH15.... **109** C5
Valebridge Rd RH15... **109** C6
Vale Ct BN41.......... **190** B7
Vale Dr
 Horsham RH12..........**36** B3
 Worthing BN14....... **163** F2
Vale Fst & Mid Sch
BN14................. **163** F2
Vale Gdns BN41....... **190** B7
Valencia Rd BN11..... **186** A3
Valentine Cl
 Shoreham-by-S BN43... **166** D1
 Worthing BN14....... **186** B7
Valentine Ct BN3 ... **191** C7
Valentine Dr RH15.... **108** E4
Valentines Gdns
PO21 .... **200** C2
Valentines Lea GU28...**51** A8
Vale Rd
 Haywards Heath RH16 ...**87** E2
 Portslade-by-S BN41 .. **190** C7
 Saltdean BN2......... **194** D3
Valerie Cl BN41....... **168** C2
Vale The
 Ovingdean BN2....... **193** E5
 Petersfield GU32.......**68** D5
Valetta Pk PO10....... **173** A8
Valetta Rd PO10....... **173** F1
Vale Wlk BN14......... **163** F1
Valewood Cl RH13......**56** D1
Valewood La RH13......**56** D1
Valewood Rd GU27.....**27** C4
Valiant Rd PO10....... **173** F1
Vallance By-ways RH6.....4 F6
Vallance Cl RH15..... **108** E4
Vallance Ct BN3 ... **191** A6
Vallance Gdns BN3 ... **191** A6
Vallance Rd BN3...... **191** A6
Vallensdean Cotts
BN41................. **168** C2
Valley Cl BN1......... **169** C4
Valley Dr BN1......... **169** C4
Valley Farm Bsns Pk
BN6 .... **107** B1
Valley Gdns BN14..... **164** A1
Valley Rd
 Lancing BN15......... **187** C8
 Portslade-by-S BN41 .. **168** A2
Valley Side GU30.......**25** B5
Valverde Ho BN3... **191** C7
Van Alen Bldg The
BN2 .... **213** C1
Van Alen Mews BN2 .. **213** C1
Vanbrugh Cl RH11......**17** E3
Vanbrugh Ct BN1... **191** C7
Vancouver Cl BN13... **185** D7
Vancouver Dr
RH11...................5 D1
Vancouver Rd BN13... **185** D7
Van Dyck Pl PO22.... **201** A6
Van Gogh Pl PO22.... **201** B6
Vann Bridge Cl GU27...**49** A6
Vanners RH10..........**18** E7
Vann Rd GU27..........**49** A6
Vanzell Rd GU29........**73** A1
Varey Rd BN14........ **185** B7
Varndean Cl BN1..... **169** E3
Varndean Coll BN1... **169** F3
Varndean Dr BN1..... **169** E3
Varndean Gdns BN1.. **169** F3
Varndean Holt BN1... **169** F3
Varndean Rd BN1..... **169** E3
Varndean Sch BN1.... **170** A3
Varsity Rd PO10...... **173** F1
Vauxhall Way GU32....**68** A3
Velyn Ave PO19....... **177** B6
Velyn Ct PO19......... **177** B6
Ventnor Villas BN3... **191** B6
Venus La PO21........ **210** E7
Veras Wlk RH20....... **122** C1
Verbania Way RH19....**10** B1
Verdley Cotts GU27.....**49** C3
Verdley Pl GU27........**49** C3
Vere Rd BN1.......... **213** B5
Veric BN3.......... **191** C7
Verica Ct PO19........ **176** B7
Verdley Fields BN13.. **185** D8
Verdley Rd RH14.......**32** A2
Vicarage La
 Bognor Regis PO22... **202** A4
 East Preston BN16.... **205** F5
 Haslemere GU27.......**26** F6
 Horley RH6.............5 C3
 Rottingdean BN2......**74** B2
 Scaynes Hill RH17......**88** F3
 Steyning BN44........ **145** D3
Vicarage Rd RH10.....**21** A8
Vicarage Terr BN2.... **193** F1
Vicarage The RH12.....**38** C6
Vicars Ct PO19..... **177** A6
Viceroy Ct BN3....... **206** E5
Viceroy Lo BN3.... **191** A6

Victor Ct RH10.............6 D1
Victoria Ave
 Burgess Hill RH15.... **108** E3
 Midhurst GU29.........**73** A1
Victoria Bldgs BN13.. **186** E2
Victoria Bsns Ctr
RH15................. **108** E2
Victoria Cl
 Burgess Hill RH15.... **108** F2
 Horley RH6.............2 A3
  Midhurst GU29......**94** E7
Victoria Cottage Hospl
PO10................. **173** B8
Victoria Cotts BN3 .. **191** B5
Victoria Ct
  Bognor Regis
 PO21................. **201** E6
  Horsham RH13.......**36** D2
  Hove BN3........... **191** C6
  Lancing BN15....... **187** E4
  Portslade-by-S BN41 .. **190** C8
  Shoreham-by-S
 BN43................. **188** E7
  Worthing BN11...... **186** C3
  Worthing BN11...... **186** C3
Victoria Dr PO21..... **201** B3
Victoria Gdns
 Burgess Hill RH15.... **108** F2
 Westergate PO20..... **179** D7
Victoria Gr BN3... **191** C6
Victoria Ind Est RH15 .. **108** E3
Victoria Lo BN11... **186** C3
Victoria Mews
 Crawley RH11.........**18** D6
 Rottingdean BN2..... **193** F1
Victoria Park Gdns
BN18................. **181** D4
Victorian Bsns Ctr
BN18................. **181** D4
Victoria Pl
  Bognor Regis
 PO21................. **201** B2
  Brighton BN1....... **191** E6
  Liphook GU30........**47** E8
Victoria Rd
 Balcombe RH17.........**41** A1
 Bognor Regis PO21... **201** B2
 Brighton BN1......... **191** E6
 Burgess Hill RH15.... **108** E2
 Chichester PO19..... **177** C7
 Crawley RH11.........**18** C6
 Emsworth PO10...... **151** A1
 Haywards Heath RH16 ...**88** A3
 Horley RH6.............2 A4
 Portslade-by-S BN41 .. **190** C8
 Shoreham-by-S BN43.. **188** E7
 Southwick BN42...... **189** D7
 Worthing BN11....... **186** C3
Victoria Rd BN3... **191** C6
Victoria Road Trad Est
BN41................. **190** C8
Victoria St
 Brighton BN1......... **191** E6
 Horsham RH13.........**36** D2
Victoria Terr
 Bognor Regis PO22... **201** F3
  Hove BN3.......... **191** B5
 Lumley PO10......... **151** C1
 Prinsted PO10........ **173** B8
 Westbourne PO10.... **151** D3
Victoria Villas BN18.. **181** A3
Victoria Way
 Burgess Hill RH15.... **108** F2
 East Grinstead RH19...**22** F7
 Liphook GU30.........**25** B4
Victor Rd PO10....... **173** F1
Victory Ct PO21... **201** B2
Victory Mews BN2.... **193** A3
Victory Rd RH12........**36** B3
Views Path RH16.......**88** B4
View The PO21........ **211** A8
Viking Terr BN17..... **204** D4
Viking Way PO18..... **175** B5
Village Barn The BN1 . **169** E7
Village Cl BN41....... **168** B2
Village St GU32........**68** D6
Village Way RH11.... **171** C6
Villa Plage PO22..... **203** A5
Villiers Cl BN1....... **169** B6
Villiers Cr BN1....... **213** B3
Vinall Gdns RH12.....**35** D4
Vinalls Bsns Ctr BN5. **125** E4
Vincent Cl
 Horsham RH13.........**36** F4
 Lancing BN15........ **187** D6
Vincent Rd PO20..... **212** C6
Vine Pl BN1.......... **213** A3
Vineries Cl BN13..... **186** A6
Vineries The
 Burgess Hill RH15.... **109** D3
  Hove BN3.......... **191** E6
Vinery Ct BN13....... **186** A6
Vinery The BN18..... **183** C8
Vines Cross Rd BN2.. **192** F7
Vine St BN1.......... **213** B3
Vinery Cl RH20....... **122** C1
Vinnetrow Farm Bsns Ctr
PO20................. **177** E3
Vinnetrow Rd PO20.. **177** E3
Vinols Cross RH19.....**42** F6
Vinson Rd GU33.......**45** C4
Visage BN1....... **191** D7
Viscount Dr PO21.... **211** B8
Vivienne Cl RH11.......5 D1
Volks Electric Rly* BN1,
BN2 .... **192** C4

Vowels Forest Wlk*
RH19..................**21** E3
Vowels La RH19.........**21** E2
Vulcan Cl RH11.........**18** C2
Vulcan Ho RH20.... **121** E1
Vulcan Rd PO10...... **173** F1

W

Waddington Cl RH11....**18** A3
Wade Ct RH18..........**23** F2
Wade End PO20....... **212** C8
Wadeway Cvn Site
PO20................. **212** C8
Wadeway The PO20.. **212** C8
Wadeys The RH14......**79** C8
Wadham Cl RH10.........6 C1
Wadhurst Cl PO21.... **201** B4
Wadhurst Dr BN13.... **186** A3
Wadhurst Rd BN2..... **185** B3
Wadhurst Rise BN2... **192** F5
Wadlands Brook Rd
RH19...................9 D5
Wad The PO20........ **196** B1
Wagg Cl RH19..........**10** A1
Wagtail Cl RH12........**36** D7
Wain End RH10........**36** D5
Wainwrights RH10....**18** D3
Wakefield Cl RH12....**36** B2
Wakefield Rd BN2.... **213** C5
Wakefield Way PO21...**36** B2
Wakehams Green Dr
RH10...................6 D1
Wakehurst Cl BN11... **186** F3
Wakehurst Dr RH10....**18** D3
Wakehurst La RH17... **110** A5
Wakehurst Mews RH12..**35** F1
Wakehurst Pl (Royal
Wakehurst Place (Royal
 Bot Gdn)* RH17.......**41** F3
Wakestone La PO20....**77** A2
Walberton & Binstead CE
 Prim Sch BN18....... **158** E1
Walberton Cl PO22... **202** B5
Walberton Dr BN11... **185** F2
Walberton Pk BN18... **180** E8
Waldby Ct RH11........**18** A3
Waldegrave Cl BN2... **194** D3
Waldegrave Rd BN1.. **170** A1
Walders Rd BN16.... **205** B6
Waldron Ave BN1.... **170** D6
Waldron Pl BN1...... **170** D6
Walesbeech RH10.....**19** A5
Walhatch Cl RH18......**23** F2
Walker Rd RH10........**19** C4
Wallace Ave BN11.... **185** F2
Wallace Cl BN11... **185** F3
Wallace Par BN11.. **185** F3
Wallace Rd BN16.... **205** C6
Wallage La RH10......**20** C3
Walled Gdn The RH14...**31** F7
Wallfield PO21........ **200** F2
Wall Hill Rd RH18,
RH19..................**23** E5
Wallis Ct RH15....... **109** A3
Wallis Ho RH19.........9 E1
Wallis Way
 Burgess Hill RH15.... **108** E4
 Horsham RH13.........**37** A4
Wallner Cres PO22... **202** C5
Wallrock Wlk PO10... **151** B4
Walmer Cl
 Brighton BN2......... **171** B1
 Southwater RH13......**58** A2
Walmer Cres PO21.... **201** B1
Walmsleys Way PO20 . **208** C5
Walnut Cl
 Horsham RH13.........**36** E1
 Worthing BN14....... **186** A6
Walnut La RH11.........5 B1
Walnut Lo BN14...... **186** C4
Walnut Pk RH16........**88** B4
Walnuts The RH12.....**36** A3
Walnut Tree Cotts
RH14..................**79** A3
Walnut Tree Cvn Pk
PO20................. **196** C2
Walnut Tree Dr PO10. **152** A3
Walnut Tree Way
BN13................. **185** B6
Walpole Ave BN12.... **185** D3
Walpole Rd BN2...... **192** D5
Walpole Terr BN2.... **192** D5
Walsham Cl PO22.... **201** F6
Walsingham Rd BN3. **190** F6
Walstead Ct BN14.. **18** D5
Walter May Ho
BN2 .... **192** F5
Walters Gn BN17..... **182** C5
Waltham Park Rd
RH20................. **119** B6
Walton Bank BN1.... **170** C5
Walton Cl RH13....... **185** F3
Walton Dr RH13.......**37** C4
Walton Heath RH10...**18** B3
Walton Ho PO18...... **175** C7
Walton La BN13...... **185** F3
Walton Lo BN13...... **185** F3
Walton Rd PO21...... **201** B6
Walwyn Cl PO20..... **197** C5
Wanderdown Cl BN2. **193** E4

Wanderdown Dr BN2 . **193** E4
Wanderdown Rd BN2 . **193** D4
Wanderdown Way
BN2 .... **193** E4
Wandle Cl RH10.......**19** C5
Wandleys Cl PO20 ... **157** F1
Wandleys Dr PO20 ... **157** F1
Wandleys La BN18,
PO20................. **158** A2
Wandleys Lane Cvn Site
PO20................. **157** F1
Wansford Way PO22.. **202** C4
Wantage Cl RH10......**19** C3
Wantley Hill Est BN5.. **125** F6
Wantley La RH12..... **121** E2
Wantley Rd BN14.... **164** A1
Warble Heath Cl
BN18................. **154** F6
Warblers Way PO22... **201** B7
Warbleton Cl BN2.. **192** E5
Warbleton Ho RH11...**17** F3
Warblington Rd PO10. **173** A8
Warborough Rd RH11..**18** A3
Warburton Cl RH19.....**23** A8
Ward Cres PO10..... **151** C3
Warden Cl RH17.......**87** A6
Warden Park Sch
RH17..................**87** A5
Wardley Cl RH17.......**47** C4
Wardley Cotts GU30...**47** D4
Ware Ct RH15........ **109** D3
Wareland Ho RH19....9 E1
Warelands RH15..... **108** F1
Warenne Rd BN3..... **168** C4
Warleigh Rd BN1.... **213** B5
Warltersville Way RH6 ...2 C1
Warmdene Ave BN1.. **169** F5
Warmdene Cl BN1.... **169** F5
Warmdene Rd BN1... **169** F6
Warmdene Way BN1.. **169** F6
War Meml Hospl
RH16................. **201** C5
WARMINGHURST **122** D6
Warminghurst Cl
RH20................. **122** F5
Warminghurst Ct
RH12..................**36** D5
Warner Cl RH10.......**19** C2
Warner Ct RH15..... **109** A3
Warner Rd
 Selsey PO20.......... **212** C6
 Worthing BN14...... **186** F4
Warner's La PO20.... **212** C8
Warnes Barn BN1.... **186** C3
Warnes BN11......... **186** E1
Warnham CE Prim Sch
RH12..................**35** F8
Warnham Cl BN12... **185** D2
Warnham Ct
 Broadbridge Heath
 RH12..................**35** D4
 Crawley RH10.........**19** B4
 Horsham RH12.........**36** B5
 Worthing BN13...... **185** D3
Warnham Manor RH12..**35** C7
Warnham Nature
 Reserve* RH12.......**36** B6
Warnham Rd
 Broadbridge Heath
 RH12..................**35** D4
 Crawley RH10.........**19** B4
 Horsham RH12.........**36** A5
 Worthing BN13...... **185** D3
Warnham Rise BN1... **170** A5
Warnham Sta RH12....**36** C8
Warninglid La RH13,
RH17..................**60** D2
Warninglid Prim Sch
RH17..................**61** A2
Warren Ave PO20.... **193** C8
Warren Chase RH20.. **121** E2
Warren Cl
 Felbridge RH19..........8 E3
 Woodingdean BN2.... **193** B8
 Worthing BN14...... **186** B7
Warren Cotts
 Handcross RH17.......**61** B8
 West Dean PO18..... **134** F6
Warren Cres BN16.... **206** A6
Warren Croft RH20... **121** B1
Warren Ct
 Lancing BN15........ **187** D5
 Southwick BN42..... **167** E1
 Worthing BN14...... **186** B7
Warren Dr
 Crawley RH11.........**18** A4
 Southwater Street RH13...**58** A3
Warren Farm La
PO19................. **154** F2
Warren Farm Pl
BN14................. **186** A8
Warren Gdns BN14 .. **186** B7
Warren Rd
 Liss GU33.............**45** E7
 Woodingdean BN2.... **193** B8
 Worthing BN14...... **186** B7
Warren Rise BN2..... **193** B8
Warren Side GU33.....**91** D3
Warren The
 Ashfold Crossways
 RH17..................**60** E6
 Burgess Hill RH15... **109** C4
 Conford GU30.........**24** E8
 Ferring BN12........ **206** F4
 West Dean PO18..... **134** F6
Warren Way
 Barnham PO22....... **180** B6

Warren Way continued
Woodingdean BN2...... 193 D8
Warrington Cl RH11 .....17 E2
Warrior Cl BN41.......168 B2
Warrs Hill La BN8 .....89 E1
Warwick Cl PO21......200 B2
Warwick Ct
 Arundel BN18 ......160 A2
 5 Henfield BN5 ......173 B8
 8 Hove BN3..........191 E7
Warwick Gdns BN11 .....186 E2
Warwick La 1 BN11 ....186 E2
Warwick Mount 2
BN2 ....192 C4
Warwick Pl
 Bognor Regis PO22 ...202 D5
 Worthing BN11 ......186 E2
Warwick Rd BN11......186 E2
Warwick St BN11.......186 E2
Warwick Wlk 3 BN43....166 F1
Washbrooks Farm Pk*
BN6 ....127 F5
Washington Bostal
RH20 ....143 D5
Washington Cotts
RH20 ....143 D8
Washington Rd
 Buncton BN44.......144 E8
 Crawley RH11 ....17 E3
 Emsworth PO10......151 B1
 Haywards Heath RH16 ...86 A5
 Storrington RH20.....121 E1
 Washington RH20.....143 A8
Washington St
 Brighton BN2........213 C4
 Chichester PO19 .....176 F7
Washington Towers Cvn &
 Camping Pk RH20.....143 E7
Wassand Cl RH10 ......19 A6
Waterbury Hill RH17 ....65 B5
Watercress Pl 3 RH16 ...36 F3
Waterdyke Ave BN42...189 C7
Waterfield Cl RH13 ....36 E3
Waterfield Gdns RH11 ...17 E4
Waterhall Rd BN1 .....169 C6
Water La
 Angmering BN16......183 F5
 Buncton BN44 ......144 C8
 Littlehampton BN17...204 D6
 Selden BN16, BN13 ....184 C7
 Storrington RH20.....121 F2
Waterlands La RH12 ....13 E1
Water Lane Ind Est
RH20 ....121 E3
Waterlea RH10 ....19 A5
Waterloo Cl 1 PO21 ...201 C2
Waterloo Ho 9 BN1.....191 D5
Waterloo Pl 1 BN1.....213 C3
Waterloo Rd PO22 .....202 A4
Waterloo Sq PO21 .....201 C2
Waterplat The PO19....177 C8
Waters Edge
 Bognor Regis PO21 ...200 E1
 Pulborough RH20......100 A1
 13 Shoreham-by-S
BN43 ....189 A6
Watersedge Gdns
PO20 ....207 E6
Waters Edge Gdns
PO10 ....173 B8
Watersfield Rd BN14...186 B5
Waterside
 East Grinstead RH19....10 B1
 Horley RH6 ....2 A5
Waterside Cl RH11.....17 E4
Waterside Dr PO19 ....176 F4
Waterside The BN17 ...204 C5
Watersmead Bsns Pk
BN17 ....204 F8
Watersmead Cl BN17...205 A7
Watersmead Dr BN17...205 A7
Waterstone Cl PO20 ...197 A7
Water View RH6 ....2 C3
Waterworks Ct RH18.....23 F3
Waterworks Cotts
BN14 ....169 A2
 Worthing BN14 ......186 C7
Waterworks Rd GU32 ...68 C6
Watery La
 Chichester PO19 .....177 A4
 Funtington PO18 .....153 A4
Watling Cl 5 BN42 .....189 E7
Watling Ct 6 BN42 .....189 E7
Watling Rd BN42 ......189 E7
Watney Cotts RH17 .....42 E1
Watson Cl RH10 ....19 C3
Watson Way PO22 .....179 E7
Wattlehurst Dr RH12....15 B7
Watts Cnr RH11........33 C7
Watts Lo RH15.........109 D3
Waveney Wlk 7 RH10 ...19 B4
Waverley Cres BN1 ....170 C1
Waverley Ct
 6 Horsham RH12.......36 B2
 9 Worthing BN11.....186 B1
Waverley Rd
 Bognor Regis PO21 ...201 A4
 Rustington BN16 .....205 D5
Wavertree Ct RH6 .....1 F2
Wavertree Rd BN1.....185 D4

Wayfield Ave BN3......168 F1
Wayfield Cl BN3 ....168 F1
Wayland Ave BN1......169 C3
Wayland Hts BN1 ......169 C4
Wayside
 Brighton BN1........169 D6
 Crawley RH11 ....17 E4
 Lancing BN15........187 C5
Wayside Ave BN13.....185 D5
Wayside Cotts GU6 .....12 F4
Wayside Rd BN16......206 A8
Way The BN16 ....206 A4
Weald Ave BN3 ....190 F8
Weald Cl
 Horsham RH13.......58 E8
 Hurstpierpoint BN6 ...127 F6
Weald Ct RH14 ....79 D7
Weald Day Hospl The
RH11 ....18 C6
Weald & Downland Open
 Air Mus* PO18.......135 C6
Weald Dr RH10 ....19 A4
Weald Rd BN44........188 F6
Wealden Way RH16.....87 D4
Wealden Cl RH13 ....81 F7
Weald Rd RH15........108 D3
Weald Rise RH16 ......87 E1
Weald Sch The RH14...79 D7
Weald The RH19 ....9 F4
Wear Cl BN13 ....185 C8
Wear Rd BN13.........185 C8
Weatherhill Cl RH6 .....2 F3
Weaver Cl 5 RH11......17 E5
Weavers Cl
 Burgess Hill RH15.....109 D1
 Midhurst GU29 ......72 F2
Weavers Ct 10 BN43....188 E7
Weavers Hill BN16.....184 A5
Weavers La BN16 .....125 E4
Weavers Mead 6
RH16 ....87 C2
Weavers Mead Cotts
BN16 ....184 A6
Weavers Ring BN16....184 A6
Webb Cl
 Bognor Regis PO21 ...211 A7
 Crawley RH11 ....18 B1
Weddell Rd RH10 ......18 F3
Wedges The RH13......56 D5
Wedglen Ind Est GU29...94 D7
Wedgwood Rd PO22 ...202 A4
Weirbrook RH17 ....19 A8
Weir Wood Resr Nature
 Reserve* RH19 ......22 D1
Welbeck Ave BN30.....190 E6
Welbeck Cl RH15 ......109 D4
Welbeck Dr RH15 .....109 D5
Welbeck Mans BN1.....190 E6
Welesmere Rd BN2 ....194 A3
Welkin The RH10 ......88 A8
Welland Cl BN13 ......185 D9
Welland Rd BN13......185 D9
Wellcroft Cotts BN2....127 C5
Welland Villas 2
BN1 ....191 F8
Weller Cl RH10 ....19 D5
Wellesley Cl BN13.....185 F2
Wellesley Ave BN12 ...185 D3
Wellesley Ct 3 BN7....204 E4
Wellfield RH11 ....23 C7
Wellfield Cotts GU31....91 D3
Wellgreen La RH17 ....172 F5
Wellhouse La RH15 ....129 C7
Well House Rd RH20 ...123 A5
Wellingham La BN13...163 E1
Wellingham Cl RH12 ...17 C1
Wellington Cl RH10 .....6 E1
Wellington Ct
 Brighton BN2........193 A3
 1 Worthing BN11....186 A2
Wellington Gdns
PO20 ....212 E8
Wellington Ho BN41....190 C6
Wellingtonia Ct 8
BN1 ....169 E3
Wellington Rd
 Bognor Regis PO21 ...201 B3
 Brighton BN2........213 C4
 Chichester PO19 .....155 A1
 Horsham RH12........36 D2
 Portslade-by-S BN41...190 B6
Wellington St RH7 ....192 C7
Wellington Town Rd
RH19 ....9 D2
Wellington Way RH6.....1 F5
Well La
 Haslemere GU27 ......27 D6
 Midhurst GU29 ......94 E4
Well Lo PO21.........200 A2
Well Rd PO21.........210 F7
Wellsbourne 6 BN2....192 F5
Wells Cl RH12 ....35 F2
Wells Cres
 Bognor Regis PO21 ...200 E4
 Chichester PO19 .....154 F1
Wellsfield PO20.......196 C1
Wells Ho GU29 ....94 E6
Wells Lea RH19........9 D3
Wells Mdw RH19.......9 D3
Wells The GU27.......27 D6
Wellswood RH16.......87 F3
Wellswood Gdns PO9...130 E3
Wellsworth La PO9....130 D3
Wellwood Cl RH13......37 B4
Welwyn Cl RH11........17 E2
Wembley Ave BN15...187 D6

Wembley Gdns BN15....187 D6
Wenban Mews 5
BN14 ....186 D3
Wenban Rd BN11......186 D3
Wenceling Cotts 4
BN15 ....188 C5
Wendover Grange 3
BN1 ....191 A6
Wendy Ridge BN10....205 B6
Wenlock Cl RH11......18 A4
Wensleydale RH11.....18 C3
Wensley Gdns PO10...151 B3
Wentworth RH6 ....2 B2
Wentworth Cl
 Barnham PO22.......180 B7
 Worthing BN13.......185 F9
Wentworth Ct
 1 West Kingston
BN16 ....206 A4
 8 Worthing BN11.....186 A2
Wentworth Dr
 Breach PO10 ....152 A2
 Crawley RH10 ....19 D7
Wentworth St BN2....213 C1
Wepons 2 BN43 ....188 F7
Wesley Cl
 Crawley RH11 ....17 E3
 Horley RH6 ....2 A5
Wessex Ave
 Bognor Regis PO21....201 B2
 East Wittering PO20...208 A4
Wessex Ct 3 BN11.....186 C2
Wessex Wlk 1 BN43...166 F1
West Ashling Rd
PO18 ....152 E3
West Ave
 Bognor Regis PO21 ...200 F3
 Crawley RH10 ....19 A8
 Lancing BN15........188 A5
 Middleton-on-S PO22...202 F6
 Worthing BN11 ......186 A2
West Bank BN1 ....181 A5
West Beach Rd BN43...188 D5
WEST BLATCHINGTON
..................168 F1
West Blatchington Inf Sch
BN3 ....168 E4
West Blatchington Jun
 Sch BN3 ....168 E4
West Blatchington
 Windmill* BN3 ....168 F2
West Ridgs BN1 ....186 D1
Westbourne Ave
 New Brighton PO10....151 C2
 Worthing BN14 ......186 D4
Westbourne Cl PO10...151 C2
Westbourne Gdns
BN3 ....191 A7
Westbourne Gr BN3 ...191 A7
Westbourne House Sch
PO20 ....177 F7
Westbourne Pl BN3 ...191 A6
Westbourne Prim Sch
PO10 ....151 D4
Westbourne Rd PO10 ...151 C3
Westbourne St BN3 ...191 A7
Westbourne Villas
BN3 ....190 F6
West Bracklesham Dr
PO20 ....208 A6
Westbrook
 Forest Row RH18......23 E3
 Saltdean BN2........194 C2
Westbrook Cl PO18 ...175 A5
Westbrooke BN11......186 D2
Westbrooke Ct 12
BN11 ....186 D2
Westbrook Field
PO18 ....175 A5
West Broyle Dr PO19...154 C2
West Burton La RH20...139 E8
West Burton Rd RH20...139 D8
Westbury Cl BN11......186 B2
Westbury Lo BN18......160 B2
West Chiltington Com Fst
 Sch RH20 ....101 E1
West Chiltington La
 Balls Green RH14 .....79 F2
 Coneyhurst RH14, RH13...80 C6
West Chiltington Rd
 West Chiltington Common
RH20 ....121 D5
 West Chiltington RH20...102 A2
West Cl
 Bognor Regis PO22...202 B4
 Fernhurst GU27......49 B6
 Middleton-on-S PO22...202 D5
Westcombe 1 BN1.....191 E7
West Comm RH16 ......87 F6
West Common Dr
RH16 ....88 A7
Westcott Cl RH11......39 C8
Westcott Keep RH46....2 C4
Westcourt Pl BN14....186 C3
Westcourt Rd BN14 ...186 C4
West Ct 3 BN43.......188 E7
West Dean CE Prim Sch
PO18 ....134 F5
West Dean Coll PO18...135 A6
West Dean Gdns*
PO18 ....135 A6
Westdean Rd BN30....186 B5
WESTDENE 169 C5
Westdene Dr BN1......169 C5
Westdene Prim Sch
BN1 ....169 C5

Westdown Ct 2
BN1 ....186 A3
West Dr
 Angmering BN16......205 D8
 Bognor Regis PO21...200 B3
 Brighton BN2........192 C6
 Ferring BN12........206 E4
 Middleton-on-S PO22...203 A5
West Durrington Sh Ctr
BN13 ....185 C7
WEST END 125 C5
West End La
 Ansteadbrook GU27,
GU8................28 D8
 Henfield BN5........125 B5
West End Way BN15 ...187 D3
Westergate Bsns Ctr
BN2 ....170 C4
Westergate Ct 2 BN2...206 F6
Westergate Com Sch
PO20 ....179 E7
Westergate Mews
PO20 ....179 D8
Westergate Rd BN2....170 E4
Westergate St PO20 ...179 D6
Westerley Gdns PO20...208 B6
Western Ave PO20 ....173 A8
Western Cl BN15......187 C4
Western Concourse
BN2 ....192 F3
Western Espl BN41 ....190 D6
Western Lo 2 BN15 ...187 C7
Western Par BN2 .....173 A7
Western Pl 1 BN11....186 C1
Western Rd
 Burgess Hill RH15.....108 E3
 Haywards Heath RH16...87 F4
 Hove, BN3..........191 E5
 Hurstpierpoint BN6 ...127 F6
 Lancing BN15........187 C4
 Liss GU33 ....45 B4
 Littlehampton BN17...204 F4
 Selby PO20.........212 E6
 Shoreham-by-S BN43...188 F7
Western Rd N BN15....187 C6
Western Row BN11 ....186 C1
Western St BN1 ....191 D5
Western Terr
 21 Brighton BN1.....191 E5
 Worthing BN15 ......186 F7
Westfield PO22 ....201 B7
Westfield Ave
 Saltdean BN2........194 D3
 West Kingston BN16...206 A4
Westfield Ave S BN30...194 D3
Westfield Cl BN1 ......170 A5
Westfield Cres BN1 ...170 A5
Westfield Ct 1 BN11...204 F4
Westfield Rd RH11.....18 B6
Westfield Rise BN2 ...194 E3
West Front Rd PO21 ...210 F7
West Furlong Ct BN6...128 A5
West Furlong La BN6 ...128 A4
Westgate PO19 ....176 E6
Westgate Ct BN12 ....185 B3
Westgate St
 BN2 ....170 C6
WEST GREEN 18 C6
West Green Prim Sch
RH11 ....18 C7
Westgrove Gdns 11
PO10 ....173 B8
West Gun Copse RH13...57 D5
Westham 3 BN1........192 F5
Westhampnett Rd
PO19 ....177 C7
WEST HARTING 91 D7
West Head BN17.......204 F4
WEST HILL 41 D1
West Hill
 Ardingly RH17........63 E8
 Dormans Park RH19 ....9 E6
 East Grinstead RH19....22 D8
 Worthing BN13.......163 E2
Westhill Dr RH15......108 C8
West Hill Pl BN1.......213 A3
West Hill Rd BN1 .....213 A3
West Hoathly CE Prim Sch
RH19 ....42 E6
West Hoathly Rd RH19...22 D4
West Hove Inf & Jun Schs
BN3 ....190 F7
Westingway PO21......201 A3
West La
 East Grinstead RH19...22 D8
 Lancing BN15........187 E7
Westlake Cl BN13......185 E6
Westlake Gdns BN13...185 F6
Westland Ave BN14 ...186 A4
Westland Cl BN41......190 A7
WESTLANDS 197 D6
Westlands
 Ferring BN12........206 E5
 Horsham RH13........36 E3
 Littlehampton BN16...205 A6
Westland's Copse La
GU28 ....49 D4
Westlands La PO20 ...197 D5
Westlands Rd
 Haywards Heath RH16...88 A4
 Hunston PO20 ......199 A8

Westloats Gdns PO21 ...201 A5
Westloats La PO21......201 B5
West Mallion RH16 ......87 F3
West Mans BN11.......186 B1
West Mare La PO20....100 F1
West Mead BN16 ......205 A4
West Meade GU30 ......47 B2
Westmead Gdns
BN11 ....185 F3
Westmead Rd PO19 ...176 C6
Westmeads RH6 ....2 C3
West Meads Dr PO21 ...200 F4
Westmeston Ave BN2...194 B2
Westminster Ct 9
BN11 ....186 F2
Westminster Dr PO21...200 C3
Westminster Rd RH10...19 C5
Westmoreland Wlk 2
BN43 ....166 F1
Westmorland Ct 16
BN1 ....191 E7
Westmorland Dr
PO22 ....202 B6
Westmount 3 BN2 ....192 C6
Westmount 2 BN2 ....189 D8
West Mount Cvn Pk
PO20 ....212 D8
Weston La PO18 ......152 F5
Weston Rd GU31.......68 C3
Westons Cl RH12 ......36 D7
Westons Hill RH13......57 B6
West Onslow Cl BN12...206 F7
Westout Cotts BN14 ...186 F1
West Pallant PO19 .....177 A6
West Par
 Horsham RH13........36 C4
 Worthing BN11 ......186 A1
West Park CE Fst & Mid
 Sch BN12...........185 D3
West Park Cres RH15...108 D4
Westpark La BN12 ....185 E3
West Park Rd
 Domewood RH10, RH7....7 F5
 Handcross RH17......61 B7
 Horne RH7..........8 B7
West Point BN43 ......189 A6
West Preston Manor
BN16 ....205 E5
West Preston Mews
BN16 ....205 E5
West Rd
 Emsworth PO10......173 A8
 Portslade-by-S BN41...190 A7
 Poynings BN45, BN6...148 E7
West Ridings BN1 .....205 F4
West Sands Holiday Pk
PO20 ....212 B8
West Sands La PO20...212 B7
West Sea Gate BN30....97 B8
West St
 Billingshurst RH14.....79 C8
 Bognor Regis PO21 ...201 C2
 Brighton BN1........213 A2
 Burgess Hill RH15.....108 E4
 Chichester PO19 .....176 F6
 Crawley RH11 ....18 D5
 Ditchling BN6........129 D3
 Dormansland RH7 ....10 A8
 East Grinstead RH19...22 C8
 Emsworth PO10......173 B8
 Haslemere GU27 ......27 C6
 Horsham RH12........36 C2
 Lancing BN15........187 B7
 Midhurst GU29 ......94 F7
 Portslade-by-S BN41...190 C7
 Rogate GU31.........70 B4
 Rottingdean BN2......193 F1
 Selsey PO20.........212 C7
 Shoreham-by-S BN43...188 E7
 Storrington RH20.....121 D1
 Worthing BN11 ......186 C1
West Stoke Rd PO19...154 C3
West Strand PO20 .....207 B8
WEST TARRING 186 A4
WEST TOWN 127 C6
West Tyne BN13.......185 D6
Westup Rd RH17........40 E7
West View
 Fishbourne PO19......176 B6
 Hove BN3...........191 C8
 Lindfield RH16........88 B6
West View Cotts
 Breach PO10 ....152 A2
 Lindfield RH16........88 B6
West View Ct 8
BN1 ....186 B2
West View Dr BN18....180 F2
West View Gdns
 East Grinstead RH19....22 E8
 Yapton BN18.........180 F1
Westview Terr BN14....163 E6
West Walberton La
BN18 ....158 C2
Westward Cl PO18 ....175 C5
Westward Ho PO19 ...176 C6
Westward La RH20 ....121 C6
Westway
 Bognor Regis PO22 ...201 D3
 Copthorne RH10 ......7 A3
 Crawley RH6 ....6 B7
West Way
 Chichester PO19 .....154 C2
 Crawley RH10 ....19 A7
 Hove BN3...........168 D2
 Lancing BN15........188 B5
 Slinfold RH13........34 D3
 Worthing BN13 ......163 D1

Westway Cl BN41 ....167 E4
Westway Gdns BN41 ...167 E4
West Wittering Parochial
CE Sch PO20..........196 B1
Westwood Cl PO10.....151 C3
WEST WORTHING
BN13 ....186 A1
West Worthing Sta
BN13 ....186 A3
Wetherdown GU31......68 C3
Weycombe Rd GU27....27 C8
Weydown Ct GU27......27 B7
Weydown Ind Est
GU27 ....27 B7
Weydown Rd GU27......27 B7
Wey Gdns GU27........26 F5
Weyhill GU27 ....27 A6
Wey Ho RH20..........100 B2
Weyland Cl GU30.......25 C5
Wey Lodge Cl GU30....25 D4
Weysprings GU27......27 A6
Whapple The 8 BN17...204 F4
Wharf Ho PO19........176 F5
Wharf Rd
Hove BN3.............190 D6
Littlehampton BN17...204 E5
Wharf The GU27........94 F7
Wheatcroft BN17......204 E5
Wheatear Dr GU31.....68 C2
Wheatfield Rd PO20...212 F8
Wheatfield Way
BN2 ....170 F3
Horley RH6 ....2 C4
Wheat Ho BN44 ....145 D2
Wheatlands Ave
PO11 ....195 A1
Wheatlands Cres
PO11 ....195 A1
Wheatsheaf Cl
Burgess Hill RH15....108 E5
Horsham RH12.........36 E5
Wheatsheaf La RH17...87 A6
Wheatsheaf Rd
Henfield BN5..........126 A8
Wineham BN5..........106 C1
Wheatstone Cl RH10....6 B3
Wheelbarrow Castle
GU29 ....73 A2
Wheeler Ct RH16......87 F2
Wheeler Rd RH10......19 B4
Wheelers Way RH19.....8 E3
Wheelwright La RH15..109 D1
Wheelwrights RH20...101 E1
Wheelwrights Lo 6
BN15 ....187 C2
Whichelo Pl BN2......192 C6
Whippingham Rd
BN2 ....193 F1
Whippingham St BN2..192 C8
Whipping Post La
BN2 ....193 F1
Whistler Gr PO19.....155 A1
Whistler Cl RH10......18 F3
Whistler Ct Yd1......169 F1
Whitaker Pl PO20.....178 B7
White Acre BN17......204 C7
Whitebeam Ct 8 BN16..87 C2
Whitebeam Mews 8
RH16 ....87 C2
Whitebeam Rd BN13...185 C6
Whitebeam Way
Middleton-on-S PO22..202 E6
Tangmere PO20.......156 D1
Whitechimney Row
PO10 ....151 D3
White City GU29.......94 E7
Whitecroft
Horley RH6 ....2 B4
7 Littlehampton BN16.205 C6
Whitecross St BN1....213 B3
Whitehall Dr RH11....17 E6
White Hart Ct RH12...36 C4
White Hart Mews
GU30 ....25 B2
WHITEHAWK 192 E5
Whitehawk Cl BN2....192 E5
Whitehawk Cres BN2..192 E5
Whitehawk Hill Rd
BN2 ....192 D5
Whitehawk Prim Sch
BN2 ....192 E6
Whitehawk Rd
Brighton BN2.........192 E6
Brighton BN2.........192 E5
Whitehawk Way BN2..192 F6
Whitehill Pk GU35....24 A8
White Horse Cnr
PO20 ....179 A8
White Horse Ct 2
RH20 ....121 D1
White Horse Cvn Pk
PO20 ....212 D8
Whitehorse Rd RH12...37 B6
White Horse Sq BN44..145 D3
White Horses Way
BN17 ....205 A5
White Horse Yd PO11..121 D1
White House Gdns
GU32 ....68 A5
White House Rd BN13..185 E9
Whitelands PO22.....202 A6
Whitelea Rd RH11....204 D6
White Lion Ct 8
BN43 ....188 E7
White Lo

White Lo continued
4 Littlehampton BN17...204 E5
Whitelot Cl BN42.....167 E2
Whitelot Way BN42....167 E2
Whitely Hill RH10.....19 F1
Whiteman's Cl RH17...86 E8
Whitemans Gn RH17...86 E8
WHITEMANS GREEN 86 E7
Whiterock Pl BN42....189 E7
White's Rd BN6........128 A7
WHITE'S GREEN 74 F7
Whiteside Cl PO19....177 B7
Whites La GU27........48 E3
White St BN2..........213 C2
White Styles Mid Sch
BN15 ....187 B6
White Styles Rd BN15..187 B7
White Styles Terr
BN15 ....187 B7
Whitethorn Dr BN1...169 B4
Whitethroat La RH11...62 D6
Whiteway La BN2.....194 A2
Whiteways PO22......201 A6
Whiteways Cl
Bognor Regis PO22....201 A6
Littlehampton BN17...204 D6
Whitfield Cl
Angmering BN16......206 A8
Bognor Regis PO22....201 C5
Whitfield Rd GU27.....27 C8
Whitgift Wlk RH10....18 D3
Whitley Cl RH10......151 D5
Whitmore Way RH6.....1 E3
Whittingehame Gdns
BN1 ....169 F3
Whittington Coll
(Almshouses) RH19...9 A4
Whittington Ct 1
RH10 ....173 B8
Whittington Rd RH10..18 E3
Whittle Way RH10......6 A3
Whitwell Hatch GU27..27 D5
Whitworth Ho 3
BN11 ....186 B3
Whitworth Rd RH11....5 D2
WHYKE 177 B5
Whyke Ct PO19........177 B4
Whyke Cl PO19........177 B4
Whyke La PO19........177 B4
Whyke Rd PO19.......177 B5
Whylands Ave BN15...185 D9
Whylands Cl BN13....185 D9
Whylands Cres BN13..185 D9
Whytemead Fst Sch
BN14 ....186 E5
Whytings RH13........59 C6
WICK 204 D8
Wickbourne Ho RH17..204 C6
Wickbourne Inf Sch
BN17 ....204 C6
Wick Ct PO22.........202 B5
Wick Ct BN17.........204 B7
Wickens Ct 2 RH16....87 C2
Wickens The RH11.....57 F1
Wickets The RH15....108 F5
Wick Farm Rd BN17...204 C6
Wick Hall BN3........191 D6
Wickham Bsns Ctr
BN17 ....204 C6
Wickham Cl
Haywards Heath RH16..87 E7
Horley RH6 ....1 F4
Wickham Dr BN6......128 C5
Wickham La BN17.....204 D7
Wickham Way RH16...87 E7
Wickhurst Cl BN41....167 F2
Wickhurst Gdns RH13..35 E3
Wickhurst La RH13....35 E3
Wickhurst Rd BN41...168 A2
Wickhurst Rise BN41..167 F3
Wick La
Bognor Regis PO22....202 B5
Midhurst GU29........73 B4
Wickland Ct RH10....18 D3
Wicklands Ave BN2...194 D1
Wickor Cl PO10.......151 C2
Wickor Way PO10.....151 C2
Wicks Cotts BN16....181 C4
Wicks Farm Cvn Pk
BN17 ....204 A8
Wick St BN17.........204 D7
Widdicombe Way
BN2 ....170 E2
Widewater Cl 1
BN15 ....188 C5
Widewater Cl 7
BN43 ....188 C5
Widgeon La PO20.....212 B8
Widgeon Way RH12....36 C5
Widworthy Mews 7
PO21 ....201 B3
Wight Ct BN17........204 D4
Wight Way PO21.......212 E5
Wigmore Cl BN1......170 B1
Wigmore Rd BN14....186 D6
Wigmore Trad Est
BN14 ....186 F5
Wilberforce Cl RH11...39 C8
Wilberforce Way RH13..58 A4
Wilbury Ave BN3.....191 C8
Wilbury Cres BN3....191 D7
Wilbury Gdns BN3....191 C8
Wilbury Gr BN3.......191 C6
Wilbury Lo 10 BN3....191 C6

Wilbury Mans BN3....191 D8
Wilbury Rd BN3......191 C6
Wilbury Villas BN3...191 C7
Wilby Ave BN42......167 E1
Wildacre Ct RH14.....31 D3
Wildbrooks Cl RH20..100 D2
Wilderness Rd BN6...128 A6
Wilderness Rise RH19..10 A6
Wilderness The RH16..88 B8
Wilderwick Rd RH19...10 A5
Wildgoose Dr RH12....35 F3
Wild Orchid Way RH13..58 A3
Wild Park Cl BN2......170 E3
Wild Park Nature Trail*
BN2 ....170 D5
Wildwood La GU6.....11 C5
Wilfrid Rd BN3........168 D1
Wilfs Copse PO20....177 B1
Wiliamson Cott Homes
BN3 ....191 A7
Wilkinson Cl
Angmering BN16......184 A5
Rottingdean BN2.....193 F3
Wilkinson Ct 4 RH11...18 B1
Willard Way
Ashington RH20......122 F5
East Grinstead RH19...9 A3
Willett Cl GU28.......117 B7
Willetts Way RH14....31 F3
William Allen La RH16..18 E7
William Cawley Mews 3
PO19 ....177 A8
William Morris Ct
BN14 ....186 F4
William Morris Way
RH11 ....39 C8
William Olders Rd
BN14 ....206 A8
William Penn Sch
BN3 ....80 E2
William Rd GU35......54 C8
Williams Rd
Broadbridge PO18....175 C7
Shoreham-by-S BN43..189 C8
William St
Bognor Regis PO21...201 D3
Brighton BN2.........213 B2
Shoreham-by-S BN43..190 B7
William Street Trad Est
BN41 ....190 A7
William Sutton Ho
BN1 ....213 B2
Williams Way RH10...19 B6
Willingdon Rd BN2...170 E1
Willington Ct 2
BN11 ....186 B1
Willoughby Ho BN11..125 A3
Willow Ave BN16.....205 E5
Willowbed Ave PO19..177 C4
Willowbed Dr PO19...177 C4
Willow Brean RH6......1 E5
Willow Brook
Littlehampton BN17...204 C7
Middleton-on-S PO22..203 A5
Willowbrook BN15....187 F4
Willowbrook Pk Cvn Pk
BN15 ....188 A5
Willowbrook Pk
BN15 ....188 A5
Willowbrook Rd
BN14 ....187 A4
Willowhale Way
BN6 ....129 A3
Willow Cl
Crawley RH10.........18 E8
East Grinstead RH19...9 D3
Hurstpierpoint BN6...127 F7
2 Lancing BN15......188 C5
Liphook GU30.........25 D3
West Chiltington Common
RH20 ....121 E6
Willowhayne Cl 4
BN16 ....206 A4
Willowhayne Cres 5
BN16 ....206 A4
Willow Ho
Billingshurst RH14....79 D8
Petersfield GU31......68 B1
Willow Mead 8 RH19..22 F8
Willowmead Ct PO20..177 E1
Willow Pk RH16......88 B4
Willow Rd
Horsham RH12........37 B5
Liss GU33 ....45 B4

Willow Ridge RH10....21 A3
Willows Cvn Pk PO20..179 E4
Willows Cvn Pk The
PO11 ....195 A2
Willows Fst Sch The
BN15 ....187 E7
Willows The
Billingshurst RH14....79 C7
5 Bognor Regis PO21..201 C4
2 Brighton BN2......213 C5
Burgess Hill RH15....109 B5
Findon BN14..........163 E6
Ford BN18............181 E5
Hassocks BN6.........128 E4
Horsham RH12.........36 D5
4 Lancing BN15......188 C5
Polbrough RH20......100 A1
Rustington BN16.....205 D5
Selsey PO20..........212 E8
Storrington RH20.....121 C1
Willow Way
Ashington RH20......123 A4
Bognor Regis PO21...200 B1
Hurstpierpoint BN6...128 D8
Willow Wlk GU28......97 E7
Willowwood Cl BN16..206 A8
Wills Cl BN18.........181 B2
Wilman Gdns PO21...200 D2
Wilmington Cl
Brighton BN1.........170 A5
Crawley RH11.........18 C1
Hassocks BN6.........128 F4
Wilmington Par BN1..169 F5
Wilmington Way
Brighton BN1.........170 A5
Haywards Heath RH16..88 A5
Wilmot Cl 6 BN43....189 C8
Wilmot Rd BN43......189 C8
Wilson Ave BN2......192 F6
Wilson Cl
Chichester PO19......176 D7
Crawley RH10.........18 D3
Wilson Ct BN18.......181 B2
Wilton 1 BN16........87 D6
Wilton Ct
Bracklesham PO20....208 C5
Partridge Green RH13..105 A3
Rustington BN16.....205 B7
Wilton Dr BN16.......205 B7
Wilton Villas RH17...41 A1
Wiltshire Croft Ct
PO20 ....212 D7
Wiltshire Rd 16 BN2..213 C2
Wimbledon Cl BN14..186 D5
Wimblehurst Ct 4
RH12 ....36 C4
Wimblehurst Rd RH12..36 C4
Wimborne Cl BN11...185 F3
Wimbourne Ho RH11..16 D2
Wimland Hill RH12....16 D2
Wimland Rd
Faygate RH12.........16 D1
Rusper RH12..........16 D1
Wimlands La RH12....16 E3
Wincanton Cl RH10...19 C6
Winchelsea Ct 9
BN11 ....186 A1
Winchelsea Gdns
BN11 ....186 A1
Winchester Ct
Southwater RH13.....58 A2
Worthing BN11.......186 B2
Winchester Dr PO19..176 F8
Winchester Ho
Petersfield GU32......68 A4
Worthing BN12.......185 A4
Winchester Rd
Crawley RH10.........18 E2
Rustington BN16.....205 E6
Stroud GU32..........67 D4
Worthing BN11.......186 C2
Winchester St BN1...213 B5
Wincombe Rd BN1...169 D1
Winden Ave PO19....177 B6
Windermere 2 BN16..205 C5
Windermere Cres
BN12 ....185 D6
Windermere Ct
9 Brighton BN2.....192 C6
Worthing BN11.......185 B3
Windermere Rd RH16..87 F4
Windlesham Ave BN1..191 E6
Windlesham Cl BN41..167 E6
Windlesham Ct
14 Brighton BN1.....191 E7
5 Lancing BN11.....186 A1
Windlesham Gdns
Brighton BN1, BN3...191 E7
East Preston BN16...206 A4
Shoreham-by-S BN43..188 F8
Windlesham Hall
BN1 ....191 E6
Windlesham Ho 15
BN1 ....191 E6
Windlesham House Sch
RH20 ....143 D3
Windlesham Mans 17
BN1 ....191 E7
Windlesham Rd
Brighton BN1.........191 E6
Shoreham-by-S BN43..188 F8
Windmill Sch BN1....191 E8
Windmill Ave BN6....128 D5
Windmill Cl
Angmering BN16......206 A8
Ashington RH20......123 A4
Bognor Regis PO21...200 B1

Windmill Cl continued
Horley RH6 ....2 B3
Horsham RH13........37 A4
Hove BN3.............168 F2
Upper Beeding BN44..146 B2
Windmill Copse RH20..121 E2
Windmill Ct
Barnham PO22.......180 B5
Crawley RH10.........18 D8
East Wittering PO20..207 F7
Tangmere PO20......156 D1
Windmill Dr
Brighton BN1.........169 C6
Burgess Hill RH15....109 A4
Rustington BN16.....205 D6
Windmill Field PO18..175 A5
Windmill La
Ashurst Wood RH19...23 C7
East Grinstead RH19...9 D3
Henfield BN5..........125 E4
Windmill Par
Burgess Hill RH15....205 C6
Southwick BN42......167 E1
Windmill Platt RH17...61 C8
Windmill Rd
Littlehampton BN17...204 D4
Southwick BN42......167 E1
Windmills Jun Sch The
BN6 ....129 A3
Windmill St BN2......213 C3
Windmill Terr 8 BN2..213 C3
Windmill View BN1...170 B7
Windrum Cl RH12......57 F8
Windrush Cl
Crawley RH11.........17 F4
Worthing BN13.......185 C9
Windsor Cl
Bognor Regis PO21...200 E4
Crawley RH11.........18 C2
Haywards Heath RH16..87 E2
Hove BN3.............169 A3
5 Rustington BN16..205 B7
Southwater RH13......58 A1
Windsor Ct
Brighton BN1.........213 A2
Brighton, Withdean
BN1 ....169 D4
3 Horsham RH13......36 F3
Worthing BN11.......187 A2
Windsor Dr
East Wittering PO20..207 F7
Rustington BN16.....205 B7
Windsor Pl 5 BN3....191 B6
Windsor Pl RH19......23 A8
Windsor Rd
Chichester PO19......177 D6
Petersfield GU32......68 B4
Selsey PO20..........212 E6
Worthing BN11.......186 F3
Windsor St BN1......213 A2
Windsor Way BN15...188 B6
Windward Cl BN17....205 A5
Windyridge RH11......18 A5
Wineham La BN5,
RH17 ....106 D5
Winfield Ave BN1....169 F6
Winfield Cl
Brighton BN1.........169 F5
Portslade-by-S BN41..168 A3
Wingle Tye Rd RH15..129 A8
Winguard Way PO19..177 A5
Winkfield St RH15....109 D1
Winnals Pk RH16......87 D5
Winner Way RH6.......5 D6
Winnet Way RH13....58 A2
Winnipeg Cl GU30...25 C3
Winston Bsns Ctr
BN15 ....187 C5
Winston Cl PO21......200 F6
Winston Cres PO21...200 F6
Winston Ct PO19......154 F3
Winston Rd BN15....187 D4
Winterbourne RH12...36 F7
Winterbourne Cl
BN13 ....185 B6
Winterbourne Ct
BN13 ....185 B6
Winterbourne Way
PO19 ....155 A2
Winterbourne Way
BN13 ....185 B6
Winterfold RH10......19 A3
Winter Gdns RH11....18 C5
Winter Knoll The
BN17 ....204 F5
Winterpit Cl RH13....59 C6
Winterpit La RH13....59 B6
Winters Cotts 8 GU29..94 E7
Winters La GU29......73 A4
Winterton Ct RH13....36 F2
Winterton Ct 7 PO21..204 E5
Winterton Way RH43..189 B6
Winton Ave BN2......194 C3
Winton Cl 4 GU32....68 B3
Winton La BN13.......185 D8
Winton Pl RH11.......186 D3
Winton Rd GU32......68 B4
Wire Mill La RH7.......8 F8
Wisborough Ct
Crawley RH11.........17 F3
Worthing BN13.......185 F4

Wisborough Gdns
RH14 . . . . .78 D8
Wisborough Green Prim
Sch RH14 . . . . .54 C1
Wisborough La RH20. . . .121 E1
Wisden Ave RH15. . . . . . .108 E5
Wisden Ct BN14 . . . . . . .186 A8
Wish Ct BN3. . . . . .190 E8
Wish Rd BN3 . . . . .190 E6
Wisley Ct BN11. . . . . .186 A2
Wisteria Pl RH13 . . . . . . .80 E2
Wiston Ave
Stockbridge PO19 . . . . . .176 E4
Worthing BN14 . . . . .186 B5
Wiston Bsns Pk RH20 . . .122 E2
Wiston Cl BN14. . . . . . . .186 B5
Wiston Ct
Crawley RH11 . . . . .17 F3
1 Horsham RH12 . . . . . . .36 D5
12 Shoreham-by-S
BN43. . . . . .189 C8
Wiston Rd BN2 . . . . .192 F6
Wiston Way BN2. . . . . . . .192 F7
WITHDEAN 169 F4
Withdean Ave
Brighton BN1. . . . . .169 D2
Worthing BN12 . . . . .185 B1
Withdean Cl BN1 . . . . . . .169 D3
Withdean Court Ave
BN1 . . . . .169 D3
Withdean Cres BN1 . . . . .169 E3
Withdean Ct 7 BN1 . . . . .169 E3
Withdean Hall 9
BN1 . . . . .169 E3
Withdean Rd BN1. . . . . . .169 E3
Withdean Rise BN1 . . . . .169 D3
Withdean Stad (Brighton
& Hove Albion FC)
BN1. . . . . .169 D3
Wither Dale RH6 . . . . . . .1 E4
Withey Brook RH6 . . . . . .1 D1
Withey Mdws RH6 . . . . . .1 D1
Withy Bush RH15 . . . . . .108 E5
Witham Ave BN2 . . . . . . .194 C1
Withylands View RH17 . . .64 B8
Witty Patch Cvn Pk
BN15 . . . . .188 B8
WITHYPITTS 21 A3
Withypitts RH10 . . . . .21 A3
Withypitts E RH10 . . . . . .21 A3
Wittering Rd PO11. . . . . .195 B2
WIVELSFIELD 109 F6
Wivelsfield Prim Sch
RH17 . . . . .109 F6
Wivelsfield Rd
Haywards Heath RH16 . . . .87 E2
Saltdean BN2. . . . . .194 C3
Wivelsfield Sta RH15. . . .109 C4
Woburn Ct BN11 . . . . . . .186 C1
Woburn Pl BN1 . . . . .170 F5
Woburn Rd RH11 . . . . . . .18 A4
Woelfs Cl RH20. . . . . .123 A5
Woking Ct BN16 . . . . . . .205 E6
Wold Cl RH11 . . . . .17 F4
WOLDHURST 199 E8
Woldhurst Ct PO20 . . . . .199 E8
Woldhurstlea Cl RH11. . . .18 A4
Wolfe Cl PO19 . . . . .154 F1
Wolseley Rd
Brighton BN1. . . . . .170 D6
Portslade-by-S BN41. . . . .190 A8
Wolsey Cl PO21. . . . . . . .200 B1
Wolsey Pl BN11. . . . . . . .186 A2
Wolstead Lo 3 RH16 . . . . .87 F3
Wolstenbury Rd
BN16 . . . . .205 C7
Wolstonbury Cl
Crawley RH11 . . . . .18 C4
Hurstpierpoint BN6 . . . . .128 B4
Wolstonbury Ct RH15 . . .109 B2
Wolstonbury Rd BN3. . . .191 E7
Wolstonbury Way
RH15 . . . . .109 B2
Wolstonbury Wlk 7
BN43. . . . . .166 F1
Wolverstone Dr BN1 . . . .170 C2
Wolverton Cl RH6 . . . . . . .1 F1
Wolverton Gdns RH6. . . .1 F2
Wood Acre Ct 9
PO21. . . . . .201 D4
Woodard Mews BN5 . . . .125 C6
Woodard Rd BN15. . . . . .187 F7
Woodards View BN43 . . .188 D5
Woodbanke La 5
RH16 . . . . .87 C2
Woodberry Ho GU28 . . . . .97 D2
Woodberry La
Rowland's Castle PO9 . . . .130 F1
Stubbermere PO10,
PO9. . . . . .151 B7
Woodbine Ct 8 PO21. . . .201 D4
Woodborough Cl
PO20 . . . . .208 C5
Woodbourne Ave
BN1 . . . . .170 A4
Woodbourne Cl GU33. . . .45 C4
Woodbridge Ct RH12 . . . .37 A5
Woodbridge Pk BN18 . . .206 A5
Woodbury Ave
East Grinstead RH19 . . . . .10 B1
Petersfield GU32. . . . . . . .68 A5
Woodbury Ct RH19. . . . . .23 B8
Wood Cl RH11 . . . . .2 A8
Woodcock Hill RH19 . . . . .8 F6
Woodcote RH6 . . . . .2 C4

Woodcote Cotts
GU28 . . . . .116 A8
Woodcote Ho 3 RH16 . . . .87 C2
Woodcote La
Fittleworth RH20. . . . . . . .99 D5
Littlehampton BN17. . . . .182 D5
Woodcote Rd RH18 . . . . . .23 F2
Woodcourt RH11 . . . . .18 C2
Woodcrest Rd RH15 . . . .108 F1
Woodcroft RH15 . . . . . . .108 F5
Woodcroft Rd RH11. . . . . .17 D4
Woodcutters RH17. . . . . . .88 F3
Woodaale La RH14 . . . . . .56 A2
Woodend
Bognor Regis PO18. . . . . .201 A4
Crawley RH10 . . . . .153 C5
Wood End RH12 . . . . .37 C5
Woodend Cl RH10 . . . . . . .19 A8
Woodfield RH13 . . . . .57 F1
Woodfield Cl
Bognor Regis PO21 . . . . .211 A7
Crawley RH10 . . . . .18 E7
Tangmere PO20 . . . . .156 D1
Woodfield Lo RH10 . . . . . .19 A8
Woodfield Park Rd
PO10 . . . . .173 D8
Woodfield Rd
Crawley RH10 . . . . .18 F7
Rudgwick RH12 . . . . .33 D7
Woodfield Terr RH13. . . . .83 E1
Woodgate Cl PO20. . . . . .179 D5
Woodgate Pk PO20 . . . . .179 D6
Woodgate Rd PO20 . . . . .179 D5
Woodgates Cl RH13. . . . . .36 F3
Woodhall Cl RH17 . . . . . . .86 F7
Woodhatch RH13 . . . . . . .57 F2
Woodhayes RH6 . . . . .2 B4
Woodhorn Cotts
PO20 . . . . .178 E6
Woodhorn La PO20 . . . . .178 D6
Woodhouse Cl BN3 . . . . .190 E7
Woodhouse La PO8,
PO9 . . . . .130 E4
Woodhouse Rd
Blendworth PO8 . . . . .130 C7
Hove BN3. . . . . .190 E7
Woodingdean Bsns Pk
BN2 . . . . .171 D1
Woodingdean Prim Sch
BN2 . . . . .193 C8
Wooding Gr 16 RH11. . . . .18 B1
Wood La BN5. . . . . .146 F7
Woodland Ave
Burgess Hill RH15. . . . . .109 C4
Hove BN3. . . . . .169 B3
Worthing BN13 . . . . .163 F1
Woodland Cl
Burgess Hill RH15. . . . . .109 C4
Five Oaks RH14. . . . . .55 E6
Horsham RH13. . . . . .37 B4
Hove BN3. . . . . .169 B2
Woodland Cotts
RH20 . . . . .122 A7
Woodland Cres RH15 . . .109 C4
Woodland Ct BN3. . . . . . .169 B4
Woodland Dr
Crawley Down RH10 . . . . .21 B8
Hove BN3. . . . . .169 B3
Woodland La RH13 . . . . . .38 C3
Woodland Par BN3 . . . . .169 B3
Woodland Pl PO19. . . . . .155 A3
Woodland Rd PO20 . . . . .212 D6
Woodlands
Crawley RH10 . . . . .19 D8
Horley RH6 . . . . .2 D4
Hove BN3. . . . . .169 C2
Woodlands Ave
New Brighton RH11. . . . . .151 B3
Rustington BN16 . . . . . . .205 C6
Woodlands Cl
Angmering BN16 . . . . . . .184 A7
Clapham BN13 . . . . .162 F1
Crawley Down RH10 . . . . .21 B7
Rustington BN16 . . . . . . .205 C6
Woodlands Cotts
BN16 . . . . .205 C6
Woodlands Ctr
(Rustington Heritage
Exhibition Ctr)*
BN16 . . . . .205 C6
Woodlands La
Chichester PO19 . . . . . . .176 F8
Haslemere GU27. . . . . . . .26 F7
Heath Common RH20 . . . .122 C3
Liss GU33 . . . . .45 D3
Walderton PO18 . . . . . . .132 B2
Woodlands Pk BN18 . . . .180 F3
Woodlands Rd
Bognor Regis PO22. . . . . .201 B6
East Grinstead RH19 . . . . .10 A4
Haywards Heath RH16 . . . .87 F4
Littlehampton BN17. . . . .204 E4
Woodlands The BN1. . . . .169 E5
Woodlands Way
Billingshurst RH14. . . . . .79 E6
Southwater RH13. . . . . . .81 E8
Woodlands Wlk RH13 . . . .59 C5
Woodland Villas
PO20 . . . . .157 F1
Woodland Way
Brighton BN1. . . . . .169 F4
Horsham RH13. . . . . .37 B4
Woodland Wlk BN2 . . . . .193 D4
Woodlark Gdns GU31. . . .68 E3
Wood Lea Cotts RH12. . . .34 F7
Woodlea Rd BN13 . . . . . .186 A4
Woodleigh Rd RH15 . . . .109 C4

Woodmancote Ct 6
RH12 . . . . .36 D5
Woodmancote La PO10,
PO18 . . . . .152 B4
Woodmancote Rd
BN14 . . . . .186 B4
WOODMANSGREEN 48 A3
Woodmans Hill RH14 . . . .18 C2
Woodpecker Cres
RH15 . . . . .108 D3
Woodpecker Ct GU28 . . . .97 F7
Woodpecker La RH20 . . . .121 E1
Woodpecker Rd GU28. . . .97 C7
Woodpeckers RH13 . . . . . .57 F3
Woodpecker Way
Turners Hill RH10 . . . . . . .21 C5
Worthing BN13 . . . . .185 C6
Wood Ride RH16. . . . . . . .87 D3
Woodridge RH16. . . . . . . .88 A3
Woodroffe Benton Ho
RH11 . . . . .17 F6
Woodroffe Wlk PO10. . . .151 B4
Woodroyd Ave RH6 . . . . . .1 F2
Woodroyd Gdns RH6. . . . .1 F1
Woodruff Ave BN3 . . . . . .169 C2
Woodruff Bsns Ctr The
PO19 . . . . .176 C5
Woodsdale Ct BN14. . . . .186 C5
Woods Hill RH19 . . . . .23 D6
Woods Hill La RH19 . . . . . .23 D6
Woods Ho
Hove BN3. . . . . .191 A8
8 Petersfield GU32 . . . . .68 B4
Woodside
Barnham PO22 . . . . .180 B6
Horsham RH13. . . . . .37 B4
Woodside Ave BN1 . . . . .169 D2
Woodside Cl
Partridge Green
RH13. . . . . .105 D4
Storrington RH20 . . . . . .121 E2
Woodside Gr 8 BN17 . . . .204 E4
Woodside La RH10 . . . . .169 D2
Woodside Rd
Crawley RH10 . . . . .18 F8
Worthing BN14 . . . . .186 B4
Woodside Road (Worthing
FC) BN14 . . . . .186 B4
Woodsland Cl BN6. . . . . .128 F4
Woodsland Cross
RH16 . . . . .64 E3
Woodsland Rd BN6 . . . . .128 F4
Woodsmill Cl BN6 . . . . . .128 F4
Wood's Mill Countryside
Ctr* BN5 . . . . .146 F6
Wood St
Bognor Regis PO21 . . . . .201 B2
East Grinstead RH19 . . . . . .9 D1
Woodstock RH19 . . . . .9 C2
Woodstock Ct RH12. . . . . .36 D5
Woodstock Gdns
PO21 . . . . .200 F2
Woods Way PO20 . . . . . .185 C4
Woodview BN43 . . . . .166 F1
Wood View BN18 . . . . . . .160 A2
Woodview Ct RH10 . . . . .170 D6
Woodview Ct 8 BN43. . . .166 F1
Woodwards RH11 . . . . .18 C2
Woodwards Ct RH15 . . . .109 B1
WOOLBEDING 72 C2
Woolbeding La GU29. . . . .72 B4
Woolborough Cl RH10 . . . .18 E7
Woolborough La
Crawley RH10 . . . . .5 F1
Crawley, Three Bridges
RH10. . . . . .19 A8
Salfords RH1 . . . . .2 B8
Woolborough Rd RH10 . . .18 E7
Wooldridge Wlk
BN17 . . . . .181 D1
Wool La GU29 . . . . .94 F7
WOOLMER HILL 26 D7
Woolmer Hill Ho GU27 . . .26 C6
Woolmer Hill Rd GU27. . . .26 C6
Woolmer Hill Tech Coll
GU27 . . . . .26 D7
Woolmer La GU30. . . . . . . .25 D4
Woolmer St PO10. . . . . . .151 A4
Woolmer Ave GU32. . . . . .68 B4
Woolstaplers The
PO19 . . . . .176 F6
Woolven Ct RH15 . . . . . . .108 E1
Woolven Row BN5 . . . . . .125 F5
Wophams La PO20 . . . . . .198 D7
Worcester Cl PO21. . . . . .200 E3
Worcester Ct 1 BN3 . . . .191 E6
Worcester Rd
Chichester PO19 . . . . . . .154 F2
Crawley RH10 . . . . .18 E2
Worcester Villas BN3 . . .190 C7
Wordsworth Cl RH10. . . . .19 B8
Wordsworth Gdns
PO22 . . . . .202 D6
Wordsworth Pl RH12. . . . .36 E7
Wordsworth Rd BN11 . . . .186 C1
Wordsworth Rise 6
RH19 . . . . .9 C1
Wordsworth St BN3. . . . .191 A7
WORLD'S END 109 F3
Worms La PO22 . . . . .202 E7
Worsted La RH19 . . . . .23 B8
WORTH 19 E6
Worth Abbey* RH10 . . . . .20 B1
Worthing Coll BN13. . . . .185 E4

Worthing Mus & Art
Gallery* BN11 . . . . .186 D2
Worthing Rd
Dial Post RH13 . . . . .103 E3
East Preston BN16 . . . . . .205 F6
Horsham RH12 . . . . .36 B1
Littlehampton BN16,
BN17. . . . . .205 B7
Littlehampton BN17. . . . .204 E7
Southwater RH13 . . . . . . .57 F2
Tower Hill RH12, RH13 . . . .58 A7
West Grinstead RH13 . . . .104 A6
Worthing Sta BN11 . . . . .186 C3
Worth Park Ave RH10 . . . .19 C7
Worth Rd RH10 . . . . .19 C6
Worth Sch RH10 . . . . .20 B1
Worth Way RH10 . . . . .19 E5
Wray Cl RH19 . . . . .23 D6
WRAYS 1 B5
Wraysbury Gdns
BN15 . . . . .187 E7
Wraysbury Park Dr
PO10 . . . . .151 B4
Wren Cl
Burgess Hill RH15 . . . . . .108 D3
Horsham RH12 . . . . .36 D7
Pulborough RH20 . . . . . .100 B2
Wren Cres PO22 . . . . .201 B6
Wren Ct RH10 . . . . .18 E3
Wren Ctr The PO10 . . . . .151 C3
Wrenfield Pl 9 PO21. . . . .201 C2
Wren St RH10 . . . . .21 C5
Wrentham Ho RH15. . . . .109 B3
Wright Cl RH10 . . . . .19 C2
Wroxham Way PO22 . . . . .201 F6
Wroxham Wlk 8 RH10. . . .19 B4
Wr Twr Bldgs 3
PO21 . . . . .201 D3
Wyatt Cl RH14 . . . . .54 B1
Wyatt Ct PO20 . . . . .207 F7
Wyatts La RH17 . . . . .86 A5
Wyberlye Rd RH15. . . . . .109 A4
Wyberton Ho PO19 . . . . .155 A3
Wychacre RH20. . . . . .190 E7
Wychcroft 4 BN17 . . . . .204 D5
WYCH CROSS 44 E5
Wycherry Rd RH16 . . . . . .87 D5
Wychwood RH14. . . . . . . .31 D3
Wychwood Cl PO21 . . . . .200 E1
Wychwood Gdns
BN11 . . . . .187 B3
Wychwood Wlk PO21. . . .200 E1
Wyck Ct BN41 . . . . .190 A7
Wycliffe Ct
Crawley RH11 . . . . .17 E3
15 Worthing BN11. . . . . .186 A1
Wyde Feld PO21. . . . . . . .200 F2
Wye Ct RH11 . . . . .39 C8
Wye Ho BN11. . . . . .186 B2
Wyke Ave 6 BN11. . . . . . .186 C2
Wyke Ct BN44 . . . . .145 D3
Wykeham Ct BN11. . . . . .186 C2
Wykeham Terr BN1 . . . . .213 A2
Wykeham Way RH15 . . . .109 C2
Wyke La N PO22 . . . . .202 E6
Wyke Vad GU30. . . . . .25 D4
Wyld Green La GU33. . . . .45 D5
Wyncombe Cl RH20. . . . . .99 B3
Wyndham Bsns Pk
GU29 . . . . .94 D7
Wyndham Lea RH10 . . . .121 D6
Wyndham Rd GU28 . . . . . .97 F7
Wyndham St BN2 . . . . . .213 C1
Wynlea Cl RH10 . . . . .21 A8
Wynnes Mews BN2 . . . . .194 C2
Wynnstay RH15 . . . . .109 B2
Wysemead RH6 . . . . .2 C4
Wyshe The BN45. . . . . . . .149 C6
Wythering Cl PO21 . . . . .210 F7
Wythwood RH16 . . . . .87 E1
Wyvern Cl PO20 . . . . .156 E1
Wyvern Ct 6 BN11 . . . . .186 C1
Wyvern Pl RH12 . . . . .35 F8
Wyvern Way RH15 . . . . . .109 C3

Y

Yachtsmens Cotts
PO18 . . . . .175 C5
Yapton CE Prim Sch
BN18 . . . . .180 F4
Yapton La BN18. . . . . .180 F7
Yapton Rd
Barnham BN18, PO22 . . . .180 D4
Climping BN17, BN18 . . . .181 C1
Middleton-on-S BN18,
PO22. . . . . .202 E7
Yarborough Terr GU29 . . . .72 A1
Yarbrook PO18 . . . . .154 E7
Yardlea Cl PO9 . . . . .130 D1
Yardley St BN1 . . . . .213 B5
Yarmouth Cl RH10 . . . . . .19 A4
Yarrow Cl RH12 . . . . .36 E5
Yattendon Rd RH6 . . . . . .2 B3
Yattendon Sch RH6 . . . . . .2 A4
Yeoman Gate BN13 . . . . .185 B5
Yeoman Rd BN13 . . . . . . .185 B6
Yeomans Acre PO21 . . . . .200 F3
Yeomans Field PO18 . . . .152 D1
Yeomans La GU30 . . . . . . .25 A4
Yeoman Way BN13. . . . . .185 B5
Yew Ct
Crawley RH11 . . . . .18 D5
1 East Grinstead RH19 . . . .9 D2
Yew La RH19 . . . . .9 B3
Yewlands Wlk RH11. . . . . .17 D4

Yew Tree Cl
Bognor Regis PO22 . . . . .201 B6
Cowfold RH13 . . . . .83 E2
Horley RH6 . . . . .2 A4
Lancing BN15. . . . . .187 E5
Yew Tree Cotts
Burgess Hill RH15 . . . . . .109 B3
3 Worthing BN14 . . . . . .186 D5
Yew Tree Ct RH17. . . . . . .86 F6
Yew Tree Pl GU33. . . . . . . .45 C4
Yew Tree Rd RH6 . . . . .4 E7
York Ave
East Grinstead RH19 . . . . .23 A8
Hove BN3. . . . . .191 E6
York Chase PO19 . . . . . . .154 F1
York Cl
Horsham RH13. . . . . .36 F3
Petersfield GU32. . . . . . . .67 F3
Southwater RH13 . . . . . . .58 A1
York Ct 13 BN3 . . . . .191 E7
York Gr BN1. . . . . .213 A4
York Hill BN1. . . . . .213 A4
York Ho
Portslade-by-S BN41. . . . .190 B8
Worthing BN11 . . . . .187 A3
Yorkhurst Hill PO18. . . . .114 F1
Yorklands BN3. . . . . .169 A4
York Lo 11 BN11. . . . . . . .186 C3
York Mansions E 13
BN3 . . . . .191 E6
York Mansions W 12
BN3 . . . . .191 E6
York Pl
Brighton BN1. . . . . .213 B3
Hove BN3. . . . . .191 E6
York Rd
Bognor Regis PO21 . . . . .201 D3
Burgess Hill RH15 . . . . . .108 D2
Chichester PO19 . . . . . . .177 C5
Hove BN1, BN3 . . . . .191 E6
Littlehampton BN17. . . . .204 D5
Selsey PO20. . . . . .212 E5
Worthing BN11 . . . . .186 E2
York Villas BN1 . . . . .213 A4
Yorkwood GU33. . . . . .45 B4
Youngsmere Cl BN1 . . . .170 B6
Young St 4 PO19. . . . . . .155 A2

Z

Zachary Merton Com
Hospl BN16 . . . . .205 D4
Zion Gdns BN1 . . . . .213 A2